WORKING THROUGH SYNTHETIC WORLDS

Working Through Synthetic Worlds

Edited by

C.A.P. SMITH
Colorado State University, USA

KENNETH W. KISIEL
Lockheed Martin Corporation, USA

&

JEFFREY G. MORRISON
Space and Naval Warfare Systems Center – Pacific, USA

ASHGATE

Published by
Ashgate Publishing Limited
Wey Court East
Union Road
Farnham
Surrey, GU9 7PT
England

Ashgate Publishing Company
Suite 420
101 Cherry Street
Burlington
VT 05401-4405
USA

www.ashgate.com

British Library Cataloguing in Publication Data
Working through synthetic worlds.
1. Virtual reality in management. 2. Virtual corporations.
I. Smith, C. A. P. II. Morrison, Jeffrey G. III. Kisiel, Ken.
658'.0568-dc22

ISBN: 978-0-7546-7712-3 (hbk)
978-0-7546-9430-4 (ebk)

Library of Congress Cataloging-in-Publication Data
Working through synthetic worlds / edited by C.A.P. Smith, Jeffrey G. Morrison, and Kenneth W. Kisiel.
p. cm.
Includes index.
ISBN 978-0-7546-7712-3 (hardback) -- ISBN 978-0-7546-9430-4 (ebook)
1. Human-computer interaction--Technological innovations--Forecasting. 2. Virtual reality--Technological innovations--Forecasting. 3. Virtual reality in management--Forecasting. I. Smith, C. A. P. (Charles Adams Plater), 1956- II. Morrison, Jeffrey G. III. Kisiel, Kenneth W.
QA76.9.H85W645 2009
004.01'9--dc22

2009026052

Mixed Sources
Product group from well-managed forests and other controlled sources
www.fsc.org Cert no. SGS-COC-2482
© 1996 Forest Stewardship Council
FSC

Printed and bound in Great Britain by
TJ International Ltd, Padstow, Cornwall

Contents

List of Figures

List of Tables

Notes on Contributors

Richard Brath is a Partner at Oculus Info Inc. He has been actively involved in the design and development of information visualization and design software over the last twenty years with an emphasis on creating innovative visual solutions that solve real-world business needs from conception and design through to full enterprise-scale implementations deployed to hundreds of thousands of users. Richard originally acquired a Bachelor of Architecture from University of Waterloo and produced international award-winning architectural designs. He transferred and extended those skills to design for special effects, information visualization and human computer interaction at the same time as acquiring a Master of Computer Science from University of Toronto. Richard is a frequent contributor to information visualization research conferences and was a recent keynote speaker at IEEE's IV09.

John W. Bodnar is a Senior Biological Warfare Analyst at SAIC, McLean, VA. His interest in analytical methods and tools for biology and for the Intelligence Community comes from previous experience conducting biological warfare analysis at the Defense Intelligence Agency, analyzing the Revolution in Military Affairs as a Navy Reservist for the Office of Naval Research and the US Naval War College, and researching and teaching biochemistry and bioinformatics at Northeastern University, the US Naval Academy, and Stevenson University.

Alexander Bringsjord is a Junior at Rensselaer Polytechnic Institute (RPI) majoring in management and philosophy, and carrying out research mostly in the following areas: advanced synthetic characters, the fundamental nature of the human mind, and the formal foundations of economics. He has a special interest in the legal and ethical aspects of autonomous agents.

Selmer Bringsjord specializes in the logico-mathematical and philosophical foundations of artificial intelligence (AI) and cognitive science, and in building AI systems on the basis of formal reasoning. He received the bachelor's degree from the University of Pennsylvania, and the PhD from Brown University in 1987, where he studied under Roderick Chisholm. Since 1987 he has been on faculty in the Departments of Cognitive Science and Computer Science at Rensselaer Polytechnic Institute (RPI) in Troy, New York, where as a Full Professor he teaches AI, formal logic, human and machine reasoning, and philosophy of AI. Dr. Bringsjord is the author of papers ranging in approach from the mathematical to the informal, and covering such areas as AI, logic, gaming, philosophy of mind, and ethics. He has lectured and interviewed in person, and on television and radio, across the globe.

Dr. Diana L. Burley is Associate Professor, Director of the Center for the Study of Learning and the Executive Leadership Doctoral Program at The George Washington

University. She holds a Ph.D. in Organization Science and Information Technology, and an M.S. in Public Management and Policy from Carnegie Mellon University. For more than 15 years, Dr. Burley has examined the social and organizational implications of new information and communication technologies. She is widely published in the areas of knowledge management, electronic government, and IT workforce development; and has received competitive research grants from several sources including the US National Science Foundation (NSF) and the PriceWaterhouseCoopers Center for the Business of Government. Dr. Burley served as an NSF program director where she managed multi-million dollar grant programs in computer science education. Based on her work, she was honored by the US Federal Chief Information Officers Council for outstanding effort toward the development of US Federal IT workforce.

John Campbell is Associate Professor of Information Systems in the Faculty of Information Sciences and Engineering at the University of Canberra. A major theme throughout his research work is how users interact through information systems in the social world and, in particular, the ways in which organizational decision-making and community interaction are enacted through collaborative technologies. He has published articles in various journals including *Information Systems Journal*, *Information & Management*, *Data Base for Advances in Information Systems*, *Journal of Organizational Computing and Electronic Commerce*, and *Australasian Journal of Information Systems*.

Robert Cox has a Masters degree in Information Technology from the University of Canberra. He has 22 years experience as an IT practitioner; in addition he has been working as a researcher and teacher for the past seven years. His research interests include Computer Games, Synthetic Worlds, Neural Networks, Soft Computing and Intelligent Agents. His avatar, Galen Garmes, has been a resident of Second Life since January 2007. With interests in artificial intelligence and role play gaming, it is hardly surprising that he imagines androids in Synthetic Worlds. He builds, scripts and teaches in Second Life and OpenSim. He is working towards a PhD.

Patricia Crowther has a BSc from Victoria University of Wellington and Master of Information Technology Degree from the University of Canberra. She has been a resident of Second Life (as Trixie Garmes) since January 2007. Her research interests include Neural Networks and Virtual (Synthetic) Worlds. She has a long time interest in role play and simulation gaming having first played Dungeons & Dragons in 1983. She has seen the transition of role play gaming from table top to computers, giving her a broad view of the origins of role playing from imagination to realization on the computer screen.

John DeBello has a degree in American History from the University of California San Diego. Over the past two decades he has helped create and design Concept of Operations models and supporting visualizations on behalf of many government agencies and partner organizations including DARPA, the Department of Homeland Security, the Department of Energy, NIMA, SPAWAR, General Atomics, Lockheed

Martin and QUALCOMM. An expert in the application of leading communication technologies, his notable achievements include producing the event that introduced digital HDTV to North America. He was recently inducted into the Silver Circle by the National Association of Television Arts & Sciences (NATAS), Pacific Southwest chapter, in recognition of 25 years of special achievement in television.

Nathan T. Denny received his Master of Science in Computer Science from Southern Illinois University in 1998 and his Bachelors of Science in Computer Science and Mathematics from Southern Illinois University in 1997. Mr. Denny has published in diverse fields such as design for testability (DFT) of very large scale integrated circuits (VLSI), information re-use in case-based reasoning, Internet spam control, automation in agricultural irrigation, peer-to-peer networking, knowledge management in global software development, and models of human motivation in social science simulations. His current research interests include distributed computing, artificial intelligence, human-machine interfaces, cognitive science, knowledge management, and collaboration in the 24-Hour Knowledge Factory. Mr. Denny currently conducts research and development at the Omaha, Nebraska office of 21st Century Systems, Inc.

Donna N. Dillenberger is the Chief Technology Officer of IBM's IT Optimzation Solutions. At IBM, she is a Distinguished Engineer, Master Inventor, Member of IBM's Academy and an Adjunct Professor at Columbia University's Graduate School of Engineering. She joined IBM in 1988 and has worked on future hardware simulations, operating systems, java virtual machines, java containers, workload management, IT optimization solutions and hypervisors.

Peter Garretson is an Airpower and Spacepower Strategist, and Grand Strategist, with interests in virtual and augmented reality, wargaming, modelling and decision support. He is currently a visiting fellow at the Indian Institute for Defence Studies and Analyses (IDSA) under the sponsorship of the Council on Foreign Relations (CFR). He served previously as the Chief of Future Science and Technology, Headquarters Air Force, Directorate of Strategic Planning, and a DARPA Service Chiefs' Liaison. A tech scout, strategist, and futurist, he leverages a diverse experience base in long range strategic planning, technology forecasting, advanced concept development, and wargaming to effect macro-level organizational transformation.

Dr. Xin Ge got her Ph.D. in Marketing from the University of Alberta. She is an assistant professor of Marketing at the University of Northern British Columbia, School of Business. Her research interests include consumer judgments and decision making, consumer information processing, constructive consumer preferences, and consumer behavior in the virtual worlds. Xin's research has been recently published in *Journal of Retailing, Journal of Virtual Worlds Research,* and *Canadian Journal of Administrative Sciences*.

Dr. Ben Goertzel is CEO and Chief Scientist of AI firm Novamente LLC, a company focused on creating powerfully intelligent NPC's for online games and virtual worlds.

He is also CEO of bioinformatics firm Biomind LLC, and Director of Research of the nonprofit Singularity Institute for AI. Dr. Goertzel is the originator of the OpenCog open-source AGI framework, as well as the proprietary Novamente Cognition Engine AGI system. A research faculty for 8 years in several universities in the US and Australasia, he remains active in the academic AI community. He is the Chair of the Steering Committee for the Artificial General Intelligence conference series, and was the Conference Chair for AGI-09 which was held in March 2009 in Washington DC. He currently serves on the Board of the World Transhumanist Association. Dr. Goertzel has authored eight technical monographs in the computing and cognitive sciences, published by leading scientific publishers, most recently Probabilistic Term Logic, published by Springer in 2008; and also edited four technical volumes. He has also published over 80 research papers in journals, conferences and edited volumes, in disciplines spanning AI, mathematics, computer science, cognitive science, philosophy of mind and bioinformatics; and has developed two AI-based trading systems for hedge funds in Connecticut and San Francisco. AI software created by his teams at Novamente LLC and Biomind LLC has been used in numerous government agencies and corporations.

Sandra K. Johnson is a Senior Technical Staff Member at IBM. She has worked as the Chief Technology Officer, Global Small and Medium Business, the Linux Performance Architect, and managing the Linux Performance, WebSphere Database Development, and Java Server Performance teams within IBM development and research organizations. She has also conducted research on computer architecture, memory and I/O subsystems, and performance evaluation. Dr. Johnson is a member of the IBM Academy of Technology, has received numerous technical and professional awards, and is a Master Inventor, with over 40 patents issued and pending. She has authored and co-authored over 80 publications, is Editor-in-Chief of the book *Performance Tuning for Linux Servers*, and is author of *Inspirational Nuggets* and *GREGORY: The Life of a Lupus Warrior*. Dr. Johnson earned B.S. (*summa cum laude)*, M.S. and Ph.D. degrees, all in electrical engineering, from Southern University, Stanford University, and Rice University, respectively. She is a member of the Institute of Electrical and Electronics Engineers (IEEE) and the Association for Computing Machinery (ACM). She is also an IEEE Fellow and an ACM Distinguished Engineer.

Kenneth W. Kisiel is Principal Research Engineer at Lockheed Martin Corporation and a Senior Technical Advisor assisting clients in applying virtual/synthetic worlds to information understanding. Mr. Kisiel was also the founder, CEO, and visioneer for WisdomBuilder, LLC which researched and commercialized advanced visualization analytical tools to both the government and private sectors. Mr. Kisiel holds patents in visualization and social network analysis. He earned a B.A.S from Florida Atlantic University and an M.S. from Johns Hopkins University.

John Light worked with John David Miller at Intel to create the Miramar 3D workspace, including preliminary studies involving novel Information Management and Information Visualization prototypes that contributed to the Miramar vision. Subsequent to that work, he researched Ubiquitous Computing concepts at Intel, including the Personal Server. Prior to Miramar, John worked for a variety of companies on products as diverse as packaged X-Window Systems at Network Computing Devices, graphics workstations and test instruments at Tektronix, CAD/CAM systems at United Computing Corporation, and operating systems at Computer Automation. He dances and meditates, both of which he believes contribute to building good user interfaces.

Dr. Joseph MacInnes is a Researcher at Oculus Info Inc. He has a degree in Computer Sciencc from the Technical University of Nova Scotia, and a Ph.D. in Computer Science and Cognitive Psychology from Dalhousie University. His specialty is computer models of human and computer cognition, and he is researching approaches with connectionist, Bayes and genetic algorithms. Dr. Macinnes' research publications include the journals of Psychological Science; Cognitive, Affective & Behavioral Neuroscience; Behavior Research Methods Instruments & Computers and conference proceedings at Computer-Human Interaction, Cognitive Science, Artificial Intelligence and Artificial General Intelligence. His most recent work at Oculus is in workflow models for adaptive interfaces and visualizations.

Dr. Judi McCuaig holds a Ph.D. in Computer Science from the University of Saskatchewan and presently holds the position of Associate Professor at the University of Guelph. Judi has a long career as an educator during which she has taught primary school, middle school, and university students as well as conducted numerous professional development seminars. Judi's academic research focus is user adaptive systems with a specific focus on determining the correct timing and modality with which to deliver personalized information to a computer user. Current projects are examining the role of adapted help and tutoring vignettes in the usability of computing systems. Judi spent four years working as a Senior Research Scientist at the Department of Energy's Pacific Northwest National Lab, in Richland, WA where she both managed and worked on several interesting research and development projects in the information processing and presentation domain.

Paul R. Messinger is Associate Professor of Marketing at the University of Alberta School of Business and IBM Faculty Fellow in the Centre for Advanced Studies program at the IBM Toronto Laboratory. He recently served as Principle Investigator of the Research Alliance "Harnessing the Web-Interaction Cycle for Canadian Competitiveness" for the Social Science and Humanities Research Council of Canada and as Founding Director of the University of Albert School of Retailing. Paul currently serves on the Editorial Board of the journal *Marketing Science* and as guest editor for a special issue on eService for the *Canadian Journal of Administrative Sciences*. Paul's research focuses on e-commerce, 3D mediated virtual worlds, service science, emerging retail formats, dynamic pricing, and recommendation systems; his publication outlets include *Marketing Science, Journal of Retailing, Journal of Economic Dynamics and Control, Journal of Virtual Worlds Research, Journal of Business Research, and Journal of Retailing and Consumer Services*. For more details, see http://www.business.ualberta.ca/pmessinger/

Anna C. Merzagora has a Masters degree in biomedical engineering from Politecnico di Milano, (Milan, Italy); she is currently working towards a her Ph.D. at the School of Biomedical Engineering, Science and Health System of Drexel University (Philadelphia, PA). Her research interests include the application of signal processing and pattern recognition methods to foster cross-disciplinary studies of neurophysiology and neuroimaging.

Dr. Joan L. Mitchell has a Physics degree from Stanford University and a M.S. and Ph.D. in Physics from the University of Illinois at Urbana. She was hired into IBM at the T.J. Watson Research Center to work on printing technologies. She is co-inventor of the ribbon technology used in the IBM Quietwriter typewriter. She then switched fields and did data compression and helped established the CCITT digital facsimile standard. She is most famous for her participation in the original Joint Photographic Expert Group (JPEG) committee for seven years, which established a continuous tone color data compression standard. She was elected to the IBM Academy of Technology in 1997. She transferred to IBM Printing Systems Division in 1999 and became an IBM Fellow in 2001. She has written books on JPEG, MPEG and mentoring. She was elected to the National Academy of Engineering in 2004. She retired from IBM in 2007 and became an InfoPrint Fellow when the Printing Systems Division became a joint venture between IBM and Ricoh, called InfoPrint Solutions Company. Her combined issued patents are over 100. She left InfoPrint in June, 2009.

John David Miller is a Principal Engineer for Intel Corp, and led the development of both Miramar and Escher. His lifelong professional quest is to create memory/cognition-augmentation systems that enable both individuals and teams to forget less, understand more, make better decisions, and achieve ever-higher levels of performance, despite the world's ever-increasing complexity.

Dr. Jeffrey G. Morrison has a Ph.D. in Engineering Psychology from the Georgia Institute of Technology; and has been a scientist, engineer and program manager with the U.S. Navy for 20 years. His work in the fields of cognition, decision support, advanced automation, and human factors has been instrumental in the success of numerous Defense Advanced Research Project Agency (DARPA) and Office of Naval Research (ONR) Programs. He has authored over 50 scientific publications, lectured internationally in 7 countries, and edited 4 professional journals and books. He is a recipient of The Dr. Arthur E. Bisson Prize for Naval Technology Achievement from ONR for developing and transitioning "Knowledge Web Technologies" and subsequently supporting Naval operations utilizing the technologies during both Operation Enduring Freedom & Operation Iraqi Freedom, as well as receiving both the American Psychological Association's George E. Briggs Dissertation Award, for original research exhibiting creative application of scientific inquiry in the area of Engineering Psychology.

Elizabeth D. (Betty) Murphy earned a Masters degree in Industrial-Organizational Psychology from George Mason University in Fairfax, Virginia, and a Ph.D. in Cognitive and Experimental Psychology from the University of Maryland, College Park. Betty holds an M.A.T. in English and Education from Wesleyan University and a bachelor's degree in English from Cornell University. She has nearly 30 years of experience in conducting human-factors studies and usability evaluations of user-interface designs for Federal agencies (e.g., FAA, NASA, U. S. Census Bureau). Betty has published in such journals as the *International Journal of Human-Computer Studies*, *Telematics and Informatics*, and the *International Journal of Aviation Psychology*. She has been a research psychologist at the Census Bureau since 1998, most recently managing staff and facilities of the Census Bureau's Usability Laboratory.

Greg Nuyens is founder and CEO of Teleplace, provider of virtual spaces for enterprise collaboration. In more than twenty five years experience as a high tech entrepreneur, he has served in a variety of executive roles. He has served as CEO of Devicescape (backed by Kleiner Perkins and August Capital) CTO of Neomar (now part of Motorola), and chief technologist at Inktomi. Earlier roles included co-founder at Ilog (now part of IBM), director at Sun Microsystems and researcher at Xerox PARC and Xerox AI Systems. Greg holds a MS in Computer Science from Stanford University and a BS in Computer Science from Carleton University.

Theresa A. (Teri) O'Connell earned a Masters degree in information science at the University of Maryland, College Park and a BS in languages and linguistics from Georgetown University. A senior usability engineer in the Usability Group at the U.S. National Institute of Standards and Technology (NIST) in Gaithersburg, MD, she researches usability metrics and evaluation methods for innovative technologies. She has led usability engineering in more than 100 software development projects in North America and Europe. Her more than 20 years of experience span both government and the private sector. She has worked, presented and published in a variety of areas, including digital native interaction with digital games; discourse analysis of gameplay chat; integrating software engineering and usability engineering processes; internationalization and localization of Web sites; and human interaction with natural language technologies, complex visualizations, analytic tools and personal autonomous intelligent agents. Journals where she has published include *Journal of Virtual Worlds Research*, *Journal of Informatics Education Research* and *IEEE Computer Graphics and Applications*.

Michael Osias is an Information Technology Architect with IBM, having joined the company in 1997 specializing in distributed computing, virtual worlds, and evolutionary holographic artificial neural networks and distributed multiagent systems.

Michael Peters is a Partner at Oculus Info Inc. responsible for commercial visualization solutions with more than ten years of experience in financial visualizations for risk management, portfolio analysis and trading systems for major financial institutions and Global F100 firms. Peters is interested in the application of visualization to commercial business needs, ranging from the best utilization of the very latest web technologies, to visual integration of disparate data and visualization of simulation models. He is also experienced in the application of visualization for supply chain management, GIS and web site analysis.

Cindy Pickering is an IT Senior Principal Engineer for Intel Corp., focusing on global team collaboration, including people, process, and technology. Her research combines needs assessment, new concept development, emerging usage-models definition, and enabling architecture and technology exploration.

Robert Rice is an author, technology entrepreneur, futurist, as well as a recognized leader and pioneer in mobile augmented reality. With more than 17 years of experience he is a passionate innovator and is continually seeking to advance the state-of-the-art of dynamic and interactive technologies. Robert collaborated on the first conversion of a single player PC game to a virtual reality game in 1992 at the first virtual reality entertainment company in the US and is currently developing a global augmented reality network platform. Over the last two decades he has gained broad and in-depth experience in design, development, production, project direction and executive management with a number of technology start-ups. Recognized as an "Internet Gaming Pioneer" by *Advertising Age* magazine in 1996, Robert was also called "a Founding Father of the Digital Nation" in 1998 by *The Raleigh News & Observer* while he was designing immersive interfaces and next-generation concepts for a 3D internet. He is an authority on mobile augmented reality, persistent immersive environments, virtual reality and worlds, massively multiuser online games, and simulations.

Brian S. Rogers holds a bachelor's degree in biotechnology from Stevenson University. After graduating from Stevenson, he worked for four years as a technician at the Wilmer Eye Institute at the Johns Hopkins University School of Medicine, where he studied oxidative stress-induced retinal degeneration. During this time, Rogers took graduate courses at Johns Hopkins University and completed an independent study project in developmental biology and bioinformatics as a Howard Hughes Digital Scholar. Rogers is currently in his third year of the MD/PhD program at the Drexel University College of Medicine.

Renate Roske-Shelton holds a Ph.D. in Cognitive/Engineering Psychology from New Mexico State University, Las Cruces, as well as an M.S. in General Psychology and a B.T. in Air Traffic Control/Education/Mathematics from the University of Alaska, Anchorage. She has over 20 years of experience working in major government research laboratories on cutting-edge technology projects. Currently she works on design and usability testing of Federal Web 2.0 spaces with the Food and Drug Administration's (FDA) Web Transformation and Communication Teams in Rockville and Silver Spring, Maryland. Renate's scholarly publications include articles on menu structures and cognitive Just-Noticeable-Differences (C-JNDs) in the *International Journal of Human-Computer Interaction* and the Human Factors *Bulletin*. In her early career, Renate conducted Aviation Safety research at NASA's Ames Research Center in their Human-Machine Interaction Group on Pilot/Cockpit Interfaces and Air Traffic Control advanced automation systems.

Dr. Maria T. Schultheis is an Associate Research Professor with appointments in the Department of Psychology and the School of Biomedical Engineering, Science and Health Systems at Drexel University. She also directs the Clinical Neuropsychology

Concentration of the Graduate Clinical Psychology Program. She receive a Masters in Biological Science, with a specialization in Neuroscience from Temple University and her PhD is in Clinical Neuropsychology from Drexel University. Dr. Schultheis' has over 12 years of clinical and research experience that has been focused on the rehabilitation of cognitively impaired populations, including traumatic brain injury, stroke and multiple sclerosis. Recently, she has focused on the development of new driving assessment protocols for individuals with disabilities. This includes research focusing on the application of Virtual Reality (VR) technology. Dr. Schultheis is also investigating the development of VR as a tool for ecologically valid assessment and retraining of everyday activities in rehabilitation. Dr. Schultheis' overall interest is in research related to the investigation and development of methodologies that have functional significance and can improve the quality of everyday life for persons with disabilities. She has published over 50 peer-reviewed publications and has recently published the book entitled *The Handbook for the Assessment of Driving Capacity*. In 2007 she received the American Psychological Association Early Career Award for Division 40 (Clinical Neuropsychology).

Dr. Lisa K. Simone has engineering degrees in Electrical and Biomedical Engineering from Rutgers University, and an MS in Management of Technology from University of Pennsylvania and The Wharton School. With 20 years of industry research and development experience, she has designed biomedical, scientific, robotic motion control, and wireless devices. Dr. Simone's research has been published in journals such as *Journal of Head Trauma Rehabilitation*, *Journal of Neuroscience Methods* and *CyberPsychology & Behavior* with funding from the National Institutes of Health. She is the author of a collection of engineering mysteries entitled, *If I Only Changed the Software, Why is the Phone on Fire?* She recently spent 2 years redesigning a college curriculum for biomedical engineering design at New Jersey Institute of Technology and consults through her company, Simone Concepts.

Vadim Slavin is a Senior Software Engineer, a Principal Investigator, and the Head of Human Systems Interaction group within Modeling, Simulation and Information Sciences Department at Lockheed Martin Space Systems' Advanced Technology Center. He graduated from Brown University with a Bachelor of Sciences in Math-Physics, Bachelor of Arts in Computer Science, and finally with a Master of Sciences degree in Computer Science. Having joined Lockheed Martin, Vadim has worked on a number of modeling and simulation projects for space industry customers as well as premier government research organizations. His research interests include human-computer interaction, immersive collaborative visualization environments, and semantic technologies for reasoning under uncertainty. Vadim serves on the board of several internal Lockheed Martin-wide working groups and has participated in NASA proposal reviews as a lead reviewer.

Dr. C.A.P. Smith has an Engineering degree from M.I.T. and a Ph.D. in Information Systems from the University of Arizona. He has more than 20 years of experience with research into decision-making in stressful conditions. He is an expert in the design of decision support systems and the application of Human Factors to Human-Computer Interfaces. Dr Smith's scholarly research has been published in numerous journals such as *Human Factors*, *Group Decision and Negotiation*, *International Journal of Human-Computer Studies*, and *International Journal of Human-Computer Interaction*. He recently spent 3 years working as a Senior Scientist for the US Navy's Space and Naval Warfare Systems Center where he managed several research and development projects.

Jeffrey M. Stanton, Ph.D. (University of Connecticut, 1997) is Associate Dean for Research and Doctoral Studies in the School of Information Studies at Syracuse University. Dr. Stanton's research focuses organizational behavior and technology, with his most recent projects examining how behavior affects information security and privacy in organizations. He is the author with Dr. Kathryn Stam of the book, *The Visible Employee: Using Workplace Monitoring and Surveillance to Protect Information Assets—Without Compromising Employee Privacy or Trust* (2006). Dr Stanton has also published scholarly articles in peer-reviewed journals, such as *Computers and Security, Communications of the ACM, Computers in Human Behavior,* the *International Journal of Human-Computer Interaction, Information Technology and People,* the *Journal of Information Systems Education,* the *Journal of Digital Information, Surveillance and Society and Behaviour & Information Technology*. He also has published several book chapters on privacy, research methods, and program evaluation. Dr. Stanton's research has been supported through 15 grants and supplements including the National Science Foundation's CAREER award.

Randy Stiles is the Deputy Department Manager for the Modeling, Simulation and Information Sciences department at the Lockheed Martin Space Systems Co. Advanced Technology Center (LMATC). A native of Montana, Randy graduated from Stanford University with a B.S.in Mathematical and Computational Sciences, and from Montana State University—Bozeman with an M.S. in Computer Science. Randy has led a variety of visualization and interaction research and development contracts involving human-autonomous systems interaction, and visualizing intelligence information and uncertainty, including the Office of Naval Research's Virtual Environments for Training (VET) project, the Intelligence Community's Advanced Research and Development Geospatial Intelligence Information Visualization (GI2VIS), DARPA Integrated Battle Command (IBC) course of action visualization, the NRO Director's Innovation Initiative Adversary Collection Environment (ACE), and a NASA Human & Robotic Technology Advanced Technology Initiative for telepresence control of adjustably autonomous systems.

Warren Tignor is a SAIC System Engineer with BA and MS degrees from the University of Maryland and American University, respectively. As part of an education and research project, he joined the International Systems Dynamics Society in 1998. Since his initial exposure to system dynamics, he has applied its theory and practice to numerous topics in the information systems field, and published results in the Proceedings of the International Systems Dynamics Society. He was selected to join the society's Policy Council for its 2007–2009 term. He recently completed a SAIC four year advanced research assignment for the US federal government where he provided system engineering and technical assistance support.

Tom Trinko received his BS from Cal Tech and his Ph.D. in high energy physics from the University of Wisconsin at Madison. Tom has worked operational research issues on a variety of programs. He has headed software efforts and worked on advanced visualization activities. He has taken time to write two programming books and a series of military and software related magazine articles. He is currently working for the Lockheed Martin Advanced Technology Centers Modeling Simulation & Information Sciences Department.

Dr. Russ Vane has a Ph.D. in Information Technology from the George Mason University. He is an expert in adversarial mathematics, extending game theory to account for limited information, as well as denial and deception. He is a follower of Jesus. He has led information fusion research projects. Russ has published in journals on decision theoretic software agents and modeling and simulation. He has delivered software in national command and control systems. Russ served as a US Armored Cavalry officer and designed commercially published board games. Previously, he earned a Masters degree in Information Sciences from University of Pennsylvania and an engineering degree from Johns Hopkins.

Ed Waltz is the Chief Scientist, Intelligence Solutions of BAE Systems Advanced Information Technologies where he conducts hard target intelligence research. He has led numerous hard target, human behavior and counter D&D studies and tool developments over the past decade for different agencies of the Intelligence Community and the Department of Defense. Mr. Waltz holds a BSEE from the Case Institute of Technology and an MS in Computer, Information and Control Engineering from the University of Michigan. He has over 35 years of experience in developing and deploying signal processing, data fusion and intelligence analysis capabilities. He is the author of *Knowledge Management in the Intelligence Enterprise* (Artech 2003), *Information Warfare Principles and Operations* (Artech 1998), coauthor of *Counterdeception Principles and Applications for National Security*, (Artech 2007) and *Multisensor Data Fusion* (Artech 1990), and coeditor of *Multisensor Data Fusion* (Kluwer 2001). He is also a recipient of the DoD Joseph Mignona Data Fusion Award (2004); he became a Veridian Technology Fellow in 2002 and a BAE Systems Engineering Fellow in 2009.

David Ward is an Advisory Software Engineer at InfoPrint Solutions Company, a joint venture between Ricoh and IBM Printing Systems Division. At IBM, he has worked on IBM's Advance Function Common Control Unit architecture. He is currently developing new technologies for the next generation of color printers. He has over 15 patents issued and pending. Dr. Ward has also conducted research in formal verification methods using Computational Tree Logic and has published several technical papers. He has a B.S.E.E degree from Rochester Institute of Technology and a M.S.E.E and Ph.D. in Electrical Engineering from Syracuse University and University of Colorado at Boulder, respectively,

William Wright is a Senior Partner at Oculus Info Inc. A researcher, innovator and practitioner in visualization since the late 1980's, he founded Visible Decisions in 1992 and co-founded Oculus Info Inc. in 2001. He works directly with major organizations in Washington, New York and elsewhere to help them apply visual analytic methods for competitive advantage. Bill has served as a DARPA and IARPA Principle Investigator on several research programs culminating in the successful transition of GeoTime, nSpace and the 4D component in CPOF. Bill was a contributor to "Illuminating the Path—The R+D Agenda for Visual Analytics". His current research interests include intelligent, mixed initiative, visual analytic systems that enhance human understanding and decision making. He has written over twenty papers on information visualization and visual analytics. Bill has a B.A.Sc. and M.A.Sc. in Systems Design Engineering from the University of Waterloo.

Foreword

You will be Superman. Or Superwoman.

That is not just wishful thinking. It is an inescapable reality. This new reality is afforded by *virtual* worlds. One of the more intriguing aspects of virtual worlds is their ability to allow you to bring together representations of the imagination with representations of reality. Within a virtual world, you *can* move faster than a speeding bullet, or use x-ray vision to see inside buildings.

Within the next twenty years we, the human race, will have attained many of Superman's powers and a number of others that he would love to have. But there is a small hitch. Once you embrace these new capabilities, you will not be able to give them up again. However, if you don't embrace them, you will find yourself as isolated as Robinson Crusoe on his island before Friday showed up. Everyone else will not just become Superman—they will be instantly and continuously collaborating with all of the other supermen in the world and you will soon be left far behind.

If you know where to look, you might notice that you are already in the process of this magical transformation—it permeates every part of your existence in some way, but you don't notice because it has been sneaking up on you over the last few decades. You may have noticed that you now have these super powers only because on occasion you find them to be missing.

How lost did you feel the last time you left your house forgetting your cellphone/ Blackberry/iPhone/laptop/Kindle? If you forgot your GPS, you may have literally become lost. Even though I know the way to my parents' house, last week my son borrowed my car (along with my GPS) and I had to actually remember how to get there. It wasn't that I didn't know, I had visited them hundreds of times without a GPS—it was just that I felt more secure knowing that I could make mistakes on the way and not be punished for it. I felt like I had my sense of location amputated, which was indeed the case.

Yes—I lost a sixth sense. It isn't built in like the others yet, but I have started to depend on knowing where I am in the world at any given moment in much the same way I depend on being able to hear what is going on around me. When humans can travel faster than a horse can run, and can fly faster than any bird, and find themselves doing this a great deal, and further find themselves almost immediately in new locations they have never been, location becomes a very important sense to have.

The kind of power that these extensions of our being give us is very much a drug and we even have withdrawal pains when we lose them. We love being superman—and we don't want to, or even can't go back to being our simple Clark Kent selves anymore. Try to give up your cell phone for a day. This is relatively easy, especially over the weekend. Try to give it up for a week or a month. Most people won't want to—or even from their point of view, they simply can't. It is essential for you to be able to perform your job, maintain your safety, or simply be instantly accessible to your spouse.

As noted by Marshall McLuhan in his book *Understanding Media*, these new ways of seeing and interacting have a profoundly deep impact on our definition of ourselves as humans. The very use of the medium changes us. The fact that I use a GPS to find my hotel is nowhere near as important as the idea that I use it to determine and understand my location and place in the world. I actually change how I think of myself and my abilities because I am using it. I understand the world around me in a much different way and so I make decisions differently. In some ways, the GPS is a tool that extends my abilities in much the same way that the first knife transformed a human's hand into an incredible instrument of destruction and creation. As noted above, however, the extension may be even deeper than just a tool. The subtitle of *Understanding Media* is *The Extensions of Man*. These technologies do indeed extend us in remarkable ways, and we easily incorporate these extensions into our lives and ourselves. Right now, I am on a flight from New York to San Francisco and not only do I have access to the Internet at 35,000 feet for the first time—including web browsing, YouTube videos and email, I have even been using a realtime 3D collaboration virtual space in a testing session with my colleagues. I think what is most remarkable was that no one else seemed to think it was all that amazing. The quality of this service is exceptional—not quite the high-speed cable connection I have at home, it does not have the same bandwidth, but the latency is almost as good as my home office, so realtime applications are quite responsive. The point is, yet another barrier has dropped in my ability to be virtually anywhere—I have added yet another super power, and over the next few months and years it will become uninteresting because I will assimilate it into how I define myself.

In 1968, Alan Kay had a vision of the future. Alan had seen the very first LCD displays—far too small to be usable, but demonstrating that they would in fact exist; he also understood Gordon Moore's law where we continue to see a doubling of the number of transistors in an integrated circuit in a fixed time for the same cost; and he may have had an even deeper understanding of Douglas Engelbart's ideas of augmenting human intelligence by bootstrapping ourselves from within a working system than even Engelbart did.

From these concepts, and a few others, Alan formed a vision of a personal computer that weighed less than two pounds, had a built-in megapixel display, and wireless connectivity. It was intended as a new kind of toy for children that allowed them to work together to explore and develop ideas. He called this machine the Dynabook, and he referred to what the children did with it as "hard fun"—a wonderful concept that Alan got from Seymour Papert. This simply meant that the children would use the system to not just learn about the world, they would use it to simulate it themselves. They would learn physics and mathematics not by reading about it, but by recreating a part of the real world inside the system with their friends and teachers. They would actually learn to understand the world they lived in by creating simulations of it. These simulations are true shared synthetic worlds.

What was most impressive however, was not just this vision. Alan and his team at Xerox PARC built what they referred to as the interim Dynabook, the Alto. Anyone who uses a PC or Macintosh today would feel quite at home working on the Alto because it is the machine that literally defined the PC and the Mac as we know them today. It had a mouse, again invented by Engelbart, it had a bitmap display, overlapping windows, pop-up menus, what-you-see-is-what-you-get text editing, laser printing, and it had ethernet connectivity. The only thing missing from this list is the Internet, but the people at PARC played a critical role there as well. In some ways, the Alto and the software behind it was even more advanced than what we use today, and this is because it fully embraced Engelbart's conception of the users being able to extend the system directly from within it. The Alto was programmed using a powerful object oriented language that was infinitely extensible and not only were the applications developed using it, the entire operating system was built with it. There were no real barriers between the applications and the frameworks upon which they ran. This was truly developing a system from the inside—using the tool to create and extend the tool itself. This is one of the things that Doug Engelbart meant by bootstrapping.

Alan Kay, and those who directly influenced him, invented the future, and it was such a powerful vision that even though many people, including Alan, are dissatisfied with the systems we have today, it has defined the greatest transformation of the way humans work and think in history.

And now we see, just over the horizon, the next big leap.

Synthetic worlds; or virtual worlds designed as augmentations to our physical worlds, will be at the heart of the next extension of a human, and humanity—in much the same way that Alan's Alto-based systems are the center of our computing world today. Our new peripheral senses, the GPS units, cell phones, computers, and the Internet will continue converging over the next years. New capabilities and extensions will be smoothly incorporated into the frameworks that we use on a daily basis—sometimes without us taking much note of them. All of these new senses will be accessed and controlled as part of an immersive synthetic world that dramatically extends our view of the world that we inhabit. Many of these extensions will simply be a far better user interface to our existing tools, some we don't have yet but are obvious, and some are simply beyond our ability to foresee.

Just as Alan and his team thought of the Alto as the interim Dynabook, I think we can describe the equivalent to the Alto for immersive collaborative synthetic worlds today—and perhaps this will allow us to understand the meaning of the "real thing" when it shows up and in so doing get a fuzzy view of what awaits us in the next transformation. Here then is a description of the system that we will all be using some day. Let's call the new system the DynaWorld.

The major components of this new system are that it augments your real world, it is implicitly collaborative, and it allows the users to dynamically create and share simulations. The actual interface to the DynaWorld is perhaps even simpler than the interface you use for your PC. The best interfaces are invisible—you don't even notice that they are there. Any interface you notice is actually a failure of design. The display of the DynaWorld will look much like a pair of wireless glasses that have the ability to project any image as an overlay on the real world—even replacing it completely if necessary.

The input from the user will come from two sources, audio and video. There won't be a keyboard or any kind of hand held device. Your voice, eyes, hands, arms, and body will be the controllers. Cameras that are mounted on the glasses will monitor both your movements and your eye motion to determine how to respond. You can select an item in your augmented reality simply by staring at it for an instant. Pointing at objects with your hand will actually have meaning, and of course you will be able to tell the system exactly what you want to do. The actual computing device will be a small unit that you might carry in your pocket, but it won't have any kind of controls itself, except perhaps a way to change batteries. In fact, this computing device only performs local computations that are required to maintain your augmented reality. Most of the heavy lifting will be performed by computation utilities, similar to water and electric utilities, that will permeate the world in much the same way the Internet has.

What is it like to use this? First, imagine every object, and every person in the world you exist in having a tag associated with it that you can access with a glance. You see someone new come into the room and immediately identify him and his relationship to your organization or to other people. When you walk by a restaurant on the street you can access its menu, specials of the day, and how it was rated by the people who just completed their meal. The system will be able to show you how to get to any location with building sized road signs and enhanced colored streets that ensure you never miss a turn.

This DynaWorld will give you x-ray vision—Superman again. You can look out at a cityscape and see where your friends and family are, and zoom in on them to see what they are up to. If you are a firefighter, you can instantly see where your fellow fireman is in a burning building. You can even jump directly into his head to see what his status is and if he needs assistance.

If you can become someone else and view their version of reality, why can't you become yourself as you were yesterday and review what you did then. Since we have built in video and audio input to this system, we can use this to record every moment of your life and play it back to you. We can Tivo your life. Beware of relying on this capability too much. As a wise person once said to me—you can be right, or you can be married.

The DynaWorld replaces your cell phone and video conferences. You can have a meeting with anyone at any time—even while walking down the street. You do this all of the time on your cell phone. Imagine contacting someone a continent away and having them join you on your walk. You can be sitting in a conference room where some of the participants are actually sitting beside you, and others are virtually present. Everyone looks like they are there, and will even make direct eye contact with you. You can even replace the real conference room with a virtual space that might contain the elements of the team's projects as well as the associated simulations. You will be able to watch as your colleagues work in this room and have the context of what they are working on and where they are focused. This is incredibly powerful, as it helps in understanding and working with that person.

But here is where it gets really interesting—and it is exactly the same vision Alan Kay had for his Dynabook. In the DynaWorld, you will be able to create synthetic worlds with your colleagues just by describing them. The system is listening and watching you, and will convert your ideas into a synthetic world as fast as you can describe it. You will define how the artifact you are creating will look, how it will work, how it will respond to external events. Once you have created it, you can actually try it out to see how it works—or doesn't. And best of all, your colleagues who are with you in this virtual space will be able to contribute ideas, make changes to your designs, and modify the system simultaneously. This act of invention is really a very high bandwidth conversation between the participants. The exchange of ideas is at a level that is profound, literally converting ideas into implementations, concepts into simulations.

Our synthetic worlds become the most powerful vehicle of human exploration and understanding ever created. The real power of this system is its ability to leverage the group, the class, the team to extend themselves far beyond what any individual would ever be able to accomplish. All of us is indeed more powerful than one of us. And if we each become a superman, then together we become something far greater.

Working Through Synthetic Worlds is an invitation to consider what the next steps might look like as we begin to use virtual worlds in real work. You will find there is no one vision, though there are converging themes and many intriguing possibilities. There is no reason to think this evolution is unlikely, or that we will not become dependent on them—no doubt being Superman will come with a cost! Enjoy the book, and join the contributors on exploring these new worlds.

David A. Smith

Preface

Working Through Synthetic Worlds. The title and the content of this book are intended to initiate a new wave of research to advance the general state-of-the-art and use of immersive worlds. Before we begin, however, we need to describe what we mean by "working" and "synthetic worlds."

Over the past several years, a number of new Internet based immersive worlds (i.e., virtual worlds) have grown in popularity. Second Life (www.secondlife.com) logs millions of simultaneous users on a daily basis. Massively Multi-User Online Games (MMOGs) such as World of Warcraft are becoming ubiquitous. It is clear that games and social interaction are greatly facilitated by virtual worlds but we believe that the time is right to start taking a serious look at the future potential of these environments beyond games and social networks. We need to ask questions like: Just what are virtual worlds good for? What value is there in these virtual communities and what potential value could there be for doing real work? Where might one strategically invest in research with these technologies to influence their development to make people more productive?

So by "working" we mean: How could virtual world technologies be used as a tool to assist in transforming the traditional workplace? How can we use them to facilitate information sharing and collaboration across a diverse workforce that might be geographically and temporally separated? What does a virtual environment afford that offers a favorable value proposition compared to the real world?

A common general term for immersive world technology is the Metaverse which can be partitioned into four sub-areas:

1. Virtual Reality—represents a fantasy world for role-playing, gaming, and social networking.
2. Mirror Worlds—provides a digital representation of the real world.
3. Augmented Reality—overlays the real-world with digital information.
4. Life Logging—stores personal real-world events for later sharing.

Unfortunately, performing "real" work does not fit completely into any of these sub-areas even though some work may rely on virtual reality or mirror worlds. The authors will introduce work environments that require complete in-world control over time, size, and levels of abstraction. These dynamically created (or synthesized) worlds will provide the foundation for extending current immersive worlds into the work domain. So how do we move from fantasy worlds to worlds for work?

While the technology of virtual worlds is rapidly maturing, research related to transforming it into a useful tool is lagging behind. Most research is documenting what has been done, or speculating what could be done, rather than asking what *should* be done. It is in this context that we asked our professional colleagues, in academia, in government, and in commercial ventures, "If you could work in a Synthetic World, what should it look like?"

We discovered immediately that our colleagues were brimming with ideas. Perhaps too many ideas! So, we started to constrain the question. We developed a set of instructions for prospective authors. These instructions included constraints on the formatting of the chapters, and the requirement to present their visions initially as a narrative. We redirected to other outlets a large number of proposals that sought to discuss gaming or social networking. About half of the initial proposals focused on the use of virtual environments for training. We encouraged these authors to look past the training or educational use of their synthetic world, towards a commercial application of the skill they sought to train. Since training is apparently a natural use of these technologies, we kept the best proposals of that genre, and we present them as one section of this book.

The result is a book that offers 20 distinct visions of the workplace of the future. And although the visions are completely original, and describe a large number of task domains, they share some remarkable similarities. We discuss one of these similarities, the ubiquitous presence of software agents, later in this preface.

We have designed this book to have a wide appeal. We expect that the information contained in this book will be accessible to academics, practitioners, managers, as well as people who are simply curious about what the future holds. Because the book deals with the application of technology to work, we expect that specific disciplines will have a special interest in the topic. These disciplines include both scientists and engineers involved with technology development (computer scientists, information scientists, computer engineers, human factors engineers, etc.) and also social, behavioral and cognitive scientists who are interested in the effects of technology on people and groups. We think this book would be an excellent resource for graduate seminars in any of these disciplines.

The format of the book was selected to maximize its accessibility to various user communities. We divided each chapter into three sections to enable efficient browsing for specific purposes. The first section of each chapter is a story about a day in the work life of a person in the year 2025. At some point in each story, the person is working in a Synthetic World. The stories present different visions of the ways that technology will influence our work lives. By browsing the stories, our readers can sample from among these visions, and decide for themselves which visions are likely to become reality. There are several common themes that emerged from these stories: What is the real value of a virtual environment for work? What roles will software agents play in this work environment? What is the unique contribution of the human?

The second section of each chapter is intended to be a scholarly examination of the vision illustrated by the story. In this section, the authors review the current literature related to the technologies described in their stories. In some cases, their stories describe tools and processes that are currently under development. In other cases, the technologies and affordances are novel. The goal is to provide the reader with estimates of which ideas are inevitable, possible, or unlikely. These second sections may be especially useful for graduate students, academics, and scientists who are looking for summaries of current research and citations for refereed publications. The references are listed at the end of each chapter.

The final section in each chapter provides prescriptions for managers, scientists, and engineers. We seek to answer the question, "How do we get there from here?" The authors provide their expert opinions regarding the relative importance of various research and development projects. To convert the visions described in the stories to reality will require expenditure of resources. Some of that effort will come from commercial enterprises, some may come from university laboratories, and some may require government support. What is the best way to allocate our scarce resources for research and development? We expect that these sections will be especially useful for managers of research and development. Finally, the story format itself was chosen to promote certain cognitive benefits. In the first chapter, we provide a scholarly essay outlining the reasons why stories can facilitate encoding and recall of detailed information.

As noted earlier, the popular use of virtual worlds has been for gaming and social interaction. Our intent is to look beyond play and entertainment to present a view of the future where synthetic worlds are being used for significant work. As such, we have selected five work thrust areas for grouping the chapters. Readers interested in specific themes may find it useful to read only a subset of the chapters.

The first section, Forecasting, explores how synthetic worlds could be used to construct and visualize possible future situations in several different business domains. Messinger and Ge begin this section by looking at how market research techniques will be impacted by making online communications more personal and vivid. This first chapter in the Forecasting group is somewhat longer than the others because we asked the authors to provide an especially detailed review of the literature. Scholars and academics may find this chapter useful as a general reference. Brath et al. explore the collaboration aspect of synthetic worlds for analyzing and making projections in the financial industry. Osias et al. presents a mirror world situation for monitoring the security of data centers. Next, we turn our attention to the physical world where Bodnar et al. address biological research and Tignor explores simulating environmental change. This section concludes with a look at synthetic worlds for working the interrelated problems of intelligence analysis, smart collection, and mission operations by Trinko et al.

The second section, Forensic Analysis, looks at reconstructing and understanding past events. Miller begins this section by presenting an environment that is rich in information providing the user with total situational awareness. What may be especially interesting to our readers is that Miller's Miramar synthetic world actually exists, albeit not in the highly developed form described in his story. Waltz follows this up with a description of recreating foreign situations to aid in national security policymaking. Rice concludes this section by combining synthetic world technology with augmented reality for crime scene analysis.

The next section, Cognitive Amplifiers, looks at how synthetic worlds can be used to enhance, augment, or otherwise expand the participant's personal skills. Kisiel leads off this section by describing how synthetic worlds can be used to gain experience in faster than real-time. Bringsjord explores using synthetic worlds for visualizing storylines so authors can directly interact with their characters during the writing process. Schultheis et al. show how synthetic world technologies can offer the opportunity for persons with disabilities to be accepted as part of the general public while minimizing the effect of the disabilities. Finally, Burley presents a case for using synthetic worlds to hone negotiating and consensus building techniques.

In the fourth section, we turn our attention to Training, an area that has already seen a lot of development over the past decade (e.g., serious games), but with a slight twist. Garretson and Denny describes a future where an airman enhances his skills using a combination of virtual and augmented reality. Goertzel and Cox et al. explore the training of avatars (supported by intelligent agent technology). McCuaig et al. conclude this section by exploring how synthetic worlds can help individuals learn and practice higher order thinking skills.

The final section, Infrastructure, takes a look behind the scenes at what it will take to ensure the security and usability of synthetic worlds. O'Connell et al. explore the future usability testing well before an actual product is built. In the final chapter of the book, Stanton reviews the history of multi-user worlds for clues to assist in identifying security issues in future virtual spaces.

One of the recurring themes that emerges in the visions for synthetic worlds is the extensive role for advanced automation, typically in the form of "agents". One of the more interesting aspects of agents, however, is that they mean different things to different people. It is worth a few moments here to consider how these different visions for agents are alike and different, how they relate to advanced automation, and ask: What should the role of agents be in synthetic worlds?

As you read through the book you will find some extremely ambitious roles for agents, they are often virtually indistinguishable from human entities working in a synthetic world. This vision of agents is not a new one, as it is a recurring theme in the science fiction literature. Unfortunately, there is still a huge leap of faith in bringing such a vision of agents into reality. On the other hand, there are other visions for agents that seem much more plausible. There are more limited concepts of agents where the agents serve as active context filters, where agents have an understanding of task context and selectively present changed information based on some level of understanding of likely relevance. Then there are agents as information gatherers; that is they are semi-autonomous constructs that look for information based upon information a user has previously used in performing a task or analysis. These agents are typically the logical products of workflow management tools.

Regardless of how we define agents, looking across the visions of synthetic worlds described in this volume, there are several issues that emerge in connection with them. The first is the relationship of the agents to the users they are working for or with. This is closely related to the work done in the late 1980's through the 1990's relating to philosophies of automation, and the appropriate degree of autonomy that should be granted to automation for various man-machine systems. Numerous attempts have been made to develop notional taxonomies for the application of automation in human-machine systems (e.g., Morrison and Gluckman 1993, Parasuraman et al. 2000, Hutchins et al. 1996). Parasuraman et al. (2000) proposed one of the first notional taxonomies for advanced automation.

In these articles, one of the recurring dimension of their taxonomies is the idea that Advanced Automation should refer to systems where the automation had equal status to that of the humans in the system, and had full autonomy to perform tasks with or without the knowledge of the human users of the system. Advanced automation gives the automation in a system the same status as the human users of that system. They share autonomy and authority.

In contrast, Decision Aiding is a concept where the automation is an active agent in facilitating the human processing of information by transforming it so as to highlight a predefined parameter of a complex system to elicit a required decision as determined by the system designer. In its simplest form, one could consider the advent of an automotive oil pressure "idiot light" as a decision aid designed to elicit a specific response from the operator as opposed to the pressure gauge that provides more subtle information. In the case of the warning light, the system designer has determined that the only thing the operator of the system needs to know is that there is a problem and the engine needs to be turned off.

Finally, Decision Support is a concept advocated in Hutchins et al. (1996), where the goal of the automation is to never take the decision-making away from the human decision maker. The goal of the automation is to get the decision-maker "in the ballpark", but never limit or force a specific decision. These differences in philosophy of automation are subtle but important. Hutchins et al. repeatedly found that effective decision support was much more accepted and useful to decision-makers in complex tactical weapons systems, even if the underlying algorithms were the same as those used in an automated or decision aiding system. In decision aiding, the automation has limited autonomy—there is usually an explicit contract between the human and the automation regarding roles and authorities. However, the automation can process data, use rules to infer new knowledge, and has the authority to take limited actions without explicitly consulting with the human users. Decision support may use many of the same underlying technologies as advanced automation, but the system is designed to never take decision-making away from the decision makers.

What does this suggest for agents? The view that agents will be synthetic, algorithmically based entities that wander around among humans in a synthetic world seems not just computationally difficult (extremely difficult), but also seems fraught with peril. It is unlikely that fully autonomous agents with equal status and authority are likely to be accepted in polite society—even a synthetic one. However, this same technology may prove critical to managing the astounding quantities of information implied by working in synthetic worlds. Agents derived from a user's activities, either explicitly created by the user or implicitly derived from workload, do seem plausible. Such agents would need to serve an advisory role where they track what has changed and perhaps seek out new information related to work a user has previously done in the synthetic world.

So, we suggest that as you read these different visions of the future, consider the implications of using automation in these various task domains. Does the use of automation create an unintended secondary task? Or, does the automation reduce the amount of low-level, repetitive work, thus freeing the human to perform more valuable tasks? We hope you derive as much enjoyment from reading this book as we did from creating it.

C.A.P. Smith
Kenneth W. Kisiel
Jeffrey G. Morrison

Chapter 1
An Essay on the Cognitive Benefits of Stories

C. A. P. Smith

A Story About Stories

A good friend of mine once told me that every good story should start with the words, "There I was…"

So, there I was, a young faculty member at the University of Montana who had through luck and slim virtue been offered the opportunity to ride aboard a Navy command ship, the *USS Coronado*. The *Coronado* was based out of San Diego, where it was the floating headquarters of the US Navy's 3rd Fleet. I had been conducting a series of studies on decision making under time pressure; this activity had led to an invitation to ride the command ship during a simulated warfare exercise.

The exercise lasted two weeks, during which I was allowed to wander freely aboard the ship, attend the various meetings and briefings, interview the fleet staff, and otherwise make a nuisance of myself. I had a wonderful time, and frankly I don't recall very much about it. But this one thing is firmly embedded in my memory: the evening meals.

For sailors, there isn't much to do aboard ship except eat, sleep, and work. I noted that the officers and senior enlisted personnel that comprised the Fleet staff tended to sleep about 4 hours per night, minimize their time spent eating, and devote the remainder of each day to work. These men and women typically had the equivalent of two full-time jobs as well as some ancillary duties. So, they didn't have a lot of time for eating. The exception was the evening meal.

Each evening, the commander of 3rd Fleet, VADM Herb Browne, would attend a formal dinner in the Flag Mess. The Navy is big on protocol; as a visiting professor, I was granted the courtesy of eating in the Flag Mess. On the first night, I showed up for dinner, and discovered that I was seated immediately to the admiral's right. We made small talk during the meal, and when the dessert was served, the admiral leaned over to take a good look at my name badge, and then he asked me something like,

> "What is an egghead from the University of Montana doing on my ship?"

I'm sure his actual words were more polite—but I got the gist. I responded in a properly sycophantic manner with,

> "Well sir, I have been conducting research on decision making under time pressure.
> And I'm here to see how the experts do it."

Everyone at the table, which included most of the senior staff, had been observing this exchange. The admiral swept his gaze around the table, and looked back to me, and said,

> "Decision making under time pressure, eh? Let me tell you a story about the time I was captain of the John F. Kennedy. There I was, …"

And the admiral proceeded to tell us all a story about a particularly hair-raising incident from his earlier career during which he came very close to sinking a nuclear aircraft carrier and creating the world's most heinous ecological disaster while sailing peacefully in the Red Sea. The admiral finished his story of near-disaster by acknowledging a variety of contributing factors to what was *almost* an example of really bad decision making under time pressure.

You see, admirals don't get to be admirals by making mistakes. In the Navy, decisions are frequently judged by the quality of their outcomes rather than the quality of their process. During subsequent meals, I came to understand that the admiral's story of near disaster was a form of organizational memory. The admiral used me as a foil to tell a story for the benefit of his junior officers. The point of the story was the self-criticism offered at the end, in which the admiral described a few things he might have done differently if he'd had the benefit of his current wisdom.

As I said, I don't recall much about those two weeks on the *USS Coronado*. But I remember the admiral's story almost word for word. This experience was an eye-opener for me. I resigned my tenure at the university, and was hired as a scientist for the Space and Naval Warfare Systems Center—SPAWAR for short. During three years at SPAWAR, I had several additional opportunities to ride ships, and visit other shore-based command centers. I repeatedly witnessed storytelling by senior officers in those mealtime settings.

For example, on another cruise aboard the *Coronado*, I was seated next to Major General Charles Bolden, USMC. The general was wearing aviator's wings; at some point I asked him if he was a fixed-wing pilot. Without missing a beat, the general acknowledged that he was a fixed-wing pilot, and proceeded to tell me some stories about his days at the Naval Test Pilot School in Paxtuxent River, Maryland. Again, the stories took the form of interesting events that were almost tragic. And although the general was talking directly to me, I know that I wasn't the only one listening because the next day a young officer approached me and asked, "Did you know that General Bolden flew four Space Shuttle missions, and was the commander for two of them?" Fixed-wing pilot, indeed.

Over the years, I've written dozens of scholarly articles about decision making and computer-aided decision support. But, I think one of the most important observations that I've ever made is one about which I've never written: the role of stories as an aid to memory. In the essay that follows, I explain some of the reasons why stories are important as a method for conveying information. And hopefully, my own anecdotes will help the readers to remember that they can always pull this volume off their shelves when they need access to the details.

Research On Storytelling

Storytelling has been used as a form of communication since ancient times, beginning with chants to convey complex multi-layered stories (Greene 1996, Cooper and Simonds 2003). The first written record of a storytelling activity was found in an Egyptian papyrus called the Westcar papyrus, recorded sometime between 2000 and 1300 BCE (Greene 1996), where King Khufu heard tales told by his sons about the wonders of other days and the doings of magicians. Nietzke (1988) calls storytelling the "ancient new method" because they have been used for centuries and teachers are rediscovering the benefits that storytelling can have for learning.

Other terms that are synonymous with storytelling include narratives, stories, histories, fables, epic, and folktales (Gudmundsdottir 1995). These all refer to a basic structure that: 1) includes accounts of action usually involving humans or humanized animals; 2) develops characters in the story; 3) has a beginning, middle, and an end; and 4) contains parts held together by a plot. A number of taxonomies have been proposed to classify the near infinite varieties of stories (Polkinghorne 1988). For example, Schank (1990) describes four types of stories. Gergen and Gergen (1986) have devised a system with three categories. Frye's (1957) story taxonomy includes 5 categories: myth, romance, high mimetic, low mimetic, and ironic.

There are a couple of important points to make about these schemes. First, the fact that scholars can't agree on a single taxonomy hints that none of these are universal for all humans across all contexts. So, the categories might be dependent on factors related to personal experiences such as culture or professional training. But, second, the consistent attempt by scholars to identify categories suggests that such categories do exist, and may be nearly universal within their target population. That is, humans in broad categories may have been exposed to certain types of stories so often that they have become able to recognize and anticipate the story elements. That is certainly the case in the military, with respect to the near-disaster story format. Aircraft pilots tell similar stories; they call it hangar-flying. Hunters and fishermen talk about, "the one that got away."

These classifications help organize the stories either in published or oral forms. We, as human beings, seem to have an instinctive desire to share our feelings and experiences (Greene 1996, Polkinghorne 1988, Schank and Abelson 1995). We tell stories in order to make sense of our world; we listen to other people's stories in order to understand them. Everyone has a story. Some researchers (e.g., Schank and Abelson 1995) postulate that virtually all human knowledge is based on stories. Stories have the power to capture and hold attention (Raines and Isbell 1994). Detailed information can be recalled from a story because individuals can internalize and identify with the story (Polkinghorne 1988).

Because storytelling is all encompassing in everyday lives, it's not surprising to find applications of storytelling techniques in various settings. For example, the court systems utilize storytelling in criminal trials to process vast amounts of information and to make complicated judgments based on governing rules (Pennington and Hastie 1995, Bennett 1997). Organizations draw on storytelling to communicate corporate cultures and transfer knowledge in the workplace (e.g., Swap, Leonard, Shields, and

Abrams 2004, Snowden 2004). Consumer marketing uses storytelling to enhance brand connection to a product (Escalas 2004). In career development, storytelling has been used to help reshape career goals (Riendeau 2004). The counseling professions use storytelling in trauma recovery (e.g., Leseho 2005), grief and bereavement process (e.g., Bosticco 2005), anger-management (e.g., Leseho and Marshall 1999) and in coping skill development of juveniles (e.g., Haggerty 2005). Medical professionals affirm the healing power of story and storytelling (McCaleb 2003, Coles 1990, May 1991). The ubiquitous use of storytelling shows its collective appeal to the workings of the human mind.

Despite its universal appeal, stories or narratives have only recently been examined in the cognitive sciences (Polkinghorne 1988, Jonassen and Hernandez-Serrano 2002). The terminology "narrative intelligence", born out of work in AI, describes how narratives intersect with intelligence (Mateas and Sengers 2006). It stresses the importance of narratives in sense making. Schank and Abelson (1995), early proponents of the importance of storytelling in human cognition, believe that it is more important to study the cognitive and social nature of storytelling than to pursue abstract, formal and compartmentalized domains of human information processing. They believe "stories about one's experiences and the experiences of others are the fundamental constituents of human memory, knowledge and social communication." (p. 1). Virtually all human memory is based on stories built around past experiences. What we know, learn, and understand is structured in stories. Human memory is a collection of thousands of stories we remember through experience; stories we remember because we heard them or stories we remember because we composed them. Our knowing is based on stories.

Cognition and Storytelling

Research in memory and learning has substantially improved our understanding of human information processing. Such research has generated a variety of theories and models describing how people process information. The capacity or resource models (e.g., Kahneman 1973, Navon and Gopher 1979, Wickens and Liu 1988) view the human system as having a limited reservoir of resources that are quantifiable, divisible, allocatable, and scarce. Multiple resource theory proposes that there are separate and finite reservoirs of cognitive resource (Wickens 1984; 2002), some of which are potentially available simultaneously for different purposes. There have been several attempts to characterize the interactions among our cognitive processes (e.g., Card, Moran, and Newell 1983). One such model that has become widely uses is the EPIC model (Kieras and Meyer 1997, Figure 1.1). The model shows various cognitive resources, including different types of memory (long-term and separate working memory stores for visual and auditory working memory), separate processors for perception, motor control, and an executive "cognitive" processor. Working memory refers to temporary or "short-term" memory that humans use to buffer our recent perceptions, or to gather our recollections from "long-term" memory.

It requires some cognitive effort to retrieve memories from long-term storage. Once those long-term memories are "active" in short-term memory, it also takes some ongoing

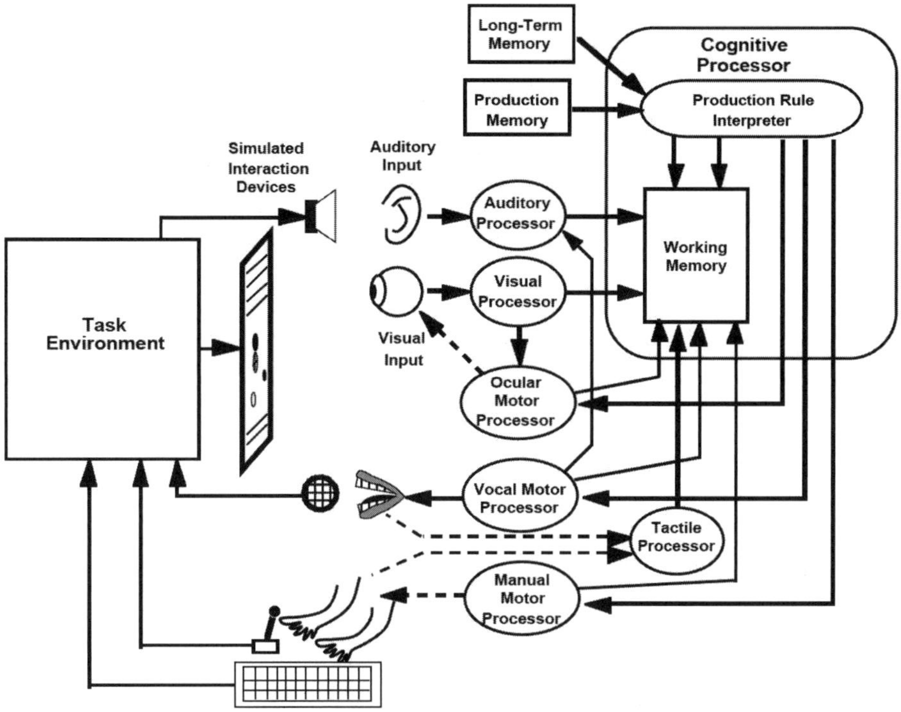

Figure 1.1 EPIC Model of Memory (from Kieras and Meyer 1997)

effort to keep them active. These efforts are expended by the cognitive processor, and are generally referred to as "attention." Humans have a finite amount of attention resource, which can be consciously directed to a variety of tasks, such as retrieving memories from long-term storage, maintaining memories in short-term storage, directing sensory activities (e.g., looking or listening carefully), and controlling motor processes. We have difficulty dividing attention among several tasks, or attending to all the information provided by the senses (Broadbent 1958, Treisman 1969). As a result, we often do not perceive most of the information that is available to us (Lavie 1995). As Nobel Laureate Herb Simon has said, "a wealth of information creates a poverty of attention." (Varian 1995). In the following paragraphs, I offer an explanation why stories have the potential to mitigate the limitations of our cognitive resources.

The presence of separate short-term memory stores has received significant recent support (Baddeley 1992; 1998, Baddeley, Chincotta, Adlam 2001, Wickens 2002, Wickens and Liu 1988). Baddeley's terminology has been generally adopted as the standard; he refers to these separate resources as "visuo-spatial" and "articulatory-loop" memory. While Chase and Simon (1973a; 1973b) adopted Miller's (1956) estimate for the size of each short-term memory store as about 7 ± 2 items, more recently, the size of the visuo-spatial store has been estimated as a maximum of 4 items (Zhang and Simon 1985, Gobet and Clarkson 2004, Gobet and Simon 2000). These limitations are additive; it is possible to simultaneously hold about 4 items in visuo-spatial memory while holding approximately 7 items in articulatory-loop memory.

The advantage of long-term memory is that we do not have to constantly rehearse information to keep it in storage. In addition, there is no practical limit on the amount of information we can store in long-term memory. To make use of this information in long-term memory, we must move it into our working memory, using a process called retrieval. The quality of retrieval in long-term memory depends on several factors including how the information was encoded, and what type of prompt is used for retrieval.

One of the most influential cognitive concepts in delineating our knowledge structure is the idea of schema (e.g., Bartlett 1932, Rumelhart and Norman 1981, Driscoll 2000). Researchers have used other terminology to denote the conceptual idea of a schema (Derry 1996), such as frame (Tannen 1993), script (Schank and Abelson 1977), and template (Gobet 2005). A number of definitions have been given varying in their specificity; schemata can generally be defined as structures or frameworks for representing the generic concepts stored in memory. According to schema theory, knowledge is put into units called schemata (e.g., Schank 1990; 1999, Schank and Abelson 1995; Brenner 1998) and that schemata are used to process incoming information and to interpret the world (Rumelhart 1980).

These schemata represent concepts related to one's environment and are built through experiences. A person's cognitive structure is organized in an interrelated network of knowledge and experiences—organized in memory through a system of categories and subcategories (Snyder 1986). For example, an individual's schema for airplane probably has "core" categories for wings, engine, fuselage, and "flies in the air." Within a category, we may have concept "slots" for additional information. New experiences are processed according to how they fit into existing schemata. What we remember is influenced by what we already know by the schemata we possess.

According to Schank (1990), schemata are dynamic. We are constantly building new and modifying existing schemata. Even when information presented is limited in detail, we can still abstract the essence of the meaning. For example, when we see a very rudimentary outline of an owl, we can recognize that it is an owl. Schemata are important not just in interpreting information, but also in encoding and decoding how that information is processed. When we attend a wedding, we know what to expect and how to behave. We have a variety of schemata—about what we should do in restaurants, classrooms, and various social interactions. We also have schema for stories (Schank and Abelson 1995, Schank 1999, Price and Driscoll 1997, Halliday and Hassan 1989).

Story schema serve to facilitate both encoding and retrieval. During encoding of the source, the schema acts as a general framework within which comprehension processes take place. This framework serves several functions (Mandler and Johnson 1977). First, it directs attention to certain aspects of the incoming material. For example, statements about the type of story, such as folktale, cue the person the expectation of the story format; they warn the listener that certain facts should be kept in mind. Second, the schema helps the person keep track of the progression of events in the story. This monitoring process creates a summary that increases the predictability of what will immediately follow. Third, the framework tells the listener when some part of the story is complete and can therefore be stored, or is incomplete and therefore must be held until more material has been encoded. All these functions help to reduce the workload on the working memory, thereby, facilitating comprehension. In summary, information that is presented as a story is easier to recall and less effortful to encode.

There is another benefit from stories: they permit rapid encoding of new information. This is a side-benefit of our familiarity with stories. That is, we are all experts with stories. It has been noted that experts in various domains vastly outperform novices in the recall of meaningful material coming from their domain of expertise. To account for this result, Chase and Simon (1973a; 1973b) proposed that experts acquire a vast database of chunks, containing, as a first estimate, 50,000 chunks. When presented with material from their domain of expertise, experts recognize chunks and place a pointer to them in short-term memory. These chunks, each of which contains several elements that novices see as units, allow experts to recall information well beyond what non-experts can recall (Simon 1974). However, recent intensive research in skilled memory has shown that parts of the original chunking model must be incorrect (Gobet and Simon 1996a). Experts can increase the size of their chunks based on new information; effectively increasing short-term memory (Gobet and Simon 1998). Gobet and Simon (1996b) have also demonstrated that the time required to encode and retrieve chunks is much shorter than previously believed. Templates allow rapid encoding and retrieval from long-term memory of more data than chunks (10–15 items as opposed to 4–5 items). Templates are retrieved from long-term memory in at least an order of magnitude less time (sometimes two orders of magnitude less time) than other long-term memory structures, i.e., 200 milliseconds (Gobet 2005). In other words, information presented in a story can be encoded at about the same rate that we can talk or read.

The fact that a story can facilitate encoding of information doesn't necessarily imply that it *will*. There are several other factors that influence encoding and recall. Nevertheless, if one is sufficiently motivated to remember something, and if the information is presented in a story format with which one has plenty of experience, then the presentation of that information in a story format should reduce the cognitive effort required to encode it into long term memory.

I assume that this is why I can remember the admiral's story after so many years. Although I have never served in the military, I have read extensively in the military memoir genre. And I happen to be a pilot, a hunter, and a fisherman. As mentioned previously, these groups tend to share stories with similar structures. I just happened to have the correct story template. So, when the admiral told his story, I was able to encode the important details in long term memory at the same rate the story was told. And besides, the admiral gave us a cue which template to expect when he began his story with, "There I was..."

And Now, the Rest of the Story

The remaining chapters of this book each begin with a story. These stories have a consistent format—they are a type of near-term science fiction. Each story describes a day in the work life of a person in the year 2025, sixteen years in the future at the time these stories were written. Sixteen years is sufficient for several cycles of Moore's law to apply: the authors were instructed to consider a near future in which computer processing power, network bandwidth, and display resolutions were vastly superior to what is currently available. Within this consistent framework, the authors were given license to imagine how work will be conducted within a virtual world. What affordances are provided by the virtual nature of transactions within the Synthetic World? What is the unique value of the human contribution in the virtual workplace? The stories provide a vehicle to illustrate our authors' answers to these questions.

Hopefully, these stories will serve their intended purpose: to facilitate the readers' abilities to compare and contrast these different visions of the future, and to provide a consistent template that reduces the effort needed to absorb the wealth of technical information provided.

Enjoy.

References

Baddeley, A. (1992). "Working Memory," *Science*, 255(5044):556–559.

Baddeley, A. (1998). "Recent Developments in Working Memory," *Current Opinion in Neurobiology*, 8(2):234–238.

Baddeley, A., Chincotta, D., and Adlam, A. (2001). "Working memory and the control of action: Evidence from task switching," *Journal of Experimental Psychology: General*, 130:641–657.

Bartlett, F.C. (1932). *Remembering*. Cambridge, UK: Cambridge University Press.

Bennett, W.L. (1997). Storytelling in criminal trails: A model of social judgment. In L.P. Hinchman and S.K. Hinchman (eds.), *Memory, Identity, Community: The Idea of Narrative in the Human Sciences*. NY: State University of New York Press.

Bosticco, C. (2005). Narratives and story telling in coping with grief and bereavement. *Omega: Journal of Death and Dying*, 51(1):1–16.

Brenner, S. L. (1998). Storytelling and story schema: A bridge to listening comprehension through retelling. *Dissertation Abstracts International Section A: Humanities and Social Sciences*, 58(12-A):4599.

Broadbent, D. E. (1958). *Perception and Communication*. London: Pergammon Press.

Card, S., Moran, T., and Newell, A. (1983). *The Psychology of Human-Computer Interaction*, Lawrence Erlbaum Associates, Hillsdale, NJ.

Chase, W. G., and Simon, H. A. (1973a). "Perception in Chess," *Cognitive Psychology*, 4:55–81.

Chase, W. G., and Simon, H. A. (1973b). The mind's eye in chess. In W. G. Chase (Ed.), *Visual Information Processing* (Chapter 5). New York: Academic Press.

Coles, R. (1990). *The Call of Stories: Teaching and the Moral Imagination*. Boston: Houghton Mifflin.

Cooper, P.J., and Simonds, C.J. (2003). *Communication for the Classroom Teacher*. Boston: Allyn and Bacon Publisher.

Derry, S. (1996). "Cognitive Schema Theory in the Constructivist Debate." *Educational Psychologist*, 31(3/4):163–174.

Driscoll, M.P. (2000). "Psychology of Learning for Instruction and Policies." *Journal of Adolescent Health*, 12(8), Special Issue: Adolescents at Risk, 630–637.

Escalas, J.E. (2004). "Narrative Processing: Building Consumer Connections to Brands." *Journal of Consumer Psychology*, 14(1–2):168–180.

Frye, N. (1957). *The Anatomy of Criticism*. Princeton, N.J.: Princeton University Press.

Gergen, K.J., and Gergen, M.M. (1986). Narrative forms and the construction of psychological science. In T.R. Sarbin (ed.), *Narrative Psychology: The Storied Nature of Human Conduct*, 22–44. New York: Academic Press.

Gobet, F. (2005). "Chunking Models of Expertise: Implications for Education." *Applied Cognitive Psychology*, 19:183–204.

Gobet, F., and Clarkson, G. (2004). "Chunks in Expert Memory: Evidence for the Magical Number Four… or is it Two?," *Memory*, 12:732–747.

Gobet, F., and Simon, H.A. (1996a). "Templates in Chess Memory: A Mechanism for Recalling Several Boards," *Cognitive Psychology*, 31:1–40.

Gobet, F., and Simon, H.A. (1996b). "Recall of Rapidly Presented Random Chess Positions is a Function of Skill," *Psychonomic Bulletin and Review*, 3:159–163.

Gobet, F. and Simon, H. A. (1998). "Expert Chess Memory: Revisiting the Chunking Hypothesis," *Memory*, 6:225–255.

Gobet, F. and Simon, H. A. (2000). "Five Seconds or Sixty? Presentation Time in Expert Memory," *Cognitive Science*, 24(4):651–682.

Greene, E. (1996). *Art of Storytelling: Art and Technique*. Westport, CT: Libraries Unlimited.

Gudmundsdottir, S. (1995). The narrative nature of pedagogical content knowledge. In H. McEwan, and K. Egan, (Eds.), *Narrative in Teaching, Learning, and Research*, 24–38. New York: Teachers College Press.

Haggerty, N.K. (2005). "Increasing Self-managed Coping Skills though Social Stories and Apron Storytelling." *Teaching Exceptional Children*, 37(4):40–47.

Halliday, M.A.K. and Hasan, R. (1989). *Language, Context, and Text: Aspects of Language in a Social-Semiotic Perspective*. New York: Oxford University Press.

Jonassen, D.H., and Hernandez-Serrano, J. (2002). "Case-based Reasoning and Instructional Design: Using Stories to Support Problem Solving." *Educational Technology Research and Development*, 50(2):65–77.

Kahneman, D. (1973). *Attention and Effort*. Englewood Cliffs, NJ: Prentice-Hall.

Kieras, D. E., and Meyer, D. E. (1997). "An Overview of the EPIC Architecture for Cognition and Performance with Application to Human-computer Interaction." *Human-Computer Interaction*, 12(4):391–438.

Lavie, N. (1995). "Perceptual Load as a Necessary Condition for Selective Attention," *Experimental Psychology: Perception and Performance*, 21(3):451–468.

Leseho, J. (2005). " 'Listen and I Tell You Something': Storytelling and Social Action in the Healing of the Oppressed." *British Journal of Guidance and Counseling*, 33(2):175–184.

Leseho, J., and Marshall, A. (1999). "Dealing with Angry Students: A Qualitative Study with Implications for School Counselors." *Professional School Counseling*, 3(2):91–100.

Mandler, J.M., and Johnson, N.S. (1977). "Remembrance of Things Parsed: Story Structure and Recall." *Cognitive Psychology*, 9(1):111–151.

Mateas, M., and Sengers, P. (2006). Narrative intelligence. In M. Mateas. and P. Sengers, *Narrative Intelligence: Advances in Consciousness Research*. PA: John Benjamins Publishing Company.

May, R. (1991). *A Cry for Myth*. N.Y: Norton Publishing.

McCaleb, J.L. (2003). "Story Medicine." *English Journal*, 93(1):66–72.

Miller, G. A. (1956). "The Magical Number Seven, Plus or Minus Two: Some Limits on Our Capacity for Processing Information," *The Psychological Review*, 63:81–97.

Navon, D., and Gopher, D. (1979). "On the Economy of the Human Processing System," *Psychological Review*, 86:214–253.

Nietzke, D. (1988). "The Ancient New Method." *The Clearinghouse*, 61:419–421.

Pennington, N. and Hastie, R.W. (1995). "Cognitive Approaches to Judgment and Decision Making." *Psychology of Learning and Motivation*, 32:1–31.

Polkinghorne, D. (1988). *Narrative Knowing and the Human Sciences*. Albany: State University of New York Press.

Price, E., and Driscoll, M.P. (1997). "An Inquiry into the Spontaneous Transfer of Problem Solving Skill." *Contemporary Educational Psychology*, 22:472–494.

Raines, S.C., and Isbell, R.T. (1994). "The Child's Connections to the Universal Power of Story." *Childhood Education*, 70:164–170.

Riendeau, R.J. (2004). "Life Storied: What are the Key Learning Schemas Shaped by Storytelling and Metaphors in Downsized, White Male Executives 45–60 Years of Age?" *Dissertation Abstracts International: Section B: The Sciences and Engineering,* 65(7-B), 2005.

Rumelhart, D.E. (1980). Schemata: The building blocks of cognition. In R.J. Spiro, B.C. Bruce, and W.F. Brewer (eds.), *Theoretical Issues in Reading Comprehension* (33–58). Hillsdale, NJ: Erlbaum.

Rumelhart, D.E., and Norman, D. A. (1981). Analogical processes in learning. In J. R. Anderson (ed.), *Cognitive Skills and Their Acquisition*. Hillsdale, NJ: Erlbaum.

Schank, R.C. (1990). *Tell Me a Story: A New Look at Real and Artificial Memory.* New York, NY: Charles Scribner.

Schank, R.C. (1999). *Dynamic Memory Revisited.* Cambridge, New York: Cambridge University Press.

Schank, R.C., and Abelson, R.P. (1977). *Scripts, Plans, Goals, and Understanding.* Hillsdale, New Jersey: L. Erlbaum Associates.

Schank, R.C., and Abelson, R.P. (1995). Knowledge and memory: The real story. In R.S. Wyer, Jr (ed.), *Knowledge and Memory: The Real Story*. Hillsdale, New Jersey: L. Erlbaum Associates.

Simon, H.A. (1974). "How Big is a Chunk?," *Science*, 183:482–488.

Snowden, D. (2004). Narrative patterns: The perils and possibilities of using story in organizations. In E. Lesser and L. Prusak (eds.), *Creating Value with Knowledge: Insights from the IBM Institute for Business Value*. England: Oxford University Press.

Snyder, B.S. (1986). *A Schema-theoretic View of Reading: An Application in a Seventh-grade Social Studies Classroom*. Unpublished Doctoral Dissertation. University of Akron.

Swap, W., Leonard, D., Shields, M., and Abrams, L.C. (2004). Using mentoring and storytelling to transfer knowledge in the workplace. In E. Lesser and L. Prusak (eds.), *Creating Value with Knowledge: Insights from the IBM Institute for Business Value*. England: Oxford University Press.

Tannen, D. (1993). *Framing in Discourse*. New York: Oxford University Press.

Treisman, A.M. (1969). "Strategies and Models of Selective Attention." *Psychological Review*, 76:282–299.

Varian, H. (1995). "The Information Economy: How Much Will Two Bits be Worth in the Digital Marketplace?," *Scientific American*, 200–201.

Wickens, C.D. (1984). Processing resources in attention. In R. Parasuraman and R. Davies (Eds.), *Varieties of Attention* (63–101). Orlando, FL: Academic Press.

Wickens, C.D. (2002). "Multiple Resources and Performance Prediction," *Theoretical Issues in Ergonomic Science*, 3:159–177.

Wickens, C.D., and Liu, Y. (1988). "Codes and Modalities in Multiple Resources: A Success and Qualification," *Human Factors*, 30:599–616.

Zhang, G., and Simon, H.A. (1985). "STM Capacity for Chinese Works and Idioms: Chunking and Acoustical Loop Hypotheses," *Memory and Cognition*, 13:193–201.

FORECASTING

Chapter 2
The Future of the Market Research Profession

Paul R. Messinger, and Xin Ge

Abstract

Like many fields, the profession of market research is being transformed by technology. The Internet has been a great enabler of market research by making distant multifaceted communications more efficient. Virtualization technologies of synthetic worlds are further changing market research methods by making online communications more personal and vivid. We begin this chapter with a vision of the market research profession in 2025, dramatized as a day in the life of a marketing research professional. We then trace how five market research methods were first influenced by the Internet and are likely to be further influenced by virtualization technologies. Finally, we describe prospective future developments assumed in our dramatization, as well as likely research directions.[1]

A Day in the Life of a Marketing Research Professional

D. Sands awoke with the morning sun and examined his day planner for Wednesday, July 2, 2025. His morning routine began with coffee on the balcony. Sunlight filtered through clouds on the mountains due east and illuminated the waterfront adjacent to the Inner Harbour. To the southeast was a partial view of the historic Fairmont Empress Hotel. A low sustained horn from the Port Angeles Ferry sounded in the distance. Not

1 The authors are indebted to Eleni Stroulia, Kelly Lyons, Stephen Perelgut, Michael Bone, Kristen Smirnov, and Run Niu for thought-provoking discussions and comments. We gratefully acknowledge funding support from an Alberta School of Retailing Research Grant, IBM, the Alberta Ministry of Advanced Education and Technology, and the Social Sciences and Humanities Research Council of Canada Initiative in the New Economy Research Alliance Program (SSHRC grant 538-02-1013). For several suggestions regarding the "Kangaroo Pocket" virtual focus group, we thank the Executive MBA class of Marketing Management at the University of Northern British Columbia who participated in a virtual world exercise in winter 2008, particularly the study group consisting of Geoffrey Clarke, Melony Forster, Kui-Ying Lin, Chris Nickerson, and Ashley Stoppler. the "Kangaroo Pocket" virtual focus group, we thank the Executive MBA class of Marketing Management at the University of Northern British Columbia who participated in a virtual world exercise in winter 2008, particularly the study group consisting of Geoffrey Clarke, Melony Forster, Kui-Ying Lin, Chris Nickerson, and Ashley Stoppler.

yet out at this hour were the newer hovercrafts beginning to be used between Vancouver and his home in Victoria B.C., Canada.

D. Sands began his workday from home. He looked over clips from his virtual meeting with Meridee the day before. When they had talked, Meridee had been communicating from her office in Canberra, Australia, and D. Sands had taken a break from a picnic in Stanley Park to communicate from his parked hybrid crossover. D. Sands now prepared a follow-up email concerning key decisions agreed upon yesterday.

Virtual focus groups Meridee represented a company nearly ready to introduce a new product, a baby sling, called "Kangaroo Pocket." With most Australian women participating in the workforce and young mothers shortening maternity leave to work from home offices, such a product was believed to have great potential.

Meridee and D. Sands had agreed that the (virtual) focus (or v-focus) groups should consist of working mothers. To set up v-focus groups, D. Sands had already subcontracted with an Australian firm that maintained a consumer panel recruited and authenticated on an on-going basis. From this panel, groups of six working mothers of various income levels and from several Australian states would be interviewed at a time. They had agreed that there should be one female moderator, a colleague of D. Sands from the Victoria office. Her avatar would be casually professional, about 38 years old, attractive, not-too-slender but fit, with a confident and nurturing demeanour. They had tested the exact avatar during the meeting. (D. Sands had used his car navigation system to display the image of the avatar moderator.) Meridee did not want to have her own avatar in attendance representing her, but she would synchronously observe (lurk) and send occasional instant messages to the moderator as needed. They had also agreed that the v-focus groups should be held in the setting of a family room that opened to an outdoor patio with a barbie ("aussie" for barbeque). D. Sands had subsequently sent schedules and participant profiles, with names removed to preserve anonymity. He had presented a list of core questions to be asked, together with some follow-up contingencies, which Meridee had modified and customized for participants from particular regions of the country. In addition, prototypes of the product had already been Fedex'ed to participants to allow them to try out the product (under close supervision) during the focus groups.

Of the v-focus group services offered, Meridee had opted for an enhanced room view, a view of (side-by-side) head-shots of the actual participants, and a hybrid view wherein the avatars' faces would consist of superimposed, video-enhanced 3D images of the webcam headshots showing the respondent's actual faces. The use of invasive or even non-invasive sensors for emotions and gestures did not seem needed or cost-effective for this project. However, Meridee did want the demo-avatar to be completely gesture-enhanced. With the human model using a full suite of sensor monitors, the demo-avatar had a nearly complete ability to virtually demonstrate to each focus group participant what the baby sling looked like, the fabric and style options, sizes (for both wearer and baby), the level of comfort and safety for the baby (including a "head-support" feature for infants), how it moved with the mother's movements, and whether it was also adaptable for use by fathers.

The first of six two-hour v-focus group meetings was planned for tomorrow. Analysis of the results would consist of interpretive viewing by Meridee and D. Sands, plus software that notes commonalities in the text, and graphical software designed to examine facial cues and gestures for nonverbal indications of satisfaction or displeasure. The final report would include tabulation of results, with descriptive quotes, video, and audio, together with a final recommendation on whether to take the product to the next level, a test market. One key advantage of utilizing the virtualization specialty of D. Sand's firm was that all this work—planning, doing the interviewing, and analysis—could be carried out at relatively low cost in less than ten days. The total fee would be CA$20K, but this included a surcharge to expedite the work.

D. Sands completed his email, clicked "send," and turned to his next call.

Virtual test market "Buongiorno Serge!" began D. Sands.

"I think you mean Buona sera, Dare! Or nearly—its 4 p.m. here in Milan. And I must say, it's all BELLA here!" Serge was one of the few work associates that used D. Sands nickname, but at least it was better than something from a Jane Austin novel. D. Sands was uncertain whether Serge's last sentence referred to the local weather, the women, or a new line of women's activewear that Lululemon designers were developing. D. Sands and Serge were communicating on Google's virtual chatroom.

The discussion revolved around two dozen Lululemon designs that D. Sands' firm was putting through a virtual test market in Second Life, Cyworld, and World of Women. The designs had been introduced in the past two weeks in various virtual stores in these worlds, together with accompanying in-world promotions and fashion shows. There had been mixed reviews, with a vocal minority raving positively about five edgy designs, together with criticisms like "Lululemon, please don't forget your mantra 'yoga-inspired apparel for healthy living'" and "Where will we dancers go for our Lulus if they become just another 'out there' outfit!" D. Sands and Serge discussed what market segment these worlds represented. They both realized that there was a need to act soon, now that they had "tipped their hat" to the competition about Lululemon's intention to introduce a new line. D. Sands recommended that Lululemon "go slow" and maintain most of their core products to keep their loyal customers happy. There was enough good news, however, for D. Sands also to recommend taking the five positively-received designs to real (non-virtual) test markets in Milan, Hong Kong, and New York.

It was clear that, while they differed on some details, Serge and D. Sands agreed on these basic points. Ever since Lululemon was founded in Vancouver B.C. in 1998 in shared retail space with a yoga studio, and later infused with venture capital in 2005, the company had had a longstanding tradition of using market research techniques to listen to the voice of the customer. As they said "ciao" to each other that day, Serge indicated that he felt that the Wilson family (who owned Lululemon) would be happy with this latest market research.

A fifteen-minute walk to work from his two-bedroom condo led D. Sands to his firm's downtown offices. Crossing the bridge on Pandora Avenue (with a view of the old train bridge) reminded him of the frontier history of the place—that prospectors headed north from Victoria to seek fortunes in Klondike gold. Now he and his colleagues were searching for gold in a virtual world. Fourteen factories had once flourished in this neighbourhood through the legal production of opium. D. Sands couldn't help wondering, along these lines, whether virtual worlds would last, and whether they brought out illusory reflections of people's fantasy selves: "Lucy in the sky with diamonds," if you will. Waking from his reverie upon entering the company offices, he was soon reminded of another practical application of synthetic worlds.

Virtual experiment and walk-through D. Sands next call was to Hank Learner, a developer in Mesa, Arizona interested in talking about the "walk-throughs" of a mixed-use retirement development consisting of numerous duplex bungalows, an assisted living facility with nursing home, retail development, and a small planned "lake" adjacent to a desert-style park. The proposed site was just off a highway, located alongside a well-known golf course with views of the valley and surrounding mountains. This was part of a major project that involved collaboration of architects, specialists in geriatric healthcare, physicians, interior decorators, landscapers, developers, store planners, retail customers, retail employees, and members of the supply chain. Virtual reality representations had been created that included landscapes, buildings, common spaces, healthcare facilities, and stores; these representations included interior decorating finishes, furniture, shelving fixtures, workstations, trees, lawns, and shrubbery. Interviews were being conducted during virtual walkthroughs with potential residents of various ages (to discuss attractiveness of the environment), employees (to discuss functionality), and members of the supply chain (to discuss desirability of logistics and of product merchandising).

D. Sands' role was relatively limited, as the "field avatar" moderator of four groups of eight avatar seniors on walk-throughs of the independent-living residences (California-style ranch houses with Spanish Colonial elements). At various points along the walk-throughs, D. Sands helped administer a survey, followed by abbreviated focus group discussions (the market research services included "field trip view v-focus groups" and "v-surveys" offered by D. Sands' firm). In this instance, the architects had already created the virtual model of the whole development; and D. Sands' firm was providing research services to learn about consumer reaction to the plan. The subjects had been asked to use a full complement of relatively non-invasive sensors, with goggles monitoring eye-movements, RFID tags taped between the inner points of subjects' eyebrows to measure interest and surprise, as well as pulse and breathing monitors. D. Sands had provided a report last week on the surveys, focus group discussions, sensor readings, and walk-through video clips. This morning, D. Sands answered Hank Learner's numerous questions about the report. Hank was preparing for a meeting with architects and planners tomorrow and wanted D. Sands' feedback.

Discussing a "netnographic study" at lunch Walking 10 minutes to the CANOE Brewpub in historic "Old Towne," D. Sands could see that the lush shoreline justified Victoria's moniker the "Garden City." His friend Seth ordered a Grasshopper beer; D. Sands ordered a cappuccino.

D. Sands talked about a planned blind date that night. His friend and colleague, Vincent Tsui, had told him about a netnographic study being conducted about the virtual community, elovesong.sl, whose real business headquarters was in Hong Kong. Branches of the virtual community were on the virtual worlds Second Life and HiPiHi. The club had local branches in each U.S. state, Canadian province, Chinese province, major region of European countries, etc. Vancouver Island had an active branch, with most real activities based in Victoria. Apparently elovesong.sl was exploring alternative business models for various services, including: (1) a single purchase price or registration fee (i.e., fixed fee); (2) fee per use (i.e., variable fee); (3) subscription-based fees; (4) advertising-based fees; (5) pay-as-you-go extras (virtual assets including clothing, land, and software); and (6) sale of real ancillary products. But the company did not know whether such business models would be at variance with community culture. Ethnographic research was being done by the firm, using graduate students employed from the University of Victoria. According to this methodology, avatar representatives would gain entrée into the community, attend various virtual events (virtual parties on Fridays, holiday gatherings, etc.), and gather field notes and observational materials about cultural practices in the communities relating to dating, consumption, and payment mechanisms.

Interesting as this was from a professional standpoint, the upshot of this discourse was that Vincent had obtained for D. Sands a free membership for six months, including dating service, real-event tickets, and compatibility match-up. Dare had formed Grace's acquaintance in the virtual worlds of Second Life and Kaneva over the past three weeks; they had exchanged photos; and tonight was to be their first in-person date. At the end of lunch, Seth, cautiously pleased for his friend, couldn't resist adding, with a wry grin, "So, maybe, you won't have to be 'Victoria's Secret' much longer!"

Shopping centre portal After returning to the office from lunch, D. Sands' colleague Zoe drove the two of them to the Mayfield Shopping Centre to meet marketing manager Geraldine Buchart. The discussion centered on the possible testing of a virtual reality version of the mall, whereby the mall website would contain a clickable portal into a virtual reality version of the mall, using the Virtual Consortium avatar standards. Shopper's avatars could visit stores and move into those stores with 3D-VR (virtual reality) sites, or they could tunnel into the stores' standard Internet websites.

The shopping centre management was interested in knowing whether setting up the needed technology would generate enough incremental (online and real) business to justify the costs. She and her colleagues also wondered whether the social influences of avatars seeing other avatars and interacting with them in the virtual mall site would generate additional excitement, satisfaction, and traffic to the online and bricks-and-mortar malls. Most importantly, she was interested in knowing whether sustainable and meaningful virtual communities of users would develop around a mall-based virtual world that would increase word of mouth and loyalty to the real mall. She knew, for instance, that her daughters were enamoured of Webkinz and the Canadian Doll virtual worlds, and she wondered whether it would be possible to transfer some of the excitement and loyalty that consumers felt for these virtual worlds to the mall that housed the stores selling the real products associated with these virtual worlds. There was clearly a complementarity of skills and interests, and, the non-verbal cues left little doubt that this sales-call was a first step in the development of an ongoing client relationship. D. Sands mind wandered, nonetheless, to his upcoming dinner date with Grace.

In-world email survey On return to the office, D. Sands checked his emails, only to find one from Dr. Jacquelyn Shan, biotech guru and emeritus CEO of Afexa Life Sciences Inc. (previously, CV Technologies).

"Prior to a v-conference, perhaps it would be helpful for me to peruse the preliminary survey results that you have. If this is agreeable to you, please forward a short report containing this information. We can reschedule after that point. Best, Jacquelyn Shan"

She had a point, and D. Sands used the rest of the afternoon to prepare and forward a two-page memo to Dr. Shan. The memo concerned a new health drink that Afexa was planning to introduce in the Nutraceuticals category, containing aloe vera and American ginseng extract. The memo was based on a general survey conducted recently concerning attitudes toward and usage occasions for health drinks, including: (i) intercepts of participants in three virtual worlds (an open-role world, a warfare world, and an educational world); (ii) an instant messaging activity to members of the virtual worlds; and (iii) a standard email survey (accompanied with a coupon for a free sample).

Dinner with Grace Earlier that week, D. Sands had proposed the Swans Wild Saffron Bistro for dinner. Grace had responded with alacrity, indicating that she loved the place, particularly the boutique art orientation of the building. She had suggested that afterward they could listen to a music group playing at the pub next door. (She had become familiar with this group in the music-oriented world vSide.)

As he walked toward the bistro, D. Sands thought of friends from his *alma maters*, U.B.C. (undergraduate commerce) and McGill (MBA), who had also gone to work in market research. Most had started in Toronto, Montreal, New York, Chicago, or Los Angeles, as had D. Sands earlier in his career. Now, by picking a company that specialized in virtualization and market research, he could do the same work for the same pay (and a partnership role) in a place like Victoria B.C., walk to work, and have immediate access to any number of charming places in old towne or near the Inner Harbour. "This has been an usually productive day," he thought. Most days involve as much work, but not usually as many tangible outcomes. Then, as he caught a glimpse of Grace on the corner waving to him, D. Sands thought that the most productive part of the day was yet to come ...

From Traditional and Internet-based Market Research to Virtual Worlds

The above vignette incorporates projections of how the market research profession will harness the potentialities of virtual worlds. This section makes our projections explicit by tracing how standard methods were changed by the 2D Internet and will likely be changed again by virtual worlds. We consider, in turn, the five key market research techniques shown in Table 2.1.

Focus Groups (and Depth Interviews)

Traditional and Internet methods Focus groups traditionally consist of group interviews of 6 to 10 individuals led by one or two moderators. This form of market research has been remarkably effective for exploratory market research—particularly for obtaining consumer feedback about planned marketing programs. The cost of focus groups can range from almost nothing to more than $3,000, and the only forms of

Table 2.1 Market research techniques: Changes associated with virtual worlds

Techniques		Standard Methods	2-D Internet	Virtual Worlds
Data Type	Focus Groups & Depth Interviews	conference rooms; living rooms; & field meetings	chat forums; online conferencing; learning systems	room view (of avatars); virtual field trips; head-shots; hybrids
	Surveys	mail; phone; mall-intercept; hybrid	adaptable web forms input to a database; email or web panels	immersive field setting; in-world panels
	Test Markets	controlled; simulated	online stores; chat forums; blog discussion	in-world roll-out of virtual products
	Observation	human observation, tracking, and video	webpage clicks; email openings; in-store sensors	monitoring of purchase behavior, consumer usage patterns, in-store kiosks, and customer traffic
	Ethnographic Consumer Research	social context of consumption	netnography assesses social context of virtual communities	moves netnography from textual analysis to examination of virtual interactions

technology present under traditional methods may be audio or video recording devices, or one-way mirrors. The moderator plays a critical role by gently probing with follow-up questions to "draw out quiet or shy participants, energize a slow group, and use innovative techniques that will delve a little deeper into the minds of the participants" (Greenbaum 1997). In total, five to ten thoughtful questions with follow-up can elicit two hours of in-depth discussion about various products or services. (For background on preparing for a focus group, see Krueger 1994.)[2]

The Internet has provided a new medium for conducting focus groups, enabled by recent advances in bandwidth and video-streaming technology. Online focus groups can take various forms: online chat forums, synchronous Internet distribution of real group interviews (Nucifora 2008), software conferencing for synchronous online interviewing (O'Connor and Madge 2003), and other learning management systems for synchronous conferencing (Turney and Pocknee 2005). One example of online chat

2 Most of the considerations for focus groups also apply for individual depth interviews. The only difference is that the "group" consists of one moderator and one participant engaged in a one-to-one discussion. Such depth interviews can be done as market research or as part of a larger service delivery system, such as for medical or financial professionals.

is www.wireclub.com. An example of video streaming distribution of real focus groups is provided by ActiveGroup. This technology permits observers to enter a password and synchronously view the proceedings and share text comments with others and to record a CD ROM for later playback. Related streaming capabilities exist for shopping mall intercept surveys and computer usability testing, which display, split-screen, user facial expressions from a camera situated above the computer monitor synchronously with the image currently shown on the monitor. An example of conferencing software for synchronous viewing is Hotline Connect. Examples of learning management systems include the Blackboard and Elluminate (www.elluminate.com) platforms, both popular at many universities and distance learning facilities.

The Internet, however, has been a "mixed bag" for focus groups, with distinct efficiency gains coupled with equally distinct losses in the quality of the information and nonverbal cues. Advantages are that it is inexpensive to reach difficult-to-access consumers (Turney and Pocknee 2005); client observation is easy (Nucifora 2008); synchronous and asynchronous recording of dialogue is efficiently done (Burgess 1995); and software exists for sorting, retrieving, and analyzing language-based data (e.g., Qualpro, Ethnograph, and Nudist; see Lim and Tan 2001). Disadvantages include lack of meaningful group dynamics, lack of paraverbal and nonverbal information about respondents, lack of accountability due to anonymity, lack of control of sample composition, uncertain participant attention, and a limited role for the moderator (Greenbaum 1997).

Virtual worlds Virtual worlds address many limitations of the Internet and improve information quality for focus groups by creating a shared perception that dispersed participants are interacting in a single locale through their avatars. We expect that virtual worlds will be used in multiple ways for focus groups, affording different views of respondents, and a given researcher may find it desirable to switch between views in the same research project, or even in a single session. We believe that at least four views will be common practice—room view, side-by-side head shots, virtual field trips, and hybrids. We summarize descriptions of these in Table 2.2.

The basic idea of the focus group is not changed except that the data collection is through virtual worlds rather than in person. In addition to conducting the interview, virtual worlds can be used directly for recruiting and debriefing. Content planning is essentially the same as with traditional focus groups. Since the data mostly consist of digitally recorded stimuli from a virtual world, the analysis can go beyond interpretive viewing by the clients and professionals, to include utilization of tools and software to analyze text, audio, and video.

Much of the above technology already exists in places like Second Life, where some firms already provide focus-group and market-test services for brands and product prototypes (Terdiman 2007).[3] Achim Muellers, head of brand relations and co-operations at BMW, stated in a conference in SL that, "Second Life is great to get

3 An early provider of such services, Market Truths Limited, won a business plan competition sponsored in Second Life by Linden Lab for its new in-world market research business consisting of conducting focus groups and other market research services. (See http://sl.markettruths.com/reports)

Table 2.2 Views of focus groups in virtual worlds

Room View	The participants' avatars interact in a room of the researcher's design; common examples include a conference room, a living room, or an outdoors furniture arrangement. The researcher designs in suitable lighting and ambient sound level. As in second life, participants can alternate between a camera view, where they see a view of their avatar interacting with the other avatars, or a screen view, where they only see the various other avatars, as the focal avatar turns its head. The focus group would permit typed chat input or audio input, from a headset with a microphone, as is used by skype. The moderator could also upload photos, powerpoint images, or 3D CAD (computer aided design) objects, as in Second Life, which would appear in pop-up windows for each of the participants. This would permit presentation of advertising copies, new product concepts, prototypes or other stimuli. Other users might also be able to post objects to pop-up windows, but there would be some control of this exerted by the moderator.
Virtual Field Trips	The participants' avatars walk, fly, or ride through a prepared environment, such as a store, shopping mall, neighborhood design, or transportation system, about which respondents could discuss their reactions as they proceed through the environment. For example, the store layout would include a virtual reality representation of the store, with shelving fixtures and workstations included. Interviews will be planned during virtual walkthroughs of existing customers, new targeted customers (to discuss attractiveness of the environment), employees (to discuss functionality), and members of the supply chain (to discuss desirability of logistics and desirability of product merchandising). As with the room view, the discussion could consist of audio, text, and posted objects.
Head-Shots (side-by-side)	A webcam records the actual faces of participants, which are displayed in a checkerboard on the screen. For example, if there are nine participants, each participant would see eight head-shots arrayed in a 2-row by 4-column fashion. The upper-left shot would be the moderator. All parties hear the audio. This technology already exists and is in use by telecommunications and Internet companies. Here, if an external input is added, this would appear in a pop-up window. This view permits close scrutinization of each individual's facial responses.
Hybrid Views	This consists of embedded head-shots with room view or virtual field trips. In particular, a webcam image would appear as the face of each avatar, together with improvements in avatar gesturing, facilitated by lightweight, wireless radio-frequency monitors taped to hands, feet, and head of the participants. This would show people as avatars in the room view or the field view, but participant faces would show their real expressions and a greater variety of gestures would be possible.

very honest feedback, more honest than in any focus group, because in a focus group, you sort of know what's expected from you. Second Life residents are more extroverted and honest about their feelings." Yet much technology is still being developed and perfected, which we will discuss in the final section of this chapter.

An important limitation concerns anonymity—that the respondent may use an unknown or fictitious identity. Such anonymity limits the ability of the researcher to apply desired recruiting criteria and may generate more fanciful responses than would otherwise occur from a fully identified individual.

Survey Methodology

Traditional and Internet methods Surveys constitute one of the most powerful and pervasive tools for obtaining quantitative and qualitative market research information. They have been used extensively in business and the social sciences. Widely-used question formats include open-ended text, numerical entry of information, ranking of items, rating items on a likert scale (rate level of agreement to a statement), single-select multiple choice, and multiple-select multiple choice. As a general principle, the best way to determine the relevant survey elements is to work backwards from the decision, considering the general issues one wants to explore, the focus, mode, schedule of data collection, and types of information desired. Multiple-choice questions are useful for insuring consistent coding of answers across respondents and for facilitating quantification of the desired concepts or constructs. Open-ended questions, on the other hand, permit respondents to identify new issues about which the researcher may have been initially unaware. Common data collection means include mail surveys, phone, and intercept surveys, each with progressively higher unit cost and response rates. Hybrids of these three are used for more complex subjects. Advances in technology have led to automated printing of surveys from mailing list databases and computer aided telephone interviewing (CATI) systems. For background on traditional survey methods see Churchill and Iacobucci (2005), Aaker, Kumar and Day (1995), Malhotra (2004), and Bradley (2007).

The Internet has added significantly to survey methodology by making survey instruments accessible worldwide. The most common platform is to place the survey text and questions on a linked series of webform pages; the webform pages are accessible on a website that resides on a local server with Internet connectivity. Answers are recorded with a mouse-click to a database such as MySQL, Microsoft Access, or Oracle. An alternative platform is to place the questions within email with clickable links or buttons that record answers to particular questions. A hybrid consists of emails with links or attachments: the link is to a webform survey, as described above, or the attachment may be a Microsoft Word document to be returned after updating (which is much less efficient).

Internet surveys look mostly like traditional surveys presented on a screen. The question formats are mostly the same, but rather than being mediated by paper and pencil, they are mediated by mouse, keyboard, and screen. Table 2.3 summarizes some advantages and disadvantages of Internet Mediated Surveys.

The ability to have an adaptive question sequence (also possible with traditional phone and intercept surveys) is a distinct advantage of Internet surveys over pencil and paper surveys. The ability to embed photo, audio, and video objects expands the domain of inquiry. The ability to give feedback to the respondents motivates respondents. And automated data entry and input validation provides a tremendous efficiency gain. The

Table 2.3 Internet mediated surveys: Advantages and disadvantages

Advantages	1.	*Can interact with the database to create a targeted questionnaire or an adaptive question sequence.* This can permit randomization of order and treatment conditions. It can also include "add-skip logic" so that respondents only answer questions that are relevant to them. It also allows more advanced adaptive sequencing whereby past answers can be utilized for generating more focused subsequent questions.
	2.	*Can include embedded objects, like digital photos, audio clips, and video clips.* The survey can ask questions about these objects.
	3.	*Can give feedback to respondent.* This can enhance respondent motivation or indicate the respondent's progress with a "percent completed bar."
	4.	*Can include input validation.* This avoids data cleaning.
	5.	*Automatically performs data entry.* This avoids data-entry expenses.
Disadvantages	1.	*Limited to respondents with Internet access, online skills, and high technology acceptance.* This may exclude lower-income participants, the very old, and the very young.
	2.	*Lack of subject accountability due to anonymity and limited control over sample composition.*
	3.	*Lack of human assistance to provide clarification of questions.*

disadvantage is that not everyone may have Internet access or skills needed for Internet mediated survey collection. In addition, there may be insufficient tech support to provide clarification about the questions in the way that a surveyor can do with phone and Intercept surveys. Probably one of the greatest disadvantages concerns lack of control over who answers, if recruitment is via a website, but the disadvantage can be limited by using standard recruitment procedures (possibly via email), assigning a password code to subjects, and only letting subjects who have this password participate in the survey. On balance, online surveys have many advantages in efficiency, availability, presentation, and dynamic sequencing of questions, and the disadvantages present are less significant and more manageable than the disadvantages of online focus groups.[4]

Virtual worlds Virtual worlds add to the already powerful Internet survey technology by providing at least six new capabilities or potentialities, described below.

1. *More advanced immersion with embedded objects.* As with the Internet, it is possible to display, within surveys, embedded advertisements and new product

4 There are a variety of companies that provide survey services to teach companies and individuals how to quickly gain full advantage of the new, relatively simple Internet survey technologies. Prominent examples include www.constantcontact.com; www.polldaddy.com; www.questionpro.com; and www.surveymonkey.com.

prototypes, but the embedded objects are 3D and can be rotated, manipulated, or tried out. More importantly, avatars can be led through an immersive environment and periodically asked to answer survey questions. Thus, participants can tour a store, shopping mall, neighborhood design, or transportation system, and subsequently be asked to take a survey (just as we indicated they could subsequently participate in an in-world focus group). Similarly, avatars can go through the process of utilizing a service delivery system, such as consumer services (e.g., medical, financial, etc.) or business services (e.g., consulting, information systems, etc.), with probing questions asked at intervals as avatars proceed through the process.

2. *Use of field avatars for content and tech support.* A second additional function that may be added to surveys in virtual worlds is to use avatar field representatives. Such field avatars can help with the recruitment; answer questions during the survey process; teach the respondents to properly make use of the automated systems; manage exceptions if systems fail or are misused; and answer questions about content respondents might have before, during, and after answering the questionnaire.

In managing this process, one needs to plan and consider the appearance of the avatar field representatives, set guidelines for avatar behavior, and manage the research collaborators who are behind the avatar representatives. Recent research on using avatar salespeople in electronic retail contexts (Holzwarth et al. 2006) indicates that more attractive avatars yield more positive responses for less expensive, low-risk purchases, and more expert looking avatars yield greater trust and more positive response for more expensive, high-risk purchases. Building on this research, it may be desirable to use avatars that are either informally or professionally dressed, depending on the context, or both. It is also reasonable to use avatars that are attractive, but not stunningly attractive or sexy (which might serve as a distraction). Lastly, one might wish to balance the gender, complexion, and race of the avatars. In our own past research (Messinger et al. 2009), we have accordingly used the four survey avatars that are shown in Figure 2.1.

It is also desirable to make a list of common questions and answers for the research collaborators who are manipulating the field avatars. Some personal chat is inevitable, and in fact it would be unnatural to stifle such communication. Collaborators should be advised to be honest, direct, explain the motivation of survey questions, if asked, reveal the name of the research group or institution, and, to the extent of their comfort level, discuss their roles. In our own work, each collaborator inevitably develops his or her personal contact and interview style, depending on what feels natural and comfortable for them. The one guideline is to suggest that answers not be too short, as to appear cursory or impersonal, and not be too long or technical, so as to lose respondent interest. Records of the chat communications should be kept in text files.

3. *Hybrid question forms.* One desirable capability of virtual world surveys is that they can be combined with focus groups. For example, a focus group moderator could elicit private responses to questions from a questionnaire, whereby

Figure 2.1 Field avatars

participants would type in their responses without talking. These responses would appear on a separate screen for the moderator, who could then call on one of the participants to elaborate on his or her view, followed by discussion. This survey/ focus group format is not so easily carried out using standard methods, although there are currently available wireless input devices that register multiple-choice answers of audience members, aggregate the responses, and display the results real-time to the audience members.

4. *Creation of in-world panels of users*. A further desirable feature of virtual worlds is that residents with similar interests form groups to pursue joint activities. Along these lines, one could form a group that would be willing to answer questions over time as a consumer panel for a reasonable fee. Indeed, in some virtual worlds residents are willing to work for a very low fee, and answering questions as a member of a consumer panel seems like an action that residents are willing to take. For example, there is already a "First Opinions Panel in Second Life," consisting of a sample of consumers being tracked periodically by a market research firm to monitor common behaviors and attitudes of SL residents.
5. *New forms of recruiting*. Another desirable capability of virtual worlds is that they permit new forms of recruiting. We will discuss recruiting later, but, for now, we note that in Second Life there is an entire island ("Money Island") featuring kiosks and billboards that link to various websites offering a menu of surveys for residents and providing Linden Dollars in exchange for each completed survey. Two large websites of this type are www.gameATM.com, a privately run site, and www.MyLindens.com, an official site of Linden Lab.
6. *New domain of questioning*. A final interesting aspect of virtual worlds is that these worlds provide several new domains of study which can be informed by in-world surveys. First, some of these worlds constitute new economies, and it will be desirable to survey to learn what in-world virtual products and services are in demand. Second, some of these worlds in the future will constitute an easily navigated environment to shop for real products and services, and it will be desirable to survey which products and services people shop for in these worlds, and what in-world store or office features best attract customer interest in shopping there. Third, for companies that provide products and services in a

> virtual world (as well as in the real-world), there is a carryover of consumers' perceptions of advertising and product and/or store experiences from the virtual world to the real world (Yee and Bailenson 2007). The advantage of virtual world surveys is that they can learn such things.

This section, thus, summarizes how the powerful tool of surveys has developed from traditional methods, to using the Internet, and now to realizing the potentialities of virtual worlds. Survey stimuli are now more multidimensional; surveys can be supported by field avatars; question forms can be combined with focus-group discussions and supported by consumer panels; recruiting can take new forms; and the question content can fully embrace the new domains of virtual world activities.

Test Markets

Traditional and Internet methods Test markets constitute an important form of field experiment involving small-scale product launches in carefully selected sectors of the marketplace in order to determine the likely acceptance of a product or service before full commercialization. Whereas focus groups are often used at the new product development stage, test markets are typically used just prior to roll-out.

Traditionally, test markets can be performed in three different formats: standard test markets, controlled test markets, and simulated test markets. By using standard test markets, the company sells new products in a number of selected stores through its normal distribution channel. In comparison, for controlled test markets, the test program is conducted by an outside service which provides guaranteed distribution and store acceptance. Lastly, in simulated test markets, instead of obtaining data of actual sales of the new product, researchers recruit consumers to participate in a study, during which time consumers are shown the new product and asked to rate its features, and/or to indicate their purchase intentions. This information is later fed into a model to predict likely sales and market share.

The Internet makes test markets more efficient and less costly in two respects. (1) With respect to standard test markets, by establishing their own online stores, manufacturers can now sell products directly to their consumers and bypass wholesalers and retailers altogether. By doing this, manufacturers can save the time and other resources that are necessary to make arrangements with the intermediaries in the distribution channel for the latter's acceptance of the new product. Instead, the manufacturer can test consumers' reaction to any new products directly using the online store in a timely manner. (2) With respect to simulated test markets, the dynamics of online communities (e.g., chat rooms and blogs) might reveal information that is otherwise not available in conventional settings. For example, market researchers can easily pitch new products in a chat room and encourage a group discussion. Alternatively, manufacturers can seek out a few blog authors and give them new products in exchange for their honest comments posted online. This is an effective way of spreading the word about new products and attracting people to volunteer their opinions about the products.

Virtual worlds In 3D virtual worlds, marketers can enjoy all the convenience provided by the 2D Internet in conducting test markets. In addition, 3D virtual worlds offer distinct advantages: they permit testing new product concepts without having to invest in costly production on a small scale. As more companies choose to open virtual stores (e.g., Apple or Nike stores in Second Life), they can roll out new virtual products with the desired amount of exposure to consumers and location of shelf displays (e.g., eye or floor level). Avatars are encouraged to try out virtual products in the store to have some "hands-on" experience and to provide feedback on a bulletin board. In addition to tracking sales, companies can monitor such things as the amount of time avatars spend inspecting the product (which reflects consumers' interest) and which generate attention, excitement, or confusion. Despite the efficiency with which companies can test out a new product concept, however, one downside of conducting test markets in a 3D virtual world is lack of protection from competitors. Because the details of the new product concept are widely available in the virtual worlds, companies need to be cautious about possible actions that their competitors might take.

It is important to point out that, whereas both the 2D Internet and 3D virtual worlds enhance marketers' ability to test out consumers' acceptance of new products by skipping intermediaries in the distribution channel, it is also critical to consider how well the retail trade will accept a new product.

Observation

Traditional and Internet methods Observational research is a naturalistic and unobtrusive technique of collecting primary data by observing people's behavior, and their situations. Observational research is especially useful for obtaining information that people are unable or unwilling to provide if asked directly. Conventional observational studies use trained human observers—researchers make records of consumers' behavior either in a natural setting such as a store or in a behavioral lab. The use of human observers induces two problems. First, it is very expensive to collect data this way, and, as a result, data are often collected on a small scale. Second, data recording can be subject to lack of objectivity due to human bias or simple negligence.

In the age of the Internet, many companies use automated proxy observers to record relevant consumer data. Cookie data is an important category of automated observation that provides information about individuals' web browsing activity, such as how often a person visits a certain website, how much time he/she spends within the site, how many links this person clicks through, and whether a recipient opens or deletes an email sent by a company. (Cookies are parcels of text sent by a server to a Web client, usually a browser, and then sent back unchanged by the client each time it accesses that server.) Other examples of automated observation include the use of (a) consumer goggles to record individuals' eye movements as they browse in a store, scan through a magazine, etc.; (b) meters attached to television sets to record the TV programs people watch; (c) in-store sensors monitoring traffic at entrances and at key store locations; and (d) RFID tags affixed to shopping carts to record in-store shopping routes of customers (and affixed to products to record selection order within the store and checkout). Early tracking devices began with point of sale scanners that could read Universal Product Codes (UPC) to record sales of products. While all these sensing devices are not a part of the Internet, *per se*, the data from these sources are often transmitted via the Internet to remote servers and centralized databases for analysis and distribution. Observational research with the aid of such devices enables significant cost reductions and data collection on a larger scale over a longer period of time compared with human observation.

Virtual worlds The advent of 3D virtual worlds has provided market researchers with more flexibility in implementing observational research in synthetic environments. Such observational research within virtual worlds can be used to examine (a) avatar's interactions with personal objects as a means of self-expression; (b) people's reactions to spatially-oriented structures such as stores, shopping malls, residential and commercial real estate, public buildings, parks, transportation systems, and other structures with particular orientations in physical space; and (c) people's use of small-scale worlds through in-store kiosks for product search and examination.

Personal objects as self-expression. Consumers are known to purchase certain products as a means of self-expression. This phenomenon can be examined in virtual worlds to ascertain whether residents of various virtual worlds acquire virtual products to reflect and build their virtual identity. Observing which virtual products acquired by residents of virtual worlds and how they use them (e.g., customize the appearances of their avatars and organize or decorate their own personal spaces) can help marketers understand consumer usage behavior and usage patterns, in general, and as a means of self expression, in particular. For example, it is found that in the real world, upper-middle-class consumers prefer to put their TV sets in the family room or recreation room (but not in the living room), and by comparison, lower-middle-class consumers prefer to put their TV sets in the living room. Such usage patterns have been learned in the real world by sending human observers to the households of their customers. By comparison, it would be less costly for market researchers to observe similar behavior patterns in a 3D virtual world setting. Such observation in virtual worlds can then be used to inspire product design and marketing communications in the real world.

Use of spatially-oriented structures. Companies can use virtual worlds to test a 3D virtual layout of a store or a shopping mall (including signage, lighting, interior decoration, and sound) to decide whether such layout is efficient by observing the on-site flow of traffic. In addition, one can learn which product categories garner the greatest interest and general customer satisfaction with the environment. Whereas in a conventional setting, such observation is only possible after a real store (or mall) has been built up, observation in a 3D virtual world enables diagnosing and correcting any potential problems with minimum costs before actually setting up the layout in a retail environment. Of course, observational research about spatially-oriented structures can also be coupled with focus groups who tour similar virtual structures in order to elicit discussion about them. This would include study of people's reactions to residential and commercial real-estate, including office buildings, public spaces, transportation systems, and other spatially-oriented structures.

In-store kiosks. A final use of virtual worlds is that retailers can include computer kiosks in their stores for consumers to construct their own customized virtual products. For example, people can search for features most appealing to them, such as particular colors, styles, sizes, and extras (e.g., monograms) in clothing and shoes. These virtual products, once designed, can then be tried on by people's avatars for further inspection. Similarly, people can arrange furniture shown on the store floor in virtual rooms, with their choice of particular size and paint/color schemes. This version of virtualization has been tried by Levi's (and then dropped) and Ikea (still in use). Virtualization for the purpose of trying on clothing will be further facilitated if people can maintain an avatar of themselves that is standardized to be portable from one e-commerce site to another. From the point of view of selling, in-store kiosks (as well as free virtual samples) can induce virtual product trial, which might be less costly than stores having to make greater use of their return policies to afford customers the opportunity for product trial. From the point of observational research to better understand people's preferences and thought processes, the analyst can examine styles and furniture arrangements that consumers considered when using the kiosks.

Overall, direct observation of usage patterns in virtual worlds is an attractive tool. To some extent it is already being used by companies to solicit feedback about products and services. For example, some businesses in Second Life provide free virtual samples, allow residents to modify the products, and invite customer reaction and comments. Thus, residents can go to the virtual Toyota dealership, buy a virtual Toyota for 300 Linden Dollars (just over US$1), show it off to their avatar friends, customize it, and provide aesthetic feedback to "real life" Toyota engineers and designers. Similarly, Starwood Hotel, the international lodging chain, has used Second Life to enable collaboration with potential customers to test their ideas involving large investments.

Ethnographic Consumer Research

Traditional and Internet methods As the influence of culture on consumer behavior has been widely acknowledged, ethnographic market research, an interpretive method which examines consumer experiences in a cultural, social, and ethnic context, is gaining increasing popularity. Ethnographers seek to understand a particular group of people through physical immersion in the culture over an extended period of observation and participation (Silverman 2000). In order to interpret the rich implications of the social fabric for consumers' perceptions, preferences, opinions, and attitudes, market researchers using ethnographic methods collect data in the field by studying consumer behavior in a natural, everyday environment, rather than in an artificial setting such as an interview room with two-way mirrors and a controlled behavioral lab. An early influential ethnographic study that focuses on the American consumers involved synthesizing the observations of Belk and his colleagues (1991) as they toured the U.S. in a Winnebago.

The Internet, which fostered the emergence and growth of a vast number of virtual communities, renders it possible to extend ethnographic research from physical space to the realm of cyberspace. Online ethnography, also referred to as netnography, was introduced as a methodology of market research for the Internet in the late 1990s (Kozinets 1997; 1998; 2002). Just as in real communities, members of virtual communities build their own cultures, develop their own social relationships, and share specific collective norms. Netnography seeks to understand such online cultures, social relationships, and norms. Such research has the added advantage of avoiding the cost of physical travel. But, though these communities lie at our fingertips, researchers must be sensitive to the rules, norms, and etiquette of virtual communities, just as they must be sensitive when conducting ethnographic research in distant lands. Some researchers even advocate that the researcher take observations from the perspective of a non-participant—called "lurking" in virtual communities (Catterall and Maclaran 2001).

Kozinets (2002) recommends five methodological steps for netnographic studies. Catterall and Maclaran (2001) expand this into a more complete eight-step procedure: Entrée, trust and rapport, ethics, fieldnotes, interviews, member checks, exit, and research representation. From another perspective, these eight steps can be organized into three stages in a temporal order: the preparation stage, the fieldwork stage, and the wrap-up stage, as demonstrated in Figure 2.2.

In addition to the advantages of speed, simplicity, and low cost, netnography enjoys two further advantages as compared with traditional ethnography: (1) Netnography permits collection of first-hand data by direct observation (lurking) in the preparation stage (as well as in the fieldwork stage). This information can then be used to decide whether the focal virtual community represents a suitable research target. (2) With netnography, researchers do not have to exit the virtual community after the fieldwork stage, because keeping presence and participation is easy in the virtual community. Netnography, thus, affords greater opportunity for verifying researchers' interpretations with online community members, incorporating members' feedback in research reports, and even planning further rounds of data collection if necessary.

Preparation Stage		*Fieldwork Stage*		*Wrap-up Stage*
Entrée *Trust and Rapport* *Research Ethics*	⇨	*Fieldnotes* *Interviews*	⇨	*Member Check* *Exit* *Research Representation*

Procedure	***Tasks***
Entrée	Selecting appropriate virtual communities for study according to the goals of research and gaining entry
Trust and Rapport	Building trust and rapport within the community under study
Research Ethics	Researchers should (1) disclose their presence, affiliation, and research intention, (2) ensure confidentiality and anonymity of respondents, (3) take a cautious position on the issue of private versus public medium usage, and (4) incorporate feedback from members of the virtual community
Fieldnotes	Making direct copy or taking observation of logs, messages, and communications among community members
Interviews	Conducting online interviews with members of virtual communities
Member Check	Presenting researchers' interpretation back to members of the virtual worlds to solicit their comments and feedback
Exit	Withdrawing presence from a community
Research Representation	Constructing a report of the research

Figure 2.2 Stages of online ethnographic research

Virtual worlds The domain of emergent behavior in 3D virtual worlds is broader than on the 2D Internet. In the early Internet—with chatrooms for instance—most activity takes the form of text messaging. As Kozinets (2002) points out, "market researchers must be conscious that they are analyzing the content of an online community's communicative acts rather than the complete set of observed acts of consumers in a particular community." With the development of Web 2.0 and social networking, web behavior goes beyond simple text messaging to include asynchronous posting of text, images, audio, and video files. With the advent of 3D virtual worlds, emergent behavior goes even further to take more human forms, including text exchange, expression of emotions, audio exchange, gestures, touching, movement, creating objects, building structures, running businesses, and purchasing products. As a result, netnography, once confined to analysis of text messages, now includes more and more of the types of analysis of traditional ethnography, embracing the gamut of human interactions—only the activity occurs in virtual worlds, not in the real world.

Recruiting and Contacting Participants

A general issue for most of the above forms of market research is recruiting and making contact with participants. In the previous sections, we occasionally alluded to recruiting participants; we develop this issue more fully now.

Traditional and Internet methods Traditional ways of recruiting research participants include mail, print media, telephone, personal interaction, and purchase-related devices. Recruiting participants through mail and print media is low cost per capita, but participation rates tend to be low. Phone and personal intercept methods, by contrast, are high cost per capita; but the cost may be justified by higher participation rates. In addition, market researchers also may use specific purchase-related devices, e.g., questionnaires inserted in packages or appended to warranty sheets. While reaching participants in such ways is easy, a disadvantage is that non-buyers of the product are not reached.

With the aid of the Internet, researchers now can reach a larger pool of potential participants by sending emails, instant messages, and using links and banners embedded in a large host websites or a small, targeted micro-sites. While many of these messages are sent via the Internet to potential respondents' personal computers, others may be targeted to telephones or cell phones, using skype or voice-over Internet protocols. These tools are efficient in terms of time and cost to the recruiter; they also facilitate easy response by subjects. An important ethical consideration concerns the generation of spam, and it is desirable to adhere to the protocols of permission marketing (Godin 1999). Another general problem of recruiting using conventional Internet tools, however, is the lack of control of the target audience, generally, and self-selection bias, in particular. For example, a recruiting message posted on a website would be globally accessible and not targeted to a single geographic area.

Virtual worlds The development of virtual communities enables greater targeting and selection of particular consumer segments for the purpose of recruiting participants for market research. In particular, a number of virtual communities serve specific demographic segments (e.g., location of residence, age, income, education) or address specific topics (e.g., beer, games, computers, books). Careful selection of particular virtual communities for recruitment, therefore, permits a tight coupling between the research purpose and the targeted audience.

Once one has chosen a particular virtual world, recruitment can be done either outside or inside the virtual world. Recruiting outside the virtual world can be done, for example, using emails, social computing sites, or auction sites. Such recruiting possesses the advantage of being grounded in reality, but an important disadvantage is that not every person encountering a recruitment message will know enough about the focal virtual world to enter for the purpose of survey collection or to answer questions about in-world behavior. Becoming proficient at navigating, interacting, and manipulating the environment, through skill-development on places like the "Newbie" islands in Second Life, may involve an investment of several hours, at a minimum. We are aware of projects that tried sending emails to a consumer panel, but these projects have basically been unsuccessful due to low response rates. We also are aware of a paid study announced on Craigslist that similarly struggled to meet the targeted sample size after several tries over several months.

In-world recruiting, by contrast, insures that the respondent has the requisite skills, knowledge, and experience to carry out the survey and to answer questions about the world, itself. Recruiting inside a virtual world can be done in one of the following ways: (a) in-world instant messaging; (b) clickable in-world banners and advertisements with links; and (c) in-world intercept-style methods using field avatars. In the latter two cases, researchers must carefully plan the placement of their recruiting messages in targeted high-traffic locales to maximize the exposure of such messages. Important considerations involve employment of suitable explanatory signage and field avatars with a suitable appearance. Concerning avatar-intercept methods, using avatar representatives to interact with other users in the 3-D virtual worlds permits "face-to-face" avatar interactions between the researchers and potential participants to regain part of the personal touch in the recruitment process.

In-world instant messaging is desirable for its efficiency and wide reach. The messages may be text or audio (analogous to traditional mail and phone contact). These can generate standard emails or skype-type phone messages if a respondent is not currently active in-world. (Note that the principles of ethical and representative recruitment applicable to traditional mail and phone also apply in-world.) Some worlds, such as Second Life, however, discourage instant-messaging or mass distribution of notecards (viewing these as spam).

In-world clickable advertisements can take the form of billboards, survey machines, or other forms of indoor and outdoor objects or banner ads with links (for an example used in Second Life, see Figure 2.3, left image).

These can automatically open a survey either in an in-world medium (such as a series of notecards in Second Life) or in a pop-up window (displaying a more standard Internet survey). Alternately, such advertisements can begin a sign-up process for a focus group, depth interview, or experiment. Limitations of using clickable advertisements for recruitment include self-selection bias and reliance of adequate avatar traffic passing the advertisement. Accordingly, we are aware of studies that used banner ads to teleport residents to survey machines where insufficient numbers of responses were generated.

Figure 2.3 Survey booth and survey avatar with sandwich board

In-world intercept-style recruiting, based on avatar-to-avatar interactions (for an example, see Figure 2.3, right image), promotes empathy and a high response rate, just as real intercept surveys do in shopping malls. Virtual-world, intercept-style recruiting, however, has some advantages over real intercept surveys because the travel time to the survey site is minimal in virtual worlds. In particular, it is possible to cover many locations with ease and low cost. Nevertheless, intercept style recruiting requires greater human resources for data collection than other in-world methods. (In the future, designing mobile "bots" to do the recruiting may reduce costs of human resources for data collection, but we have found the "personal touch" effective, thus far.)

Conclusion: Future Research and Development to Make the Story Become a Reality

Many changes that enhance the usefulness of virtual worlds for market research applications will inevitably occur by 2025. We describe below likely changes (summarized in Table 2.4), many of which were assumed in our opening vignette. We also provide recommendations.

New Practices

We expect to see new standards and institutions that support content development.

3D web standards A Web3D Consortium has been recently formed to provide a forum for the creation of open standards for Web3D specifications, called X3D specifications, designed for communicating 3D on the web. There are multiple related goals. One goal is to permit a person to move his or her *same avatar* between multiple 3D worlds, such as Second Life, World of Warcraft, Entropia Universe, Kaneva, There, Lively, RuneScape, Webkinz, Habbo, Club Penguin, Ty Girlz, Neopets, and Whyville. Another goal is to move between platforms for PCs, laptops, cell phones, or automobile navigation systems. Yet another goal is to permit people to move their avatars between 3D and 2D worlds, to provide "inter-dimensional compatibility." We think all of these

Table 2.4 Future development for market research in virtual worlds

Area	Topic	Future Developments
New Practices	Standards	3D web standards Standardized avatars across virtual worlds
	Institutions	Guaranteed security of identity Protection of intellectual property rights Norms for research ethics Methods for assuring data validity
New Technology	Human-Computer-Avatar Interface	More expressive avatar faces and gestures Better sensors and input devices
	Market research software	New methods for recording group interactions New survey technology
	Infrastructure	Scalability Affordable modular virtual world servers Enhanced usability of hand-held devices Improvements in 3D recording and 3D projections
New Research	Analysis tools and models	New methods for analyzing different types of data Classification models Choice models Data extraction software from audio and video
	Behavioral Research	How people use virtual worlds Carry-overs between virtual and real worlds Effects of avatar appearance
	Applied Research	Applications for retailing, service delivery, and advertising
	Basic Research	Implications for social sciences and humanities

are laudable goals. Standards also do not yet exist for unified in-world 3D object coding and scripting languages, and for common communication protocols. For market research, filling these gaps would facilitate doing focus groups, surveys, test markets, consumer observation, and ethnographic studies across multiple virtual worlds.

Institutions Important practices also are lacking in a 3D context concerning insuring security, intellectual property rights, research ethics, and data validity. From a privacy standpoint, security on servers and databases is critical. From a legal standpoint, key issues involve intellectual property law and dispute resolution (within a virtual world, and between individuals in different virtual worlds, and between different virtual worlds, themselves). From the standpoint of research ethics, new standards for market research and spam are yet to be developed, agreed upon, and enforced. From the standpoint of validity of data collected in virtual worlds, several practices would be helpful. These include practices that to authenticate the members of a research panel or focus group as representative of particular demographic or customer groups, new protocols for virtual meetings, and new work values that facilitate people participating from remote locations.

Recommendations To progress further, we recommend four things:

1. The community should follow through with its goals of establishing standards across different virtual worlds for coding of avatars, 3D objects, animation scripts, and communications protocols. This would enable movement of avatars, and transfer of content among virtual worlds and between 2D Internet and 3D environments. This would also create incentives for content creation of all types, but a key use for our purposes would be to create greater incentives to create market research tools that could be used across multiple worlds. Thus, a firm investing in developing market research capabilities for focus groups, surveys, test markets, consumer observation, and ethnographic study in one world, could transfer these same capabilities to other worlds.
2. National and international institutions should be solidified to protect intellectual property and to secure a firm's rights to data that it creates. This would support content creation of all types, but for market research in particular, it would increase a firm's incentives to invest in capabilities to do market research, knowing that any value that they created would be secure.
3. As regards rights to privacy and research ethics, it is critical for international standards to be created to clearly define where the separation line exists between the rights of the individual (to both privacy and being fully informed before providing data) and of the market research profession (to have the ability to obtain valid and important marketing data for commercial enterprises). Clearly defined rights for both sides in advance can avoid infringing on individuals' rights and commercial investment in activities that turn out later to cross the line.
4. Concerning data validity, we suggest that there is an opportunity for private companies to be formed to authenticate members of virtual research panels, from whom data would be collected using focus groups and surveys. This allows firms to leverage virtual worlds for focus groups and surveys in a way that avoids anonymous consumers being remunerated for providing poor information.

New Technology

We expect to see new technologies, involving both hardware and software, and new infrastructure.

Human-computer-avatar interface The expressiveness of avatars' faces, body language, and non-verbal communications is currently limited. In most worlds, the most that can be done to establish eye contact is to rotate an avatar's body 360 degrees, and to look up or down. There are very limited non-verbal body-modalities such as facial expressions, eye movements, hand gestures, body postures, and walking styles, although it is possible to write scripts to alter these.

To support easy, independent control of facial, eye, and body parts, of course, one needs improved human-computer interfaces for virtual applications. Toward this end new multimodal hardware and software are beginning to emerge involving sensors and input devices. Sensors would include webcams, eye-trackers, microphones, wireless motion-monitors and other gestural interfaces for enhanced abilities to convey facial expressions and body gestures, and biosensors of pulse, blood pressure, breathing rate, and the distance between the innermost edges of the eye-brows (a measure of emotional response). For navigating gestures, enhanced input devices would include new joysticks, mouses, touchpads, "walkpads," and devices related to those currently used for Nintendo Wii games for throwing objects and swinging objects like golf clubs. Some of the applications, such as for work-out machines, could permit enhanced in-world dancing or sports, and even could involve forms of bio-feedback. There is also a need for enhanced computer-vision approaches to gesture recognition. Enhanced monitors could also show improved representation of people's internal emotional state. (We would not advocate more invasive sensors, such as those involving implants. Indeed, we would favor laws that prohibited frivolous use of invasive sensors.) Enhanced cell phones with digital cameras (and car navigation systems) may also serve as flexible and mobile input devices. Overall, improved avatar expressiveness, sensors, and input devices will greatly facility focus group and observational research in virtual worlds.

Market research software In the vignette, we assumed development of market research software for: (a) focus groups that easily records and moves between room view, field trip view, head-shot view, and hybrid view; (b) survey technology that seamlessly links the avatar's experience within the virtual world, the survey questioning platform, and a database; and (c) remote monitors that tabulate sales from the stores participating in a test market or in measurement of some other observational variable. These applications all build on basic technology nodes that already exist; all that needs to be done is to write and popularize applications that "connect the dots."

In addition, the technological building-blocks already exist for another type of market research software involving market forecasts. In particular, after calibrating individual models for responses of particular subjects to various stimuli (e.g., involving various combinations of attribute offerings) it is possible to project individuals responses to a particular offering (either a new product, a new store or service, or the location of a store). Then one can aggregate across all individual responses to provide an aggregate design and forecasting tool. In principle, one could alter the size or location of a virtual store and then obtain immediate forecasts of resulting changes in traffic, sales, and profits.

Infrastructure Current infrastructure is challenged for both large synthetic worlds and for micro-worlds. Even the most widely used Massively Multiuser Online Games (MMOGs) often reach peak loads and experience crashes and down time. Not all of the technology is scalable. New computing and communications paradigms, hardware, software, languages, and scripts are being developed to address these service breakdowns. These must attend to the need to do multicasting, inter-avatar communications, and zoning within the environment. Replacing a given server is often not possible, so adding servers with load balancing, added memory, and tolerance for errors are all necessary.

Commercially developed capabilities for modular virtual world servers and software are, thus far, relatively limited in the support of micro-worlds for retail or shopping mall applications (like Mayfield Shopping Centre example in the vignette) or architectural design applications (like the Verde Adult Community in Mesa Arizona in the vignette). Some of these (such as the latter) can be handled on private islands within massive virtual worlds like Second Life; but some of these (such as the former) require a stand-alone space, with proprietary ownership, control of management policy, and security.

Other desirable new infrastructure technologies could include (a) improved usability of hand-held devices (like cell phones) for video capture and for navigating in virtual worlds; (b) improved methods for photographing, scanning, and recording real 3D environments and rendering them in virtual worlds; and, even, (c) improvements of three-dimensional "replicators" to mold, cut, or shape figurines out of various materials that are designed with CAD (computer assisted design) systems.

Recommendations To progress further, we recommend several things:

1. A consortium of virtual worlds should develop universal enhanced coding of avatars that provides easier independent control of avatar's faces, body language, and non-verbal communications. This would include non-verbal body-modalities such as facial expressions, eye movements, hand gestures, body postures, and walking styles. This requires expanding the avatar-design palate and better automated control puppetry for avatar movements. Having the capability of recording these features in new forms of animated videos would also be desirable.
2. In order to better control avatars, it will be important to develop a new suite of easily used (and worn) input devices for facial and body parts. Some of these input devices will use enhanced sensing devices. For example, enhanced eye-tracking devices could help control avatars' eye movements, and motion detectors for arms and head could be useful for controlling the arms and head of the avatar. This would better facilitate nonverbal communication, so important to focus groups and individual interviews.
3. In order to record emotional responses of subjects, the industry will need to develop better sensing devices. When possible, these should be wireless, lightweight, and non-invasive. In addition to devices that monitor eye, facial, and body movements, biological sensors would also be useful. Then, emotional responses of subjects to certain issues under discussion in focus groups, individual interviews, and surveys, could be monitored more precisely.
4. New computing and communications paradigms, hardware, software, languages, and scripts should be developed to better support Massively Multiuser Online Games (MMOGs) to avoid crashes, down time, or other degradation of service during peak loads, to make systems more scalable, and to add to load balancing across services and to afford greater tolerance for errors. This is important for supporting development of the constellations of virtual worlds generally.

5. In order to support micro-worlds for retail or shopping mall applications or architectural design applications, developers should create modular virtual world servers and software, and an industry consortium (with government support) should provide incentives to commercialize these.
6. Software should be created specifically for gathering market research data. First, software should be created to conduct and record focus groups in multiple views. This should permit simple switching between room, field trip, head-shot, and hybrid views. This should also permit easy replay and analysis of focus groups, after the fact. Second, survey technology should be developed that seamlessly links the avatar's experience within the virtual world, the survey questioning platform, and a database. Third, remote in-world monitors should be developed that tabulate sales from all stores participating in a test market or some other observational variables (such as store traffic, or even customer conversations with service personnel).
7. Software should also be created to provide for rapid market forecasts of changes in market offerings. This will enable practitioners to better visualize the impact of altering their offerings in terms of sales and profits.

New Research

Lastly, we expect to see new tools, models, and research.

Analysis tools and models To harness data that becomes available from virtual worlds, new analysis tools and models will be needed. Models are now only beginning to combine physiological, performance, and subjective attitudinal measures, three-dimensional imaging, in-store navigation trackers, in-world traffic flow data, and knowledge extraction from textual sources, audio, video sources, and multimodal sensor-based sources. We also are seeing the development of behavioral measures for such things as truthfulness, interest, and satisfaction.

Behavioral, business, and social science research In order for us to interpret market research in virtual worlds, we need a better understanding of how people use virtual worlds, who uses which worlds, and the extent to which information provided is representative of behavior in the real world. We also need to determine what subject areas can be usefully studied in the context of virtual worlds. A natural line of inquiry concerns the best ways to utilize virtual worlds for commercial purposes. Another important line of inquiry concerns how to best utilize virtual worlds for education. A final line of inquiry concerns the implications of virtual worlds for social sciences and humanities.

Recommendations To progress further, we recommend several things:

1. Researchers in computing, business, and behavioral sciences should develop new analytical models for fast analysis of the emerging data coming from a world of unlimited bandwidth, with monitoring devices and triangulation between physiological, performance, and subjective attitudinal measures, three-dimensional imaging, in-store navigation trackers, and in-world traffic flow data. It would also be desirable to develop fast classification models that use such data to develop measures for such things as truthfulness, interest, and satisfaction.

2. Statisticians and researchers in the business and economics should develop improved statistical analysis techniques for choice data, sales data, and customer tracking data that builds on past research in marketing and economics.
3. Work in machine learning and other areas of computing science should develop improved methods for knowledge extraction from textual, audio, video, and multimodal sensor-based sources. This involves classification, clustering, and extraction methods, utilizing time-dependent and space-dependant data, ontology generation, speech processing and understanding, image and video analysis, grammar generation, and semantic speech decoding. Also important are formal representations of knowledge that incorporate domain-specific information, with browsing and navigation capabilities, search, and permission policy for shared information, all of which are useful for building social networks linking people and resources. Such tools would be invaluable for analyzing market research results.
4. Core research questions should be addressed by behavioral researchers to ascertain how people utilize virtual worlds. Relevant questions include the following. What is the extent to which (and the conditions under which) consumers provide true information in virtual worlds about their behaviors in the real world? Are people's behaviors in virtual worlds different (e.g., less inhibited) from their behaviors in the real world? What are people's motivations within virtual worlds? Do people make the appearance of their avatars similar to or different from their real selves? What are the lifestyles of and personality traits of people who choose to participate in virtual worlds? Do virtual worlds reflect consumers' self-concept or role identity? These questions are particularly relevant to assessing market research results.
5. From the perspective of applied topics for study, market research about consumer attitudes should be conducted to address questions relating to practical and effective ways to commercially utilize virtual worlds. Such applied questions include the following. What is the best way to communicate with consumers in online environments? For media placement, what are the demographics, psychographics, geographic characteristics, membership sizes, and participation levels of various virtual worlds? Will exposure to advertising messages and positive virtual service encounters carry over to change real purchase and consumption behavior on the part of consumers. What product or service attributes can be best experienced and marketed virtually? For what virtual services and products are people price sensitive? How should an avatar sales agent's appearance be designed? Will virtual worlds support themselves with a single up-front fee, periodic subscription payments, advertising, pay-as-you-go extras, or sales of real ancillary products? How can virtual worlds be used for virtual customer relationship management? For corporate training? To facilitate collaborative design? To create productive virtual workspaces?
6. Market research should also be done to assess how virtual worlds can best be utilized for education and distance learning. Related questions include the following. What are the comparative advantages of learning in virtual worlds verses traditional classroom environments or the Internet? What topics are

particularly suitable for classes in virtual worlds? How should teaching pedagogy be adapted to a virtual classroom? How does the instructor avatar's appearance influence student motivation?

7. Finally, consumer research should be done to address important questions in the social sciences and humanities. These include the following. How are norms and standards of social behavior in virtual worlds different from those in the physical world? Does the time spent in a virtual world serve a desirable function, or are virtual worlds an unproductive distraction, even to the point of being an addiction? What is the extent of self-governance in virtual worlds? How do existing governments and political campaigns utilize virtual worlds? Should virtual worlds be regulated (as compared to regulation of internet service providers)? How will laws and regulation influence creativity and productivity in VWs? What are the implications of monetary systems in various virtual worlds? Is there a new form of art emerging in virtual worlds? How is sexuality expressed virtually? Does a virtual sexual relationship constitute infidelity?

Conclusion

Overall, virtual worlds, where thousands of people can interact simultaneously within the same three-dimensional environment, represent a frontier in social computing with critical implications for how market research will be conducted. In this chapter, we fast-forward to 2025 and offer a vignette as one possible view of the future of the market research profession. We then trace the past, present, and future of market research techniques, with particular emphasis on focus groups, surveys, test markets, observation, and ethnographic research. We, lastly, identify likely future developments and research directions for virtual worlds relating to new practices, new technologies, and new research. Many of the anticipated new practices and technologies are assumed in our opening vignette.

Perhaps not all of the changes envisioned in the opening vignette will come true. Nevertheless, virtualization technology is challenging standard assumptions and freeing practitioners from conventional constraints of geography, low bandwidth, and the impersonal nature of the Internet. The virtual stage is now set, and accolades will go to those players that soonest understand the new script. Marketing professionals and business scholars must come to terms with virtualization applications because we are not talking about some science fiction dream but a transformation already in progress.

References

Aaker, D., Kumar, V., and Day, G. (1995). *Marketing Research*. 8th Edition. New York: John Wiley & Sons.

Arrington, M. (2008). *Google Launches Virtual World Called Lively*. [Online]. Available at: http://www.techcrunch.com/2008/07/08/google-launches-virtual-world-called-lively [accessed: 14 July 2008].

Belk, R.W. (1991). *Highways and Buyways: Naturalistic Research from the Consumer Behavior Odyssey*. Provo, UT: Association of Consumer Research.

Bradley, N. (2007). *Marketing Research. Tools and Techniques.* Oxford: Oxford University Press.

Burgess, R.G. (1995). Introduction, In *Studies in Qualitative Methodology: Computing and Qualitative Research*, edited by R.G. Burgess. Greenwich, CT: JAI, ix–xiii.

Catterall, M., and Maclaran, P. (2001). Researching consumers in virtual worlds: A cyberspace Odyssey. *Journal of Consumer Behaviour*, 1(3):228–237.

Churchill, G. A., and Iacobucci, D. (2005). *Marketing Research: Methodological Foundations*. 9th Edition. Mason, OH: Thomson South-Western Publishers.

Craigslist Fact Sheet (2008). [Online]. Available at: http://www.craigslist.org/about/factsheet.html [accessed: 29 May 2008].

Dillon, W.R., Madden, T.J., and Firtle, N.H. (1993). *Essentials of Marketing Research*. 1st Edition. Homewood IL: Richard D. Irwin, Inc.

Forrest, E. (2003). *Internet Marketing Intelligence: Research Tools, Techniques and Resources*. Boston: McGraw-Hill/ Irwin.

Godin, S. (1999). *Permission Marketing: Turning Strangers into Friends, and Friends into Customers*. New York: Simon & Schuster.

Greenbaum, T. (1997). Internet focus groups: An Oxymoron. *Marketing News*, 3 March, 35–36.

Greenbaum, T. (1998). *Internet Focus Groups Are Not Focus Groups – So Don't Call Them That*, [online]. Available at: http://www.groupsplus.com/pages/qmrr0798.htm [accessed: 30 June 2008].

Greenbaum, T. (2002). *The Case Against Internet Focus Groups*, [online]. Available at: http://www.groupsplus.com/pages/case2.htm [accessed: 2 July 2008].

Holzwarth, M., Janiszewski, C. and Neumann, M.M. (2006). The influence of avatars on online consumer shopping behavior. *Journal of Marketing*, 70(4):19–36.

Klassen, R.D., and Jacobs, J. (2001). Experimental comparison of web, electronic and mail survey technologies in operations management. *Journal of Operations Management*, 19(6):713–728.

Kozinets, R.V. (1997). "I want to believe": A netnography of the X-philes' subculture of consumption. *Advances in Consumer Research*, 24:470–475.

Kozinets, R.V. (1998). On netnography: Initial reflections on consumer research investigations of cyberculture. *Advances in Consumer Research*, 25:366–371.

Kozinets, R.V. (2002). The field behind the screen: using netnography for marketing research in online communities. *Journal of Marketing Research*, 39(2):61–72.

Krueger, R.A. (1994). *Focus Groups: A Practical Guide for Applied Research*. 2nd Edition. Thousand Oaks, CA: Sage.

Lim, P.C., and Tan, S.C. (2001). Online discussion boards for focus group interviews: An exploratory study. *Journal of Educational Enquiry*, 2(1):50–60.

Malhotra, N. (2004). *Marketing Research: An Applied Orientation*. 4th Edition. Upper Saddle River, NJ: Pearson/Prentice Hall.

Messinger, P.R., Stroulia, E., Lyons, K., Bone, M., Niu, A., Smirnov, K., and Perelgut, S. (2009). Virtual worlds—past, present, and future: New directions in social computing. *Decision Support Systems*, in press.

Messinger, P.R., Stroulia, E., Lyons, K., Bone, M., Smirnov, K. and Perelgut, S. (2008). Designing a survey tool for virtual worlds: An experience report. Working Paper.

Nucifora, A. (2008). *Internet is Revolutionizing Use of Focus Groups*, [online]. Available at: http://www.nucifora.com/art_146.html [accessed: 14 July 2008].

O'Connor, H. and Madge, C. (2003). "Focus groups in cyberspace": Using the Internet for qualitative research. *Qualitative Market Research: An International Journal*, 6(2):133–143.

Silverman, D. (2000). *Interpreting Qualitative Data: Methods for Analysing Talk, Text and Interaction*. 2nd Edition. London: Sage.

Silverman, G. *Why You Should Probably Not Do Online Focus Groups: A Comparison between Face-to-Face Focus Groups, Telephone Focus Groups, and Online Focus Groups*, [online]. Available at: http://www.mnav.com/online.htm [accessed: 9 July 2008].

Turney, L. and Pocknee, C. (2005). Virtual focus groups: New frontiers in research. *International Journal of Qualitative Methods* [online], 4(2), Article 3. Available at: http://www.ualberta.ca/~iiqm/backissues/4_2/html/turney.htm [accessed: 2 July 2008].

Yee, N. and Bailenson, J. (2007). The Proteus effect: The effect of transformed self-representation on behavior. *Human Communication Research*, 33(3):271–290.

Chapter 3
Synthetic Worlds and Financial Services

Richard Brath, Mike Peters, Joseph MacInnes, and William Wright

Abstract

Collaborative interactions and transactions among traders, portfolio managers and risk managers can be transformed with synthetic worlds. It is easy to anticipate that by 2025, the reports, analyses and projections from financial industry participants exist in a shared workspace for dissemination and collaboration that is flexible, adaptable and with high visualization capabilities. This chapter describes a scenario with a futuristic portfolio analysis and planning process that is distributed in a global organization. It is made possible by powerful computer graphics hardware, advanced computational industry risk models and perceptually correct, cognitively enhancing, visual analytic user interfaces.

Scenario: Sambborra Resources Inc. Project Portfolio Analysis

Imagine in 2025, an asset management portfolio analysis scenario, in which dynamic and collaborative meetings can take place between disparate groups and specialists within the group, each bringing their own expertise, data, and point of view to the discussion. In a large multi-national company with global operations, meeting, working and developing financial ideas in their synthetic financial world is the new workplace.

Our story is set in Sambborra which is a large, multinational mining and resources firm based in Singapore that meets quarterly for business planning and to discuss options and review possibilities. The ever changing prices of resources, mine capacities, competitive landscape and global market, political and economic risks are all evaluated at these meetings. At these meetings the senior management employs a cadre of specialized risk analysts to analyze many different possible choices and scenarios. These can be as diverse as tripling copper production to serve rapidly expanding Chinese and Indian industrial production, moving offshore oil rigs into untapped ultra-deep waters, or establishing a new diamond mine in an emerging Third World country. The risk analysts frequently have their own highly complex software models, using different assumptions, simulations and inputs. However, because of the complexity and diverse inputs to the models, and inherent uncertainty involved for each scenario, they require a significant level of examination and vetting, often by several analysts. Explaining the models and their implications to the CFO and other senior risk executives is a frustratingly difficult task; reams of tabular data and multi-page PowerPoint presentations have proven woefully insufficient to explain the models and their outcomes to time-constrained senior executives. Additionally the computational models need to be robust enough to address a diverse range of questions from the executives.

Emily is one of the senior risk analysts at Sambborra and has been tasked with using her model to study fifteen diverse scenarios. She has created and refined her model over the many years she has been working with the company, tuning it as new methods, and new business climates have been evaluated by it. Her model outputs data to a data repository, which is then visualized in a visualization room in a synthetic world like Second Life (Figures 3.1, 3.2 and 3.3). To help manage the overwhelming complexity, her visualization combines performance data metrics and project financials (like market capitalization, cash flow) with geographic overview of project performance to help clarify how different geographically situated projects are performing at a glance. These different elements can be selectively layered on, depending on the level of analysis or audience to whom she is presenting.

In appearance, her visualization takes the form of a "room" with a floor and two or three walls. The floor displays the primary data of interest and the walls are reserved for supporting data.

Emily and her colleagues work with the room using either mobile wearable eyewear displays or by using high resolution wall sized, multi-projector wall displays. The mobile projection eyewear is invisibly fitted into fashionable see through eyeglasses. They use dual ultra miniature display engines worn on the belt and with special optics

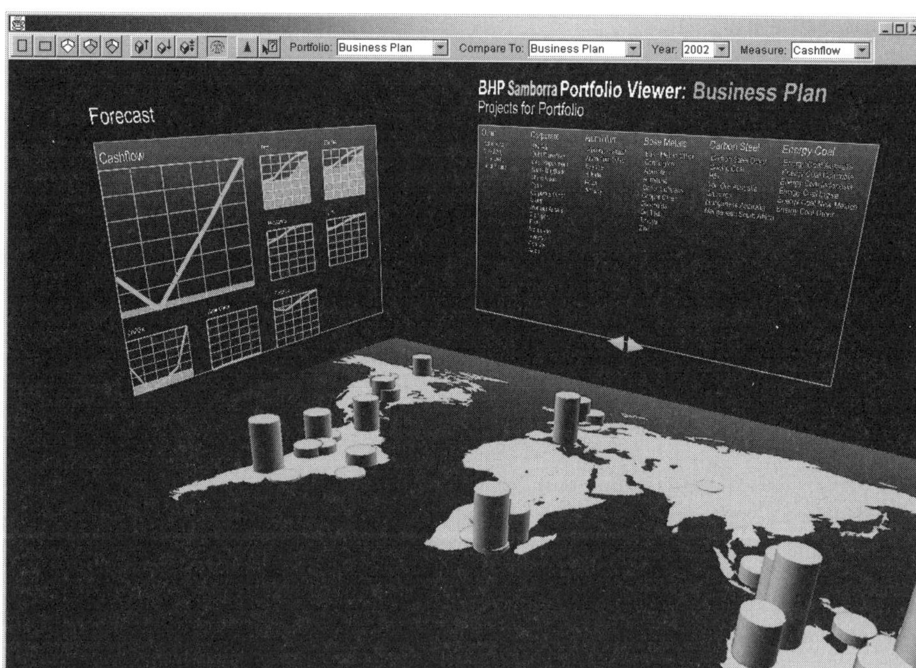

Figure 3.1 Sambborra model viewer: Global project overview

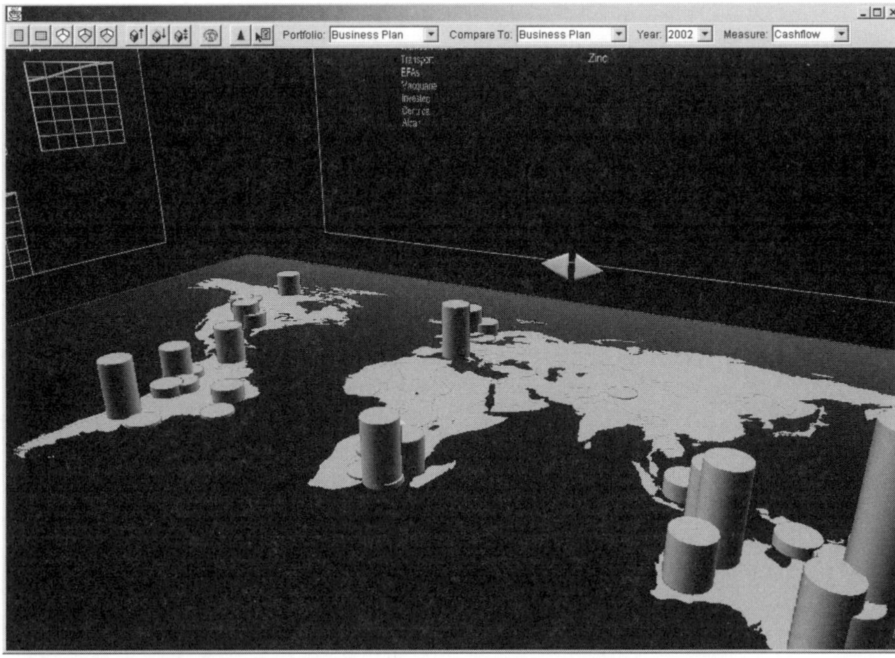

Figure 3.2 Zooming in to the projects in the southern hemisphere

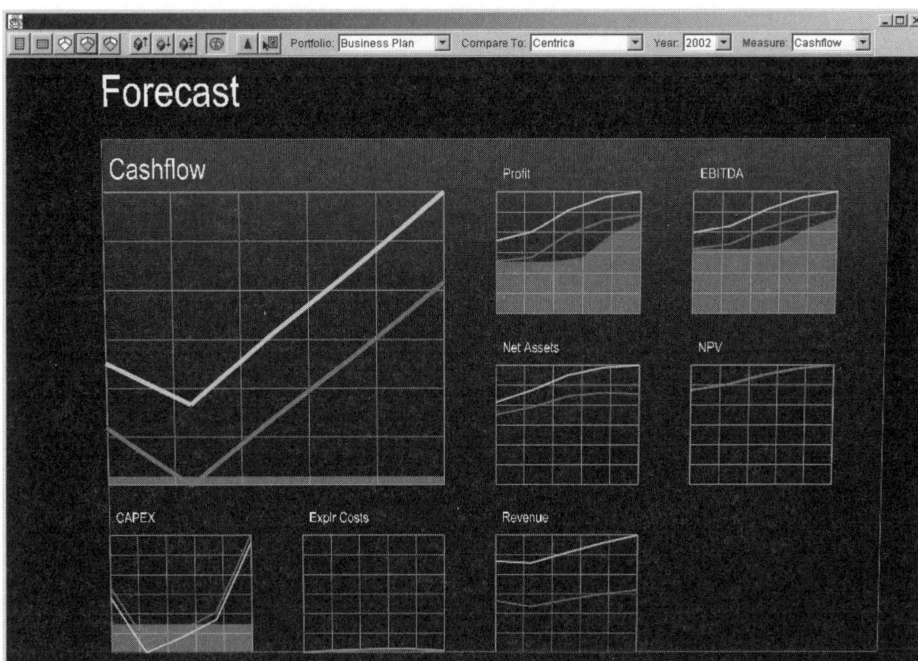

Figure 3.3 Metrics comparing the selected scenario to the baseline "business plan" model

embedded into the eyeglasses, giving each eye a smooth, moving image, and a perfect stereoscopic effect. The wall-sized display provides an even higher resolution and can leverage multiple graphics processing units (GPUs) from several systems.

Emily's model is connected to the visualization room visuals, and by toggling different switches, she can cycle through the models she has been tasked with analysing. Additionally, she can turn on and off different projects on the back wall to illustrate how those projects contribute to the overall performance of Sambborra. However, before she can present her models at the quarterly meeting, she needs to have her research staff review her model, and add their contributions to help increase the precision of some of the scenarios. Phil and Tim are analysts that work out of the London and New York offices of Sambborra respectively. Phil has extensive expertise in Net Present Value (NPV)-at-Risk models, and Tim has been working on models that forecast out commodity prices up to ten years in the future. To improve the overall veracity of her model, Emily has decided to incorporate the NPV at-Risk model and use Tim's most recent forecast data (Figures 3.4, 3.5 and 3.6). As a starting point, the dozens of projects currently in production and planned at Sambborra are displayed on a large, interactive wall display, plotting each project on an Efficiency Frontier display. This helps screen out the more risky projects, as it plots each project in terms of its NPV and its corresponding risk.

Once the team is satisfied with the results, visuals and the interactions with the underlying model, Emily arranges a meeting with the senior risk team members at Sambborra. They can all join the meeting in the synthetic world and physically walk through it, asking questions and drilling down into different components of interest in the model. Instantly, different scenarios can be defined, compared and contrasted with each other, with Emily on hand to further explain details about the results.

Her work is interrupted with a request from Carl, the CFO at Sambborra, "Due to ongoing concerns about the environmental impact of coal-fired generating plants, we may need to divest ourselves of most of our large coal mines in the southern hemisphere. This is a critical situation, and, as is well known, Sambborra generates substantial revenue from those coal mines, and we haven't had any reason to not count on this revenue in the future. Can you please show me how that would affect our overall performance metrics. And give us some options! We need to know what would happen if we cease production over the next year, or phase out this plan over the next two or three years."

Emily walks through the global map view with Carl, to show him where the largest coal mines are currently operating. They can stroll through projects, at a macro level, stepping from continent to continent, or drill down instantly to an individual facility. Carl and his staff decide on a case by case basis which mine should be closed, and which should remain open, while Emily toggles those projects on or off, temporarily removing them from the project portfolio. As each project is reviewed, the portfolio is instantly updated, triggering a model regeneration, and instantly updating the visuals. The effect is startling. As massive projects are cut or added, the Sambborra financial forecasts change significantly, triggering changes in short-term cash positions and long term profitability. Emily can easily illustrate the differences between the myriad scenarios with Carl, capturing each one as a snapshot, saving the data and visuals, and other notes off to the side. By grabbing two very similar scenarios, and performing

Figure 3.4 NPV-at-Risk model for a given scenario

a delta, the group can instantly see the subtle differences in the model results, and make accurate comparative decisions. After the initial analysis, the group breaks into multiple teams, and dozens of ad hoc scenarios are created. Phil and Tim, the analysts from London and New York, are brought in during the exercise, but due to the extreme sensitivity of the options being discussed, have a limited view of the room. In fact, their own view of the model is constrained to four scenarios, and they work in an isolated area, away from the management team. They are using their expertise to model different options around very fine-grained details. For example, two mines in Argentina are currently in the process of undergoing a "greening" modernization, at considerable expense to Sambborra. Using another "room", analysts can view the progress of the construction, and bring in engineers and project managers to discuss the current state of the modifications, and see a live feed of the construction crews, busy at work. Upon closer inspection, the executive team considers the option of holding on to these mines at the expense of closing several North American mine sites.

The overall workflow is as follows. The global view of all projects for the next 10 years appears like a matrix of bars, with each bar representing the intersection of Time and Resource (Figure 3.5). The CEO and CFO can walk around this matrix, getting an idea of the overall business from a high level. Emily is able to illustrate that the new scenario does have an immediate impact on cash flow, but due to the diminishing returns at several of the older selected mines combined with increasing mining costs several years in the future, and the hedging provided by the diverse portfolio of projects, specifically in the oil and renewable sectors, this new ad hoc plan still points to acceptable levels of profitability for Sambborra.

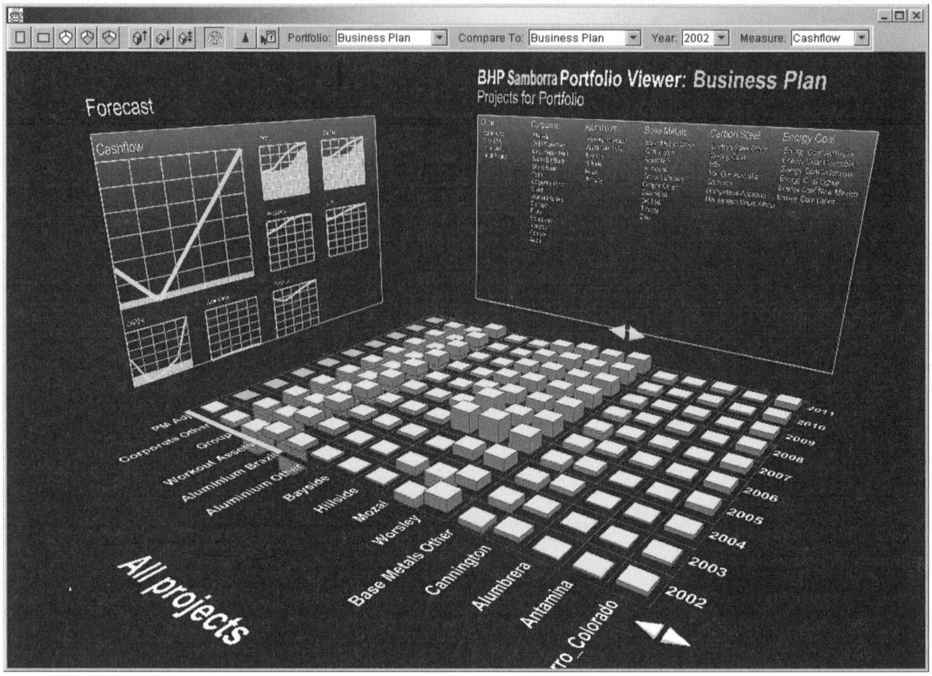

Figure 3.5 All projects displayed are forecast ten years into the future. The back wall displays the selected projects that are in the portfolio

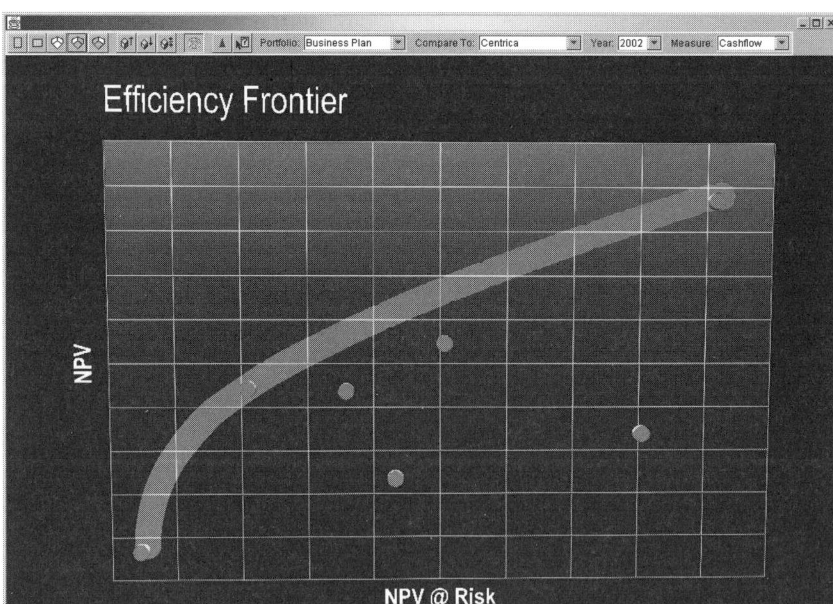

Figure 3.6 NPV versus NPV-at-Risk scatter plot. Each project is displayed as a marker and its contribution can be clearly compared to other projects

The visual room has other diverse uses at Sambborra. Confidential forecast information can be selectively hidden when outside parties are brought on to establish the legal implications of different merger and acquisition plans, product extensions under consideration or the dropping of existing or planned projects. External participants can be drawn upon, using the room concept as well. Private data or proprietary models can be shielded, while publicly available data can be exposed for potential legal, political or business decision ramifications. It is a flexible environment and is able to work with varying levels of confidentiality and permissions.

The Sambborra scenario illustrates how analysts can present a current snapshot of many different projects, looking at historical data over a recent timeline, using existing data sources augmented with multiple financial models, all integrated in an interactive 3D visual model of financial and project performance. Other specialists do collaborative work on the visual financial system, filling in missing pieces or validating possibly suspect data. As the model is evolving and becoming more complete, ancillary components can be added on as separate visual analytical constructs. For forecast data, more participants can join in, potentially with their own models and supporting data. These models may have different projections and outcomes, which can all be viewed and compared simultaneously. In this way multiple different hypotheses can be collaboratively created, debated, selected and then planned. For example, a line of business can be examined in minute detail and complex different scenarios (merger and acquisition, product extension, dropping a product line, etc.) can be studied and explored. In the financial synthetic world, the advantages and risks of complex investment decisions are immediately apparent to everyone in the group. Decision-making, ROI, risk management and consensus are all improved. This is not just social networking. This is corporate networking at an entirely new efficient and productive level. Sambbora continues to achieve high growth performance.

Technology Enablers and Research Issues for Synthetic Worlds in Financial Services

Collaborative interactions and transactions among traders, portfolio managers and risk managers can be transformed with synthetic worlds. The Financial Services industry provides venues for creating and managing transactions between parties and intermediaries in a framework of trusted relationships. Many different roles and people are involved in these processes such as data sourcing, collection and validation, model building, risk and portfolio analysis, planning and operations. It is easy to anticipate that by 2025, the reports, analyses and projections from participants exist in a shared workspace for dissemination and collaboration that is flexible, adaptable and with high visualization capabilities. Financial professionals would be able to perform tasks such as super-imposition of two analyses to validate findings, identify anomalies, use synthetic world constructs to create new synthetic financial instruments and interactively collaborate with other financial professionals to conduct analysis, creature new transactions and present proposals. Furthermore, within the analytic frameworks and visual representations (e.g., 3D customer segmentation tree-plots; 3D credit loss surface, what-if market risk analysis, news monitoring alerts), individual financial entities can be represented as virtual synthetic entities, whether individual people or corporate entities (e.g., John Smith or IBM or crude oil). The live status of any virtual entity, such as online banking, interaction with a call-center agent, or seminar presentation, represents both a data stream and a potential for interactive engagement. This new financial synthetic world collaborative workspace provides an increased pace for validation, idea generation, data validation, decision making and dissemination; as well as entity navigation for finding and communicating directly with counterparts.

Among other early examples (Wright 1995, Wattenberg 1999), a notable 3D display of the financial markets was the New York Stock Exchange's (NYSE) virtual reality trading floor. It is a large scale, real-time, 3D multi-dimensional synthetic environment originally conceived and proposed by Richard Brath in collaboration with NYSE in 1996 and then subsequently refined and implemented by Security Industry Automation Corp (SIAC), Asymptote Architecture and Silicon Graphics (SGI) for the NYSE's operations group in 1998. This virtual environment system displays financial market and trading systems infrastructure information. Flexible controls and interactions allow adjustment of time and space for trading and news events in order to monitor and correlate the stock exchange's daily trading activity. Alert agents monitor both the markets and the associated computer communication infrastructure systems. The system consolidates data streams from several floor trading systems into one interactive 3D system allowing NYSE system operators to intuitively and quickly understand complex business transactions and to see market and systems problems at a glance. Real-time visualization of thousands of equities and millions of daily transactions is provided. When originally conceived, the implementation required six SGI visualization supercomputers to generate the completely interactive virtual representation of the trading floor. Today, such a visualization system can be delivered using normal desktops and laptops. The fully immersive approach used by the NYSE system would today employ combined immersive and focused workspaces. The 3D views would use techniques providing less occlusion, more precise comparison and improved perceptual methods. A networked approach would be used to allow broader participation and utilization of the system's capabilities. It is instructive to reflect on what it was and what it achieved with a synthetic world approach.

Experience with the NYSE trading system as well as the Sambborra scenario illustrates the potential for synthetic worlds but a number of issues and opportunities need to be investigated in order to realize this potential. The following describes important technology enablers and research issues required to realize the potentials of these scenarios.

Ubiquitous Computing

Financial services are already one of the most connected professions and continue to quickly adapt to new technologies. Financial markets move quickly and it is necessary to have multiple channels of communication to a counterpart quickly and immediately. The financial service sector has been an early adopter of telephone turrets, instant messaging, video conferencing, email, cell phones, smart phones, and real-time networks. It is reasonable to expect that this community will be one of the earliest adopters of synthetic worlds as a business networking tool.

Emily, Phil, Tim and Carl are geographically dispersed and in different time zones. While Emily is at the office, Phil may be at breakfast or on a train into the city and Tim may be in an airport or the back of cab. Emily, Phil and Tim need to be able to collaborate even though they do not have access to the same device at the same time. First, consider some of the devices they have at their disposal.

Mobile Screens

Mobile world: The future of computing will reach far more people with small inexpensive mobile devices rather than with desktop screens as the mobile phone growth throughout the world shows.

Hand-held screens: Interaction with virtual worlds from small screens on mobile devices will be an opportunity (Figure 3.7). The newest, most powerful devices may well provide fully interactive 3D immersive scenes. However, some screens, such as those found on mobile phones today and on the free devices given away by banks in 2025 with a new account, will have limited computing power and limited resolution. Perhaps there are massive compute grids that render Tim's virtual world in the cloud and deliver the result as streaming video which Tim's free device is capable of displaying. Or, this may represent a unique opportunity in interaction and abstraction of 3D worlds: perhaps Tim can see preset viewpoints (top-down view of the floor); or, more challengingly, perhaps there are software techniques to abstract the complex 3D world down to a simpler 2D world. Our children willingly engage with a pixilated 2D Mario from 1985 as much as they engage with beautifully animated 3D Mario in the latest games. So, there may be conventions for depicting 3D worlds in simple, 2D interfaces for small mobile screens.

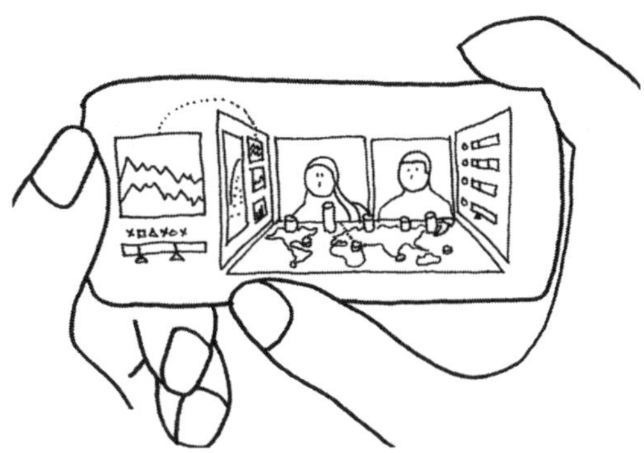

Figure 3.7 Tim's handheld view on the Sambborra risk room

Other mobile screens: Besides handheld, hand-sized devices, other opportunities for mobile virtual world access exist in 2025.

- Virtual Reality (VR) glasses: Specialized glasses provide a novel way to provide high-resolution worlds to mobile users although new interaction techniques are also required.
- Borrowed displays: Tim may find at airports in 2025 that he can simply borrow a nearby high-resolution wall screen, or use a micro-projector to display highly confidential information on his hotel suite wall.

- Wrist watch display: A wrist watch display may be tiny, but could be indispensable for quick, discrete communications to relay rumors overheard by Tim at a breakfast meeting moments before the firm is about to announce an acquisition, or instantly give Emily price updates for the commodity futures market.
- Tablets into newspapers: Phil, sitting on the train, has the opportunity to use much more space. Phil could be using a derivation of today's tablet computer combined with electronic paper, providing him with a screen the size of an opened newspaper which rolls up (or folds up) to a size smaller than a briefcase when not in use (Figure 3.8).

No screen: There will be instances, such as when Tim is driving, that there will be no screen at all. Tim will still need to participate in the virtual world, through his avatar, but his interactions will be more limited to verbal communication and simple commands such as requests for the avatar to fetch and dictate data values in a portion of the visual representation: "Avatar, what is the revenue forecast for year 2027 as currently shown on Emily's forecast chart?"

Figure 3.8 Phil's folding tablet view on the Sambborra risk room

Large Screens

Large screens: There will be the need in some financial applications to explore large amounts of complex data—more data elements than all the pixels available on the typical desktop display today of two to four mega-pixels. It is not uncommon to see traders in financial services firms today with four or six or more monitors to display large amounts of data. There are research applications today that provide more than 100 megapixel displays. By 2025, will 100 megapixels be a standard resolution available to average users? And what new visualization techniques will such a large number of pixels enable? For Emily, the large, screens deployed to the Sambborra conference room have enabled her to display her visualizations at C-level meetings with unprecedented crispness and clarity. She can partition regions of the screen and "flatten" her visualization, into a format more suited for presentation, and reserve other regions to display associated documents and tables for reference (Rusell et al. 2004).

Immersive screens: Today's Cave Automatic Virtual Environment (CAVE), the virtual reality environment whereby the walls and floor of a room are projections of the virtual world, will have variants by 2025, some useful for typical office and cubicle environments. Smaller versions of the Electronic Visualization Laboratory (EVL) of the University of Illinois at Chicago's ImmersaDesk are one possibility. Another alternative is a simple pairing of large high-resolution displays that make up Emily's desk in 2025: one is the horizontal work surface and the other is a vertical surface at the back of the desk (Figure 3.9).

Figure 3.9 Emily's immersive desk view on the risk room

Any Data, Any Model, Any Service

Data sources, data types, and methods to retrieve data continue to expand. Financial applications in 2025 will need to work with many types of data and sources.

Data

Without quality data, decisions are riskier and visual decision support tools need to include uncertainty metrics. In addition, in 2025, Emily will have access to massive quantities of data from her own model, and models generated by her associates. She also has access to historical data, captured by Sambborra over many years of business. Scalable visual and analytical techniques will be required (Eick and Karr 2002).

Big data: Financial services thrives on data and timeliness. Today, there are more than 150,000 stocks traded around the world. An active stock, such as Microsoft, may have more than 200,000 trades in one day. A bank will have millions of credit card accounts, with thousands of data attributes per person (age, income, number of cars, average balance, etc.) and thousands of transactions per person with multiple attributes per transaction. By 2025 the quantity and granularity of this information will increase by several orders of magnitude

Scope of data: Today, Emily's counterpart would have access to all the data stored in the SAP system available as input into her models. Emily's simulation, in today's terms, may generate thousands of scenarios across thousands of assets across hundreds to thousands of time steps. By Emily's time, she will have access to much more data available to her, such as:

- News, politics and economic data from different regions to understand the impact on local production and wages.
- Competitive intelligence, such as leaked emails, satellite photos, surveillance video and blog gossip, to assess aspects such as the financial health, management turmoil and pricing of her competitors.
- Simulation data from the R&D group providing better estimates on the potential value of each asset.
- Real-time data beyond market data, to include real-time sales and forecasting rather than end of quarter.

Underlying data infrastructure: Data services play a crucial role in making powerful applications like Emily's possible. Emily needs to easily gain access to this data through easy-to-use and easy-to-access real-time data distribution networks and transaction databases, multi-dimensional data management, and interfaces to web services for various models and data sources.

Models, Applications and Services

Integration of diverse analytical models will be required to maximize the new synthetic decision environment. Service oriented architectures (SOA) will need to be extended to support a broad range of informal and formal model services and their properties.

Computational models: Computational financial models are critical to the financial services industry: research analysts use models to estimate the profits of a company; ratings firms use models to estimate the likelihood of default; risk managers use models to estimate the potential for losses; portfolio managers use models to evaluate optimal combinations of assets; and traders use models to evaluate the appropriate price for an asset relative to other assets. Statistical models for aggregation and correlation are used for retail banking customer analytics.

Model location: Some of these models reside in spreadsheets, where numbers are changed and the spreadsheet recalculates on-the-fly for a quick "what-if" scenario. Other models may exist in a database or web service, accessed through a complex API interface and potentially returning results nearly immediately or over a few hours. And some models will reside with certain people: for example the best estimate of the expected outcome of an ongoing legal case may be from a lawyer closely involved in the case rather than any computational model. Emily, Phil and Tim store their data in self describing data structures, that contains both the data and the syntax of its data model. This way, they can share their data without needing to pass through many layers of conversion.

Data integration: Spreadsheets are ubiquitous in financial services today. A modern spreadsheet is a powerful tool to complete sophisticated tasks for collecting, analyzing and summarizing data from multiple sources; and at the same time it is an easier environment to use than programming. Emily also needs an easy-to-use means to connect elements of data together, possibly via sophisticated, next generation spreadsheets, capable of manipulating tables, vectors, arrays and models as easily as individual cells are manipulated today, or perhaps some new form of semantic dataflow programming or workflow modeling will emerge.

Representations

The challenge and opportunity for virtual worlds is how to gain value from all the available data and models within a virtual environment. How can all the salient pieces of information hidden in this vast collection be found, connected, understood, repurposed for use in Emily's simulations, and then adequately explained to Carl in a brief meeting? These are issues of representation, interaction and workflows. What should a virtual world of financial data look like? The data is completely abstract without a real-world analog: there is no need for the data to look like a building or island. This is the question of representation.

Data Representations

One of the grand challenges for financial visualization in virtual worlds is visual expression through geometrical representations. There are many potential visualization techniques beyond bar charts, scatter plots and heat maps that have yet to be discovered that build on existing techniques (Bertin 1983, Healey 2007, Lohse 1991, Ware 2004) or invent wholly new ones (Harper et al. 2008, Horn 2002, Reijner 2008, Ziegler et al. 2008).

Scaling up representations: New high-level questions emerge, for example: When 100 megapixel displays are available, is it better to make a bar chart with 1000 bars, or is it better to use the concept of small multiples and create clusters of bar charts? Will heat maps (such as SmartMoney's Map of the Market) be effective when looking at 150,000 stocks?

Intuitive representations: Some visualization representations are powerful, such as parallel coordinate displays, wormplots and rugplots, but are not as common as other representations, perhaps because they are difficult to comprehend for new viewers. Are there visual enhancements that can improve the comprehensibility of these representations? Emily is comfortable with very sophisticated visualization metaphors, but she knows that Carl has a much more limited visual vocabulary. As such, she can apply different "templates" to the visuals, adapting it for different audiences, or as the level of complexity of analysis dictates.

Visual attributes: But even more importantly, the low-level underpinnings of visualization are not yet fully understood. For example, much research has been done regarding visual attributes such as color, but far less has been done in texture and shape. The interaction of these different variables is also not fully understood: which combinations work best under which circumstances? New research in neurophysiology, visual perception, vision systems and graphic design all provide valuable input into possibilities for new useful visual representations.

Beyond icons: Emily's visualization includes a map with markers for each location of Sambborra. A simplistic approach uses attributes such as size, color, shape and labels to convey information. Or, alternatively icons are used. How can icons be extended to show 5, 10 or more attributes? How does someone make sense of an icon with 50 attributes? How can one use and learn icons quickly, without training, rather than learning the hundreds to thousands of icons available in military 2525B symbology for example? Phil's model takes a level-of-detail approach, allowing a visual to be represented as a simple bar at a high level, but represents it as a complex cluster of very detailed visuals upon close inspection. In this way, he doesn't overload the user with too much information when a casual overview is required, but is able to present considerably more detail as the element is "zoomed-into".

Efficient layouts: Newspaper illustrations today are beautiful hand-crafted combinations of graphics and text, well composed and set out, with labels and whitespace. With 100 megapixels, can visualizations automatically organize content and layouts so that regardless of where you may be standing within a virtual room, elements can be organized and tweaked to minimize issues such as occlusion and poor legibility and maximize emphasis to optimize the user's attention?

Visual fusion: Attempting to understand many different attributes at once remains a challenge. Many visualization approaches today attempt to solve this by marshalling several coordinated visualization components into a larger framework. Interaction with one component updates the corresponding data point in other components. The problem with this technique is that a user becomes overloaded by the need to visually coordinate one data point across several simultaneous representations. Visual fusion is the attempt to represent the many different attributes per each data point within a single display. However, this requires research and design, working through concepts in visual attributes, icons, labeling and layouts to create effective visual fusions of data.

Avatars

Seamless avatars: As previously noted, financial users will need to access the virtual world from various devices. An avatar must be able to act as a proxy for a participant who may only be participating via phone. Or, for some of the small screens, avatars may be better represented as an abstracted 2D comic.

Telepresence: At the other end of the spectrum, for important decisions, directly seeing the facial expressions and body language of the participants may be critical to reach an agreement. These avatars may be an extremely high-fidelity representation of their human counterpart or a direct high-definition video of the human participant. At the extreme, it could it be similar to the virtual sets used during the CNN 2008 US presidential election results television broadcast; although simpler desk-sized and board-room-table sized virtual sets may be more likely utilized in a workplace.

Visual Analytics

Visual analytics: Visual analytics is the combination of visualization interfaces with analytical computational models (Thomas and Cook 2005). Visualization of these models provides a means for rapidly assessing the information generated by the models; as well as a natural interface for exploring the model by adjusting parameters or interacting subsets of results. By tightly coupling the visualizations to the models the users of this information have an environment for quickly constructing and revising models and assumptions as well as evaluating the results. This faster cycle of analysis permits more alternatives to be considered in a shorter time span increasing the opportunity for profitability and productivity. For example:

- Emily may want to override Tim's commodity price forecasts and directly adjust the underlying assumptions. She can drill into Tim's model, then click and drag the setting for price volatility. Increasing its value by two or three times shows Emily how the dramatic market swings back in 2008 would impact the company if they were to happen again now.

- Carl may want to gain a rapid understanding of the geothermal power generation market, a new line of business that Sambborra is considering. Using the vast amounts of high-dimensional data available, Carl is slicing and dicing the data with statistical algorithms to see correlations between the geothermal power market in general as compared to power generation in coal, oil, gas, nuclear, wind and solar. He is also looking for quality of fit with Sambborra's existing operations, so that Sambborra could quickly divest of non-strategic assets to reduce his acquisition costs.

Data objects: Data integration is a desirable task to achieve directly in the virtual world. If Phil has a new spreadsheet model, he wants to bring it to the virtual world meeting and re-integrate it there—not back on his desktop. Models can become tangible objects manipulated directly within the virtual world. Some are like spreadsheets, visually revealing the data with a click and drag of a group of cells in one application over to another application creating a link between the two applications. Others are represented as electronic components visually revealing their connectors and integration is click and drag assembly of components. Still others are represented like charts and graphs, or other abstract visual constructs, depicting the data and providing connection via click and drag on bars (for a data series), axes (for a range of values), or labels (for categories).

Adaptive analytics: Visual analytics can go further still. Considerable time and effort is currently dedicated to get our software tools to do what we want. Early cars required drivers to handle a plethora of gadgets (chock levers, engine cranks, clutch and gear shifts, etc.). All these gadgets took time away from the primary task of driving. Future cars may be designed to realize the primary task is to reach a destination and change what we consider necessary for driving. Similarly, future visual analytics software will sense the task, the tool and the context. Reasoning services will work with tool and task models to make recommendations on useful operations and tasks to do as well as how and when to best show those recommendations to the user.

Interaction, Workflow and Adaptation

Input

We can see precursors to tomorrow's input devices in today's objects like the Nintedo Wii game controller, Sony's Eyecam and Apple's iPhone.

Gestures: Gesture-based interfaces, popularized by the iPhone and other multitouch interfaces, have the potential to make navigation of visualizations more intuitive. For example, in a 3D visualization today, if something in the background is occluded by the foreground, the viewer must change position or rotate the scene to see around the offending object. In a gesture based interface, one could simply brush the foreground aside. Our interaction vocabulary will need to be expanded for a wide variety of gestures. For example, if Tim uses 3D scatter plots to review price data, then interactions such as stretching, rotating, clustering, sorting, splitting, ranking and expanding will be necessary to work with subsets of the data. Research is required to create a language of gestures for navigating and interacting with 3D spaces.

Phicons: More complex interactions can be achieved using phicons: an intuitive means of interaction with 3D environments through grasping and manipulating real-world objects (e.g., a Wii controller) that corresponds to a virtual world object (e.g., a tennis racket). For example, trying to rotate and move a 3D object with a 2D device (e.g., a mouse or a gesture) can be challenging. However, a phicon can be physically grasped and twisted to easily and simply define six attributes of position and orientation. Furthermore, you can use a number of specialized phicons: phicons for avatars (to move around); for models (to adjust parameters); for assets (drag assets from a portfolio to a broker to sell them); or for navigation (e.g., to change the orientation of a portion of a scene).

Heads-up: Transparent overlays across a 3D scene providing a "heads-up" display are common in many games today. Within financial services there is much additional information about people and objects in the world that need to be easily accessible to subsets of participants. Note that Phil and Tim cannot see everything that Carl and Emily can see. The extra information could be provided in the heads-up display without compromising the core visualization that everyone can see. Similarly, Phil may be an outside consultant with access to additional information that only he can see. The concept of the heads-up display augments the common virtual world with private information.

Lens: Heads-up displays can be extended with the concept of the "see through interface" popularized by Bill Buxton in the 90's. A viewer can move a lens over any part of the scene to reveal additional information and provide additional interactions. Imagine Emily has a magnifying glass with X-ray capabilities that shows hidden details such as the data source, when moved over a bar. Now, with the X-ray view, the internal details can be adjusted, and the visualization updates. Phil also has a magnifying glass, but his magnifying glass only works on his spreadsheet while Emily's model remains opaque to Phil. Similarly, Donovan, the CEO of Sambborra, can walk into a meeting, and use a lens to reveal the names and affiliation of Tim and Phil since he is not familiar with them and frame his comments as needed.

Coordination and Workflow

Multiple simultaneous collaborators: The collaborative world that Phil, Emily and Tim work in will result in greater productivity and more accurate forecasts. But what happens when both Emily and Tim want to adjust the volatility parameter at the same moment: does it lock onto the first participant to reach it? Or, what happens when Emily changes the volatility assumptions at the same time that Phil adjusts some cash flow assumptions: does Emily see only the impact of her change, or both? If she sees both, then how can she know what the contribution of her modification is to the overall result? If each participant has to wait, productivity goes down. If each participant acts independently and has separate versions, then they are no longer referring to the same common model. Techniques are required that enable each person to work independently, then bring their results back together and easily overlaying two versions to see and resolve the delta between them as Emily has done. This implies tremendous complexity: the changes may be in the input data, the assumptions, the models or the output data. Drawing comparisons and finding differences between two or more highly similar models is always a challenge. Sometimes Emily pairs two models together, side-by-side, so that a quick comparison can be made. On other occasions, she takes several models, makes them translucent, and overlays them together in the same 3D space, so that subtle differences can be visually extracted. When multiple models are being compared, she can even play back these models as though they were frames in a movie, detecting subtle differences as minute flickers, the way an astronomer uses multiple images of the night sky to search for stellar objects.

Multiple worlds: Participants act in several markets with different people and different contexts. Phil works with an outside consulting firm and several times in a day needs to participate in another virtual world with a large bank. Carl works closely with this forecasting group but also with the VP of Sales and at times wants to overlay the work from the sales forecasts against the risk forecasts from Emily's group.

Workflow: The synthetic virtual worlds of 2025 have semantic understanding of a user's task and data, enabling them to recommend new tools, related information or even other people that might be useful for the current task. Solutions may be created as task models authored by experts or use some form of automated workflow mined from the history of past workflows. Questions for extending these techniques will include how to infer task without any authored input and how to model workflow in a multi-tasking, multi-user environment.

Situation awareness: Movement between worlds must provide intuitive representations for rapid situation awareness. Not only does the system need to understand the context changes a user undergoes as their workflow progresses, but it must project those changes to the user in a way which promotes understanding. Data, applications, screen real estate and the nature of the problems themselves will increase by an order of magnitude for future users leaving little time for tweaking one's own interface.

Recording: Any of these tasks may be recorded. Not only is this a recording of the particular analysis, but it can also be a template for future analysis. All the captured interactions and intents can be reapplied in the future, with newer data and different participants. Since the data is now different and the results are different, the users can step back through the template and adjust assumptions that may no longer be valid; at the same time as gaining the benefit of the all the other steps done in the earlier review which are still valid. But how is the intent captured and clarified: does clicking on the tall left bar on a chart mean that the user is selecting the tallest bar or a specific category?

Adaptive Interfaces

In the face of complex, massive data as well as sophisticated computational models and powerful graphics engines, automatic intelligent agents will be working to help harness the value in the data, to present it in the right way at the right time and to make the most of the medium. Synthetic world environments will automatically adapt to factors such as individual users, tasks, the data and the context. The cognitive load of a task can be reduced by techniques such as scaling task complexity, scaled automation, attention management and clarifying meaning. Emily is well aware of cognitive overload. While she has many years of experience with her model, she knows how overwhelming it can be to the uninitiated. To help reduce this, she starts with reviewing the entire model at a geographic level, to help cement the concept that her various modeling elements map to real, physical locations. From there, she can expand on a region, sector, or timeline, using abstract visuals to represent financial metrics. Different layers, walls, and visual elements can be selectively overlaid, depending on the complexity of the analysis, or what is required to effectively describe the scenario.

Adaptive synthetic world visualizations will require user models, task models, context recognition, data awareness, visualization composition grammars and effective machine reasoning methods. Visualization techniques may use automatic abstraction and automatic composition agents to help the user make sense of the data for the task. In Emily's case, to visually inspect and tune their models, Emily and the analysts have several meetings in a synthetic world environment to review the models and discuss how to best integrate new elements and come up with options. Automatic intelligent agents mediate this process by making suggestions to correct errors, to fill gaps, to extend coverage and to test operation of the models.

Usability issues with adaptive systems will need to be resolved. For example, the complexities of machine inference and decision processes contradict the usability goals of predictability and comprehensibility. The implicit or explicit acquisition by the system of information about the user as well as the seizure of work from the user contradicts usability goals of controllability. In your face, anthropomorphic appearances of software agents are the opposite of unobtrusiveness. Usability of adaptive systems is not a solved problem but there are promising improvements such as inspection of user models, explanation of system action, making requests for approval and adapting timing of messages to the user's context and activity (Jameson 2005). When Emily and her associates meet in their synthetic world, the environment is responsible for coordinating communication and control between different parties, for instance, allowing only those users who should have the ability to make changes to actually be granted that control.

Experimental Assessment

Information visualization and visual analytic techniques for immersive synthetic worlds can provide rapid and insightful understanding of complex situations, Some performance factors are measurable (e.g., speed, accuracy, errors, comprehension) but the more important factors (e.g., creativity, consensus, divergence) are subtle and experiments are needed to understand how they are related and the principles underlying them (Brath 1997). For 3D virtual worlds to generate business value in a financial context, the right visualizations and interactions need to be used to improve speed of analysis, reduce rate of errors and improve quality of decisions. Various formal and informal studies and experiments need to be performed to observe, collect data and generate feedback to validate performance claims, to understand performance tradeoffs and to more clearly establish performance principles.

Social Issues

Social issues and the technological implementations to address those issues could dominate the acceptance and broad participation in financial synthetic worlds. Individual issues include user acceptance, willingness to learn and willingness to participate in the virtual world. Privacy and personal information will become increasingly contentious: the right to privacy and the right to act anonymously will conflict with computational abilities to aggregate personal information from a multitude of sources combined with interactive real-time analytic forecasting continuously updating throughout a conversation. New fraudulent techniques will emerge so new synthetic analytic worlds specifically for fraud prevention will also be required.

Priorities

There is still much that we do not know about effective visual representations, intuitive interactions, enhancing the coupling between visualization and analytics and aiding workflows. This research needs to occur at different levels: Some research will be conducted by the financial community, some by the visual analytics community and some by the human information interaction university research community. Who does what depends on payoff and the perceived addressable challenges.

Methodical investigation Required into the underlying representation and interaction techniques. Findings from related research areas, such as perceptual psychology and neuroscience inform potential techniques. As discussed above, our understanding of visual attributes, moving beyond icons, and understanding how to fuse many variables into one effective display are deep research issues on visual representation. Interaction techniques that combine gestures and phicons with layered displays require research.

Design and experimentation At a higher level, there is a need to create new ways of abstracting and representing information informed by the lower level investigations. The scale of the design space is enormous: there are many novel techniques for representing and interacting with information to be discovered. These designs need to be evaluated through experimentation and feedback. Our evolving virtual worlds can play a valuable role as a forum for potentially conducting these experiments. As these techniques evolve, they need to be classified and organized into design patterns so that the most effective techniques can be learned and reused.

Real-world applications Some design experiments may focus on evaluating a visual technique in a limited controlled setting. Also important is to apply the technique in real-world applications: does the technique work when applied to a real-world application or are there additional gaps that inform future improvement?

Conclusions

There is much exciting potential in virtual worlds for the financial industry. There are many research issues to be defined and tackled. Some have been identified here and many more are yet to be defined. For the financial industry though, the motivation to innovate and adopt new capabilities is based on the benefits to be gained.

The benefit of any new technology must be measured in its usefulness to the final user, so how will these advances impact the actors of our scenario? Phil and Tim's main goal is to provide solid financial advice to Emily in a way she will understand and appreciate. Synthetic worlds provide a sense of presence which allows them to interact with Emily despite the fact they are on a different continent. Their adaptive visualizations of complex data allow them to efficiently provide rich information as it needed.

Emily's job is not only dealing with extremely complex data, but also creating and incorporating complex models and predictions of that data. Her chosen visualization of work environment allows her to work with the models directly as opposed to through a collection of disparate and cumbersome tools. She can draw on other team members and experts, allowing her model to be tuned and enhanced with their specialized knowledge Her presentation is both intuitive and interactive, giving her superiors a deep level of understanding the data as well as engaging in their own "what-if" scenarios. She is able to get the results she needs faster and get them to the people that need them.

Carl knows his detailed financial models but worries that his team hasn't covered enough scenarios with adequate precision. Sambborra's financial synthetic world gives him confidence that the decisions he recommends to the board of directors mitigate Sambborra's risks and optimize its growth.

References

Bertin, J. (1983). *Semiology of Graphics*. Madison, Wis.: University of Wisconsin Press.

Brath. R. (1997). Metrics for Effective Information Visualization. *Proceedings of IEEE Symposium on Information Visualization '97*, 108–111.

Eick, S and Karr, A. (2002). Visual Scalability. *Journal of Computational and Graphical Statistics* 11(1):22–43.

Healey, C. (2007). Perception in Visualization. www.csc.ncsu.edu/faculty/healey/PP/index.html

Harper, R., Rodden, T., Rogers, Y., and Sellen, A. (2008). *Being Human: Human-Computer Interaction in the Year 2020*.

Horn, R. (2002). Visual Language and Converging Technologies in the Next 10–15 Years. *Converging Technologies for Improving Human Performance,* 141–149.

Jameson, A. (2005). User Modeling Meets Usability Goals, *Proceedings of User Modeling 2005*, 1–3.

Lohse, J. (1991). A Cognitive Model for the Perception and Understanding of Graphs, *Proceedings of ACM Conference on Human Factors in Computing Systems 1991* 137–144,

Reijner, H., (2008). The Development of the Horizon Graph. *Vis2008 Workshop.*

Russell, D.M., Trimble, J.P., and Dieberger, A. (2004). "The Use Patterns of Large, Interactive Display Surfaces: Case Studies of Media Design and Use for BlueBoard and MERBoard." *Proceedings of the 37th Hawaii International Conference on System Sciences,* 98–107. (*)

Thomas, J., and Cook, K. (2005). *Illuminating the Path: The Research and Development Agenda for Visual Analytics*. New York: IEEE Press.

Ware, C. (2004). *Information Visualization: Perception for Design*. San Francisco, CA: Morgan Kaufmann.

Wattenberg, M. (1999). "Visualizing the Stock Market." *Proceedings of SICGHI '99 Extended Abstracts,* 188–189.

Wright, W. (1995). "Information Animation: Applications in the Capital Markets." *Proceedings of Information Visualization 1995.*

Ziegler, H., Nietzschmann, T., and Keim. D. (2008). "Visual Analytics on the Financial Market: Pixel-based Analysis and Comparison of Long-Term Investments," 2008, *Proceedings 12th Conference On Information Visualization.*

Chapter 4

A Day at a 3D Datacenter

Michael Osias, Joan L. Mitchell, Donna Eng Dillenberger, David Ward, and Sandra K. Johnson

Abstract

The 3D datacenter brings together data from customers systems and renders the many dimensions of the datacenter in ways that are not possible with 2-dimensional business applications. The integrated and consolidated view of the datacenter provides enhanced situational awareness of multiple facets of the center, leading to improved operational efficiencies and new insights into the business. A 3D datacenter is customizable and versatile, both in the data it receives and the layout and function of the datacenter. This customization is useful when managing live systems, but especially if the tool is used to perform simulations for planning such as space, thermal, power, or other planning needs. Or if the business is oriented toward marketing and branding, customers can include their own brand images, products, and equipment in the center for sales and marketing purposes such as demonstrations. A 3D datacenter also extends the business value of previous investments, by leveraging and extending existing systems management and monitoring infrastructure.

A day in the life of a system administrator in a 3D datacenter consists of teleporting their avatar into the synthetic datacenter. Walking, and flying, through the synthetic datacenter to check on status or clicking on physical systems to move their workloads to another part of the 3D datacenter. What happens in the virtual world will be mirrored in the physical world and vice versa. Moving virtual machine images in the synthetic world will be a control for global workload load balancing. Other avatars could teleport in for collaborative debugging, training and capacity planning sessions. Physically, the experts would come from any corner in the world where there is internet access. No one need board a plane that may get delayed or drive on a freeway that freezes up or leave the comfort of their families to help colleagues provide a global IT operations.

1.0 Story

Grant squinted in the morning light as he opened the rustic wooden door of his log home. The chill in the early morning air made the far off snow covered peaks sharp like razors, while the sunbeams cascaded through the clear air and into his sleepy eyes. He looked down the hill where the livestock were, and saw the animals lightly grazing. Living on this remote mountain farm in the modern era was afforded by the pervasive global information grid. This allowed Grant and most of the worlds' population to "plug in" to the grid, sometimes called cyberspace, from any location. It was time to plug in to the grid and check up on the business, so he headed up to his office.

The business Grant had constructed was a purely virtual business in cyberspace and provided various kinds of services to customers on the grid such as 3D Datacenter management, AI, and economic services. The massive buildings, machines, and square miles of land Grant owned in cyberspace, would be a large city in the real world. Yet he was able to coexist with nature on this small farm, emitting a carbon footprint less than zero, and enjoy the beauty and seclusion of his home.

Grant did most of his work from the office on the second floor, which was a hexagonal room with large windows on each side. While offering a stunning panoramic view, it also served as a weather station and observatory, and with one thought could be shuttered tight or shaded. He willed the shades shut, and activated his grid link.

He chose a nondescript grid link, a small plastic one that fit behind his ear, model TM20. Even though he as always tried to stay as "natural" as possible, he did elect for the electromagnetic implant option. A small syringe of nano-solution was injected, and a swarm of nanobots converged on certain points of the neocortex and built molecule sized electromagnetic receptors which became embedded wetware for use in conjunction with the TM20 or other grid links. He affixed the TM20 behind his right ear and with a thought powered it on and established a link with the grid. Within a few seconds the TM20 configured an electromagnetic mesh field around Grant's skull, and brought his internal wetware online. The effect was sort of like switching from one frequency to another, except for all of the senses, and even some senses humans do not posses in the real world. With a flash and bit of static, Grant teleported into his command center.

The digital structures formed before him, porcelain white digital stone, carved in the mind of the machine towered before him. Brilliant white spires of data towered above fields of virtual software and hardware machines of which Grant currently had under contract. From his location on level 3 he could see nearly all of the projects, and saw some alert activity over near one of the government accounts. Beacons were flashing and he could faintly hear the sirens above the gentle breeze. Grant pulled up the map and saw that his partner Jimbo had already teleported over and was looking into the situation. Grant decided to teleport to the bridge and begins a shift of work.

Even though Grant serviced many customers, mainly looking over their physical infrastructure and health of applications, his 3D datacenter and operations center allowed him to merge the disparate heterogeneous resources and applications into a single entity that allowed him to manage it as a whole. This also includes the suites of AI agents which perform optimization and grid reconnaissance operations for him. For some of his accounts, he is only brokering resources by optimizing the cost and provisioning of clouds, e.g., virtual appliances to grid services that customers run. A lot of this has been automated but there is always some critical situation that comes up and requires Grant or Jimbo to intervene.

Grant's communicator beeped and Jimbo spoke. "You better come look at this; we may be facing a weather event." Grant hit teleport on the in-world communicator and teleported to Jimbo's location. He was on an observation platform above the region of

Figure 4.1 Overlooking the Operations Center

systems for some global government applications. These applications were related to the automated remote grid processor nodes that were deployed in the wastelands. There appeared to be some odd patterns in the workload indicators across the field. The alarms that had sounded for this sector were the workload entropy scanners, part of the security subsystem.

These grid nodes the government is using are small solar powered processors which are manufactured and deployed in the desert. Since they are deployed in the desert, actually on the desert floor, there is plenty of radiation hitting the surface which these devices can convert to processing power. Long gone are the days of air conditioning and water cooling. Soon after the first decade of the turn of the century, legacy datacenters generated a carbon footprint which exceeded the airline industry at the time. The green period, which sought to reduce energy consumption and optimize resources, could not keep pace with the exploding demand for computational capacity. No matter how the energy was shifted, from the superheated processors to the water chillers, no one could circumvent the laws of thermodynamics. All terms of the equation must equally balance over time.

These nodes are manufactured from the sand in the wasteland, by a continuous large scale nano-reaction. When one observes such a complex first hand, they see tens of thousands of small shimmering cubes just lying on the desert floor, sprawled out in a grid fashion. Each of these grid processors has standard components, but they can be custom built to take on certain characteristics of the ever changing workload characteristics seen on the grid. Redundancy is cheap, and advanced algorithms distribute workload and data in an operating context where failure of nodes is guaranteed. These complexes are highly resilient in the face of hardware faults by sheer redundancy and autonomic algorithms.

"Let's teleport to the situation room and perform some analytics." Grant suggested. Grant and Jimbo teleported into the situation room, an area above the operations floor,

Figure 4.2 Situation Room

consisting of a large map of the world on the floor, and a semi-transparent observation platform. Grant walked across the platform to the map control console, and selected a filter based on the account. He selected seismic, weather, and electromagnetic filters. On the map room floor, several layers of holograms appeared over the map. Each layer represented one of the data points on the filter, starting with seismic, weather, and electromagnetic. Off the coast of the desert land where the processing center was located, a line of small red dots was scattered in a random but semi-linear pattern. A pressure trough was also visible, indicated by the thermal lines in the weather layer. There were also some odd patterns in the electromagnetic field above the seismic and weather activity.

"This does not look good." Grant said, as he and Jimbo walked across the map to the area. "This seismic activity, the red dots, is exhibiting a pattern which follows this continental shelf. Computer, generate seismic relief." As Grant issued the command, the map was transformed into a seismic relief map, and sure enough, there was a large shelf on the ocean floor which spanned hundreds of miles. "This could be a tsunami situation. The entropy scanners at the processing facility are probably sensing the fluctuations of the EMF as a result of the stresses on the fault."

"Do we have enough data to run some simulations?" Jimbo asked.

"We do not have those data feeds, but I think running a simulation is a good idea. Let's task an agent to assemble an application to perform the services integration and fusion." Grant summoned an agent using his in-world communicator. The agent materialized before Grant and Jimbo. This version had some enhanced algorithms regarding data recon and optimizing provisioning of those services based on quality and economic metrics. The agent's appearance was driven by its function, with small propulsion motors, a core AI housing, a sensor complex with various spatial, visual, and data sensors, and two seats in case an avatar such as Grant wanted to ride along on a mission. Grant then tasked the agent in natural language. "I want to run tsunami simulations based on the data in the map. Provision for me data services, processing algorithms, and enough computational capacity to run real-time simulations. Corroborate findings with the Global Weather Service, and if necessary alert them and provide them with the simulation data."

"For what duration and cost?" the agent asked.

"I want to run simulations for 15 minutes at no more than $100 per simulation." Grant replied.

"Ok" the agent confirmed, as it launched high into the command center and out one of the grid portals. "While that's happening, let's begin to locate backup capacity in case we need to shut down alpha plant." said Grant.

"Why will we need to shut it down?" asked Jimbo.

"If a tsunami hits, it will likely submerge the facility. The processors can operate under water, but if the entire population is swept away, they will loose processing coherency and eventually power if they are underwater for too long. We need to plan for a backup site for this workload in the event this seems likely. We'll know more after we run the simulations. Jimbo, please use the global grid workload simulator to find a backup site. Spread it across multiple sites in the grid if needed. After you have identified the candidate 3D datacenters, task an agent to optimize the operational and financial SLAs so we minimize the impact to us and the customer".

"I'm on it." said Jimbo, and he teleported back up to the observation deck to work with one of the consoles. Grant began configuring a composite simulation that would combine the tsunami scenarios with the datacenter relocation work that Jimbo was performing. The trick is to calibrate the simulation systems so all of the data is synchronized, and can be rendered in the map room of the command center so they could see exactly what is happening with the different scenarios.

As Grant was finishing the simulation integration, the agent returned and gave a report. "All services have been provisioned within the requested parameters. Cloud resources have been configured and are ready to execute."

"Let's start the tsunami simulation" said Grant. With the command, the agent took control of the map apparatus, and began rezzing, or manifesting the 3D elements. The datacenter in jeopardy appeared as a small 3D structure on the map, while the seismic, weather, and electromagnetic layers rezzed above it. "Running simulation epoch 0" said the agent.

The seismic simulation layer began to jitter, and suddenly shifted and split along the oceanic shelf, leaving a fifty meter difference in height along the fault line. An image of a high energy waveform developed along the ocean floor. Grant watched as it rippled away from the epicenter, and noticed the amplitude waveform heading straight for the datacenter. As it approached land, a one hundred meter wall of water washed over the coastline, and crashed nearly 150 miles inland. He became alarmed as this easily wiped

Figure 4.3 Visualizing the datacenter simulation

out any trace of the datacenter. He was glad he performed the simulation, and would now have enough time to take preventative measures.

"Jimbo how are you doing with your models?" Grant asked into his communicator. "It looks like we are going to take the hit in a bad way."

Jimbo had constructed a 3D datacenter on the fly, drawing resources from the datacenter in the tsunami path as one set of systems, and an inventory of capacity which were owned by the company and situated throughout the grid. At his command console, he entered a request to filter servers by service criticality. Instantly, all the high priority servers glowed a bright hue of yellow. Jimbo flew over to the first group, and touched the button on the rack to bring up the rack control center. A screen popped up above the rack, and indicated the nature of the critical applications and data running on the group of systems. He flew up a bit more and inspected the field of reserve capacity, and issued a query for an equivalent set of resources. The compatible reserve systems lit up with gold beacons. With that, Jimbo pulled the applications and data from the running datacenter and into his virtual inventory, and deposited them onto the identified reserve systems, effectively performing a data and workload migration. However, this being a simulation, no actual operations were taking place. Rather, as the simulation ran, the steps were recorded into a script, which Jimbo planned to execute once all the critical elements were identified and operations deemed valid.

"I am using the 3D datacenter to identify critical applications and remote reserve capacity on the grid. I've started to build a migration script that will move the data and applications." Jimbo reported.

"Please continue, we are definitely going to have a full outage on this underwater datacenter. I have already dispatched the results of the tsunami models to the customer. The priority is critical applications and data have no service interruption." Grant said.

As Jimbo was inspecting the datacenter and moving critical applications, one of the government customers, Ian, teleported in. "Hi, my CIO sent me here to monitor the migration and report on the risk of outage from the tsunami" he said to Jimbo.

"That is great; you can help me with this. I am preparing a script to move these systems to other grid nodes." Jimbo granted access to Ian so he could begin to interact with the 3D servers and help make decisions. The collaborative capabilities offered by the 3D datacenter will reduce the cycle time between customer communications and help Jimbo move the data and applications faster.

When they had finished simulating the migration, Jimbo notified Grant. "We have a script ready to go to shut down the datacenter and migrate the workload. Based on the forecasts, we expect zero downtime for the critical applications. Just give me the word and I will execute it."

"Make it so" said Grant.

Jimbo went back to his console, and bespoke the commands to the computer to execute the migration plan they had just constructed using the 3D datacenter. Sirens blared and alert lights began flashing, indicating a major 3D datacenter operation was underway. Above the live systems and reserve systems, beams of light connected from source to target resource migration. The color and thickness of the beams indicated the rate of transfer and overall status. Ian and Jimbo flew high above the 3D Datacenter and observed the matrix of light as it ebbed and oscillated based on the state of the migration. When systems were finished, the light link would disappear, and the source system would turn grey and semi-transparent, indicating it was offline.

Grant flew up next to where they were hovering, just as the last of the migrations were complete. Ian accessed his communicator, and opened an ad-hoc holographic group chat with his CIO. "Good news boss, the 3D datacenter tool allowed us to quickly create and execute a mitigation plan. Our applications and data are online and no longer in jeopardy from the tsunami."

2.0 Technology

The Grid

A globally connected grid, or Intergrid consisting of independent but interlinked grids, is the foundation for much of the technology discussed. A grid is nothing more than an array of general purpose computing resources which can be tasked/provisioned/managed as a single entity. The emergence of grid technology centered around massively parallel processing applications in supercomputing centers around the world. We will see that parallel processing is a key aspect of the next evolutionary step of the 3D virtual worlds, as these services are provided by instances of simulators which run in parallel in grids or virtualized within a grid as a cloud. One could argue that the Internet is a loosely coupled collection of parallel processes, namely web servers.

The Internet today is a globally distributed and connected computing platform. Services operating in this hardware footprint are mostly those which provide web services for applications internet applications. These include presentation services such as web sites and portals, infrastructure management services, and information services from databases, backend systems, or real-world sensors. The new applications that are coming, the 3D simulators, are also parallel applications, but have quite different workload characteristics which complement virtualized distributed parallel processing grids.

The Simulators

The simulator is the 3D equivalent of the 2D Internet web server in the sense that it serves content, manages client sessions and network connections, and other services to 3D clients. The simulator serves up the virtual world to 3D clients. This means that the land/terrain, buildings, object, and user sessions/avatars are all managed by the simulator server. And just because it is commonly referred to as a simulator, does not mean the activity in the virtual world is not related to real world operations. As an example, simulators have data integration interfaces that can integrate data from management systems or distributed sensor networks.

Another characteristic of simulators is the rich in-world programming models, which allow users to automate aspects of the 3D environment with various scripting languages. A script object can be associated with a 3D object, which creates a containment association; conceptually equivalent to the 3D object becomes a runtime container for the scripts. These scripts can manipulate the 3D object by location, scale, color, and many other attributes. They can send and receive messages, and perform other functions related to the simulator. A very important construct emerges here, which is the notion of a state based autonomous asynchronous execution environment, which lays the foundation for some of the artificial intelligence subsystems.

AI Subsystems

The artificial intelligence scenarios described utilize the characteristics of the interconnected simulator grid. These include perceptors regarding proximity and in-world data communications, effectors, and autonomous state management. The programming model described above allows a variety of AI algorithms to be implemented for specific behaviors, and more complex agents can be constructed by partitioning perceptive, reasoning, and measurement systems into layers with different objects such as the subsumption architecture. Within this fertile environment for multiagent systems are many possibilities. Since we are discussing stateful asynchronyous entities which are mobile across the grid, essentially a large interconnected computing space, it provides a rich platform for distributed agent based computing. Scenarios range from personal information assistants to populations of trained agents which perform complex dataveillance or control tasks across the grid.

Cognitive UI

As operating in the 3D environment has many advantages as a new user interface for general purpose computing, so are emerging control interfaces which improve efficiency. The emerging trends in this area are focused around reading electromagnetic signals from a person's brain using a hardware apparatus which fits on the person's head like a hat. Software is used to correlate the signals read with some operation to be performed on the system. Basic thought commands can be merged into strings of complex operations. As this technology matures, applications will become increasingly more sophisticated as users learn to vibrate thought forms and the software performs corresponding actions in the system. These include moving the operators' avatar as if they used a mouse, manipulating objects in the world, and at some point potentially sending thought messages through the system to other users on the grid without the use of voice or text.

Tying it all Together

When all of these elements are combined, a new computing model and infrastructure emerges that is evolutionary from today's technology but introduces a number of discontinuities which dramatically change how the system is accessed, how applications are developed, and how data is processed. In time the simulators themselves are likely to become operating systems which fulfill sort of a holy grail of the network operating system, but instead as a grid operating system. This was demonstrated with technology such as Doom OS where the simulator was the operating system, no DOS or Windows required. In a grid environment, simulators like Doom OS would incorporate grid and local infrastructure and management services into an integrated software platform. Even middleware components that manage grid-wide concerns can be built inside of the simulator virtual world.

Prescriptions to Managers and Research Sponsors

Many of the technologies described to support the scenario are available today and are at various levels of maturity. Simulators such as the OpenSimulator project and various 3D engines are available for production use today. Some have included a grid architecture as part of the foundation such as OpenSimulator and OptimalGrid. Users can get started on these platforms and learn about the content pipeline, simulator operations, and applications in virtual worlds. However, much work needs to be done on standardizing grid architectures to address infrastructure management issues, and more importantly interoperability of services within and between grids that support virtual worlds.

A phase shift of application function, logic, and processing will occur as people begin to use virtual worlds for real world business applications, as foreseen by the story. There will still be pure middleware and some web services elements of the architecture for quite some time. However as the phase shift progresses, these will migrate into the new 3D virtual world platform and begin to evaporate from the architecture as this refactoring occurs. Users should always question, "if" they leave the virtual world to perform some function, what is missing from the virtual world that causes them to go outside and seek a web or script or other type of solution? These are important research topics.

The notion of the virtual world platform as a network or grid operating system is a research area with a great deal of potential. This 3D grid operating system will have specialized in-world applications and interfaces and hardware drivers, and the line between the virtual world of today and the operating system will be pushed very close to the hardware layer. One can envision what the management interface to the drivers for a high performance storage subsystem attached to a grid hardware node might look like in the virtual world.

New ways to interface with the virtual world are available today. Emotiv has developed a commercially available neuroheadset that detects and maps brainwave signatures into system commands. Instead of the user thinking to physically move her mouse and click on something, she may will her avatar to walk over to a 3D virtual terminal and press a button. The applications of such capability are very compelling, but there are issues to be worked out. These include the safety of the devices, the privacy of the user, since we are now essentially reading his thoughts and streaming them into a computer, and long term usage consequences. There are opportunities for both cognitive and computer science research in this area.

From the artificial intelligence perspective, the environment described provides a rich "aether" or "fabric" where autonomous intelligent software machines can operate and even coexist and communicate with human based entities in the environment. The feasibility of the application of much of the prior generation of AI technology, specifically systems of distributed agents, should be reviewed in light of this emerging computing environment. This can lead to resolution of some difficult problems faced in classical agent environments, reinforce robust patterns, and provide insight into new generations of AI technology.

References

Gelernter, D. (1991). *Mirror Worlds*. Oxford University Press.

Weiss, G. (1999). *Multiagent Systems: A Modern Approach to Distributed Artificial Intelligence*. Cambridge, MA: MIT Press.

Foster, I., and Kesselman, C. (2004). *The Grid 2: Blueprint for a New Computing Infrastructure*. Elsevier.

Emotiv neuro headset. http://www.emotiv.com

Roco, M.C., and Bainbridge, W.S. (2002) Converging technologies for improving human performance: Integrating from the nanoscale. *Journal of Nanoparticle Research*, 4(4):281–295.

Osias, M.J., Tolk, A., and Darden, R.L. (2005). A grid enabled modeling and simulation prototype. IEEE ISPDC05.

Chapter 5
Hypothesis-Testing in a Biological Cartographic Virtual World

John W. Bodnar, Russ Vane, and Brian Rogers

Abstract

The biological sciences are at a watershed where the technological advances in data collection and database populating are leading toward a new era in understanding living organisms. The newest biological disciplines, bioinformatics and systems biology, hold the key to the next level of understanding. There are multiple challenges that must be met before biologists can build a virtual world in which they can study, analyze, visualize, and simulate both organismal behavior, the goal of systems biology, and the evolution of life, the core of bioinformatics. The addition of GPS- and Mapquest-driven cartographic virtual worlds on our car dashboards has revolutionized the way we navigate. We believe that the next revolution in systems biology and bioinformatics will come from adding a similar set of cartographic virtual world tools to the biologist's toolbox. Here we focus on some of the visualization challenges required for a biologist to plan in silico experiments for hypothesis-testing while na01vi0gating a cartographic virtual world in which playing field size can vary by fifteen orders of magnitude.

> The time is May 2025, and we are in a college freshman biology virtual classroom. The teacher, screen name MsDNA, has logged onto the projector screen; also logged on at individual workstations are NewBee, whose avatar is in the back row, PixieGirl is—as always—in the front row, while CaptainCrunch and CyberFemme are sitting together in the second row.
>
> "Welcome to our experimental *CootieWorld*[1] version of advanced introductory biology. Due to our success in using *CootieWorld* as a research tool and support tool in upper level biology classes, this year you are part of a nationwide experiment to use *CootieWorld* as a primary teaching tool all the way through your college career. The four of you have been chosen from all our freshmen to help us in this experiment because you all have had extensive experience with *CootieWorld*.

---

1 *CootieWorld* is a multi-dimensional virtual world based on the "Cootie" game. One wins the "Cootie" game in a simple biological virtual world by recognizing the simple modules that comprise the "cootie bug" and assembling them into a viable organism with all required body parts.

Remember on orientation day when we asked you for your *CootieWorld* screen name and asked your permission to get your profiles from NCBI?[2]" {All nod.} "We checked all the screen names and found that of all the incoming freshmen, about half already have *CootieWorld* screen names and avatars, but you're the only ones who have already advanced to green belt in the training modules. We hope you all will advance to black belt this year, so you can begin your careers as experimental scientists in the new series of labs next year." {CaptainCrunch looks distressed and raises his hand}. "Yes, CaptainCrunch, I know you're in Naval ROTC and hope to be a nuclear submarine officer when you graduate. But, when I say 'scientist,' I mean 'anyone who uses the scientific method.' And engineers, naval officers, and even historians are 'scientists' by my definition because they all employ the scientific method in their work." {He smiles and puts his hand down.}

"We're going to do your first *in silico* research project over the next three classes. Remember, *in vivo* projects are ones you do in the field or wet lab, *in vitro* projects are ones you do in the test tube. *In silico* ones are ones you do inside the virtual world inside the computer." {Blank stares all around}. "Please explain what we mean by the scientific method?"

CyberFemme: "It's a systematic way of finding answers to research questions. You start with a hypothesis, design an experiment, do the experiment, compare the results with your hypothesis, then refine your hypothesis based on what you see. AND go around and around until you're sure your hypothesis is true (or really, not false), to the best of your ability."

MsDNA: "And when you're done you have a theory—that's what we call a hypothesis supported by experimental evidence—and you write up your theory in a paper. EVERYONE who uses the scientific method does that. Scientists—like you want to be *NewBee*—publish in journals; naval officers—*CaptainCrunch*—write technical manuals and operation orders. Historians write books. Doctors and nurses—like you want to be *PixieGirl*—write prescriptions or clinical papers based on their research, but their research goes by the name of diagnosis. And intelligence analysts—like you want to be *CyerFemme*—write assessments for the president or the Pentagon, but their research goes by the name of analysis. SO… today we will teach you how to use *CootieWorld* to do research or diagnosis or analysis—whatever your particular career field calls it. Next week we'll teach you how to use all the *CootieWorld* navigation and hypothesis-testing tools to build a theory from a hypothesis, and the third week to integrate all that research into a coherent story ready for publication. Think of these three classes as a career counseling session on how *CootieWorld* can be an integral part of the rest of your careers.

2 NCBI is the National Center for Biotechnology Information. We believe that by 2025 some version of what we call *CootieWorld* will be added as another resource to the NCBI website [http://www.ncbi.nlm.nih.gov/] and integrated with the growing number of NCBI data-recall, bioinformatics, and systems biology tools for seamless "pivoting" among the applications.

When I mentioned doing experiments *in silico*, I saw you, *CyberFemme*, rolling your eyes because I know you were thinking 'How the heck can I do an experiment in a computer?'" {*CyberFemme* blushes.} "That's a pretty usual response. But get used to it. Intelligence analysts do ALL their experiments *in silico*. That's why our first *in silico* research paper to will be right up your alley.

Today we've got two aims. Number one is learning how to get past the Drill-Down Dilemma and be able to frame a biological hypothesis in a manner that encompasses all the different biological disciplines, and number two is to practice doing hypothesis testing *in silico*. Both are challenges faced daily by biologists that require new ways of visualizing the world and how we think about the world.

Here we are on my default *CootieWorld* homepage… All of you logon and find your *CootieWorld* homepage." {Lots of clicking. The clicking stops and all the students look up}. "Good. Now, get into your mini-sub, and select HOME Level, then submerge your mini-sub and leave the docking bay.[3] You should start looking over the shoulder of your default avatar—mine's a fruit bat. Follow along with me as we navigate, not only for practice but because I'll want each of you to collect at least one Time-Arrow for your homework assignment." {We wait while the students get set.}

"All set?" {Nods all around} "Here we all are on our way out of the docking bay. We just call this HOME Level but it's really the ZoomLevel-Zero. *NewBee*, do you know why?"

NewBee: "Oh yes, that's because the screen size is ten-to-the-zero meters across."

MsDNA: "Exactly! Ten-to-the-zero is one, so your *CootieWorld* mini-sub viewscreen presents what you can see if that viewscreen is one meter-by-one meter in dimension. Now in the default NAVIGATE mode[4] you're looking out that one meter window just as you would if you are a Player in the game. Now, everyone click the OBSERVE mode button in the menu at the top… Here instead of looking over the shoulder of

3 *CootieWorld* is a navigational virtual world where level-jumping is done in a miniaturizable atomic-submarinea in the Isaac Asimov book *Fantastic Voyage* and the 1968 movie of the same name.

4 *CootieWorld* has multiple modes: Navigate games (where one navigates an avatar owl, bat, fly, yeast cell, or bacterial cell as one would in Second Life); Emulate games (where the viewscreen converts to what would be seen by the avatar owl navigating only by sound or the avatar yeast navigating only by taste); Observe games where the biologist can back off and hover various distances over the playing field to watch organismal behavior (as we will do in the narrative); and Analog games (where engineering analogs are used to teach how the analog biological systems work such as a submarine game that parallels the owl hunting by passive sonar and the bat hunting by active sonar or the submarine diesel-electric engineering system that parallels the aerobic-anaerobic metabolism of the yeast cell). First generation versions of the *Fly-Web* and *Yeast-Life* manual games and the *CootieFly* and *CootieBeetle* games for MacIntosh are available at http://www3.vjc.edu/academics/faculty/bodnar_john/

my fruit bat avatar, I'm flying in space directly above the bat. *PixieGirl*, you should be looking down on your *CootiePig*, and the rest of you on your favorite organism. In the OBSERVE mode, I detach myself from the avatar and can roam the entire *Cootie* virtual world at will. Now if I zoom out, how far do I need to go to encompass the entire range of biological sciences? *CyberFemme*, if you end up as an intelligence analysis and have to study an influenza pandemic or model a worldwide smallpox attack, how big an area do you have to study?"

CyberFemme: "The ENTIRE Earth!!?!"

MsDNA: "Absolutely. Now, if we're going to assign a *CootieWorld* Level Number to the biggest computer screen we need to use, the Earth is about twenty-four thousand miles in circumference or roughly a hundred thousand kilometers or about a hundred million meters. So that's the top *CootieWorld* Magnifier or Zoom Level of ten-to-the-plus-eight or just ZoomLevel-Plus-Eight. If we're going to study a mutation in the genome of that influenza or smallpox virus as a single change to a nucleotide in the viral DNA, that change happens on the atomic level. Atoms are about one Angstrom across. That's one times ten-to-the-minus-tenth meters or a ZoomLevel-Minus-Ten.

Now, rather than switching to some bioweapon like smallpox, let's take a look at a very similar problem that applies to all you students and which will be your first *in silico* research project. I'm thinking of a growing worldwide epidemic that might turn into a pandemic that not only can kill people but is killing owls and bats all over the world and is spreading across the United States."

PixieGirl: "You must mean West Nile Virus! It's killing birds all over Maryland. And it's starting to kill people all over the world… And even some pigs and ponies."

MsDNA: "Right on! On one hand epidemiologists and biologist have to care what's happening all over the world… that's ZoomLevel-Plus-Eight. But, does anyone remember what virologists have to do to design and build vaccines?"

NewBee: "Yes! They have to find some kind of atom or molecule on the outside of the virus then change it… that's a mutation, right?" {*MsDNA* nods.} "Then they can shoot you up with the mutated virus, and you get a little sick but you don't ever catch that virus again."

MsDNA: "Yes indeed! That mutated virus is the silver bullet to combating most every kind of viral disease. On the other hand virologists and molecular biologists have to care about the individual atoms that show up on the outside of a virus… that's ZoomLevel-Minus-Ten. THAT's what makes biology so different from all other sciences that most folks totally miss why being a biologist… and why building and using *CootieWorld* is SO HARD!

We have to have a zoom lens that can go all the way from ZoomLevel-Plus-Eight—that's the WHOLE WORLD—all the way down to ZoomLevel-Minus-Ten—that's the DIAMETER OF AN ATOM."

{*MsDNA* then projects a slide. (Figure 5.1).}

CootieWorld Magnifier Summary

Zoom Level	Science	Multiplier	Windshield Size	Visible thru Windshield
+8	Epidemiology	1E8	100,000 km x 100,000 km	the entire earth
+5	| Ecology	1E5	100 km x 100 km	ecosystem
+4	|	1E4	10 km x10 km	
+3	| Population Biology	1E3	1 km x 1km	community
+2	|	1E2	100 m x 100m	blue whale, Sequoia
+1	| Zoology/Botany	1E1	10 m x 10 m	elephant, maple tree
HOME	|	1E0	1 m x 1 m	owl, mouse
-1	|	1E-1	10 cm x 10 cm	
-2	| Developmental Biology	1E-2	1 cm x 1 cm	fruit fly, human embryo
-3	|	1E-3	1 mm x 1 mm	nematode (small worm)
-4	|	1E-4	100 mm x 100 mm	
-5	| Cell biology	1E-5	10 mm x 10 mm	yeast cell
-6	| Microbiology	1E-6	1 υm x 1 υm	bacterial cell
-7	| Molecular biology/Virology	1E-7	100 nm x 100nm	DNA, virus
-8	| Biochemistry	1E-8	10 nm x 10 nm	protein
-9	|	1E-9	1 nm x 1 nm	amino acid, sugar, nucleotide
-10	| Chemistry	1E-10	1 A x 1 A	atom

Figure 5.1 *CootieWorld* Magnifier Summary

MsDNA: "Here's a summary of all the *CootieWorld* ZoomLevels we have to consider in building and using *CootieWorld.* Let's look at them one at a time as we would in studying any epidemiology or biological warfare problem. The West Nile virus was introduced into the US a couple decades ago[5] and has spread throughout bird populations and has jumped the species barrier into people and horses, and bats, and even pigs. For you *CyberFemme* and for you *CaptainCrunch*, it's a very good model for a flu pandemic or biological

5 Obviously, we do not have West Nile virus data for the year 2025, so all slides presented here are taken from publications with data relevant to hypothesis testing in 2008.

warfare attack. For you *PixieGirl*, it's a viral infection you're possibly going to see in your clinic in the future. For you *NewBee*, just think of all the systems biology models and visualization tools you'll need to be able to model the spread of the infection from the initial virion infecting the index case to a pandemic worldwide. Oh yes, remember that it only takes a few—sometimes only one virion particle infecting one cell in a susceptible host organism to start a lethal infection, and that it only takes one infected person—what the epidemiologists call the index case—to trigger a pandemic.

Our first research project involves the West Nile Virus. About twenty five years ago there was a West Nile epidemic in the US, and many people thought it might have been a biological warfare attack by Al Qaeda or some other Islamic terrorist group. We're going to address that issue by a technique for doing the scientific method *in silico* we call the method of Alternative Competing Hypotheses or ACH for short. First thing we need is two or more rational hypotheses about the same question. Here my hypothesis-one is, 'The introduction of West Nile Virus into the US was a natural epidemic.' My hypothesis-two is 'The introduction of West Nile Virus into the US was a terrorist biological attack.' In most cases, you'll have more hypotheses, but for practice, we'll only use two. We are going to start today doing experiments and collecting data that is evidence for and against those competing hypotheses. For homework, you're each going to collect additional evidence. Next week we'll learn how to pivot that evidence into *HypothesisWorkspace* to be able to build a coherent theory based on your hypotheses. Then, in week three we'll learn how to marshal that evidence to write a paper that we'll call 'West Nile Virus: Epidemic or Biological Attack?'

Now let's start with an epidemiological map for West Nile virus. (Figure 5.2).[6]

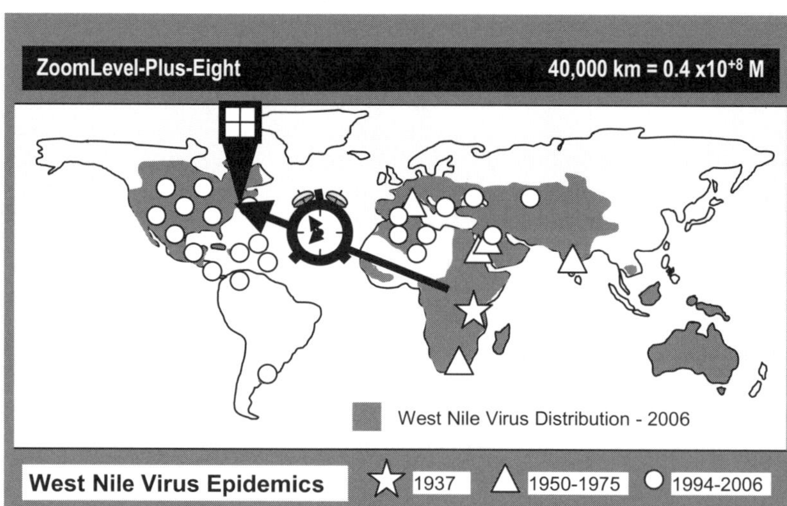

Figure 5.2 Visual drill-down on West Nile Epidemiological data

6 Figure compiled from Gubler (2007).

EPIDEMIOLOGY. That's ZoomLevel Plus-Eight. Using the controls on your mini-sub dashboard, let's first take a time machine and follow the data back to the initial West Nile Virus epidemic somewhere in East Africa in 1937. The epidemic spread needs to be studied at ZoomLevel-Plus-Eight, but the first epidemic most likely started at ZoomLevel-HOME in a single bird that was infected with a West Nile virus particle at ZoomLevel-Minus-Seven that was neurovirulent—that infects brain cells—due to a DNA mutation at ZoomLevel-Minus-Ten.

If we divide our ZoomLevel-Plus-Eight viewscreen into pixels small enough to find that mutation at ZoomLevel-Minus-Ten, that's EIGHTEEN orders of magnitude. So, the number of pixels we need to consider at this scale is ten-to-the-eighteenth times ten-to-the-eighteenth or ten-to-the-thirty-six!

That's not billions AND billions AND billions.

That's billions TIMES billions TIMES billions TIMES billions!

Now if we zoom our time-machine ahead to today, we can see how far the West Nile Virus epidemic has spread. In this case we still care about zooming down to ZoomLevel-Minus-Ten because there's a molecular biologist out there finding the single best amino acid to mutate by bioengineering to make a non-deadly vaccine strain of West Nile Virus.

But first, we need to collect evidence pro- and con- for each one of our hypotheses. Take a look at the spread of West Nile Virus. *CyberFemme*, you're our primary epidemiologist and Intel analyst. Your task is going to be to write the epidemiology paragraphs in the final paper starting on ZoomLevel-Plus-Eight. When starting top-down like you are answering 'Where?', "When?', and 'Why?' are the best places to start. 'Where?'—in general—is easy. We already said we're writing about the first West Nile Virus epidemic in the United States. But we need to be more specific. In every epidemic or biological attack, there is always an index case. Your job is to find the first organism in the US that was infected in the US and when exactly that was. But first, let's get you started on your 'Why?' question. Why did the virus enter the US? Was it natural or was it intentional? What does this slide tell you?"

CyberFemme: "Well…Umm… OH! It looks natural. See how the first epidemic is in Central Africa in 1937 then radiates like a spilled glass of milk outward and doesn't cross the Atlantic until 1994. That's pretty usual for a natural epidemic."

MsDNA: "But suppose it was an Al Qaeda attack. One of their operatives could have taken virus in Afghanistan and hand-carried to the US and sprayed it on the Washington DC Mall or throughout the World Trade Center in New York. That's why we need to know exactly 'Where?' and 'When?' for the index case. But that would suggest there has to be something different in the viruses themselves. *NewBee*, systems biologists need to know about viruses. You're going to be our systems biologist. Any ideas what would be different in the viruses between the two hypotheses?"

NewBee: "Yes. If the first… oops!... index case in the US was natural, it should have spread across the Atlantic on a bird or animal on a freighter or something like that. The DNA sequence of that virus should be like the one in Western Europe at the same time. But if it was flown in directly from Afghanistan by a terrorist, the DNA sequence would match the one there."

MsDNA: "Excellent! Both of you! And note that while you're finding out WHAT virus was involved, you'll also be learning HOW it got there. Now you each need to document what you said for the paper. In *Hypothesis Workspace*, we will document what we have learned with references. On the screen, I've already recorded *CyberFemme*'s and *NewBee*'s observations into our first set of Time-Arrows… those are an easy way we have to document evidence for or against our hypothesis.

First, I double-click on 1937 data point in Africa, then on the 2002 point. When the Time-Arrow appears, I type in my evidence… Here… '1937 West Nile epidemic time travels to 1994–2002 North American epidemic.' How many of you learned the three-by-five card method of report writing?" {All raise their hand}. "What I have just done is to build *CyberFemme* her first three-by-five card as a Time-Arrow which will end up as a single evidence nugget for our paper. AND because they're linked to referenced entities, we can always go back from our card to find and read the original reference. PLUS they automatically save the complete reference for our bibliography. PLUS we can search and sort several thousand Time-Arrows as fast as you used to sort a couple dozen three-by-five cards when it was time to write the paper.

PixieGirl: "That's WAAAAY COOL! The worst parts of paper writing are finding the best three-by-five cards to tell the story and finding all the references when you're done."

MsDNA: "That's the plan! We're aiming at telling a story just the way you've always done. We'll show you how to use the Time-Arrows next class when we start compiling evidence for and against our competing hypotheses.

I also built two Time-Arrows for *NewBee* based on his questions." {MsDNA clicks on pull-down menu at the top and finds the 'BIO101-West-Nile' folder on the shared drive, finds the "Time-Arrows" in the folder and opens it.}

"*CyberFemmes's* Time-Arrow is here plus a few more. Here are the Belief-Statement Time-Arrows I built for *Newbee*. *Newbee-One* is, 'If AQ attack, US West Nile sequence is the same as Afghanistan sequence,' and *Newbee-Two* is, 'If natural epidemic, US West Nile sequence is the same as West Europe sequence.' Now *Newbee*, when you start your research, you can remember what you were just thinking when you're ready to do some detailed research on those competing mini-hypotheses.

Is everyone clear why and how we use Time-Arrows and Belief-Statements?" {*CyberFemme* turns to *CaptainCrunch* and whispers, "Maybe you can help me later at the Student Union." Then all nod.}

"Good! Now let's return to hypothesis testing. We just figured out that the best way to tell the difference between natural epidemic and bio-attack is to find the index case organism and virus in the US. To do a level jump in your mini-sub, first find the Level-Zoom control on your mini-sub dashboard. Remember that you pivot out to NCBI research tools and hypothesis-testing tools on the top menu and navigate your mini-sub using the bottom dashboard.

So, let's rev up our mini-sub, hit the Zoom-In button, and miniaturize ourselves down to ZoomLevel-Plus-Six. Center your Zoom-Level crosshairs on New York City on the world map (Figure 5.2) and hit ZOOM. That's ZoomLevel-Plus-Seven. Center on New York again and hit ZOOM.

ECOLOGY. That's ZoomLevel-Plus-Six in which the ecosystem is 1000 km on a side (Figure 5.3).[7] At this level we can see the distribution of West Nile Virus in the Northeast United States. There were almost thirteen hundred birds reported infected here in Maryland by 2001. *CyberFemme*, as our epidemiologist, you start with your Time-Arrow and work down from the top ZoomLevel through ZoomLevel-Plus-Seven.

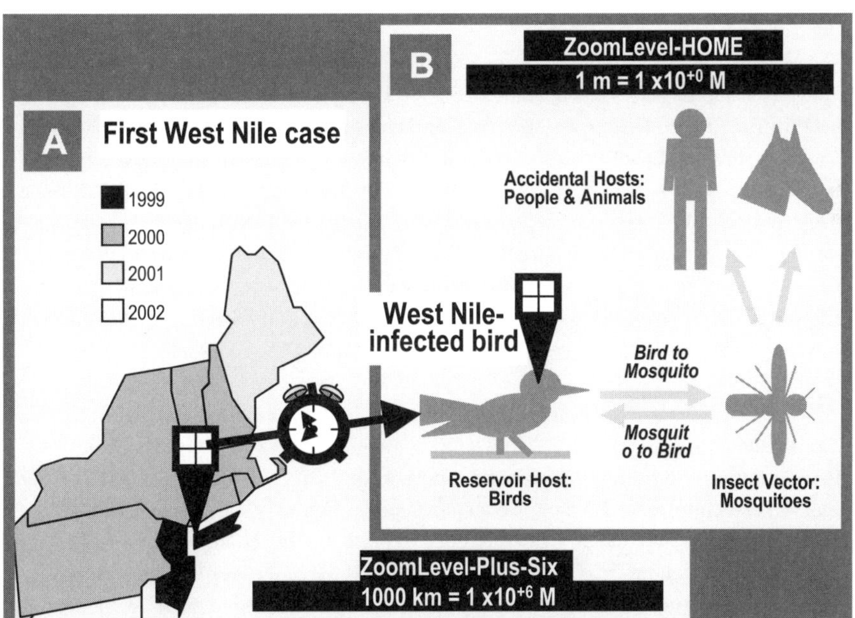

Figure 5.3 Visual zoom-in on West Nile Virus Ecological and Zoological data

7 Adapted from *Equine Disease Quarterly* (2001) and Dudley (2003).

You're up next *CaptainCrunch*. You're going to be our ecologist and population biologist. You've got ZoomLevel-Plus-Six down to—Plus-Three. That's about as big as a submarine operating area. At this level, the best place to start is usually by asking 'How?' To discriminate between the natural epidemic and bioattack hypotheses, we need to figure out HOW the virus got into the US. Here *CaptainCrunch*, I've done two Belief-Statements for your homework." {*MsDNA* opens up the Belief-Statements as before.} "*CaptainCrunch-One*, 'Natural epidemic started with West Nile-infected European birds entering Port of New York in cargo,' and *CaptainCrunch-Two*, 'Bioattack started with West-Nile aerosol sprayed in ventilation system of New York building.'

Now, if you take a look at the viewscreen (Figure 5.3), we can start with *CyberFemme's* Time-Arrow which we did before we zoomed down. Any idea on how you'll test each of those mini-hypotheses, *CaptainCrunch*?"

CaptainCrunch: "Let me see… Hmmm… If it was the bio-attack scenario, I should be able to zoom-in on the New York cases and see if the first ones were human or maybe in rats that could have been in the World Trade Center or other important targets at the time of the attack. And if it's a natural epidemic, the index case should be a bird somewhere near a New York seaport or airport."

MsDNA: "Very good. Now, after class, add those observations to your Belief-Statements in the 'Comments' section so you don't forget them by the time you start your homework.

Now, let's skip through the Population Biology Levels and go zoom all the way in on a single infected bird. That means six ten-fold miniaturization jumps for the mini-sub all the way down to ZoomLevel-HOME. Everyone watch while I center my ZoomLevel crosshair on New Jersey, then Jump to ZoomLevel-Plus-Five. Then switch to time-machine mode back to 1999 which is the first year with West Nile cases in New Jersey. Then center on the highest concentration of cases. Then do five more zoom-jumps: center-jump, center-jump, center-jump, center-jump, center-jump, and here we are at ZoomLevel-Zero (Figure 5.4A). Don't get nauseous *PixieGirl*. I realize all this level jumping and time traveling sometimes as disorienting as watching *The Blair Witch Project*.

ZOOLOGY. That's ZoomLevel-HOME (Figure 5.4A; Sonoma County, 2008). We can see that birds are infected by mosquitoes and mosquitoes pass the West Nile Virus to other birds—and sometimes humans and horses. *PixieGirl*, you're going to be our biologist and physician. As a physician you should obviously start with 'Who?'. If the natural infection hypothesis is good, clinical reports in 1999 should start in veterinary journals and then later on some human infections. If the bio-attack hypothesis is good, either there are going to be veterinary cases that can be traced back to the World Trade Center… *CaptainCrunch* is following that… or a small pocket of human cases reported in medical journals followed by mosquito-born spread to animals and birds. Your two Belief-Statements are posted but you should add comments, too, right after class.

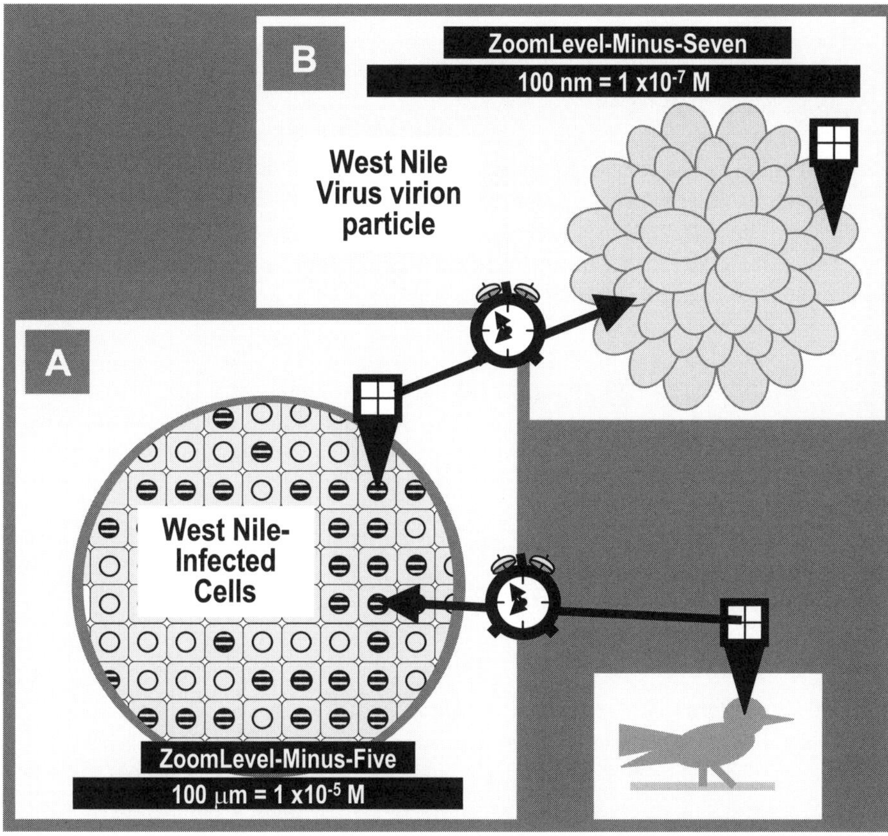

Figure 5.4 Visual zoom-in on West Nile Virus Zoological and Cell Biological data

PixieGirl: "Let me jot those down. If it's natural, the progression should go from index case—probably a bird—to mosquito pool, to pigs and horses, then to humans. And if it's a bioattack it should either be people first or rats within the attacked building or subway, then onward to mosquitoes, birds, and animals. But that would mean that the bioattack was a flop since there were no reports of terrorists hitting the US with biological weapons until the 2001 anthrax attack. Or that the terrorists were trying to kill birds."

MsDNA: "FABULOUS! Write those down, too. This shows the power of the ACH method! Note that every time we looked at data, we saved what we could conclude from that one screen as a set of Time-Arrows, and then we write up more focused hypotheses under each one as a Time-Arrow to come back to later." {*PixieGirl* jots down her notes and nods to *MsDNA* she's ready.}

"Next, we need to pick up one of the dead birds, and find the infecting West Nile Virus particle—we call those virions. First, we do an autopsy at ZoomLevel-HOME and find the infected organs. There are many that are necrotic, but we pull out a kidney, cut it open—carefully with gloves under a clean-room hood. We then cut a piece and look at it under a scanning microscope and find a piece that looks infected. Everyone sit back and watch while we zoom-jump.

PHYSIOLOGY. That's ZoomLevel-Minus-Two. We'll skip that slide and zoom-in three more levels—that's another thousand-fold magnification to…

CELL BIOLOGY. That's ZoomLevel-Minus-Five (Figure 5.4B; adapted from Ganz et al. 2006). Here we can see the kidney cells and if we look closely—as shown by the arrows—we can see infected deformed cells.

Remember *PixieGirl*… Physicians and veterinarians look at all the patients that come into their clinic—that's ZoomLevel-Plus-Two down thru what they can see through a light microscope at ZoomLevel-Minus-Five. So start with your Time-Arrows and work down to here.

Now, we pick out an infected cell and set the mini-sub magnifier for another couple jumps. But theses next couple can be deadly!"

{The screen goes black!}

"Uh-Oh. The lights went out. Anyone know why? {All the students shake their heads.} Well, that's because our mini-sub is now smaller than a single wavelength of visible light. Light waves diffract off objects that small, and you cannot make an image. {Blank stares all around.} Remember when we used the microscopes to look at amoebas and other single-celled organisms? How many different lenses did we have?"

NewBee: "There was a ten-X, hundred-X, and four hundred-X. Oh-my-Gosh! Four hundred-X is ZoomLevel-Minus-Two-Point-Four."

MsDNA: "Not exactly, but close enough. And remember how hard it was to see things in four hundred-X?"

CaptainCrunch: "Yes Ma'am. We made a mess of all the microscopes with that special oil we had to put under the lens."

MsDNA: "That's because the light is already scattering at that magnification, and you need something to keep it from diffracting away from the lens.

What that means is that for anything smaller than ZoomLevel-Minus-Five, you need to use special tools like an electron microscope. So, you cannot take pictures anymore. You have to reconstruct what's there using mathematical tools.

Anyway, here we zoomed down to ZoomLevel-Minus-Seven. In the real world we couldn't see anything, but in *CootieWorld* OBSERVE mode, if we wait, our mini-sub viewscreen automatically turns into an electron microscope—with all the shielding we need not to get burned—and we mush onward and downward." {A new image, an electron microscope image of a West Nile Virus slowly appears on the projector screen}. "*NewBee*, you're up again. Systems biologists get stuck tying together everything from top to bottom.

VIROLOGY. That's ZoomLevel-Minus-Seven. Here we see the virion coat of a West Nile Virus. Now we're getting close to being able to work on the vaccine."

NewBee: "MsDNA! Why are we drilling down further? We all have our individual Belief-Statements and Time-Arrows for homework. What else do we need to know that will help solve our problem?"

MsDNA: "Ah! If you find there are differences in the DNA sequences between the New Jersey index case and either the West European or Afghan virus, how are you going to know WHAT those differences do? {*NewBee* turns red and sinks down in his seat.} But that IS an excellent question. {*NewBee* perks up.} Remember we said there's always a link between epidemiology at the top ZoomLevel and molecular biology at the bottom ZoomLevel. It's your job to find that… and here's how."

{MsDNA continues to zoom down. She stops at:

BIOCHEMISTRY. ZoomLevel-Minus-Eight. The mini-sub viewscreen is now only 10 nanometers across, and she explains how the 3-D structure of the West Nile Virus E Protein affects how it can infect different cell types.

ORGANIC CHEMISTRY. ZoomLevel-Minus-Nine. The mini-sub viewscreen is only one nanometer—or ten Angstroms—across, and she explains how the individual amino acids in the E Protein affect its function.

CHEMISTRY. That's ZoomLevel-Minus-Ten. The mini-sub viewscreen is only one Angstrom across—the diameter of a single atom. Then she continues..}

"Here's where we biologists say, 'ENOUGH! Let the chemists and physicists explain that. All we need to know is that the oxygen atoms form two covalent bonds and are highly electronegative and, therefore, very reactive.

But, *NewBee*, let's go back up to ZoomLevel-Minus-Eight and find the Belief-Statemetns I set up for you. All the virological and molecular biological data suggest that mutations at or near the asparagine-154 in the West Nile virion particle E protein cause very large changes in whether the virus attacks the brain or just other organs. So, when you find the data to compare the DNA sequences of the viruses from New Jersey, Western Europe, and Afghanistan, any of the mutations that change that particular region probably had very large effects on the epidemic. Here are your Belief-Statements. *NewBee-One*, 'The 1999 New Jersey West Nile Virus E Protein DNA sequence is the same as the West Nile

Virus E Protein DNA sequence from Western Europe.' And *NewBee-Two*, which is the same except for here… 'from Afghanistan.'"

NewBee: "OK, I've got those. Gosh! *PixieGirl*'s not the only one that's nauseous. This eighteen-level zoom is a wild roller-coaster ride! But I do see why all the biology and chemistry I've already learned is important, but that we've all got a bunch to learn in college and graduate school."

MsDNA: "If you listen to an epidemiologist and virologist talking about West Nile Virus—or smallpox—or Ebola—or especially influenza that mutates so much—they can zoom all the way from the worldwide epidemiology down to the specific protein mutations involved in a single sentence—without any visual aids! The ZoomLevel setup in *CootieWorld* is necessary to systematically move in space and time at all required levels of precision. But hopefully by the end of this year, you won't even need the slides to do that eighteen-level zoom because you'll be able to zoom wherever you want in your head then click directly there.

Now you've all got your research assignments as Belief-Statemetns on the shared drive. For homework you'll need to document evidence that supports or refutes each of those Belief-Statements and Time-Arrows. The last thing we need to do today is to consider some of the other kinds of data biologists need to consider when modeling and combating epidemics and bioterrorism attacks.

Indeed the methods for biological and forensic analysis of determining epidemic or bioattack index cases have improved markedly since the 1999 West Nile outbreak. I've assigned you the 'textbook' West Nile scenario because it's 'old' and the answers are already known. I'm not going to ask you to find the name of the person or pet that was the West Nile North American index case. The epidemiologists, doctors, and law enforcement officials never went that far because doing so had no 'actionable' reason for that individual case: for the epidemiologists and doctors, digging that deep would not help them cure any patients of that particular outbreak, and for law enforcement, the conclusion of 'not criminal' and 'not terrorist-linked' meant their job was done.

But sometimes biologists have to dig deeper and correlate other kinds of data. One of the classic textbook examples here is the anthrax outbreak in Sverdlovsk, Russia in 1979. Almost a hundred people died and the entire city was in a panic. There was speculation that the epidemic was an accidental release from the military's Compound Nineteen which was believed to be a Soviet Biological Warfare production facility.

The 1979 Sverdlovsk Anthrax release was quote-proven-unquote" {*MsDNA* does air quotations marks by her face} "to be an accidental release of weapons-grade anthrax from a Soviet Biological Warfare production plant.[8] Why did I use quotes on the word 'proven.'?"

8 The reconstruction of the 1979 Sverdlovsk anthrax incident is detailed in Guillemin (1999). [This is an outstanding case study on how epidemiologists collect and integrate biological

CyberFemme: "Because hypotheses can never be proved, only falsified."

MsDNA: "Exactly. When we use ACH, we work exactly like Sherlock Holmes." {She mimics smoking a pipe and adopts a British accent.} "'When you have eliminated all which is impossible, then whatever remains, however improbable, must be the truth.'

In ACH we use all possible tools and evidence to blow away all our possible hypotheses. When we show all the ones that are impossible, what's left is PROBABLY true.

For the Sverdlovsk anthrax outbreak, the evidence can be visualized on a very convincing *CootieWorld* slide (Figure 5.5; Guillemin 1999) compiled by a US-Russian epidemiology team. They were able to 'map' the borders of an accidental release of weaponized anthrax from a Soviet BW production plant on the afternoon of 2 April 1979 through the consolidation of non-visual data.

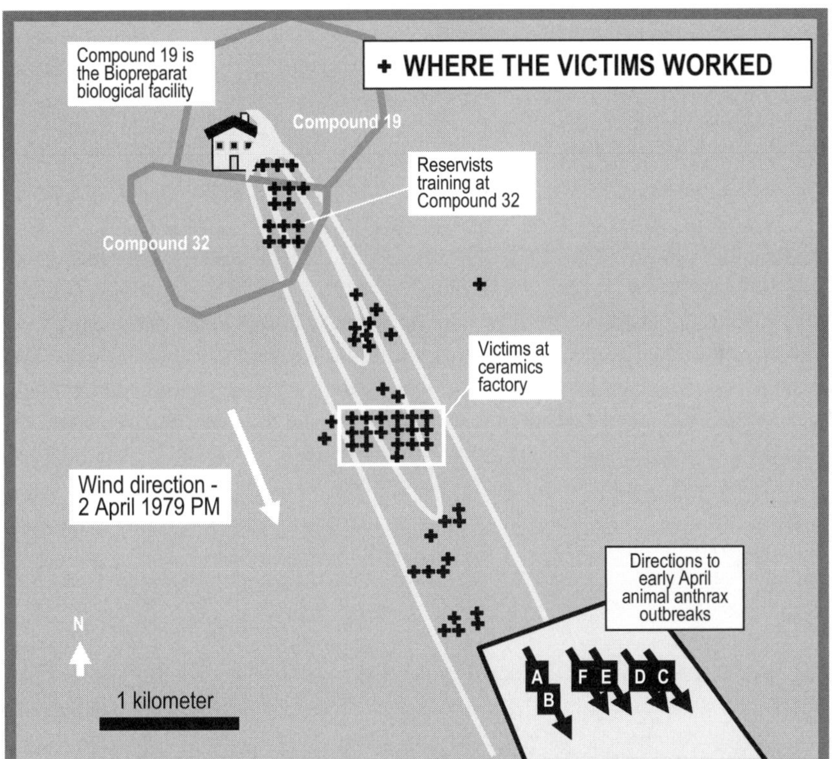

Figure 5.5 Human and Animal Infections: Sverdlovsk BW Plant Anthrax Release, 2 April 1979, afternoon

---

and sociological data—most of it non-visual—from ZoomLevel-Minus-Eight thru ZoomLevel-Plus-Five into a visual "story"].

Let's point out a few things here and add some other non-visual data plus the ZoomLevel at which the investigators had to work to find it…

Here are the relative locations of Compound 19—the biological warfare plant." {She points on the screen}. "Compound 32—an Army reserve training facility. A ceramics plant. This is at ZoomLevel-Plus-Three.

Reconstruction from hospital and autopsy records and known gestation time for anthrax infections showed that the epidemic was indeed inhalational anthrax and began on the afternoon of 2 April 1979. That's ZoomLevel-Minus-Five thru ZoomLevel-Plus-Two.

Here's the wind speed and direction on the afternoon of 2 April 1979 from records at the Sverdlovsk-Koltsovo airport. That's ZoomLevel-Plus-Two.

The investigation team first found the names of all victims of the outbreak from headstones in the cemetery set aside for incident victims and then did interviews with family and coworkers determine where all victims were during the course of the day on 2 April 1979. If we plot the position of their homes, where we'd expect they'd be during the evenings and early morning, they're scattered all around the city." {She switches slide to show that.} "But the small circles on this plot (Figure 5.6) are the work places of all the victims. Most victims were either reservists training in Compound 19 or workers in the ceramics plant. That's work at ZoomLevel-Plus-One thru ZoomLevel-Plus-Three.

Down on the right-hand corner of the plot are the Time-Arrows documenting the directions to animal deaths from diseases with anthrax symptoms in early April 1979, again determined from interviews. The epidemiology team went much further afield here because they knew that animals are much more sensitive than humans to anthrax infection, and any wind-blown anthrax spores would kill animals much further downwind. That's tough work at ZoomLevel-Plus-One thru ZoomLevel-Plus-Five.

On the basis of the above data, an anthrax 'plume' could be modeled that was consistent with the data. And all the evidence points the plume originating about two o'clock in the afternoon on April Second 1979 from… drum role please…"

CaptainCrunch: "The Russky BW Plant. When you put the evidence together like that, it's obvious! But, *MsDNA*… You plotted all those evidence overlays on a satellite photo of Sverdlovsk, but as you went along you left the overlays and deleted the satellite photo. Why is that?"

CyberFemme: "Because, Mr. Technology Guy, the satellite photos are pretty but just window-dressing. In biology we get answers the hard way. Ecologists and population biologists stomp around in the field in hip waders. Epidemiologists interview sick people and families of dead people. Doctors and vets do autopsies. Molecular biologists do lab experiments. It's only when we have data in hand that we sit down and graph it to make sense out of everything." {*MsDNA* nods, but doesn't interrupt.}

"But, MsDNA… All the cases you gave us, all the people and animals were dead before we found the answers. Shouldn't we be SAVING lives?"

MsDNA: "Absolutely. Sverdlovsk 1979 and West Nile 1999 are ancient history from back-in-the-day before *CootieWorld* was started. In 2002, the state-of-the-art in biology got better so that when the SARS virus was first discovered, a worldwide epidemic was headed off because the biologists, doctors, and public health officials used all these methods in real time to identify and sequence the viral DNA, diagnose the symptoms and effects, and quarantine all the appropriate places. Even then, over eight thousand people were infected in twenty-seven countries, and almost a thousand died.

Thanks for the great lead-in to your homework, *CyberFemme*…

Next week we're going to learn how to build and use Time-Arrows so we can't really get started on the nitty-gritty West Nile research project yet. For next week, I want each of you find one case where an epidemic was stopped or a bioattack was thwarted between these textbook examples back-in-the-day and today in 2025. Then find a good review article, summarize the evidence for how the problem was found and cured, then list at least ten evidence Time-Arrows…only as PowerPoint slides for now…and what ZoomLevel they were done at.

This has been a great start. Finish off the comments on your Belief-Statements… Then I'll see you all next week."

We fade out as the students start their first *in silico* biology experiment…

Discussion: How Do We Get There From Here?

We believe a *CootieWorld* virtual world can become a viable research environment for systems biology and bioinformatics that can be built with today's technology.

All the technology for building *CootieWorld* is already in hand.

BUT

CootieWorld can only become a reality if we choose the appropriate virtual world paradigms.

We do not have to build any new paradigms… only focus on using the proper old paradigms.

From Google Earth to Mapquest: From Precise Photographic Virtual Worlds to Accurate Cartographic Virtual Worlds.

The reality of the photographer is to re-present the world, to "see" it as our eyeballs see it.

The reality of the cartographer is to represent the world, to “see” it in our mind’s eye.

On a photograph, we see the world precisely as our eyes see it.

On a map, we see the world as accurately as the cartographer can see it.

The purpose of a photograph is to capture an instant in time.

The purpose of a map is to help the navigator reach the destination safely.

Consider the differences between Google Earth, a photographic virtual world, and Mapquest, a cartographic virtual world. Let’s investigate how easy and well you can use those two kinds of virtual worlds in “biological” problem-solving. In our narrative, we were getting “driving directions” in the form of Time-Arrows (the “road-trip” of West Nile Virus in 1937 East Africa to West Nile virus sometime-around-2000 in North America) then zooming in at evermore precise ZoomLevels and readdressing the same question (the “roadtrip” of West Nile Virus from nose to brain inside a bird) for eighteen different level-jumps. Similarly, you all can be *Newbees* and I’ll play *MsDNA* as we plan a road trip from home in Annapolis, MD to the Bronx Zoo—just another road-trip.

Call up Mapquest and Google Earth as alternate windows in your browser. The images on Google Earth are very precise; you see precisely what the satellite photographs at a given level of magnification. The images on Mapquest are very accurate; you see a distorted depiction of the world with the best landmarks chosen by the cartographer. Compare side-by-side the first level images: Google Earth gives you a satellite photograph; Mapquest give you a map. On Google Earth, you cannot even see Interstate highway I-95 because it’s only about fifty feet wide (less than the width on a single pixel at this scale). On Mapquest, I-95 is very prominent and easy to see, even though the cartographer has made it several miles wide on this map scale. Google Earth has back-fitted cartographic symbols where necessary because, for those navigating from here to there in space (whether it’s you, the biologist, or the West Nile Virus going along for the ride), it’s more important to have an accurate cartographic image of the most important landmarks than a precise photographic image of the same world.

In short, for those planning a road-trip from here to there and now from until then—be it for planning an excursion to the zoo, testing a biological hypothesis, making a medical diagnosis, or writing an intelligence assessment—it’s better to take that road-trip in an accurate cartographic virtual world than a precise photographic virtual world.

From Vesalius to Systems Biology: From 2-D Black-and-White Engravings to N-D Color Videos

Biologists have always used virtual worlds to record their road-trips of discovery and have used those worlds to systematically build a navigable environment to teach future scientists and students what they learned on those expeditions. The gold-standard in biology at ZoomLevel-Home for the last half-millennium has been *De Humani Corporis Fabrica* by Andreas Vesalius, published in 1542 (Figure 5.6), which details the physiology of the human body in a series of hand-drawn “maps.” At ZoomLevel-Minus-Five, it has been Robert Hooke’s *Micrographia* (1665), which first drew and

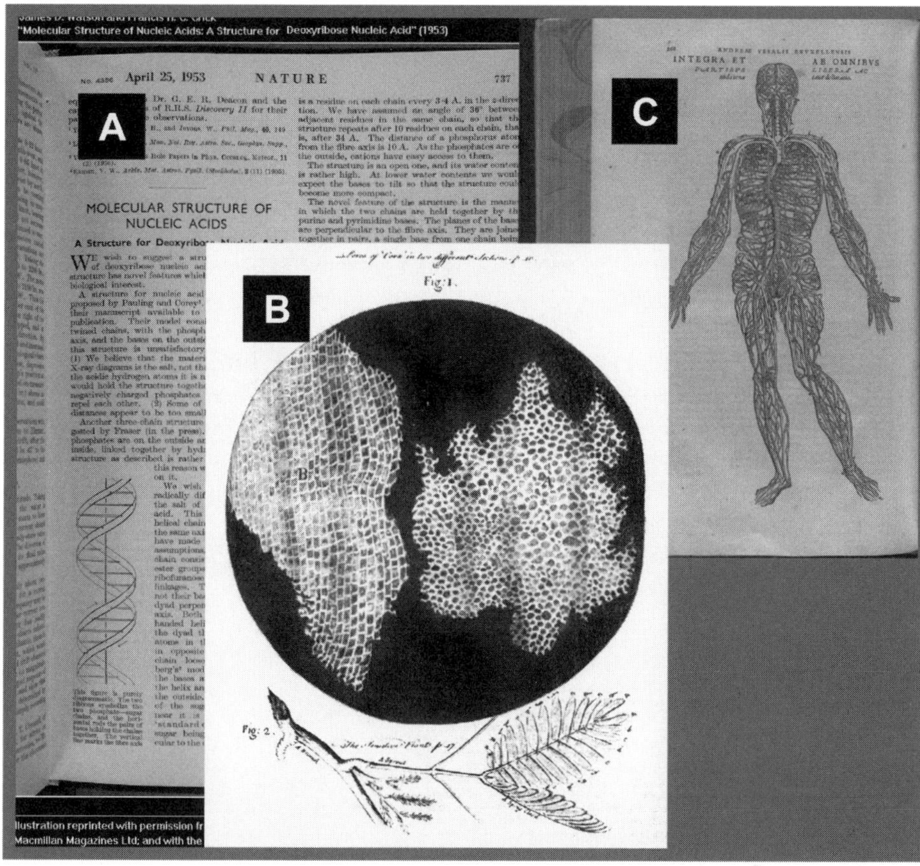

Figure 5.6 Visualizations of Biological Virtual Worlds in the Age of Printing

documented cells, and at ZoomLevel-Minus-Nine it's Watson and Crick's hand-drawn diagram of a cardboard-and-stick model of DNA in the journal *Nature* (1953). Biological virtual worlds are designed to be super imposable on the real world where one first views the real and virtual images side-by-side then uses the virtual images as "Time-Arrows" in the future. Each one of these "Mapquest" virtual worlds has been taught to new generations of biologists because they are accurate distortions of reality that allow biologists to navigate around the *CootieWorlds* that exist in all their heads.

With the new computer technologies that we now have that Vesalius, Hooke, and Watson and Crick did not, biologists are building a collaborative virtual world, but so far only below ZoomLevel-Minus-Five. Remember that the lights went out on our *CootieWorld* explorers when they did a level-jump across ZoomLevel-Minus-Five, the lowest ZoomLevel for which the light microscope works and for which we can use photographs. Everything below that level is done bottom-up by modeling the biological world from indirect non-visual data such as DNA sequencing, electron microscopy, and protein crystallography. Therefore, everything in the biologist's world being built bottom-up is cartographic. While we will not discuss these new virtual worlds in systems biology and bioinformatics, we invite the reader to examine the references in the annotated bibliography that indicate the new directions and tools biologists have for navigating at the bottom end of the eighteen-level zoom.

Most biologists and physicians already have digitized full-color versions of Vesalius's work available to navigate, and doing virtual autopsies is already possible. Unfortunately, tools limit what we can do. Even in this chapter, we had hoped to be able to do several virtual road-trips in full-color multi-zoom on several biological problems. But alas, the current state-of-the-art is still bound books with black-and-white figures. Therefore, here we are limited to the half-millenium-old technology of 2-D black-and-white engravings that Vesalius used. In the future, we envision a *CootieWorld* that will be a 6-dimensional full-color world with eighteen ZoomLevels and a time-machine that can go back four billion years to study the first living cell as a *CootieProtoCell* game.

In short, biologists need *CootieWorld* development tools that work at the top end of the eighteen-level zoom that have the same cartographic accuracy is those they are currently building at the bottom-end of that zoom.

From Second Life to GPS: From Living Immersed in a Virtual World to Using a Virtual Planet Earth to Live on Planet Earth

In Second Life, you sit in front of a computer monitor immersed in that virtual world to the exclusion of the real world.

With GPS, you sit in the driver's seat of your car immersed in the real world through your windshield and occasionally monitor the GPS virtual world when it can help you navigate in the real world.

In Second Life, one lives totally immersed in a virtual world.

GPS is a virtual Planet Earth to be used by a driver who lives on Planet Earth.

In Second Life, it's best to have as much photographic precision as possible on the computer monitor.

With GPS, it's usually best to turn on the audio and have the computerized tour guide tell you when your turn is coming up so that you don't have to take your eyes off the road.

While computer animated virtual worlds have been around since George Lucas's *Star Wars* movie trilogy, there was no way to turn a Mapquest visual Planet Earth into a viable navigation tool until the navigational technology was sufficiently sophisticated such that the local position of your car could be accurately determined on the map on a continuous basis. This meant that the GPS system needed to be able to tell you which highway you were on precisely enough to tell you of upcoming exits within seconds of when you would need that information.[9] This Space Age technology thus afforded motorists the same level of navigational accuracy that mariners (who navigate slower in a wider shipping lane) have had since the 1960s.

9 A highway lane is about ten feet wide; therefore, any usable navigational tool for auto road-trips needs to be precise to less than ten feet. A car at 60 mph travels 880 feet (0.16 miles) in 10 seconds; therefore, if that system cannot update more frequently than once every five seconds, it cannot give more than five second notice of an upcoming exit.

While navigating in *CootieWorld*, each ZoomLevel has a required level of precision that allows them to "stay on the road" and not "overshoot the exit." The epidemiologist at ZoomLevel-Plus-Eight needs to track viral spread across continents over decades; the ecologist at ZoomLevel-Plus-Five track viral spread across states over weeks; the physician or veterinarian tracks viral spread at ZoomLevel-Home from organism to organism over days; and at ZoomLevel-Minus-Five from cell to cell over hours. Each ZoomLevel has a required precision in both space and time that parallels both navigational events and processes at that level. Plus, biologists at every level require a tool to detect the boundaries of that "lane-in-the-road:" uninfected versus infected continents, states, populations, organisms, organs, or cells.

In short, *CootieWorld* is a virtual Planet Earth. Biologists want to build virtual worlds that have GPS tools that provide positional feedback to correlate position and momentum in the virtual Planet Earth with the real Planet Earth.

From Second Life to GPS: From Tools as Toys to Toys as Tools

The tools of the Space Age have been used to build a toy called Second Life.

The toys of the Space Age have been used to build a tool called GPS.

Can pigs fly?

In the real world they cannot.

In a virtual world they can—if the world designer says they can.

Designers of Second Life have taken the Space Age tools and built a world in which pigs can fly. If the island becomes too small, it can be virtually expanded, and there is no need to worry about West Nile virus because the designers never wrote it into the code.

Designers of GPS have taken Space Age toys and built a virtual Planet Earth in which pigs cannot fly, and the size of Manhattan island only changes by massive and expensive landfill operations.

Second Life is a toy built with Space Age tools in which players can escape reality by building their own.

GPS is a Space Age tool by which the Mapquest and GPS team can build a virtual Planet Earth that has laws so close to that of the real Planet Earth so that navigating in the virtual Planet Earth allows the motorist to navigate better in the real Planet Earth.

In short, *CootieWorld* is a virtual Planet Earth. Biologists want to build virtual worlds in which flies and bats can fly but pigs cannot.

Conclusion

Cootieworld will become a reality when students of science learn that various aspects of biology are programmable and that this allows for the creation of virtual worlds that are useful not solely for entertainment (like in video games) but for hypothesis testing in research. When people realize the utility of having a "virtual lab" inside their PC, the demand for such tools will increase, and supply will follow as biologists and computer scientists work together to merge their disciplines.

References

References were selected to provide a reading list accessible at a layperson's experience for those who wish to explore the unique visualization and modeling challenges faced by systems biologists, bioinformatics specialists, and biological librarians.

Barrett, C.L. et al. (2005). If Smallpox strikes Portland. *Scientific American*, March, 55–61. Available at http://www.idready.org/webcast/spr05_cider/2005-03-15/Episims-March2005.pdf [accessed 28 March 2009]. [A *CootieWorld*-like simulation of a biological attack on Portland, Oregon that encompasses ZoomLevel-HOME thru ZoomLevel-Plus-Five.]

Bier, E.A. et al. (2008). *Entity-Based Collaboration Tools for Intelligence Analysis.* IEEE Symposium on Visual Analytics Science and Technology (VAST 2008), Oct 2008. [One version of a hypothesis-space that is built to pivot data visualizations into a hypothesis-space.]

Bodnar, J.W. (2005). *Making Sense of Massive Data by Hypothesis Testing.* 2005 M MITRE Conference on Intelligence Analysis, May 2005. Available at https://analysis.mitre.org/proceedings/Final_Papers_Files/124_Camera_Ready_Paper.pdf [accessed 28 March 2009]. [Notional model for hypothesis-testing that can serve as a basis for building sensemaking tools.]

Boogerd, F., Bruggesman, F., Hofmeyr, J.-H., and Westerhoff, H. Afterthoughts as foundations for systems biology, in *Systems Biology: Philosophical Foundations*, edited by F. Boogerd et al. New York: Elsevier. Xx–xx. [Excellent definition of systems biology and its functional and mechanistic approach.]

Cavalier-Smith, T. (2006). Rooting the tree of life by transition analyses. *Biology Direct* 1:19. [Bioinformatics visualizations and methods to study the evolution of biological systems.]

Dudley, J.P. (2005). *West Nile Virus Overview: August 2003 Update.* [Online Headquarters U.S. Army/Office of the Director of Environmental Programs.] Available at http://www.afpmb.org/bulletin/vol25/West%20Nile%20Distribution.pdf [accessed 28 March 2008]. [Epidemiological reporting for virus spreading at ZoomLevel-Plus-Five.]

Gancz, A.Y. et al. (2006). Pathology and tissue distribution of West Nile virus in North American owls (family: Strigidae). *Avian Pathology.* 35(1):17–29.

Gubler, D.J. (2007). The Continuing Spread of West Nile Virus in the Western Hemisphere. *Clinical Infectious Diseases*. 45:1039–46. [Multilevel epidemiological tracking of a disease outbreak]

Guillemin, J. (1999). *Anthrax: The Investigation of a Deadly Outbreak.* Berkeley, CA: University of California Press. [Multilevel epidemiological reconstruction of a biological weapons accident.]

Hooke, R. (1665). *Micrographia: Or, Some Physiological Descriptions of Minute Bodies Made by Magnifying Glasses.* London: J. Martyn and J. Allestry. [The first virtual "Fantastic Voyage" through the microscopic world. See http://archive.nlm.nih.gov/proj/ttp/flash/hooke/hooke.html]

Howe, D. et al. (2008). Big data: The future of biocuration. *Nature* 455:47–50. [Challenges in building and maintaining biological databases.]

Kellis, M., and Galagan, J.E. (2008). *Computational Biology: Genomes, Networks, Evolution.* [Online Massachusetts Institute of Technology]. 6.047/6.878 Available at http://stellar.mit.edu/S/course/6/fa07/6.047/ and http://stellar.mit.edu/S/course/6/fa07/6.047/materials.html#topic2 [accessed on 28 March 2008]. [Student material from an undergraduate primer on bioinformatics.]

Moreno, A. A systematic approach to the origin of biological organization, in *Systems Biology: Philosophical Foundations*, edited by F. Boogerd et al. New York: Elsevier. Xx–xx. [Visualizing and modeling biological systems as evolving autonomous systems.]

National Center for Biotechnology Information (NCBI) Website. Available at http://www.ncbi.nlm.nih.gov/ especially http://www.nlm.nih.gov/bsd/disted/pubmed.html [accessed on 28 March 2008]. [Bioinformatics and biodata databases, tools, and applications; especially see NCBI PubMed tutorials that show how to forage and assemble biological data.]

Richardson, R., and Stephan, A. Mechanism and mechanical explanation in systems biology, in *Systems Biology: Philosophical Foundations*, edited by F. Boogerd et al. New York: Elsevier. Xx–xx. [Visualizing levels of organization and degrees of resolution.]

Sauer, U., Heinemann, M,, and Zamboni, N. (2007). Getting closer to the whole picture. *Science*, 316(5824):550–1. [Systems biology flow charts and graphs to describe functional inter-relationships in biological systems.]

Shaffner, K. Theories, models, and equations in systems biology, in *Systems Biology: Philosophical Foundations*, edited by F. Boogerd et al. New York: Elsevier. Xx–xx. [Electrical engineering circuit diagrams as analog models for biological systems.]

Snoep, J.L. et al. (2006). *Systems Biology: redefining BioThermoKinetics.* 12th BTK Meeting, September 2006. *IEE Proceedings*, 153(5):312. [Systems biology methods to visualize and model metabolism, thermodynamics, and chemical kinetics.]

Sonoma County Department of Health Services. (2008). West Nile Virus Information. [Online] Available at http://www.sonoma-county.org/health/ph/phpreparedness/wnv/ [accessed on 28 March 2008]. [Study of viral epidemiology, especially at ZoomLevel-Home.]

Vesalius, A. (1542). *De Humani Corporis Fabrica (On the Fabric of the Human Body).* [The first "virtual" autopsy. See http://archive.nlm.nih.gov/proj/ttp/flash/vesalius/vesalius.html.]

Watson, J.D., and Crick, F.H.C. (1953). Molecular Structure of Nucleic Acids: A Structure for Deoxyribonucleic Acid. *Nature*. April 25. Available at http://osulibrary.oregonstate.edu/specialcollections/coll/pauling/dna/papers/corr68.11-reprint-19530425.html [accessed 28 March 2009]. [First visualization of DNA.]

Westerhoff, H. and Kell, D. The methodologies of systems biology, in *Systems Biology: Philosophical Foundations*, edited by F. Boogerd et al. New York: Elsevier. Xx–xx. [Hierarchical flow charts in biological models.]

Chapter 6
System Dynamics and Synthetic Worlds

Warren Tignor

Abstract

For a system dynamicist, a 21st century challenge is to make sense of the accelerating changes in technology, population, economics, and environment. Changes in these domains may enhance our lives, or on the other hand may threaten our survival. To our dismay, most of the changes that confront us as challenges are the consequences of humans' past actions. Our ability to learn from the past and to project change needs our focused attention to avoid a tipping point that may carry us beyond our capacity to recover; this is a role for System Dynamics and synthetic worlds. Through the use of synthetic worlds, system dynamics methodologies and tools will facilitate our learning process, demonstrate potential benefits of policy change, i.e., a decision-making rule (Forrester 1961), and highlight their intended and unintended consequences for professional and public scrutiny to avoid disastrous tipping points.

Part 1: Introduction—The System Dynamics and Synthetic Worlds Vignette

Today is starting as a typical work day for me. Public policy is to preferably stay inside, use public transport if going outside, or telecommute via synthetic worlds. I bend the rules a little and will occasionally walk or jog to my corporate office; otherwise, I work from home. It's my job to prevent any further deterioration of the environment; this requires constant monitoring of dynamic and often volatile environmental situations to control greenhouse gases to prevent a possible environmental disaster.

"Please enter your cyberid," says the door monitor agent. I turn to face the screen and look directly into it. The cyberid device does a retinal scan while I place my fingertips on a touch pad for further verification of my identity. "Welcome, Ryan," it says and the door lock releases for my entry. There are the normal duties to perform first: email, time log, loyalty refresher, and then the real work. I detest the administrative side of my job, but they pay me to do it.

Sensor check time! The sensors are global, real-time and ubiquitous. Our lives and our futures depend upon them. I measure and model carbon dioxide (CO_2) globally using billions of sensors of various types. There are millions of parameter in the models that run on a distributed cellular automata architecture system to conserve power and space (Hoseini, You and Pavicic 2008: 305–306). Without synthetic worlds, it would not be possible to keep up with the dynamic effects globally of weather, natural events (e.g., volcanic eruptions), man-made events (e.g., wars), accidents (e.g., oil tanker ship collisions), and population changes (e.g., pandemics) that have an effect on the environmental health of the planet.

To work in synthetic worlds has taken a long time to achieve, even after the difficult lessons learned in 2010. Oh, the technology was available, but we lacked the will to use it until a disaster happened in 2010: a global environmental collapse. Now, we better appreciate that earth is a shared resource among all nations; to ignore this fact means tragedy for us all. We appreciate now that what happens in one area of the world has an effect in another; and the effect could be immediate or delayed. Shifting the burden of responsibility for environmental carelessness from one nation or industry to another is unacceptable. We've learned that it is no longer acceptable to ignore ones own environmental policies for profit at the expense of the world's environment. The age of shifting the burden of responsibility for pollution to another person, company, or country is over. The "not my problem" policy has ended.

My work goal is to maintain the current CO_2 level globally and, over time, improve it to possibly early Anthroprocene levels. Sounds simple, but the system dynamics are complex and the algorithms and appropriate sensors are still emerging. These are lofty goals, but important for human and other species survival in the Sunthetoscene era, now that we recognize our interdependency on the environment as a global commonly shared resource that must be "healthy" for our mutual survival.

Let me change my synthetic world decision trajectory and try to explain with an illustrative 2010 MindSnap, a computer snapshot of all the data, images, video, and algorithms used during the analysis of that catastrophic event. From a simplistic point of view, the earth can be envisioned as a large bathtub (Senge, Smith, Kruschwitz, Laur, and Schley 2008a: 29). We have an idea of the capacity of the bathtub to "hold" CO_2 but the actual capacity level (i.e., when it's full) is unknown; that's part of the problem. Let's say that the CO_2 in the bathtub is equivalent to the earth's atmosphere. The bathtub has a drain in the bottom, something like an entry into the oceans that eliminates the CO_2. We have an idea of the rate at which the earth is able to absorb $CO_{2,}$ but the actual rate is unknown; that's another part of the problem. In roughly 2010, the bathtub overflowed, and we had an environmental collapse, resulting in unprecedented death and destruction. The actual tipping point occurred approximately a year or two before the collapse; we are still researching the data to pinpoint this phenomenon. There was atypical environmental change globally, e.g., severe and frequent storms and droughts preceding the collapse.

As a reminder and for research, I created a MindSnap of that episodic event and reload my synthetic world (SW) to rewatch the scenario unfold as the limited instrumentation tells the story of overshoot and collapse, over and over. Here are a few of the MindSnap highlights and conditions from that time when the global climate changed:

1. The human population was approximately 7 billion people.
2. The atmospheric CO_2 concentration approached 400 parts per million.
3. The global air temperature near the earth's surface increased approximately 1.8 degrees Fahrenheit.
4. The average temperature of the North Pole was approximately 4.5 degrees Fahrenheit.

The combined effect of the reinforcing feedback loops resulted in a dynamic system that was out of control; the natural equilibrium of the earth's environment was lost. Like the sound of a microphone's feedback to an amplification system, there was a global scream of agony. My SW MindSnaps recreate the devastating global scenes forensically for me to recall and study, for example:

1. Mountain glaciers melted almost completely.
2. Hurricanes and cyclone frequency nearly doubled.
3. Arctic ice melted and the Northwest Passage was opened.
4. West Antarctica collapsed into the ocean.
5. Flooding changed coastal geography, perhaps forever (Gore 2006: 196–209).
   - Florida from Ft. Myers south disappeared.
   - The Netherlands disappeared.
   - Coastal Beijing evacuated more than 20 million people.
   - Calcutta and Bangladesh had 60 million people displaced.
   - The World Trade Center Memorial in Manhattan, New York went underwater.

Since the 2010 global climate crisis, the world's economy has changed to revolve around CUs (carbon units) as a measure of global economic and environmental sustainability. CUs are the de facto global currency of the Sunthetoscene. Today, everyone has a physical CU certificate badge, issued at birth as part of the licensing process, on their person for identity, business and sustainability measurement. The CU certificate units are monitored by debit or credit throughout each person's life. If there is a chance by calculated probability that one is using the CUs at an unsustainable rate, counseling is provided. Monitoring the global CU status is another one of my responsibilities.

"Alert, alert!" announced the monitor.

"Ryan, this is Mission Control (MC). The system has detected a rapidly increasing CO_2 level at London's Heathrow airport. Sensors indicate that there is a particulate and gaseous vapor present."

"Roger MC," I replied. "I see the plume in my SW and I'm tracking it now. It is growing rapidly, according to my sensors. The tracking algorithms have its geolocation (59º 28' 39" N by 000º 27' 48" W) and runway 09L/27R. This is very weird! Oh, the first order analysis indicates that it may be a ground source at the airport!"

"Keep trying and identify it!" MC replied.

"Roger! I see it on infrared and I am scanning with the visual spectrum cameras now," I said.

"Its source is on the ground, just short of runway! How is that possible? What could generate a carbon plume like that?" I exclaimed in frustration and anxiety.

"Ryan, this is MC. Do you have a visual?"

"Yes, I do! I am repositioning the cameras for a better angle; there is some low cloud cover! I'm switching to forensic mode for a better view and will reverse time by one minute increments. Standby!" I said.

"There are visuals of numerous flights in the area for the past ten minutes! I'm switching my SW decision space to radar scan. There! A large plane has crashed!" I yelled.

"I'm activating the Synthetic World Agents (SWA) to check passenger manifestoes and bills of laden for flights in the area at that time," said MC. "We can't risk having an uncontrolled CO_2 plume with possible negative environmental consequences!"

I watched the SWA activation order on my monitor. We'd performed similar scenarios as exercises in the past, but I never thought an aircraft would be part of a situation like this one. So far, the scenario was going according to plan. Counter-environment aircraft and ground units (CEAs) were launching with atmospheric seed pods and other sensing and environmental counter-measures.

"Ryan!" MC boomed. "The initial SWA reports indicate that a DHL jumbo jet loaded with laser printer ink cartridges has crashed!"

"Based on all the model results, I am declaring this a Category 5 (CAT 5) event," he said. "Activate the Climate Impact Assessor (CIA)!"

This meant that, considering the global state of CO_2, there was grave environmental risk. We could experience another climatic tipping point like 2010 if we failed to control this CO_2 plume! I activated the CIA, knowing that the results could have life or death consequences. My entire decision space dimmed as CAT 5 was initiated. All unnecessary processes were instantly halted. Globally, all available processors were online to assist as necessary.

On the CIA synthetic world screen, I selected Option 1 for a square-mile area around the carbon plume for air and land seeding scenarios by the CEAs. Next, future time options in years were checked: 1, 5, 10 and 50 years. I selected the appropriate parametric values based on the sensor data for the plume. The carbon volume and vaporization rate were calculated based on the bill of lading information and the estimated fuel remaining on the jumbo jet that could burn and vaporize the carbon. The dynamics of the system were simulated to estimate future global climate consequences at that location as well as globally, based on the state of the environment worldwide.

The sensitivity of the environment had to be assessed and the appropriate action taken. The CIA had to answer the questions:

1. What was the future impact, possible "butterfly effect," of the current carbon plume?
2. Was there sufficient carrying capacity to absorb this event's CO_2 footprint? How long might it take?
3. What seasonal variations might be caused?
4. Was a "tipping point" imminent that could drive more species toward extinction, including humans?
5. What was the expected carbon event's "lifespan" prior to seeding and what were the likely species that might be extinguished in that timeframe and during the seeding to neutralize it?
6. What seeding concentration of sulfur dioxide (SO_2) was needed to restore equilibrium (Mooney 2008)?
7. How did this event and its hypothesized solution integrate with the current global environmental activities, and were there any possible interactive impacts?

The CIA analysis results were vetted and implemented within five minutes of the incident. The plume was neutralized by SO_2 seeding, and any further danger to the environment avoided. A MindSnap of the event was recorded. The entire episode was stored for possible future analysis. Forensically, the episode could be reanalyzed for possible future process improvements. Lastly, the event could be recreated to reassess long-term effects that the SO_2 might have on the area climate. Transportation policy and other regulation changes could be examined to prevent the recurrence of a critical mass of carbon from being transported in a like manner in the future.

Part 2: Analysis—Global Climate Collapse and Synthetic Worlds Technologies

Introduction

Our willingness to learn from past environmental experiences, research, and writings has been lacking. Meadows, D. H., Meadows, D. L., Randers, and Behrens (1972) gave us a comprehensive look at the impacts to our environment and their possible consequences. Meadows, D. H., Meadows, D. L., and Randers (1992) updated and revised their assessment of environmental impacts; the original assessments were essentially unchanged. Gore (2006) presented a more graphic picture of environmental impacts than those hypothesized by Meadows et al. (1972, 1992). But, our will to act to protect and preserve our environment continued to be lacking. Before we run out of time to act, we need to focus our attention on global environmental issues. Otherwise, we may not be able to avoid an environmental tipping point (Gladwell 2002) that may cause environmental collapse and carry us beyond our capacity to recover.

Today, our systems, tools, and policies to monitor the environment, project change, and take action to avoid disaster are limited in scope. Some nations like the U.S. have resisted international environmental cooperation for various economic and political reasons. Other nations like the United Kingdom (UK) have agreed to limit greenhouse gases and are moving forward. Unfortunately, individual nation state efforts lack the global reach necessary to balance environmental impacts and manage their own interests. To preserve the environment, we need to consider it as a globally shared resource, essential to every creature on earth.

System dynamics is a methodology for studying and managing complex feedback systems such as the environment, e.g., weather, natural disaster, man-made pollution, and population growth. Synthetic worlds, an integration of the real world and virtual worlds, offer the opportunity to globally integrate environmental data, models and public policies to address the complexities of the environment as a whole. Together synthetic worlds and system dynamics provide a venue and methodology for global environmental analysis in contrast to many limited national stovepipe approaches currently at hand. Using the methodologies and tools of system dynamics in synthetic worlds will facilitate a holistic learning environment for the analysis of environmental policy (Forrester 1961). Working in synthetic worlds, system dynamicists will be able to evaluate environmental policy in real time to show potential benefits and possible negative, unintended consequences. Predictive analysis of possible environmental events and planned policies that will potentially mitigate them will be available for professional and public scrutiny, as well as forensic analysis.

Background

Thomas Malthus (1798) wrote that the power of population was vastly superior to the power of the Earth to produce subsistence for man. Consequently, he postulated that premature death must in some shape or other visit the human race. The Mayans of Central America, the Anasazi of the U.S. Southwest, and the people of Easter Island are possible examples of societies that have suffered a Malthusian crises. Are we destined to repeat their experience?

The Malthusian pattern of the power of population was reaffirmed in 1972 when the Club of Rome published *The Limits to Growth*. Meadows, D. H. et al. (1972: 23) wrote, "If the present growth trends in world population, industrialization, and resource depletion continue unchanged, the limits to growth on this planet will be reached sometime in the next 100 years."

To counter the various claims of imminent doom, past scarcity of resources have led to higher prices, and higher prices eventually resulted in some conservation or innovation that alleviated the risk of reaching a tipping point and subsequent collapse. For example, whale oil was a popular source of lighting in the 19th century. Prices soared in the middle of that century, and people sought other ways to fuel lamps. In 1846, Abraham Gesner invented kerosene, an alternative to whale oil. By the end of the century, whale oil cost less than it did in 1831 according to Lahart, Barta, and Batson (2008). Will we find a similar alternative to crude oil in time?

If there is a global environmental collapse, would a scenario similar to the 19th century whale oil scenario be feasible? Will economic forces alone be able to fix the problems we might face? Will societies as diverse as the U.S. and China face political resistance to boosting water or oil prices to encourage efficient use? When water resources are shared across borders, who will establish and maintain a pricing framework? Will food-subsidy programs make it less likely that rising prices will spur change? Working in synthetic worlds using system dynamics, there is an opportunity to test these global issues with alternative policies and real world parameters, and produce scenarios for international dialog. Working in synthetic worlds will enable global access to a decision space of models, data, simulation results, modeler assumptions, sensor data, and their effects for discussion, debate, and facilitation.

Interestingly, Adams (1918) formulated the Law of Acceleration to describe the exponential growth during the Industrial Revolution of technology, production, and population that made the economic basis of colonial America obsolete. Adams described the need for a new "social mind" to accommodate the radical changes in society that resulted from the industrial revolution. He believed that the human mind had adjusted quite well to change for the last 5 to 10,000 years; but going forward, he believed that the mind would need to "jump" in order to keep up with the every increasing complexity of change he observed as a result of the Industrial Revolution. This is another reason for working in synthetic worlds: to help facilitate the development of a new "social mind."

Meadows, D. H. et al. (1972) presented an "urgent" message that the earth's interlocking resources probably could not sustain then present rates of economic and population growth much beyond the year 2100. The results of the project were illustrated with static 2-D graphics. Making sense of the nonlinear results as illustrated in Figure 6.1 was and still is difficult. Deciding what to do, or not to do from the illustrated figure is challenging. To a degree, the impact of the message was obscured by the technical detail and complexity. As a result, perhaps the ability of Meadows, D. H. et al. (1972) to influence environmental public policy was minimal at the time.

Professional and public dialog about the environment was lacking when the time to take action was more opportune than now.

Hansen, Johnson, Lacas, Lebedeff, Lee, Rind, and Russell (1981) concluded that CO_2 in the atmosphere would lead to global warming. They also predicted that it would be difficult to convince stakeholders to take action. They saw the potential effects on environment in the 21st century to include the creation of drought-prone regions in North America and Central Asia, and the erosion of the West Antarctic ice sheet, which would raise sea levels worldwide.

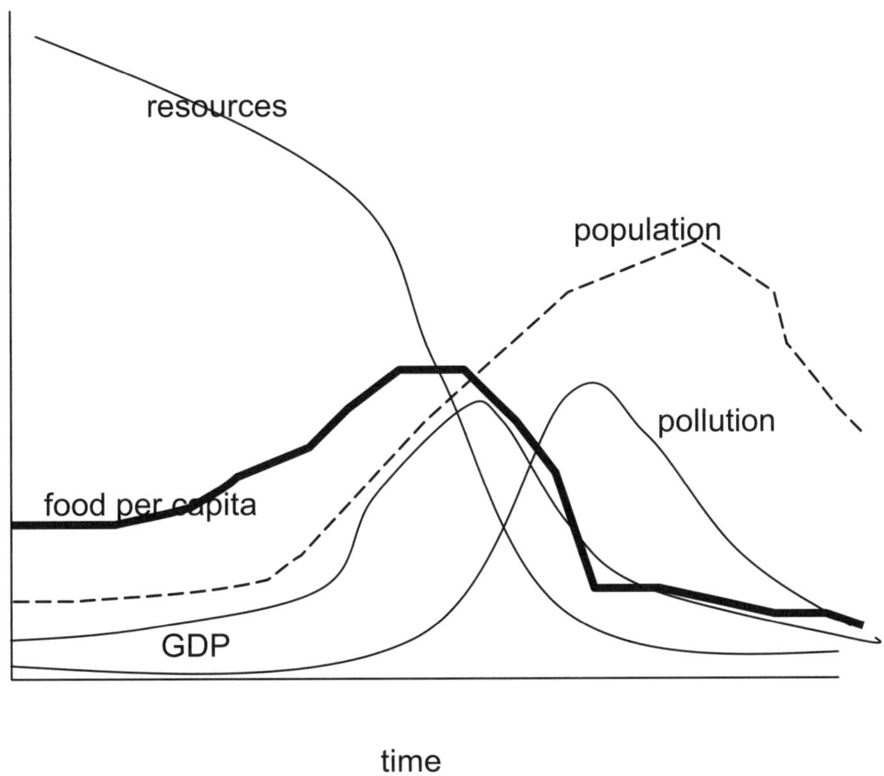

Figure 6.1 An illustration of limits to growth product by 2-D graphics inspired by Meadows, D. H. et al. (1972)

Sterman (2000: 34) anticipated the role of virtual worlds as a tool for system dynamicists. Perhaps this was the first use of the first generation of synthetic worlds to improve our learning process in complex systems, Figure 6.2. To Sterman, virtual worlds, based on the work of Schön (1983), are formal models, simulations, or "microworlds" in which decision makers can refresh decision-making skills, conduct experiments, and play (Papert 1980). Sterman envisioned virtual worlds as physical models, role models, or computer simulations.

Gore (2006) moved closer to synthetic worlds via multimedia graphics, images and video, even though he presented a similar message to Meadows, D. H. et al. (1972, 1992). Gore (2006) illustrated his message with realistic graphic images and video of real-world consequences about questionable environmental policies. The visual impacts of *An Inconvenient Truth* were significant, for example, the iconic polar bears stranded on a tiny ice floe in search of food leaves a lasting impression (Gore 2006: 147).

Although there is substantial debate about the "cause and effect" elements of the environmental issues documented by Gore (2006), they are supported in many cases

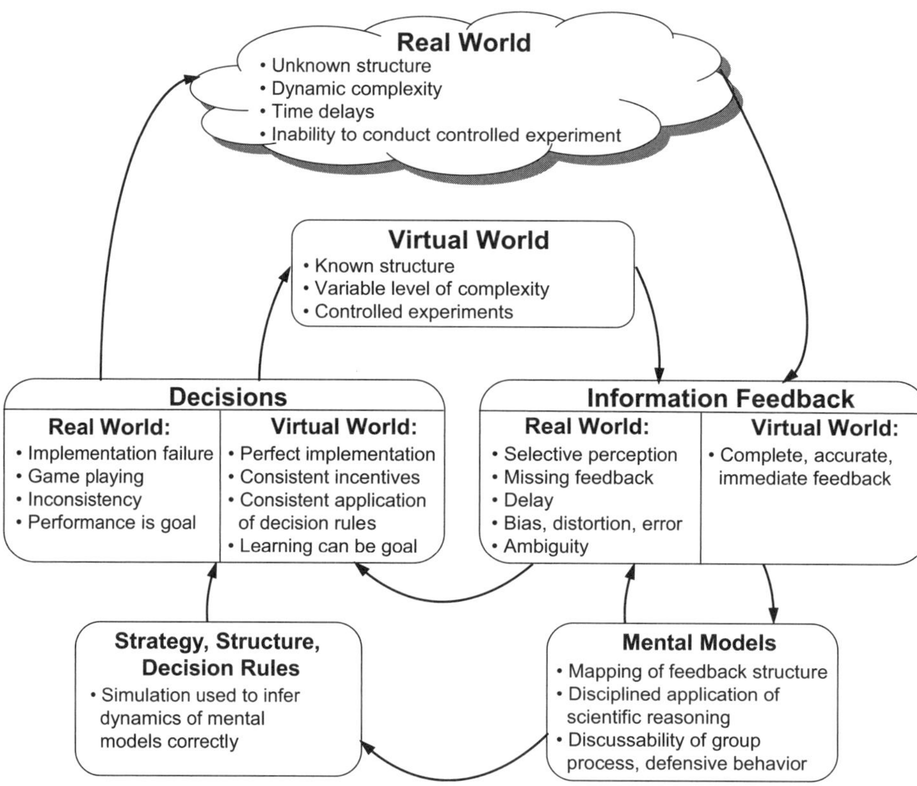

Figure 6.2 Early recognition of virtual worlds and the role in the working world of a system dynamicist

Source: The McGraw-Hill Companies, Inc., *Business Dynamics*, John D. Sterman.

by the Intergovernmental Panel on Climate Change (IPCC 2007) report. Clearly, the Norwegian Nobel Committee and the public resonated with Gore's (2006) message as evidenced by the 2007 Nobel Peace Prize award. The recognition of the work of Gore (2006) and the IPCC (2007) has resulted in movement toward global environmental preservation; however, a ground-swell global commitment to environmental preservation is still lacking.

Present Update

We need a synthetic world view of the global environment because human activity appears to be overwhelming the earth's resources. Lahart et al. (2008) wrote that the United Nations projects world population to be 8 billion people by 2025 from 6.6 billion in 2008. The middle class is growing in China, with a population of 1.3 billion people, and in India, with 1.1 billion. The new Chinese and Indian middle class are adopting the high-protein diets, personal cars and electric gadgets like developed Western nations. Projections are that, in the near future, the average middle class person will consume more food, water, metal and power than today.

The IPCC (2007) described progress in understanding the technological, human, and natural drivers of climate. Some root causes that stakeholders need to address follow: fossil fuel usage, land use, and agriculture. The IPCC (2007) concludes from ice cores spanning many thousands of years that human activities since 1750 have markedly increased the global atmospheric concentrations of carbon dioxide (CO_2), methane (CH_4), and nitrous oxide (N_2O), Figure 6.3. Increases in carbon dioxide concentration are due primarily to fossil fuel use and changes in land use. Increased methane and nitrous oxide are primarily due to agriculture. They conclude with *very high confidence* that the global average net effect of human activities since 1750 has been one of warming (IPCC 2007: 3).

Currently, we appear to be in the middle of economic turmoil after reaching a tipping-point in the global financial and banking system. According to Grynbaum (2008), the Volatility Index, VIX, illustrates the tipping point. The Volatility Index, VIX, is a popular measure of the implied volatility of McGraw-Hill Inc's S&P 500® (also known as the Standard & Poor's 500). As an indicator of collapse, the Standard & Poor's 500 has extended its 2008 retreat to 39 percent and stands poised for its worst performance since 1931 (Stanton 2008).

What if there were an environmental crisis that struck globally? Would it make the current economic crisis pale? Would there be any possibility of "recovery" for something that could take hundreds of years or longer to repair naturally? What are the parameters that should be monitored to avoid reaching an environmental tipping point and collapse? Working in synthetic worlds and monitoring global environmental parameters such as CO_2 levels offers hope to avoid a global collapse of the environment, if we act now.

If global environmental changes were detected in synthetic worlds, they would be captured in time, Figure 6.4, Morrison (2008: slide 16). According to Morrison (2008) a synthetic world would be based on a virtual and real representation of the world, and automatically updated by live data and events occurring in the real world. The synthetic

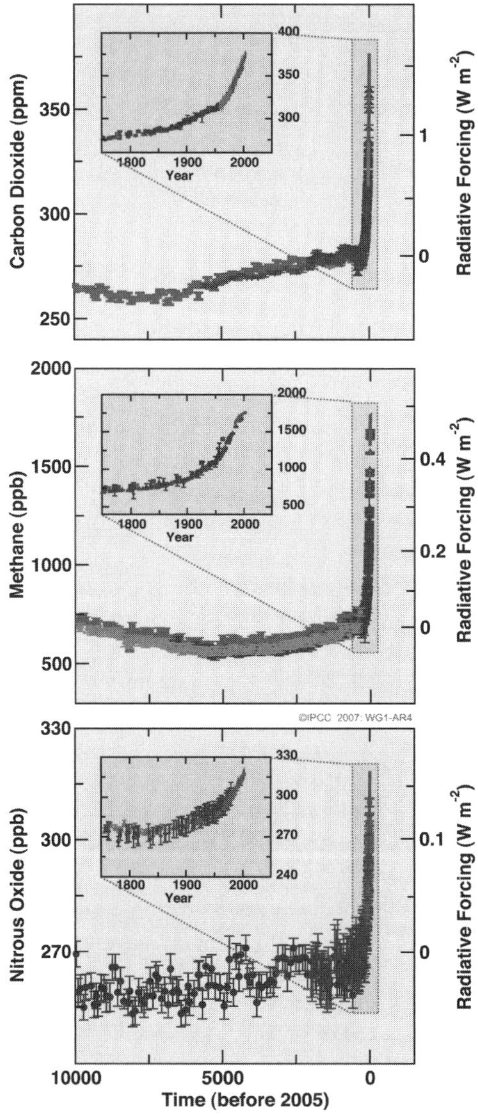

Figure 6.3 IPCC Greenhouse gas measurements showing marked CO_2 increase since the 1800s

Source: Climate Change 2007: The Physical Science Basis. Working Group I Contribution to the Fourth Assessment Report of the Intergovernmental Panel on Climate Change. Figure SPM.1. Cambridge University Press.

world would provide a way to structure live sensor and analytic data around time and place. A system dynamicist could vary a synthetic world analytic model where the version of the world being viewed could be decoupled from the live, persistent and shared synthetic world.

Figure 6.4 Conceptual representation of synthetic worlds for system dynamicist with time, sensors, models and live data converge

Source: Courtesy of Dr. Jeffrey G. Morrison, Ph.D.

Additionally, if there were other changes, e.g., in data or assumptions, alerts would be available to the system dynamicist when revisiting decision space models in synthetic worlds. These alerts would be brief abstractions of the changes in state of the models or data captured with MindSnaps, Figure 6.5, Morrison (2008: slide 21). The decision space synthetic world would allow system dynamicists to explore their own analytic processes. Decision nodes would be graphically represented as MindSnaps that reflect *changes in states of thinking* about an environmental topic. MindSnap nodes could be organized around scenarios within a model related to an environmental topic with the ones near the front representing more current decisions than the ones in the back. The system dynamicist would be able to update the model results based on new data changes identified, and a new version of the model and its results would be captured for future reference.

When there are model and simulation results that indicate actions that need to be taken, synthetic worlds would support exploration of changes that may result from implementation of the actions prior to their introduction into the real world. This may be the most important aspect of synthetic worlds as a way to mitigate policy resistance—a major cause of failed good intentions. Policy resistance to change is well recognized by system dynamicists as a phenomenon behind well-intentioned efforts to solve pressing

Figure 6.5 A conceptual MindSnap decision space for system dynamicists where models, results, and collaboration are activated

Source: Courtesy of Dr. Jeffrey G. Morrison, Ph.D.

problems that are stymied by delays, dilution, or defeated by unforeseen reactions by other people (Sterman, 2000).

Today, José Achache is networking the world's environmental sensors from polar-orbiting satellites to instrumental buoys (Tabor, 2008). Achache notes that we spend billions per year on observation systems but our approach is fragmented and suboptimal. The objective of his work is a Global Earth Observation System of Systems (GEOSS), which is a 10-year project to link the data collection of 74 nations. In 2015, Achache expects that we will use GEOSS to create better climate models and forecast imminent natural calamities, i.e., the world's Emergency Alert System (Tabor 2008). Will it be in time?

Getting good data and models will require oversight and diligence. Biello (2008) reports that the United Nations Framework Convention on Climate Change (UNFCC), charged with overseeing global greenhouse emission reduction, found that between 1990 and 2006, the overall emissions dropped by approximately 894 metric tons, but grew by 403 metric tons from 2000 to 2006. The overall decrease was attributed to a decrease in manufacturing in the European Eastern bloc countries after the 1989 fall of communist governments (Biello 2008). Since 2006, they have recovered, and the greenhouse gas emissions have probably increased. The UNFCC cautions that the emissions may even be worse now due to the data being old and the fact that the expert review teams needed two years to verify the data, partly caused by the necessity to travel to each country concerned; this is something that working in synthetic worlds could remedy. Can we wait this long in the future for data collection?

To help gather accurate environmental data, the UK has announced a new standard to inform customers about the amount of CO_2 emitted during the life cycle of a range of products. The UK Publicly Available Specification (PAS) 2050 (carbon footprint) will be managed by BSI British Standards (Kinver 2008). This is the first time that businesses have a robust standard to measure the carbon footprint of goods and services. Despite the increased political interest in the carbon footprint agenda, a survey by the British government funded by the Carbon Trust found that only approximately 1 percent of the firms questioned knew the size of their operation's carbon footprint (Kinver 2008).

Although PAS 2050 has started as a standard in the UK, it is another question as to how to address regulating greenhouse gases globally to ensure that legal limits on emissions do not put local businesses at a disadvantage to their foreign competitors (*The Economist* 2008g). Without careful consideration, the cost of compliance with PAS 2050 or a similar regulation could put businesses out of business when competing with others who do not comply, yet the environmental impact stays the same.

To avoid having international business competition leading to an environmental disaster, Senge et al. (2008a: 9) invites us to step out of our current Industrial Age bubble and into a sustainable 21st century future. To create this future, he offers these guiding ideas:

1. A viable future must account for future generations.
2. We must act interdependently.
3. We must change our current ways of thinking and perceiving.

Senge et al. (2008a: 11) says that the core capabilities needed to step out of our bubbles requires seeing systems, collaborating across boundaries, and being creative. Working in synthetic worlds is a way to help make these steps into the future possible.

Similarly, Scharmer (2007) proposes global actions to address core issues like the environment by collectively enacting and coordinating global systems, technological and human. He addresses the dilemma of current leaders who are forced to operate in dysfunctional systems that are highly resistant to change. Scharmer (2007: 327) indicates that we are trying to solve many problems at the symptom level and not identifying the root issues. He gets at the root causes through cross-institutional collaboration and innovation.

To get at the root issues, Scharmer (2007) advocates that we recognize that "unilateral" communication sets the agenda and manipulates stakeholders to behave accordingly; this often excludes other voices from the discourse. Scharmer (2007: 338) cites the work of Mancur Olson, *The Logic of Collective Action*, that small groups can organize themselves around special interests more easily than large groups can. Subsequently, there are political, industrial, civil, or other processes that are driven by well-organized special interests at the expense of promoting the interests and integrity of the whole. The voice of the majority needs to be heard over the special interests.

In the very near future (2012), the signatories to the Kyoto Protocol have to prepare for greenhouse-level compliance. At that time, if they exceed their limit, they will not be eligible for international carbon trading, purchasing cheaper emission reductions from developing countries instead of reducing their own. Also, they will be penalized by a 1.3 factor increase in reduction goals for future years (Biello 2008). Will synthetic worlds offer the opportunity to holistically "view" complex systems from many perspectives (remotely and directly), ranging from the academic laboratory experiments to public debate on the evening news in time for the next set of Kyoto Protocols? Will working in synthetic worlds provide hope that the complexity of the world we inhabit can be scientifically analyzed and the results presented in a timely way that is comprehensible to the majority of the worlds' citizenry? Synthetic worlds could help to enhance the science behind the policies of government so that decisions are coherent, manageable and beneficial to the global public, not just to the special interests.

Challenges and Opportunities

Lahart et al. (2008) report that Dennis Meadows was too optimistic in assuming that the environment would recover, if humans stopped harming it. Lahart et al. (2008) write that Dennis Meadows indicates, according to some models, that once tipping points are passed an environmental catastrophe may be inevitable.

A major challenge is convincing skeptics that the premise of the pioneering work of Meadows, D. H. et al. (1972, 1992), and Hansen (1981) has value, and that their theories can be developed, tested, validated, and used in synthetic worlds for real problems with real data. For example, Lahart et al. (2008) reports that just thirty years ago economist Joseph Stiglitz felt there was no persuasive case to be made that we face a problem from the exhaustion of our resources in the short or medium run. This sentiment is held by many today as was the thought that the U.S. banking system could never fail again like it did in 1932.

To the contrary, Espinoza (2008) says that the way we are acting, environmentally, is similar to our financial institutions' performance, seeking immediate gratification without regard to the consequences. According to Espinoza (2008) the "Living Planet Report" published by the World Wildlife Fund (WWF) on October 29, 2008, says that the consequences of a global environmental crisis are even graver than the current economic crisis. The WWF report strives to bring attention to the abuse of natural capital just as there is attention today to the abuse of financial capital.

Lahart et al. (2008) sees an even worse scenario that rather than defining internationally acceptable plans for global solutions to resource constraints, governments will concentrate on grabbing share and avoiding any constraints, for example:

1. China has funded African development for access to natural resources.
2. India trades with Myanmar after recently labeling them undemocratic.
3. The U.S., European Union, Russia and China are vying for natural-gas in politically unstable Central Asia.
4. A record drought in the U.S. intensified a dispute between Alabama, Georgia and Florida over water from a federal reservoir.
5. A long-running fight over Cauvery River water rights between the Indian states of Karnataka and Tamil Nadu led to 25 deaths in 1991.

In summary, the hypothesis of this chapter is that working in synthetic worlds will leverage the assets of the real world and synthetic worlds, and use the power of system dynamics methodologies to: harness robust models, apply data from real-time global environmental sensors, and create compelling cases to facilitate environmental integrity for the future. Green revolutions are possible. Real communications to solve environmental problems are feasible. Working globally in collaborative synthetic worlds will provide an overarching framework to manage complex environmental systems. We will be able to achieve environmental equilibrium and prevent a tipping point that could lead to environmental collapse.

Part 3: Research—A Prescription for Future Research

There is a broad domain for research that is relevant to solving global complex environmental problems with respect to accelerating changes in technology, population, economics, and environment (Reiss 2008). Today, research is needed to resolve whether systems dynamics and synthetic worlds could make more compelling the consistent messages of past and present research: that the earth cannot sustain the current use of its resources and that the possible consequences of continuing business as usual could be devastating (Schwartz 2008). The IPCC (2007) report documents the state of many greenhouse gas variables. The observed changes, causes, and projected impacts of the gases need continuing research, including better global sensing capabilities for data analysis, international collaboration, scientific models, and theories.

One important system dynamics and synthetic worlds research area pertains to dynamic 3D worlds with global real-time environmental and economic sensor data. The research materials published by Meadows, D. H. et al. (1972, 1992) provide a foundation for further exploration to motivate the global public and their policy makers to make changes to the benefit of the environment. Gore (2006) provided a dramatic use of media (text, images, and video) to bring the point home that the public and policy makers must began to get the message: our environment and our current way of life is in jeopardy. If the public and policy makers on a global basis decide to work together for the benefit of the environment, Morrison (2008) gives us an excellent vision of how that might happen by working in synthetic worlds. Research regarding Morrison's vision using system dynamics methodologies in synthetic worlds is essential for a global perspective of the environment.

Research is needed using system dynamics and synthetic worlds to facilitate a change in mind-set or "social mind" (Adams 1918) to accommodate the radical global societal changes needed now to sustain our current way of life as much as possible. Research is needed to promulgate Scharmer's (2007) Theory U into a global dialog to facilitate achieving Adam's (1918) "social mind" to address the hard problems of global environmental management and what Senge et al. (2008a) refers to as a necessary revolution to make environmental science effective. The best science in the world without an equally compelling social mind to accept and make it effective will be for naught.

Research is needed to make the bathtub model (Senge et al. 2008a) or others like those in IPCC (2007) reports operational in synthetic worlds with global sensors providing real-time inputs for policymaker decisions, e.g., CO_2 levels, Gross Domestic Product, population trends (Steffen 2008). There needs to be research to determine in synthetic worlds the real-time environmental impacts of hurricanes, volcanic eruptions, tsunamis, and the like to avoid reaching tipping points that could cause great human suffering and require long time spans to repair. The work of the IPPCC (2007) and Achache (Tabor 2008) need unification where possible and coordination overall.

Research needs to address what we know about algorithmic ways to deny problems. We need more research into social denial and acceptance of global issues like those identified by Senge et al. (2008a, 2008b): shifting the burden of responsibility; participating in the tragedy of consuming common resources; and expecting unlimited growth.

We need to develop research programs that address strategies that will enable answering correctly questions like (Warren 2008, Senge et al. 2008a; 2008b): 1. If we cut the use of fossil fuels by 10 percent, greenhouse gas levels will [a] fall; [b] stay the same; or [c] go on rising? and 2. Will government policy proposal X, if passed, be supported by a validated and publicly available algorithm and sensor capability that demonstrates solving policy objectives and avoiding adverse consequences?

Malczynski (2008) suggests that research is needed to enable politicians to regularly speak of "systems," "feedback," and "delay" in public speeches. Research into using system dynamics and working in synthetic worlds could help to determine whether it is feasible to create stories that will augment political rhetoric with verifiable information content (*The Economist* 2008c).

Crowe (2008) poses a number of significant questions that integrative cross-discipline research in system dynamics and synthetic worlds could examine: 1. What is the relationship between global warming, economic growth and quality of life?; 2. Is there an optimum replacement rate of hydrocarbon energy sources by alternative energy sources?; 3. How should energy strategies vary by country or region?; and 4. What alternative strategies will impact the accumulation of greenhouse gases and other pollutants?

There is a need for research into the role information technology will play as an environmental preservation enabler like the research by Dr. Neil Gershenfeld to determine the impact of intelligent building infrastructure on energy efficiency (MIT 2008). Information technology could enable "smart buildings" to manage lighting and ventilation depending on occupancy (*The Economist* 2008f: 78). This research is needed to make possible the integration of intelligent building technology into global environmental sensor systems.

Research into information technology in synthetic worlds as a disabler is needed, too. Research could help determine the degree that information technology continues as a major source of environmental pollution, currently on the order of aviation (*The Economist* 2008a, 2008b and 2008f). Research could help to identify mitigating alternatives to reduce information technologies' environmental impact.

Additionally, research could inform how working in synthetic worlds could reduce carbon emissions by improving global logistics, e.g., identifying delivery routes, using data networking inside electrical grids to manage demand (Mankoff, Kravets, and Blevis 2008: 103), and reducing unnecessary energy consumption (Bullis 2008).

Developing policies to more effectively manage global commons and monitoring them in synthetic worlds is another area that could benefit from research. For example, 70 percent of the earth's surface is ocean that is beyond national jurisdictions. The Antarctic is a global common area. The high atmosphere and outer space are our newest frontiers of the commons. Complex environmental life-support systems of the earth have common attributes. What are sustainable policies and how do we monitor policy compliance for resources that no one owns but we all share?

Considering the governance and policy domain, research is needed into using system dynamics in synthetic worlds to develop greenhouse gas policies and to monitor legal limits on emissions (Biello 2008). Oversight and compliance is essential to balance the competition between those who follow the regulations and those who do not (*The Economist* 2008g: 88; 2008d). The policies and the monitored results will help bridge possible gaps between rich and poor nations to meet the challenges of achieving a sustainable world. Standards like PAS 2050 (Kinver 2008) will need oversight for equitable compliance. We need to identify innovative ways to inform policy makers and the public of the state of the environment. Possibly an index like the VIX (Grynbaum 2008) could be developed as an environmental index, for example, EnVIX.

Economics is another possible research area for system dynamics and working in synthetic worlds as a way to plan for the end of fossil-fuel economies and the beginning of alternative fuel economies. We need to better understand how to tax carbon footprints and remove subsidies for fossil fuel, while encouraging transition to alternative fuels

(*The Economist* 2008e: 17). System dynamics and synthetic worlds research is needed to identify ways to promote the "greening" of the market system. According to Senge et al. (2008a: 212), we need research to support the creation of a "circular economy" with no waste. We need to identify ways that system dynamics and synthetic worlds can help this happen. Senge et al. (2008a) describes a no-waste circular economy as one that would have "natural nutrients" that are biodegradable by-products of industrial processes and "technical nutrients" that circulate back into the creation or use of other products—zero waste.

In summary, system dynamics and synthetic worlds is a broad field for research. Creative research is needed, for example, to monitor the environment, sense global impacts, control pollutants, convince governments and the public to stop polluting, provide meaningful oversight and compliance to environmental regulations and laws, and change our economic life-pattern. The hope is that, just as the research possibilities are challenging, they will spark the imaginations of us all to achieve a prosperous, environmentally balanced future.

References

Adams, H. (1918). The law of acceleration, in *The Education of Henry Adams*, edited by H. C. Lodge. Boston: Houghton Mifflin [Online: 27 October 2008]. Available at: http://www.bartleby.com/159/34.html [accessed: 27 October 2008].

Biello, D. (2008). From bad to worse: Figures on global greenhouse gas emissions. *Scientific American* [Online: 23 November 2008]. Available at: http://www.sciam.com/article.cfm?id=from-bad-to-worse-with-greenhouse-gas-emissions [accessed: 23 November 2008].

Bullis, K. (2008). A cheap CO_2 trap. *Technology Review*, 111(3):26.

Crowe, B. (2008). "REPLY Society Strategy Development (SD6924)." [Online: 13 April 2008]. E-mailed to Warren Tignor. 14 April 2008.

Espinoza, J. (2008). Environment faces its own credit crunch, in *Forbes* [Online: 30 October 2008]. Available at: http://www.forbes.com/facesinthenews/2008/10/30/wwf-environment-crunch-face-markets-cx_je_1029autofacescan01.html [accessed: 30 October 2008].

Forrester, J. (1961). *Industrial Dynamics*. Portland: Productivity Press.

Gladwell, M. (2002). *The Tipping Point: How Little Things Can Make a Big Difference*. USA: First Back Bay.

Gore, A. (2006). *An Inconvenient Truth*. New York: Rodale.

Grynbaum, M. (2008). On Wall Street, eyes turn to fear index. *The New York Times* [Online: 23 October 2008]. Available at: http://www.nytimes.com/2008/10/20/business/20vix.html?hp [accessed: 23 October 2008].

Hansen, J., Johnson, D., Lacas, A., Lebedeff, S., Lee, P., Rind, D., and Russell, G. (1981). Climate impact of increasing atmospheric carbon dioxide. *Science,* 213(4511):957–966.

Hoseini, M., You, C., and Pavicic, M. (2008). A Cellular Automata ASIC for Conformal Computing. *Proceedings Engineering of Reconfigurable Systems and Algorithms*. 305–306.

IPCC (2007). Summary for Policymakers. *Climate Change 2007: The Physical Science Basis. Contribution of Working Group I to the Fourth Assessment Report of the Intergovernmental Panel on Climate Change* [Solomon, S., D. Qin, M. Manning, Z. Chen, M. Marquis, K.B. Averyt, M.Tignor and H.L. Miller (eds.)]. Cambridge University Press, Cambridge, United Kingdom and New York, NY, USA.

Kinver, M. (2008). UK unveils CO_2 footprint standard. *BBC News* [Online: 29 October 2008] Available at: http://news.bbc.co.uk/go/em/fr/-/2/hi/science/nature/7694212.stm [accessed: 29 October 2008].

Lahart, J., Barta, P., and Batson, A. (2008). The new limits to growth revive malthusian fears. *The Wall Street Journal* [Online: 26 October 2008]. Available at: http://www.peopleandplanet.net/doc.php?id=3249 [accessed: 26 October 2008].

Malczynski, L. (2008). "REPLY Society Strategy Development (SD6917)." [Online: 12 April 2008]. E-mailed to Warren Tignor. 13 April 2008.

Malthus, T. (1798). An essay on the principle of population [Online: 27 October 2008]. Available at: http://socserv.mcmaster.ca/econ/ugcm/3ll3/malthus/popu.txt [accessed: 27 October 2008].

Mankoff, J., Kravets, R., and Blevis, E. (2008). Some computer science issues in creating a sustainable world. *Computer*, 41(8):102–105.

Meadows, D. H., Meadows, D. L., Randers, J., and Behrens, W. (1972). *The Limits to Growth*. New York: Universe Books.

Meadows, D. H., Meadows, D. L., and Randers, J., (1992). *Beyond The Limits*. Vermont: Chelsea Green.

MIT (2008). Intelligent infrastructure for energy efficiency. *MIT Plan 68* [Online: 28 November 2008]. Available at: http://sap.mit.edu/resources/portfolio/intelligent_infrastructure/ [accessed: 28 November 2008].

Mooney, C. (2008). Climate repair made simple. *Wired*, 16(07):128.

Morrison, J. (2008). Analyst workspace for exploitation (A-SpaceX) & MindSnaps: "Synthetic worlds for analysis." [Online: 29 October 2008]. Available at: https://www.fbo.gov/ at IARPA, at A-SpaceX Industry Day, at aspacexbriefing.pdf [accessed: 29 October 2008].

Papert, S. (1980). *Mindstorms*. New York: Basic Books.

Reiss, S. (2008). Inconvenient truths. *WIRED*, 16.06, 148–164.

Senge, P., Smith, B., Kruschwitz, N., Laur, J., and Schley, S. (2008a). *The Necessary Revolution*. New York: Doubleday.

Senge, P., Smith, B., and Kruschwitz, N. (2008b). The next industrial imperative. *Strategy+Business*, 51:45–55.

Scharmer, C. (2007). *Theory U*. Massachusetts: The Society for Organizational Learning.

Schön, D. (1983). *The Reflective Practitioner*. New York: Basic Books.

Schwartz, P. (2008). Cooling the globe? Been there, done that. *Wired*, 16(04): 25–26.

Stanton, E. (2008). U.S. Stocks Tumble, S&P 500 Drops to Lowest Level Since 2003. *Bloomberg.com* [Online: 27 October 2008]. Available at: http://www.bloomberg.com/apps/news?pid=20601087&sid=avDbpuPkgGog&refer=home [accessed: 27 October 2008].

Steffen, A. (2008). It's not just carbon, stupid. *Wired*, 16(06):165.

Sterman, J. (2000). *Business Dynamics: Systems Thinking and Modeling for a Complex World*. USA: McGraw-Hill.

Tabor, D. (2008). Captain calamity. *Wired*, 16(11):34.

The Economist (2008a). Buy our stuff, save the planet. *The Economist*, 387(8581): 19–20.

The Economist (2008b). Down on the server farm. *The Economist*, 387(8581):83–84.

The Economist (2008c). China, India and climate change-melting Asia. *The Economist*, 387(8583):29–32.

The Economist (2008d). Measuring deforestation-spot the rancher. *The Economist*, 387(8583):50.

The Economist (2008e). The future of energy. *The Economist*, 387(8585):17.

The Economist (2008f). Computing sustainability. *The Economist*, 387(8585):78.

The Economist (2008g). Economics Focus: Carbon pricing and protectionism. *The Economist*, 387(8585):88.

Warren, K. (2008). "REPLY Society Strategy Development (SD6903)," [Online: 10 April 2008]. E-mailed to Warren Tignor. 11 April 2008.

Chapter 7
Analytical World Environments

Vadim Slavin, Randy Stiles, and Thomas Trinko

Abstract

It is hard to imagine the future of humanity without computers. With advances in computing power and algorithms machines will become more and more sophisticated in the way they process and use information. Advances in human-system collaboration follow this natural evolution of the machine. Sophisticated reasoning, input and output technologies will reduce the impedance between human and machine allowing a broader domain of individuals to tap into the full power of sophisticated tools tailored for critical applications. One such application is a virtual mixed-initiative[1] environment for analysis of intelligence data. One can imagine how a human and a machine will work together in the near future to collaboratively solve problems based on the current vision for the future and supported by ongoing research efforts. To illustrate the possibilities we provide a day-in-the-life of future intelligence analysts who are working to understand patterns in intelligence data.

The Future

Joe walks into his darkened work space. When his thumb lands on the small pad on the left of his clear desk the angled monitor wall lights up. A virtual keyboard appears projected onto the desktop which itself is touch-screen surface. The keys protrude from the desktop as if pushed out from underneath—a haptic interface that can take the physical shape of displayed objects. Joe glances to make sure his coffee machine is starting up as the work space loads all of his preferences, and touches the email button. His emails appear in the center of the wall screen, prioritized by his key objectives. The first one indicates that Sandra, a junior analyst, has noticed interesting communications patterns near the Russian-Georgian border.

Sandra didn't know that Joe would be interested, but Joe had specified a search agent to look for any sign of correlations between Russian communications and activities in the breakaway regions. The agent has found Sandra's report and compared it to a behavioral model for the activities of extremists in the breakaway region. Months of monitoring their actions helped Joe develop a story for how they operated. It was like

1 A mixed-initiative system is one which enables a human and a machine to work together towards a common purpose utilizing the best abilities of a human (nondeterministic reasoning, domain expertise) and those of a machine (pattern recognition, automation, and modeling).

building up a Hollywood script, initially disconnected elements slowly evolved into a thread which could describe how the extremists operated.

Joe clicks on the agent icon which has been embedded in the email and a virtual human appears.

"Good morning, Joe. I trust you slept well last night?"

"Yeah. Why do you believe that the breakaway extremists are about to do something?" asked Joe. He has always been cynical about how the virtual avatar talked with fake, albeit humanlike, emotions. Abstractly, he knew some people liked this, but it was just computer software.

"Well, Joe," a storyboard appears on the left side of the large screen, "your model shows that whenever a new Russian mechanized infantry unit moves into North Ossetia it lays a land line to the main telephone network. We also know that a significant number of calls go from that unit to a variety of numbers in the break away region."

"So?" Joe is reluctant to sift through the storyboard himself and decides to let the "software" explain it instead to refresh his memory.

"Well, if you look at the left of the model you'll notice the likeliest hypothesis is that an increase in phone calls precedes a border foray by the extremists."

Joe knows that it is easier for him to check it out himself instead of relying on the virtual agent to explain it well. It will be faster at least. With one smooth motion of the left index finger, Joe drags the story board from the vertical screen onto his desktop. Immediately, the desktop eases into a slightly tilted position as the keyboard keys retract back to leave the display surface smooth. Now with the model within his main view, he can zoom in and out, scroll through the storyboard, review collected materials, and queue up collected evidence. He does this seemingly effortlessly by touching the desktop display with his fingers.

"Do we know what numbers the Russians are calling? Are they calling the numbers that we know the extremists use?"

"I can't determine that. I could not find any data source that contains the extremists' phone numbers."

"Open collection agent," says Joe slowly shaking his head.

A different avatar, one customized by Joe months ago, says:

"Yes, Joe?"

"Please add a request for collection of the telephone numbers used by the breakaway region extremists."

"I'm not sure I can do that Joe. Would you like to talk to the expert?"

"Yes," asserted Joe.

Another human face pops up on the wall monitor. It looks more real, and less clean shaven than the faces Joe has seen so far today.

"What do you want now, Joe?"

"Phone numbers for the South Ossetian extremists."

"Nearly impossible. They use disposable cell phones and change them regularly. We really have no way to pin them down."

"How do we know they get calls before they start an operation then?"

"Heck if I know."

"Excuse me, Joe," the first avatar intervenes, "may I interrupt you? That information was based on video analyzed using computer vision algorithms for body motion. The algorithm's showed that certain known targets exhibited body postures and motion profiles correlated to cell phone calls."

"Okay Joe, do you mind if I get back to business?"

"Sure Steve. Thanks for your time."

Something doesn't feel right to Joe. He just can't put his finger on it. After a few minutes of staring at the screen, Joe addresses the agent again, "Agent, run a sensitivity analysis to identify the most likely correlation between increases in Russian phone communication and the extremists' movements."

"What sample data should I use?"

"Use the most recent collected observations," says Joe rolling his eyes.

"One moment, sir," replies the avatar as it seems to be idling for a few seconds.

"The hypothesis is most sensitive to the collected video results of the analysis confirming extremists' cell phone. On the screen are the relationships between the hypothesis and supporting evidence."

A three dimensional graph of icons and links between them springs on the screen. It is dense and hairy and clearly requires some manipulation to make sense of it.

"Show me the breakdown of the supporting observations with their respective reliabilities," Joe says. He thinks he is on to something here.

A simpler, graphic table appears alongside the graph, the latter receding into the background. The tables shows the breakdown of all the evidence, analysis and observations which has gone into the conclusion that the extremists use cell phones. The table also contains data on how relevant the different parts of the analyses have been to the conclusion at the center of Joe's attention at the moment. Each cell could be expanded with a simple touch to show supporting artifacts in the form of collected reports, data feeds, and other subjective evidence, all fused together using narrative models.

Joes notices a few interesting things. There are reports of electronic intelligence with radio signal signatures matching cell phone communications. However, the reports are not weighted as relevant as the results of the computer vision algorithm that concluded the folks on the collected video were talking on cell phones. Joe thinks to himself that this is why the agent mentioned only this supporting evidence—it is statistically the most relevant to the conclusion.

"What is the reliability of this evidence?" inquires Joe pointing to the i.d. number of the vision algorithm's supporting evidence.

"The reliability of evidence K96GXF is 67 percent and meets your threshold," answers the agent.

Now Joe is getting to the point. 67 percent is entirely reliable to the computer. After all, the threshold was set such that anything above 66 percent was "fairly certain". It takes more than that to convince Joe, however.

"Show video feeds used for analysis resulting in this evidence", Joe persists.

A hazy video feed starts playing, showing a satellite view zoomed in on what looks like human figures walking on the ground.

"And what is the cloud cover percentage?" Joe has seen enough.

"70 percent. The video feed has been processed to enhance the quality."

Joe is not convinced. Still, trusting such an important discovery to supporting evidence which hinges on the results of a software algorithm analysis is something that he would get scolded for at the review. Joe anxiously touches the table to override the default reliability and correctness likelihoods of these results to something more realistic to him, 40 percent. He swipes his finger on the screen to update the results and to his surprise notices that the likelihood of the hypothesis he was digging through goes down by only a few percent. This means that the sensitivity of the hypothesis to the video feed analysis did not play as big of a role as Joe feared. Furthermore, the sensitivity of the hypothesis to the supporting evidence is now more evenly distributed so no single faulty evidence can have a big impact on the model's correctness. Joe breathes a sigh of relief, he is ready to proceed. His reasoning is solid so far.

Joe reaches to his right to switch on what appears to be a table top slightly raised above his own desktop. He pulls it closer and adjusts the lever to fix it in a convenient position. The volume of air above this surface starts to flicker and emit light. Within a few seconds, the earth globe appears spinning above the surface. This new visualization interface has always reminded Joe of movies he saw when he was a kid. Something about a galaxy far, far away where aliens battled each other and planned their missions while using flickering holograms like this one. Joe's holographic display no longer flickers because the office manager updated it to a new model. Joe also remembers when he used to have to wear goggles to see the three dimensional image floating above his surface top.

"Correlate the arrival of new Russian units within 150 km of the Georgian border with extremist raids into Georgia proper."

A two dimensional plot appears on his main desktop showing a strong correlation between extremist raids and Russian deployments.

Joe grabs the plot with his fingers and drags it over to the right letting go with a brisk motion of his wrist as if flicking a card on the table. As Joe lets go, the two dimensional plot continues to slide over until it reaches the edge of the desktop and the holographic environment. Suddenly, the floating globe disappears and the plot comes up above the table floating in mid air. Only it looks a little spiffier. The ridges of the plot are now raised to reveal another layer of information hidden from view in a two dimensional projection of the plot.

"Do we have a behavioral model for Russian mechanized infantry brigades?"

In response a story board shows up with several menu items back on the main desktop. Joe clicks on the "After a Deployment" option and a timeline appears on the floating graph showing what the unit normally does. As Joe pinches the edge of the floating graph to move it relative to him for better viewing, he can see that a unit starts out raring to go but that over time its ability to respond rapidly goes down.

"Correlate the extremist attacks with the behavioral model."

"Which behavioral model, Joe?"

Even as he arches his eyes in disgust (will they ever improve this algorithm?), Joe says:

"The Russian mechanized brigade one. Use time zero as the recorded deployment time."

The two story lines, one for the Russians and one for the extremists show up together on the right with lines showing the temporal correlation. The graph is now superimposed on the map of the area near the border between Russia and Georgia. It's very clear now that the extremists cross border attacks occur when the Russian units are at peak readiness. Joe flicks his hand over the hologram marking the cross border attack times.

"Do we have any imagery of the Russian units at these times?"

After a few seconds a series of image thumbnails appear hovering over the map as if to show which geospatial location the images correspond to. Joe touches one and it expands. Joe can see that the Russian "Bronevaya Maschina Piekhota", or BMPs for short, are loaded on transporters. Several images at various times show similar situations. Joe looks at the Russian behavioral model and notes that at those times the BMPs should have been parked in the main compound, not on transporters.

"How far, by road, from the Russian compounds to South Ossetia?"

As a map appears showing the fastest route, Joe makes a mental note to remember to get directions to that new Chinese restaurant everyone is raving about.

"Approximately 150 km, Joe."

"What's the shortest road march where the Russians will load their BMPs on transporters?"

"It depends on the commander. Do you want me to run the behavioral models for the six Russian commanders stationed in this region?" the map zooms out slightly and a certain area of southern Russia starts blinking. "I don't have any models specific to the commanders who have been in the Georgian area."

"Just give me the baseline value."

"85 km."

Joe makes a hand gesture to change the view presented to him in the hologram. Now he can see the Earth globe again hovering and rotating slightly. With a smooth motion of both of his arms he zooms in first to the European continent then quickly to the Black Sea and finally to South Ossetia. The view presented to him is a photorealistic relief map as seen from a reconnaissance satellite which undoubtedly mapped this view.

"I want to fly the route."

The map shifts slowly to a starting location as Joe shifts his body closer to the hologram. The map renders the fly over along the route from the Russian base to the breakaway region as if Joe was a giant flying through the area himself.

"Show me the location of the cross border attacks. Get me Major Peters."

After a minute Joe hears,

"Hey there Joe, how's things?"

"Ok. I was wondering if you could turn on your holodisplay and fly with me for a minute. I need your opinion."

"I've got a meeting in 30 minutes but I can squeeze you in until then."

"Great!"

Joe quickly brings up the keyboard again and types a few commands. After a moment Joe sees Peters's avatar appear on his hologram.

"What are we looking at here, Joe?"

"Here's the deal. If the Georgians respond to border forays at these locations"—the points respond to Joe's gesture by brightening—"would the Russian units here be in a good position to whack them?"

"Roger that. Based on what I can tell from the historical data the extremists tend to run parallel to the border as they retreat. The Russian unit would be ideally positioned on the high ground to take the Georgians from the side."

Joe sees the ground around the road that Peters has most likely indicated change colors.

"This means," continues Peters, "that if the Russians took out the lead and the tail vehicles the rest would be stuck since they couldn't move off road without bogging down. It gets better, Joe. The range is such that the Russian's will be able to punch holes through the Georgians side armor but the Georgians will have real trouble with the front armor of the Russian tanks."

"Well Major, what are the odds that such a perfect setup would happen by accident?"

"Zillion to one. What we're seeing would require a great deal of planning. People walking the terrain probably."

"Well thanks, Major."

"Care to fill me in on what this is about?"

"Need to know."

"Well you better buy me lunch then. Ciao!" the Major's avatar disappears.

Joe clicks another virtual button and drags all of the inputs he's gotten, including a recording of the Major's comments, into a new document. He takes a moment to clear the Major's lunch request. After all, the guy is good, and he'll need his help again. He then moves the items around and calls up standard format. After adding some words he instructs the computer to build a new signature report and a critical intelligence bulletin.

An older woman appears on Joe's screen, Hazel.

"What do you have that's so important, Joe?"

"I think I have clear evidence that the Russians are using the extremists in South Ossetia to bait the Georgians."

"Why? To give a rationale for a Russian invasion?"

As Joe waits he can see that Hazel is bringing up the data embedded in his report.

"From what I can see your reasoning is sound but we need to drill through this together. Did you perform a thorough sensitivity analysis this time? And where are we in the cycle, Joe?"

"Yes, the main model's sensitivity is well spread over supporting evidence. I learned my lesson from last time. Based on the timelines I've seen we've got 2–3 days before anything should happen."

"Alright. I'll authorize this as an urgent report. Hold a minute."

While Joe waits he figures that for once Hazel wasn't questioning everything he did as thoroughly so maybe he'll get a better review this year.

"I've set up a meeting for 1130 with DoD and State. If this is right then we need to make sure the Georgians know."

"Hazel, can you give me a priority collection authorization?"

"For what?"

"I think we should monitor the Russians in real time, particularly their communications, and if they start to move toward the border we should hot line the Georgians."

"Sounds reasonable. You've got your ticket. See you at 1130. Good work!"

Joe summons the collection agent and using his ticket schedules regular collects on the most dangerous days. This takes only a few minutes since the algorithm takes care of scheduling the right assets available in the area during the requested times. All Joe has to do is input what activity he wants to collect on and subsequently approve the collection strategy presented to him. Then he finally has time to get that coffee and look at the second email.

Relevant Technologies

This chapter describes the use of analytical, synthetic world environments for the interrelated problems of intelligence analysis, smart collection, and mission operations. These are related in complex ways. Analysis is the reason for collection and mission operations, much of which can be overcome by events. Some types of analysis are tactical and short term, and other types can be topic oriented and long term. All require ongoing synchronization with real world events and vary in the frequency and detail of the information.

Collection strategies and mission operations are enablers for doing effective analysis, and tacit knowledge from the analyst is often needed to derive effective data collection strategies and mission operations. Furthermore, the synthetic visual environment in which the intelligence analysis takes places binds together the workflow to enhance user's situational awareness of their collected data, information and knowledge, their process, reasoning and available resources.

Recent advances in the above technologies have already enabled early prototypes of the tools used by the analyst in the story above. Joe's "day in the life" is a vision based on the extrapolation of current research and development efforts at advanced technology centers around the world in the area of enhancing intelligence analysis.

The three important pillars of successful situation awareness for the intelligence analysis are Perception, Comprehension, and Prediction (Endsley and Garland 2000).

Perception enables analysts to perceive the current context of the information presented to them as they must be aware of the relevant facts related to their problems. One of the key virtues of synthetic environments is clarity by abstraction. Background information can be shown abstractly so as to highlight important information in scenes. Different analysis tasks require different levels of abstraction, but all are grounded in real world problems such that synchronization of the synthetic analytic environment with the real world is essential.

Comprehension is the adequate perception of the context. The analysts must comprehend the significance and relationships of events, people and objects, and what role they have played in the current context. Comprehension arises when data is converted into knowledge and information such that the meaning of the data becomes clearer and more useful towards subsequent analysis, resulting in Prediction.

Prediction is the perception of the unfolding events with intelligent projection into the future. Once information and knowledge arise from analysis, the next stage is fitting these to an unfolding effect or set of effects desired by the adversary. Predictive physical, economic, social, and information models can aid in this analysis. Many plausible outcomes are suited for display and interaction in a synthetic environment.

There are many key supporting technologies which should make the above vision of intelligence analysis possible. They can broadly be categorized into the following themes:

- Immersive, collaborative, interactive graphical environments for *visual fusion*,
- Adaptive *information optimization*, and
- *Supervised adjustable autonomy*.

Visual fusion Visual fusion is the process by which human analysts can use visual scenes to interactively perceive, comprehend and predict the activities and intent of others. Sometimes this is referred to as visual analytics, yet the term of visual fusion is more descriptive about the process that is going on. There may be underlying machine fusion of data in support of visual fusion by human analysts and decision-makers.

Visual Fusion is supported by a visual environment where a user can interact with the machine for a variety of tasks from data acquisition to simulation of predicted outcomes. It is the interface to the machine whose major function can be to synthesize a world environment. The latter is a notion which transcends a mere simulation of the physical realm. Various additional facts about the world comprise such a world environment: the notional information, metadata, future projections, and causal relationship between events—the list can go on and on. The limiting factor is not only the computing capacity but also the limit of human absorption of information.

Joe uses his display environments (the screen surfaces and holodisplay) as a synthetic metaphor of a physical workspace. He can drag items between various locations; bring some into view while dismissing others to the periphery. He can move items between specialized visualization environments; summon a collaborative review and assemble a report from artifacts at hand. By having such an untethered interface he can concentrate on his task at hand. His mental capacity previously devoted to operating the machine is freed up. Driving a car can serve as an analogy. Instead of concentrating on how the car wheels turn which affects the direction of car movement, a driver instead turns the steering wheel. All the car's inner workings are encapsulated away from the driver who can then concentrate on safely avoiding hitting other cars.

The information visualization and the interface to the visualization are equally important. The holodisplay greatly enhanced Joe's understanding of the data. The three-dimensionality conveyed important qualities of the graph he was viewing and the 3D map of the world he was using for analysis. Seeing the virtual objects floating in front of him Joe was able to perceive shapes as if they were real, tangible objects; objects he could drag, rotate, and otherwise manipulate to his advantage. He was able to do just that feeling the effect of the haptic feedback. This is the ultimate intuitive interface: to treat virtual objects as Joe was used to treating real, physical ones.

A seamless, intuitive interface, as was available to Joe, contained a collaborative aspect. Summoning another user created a shared space. The physical metaphor holds true here as well. The virtual objects were presented to two parties rendered in two locations simultaneously. Two holodisplays synchronized displayed data and interactions of the users in their respective work environments. Furthermore, the effects of the other side's action were conveyed using the physical metaphor as well: the users were aware of each other's point of view through the use of avatars.

People use visual representations to enhance their memory, to recognize patterns, and to organize their plans. The presentation of information at the right level of detail and with the right associations is key to using synthetic environments effectively for analysis.

Beyond presentation of information and depiction of story events in synthetic environments is the capability to view the situation from various contexts, to revise parameters related to the environment, and to generate alternative outcomes. Even more important is the need to collaboratively discuss and modify hypotheses, observations, and other parameters.

According to the theory of recognition primed decision making (Ross, Klein, Thunholm, Schmitt, and Baxter 2004), people attempt to fit a series of events to a storyline that explains past observations, provides information on intent, and can help to predict future outcomes. Each story then is a composite hypothesis, consisting of hypotheses about each event. Usually people only consider at most one or two possible stories to explain events. A key element of synthetic environments for analysis is the potential to help analysts and decision-makers evaluate a larger set of potential stories in a game-like context. This evaluation follows the information optimization performed by the machine.

Information optimization Mission operation is the process of collecting intelligence, creating knowledge from data and information (Ackoff 1989). Often an understanding of the reason for collecting the intelligence, and relative priorities, are necessary for decisionmaking during collection. In the HUMINT[2] domain this can mean interacting with data sources on an ongoing basis to direct their attention to particular elements in their environment. In the CYBINT[3] domain this can mean assessing what has been uncovered on a remote computer and directing the search for related information. For airborne and space collections of IMINT,[4] SIGINT,[5] and other domains this can mean understanding the areas covered, mitigating events, system performance parameters, and directing these resources on an ad-hoc basis. Many collection sensors interact with their environment in complex ways at the intersection

2 HUMan INTelligence is intelligence gathering by means of interpersonal contact.

3 CYBer INTelligence is intelligence gathering by cyber means through computer networks.

4 IMage INTelligence is intelligence gathering by collecting information via satellite and aerial photography.

5 SIGnals INTelligence is intelligence gathering by collecting information by interception of signals whether between people or between machines.

of multiple disciplines of physics, information and social constructs. Across these constructs a model can be developed which represents understanding of the chain of events and their most likely outcome. The synthetic environment is then the container for the model responsible for its visualization and simulation given the right tools.

The model that Joe developed was based on a series of hypotheses he developed through intuition from domain experience. These hypotheses had supporting evidence which reduced uncertainty about the hypotheses. Additionally, as observations came in, some were credible but not as relevant, some—the other way around. The ability for analysts and their customers to adjust these values interactively based on their evolving knowledge is important and can be supported by a synthetic environment that provides the other context necessary for such decisions. Joe did just that: he checked the relevance and credibility of the incoming evidence as it related to the model he had constructed.

One key aspect of synthetic environments, or serious games (Michael 2006), is that abstraction of context can illuminate the relevant context. Adjusting the level of abstraction within the synthetic environment is a useful exploration of the setting, seeing if hypotheses still make sense at a different scale. A key context for our memory and pattern recognition is the spatial and temporal properties of a given observation. An event in one place can be interpreted entirely different from one later or in another location. Cause and effect can start to be associated to make elements of a story that fit the events. Even deeper than the use of spatial-temporal events to understand cause and effect is our cognitive use of context for "sensemaking". We remember facts based on where we are, and we most certainly associate abstract thoughts with concrete locations (Kitchin and Freundschuh 2000). This geo-temporal context was made visible in Joe's model which enhanced his ability to recall and piece together facts as well as understand the most likely chain of event and their projected course into the future.

With many potential hypotheses it becomes necessary to compare one against another to determine the most dangerous, most likely, and the order of the others. Synthetic environments can provide drill-down capabilities with context to allow analysts to understand the preconditions, observations, and ranking of a given hypothesis when compared with others.

With a perception of the unfolding events, a comprehension of which ones are significant, the next stage is fitting these to an unfolding effect or set of effects desired by the adversary. Predictive physical models, economic models, social and information models can aid in this prediction and the many plausible outcomes are suited for display and interaction in a synthetic environment. Physical models of infrastructure, information, and the relevant system nodes are a baseline upon which the other models can be built (Snyder 2006). Knowing the physical limitations of troop movement by ground and armor strength informed an understanding of why an adversary most likely would resort to a plan as mentioned in Joe's report. Modeling these physical elements in a synthetic environment helped him manage a large amount of physical context he may have otherwise forgotten in his analysis (Kott and McEneaney 2007).

The interplay of human actors with each other and their environment is quite complex. In the domains of politics, military, and information systems, some elements may have a profound effect on the nonlinear behavior of the system as a whole. A new idea promulgated by one well connected person can change the direction of a nation-state.

In Joe's model, there was expected to be a dynamic adaptation of collection of evidence as events at the border unfolded. Joe's collection strategy resulted not from long term requirements, but instead was based on effects-based analysis and fusion, where effects, actions, and nodes in the system were evaluated to reduce uncertainty. The collection strategy Joe asked the agent to implement was multi-INT by virtue of addressing the elements supporting a hypothesis. He used the synthetic environment to automatically construct, execute, and monitor a collection strategy across multiple disciplines, not solely within one discipline such as SIGINT. When information optimization was accounted for, the generation of relevant collection strategies was complex, both within disciplines such as HUMINT and across disciplines, and had to accommodate situations where ad-hoc and dynamic retasking could take place. Furthermore, a collaborative interaction between Joe and the agent during the course of the collection would be required through the synthetic environment to communicate unfolding collections in the context of the relevant analysis model.

Supervised adjustable autonomy There are different ways to present the information to the user and take input from the user. Collectively, this experience, from user's perspective, is called interaction with a computer system. Certain autonomic tasks can be performed without human user's involvement when a sufficient level of autonomy is achieved by the computer system. The purpose of the user is then to supervise, or guide the system's autonomy towards completing its objectives with maximum value to the user (Siekmann 2004).

An example of supervised autonomy is Joe's interaction with the collection agent to task appropriate resources for scheduled collection of intelligence information. While the collection agent is capable of autonomously constructing the collection schedule, Joe decides to double check the results before submitting them. He was effectively supervising the autonomous agent in its duties.

Joe's interaction with the system by supervision was made possible through several advanced techniques employed by the artificial intelligence of the agent and the unique interface through which the human communicated with the machine. As Joe was communicating with the machine a dialog was taking place. Context and meaning was exchanged as Joe shared his intent with the synthetic agent. Because the agent was made to represent a human it was easier for Joe to conduct the dialogue as if with a human. This was why the agent was programmed to respond with human-like courtesy, have a human visual representation (the avatar), and otherwise reflected the social cues fitted to the user, in this case Joe (Herman 1999, Johnson, Rickel, Stiles, and Munro 1998).

Context was maintained throughout the conversation. As Joe referred to a model artifact or issued a command the agent knew what was meant. Joe did not have to repeat all background information in his queries. Furthermore, the synthetic agent was able to disambiguate the spatial cues such as "here" and "there", or "that one". The two were maintaining a spatial dialog (Green, Richardson, Slavin, and Stiles 2007).

The presented example of autonomous reasoning also provided a service for piecing together data into a coherent model based on the semantics of the seed model Joe had configured days before. This level of artificial intelligence is potentially very dangerous to the decisions that are based on machine's conclusions. This is why the notion of adjustable autonomy—the process of checking machine's correctness—is crucial to building the trust necessary to let the autonomous system offload its human partner. This human-on-the-loop interaction, where a human can monitor and refine the system's decision-making, was exemplified by Joe's interaction with the synthetic agent.

Prescription for Future Research

The vision presented above through a day in the life of an intelligent analyst is that of a future synthetic environment enabled by advances in two major technical areas: human-computer interaction and artificial intelligence enabling autonomous reasoning.

The world has already seen a number of touch screen technologies which allow for multi touch surface interaction. They vary in size from a mobile platform to a wall-like environment. What they lack is seamless interoperability. To unconstrain the user from the bounds of the frame would mean to allow stitching such surfaces together such that dragging an object from one surface would make it appear on another similar to how a multi-monitor desktop computer operates currently.

However, the biggest leap in personal computer interaction will not come from multi-touch capabilities but from multi-gesture ones. Computer interfaces could be called "intuitive" only when the adoption curve to using them is virtually nonexistent. A good general approach is to model these interfaces on the interfaces to human-human interaction (Jacko and Sears 2003) which is multi-modal in nature. People communicate with each other through a variety of means some of which are verbal and gestural. A good human-computer interface would have to borrow from these.

The display media should expand into the third dimension with the advent of 3D imaging. Currently special head mounted displays (HMDs) are required to overlay the virtual objects over the physical ones for the effect of augmented reality. There, objects can be floating in mid air and are rendered such that one can go around and view the object from different sides, angles. As the technology matures, one can expect the HMDs to disappear for a truly volumetric, three-dimensional display environment as the one used by Joe (Dodgson 2005).

The interfaces for using such a display environment should stay not too far behind. Already one can use gestures to interact with the computer yet the feedback from those gestures is still mostly visual. What if the user could feel the surface of the image floating in the midair above the desktop? Poking the space inside the image would produce the effect of a real, tangible floating object (Fruhlinger 2008). Then the interaction with such an image would be natural. One would grab the object, rotate it, and select actionable parts of it which would translate into desired effects.

Because this synthetic environment is reproducible in multiple locations it is adoptable for collaborative use. Users in remote locations should be able to view the same virtual world simultaneously while sharing information about each other's actions over a network. When one user can sense the effects on the system by the other, remote user, the environment is collaboratively affected. This is a must for an application which depends on multi user contingency and multiple user inputs across time and locations (Churchill, Snowdon, and Munro 2001).

One has to keep in mind the content of the synthetic environment as well. The amount of information available to a user is only going to grow with the advancements in information gathering techniques and artificial intelligence. The methods for presenting such vast amounts of information to the user have to keep up. New data visualization techniques should be adopted for multidimensional environments. Given a third spatial dimension, data visualization should effectively use the spatial cues that will now be available to the user: depth perception and motion parallax being at the top of the list (Bystrom, Barfield, and Hendrix 1999).

There are many directions along which artificial intelligence will progress in the near future. One of these is the increasing amount of semantic metadata associated with data stored in electronic format. Once meaning is associated with data it opens opportunities for machine reasoning through this data and ultimately creates a need to present the results of this reasoning to a human user (Berners-Lee, Hendler, and Lassila 2001). Uniting complex concepts across many disciplines and helping the user discern their relationships will require further advances in information visualization. Algorithms and methods for effectively presenting information to the user will have to borrow from storytelling and filmmaking techniques and leverage what we know about the human brain and its ability to absorb information (Bloch 1988). Certainly, the extra visual dimension will open the venue for new ideas and techniques.

The information presentation will not need to be purely visual. As mentioned before, to borrow from human-human interaction analogy a machine will have to have human traits. This includes both information presentation and behavior. Maintaining an intelligent dialog with the user will require advances in artificial intelligence just as well as in the speech recognition and speech synthesis. Recognizing speech tonality will help the machine to cater to certain human moods and discern the non verbal communication patterns used by humans instinctively. Vice versa, the machine will have to learn to communicate the same through its speech synthesis.

Spatial cues, which are part of speech gestures employed by humans in a dialog, carry important connotations as well. For example, pointing at an object that is closely related to the conversation can help disambiguate the meaning and intent of the human speaker. A machine, therefore, will have to learn to maintain this form of spatial dialogue by both parsing such spatial cues and then using them for information visualization.

As the computer algorithms evolve to give more intelligence, even personality, to the machine the inevitable trust barrier will arise. Trusting the machine to make decisions with potentially great consequences will be hard for the human to accept. For this reason, the notion of adjustable autonomy will have to play a greater role in the multimodal human-computer interaction (Kaiser et al. 2003).

The notion of human-on-the-loop, where human observer can monitor the machine's autonomous decision-making cycle and refine it, is feasible. Humans operate in the context of supervision, and therefore this is a necessary condition of machine reasoning. Effective techniques for varying the degree of autonomy are crucial for evolving machine autonomy and installing the trust in the correctness of the synthetic world created by an artificial intellect.

Given the momentum of research and development efforts across the world, the future looks bright for synthetic worlds where humans and machines interact, communicate and collaborate with each other and their peers. One can look into the near future but the vision gets hazier with each extra decade. The accelerated nature of technological research has robbed all but true visionaries of the long term insight into how humans and computers will co-evolve together. Yet those standing at the forefront of this research are in fact preaching a self fulfilling prophecy.

References

Ackoff, R. L. (1989). From Data to Wisdom. *Journal of Applies Systems Analysis*, 16: 3–9.

Asimov, I. (2004). *I, Robot*. New York: Bantam Books.

Berners-Lee, T., Hendler, J., and Lassila, O. (2001). The Semantic Web. Retrieved February 16, 2009, from *Scientific Marican*. http://www-personal.si.umich.edu/~rfrost/courses/SI110/readings/In_Out_and_Beyond/Semantic_Web.pdf

Bloch, G. (1988). From Concepts to Film Sequences. *Proc. User-Oriented Content-Based Text and Image Handling* (760–767). New York: ACM Press.

Bystrom, K.-E., Barfield, W., and Hendrix, C. (1999, April 1). A Conceptual Model of the Sense of Presence in Virtual Environments. *Presence: Teleoperators and Virtual Environments*, 241–244.

Carbonell, J. G., and Siekmann, J. (2004). *Adjustable Autonomy Challenges in Personal Assistant Agents: A Position Paper*. New York: Springer Berlin/Heidelberg.

Churchill, E. F., Snowdon, D. N., and Munro, A. J. (2001). *Collaborative Virtual Environments: Digital Places and Spaces for Interaction*. New York: Springer-Verlang.

Dodgson, N. A. (2005). Autostereoscopic 3D Displays. *Computer*, 38(8):31–36.

Endsley, M. R., and Garland, D. J. (2000). S*ituation Awareness: Analysis and Measurement*. Mahwah, NJ: Lawrence Erlbaum Associates.

Fruhlinger, J. (2008). Airborne ultrasound tactile display creates haptic 3D objects you can poke. Retrieved January 30, 2009, from Engadget. www.engadget.com/2008/09/03/airborne-ultrasound-tactile-display-creates-haptic-3d-objects-yo/

G.A., K., Calderwood, R., and Clinton-Cirocco, A. (1985). *Rapid Decision Making on the Fire Ground*. Fairborn: Klein Associates.

Green, S., Richardson, S., Slavin, V., and Stiles, R. (2007). Spatial dialog for space system autonomy. *ACM/IEEE International Conference on Human-Robot Interaction* (341–348). Arlington: ACM.

Herman, D. (1999). Spatial cognition in natural-language narratives. *Narrative Intelligence Symposium* (25–31). Menlo Park: AAAI Fall Symposium Series.

Jacko, J., and Sears, A. (2003). *The Human-computer Interaction Handbook: Fundamentals, Evolving Technologies, and Emerging Applications*. Mahwah, NJ: Lawrence Erlbaum Associates.

Johnson, W. L., Rickel, J., Stiles, R., and Munro, A. (1998). Integrating Pedagogical Agents into Virtual Environments. *Presence: Teleoperators and Virtual Environments*, 523–546.

Kaiser, E., Olwal, A., McGee, D., Benko, H., Corradini, A., Li, X. et al. (2003). Mutual disambiguation of 3D multimodal interaction in augmented and virtual reality. *Proceedings of the 5th international Conference on Multimodal Interfaces* (12–19). New York: ACM.

Kitchin, R., and Freundschuh, S. (2000). *Cognitive Mapping: Past, Present, and Future*. London, New York: Routledge.

Klein, G. A. (1992). *Decisionmaking in Complex Military Environments*. San Diego: Control and Ocean Surveillance Center.

Kott, A., and McEneaney, W. (2007). *Adversarial Reasoning: Computational Approaches to Reading the Opponent's Mind.* Boca Raton, FL: Chapman and Hall/CRC.

Lucas, G. (Director). (1977). *Star Wars* [Motion Picture].

Michael, D. (2006). *Serious Games: Games that Educate, Train and Inform*. Boston: Thomson Course Technology.

Ross, K. G., Klein, G. A., Thunholm, P., Schmitt, J. F., and Baxter, H. C. (2004). The Recognition-Primed Decision Model. *Military Review*, 6–10.

Snyder, D. (2006). *Exchanging PMESII Data to Support the Effects-Based Approach (EBA) to Operations*. Mclean: Booz-Allen and Hamilton Inc.

Spielberg, S. (Director). (2002). *Minority Report* [Motion Picture].

Vance, A. (2009). Microsoft Mapping Course to a Jetsons-Style Future. *NY Times*, B1.

FORENSIC ANALYSIS

Chapter 8
Smart, Collaborative Workspaces in the Information Ecology

John Miller, Greg Nuyens, John Light, and Cynthia Pickering

Abstract

As with the evolution of computer displays from character terminals to bitmapped graphics, the transition to 3D graphics offers a unique opportunity to rethink the human-computer interface. Much has changed since the inception of the 2D windowing interface, notably the rise of the Internet, with all its data and connectivity to people and machines, and the abundance of CPU power, ever increasing, as predicted by "Moore's Law."

By rethinking the boundary between application and data, we can move information out of silos into a common sandbox, where it can be freely morphed and amended in a mash-up of information that better fits the messy business of human sense-making and understanding. By rethinking the user-interface, we can raise the level of human-computer interaction from one-way direct-manipulation to bi-directional visual discourse—making computers smarter to make us smarter.

In this paper we examine an implementation of this philosophy. A specialized 3D virtual world is the collaborative, graphical front end to a highly-expressive data layer, where disparate information is collected into a single place for use by users and software agents acting on their behalf. Usage models depicted in Part I are decomposed into system components in Part II, with Part III looking at some of the many challenges remaining.

Part I: A Day in the Life

In Part I, we lay out a vision for a smart, collaborative, personalized information system in the form of story vignettes—a day in the life of a knowledge worker in the not-too-distant future. Part II presents a look at some relevant work that has been in this area, while Part III looks at some of the work remaining to realize the vision.

Before Work

Mark rolls out of bed and gets ready for work. The mirror-display in his bathroom briefs him on what's happened while he was sleeping and reminds him of his plans for the day. News headlines flash on the glass, automatically selected and sorted by their relevance to his interests. One particularly interesting story, about a new product announcement from Acme, catches his attention. Mark likes to keep up with what other companies in his industry are doing, even in areas that are not directly related to his. By paying attention to which stories he is interested in, Mark's "smart information system" has learned this about him, and thus presents him with those stories as part of his personalized news.

"Say more," he says, and the story plays. Mark just got out of bed, and his biosensors indicate that he's not quite awake yet. To match his level of alertness, the system is careful to present the story in calm tones, and paced a little slower than normal—at least until his coffee kicks in. "Flag it," he barks, "and send to René as 'Important but not Urgent'."

By flagging the story, Mark has reinforced his system's belief that he is interested in these types of stories. By asking that the story also be sent to René, he makes sure that it is also in her queue, where her system can present it at the right time and in the right way for her. After all, René's system prioritizes and filters information, too. The prioritization Mark chose when he sent the story to her will factor into those decisions, raising the likelihood that the story will come to René's attention soon—but, it's only a hint, and may be trumped by something deemed more urgent or more important to her. (As René is Mark's boss, there may be any number of things more urgent or more important.)

Several other stories look worthwhile, but Mark has to get going on the rest of his day. He points at the stories and says, "Send to workspace," on his way out the door. The stories are added to his queue in the appropriate workspace, to read later—if he has time.

Command Central

Mark sits down at his desk and starts his workday the way he always does: in "Command Central," his personal 3D workspace, which presents him with a high-level view of all his projects and anything else deemed critical to his overall "situation awareness." To a pilot, situation awareness, or SA, means knowing what his airplane is doing, the airplane's relation to the ground, what other airplanes around him are doing, and so on (Endsley 2000). To Mark, it means knowing the status and history of each of his projects, knowing what he needs to do next, and knowing what's coming up. To this end, Mark has set up this space with numerous 3D visualizations and information objects, which, taken together, form his Big Picture. A timeline shows a high-level view of all the active threads in Mark's life, from projects and interests to emails waiting for a response. A "radar" view summarizes upcoming deadlines and activities, converging on the center as their time comes nearer. Their color-coding tells Mark at a glance that things are on track—or have issues. A network graph shows the interconnected relationships of projects and people, with Mark himself at the center.

These and other information visualizations are scattered around Mark's workspace, which resembles a 3D desktop of sorts. However, instead of drawers and legs, Mark's 3D desktop is a large, open patch of ground in the middle of a valley, surrounded by mountains. The scenery is more than aesthetic eye candy; it helps Mark remember details and locations of items in his workspace. Ambient audio or visual cues can also communicate ancillary information subtly and unobtrusively: Mark notices a rainbow in the blue sky and smiles to himself, "Looks like stocks are up today!"

There is an inbox here, of course, but a very different one. Rather than piling all of Mark's communications into one big inbox, his system automatically sorts it according to context. Messages pertaining to each of his various and sundry projects are routed to the inbox specifically for that project; what remains is found here at the top level. Mark can handle even massive quantities of email, now that he has smart, visualization-based tools to help him filter out the noise and concentrate on what's most important. But it isn't just greater email-dispatching efficiency; with a level information playing field, email is now just part of the larger context of Mark's workflow, along with people, plans, notes, actions, outcomes, and work product. Where before he would have had to deal with separate views for each silo application, Mark now has an integrated view of virtually everything that has transpired and is planned, giving him much greater situation awareness with much less effort.

Much of what used to be communicated in text form is now sent as data, directly usable by Mark's system to update status indicators in his timeline and radar views. For example, the equipment he just ordered is being tracked as a thread in his timeline, with events for when he placed the order and status updates from the shipping company. If he needed to see the order's history, Mark could expand that thread to see the research he did on the product before placing his order, such as brochures and specifications, customer reviews, and price quotes from different vendors.

From his perch here in Command Central, Mark can not only see when something needs his immediate attention, but can plan and strategize his work, keeping the urgent from crowding out the important. Here, Mark sees that René saw his message from this morning and has asked Mark to look into Acme's new product and report back to him later this week. Mark begins by creating a new Command Central workspace specifically for that project, where he'll gather the information he needs. Later he'll present the report-out to René there, too, directly within the workspace, saving him the time and effort of creating a completely separate artifact.

From Command Central, he drags the calendar appointment for the presentation into the new workspace, along with the original email request from his boss. Before entering the new workspace, he grants access to his co-worker, Emily, who will help him do the research and create the presentation.

The Workspace

The new 3D workspace Mark that created for the Acme product research acts as a virtual project room, where he and Emily can meet and work on the project, whether individually or together. With no walls, it feels open and spacious, with a grounded work surface the size of a square football field—plenty big enough for work, but not big enough to get lost in. In this place, information objects float in mid-air, unconstrained by walls and gravity. Translucent bulletin boards collect groups of documents. Lines link pairs of objects together, representing the relationship between them. Doorways lead to other workspaces, while another workspace rests, in miniature, on a pedestal.

A Command Central workspace is a virtual world of sorts, but one that's designed literally from the ground up for work. It isn't a visualization; it's a *place* for visualizations and other information objects, representing documents, snippets, media, notes, concepts, facts, and so on. New information types, as well as new visualizations and data accessors, are added to the system as plugin modules, extending the system with new capabilities. As an extensible environment for documents and information, Command Central is the smart, 3D, collaborative equivalent of today's 2D windowed environments—the 3D user-interface to Mark's smart information system, which together assist and personalize his access to the rest of the information world.

Back in the workspace, Mark doesn't have to start from scratch: when he flagged the Acme story this morning, his system took the initiative to start searching for other, relevant information. With a thumbs-up or thumbs-down, Mark both accepts or rejects each piece and refines the search agents' understanding of what he's looking for.

Mark combs through documents and databases, pulling pieces and fragments into the workspace, taking advantage of the space to group, arrange, link, and annotate them. With each new search, he makes a selection from a palette of tools and drags it out onto the workspace floor. From that spot, a 3D visualization springs forth, and the query results fill it with brightly-colored dots, each one a piece of relevant information. Interactive controls let Mark come at the results from different angles, until he finds pieces worthy to add to his collection.

As the results pile up, Mark enlists the help of other visualization tools to show the query results from a different perspective. Mark controls the workspace in a symphony of information, turning the dials and pressing the buttons of a device on his desk to adjust the view parameters, all visualizations responding as one. As Mark turns the "date" dial, the timeline filter weeds out old items and shows a string of information building up to yesterday's Acme press release: prior Acme press releases, analyst predictions, and so on. Another visualization gauges the positive/negative response in the press, and other details, such as how many outlets simply ran Acme's press release versus which ones wrote their own story.

Mark has a whole arsenal of tools for querying, extracting, and viewing information. Importantly, the data from one can be used by another. For example, Mark can select items from, say, a timeline, and drag/drop them onto a map, giving Mark a view, in this case, of these items in both time and space. This interactivity and ability to see things from multiple perspectives, makes the workspace an incredibly powerful tool for analysis, sense-making, and understanding, limited only by the availability of the right algorithms and new tools.

Emily joins Mark in the workspace, and together they continue the research. Though Emily and Mark sit thousands of miles away, they work together in the virtual space much as if they were in the same room. Along the way, they capture their findings and thoughts, excerpting and annotating documents, and creating links between the various knowledge nuggets. As they work, the Acme project workspace fills with views, documents, and other artifacts that they've assembled, to where the workspace itself becomes the artifact.

The Context Switch

Mark's phone rings—it's Dennis calling about the Zeta project. Mark brings up his workspace list and selects Zeta. In an instant, he's in the Zeta workspace, surrounded by its documents and information. Subtle cues indicate that many individual objects have changed, and that several are completely new.

Mark follows one link to the project specification and opens it. The specification tool opens up with the familiar timeline and concept map. In addition, a 3D chart appears, showing the implementation status of each requirement.

Using these tools, Mark answers Dennis's questions about the Zeta project's current status, but Dennis is still struggling to understand how things have changed since he last visited the workspace. Mark uses a slider to roll back his own view of the workspace to what it was when Dennis last saw it. Seeing the two states in overlay, Mark now understands what Dennis is missing and can bring him up to date.

As he hangs up the phone, he clicks the Back button on his workspace browser to return to the Acme workspace, restoring his entire work context, documents, and applications just as quickly as he left it. He smiles to himself as he recalls "the old days," when the dozens of application windows from everything you were doing piled on top of each other in a jumble....

Back at Acme

Back in the Acme project, Mark resumes his collaborative work with Emily. As in the Zeta project, he can easily see what she has done while he was away.

With the amount of information they're compiling, they start to use queries and visualizations with the workspace itself as the source. Through these tools and the arrangement and link structure they've built up, they can see the Big Picture of the Acme announcement and contemplate it within a larger scope. With these artifacts in front of them, they begin to formulate how they will explain their findings to René and others. As they continue to add to, edit, and annotate objects in the workspace, they place location markers at key points. The documents and information that come into view at each marker, together with the notes and annotations of the marker, will serve as "slides" as they make their presentation. They further collect the markers into a guided tour, complete with voice- and video-narration.

The Presentation

It's the day of the briefing, and Mark and Emily are all set to go. In times past, they would have agonized over the order of their slides; briefings were linear—or at least the tools were, so they had to get the order just right. More often than not, during the actual presentation someone would ask a question two slides in, and the presenters would have to flip through their slides trying to find the answer, knocking the whole presentation off track. Worse, the data and information on the slides was static, severely limiting the level of interactivity and "what if" questions they could field from the audience. Now, by presenting in-workspace, Mark and Emily have plenty of information to handle whatever questions get thrown their way. In fact, the interactive tools and graphs in the workspace actively encourage real-time exploration by the audience—who can now rightly be called participants. Mark and Emily do have a well thought-out order in which they plan to present the material, but if need be they can access any location marker in any order, or for that matter, any other information in the workspace.

As Emily and Mark lead the group around the workspace, each person has the option of seeing an enhanced view of the information, tailored to their own knowledge and expertise. The more that person is knowledgeable in an area, the less background information they are shown, reducing clutter and holding their attention. Likewise, if they are less knowledgeable, their view presents explanations of terms and such, thus keeping them interested and engaged by not being overwhelmed.

These differences make it possible for Mark and Emily to actually engage their superiors and decision-makers, rather than the more defensive posture that comes from presenting something as a complete, finished story. The result: better informed superiors and better overall decision making—not to mention less time spent by the presenters on polishing style over substance.

Keeping an Eye on the (Even Bigger) Picture

Command Central gives Mark a vantage point from where he can see and manage what's going on in his world, with project spaces to manage his projects and do the actual work. But Mark also uses his system to gather and track things that aren't yet a part of that world—ideas, interesting facts, documents and knowledge of many sorts get tossed into Mark's information "shoebox" for safekeeping, as Mark's personal library of knowledge.

When Mark finds a piece of information he finds interesting, a push of a button "clips" it and sends it to the shoebox. There, it is analyzed and related to other information he has seen. This way, Mark doesn't have to think of how he might want to find it again later. He doesn't have to come up with a file pathname, or a set of tags. Then, instead of having to remember an exact path, Mark can recall the information by any attribute he can remember about it—where it's from, when it was created, when it was clipped, what it's about, how it was used, and so on.

Items from the shoebox may turn up unexpectedly, such as when he's searching for something else, or when he takes the time to browse through his shoebox collections, stepping back to see the forest and not just the trees, as it were. In the process he refreshes his memory, and further refines his knowledge. He's genuinely smarter for having the shoebox: he's forgetting less and remembering more, now that random, sundry bits of information have somewhere to call home.

Part II: Relevant Work

The story you just read in Part I is a dramatization of technologies we expect to be broadly available sometime in the not-too-distant future. Of course, the future is always uncertain, so no one can say *when* these things will be available, but we believe that at some point they *will* be. We can say this with some certainty, since Part I is largely a plausible extrapolation of technologies we have seen and/or developed ourselves in our labs. In fact, it is essentially a vision vignette of usage scenarios we are working towards.

Perhaps the biggest leap of faith is that it will someday all hang together as a cohesive unit, though almost certainly not as one, single, large product or even from one single vendor, but rather like tools in a carpenter's belt: the hammer need not be made by the same vendor as the wrench, yet they all "hang together" in support of the craftsman's work.

Here in Part II of this chapter we examine the scenarios of Part I through the lens of systems we have built. In Part III we look at what work remains to be done.

The Information Ecology

The *Information Ecology* (see Figure 8.1) describes the natural flow of information, from the act of acquiring it (*Find It*), to storing it (*Keep It*), then the combining of it with other knowledge and ideas (*Build on It*), to communicating it to others (*Share It*), where the cycle begins again with someone else. Independent of any particular technology, the ecology applies equally to written notes and the spoken word as it does to software. Thus, we've been using it since early 1993 as a yardstick for information systems and tools, to see where they are strong and where they have gaps. For example, today's Internet search engines can *Find* information incredibly fast, but they lack any

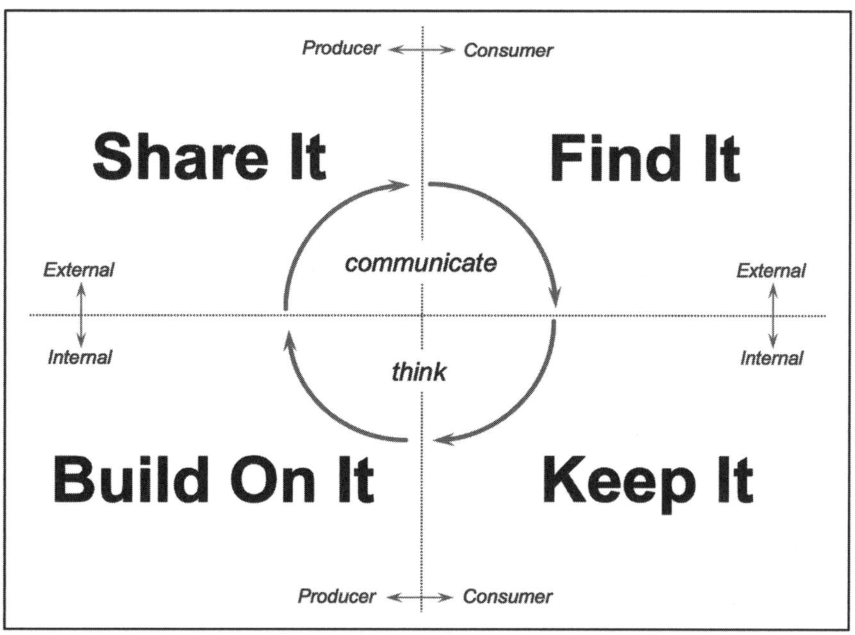

Figure 8.1 The Information Ecology

real way of *Keep*'ing those results, let alone in any kind of structure where I can *Build* on them with my own annotations and links—no way for me to build my own forest, no matter how many trees; and *Sharing* is still a cumbersome undertaking

Such a forest is really an external memory—context useful not only to me as a browsable, breathing body of knowledge, but as context for information agents working on my behalf.

Personal Newsreader

In the first vignette, *Before Work*, we see our protagonist, Mark, waking to a personalized newspaper, incorporated into his morning routine at the bathroom mirror. The mirror-display and voice input may be the first things you notice (Philips Electronics N.V. 2003), but it's actually the personalization that makes this system more valuable to Mark than a traditional newsprint newspaper. By learning Mark's interests by watching him read the news, it filters and prioritizes the potentially limitless amount of news to fit within Mark's very limited time. The voice-command input and bathroom mirror display adapt it to Mark's environment, but the personalization adapts it to Mark.

Mark's personal newsreader is similar in function to several such systems built at Intel Architecture Labs (IAL) and others in the mid 1990's (Miller 1998, Millier, Pandit, and Miller 1999, Chesnais, Mucklo, and Sheena 1995). The key element in those systems was the relevance engine, which calculates a score for each incoming news article, according to the terms and features (percepts) it contains.

In the IAL newsreader, the user dismisses each story they read with a "thumbs up," "thumbs down," or "neutral" button, thus providing feedback to the system as to the kind of articles they are interested in. Terms that occur more often in "thumbs up" stories take on a positive weight score in the user's profile; terms that occur more often in "thumbs down" stories take on a negative weight. Thus, the score of an article is the sum of its positive and negative terms and features, multiplied by their respective weights in the user's profile.

When Mark forwards a story to his boss, it doesn't just fall into her email, where she's forced to read it, whether or not she's interested in it or has seen it before. Instead, Mark's recommendation gets attached as just another percept to the story; René's personalization system decides how to factor that in to the story's rank—based, of course, on René's previous reaction to Mark's recommendations.

Miramar

Miramar (Light and Miller 2002) is the internal code name of a Command Central-type environment created by Intel as a research vehicle for next-generation user-interfaces. We had spent the earlier part of the 1990's developing algorithms for analyzing documents and information, and new 3D visualizations to interact with them. The 3D space, we intended, would give us a bigger place to put them, combining multiple visualizations, documents, and links into a persistent work context. We felt that the standard "desktop" interface was a limiting paradigm, for all the reasons outlined in

"The Anti-Mac Interface" (Gentner and Nielsen 1996),[1] and others. With Miramar, we aimed to go beyond WYSIWIG[2] by combining the look of a STARLIGHT (Risch, Rex, Dowson, Walters, May, and Moon 1997)-type interface with the feel of autonomous computer agency (Minsky 1987), raising the level of human-computer interaction from one of direct manipulation (Shneiderman 1983) to visual discourse (Zhou and Feiner 1997), where the computer plays an active role in acquiring, organizing, analyzing, and reformulating information.

For this to occur, we needed new, expressive information storage (see *Escher*, below), a layer of intelligence on top of the information, and a new user-interface to communicate between that layer and the user. We chose to build the new user-interface in 3D for two reasons: one, it was big enough to contain and give definite "place" to our 3D visualizations, documents, and the links between them; second, being a new medium, it was freer from the historical baggage of user's pre-existing expectations of how a user-interface works.

Figure 8.2 shows the initial pencil sketch of the Miramar concept. Notice the palette of tools in the foreground, with 3D icons for preferences, search, timeline, maps, visualizations, and calendar. The simple, open look is reminiscent of Xerox PARC's Web Forager (Card, Robertson, and York 1996) and MAYA Design Group's

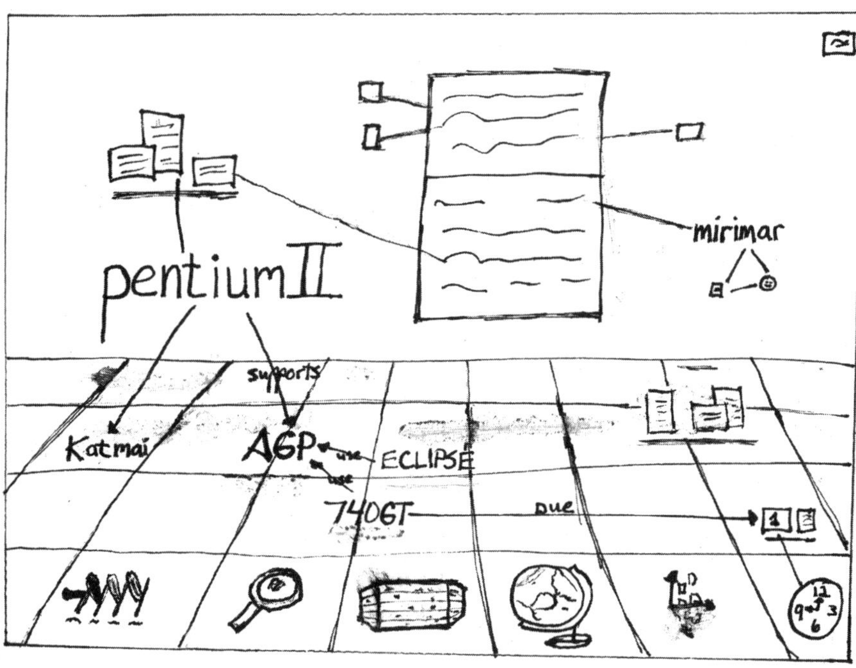

Figure 8.2 First Miramar pencil sketch, October 1997

1 Which, counter to its name is not against the Mac interface, per se, but outlines potential improvements.

2 "What You See Is What You Get."

WorkScape (Lucas and Schneider 1994). The alive, organic feel was heavily influenced by work at John Maeda's Aesthetics and Computation Group at the MIT Media Lab (MIT Media Lab 1997). The Miramar concept developed through a series of prototypes and then several major iterations, each with formal usability testing and architectural review, feeding forward into the next iteration (Miller and Pickering 2007).

As a 3D user-interface, Miramar sits atop an object database that is replicated to support collaboration with other users. Documents in the workspace are kept in a separate repository, referenced by document objects in the database. This separation of data and interface is a critical distinction, as means that users' precious documents are safe, no matter what happens to the 3D environment. As a practical matter, it also means that documents can be accessed outside the Miramar environment, e.g., when using an impoverished device.

Figure 8.3 Miramar as collaborative work environment

So far, Intel has used Miramar in applications ranging from personal productivity and collaboration to factory equipment monitoring and datacenter control. In addition to its normal role as a "window manager"-like shell for documents, 2D/3D applications, and visualizations, it has also been used directly *as* a visualization, using its APIs[3] to create and manipulate objects.

Miramar has recently been ported to Qwaq Forums (Qwaq, Inc. 2009), a Croquet-based (The Open Croquet Consortium 2004) virtual collaboration environment for enterprise (Qwaq, Inc. 2007). There it complements the Forums virtual world as an

3 Application Programming Interface.

"information space," with artifacts and operations supporting individual and group knowledge work.

Rather than beginning life as a virtual world, Miramar was created first and foremost as a work environment, for working with documents and visualizations the same way you work with windowed applications and files in Microsoft Windows™ or Macintosh OS X™. Virtual world-like scenery was added later, to provide additional grounding and visual context. We were subsequently surprised to observe *focus of loci* effects in the Miramar user testing and in our own daily usage, with users frequently recalling the location of a document by referring to the workspace theme and proximity to scenery objects, as in "the desert project, next to the cactus," or "in the fjord workspace, near the sailboat."

Escher

Early versions of Miramar prototypes were built on top of our *Escher* object-oriented database system. Escher, first publicly shown in December 1996, is a personalized, multi-purpose "shoebox" for information, including documents, web pages, email, calendar events, contacts, concepts, facts, and so on. Information is taken out of the silo applications and unified as objects, adorned with metadata properties to capture attributes as name/value pairs. Normalizing the data in this way creates a level playing field where any data can be linked to any other data, both by the user and by Escher software agents (Minsky 1987, Nwana 1996).

This flexibility in objects and structure is remarkably powerful: whereas relational databases are designed for thousands or even millions of identical records, Escher can capture tidbits of information and ad hoc relationships—well-suited, in other words, for the messy, incremental nature of human knowledge.

At any one time, approximately twenty Escher agents are cooperating to analyze, organize, relate, remember, and recall information, with communication to and from the user via numerous visual interfaces and visualizations. While the user works, browsing the web, editing documents, reading email, and so on, the system of agents observes the user's actions and analyzes the information they touch. As a continuously-running information retrieval system, Escher is similar to MIT's Remembrance Agent (Rhodes and Starner 1996); both attempt to bring the user's relevant information to them, based on observed user actions. Instead of a textual list of emails, however, Escher covers many types of information and communicates the real-time, constantly evolving search results through 2D and 3D graphics.

Escher provides long-term, persistent object storage, where information and documents are stored and retrieved by what they are about, not where they are physically located, similar to a semantic file system. (Gifford, Jouvelot, Sheldon, and O'Toole Jr 1991). In addition, a short-term, "working memory," is shared between the agents, such that the observations and postulations by any given agent can be observed by other agents, who postulate *their* assertions, and so on. This blackboard system (Russell and Norvig 1995: 770) allows agents to feed off each other in a manner inspired by Neisser's model of the human perceptual cycle (Neisser 1976: 21), or *information*

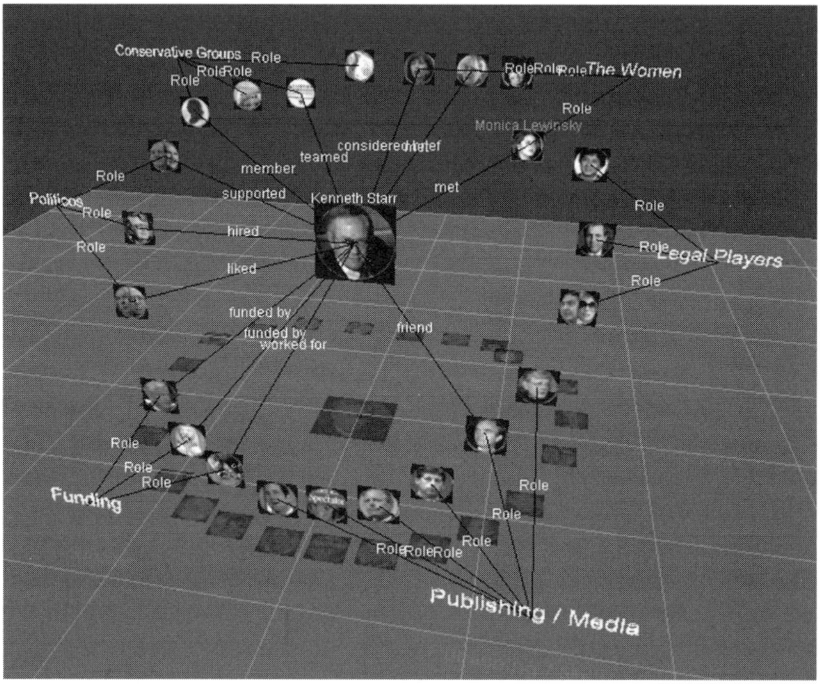

Figure 8.4 An Escher visual interface

pickup:[4] what you are thinking of indirectly causes your eyes to look for it, and by the same token, what you see causes you to think about it. Thus it is in Escher, where with no direct connection between them, quite useful behavior emerges from a set of simple, autonomous agents, each with a very specific job to do, ranging from watching mouse clicks, window activations, document openings, and so on, to computing relevance or document similarity, to generating visualizations and user-interface.

In some ways, Escher is really a scaled-up version of the personal newsreader architecture, with multiple information sensors, multiple analysis algorithms for contextual relevance, similarity, clustering, topic identification, and so on, and multiple visual interfaces to the information. However, where newsreaders tend to work in batch-oriented sessions, the continuous, emergent behavior of Escher imparts a lively, "organic" quality to it, as Escher agents, running in parallel, put forth their findings, and 3D visualizations animate to show them.

A user can think of Escher as a "magic shoebox" of virtual 3x5 notecards—when they find something of interest, be it a fact, web page or entire document, they capture it on an Escher "card" and toss it into the shoebox for safekeeping. There, they may add property metadata to the card to capture additional attributes, and link the card to other cards to express relationships between them. Meanwhile, Escher agents work in the background to analyze the card and its contents, and add metadata and soft links to

4 Pickup as in transducer, not motor vehicle.

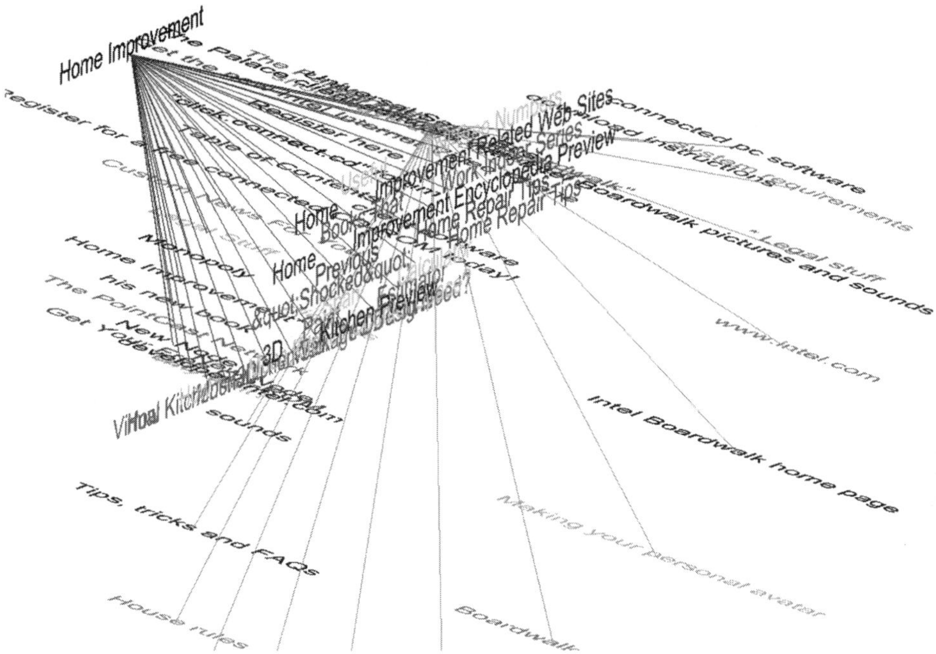

Figure 8.5 Escher version of Miramar, with semantic links

other cards. As users go about their business, working with their favorite applications, Escher agents continuously retrieve and refine a connected web of information and present it via one or more visual interfaces, stimulating the user's own memory and helping them make sense of, and understand The Big Picture.

For example, Figure 8.4 shows an Escher visualization of documents related to the current web page, "Home Improvement." Two levels of documents and pages related to this page are also shown, connected by links. Links in one color depict embedded hyperlinks in the HTML; links in another color show relationships derived by agents from the content and other features.

Weaving information in this way creates an information structure that is not only searchable, but browseable. Browsing data—especially one's own data, lets you see the forest for the trees, as it were, to help you really see what it is you know. This act of seeing, editing, and contemplating The Big Picture helps refine your understanding, and helps you "gather up your notes" and create new artifacts.

Collaboration

The goals of virtual worlds are sometimes in opposition to the goals of a collaborative information workspace such as Miramar or Command Central (Gutwin and Greenberg

1998). While virtual worlds are often judged by their degree of realism, a high-function 3D UI is often deliberately *un*realistic, for the sake of better communication of information. For example, in Miramar, shadows lay directly underneath objects, regardless of the object's height above the ground plane. In the real world, shadows convey information about the light source as well as the object under illumination, but in Miramar, shadows convey only information about the object. Specifically, Miramar shadows are always directly beneath the object, regardless of altitude or relative position of a light source. While less realistic than a true shadow, Miramar shadows better serve their informational purpose: namely, giving the user accurate cues to the object's location.

A similar situation exists with collaboration fidelity: guaranteeing that every person in a 3D space always sees exactly the same thing, in the same way, makes that aspect of the experience more like the real world, but that synchronization adds latency, making for potentially sluggish interaction, especially as the network distance increases. Optimistic synchronization, on the other hand, relaxes the ordering constraint, thereby allowing the user to make changes immediately and *then* synchronize with everyone else. This ensures low-latency, high frame-rate interaction because the user-interface doesn't have to wait for synchronization before acting. The trade-off is that users may see events occur in somewhat different order, and as a result, there must be ways of dealing with ordering conflicts when they pop up. In practice, such conflicts happen infrequently in synchronous collaboration. Further, resource-locking transactions reduce the number of conflicting state changes that can occur in a purely optimistic model, such that conflicts become easy for users to resolve directly via the user-interface. We created a novel user-interface that solved the most common case: when two users move the same object at the same time (Hancock, Miller, Greenberg, and Carpendale 2006)—but a general solution that makes it easy to resolve more complex conflicts (e.g., changing multiple objects, or non-positional attributes) remains a research problem.

A hybrid model may help Command Central designers retain a smooth, lively, and responsive user experience, yet achieve simulation-grade collaboration fidelity when needed, by adapting to the level of fidelity required by the task being performed, and the degree to which the technology infrastructure (particularly the network) can support it at that particular moment.

Part III: Work Remaining

In this section we look at just a few areas for further research and improvement. We'll discuss the technologies first, and end with a roadmap for pulling it all together.

Data Layer

In any information system, data is the heart of everything. Without interesting data, an information system isn't very interesting or, more to the point, useful. We believe that an *Escher*-like data layer, extended to support mobile computing and collaboration, would be a solid foundation for any sense-making and understanding platform, whether for general knowledge or work-domain focused *visual analytics*. Though that term didn't exist when we created Escher and Miramar, our intentions were rather the same, as seen in Recommendation 5.3 in (Thomas and Cook 2005: 144):

> "Create visual analytics data structures, intermediate representations, and outputs that support the seamless integration of tools so that data requests and acquisition, visual analysis, note-taking, presentation composition, and dissemination all take place within a cohesive environment…."

Another example of an Escher-like object storage is MAYA Viz's uForms (Lucas and Senn 2002), which is used by the US military in the "Command Post of the Future" (CPOF) (Thomas and Cook 2005: 139). Note that uForms is storage; it still needs an information analysis and user-awareness layer, preferably along the lines of Escher's blackboard system of loosely-coupled agents.

Mobility Enhancements to the data layer are necessary to enable users to work offline and resynchronize later. In non-collaborative information systems, this is mostly an issue of cache management; when you add collaborative changes by other people—or changes by the same person on multiple computers—more robust state management is required, and it becomes necessary to provide tools that help users resolve the inevitable conflicts. As mentioned in Part II, this can quickly grow complicated and unwieldy, as the number and/or complexity of differences grows. Fortunately, the same tools and techniques required for explaining these conflicts to users (i.e., the current state and how it got that way) are also useful to anyone looking back over the history of the workspace to understand how the knowledge grew and changed over time.

Collaboration A large challenge for a collaboration-supporting data layer is scope control for security and privacy, allowing users to control how much of their knowledge-base becomes part of the shared context, i.e., what pieces remain mine, and thus private, versus shared with others in the collaborative workspace. As one simple example, when sharing an address book with a project workgroup, it may be necessary not only to specifically include or exclude contacts, but also individual fields and links to other information, such as private meetings or phone calls. As in merging conflicting changes, the challenge will be not only in the careful design of the data layer to accommodate these capabilities, but also in the user-interface, such that users can readily understand and control how much of their information and linked knowledge they wish others to be able to see, while retaining all the interconnectedness in their own use.

Adaptive explanations One application that we'd really like to see is the explanation system seen in the group presentation of Part I, where each participant can see and access additional information to supplement their own understanding. This, of course, could also apply to most any information, not just the node-link structures of that example. We see the seeds of explanation systems in the automatically-generated hot links sometimes found on informational web pages, where the reader can click on an underlined term to see a definition. While sometimes useful, these links are more often distracting or ignored, as the reader's knowledge is not taken into account. If, instead, the information were dynamically compared to a knowledge representation of the reader's understanding, the results would be focused, personalized, relevant, and much more useful. Readers would probably be much more likely to click on a link too, if they knew that it would help them understand the material, rather than waste their time. Going one step further, rather than automatically generating hot links, authors might also create content specifically for use by such personal explanation systems, flagging important topics and otherwise providing relevant background material for any reader who needs it.

User-Interface

3D space has a powerful psychological effect. It taps into millions of years of human evolution, utilizing visual bandwidth and spatial memory in ways that 2D simply can't do (Tavanti and Lind 2001). That said, the debate rages on as to whether or not virtual 3D is "better" than 2D for information interfaces (Cockburn 2004), mostly due to the fact that a 3D virtual world is obviously *not* the "real world," and users sometimes do not find it natural, intuitive, or even pleasant. For one thing, it is much more difficult to perceive distance and move around in virtual worlds than the real world, in part because of the comparatively impoverished visuals, but mostly from the basic fact that, while our mind may be in virtual space, our bodies are not, and that deprives us of important cues of motion and proprioception. If 3D interfaces are ever going to go mainstream, the challenges and discomfort that some users have in 3D will need to be overcome.

Sonification One largely overlooked modality in 3D user interfaces is sound. In addition to better, more natural spatialized audio for acoustic localization and effects, future work in *sonification* could offset some of the perceptual information we lack in virtual space. For example, we've used pitched audio to convey the relative position of two objects, allowing much finer, faster and more accurate positioning than visually (Miller 2001). Sound and imagery can also communicate information ambiently (Ullmer and Ishii 1997), so that the user doesn't directly notice it unless they choose to pay attention to it, as in the stock price example in Part I.

Software development tools 3D presents challenges to software developers, too. Some of these, such as the scenegraph and matrix math, are somewhat more complicated than their 2D WIMP counterparts, but mostly are manageable adaptations. The biggest challenges, however, lie in the fact that you now have to take into account the location and orientation of the user within the 3D space (or users, in the case of a collaborative application), in addition to the location and orientation of any objects being displayed. This complexity is manifest in all three aspects of a 3D user interface: *presentation* (what the user sees), *locomotion* (how the user moves within the 3D space), and *manipulation* (how the user interacts with objects in the 3D space). Making things that much harder for user and programmer alike is that no real or de facto standards for these things have yet taken hold, so every system is a new adventure.

For over 25 years, the primary interface to the computer has consisted of two-dimensional, overlapping, rectangular windows. In the early days, there was precious little more than that (Pike 1983); then the so-called WIMP (windows, icons, mouse, pointer) interface, first mainstreamed by the Apple Macintosh (Williams 1984) provided visual constructs and gestures that are now second-nature to us. As we work towards new, powerful 3D interfaces, it's easy to forget that we didn't always have menubars, scrollbars, icons, pop-up menus, dialog boxes, double-click, drag/drop, cut-and-paste, and so on in our 2D windowed environments, and that equivalents will need to be adapted to or reinvented for 3D, and packaged in easy-to-use toolkits like today's developers are so accustomed to.

Not everything needs to be re-invented, of course. For one, we found that our take on the good ol' Model-View-Control architecture (Goldberg and Robson 1983) served us extremely well in Escher and Miramar—part of that separation of data layer and user interface. For information systems, this enables multiple, simultaneous, coordinated visualizations of the same data, which leads to better and quicker understanding (North and Shneiderman 1997).

Input devices The control portion of the UI, which includes input devices of all kinds, is another area ripe for exploration and improvement. As it is now, most users have to navigate three dimensions with a two dimensional input device, i.e., the mouse. This is analogous to the early days of Windows™, working without a mouse, just the keyboard. It's not just a question of three dimensions versus two; each axis also has rotation, yielding *six* degrees of freedom. And remember, 3D applications have to account not only for the objects under display but the user, too, each of which is in three-space—no wonder some people have difficulty using 3D applications with just a keyboard and mouse! Even with rational constraints (e.g., keeping users upright) and assisted navigation techniques, a 2D mouse may not be enough. Just as the mouse made 2D user interfaces feasible, 3D input devices will likely help 3D applications.

But which 3D input device will become the new, de facto standard? In the early days of WIMP there was extensive research and experimentation to find the optimal pointing device (Moggridge 2007); similar work should be done for 3D input devices. Perhaps multi-touch screens are the answer (Apple, Inc. 2007, Perceptive Pixel 2007)—or not (Hornecker 2008); they certainly show promise for some operations, especially object manipulation. For navigation, however, the six degree-of-freedom (6DOF) "puck mouse" device (3DConnexion 2007) is our current favorite.

Head tracking is another input technology with much potential. While early systems required sensors in the ceiling, tracking reflectors worn on the user's head, newer systems work surprisingly well using a standard webcam, tracking IR-emitters on a pair of eyeglasses (Lee 2007), or even through facial recognition via the video image. Using head tracking to control the movement of the user's "head" in the virtual space, the user can see around objects. Perhaps more significantly, the user gets a very strong sense of immersion within the 3D space, as moving one's head now results in motion parallax cues similar to what we get in the real world.

A completely different kind of input device—physiological sensors—can help make computers smarter about the user's context. In Part I, we saw how such sensors helped Mark's personal newsreader adapt to his level of alertness. Much more remains to be done, leveraging work at MIT Media Lab on sensing human emotion (Picard 2000) and at Stanford (Reeves 2003) on the psychology of how people relate to machines. Taken together, a physiological sensor-enabled user interface could respond appropriately to mitigate a user's stress—and help keep the system from *causing* them stress.

Conclusions

Our hope and vision is that these systems can rise above the bits and bytes to become indispensable tools of human knowledge, supporting all aspects of the information ecology for both individuals and groups, helping us learn and understand more, and forget less. Tools with fine-grained information and a context centricity, not just applications and documents. In other words, tools that directly support the messy business of sense-making and understanding.

In order for that to happen, they first need to support the usage models of the tools they replace. Specifically, socially-oriented virtual worlds can evolve to virtual collaborative work environments by explicitly supporting the artifacts (typically files, such as word processor, spreadsheet, and presentation) and operations (create, edit, share) that users currently expect, using off-the-shelf office productivity tools.

Furthermore, developers of collaborative work environments should review the rich body of hard-won knowledge that's been produced over the past several decades in the domain of computer-supported collaborative work (CSCW). Implementing their findings, much of it supported by empirical studies, would greatly improve the utility and usability of any collaborative work environment—and practically none of it is embodied in the current implementations.

To bring visual analytics to virtual worlds, start with visualization, preferably with one of the excellent toolkits available, such as prefuse (prefuse.org), Processing (Processing.org), and VTK (VTK.org). At present, none of these directly support real-time collaboration; to add it, a single instance will need to be shared, or multiple instances will need to be synchronized. Of course, any information visualizations will benefit directly from the earlier efforts to support documents and legacy applications.

Finally, we arrive at knowledge structure and agency by enriching the data layer to provide a level playing field of information and a sandbox for information agents. This is more than adding support for links and notes; fully realized, the system becomes a memory prosthesis, amplifying the users' own memory much like eyeglasses improve their vision.

We've got all the right pieces: rich information storage to augment our memory, heuristic and analytic methods to augment our cognition, and highly-visual, organic user interfaces for a high bandwidth pathway between the human and the machine. It's high time we put them all together and moved them out of the lab and into the real world. Think how much time is being wasted doing things the old way!

References

3DConnexion. (2007). *3DConnexion home page*. Retrieved Mar 6, 2009, from 3DConnexion: www.3dconnexion.com

Apple, Inc. (2007). *Apple iPhone*. Retrieved Mar 6, 2009, from Apple Inc.: http://www.apple.com/iphone

Apple, Inc. (2008). *Time Machine*. Retrieved March 5, 2009, from Apple: http://www.apple.com/macosx/features/timemachine.html

Card, S. K., Robertson, G. G., and York, W. (1996). The WebBook and the Web Forager: An Information Workspace for the World-Wide Web. *Proceedings of the SIGCHI Conference on Human Factors in Computing* (pp. 111–117). Vancouver, BC: ACM.

Chesnais, P., Mucklo, M., and Sheena, J. (1995). The Fishwrap personalized news system. *Community Networking. Proceedings of the Second International Workshop on "Integrated Multimedia Services to the Home"*. May 31, pp. 275–282.

Cockburn, A. (2004). Revisiting 2D vs 3D implications on spatial memory. *Proceedings of the Fifth Conference on Australasian User Interface* (pp. 25–31). Darlinghurst, Australia: ACM.

Endsley, M. R. (2000). Theoretical Underpinnings of Situation Awareness: A Critical Review. In M. R. Endsley, and D. Garland, *Situation Awareness Analysis and Measurement*, pp. 3–32. CRC Press.

Gentner, D., and Nielsen, J. (1996). The Anti-Mac interface. *Communications of the ACM*, 39(8):70-82.

Gifford, D., Jouvelot, P., Sheldon, M., and O'Toole Jr, J. (1991). Semantic file systems. *ACM SIGOPS Operating Systems Review*.

Goldberg, A., and Robson, D. (1983). *Smalltalk-80: The Language and its Implementation*. Boston, MA, USA: Addison-Wesley.

Gutwin, C., and Greenberg, S. (1998). Design for individuals, design for groups: tradeoffs between power and workspace awareness. *Proceedings of the 1998 ACM Conference on Computer-Supported Collaborative Work* (pp. 207–216). Seattle: ACM.

Hancock, M., Miller, J., Greenberg, S., and Carpendale, S. (2006). Exploring visual feedback of change conflict in a distributed 3D environment. *Proceedings of the 2006 Conference on Advanced Visual Interfaces (AVI 06)*.

Hornecker, E. (2008). "I don't understand it either, but it is cool"—Visitor Interactions with a Multi-Touch Table in a Museum. *Proceedings of the IEEE Tabletop 2008*. IEEE.

Lee, J. C. (2007). *Johnny Chung Lee—Projects—Wii*. Retrieved Mar 6, 2009, from Johnny Chung Lee projects: http://johnnylee.net/projects/wii/

Light, J., and Miller, J. (2002). Miramar: A 3D workplace. (pp. 271–282). IEEE International.

Lucas, P., and Schneider, L. (1994). Workscape: A scriptable document management environment. *Proceedings of the SIGCHI Conference on Human Factors in Computing Systems* (pp. 9–10). Boston: ACM.

Lucas, P., and Senn, J. (2002). *Toward the Universal Database: U-forms and the VIA Repository.* Retrieved March 6, 2009, from MAYA Design: http://www.maya.com/file_download/35/maya_universal_database.pdf

Miller, J. D. (1998). Information Evaluation, *Patent No. 5,799,304.* USA.

Miller, J. D. (2001). Method and Apparatus for Audibly Communicating Comparison Information to a User, *Patent No. 6,184,876 B1.* USA.

Miller, J. D., and Pickering, C. K. (2007). From One to Many: Transforming Miramar into a Collaboration Space. *Proceedings of the Fifth International Conference on Creating, Connecting, and Collaborating Through Computing* (pp. 109–116). Kyoto, Japan: IEEE.

Millier, M. A., Pandit, M. S., and Miller, J. D. (1999). *Patent No. 5,899,995.* USA.

Minsky, M. L. (1987). *The Society of Mind.* New York: Simon and Schuster.

MIT Media Lab. (1997). *ACG Projects.* Retrieved March 8, 2009, from MIT Media Lab: http://acg.media.mit.edu/projects/

Moggridge, B. (2007). The Mouse and the Desktop. In B. Moggridge, *Designing Interactions* (pp. 15–22). Cambridge, MA, USA: The MIT Press.

Neisser, U. (1976). *Cognition and Reality.* San Francisco, CA, USA: W.H. Freeman and Company.

North, C., and Shneiderman, B. (1997). *A Taxonomy of Multiple Window Coordinations.* Retrieved March 6, 2009, from University of Maryland HCIL: http://hcil.cs.umd.edu/trs/97-18/97-18.html

Nwana, H. S. (1996). Software Agents: An Overview. *Knowledge Engineering Review*, 11(3):205–244.

Perceptive Pixel. (2007). *Perceptive Pixel.* Retrieved March 6, 2009, from Perceptive Pixel home page: http://www.perceptivepixel.com

Philips Electronics N.V. (2003). *Philips MirrorTV.* Retrieved March 8, 2009, from Philips Research Technologies: http://www.research.philips.com/technologies/projects/mirrortv.html

Picard, R. (2000). *Affective Computing.* Cambridge, MA: The MIT Press. p. 304.

Pickering, C., Miller, J., Wynn, E., and House, C. (2006). 3D Global Virtual Teaming Environment. *Proceedings of the Fourth International Conference on Creating, Connecting and Collaborating Through Computing (IEEE C5'06).*

Pike, R. (1983). The Blit: A Multiplexed Graphics Terminal. *Bell Labs Technical Journal*, 63:1607–1631.

prefuse.org. (n.d.). *prefuse home page.* Retrieved March 8, 2009, from prefuse: http://www.prefuse.org

Processing.org. (n.d.). *Processing home page.* Retrieved March 8, 2009, from Processing.org: http://www.processing.org

Qwaq, Inc. (2009). *Qwaq Forums: Virtual Worlds Collaboration Solutions for Program Management, Virtual Operations Centers, Virtual Offices, Corporate Training, Facilitated Meetings.* Retrieved March 5, 2009, from Qwaq, Inc. web site: http://www.qwaq.com

Qwaq, Inc. (2007). *Qwaq, Intel Collaborate on Enhanced Virtual Workspace Product.* Retrieved March 5, 2009, from Qwaq Forums: News Room: http://www.qwaq.com/company/press_releases/pr-2007_09_20.php

Reeves, B. (2003). *The Media Equation: How People Treat Computers, Television, and New Media Like Real People and Places*. Stanford, CA: CSLI Publications/Cambridge University Press. p. 305.

Rhodes, B. J., and Starner, T. (1996). Remembrance Agent: A continuously running automated information retrieval system. *AAAI Technical Report, SS-96-02*, pp. 122–125.

Risch, J. S., Rex, D. B., Dowson, S. T., Walters, T. B., May, R. A., and Moon, D. B. (1997). The STARLIGHT Information Visualization System. *Proceedings of the IEEE Conference on Information Visualization.* IEEE.

Russell, S., and Norvig, P. (1995). *Artificial Intelligence: A Modern Approach.* Saddle River, NJ, USA: Prentice-Hall.

Shneiderman, B. (1983). *Direct Manipulation: A Step Beyond Programming Languages.* College Park, Maryland, USA: Department of Computer Science, University of Maryland.

Stefik, M., Bobrow, D. G., and Foster, G. (1987). WYSIWIS revised: Early experiences with multiuser interfaces. *ACM Transactions on Office Information Systems*, 5(2): 147–167.

Tavanti, M., and Lind, M. (2001). 2D vs 3D, Implications on Spatial Memory. *Proceedings of the IEEE Symposium on Information Visualization.* IEEE.

The Open Croquet Consortium. (2004). *Main Page—Croquet Consortium.* Retrieved March 5, 2009, from Croquet Consortium web site: http://www.opencroquet.org

Thomas, J. J., and Cook, K. A. (2005). *Illuminating the Path: The Research and Development Agenda for Visual Analytics.* (J. J. Thomas, and K. A. Cook, eds.) IEEE.

Ullmer, B., and Ishii, H. (1997). Tangible Bits: Towards Seamless Interfaces between People, Bits, and Atoms. *Proceedings of the SIGCHI Conference on Human Factors in Computing Systems* (pp. 234–241). Atlanta: ACM.

VTK.org. (n.d.). *VTK, The Visualization Toolkit.* Retrieved March 8, 2009, from VTK.org: http://www.vtk.org

Wikipedia. (2009). *Revision Control.* Retrieved Mar 5, 2009, from Wikipedia: http://en.wikipedia.org/wiki/Revision_control

Williams, G. (1984, Feb). The Apple Macintosh Computer. *Byte*, pp. 30–54.

Wright, W., Schroh, D., Prouix, P., Skaburskis, A., and Cort, B. (2006). The Sandbox for analysis: Concepts and methods. *Proceedings of the SIGCHI conference on Human Factors in Computing Systems* (pp. 801–810). Montreal, Quebec, Canada: ACM.

Zhou, M. X., and Feiner, S. K. (1997). Top-down hierarchical planning of coherent visual discourse. *Proceedings of the 2nd International Conference on Intelligent User Interfaces* (pp. 129–136). Orlando: ACM.

Chapter 9

Synthetic Worlds in National Security Policymaking

Ed Waltz

Abstract

Over the next 20 years, synthetic worlds will increasingly represent the non-physical, intangible aspects of life, moving beyond the 3 dimensions of the physical world. The behaviors of economies, information flows, human attitudes, cultural trends, and other intangible systems will be synthesized in models to allow users to explore the behavior of humans directly interacting with others (social systems) and humans interacting with technical systems (social-technical systems). Perhaps the most critical application of such worlds will be the use by policy makers who seek to understand, avoid, or avert global crises.

Today, we employ computer models to track the behavior (in the physical world) of aircraft, ships and trucks, and provide tactical users an ability to predict their near-term future trajectories; we envision a future where computer models will track the state of the intangibles of the world and enable strategic policymakers to discover potential flashpoints, focus on their modes of causality, and explore the effects of alternative policies and the course of action that implement them.

This chapter illustrates the future use of synthetic worlds in support of national security policymaking at the highest levels of government (e.g., National Security Council, Department of Defense, Department of State, and National Intelligence Council). The chapter complements other chapters on intelligence by illustrating how policy analysts will use the best estimate of foreign situations that are provided by intelligence in the form of synthetic worlds, to explore the effects of potential policies.

We begin by presenting the use of synthetic worlds in an 18 hour crisis situation that challenges policymakers to understand the complex dynamics of an emerging foreign crisis in the small, but potentially strategic area of the fictitious country of Cutanea. Policy makers, and their supporting analysts and planners will use their synthetic world models to both understand the emergent crisis phenomena of the situation, and to evaluate the range of effects of candidate US policies, illustrating the key role of synthetic worlds as an intermediary between intelligence and planners to support national policymaking.

The Crisis in Cutanea

[0415 Tuesday morning 2025; Washington DC]

Tom Pendleton woke to the crisis ringtone of his national security pager, and glanced at the clock. Another drill, he thought. But a quick view of the pager assured him this was not a drill. "Raven Real", was spelled in red on his pager display. Everyone on the National Security Council (NSC) staff knew this code: it indicated that the Raven system had identified a level 5 threat. Tom debated—work from the virtual secure facility in his den, or meet the old-fashioned way at the situation center? He dressed and ran to the car already in his driveway that waited to take him to the situation room. Across town, Gail McCreary was also headed to the situation room where the watch staff analyst was waiting to brief them.

This was the first level 5 crisis for Pendleton and McCreary; they were junior officers throughout the brief 2019 Middle East nuclear exchange but the re-runs of that situation were enough to make everyone in the situation room pale.

When they arrived, the Raven had already filled the wrap-around room displays with ominous trajectories of potential outcomes.

In the early hours, far away in Cutanea, a strange and ravenous outbreak of disease had begun taking a toll of human life at an infection rate not observed since the plague swept Europe.

Because of air travel, infections were already being reported across Europe, in China, India, and in the Americas. The NSC displays summarized the current situation in brilliant graphics, but the text summary was stark:

- Issue: Pandemic toxin spread, followed by threats from K54 terrorist groups to repeat the outbreak at "already emplaced distribution sources all across America".
- Probable Chain of Causality:
  1. Nano-distributed toxin agents [Necrotoxin];
  2. Distribution mechanisms [Nanotransport and dispersal];
  3. Nanotech mechanisms proliferated by Irdicia, or JHANI scientists;
  4. Nanotechnology derived from commercial agricultural distribution mechanisms widely available.
- Source of distribution: Cutanea [Mandelisi, Jucandia, trans-ported from the mountainous western provinces] (Figure 9.1).

Analysts Pendleton and McCreary knew their challenge: refine the situation to understand the causal chain that led to this situation, and project the effects of alternative measures that could be used to mitigate the pandemic and counter the threat to unleash the nano-enabled plague on the homeland. As experts on the Raven synthetic world simulation system, they slid into their cocoon-like workstations and got to work. Before they arrived, the watch staff issued a Raven "Focus" order for the Raven system to review the past 30 days of Cutanea data and refine the current model of power structures (government, political organizations (legitimate, and illegitimate), social population, etc.), economic behaviors, criminal behaviors, etc.

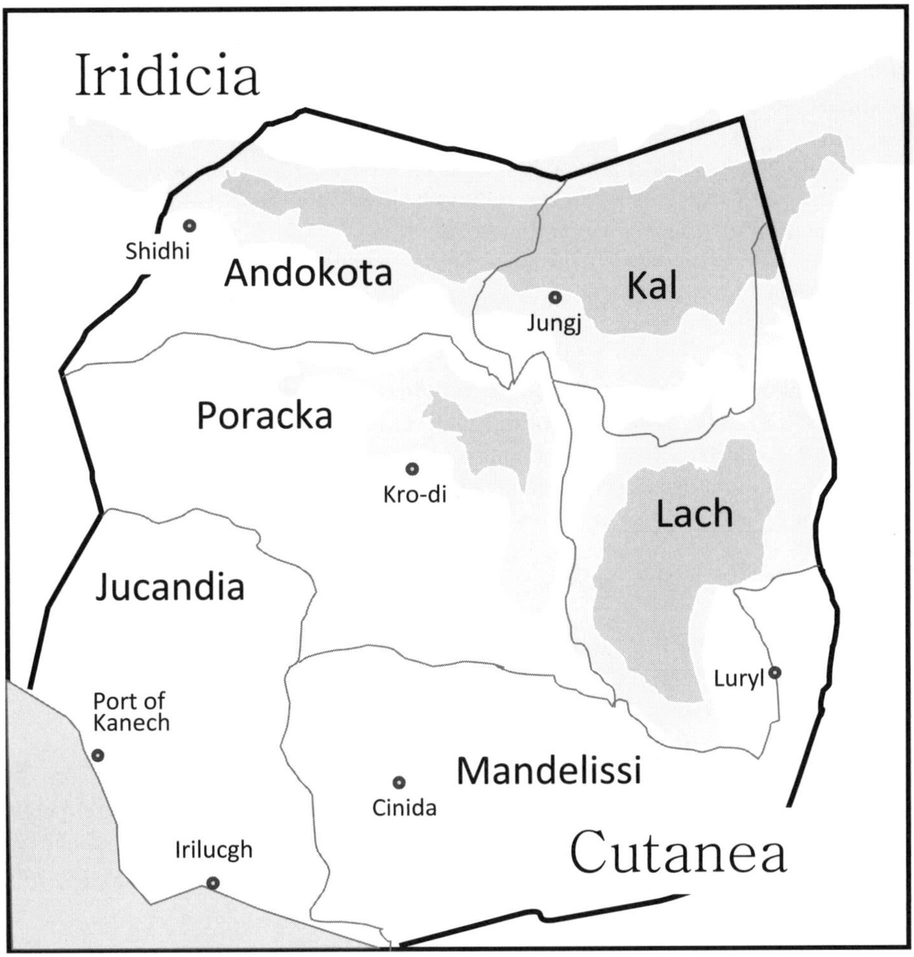

Figure 9.1 Cutanea and its Northern neighbor, Iridicia

(Raven normally used less than 25 percent of the collected worldwide intelligence to continually update models of all of the countries of the world at a uniform level of granularity; a Raven Focus event refined the specified country model using over 75 percent of the available data at a much higher than normal level of causal granularity. It also managed a wide range of uncertain factors, and created a massive space of behaviors for Cutanea alone.)

By 0600, Raven was focused and ready for Pendleton and McCreary.

[0615 Tuesday morning; Begin Situation Assessment]

The first task was an assessment of the Cutanean situation: How did we get here? Why was this the first target? Who are the probable perpetrators? The analysts ran the Cutanean synthetic world backward from the evening before through preceding days, following the dynamics in the country. The simulation allowed them to run backwards, pause, then move forward again—thinking through patterns of cause and effect. They could "see" intriguing activities (and patterns) in the synthetic world, derived and extrapolated from both open and deeply closed intelligence sources:

- K54 operatives have moved back and forth between Cutanea and Irdicia.
- Organized criminal elements within Cutanea have penetrated the ministry of interior and influenced export policies.
- Subtle increases in the black market have occurred at rates comparable to "black internet" campaigns against the government and violence against democratic institutions.

Tom focused on looking at the model activities and the specific reports that Raven used to instantiate the model—verifying each intriguing lead from synthetic causality to supporting evidence. He prepared causal link graphs that were immediately posted in the situation room displays to expose his thinking in real time. Gail began to explore the trajectories of outcomes of the current pandemic situation if it continued without intervention; she also simulated the compounding effects of the threatened dispersals within the U.S. at 2, 8, and 16 cities.

[1223 Tuesday Lunchtime; Assess Policy Concepts]

The Situation Room staff received the first formal strategic guidance from the National Security Council, now meeting in a separate secure location:

- Mitigate the spread of current infection in the Americas.
- Identify the source, perpetrator and credibility of the threat of distribution in the US homeland.
- Identify social, economic, and infrastructure effects of current and projected threats on US, EU, and allied nations.

While eating a brief lunch in her workstation cocoon, Gail assigned specific courses of action for each guidance bullet, and ran the Raven through predictive analyses of the effects of the potential US courses of action. As she expected, there were no good global population perception effects, and only dire economic outcomes. Anything we do might dump the global economy! she realized. Worse yet, she thought, if K54 can pull off even a few of these toxin releases within the US, this will be disaster.

[1345 Tuesday afternoon: Cutanea Portal Opened]

Tom signed off the current synthetic model and issued a release to the NSC Staff portal, allowing Department policymakers (Departments of State, Defense, Treasury, Justice, Transportation and others) to being conducting their own "what-if" analyses with the baseline simulation of Cutanea, the region and (at a more coarse level of causality) the world. (Defense assessed impact of military actions, Transportation and Treasury assessed the impact on global transport and economy, State assessed the political effects on the fragile states around Cutanea.)

[1452 Tuesday afternoon; Assess Impacts of World Reactions]

Throughout the morning intelligence analysts began bringing in reports of the responses of other nations: EU nations are forward deploying troops to close borders, banks are tightening financial activities, a Middle Eastern country has threatened WMD retaliation if K54 nanotoxin outbreaks occur within their borders, and K54 has issued another threat to the US. Gail entered each of these events into the Raven timeline tool while Tom ran the effects simulations to update the impacts of these activities on each of the US alternative course of action.

At exactly 1500, Tom instant messaged Gail to look at the Raven outcome indicator that read "12". The gesture interpreter in her cocoon observed her nod of acknowledgement and Tom received the "Gotcha" message. By now the range of possible outcomes, explored across the range of alterative U.S., E.U. and K54 courses of action (and the uncertainty in the current situation) had reached 1012. Raven automatically clustered and ranked these outcomes into 12 nice bins—and for each bin, Raven already identified several promising courses of action to mitigate the threat. To Tom, these outcome bins seemed to range from "ugly" to "global catastrophe" if actions were not taken soon.

[1822 Tuesday evening; The Search for Something Better]

As the U.S. policy options were explored, the Raven simulation auto validation process proceeded through the day in the background to refine Cutanean behaviors (compared to historical and current emerging real-world data). Tom watched the Raven validation index throughout the morning move from 0.35 (yellow) to a pretty good value of 0.77 (light blue) by 1800; he decided to seek a "Prime Radiant" solution. As an alternative to the policies developed from strategic guidance, the prime radiant process searched across the massive behavior space of the synthetic world for combinations of policy solutions that optimize objective functions derived from policy guidance. But even in this age of ubiquitous computing, the Raven consumed enormous resources to search for the many local, sub-optimal solutions within the space of behaviors. Within ten minutes Raven began reporting many areas of the behavior space that are slightly better than the "ugly" category, and a few that were drastically better at identification and mitigation.

[2130 Tuesday night; Showtime]

Tom and Gail emerged from their cocoons perspiring, as if two pilots from the bygone era of manned fighter jets emerging from their cockpit simulators. After 12 hours of sustained immersive simulation in their Cutanean, regional and global synthetic worlds, they were prepared for the Presidential briefing with their synthetic world—the dynamic tool to show the contributors and causes of the current situation, the potential effects of the high-level NSC strategic guidance and the responses of other worlds powers, and the more subtle, but drastically improved effects of the solutions derived by the Raven's prime radiant search for combined diplomatic, information, security, and economic actions.

Tom, Gail, and the Raven completed their work by showing how the world would play out—explaining what happened, the dynamics of the situations, and the complex effects of a range of policy options. They even ran a few "what-if" excursions for the President, a "best-case" for the Secretary of State, and a "worst-case" for the Secretary of Defense. Now it was up to the wisdom of the men and women on the National Security Council and the President to choose the best policy goal and the means to achieve it.

Postscript: This story is a vision of a real future, not an effort at science fiction. But most science fiction aficionados will recognize that the Raven in this scenario harkens to the nickname for the fictional scientist, Hari Seldon, of Isaac Asimov's classic Foundation Series. A mathematics professor, Seldon developed the methodology to model the aggregate behavior of populations in their complex environments (the Galactic Empire), based on historical knowledge of human behavior, social science theories and statistical analysis. Indeed, Seldon's predictive capabilities of collective behavior foreshadow the capabilities descried in our scenario.

Challenge Assessment

The U.S. Director of National Intelligence has described a vision for future national security capabilities in 2015, envisioning a capability as described in our scenario to provide global awareness of a future, more chaotic global environment:

> "Our anticipated strategic environment models closely on chaos theory: initial conditions are key, trends are nonlinear, and challenges emerge suddenly due to unpredictable systems behavior. In this environment, one prerequisite for decision advantage is global awareness: the ability to develop, digest, and manipulate vast and disparate data streams about the world as it is today. Another requirement is strategic foresight: the ability to probe existing conditions and use the responses to consider alternative hypotheses and scenarios, and determine linkages on what may surprise them, if we are capable of placing such inputs in a larger context and demonstrating rigor in our analytic approaches to complexity."[1]

The challenges to meet this 2015 vision and to implementing the envisioned operational scenario are manifold. Enabling them all are a projected growth in computing storage and processing power that will enable large-scale simulated global scale synthetic worlds, and ubiquitous collection of current information about the intangibles that will enable synthetic worlds to track the real world, and learn about the changing real-world behavior. Hinting at these capabilities in the "new intelligence analysis", Carmen Medina, the Director of the CIA's Center for the Study of Intelligence, recently wrote:

> "There should be an active debate among practitioners and users of how the 'new analysis' should meet the demands of a new customer base and exploit the new technologies now available. For, when the transition to the new analysis is completed, the work of intelligence analysis will little resemble what they do today. Although

1 Vision 2015, Office of Director of National Intelligence, Washington DC, July 2008, p. 9.

> there will always be prose, there will be even more graphic demonstrations, geospatial models, interactive maps, and virtual world simulations.[2]

To achieve the envisioned capabilities, seven key technology and methodology challenges must be addressed to develop the core capabilities within the vision. The following paragraphs describe these challenge capabilities and the current state of the art (in science and implementing technologies) in each area.

1. *Ubiquitous sensing and collection*—Even as the world moves toward increased transparency and the availability of information on global networks, new modes of sensing and collection will be required to accurately measure the intangibles described in our scenario.[3] From Plato to Churchill (philosophy to politics) the intangible states of human beliefs and attitudes, social behaviors, and culture have traditionally been descried in narrative. Simulations of social behavior will require these intangibles to be inferred from sensed observations of human behavior and quantified.

Today, intangible model variables are derived by subject matter experts' SME) estimates, based on their experience and observations. For example, in a simulation of Baghdad's social populations, the relative social cohesion between Sunni's and Shia's in Baghdad's Mansour district (shared values, acceptance, cooperation and participation), might be represented by a single value (e.g., 0.45, where 0 refers to no cohesion and 1 refers to fully share values; fully cooperating). Today, the values of these intangibles are based on empirical observations of SME's of their behavior.

In the future, new collection means will be required to monitor and update synthetic worlds with accurate up-to-date estimates that can be reviewed by SME's. Consider a basic taxonomy (Table 9.1) of four categories of representative sources for collecting information to infer the intangibles, distinguished by two types of sources: (Open, civil sources of information in the media, available from government or private sources and technical sensors) and the means of collecting from the sources (passive observation and active stimulation of a subject to evoke a measureable response).[4]

The prospects for ubiquitous reporting and technical sensing of human behavior are good; the challenge of deriving accurate, meaningful measures of the intangibles is more severe. Widespread distributed urban area technical sensing capabilities are already emerging to provide passive observation of human movements, activities and deviations from normalcy; these capabilities may provide data to infer intangibles, such as sentiment toward object such as the government, economy, current situations, news stories, etc.[5]

---

2 Medina, Carmen, "The New Analysis" in George, Roger Z. and Bruce, James B. (eds.), *Analyzing Intelligence: Origins, Obstacles, and Innovations*, Washington DC: Georgetown University Press, 2008, p. 247.

3 For one view of increasing transparency in society, see David Brinn's *The Transparent Society*, NY: Perseus, 1996.

4 Based on the taxonomy developed by the author in and earlier study, Urban Sunrise: Synthetic Urban Networks and Relationships *Intelligence and Simulation Environment* Final Report, DARPA, 28 Nov. 2003, pp. 54–57.

5 Cuff, Dana; Hansen, Mark and Kang, Jerry, "Urban Sensing: Out of the Woods", *Communications of the ACM*, March 2000; Vol. 51 No. 3, pp. 24–33.

Table 9.1 Taxonomy of sources of intangible information (and examples)

		Types of sources	
		Open, civil sources of information in the media from government or private sources	Collection from technical sensors
Means of collecting from the sources	Passive observation of a situation	Local Media reports Government, private economic indicators Letters to editor Sentiments and attitudes expressed in blogs and other online forums	Human behavior monitors in urban marketplaces Information traffic monitors-via open or Computer Network Exploitation (CNE) Monitoring of communication channels (chatter, buzz, current interest)
	Active stimulation of a subject to evoke a measureable response	Results of Polls (that actively elicit information) Published reactions to Media Campaigns Reactions to political, economic, security and other actions	Use of the above monitors to observe the response to political, economic, media, security, or other actions

2. *Construction*—Current modeling practice requires careful construction of individual (or component) computational models of intangibles and behaviors characterized by an underlying (general) theory of causality and an instantiation of the properties of the (particular) situation being modeled. For example, a human terrain environment model of a tribal population sentiment in a foreign area is based on a (general) tribal social behavior model which is instantiated with the (particular) attributes or parameters for that given tribal group. The construction process is largely manual, selecting the appropriate tribal social behavior model (tribal behavior under duress, or in urban transition, or in inter-tribal conflict, etc.) and then obtaining the properties that represent the particular tribe being modeled.

The modeling process moves from qualitative-to-quantitative-to-qualitative forms (Figure 9.2). Narrative assessments of the situation by subject matter experts are the basis for development of (static) conceptual models, which are then translated to quantitative computational models that simulate the behavior of a situation. The exploration of the quantitative results of these simulations reveal the dynamics are compared to empirical data to refine and validate the behavior, and the sensitivities of outcomes to the driving factors and assumptions in the model. The quantitative results are then interpreted back into narrative forms for subject matter experts most accustomed to this form.

To achieve our vision, we will need two capabilities:

1. *Causal and behavioral theories*—The ability to select from a more mature set of theories, derived by machine discovery and validated by subject matter expert review and refinement—each characterized by the range of conditions (cultural,

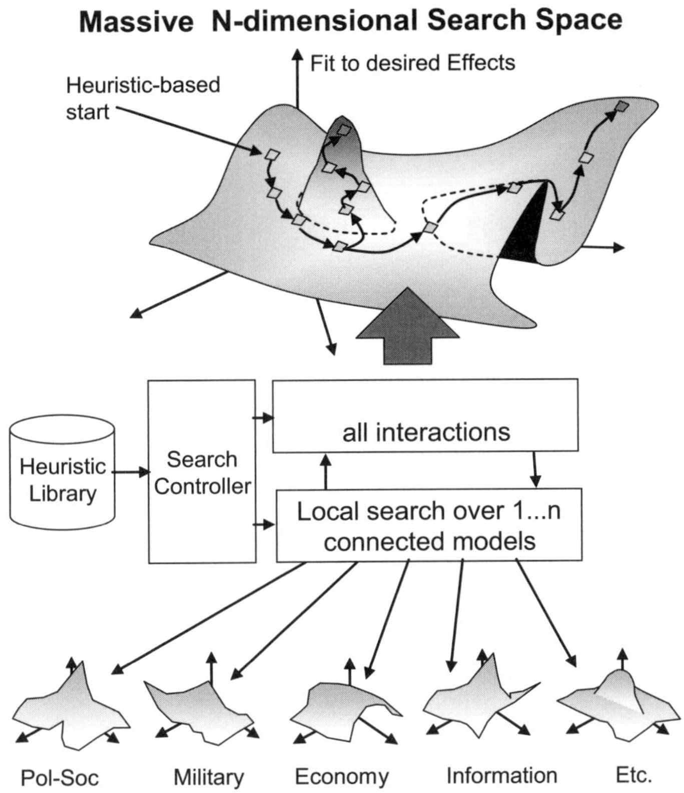

Figure 9.2 Computational modeling and analysis process example

situational, other contextual categories) under which the theory applies. Each theory is an abstract description of the major entities and influences that enable and drive the dynamics of *the current situation*. The description includes entities (people, places, things, resources, etc.), relationships and their environment.

2. *Model instantiation*—The ability to automatically learn and track the changes in the parameters that instantiate the causal models for a particular situation. The theory is instantiated as a social narrative for THIS specific situation, in THIS specific context, at THIS Specific period of time, with THESE specific actors.

3. *Composition*—The integration of different component models, instantiated by available empirical data sources into large-scale synthetic world is the next challenge to achieving the vision.[6] Consider, for example, the challenge of composing component models that represent the intangible dynamics of the Cutanean political-social power

6 For a detailed description of the model composition challenge, see Davis, Paul K. and Anderson, Robert A., *Improving the Composability of Department of Defense Models and Simulations*, Santa Monica: RAND, 2003.

struggle into a federation of models that make up the Cutanean synthetic world. The computational model must explicitly represent the intangible political structure of actors, relationships and behaviors within the context of the Cutanean physical world (e.g., economy, infrastructure, resources, security, disease migration, etc.). This federated world must include:

- Actors (Elites or leaders, institutions, or populations) and their perceptions of the relative power of others, their goals, and decision-making calculus (this presumes a rational, conscious calculation of alternatives and advantages by the actor).[7]
- Capital, an abstract measure of power maintained by each actor at any point in time. The capital is generally referred to as "social capital", a resource for instrumental action by actors within a social system which is jointly owned by actors in relationships. Such capital is fungible (interchangeable with other type of capital) within limits and constraints. The capital can include specific categories:
  - Political capital—a resource from which a political actor can derive benefit, whether it be the popularity of its own course, or the unpopularity of an opponent.
  - Economic Capital—a resource that can be translated to goods or services that can be translated to other forms of capital (e.g., purchase of arms, purchase of TV air-time for political announcements, payment to other actors to build political or social capital).
  - Social capital—a resource of cohesion based on personal trust, confidence, cooperation, commitment, information exchange, and authority between actors.
  - Armed capital—a resource to threaten violence and carry out physical defense or aggression.
- The political structure or social network that defines the relationships between actors, characterized by different degrees of influence; this influence is based on the exchange or transfer of power between actors. A line of influence between actors is directional and allows the transfer of any of the categories of capital; therefore actors may have multiple lines of influence.
- Synthetic physical world, or the physical context within which the power struggle occurs, including all relevant economic, infrastructure and services, information, military, and cultural factors. This world may be represented by dynamic models (e.g., economic models) that interact with the actors in the following ways:
  - Actors can influence the synthetic world models (e.g., influence economic processes, or translate economic power to increased security).
  - Actors can receive capital from the synthetic world (e.g., increased security and justice can translate to greater political and social capital for the

7 The actor represents a polity, or a politically independent or autonomous social unit, that may comprise many lesser dependent components.

government actor from civil population actors who consent to government authority) .

- Simulation of the dynamics of interaction between actors including the following kinds of processes:
  - Influence between actors based on the transfer of capital.
  - Negotiation between actors to achieve individual goals or common goals.
  - Formation of alliances (power sharing subnets) to complete against individual opponent actors or opponent alliances.
  - Translation of abstract capital stocks between the actors and the synthetic physical world.
- Competitiveness (and "winning") is related to the relative value of capital of actors at any point in the competition. Relative power of legitimate and illegitimate actors can be compared to assess their "position" in the struggle.

It is important to note that such a power struggle model should be able to operate in two modes:

1. Actors interacting without the synthetic physical world context to include only the dynamics of the power flows, and
2. Actors interacting within the more complex, context-setting synthetic physical world.

Table 9.2 provides a typical list of the essential actors and synthetic physical world elements included in a representative power struggle model. We adopt the following modeling distinction:

- Humans (individuals, institutions and social populations) are represented as actors (implemented as autonomous decision-making agents in the computational simulation).
- Processes and activities in the physical world (including aspects of the economy) are represented as the synthetic physical world (implemented in a variety of agent or non-agent modeling paradigms in the computational simulation).

Three major alternatives exist to computationally model the complexity of political power struggle strategy and actions:

1. Game theoretic simulations apply techniques from game theory to frame a competition as a set of agents reasoning about one another based on their perception of competitors and quantitative payoffs for each alternative action (move) as a function of opponent's moves. Such decision-theoretic game-playing simulations focus on the rational computation of estimated payoffs across the space of alternative moves to optimize the agent's expected payoff.[8]

8 See, for example, the classic, Schelling, Thomas, *The Strategy of Conflict*, Boston: Harvard University Press, 1960 and 1980.

Table 9.2 Typical modeled elements in the simulation of a power struggle

Category	Functions-Factors Modeled	Factors included in Representation
Synthetic World Actors in the Power Struggle	Political leaders, parties and Cadre (party-militants) actors.	Political actors that seek to establish policy and governance, their lines of influence and political capital.
	Auxiliaries (active supporters).	Actors (groups) that provide sources of support to political actors.
	Criminal and Insurgent Actors.	Principal insurgent actors, their goals, relationships, leadership abilities, capital (relative economic, political, social and armed power) and resources.
	Combatant Actors.	Armed actors and capabilities of the military arm of the insurgency, their goals, resources and targets.
	Civil Population Group Actors.	Population groups, goals, beliefs, and behaviors representative of demographics for the are modeled; relationships between groups represented according to influence, attraction, economics, etc.
	External Influence Actors (Regional, Int'l).	External sources of ideological, financial, and material resource influence.
	Non-government organizations (NGO's), neutral populations, etc.	Goals, activities and influences of neutral organizations, institutions and populations.
	Diplomatic Actors; Intermediate parties providing mediation.	International and domestic personnel, institutions and forums for mediation between political actors of opposing parties.
	US and other external international Coalition.	Goal, will, determination and direction of US and coalition leadership; support, and attitude of US population support for US role in support of host government; attitude toward legitimacy of hot government and the insurgency; attitude toward justification and morality of war effort.
Synthetic World Factors and Models of Contextual Influence on the Struggle	Environment—Geography.	Geospatial area representation with key features, locations of fixed entities, lines of communication, infrastructure, etc.
	Environment—Legitimate meso-economy.	Major sectors of the legitimate economy of state (e.g., manufacturing, minerals-oil, banking, etc.).
	Environment—Underground (illegitimate economy).	Sectors of the black economy; especially those that support criminal or insurgent elements.
	Environment—Seasonal factors.	Seasonal factors due to weather, climate, culture (events), etc.
	Information Environment.	Media channels from sources to targets (sources, messages, media channels, targets); effectiveness of information transfer and influence tone of news, belief in situation, and spread of positions or ideology.
	Environment—Rule of Law.	Level of rule of legitimate authority; effectiveness of government services (Security, justice and imprisonment) as a function of extent of corruption and its influence across actors and institutions.
	Environment—Food, Health and human services.	Processes that provide for basic human needs; food production, distribution, clean water, wastewater, medical care.
	Environment—Physical Services.	Electrical power, Petroleum-oil-lube (POL), natural gas, Transportation.
	Environment—Information Services.	Telecommunications and the effects on civil society social behavior, economy and conduct of government.
	Environment—Regional Economic base.	Strength of economic base in the region and major trade partners.

2. System dynamics simulations represent interconnected processes (physical or human activities) in terms of two fundamentals; commodity stocks and the flows of those stocks. The flow of stocks is described by coupled differential equations; the interaction between processes (including feedback loops) is iteratively solved to simulate the aggregate dynamics of the system.[9]
3. Agent-based simulations represent the cooperative or competitive domain as a set of autonomous agents, interacting with other agents in goal-directed behaviors. The behavior of the system emerges from the interaction and cannot be predicted by the direct combination of the individual agents. Each agent independently perceives the world context and the activities of other agents, before developing strategy and implementing mechanisms to take actions to achieve power goals. This approach provides an aggregate behavior that is complex and ordered, although not predictable and stable (i.e. it does not necessarily reach a state of equilibrium as in game theoretic approaches). Actors continually adapt their strategies; they are unable to .choose an optimal strategy because optimal strategic responses cannot be predicted or, in some cases, even imagined in the time available over the expanse of options and uncertainty.[10]

To provide representative competitive behavior, the fidelity of perception, decision and action within future synthetic world models must provide an acceptable level of political sophistication—a measure of the quantity and organization of the actors' political cognitions.[11] Consider seven levels of increasing sophistication of behavior that may be required for realistic competitor actors (Table 9.3).

Notice that the first level requires that actors have a fundamental understanding of the political competition, their relative power and, (by inference), the threats they pose. Higher degrees of perceptions are required to complement each successive level of political sophistication; this increased perception requires the ability to infer and even anticipate the adversary's perceptions, intents and actions. These more sophisticated

9 See Forrester, Jay W. "Counterintuitive Behavior of Social Systems", *Technology Review*, Massachusetts Institute of Technology, January, 1971.

10 See Axelrod, Robert, *The Complexity of Cooperation: Agent-Based Models of Competition and Collaboration*, Princeton: Princeton University Press, 1997. For a practical agent-based implementation of the political power struggle example, see Taylor, Glenn, Bechtel, Robert, Morgan, Geoffrey and Waltz, Ed, "A Framework for Modeling Social Power Structures", *Proc. of Conference of the North American Association for Computational Social and Organizational Sciences*, June 22–23, 2006; and Taylor, Glenn, Bechtel, Robert, Waltz, Ed, and White, Jeffrey, "PSTK: A Toolkit for Modeling Dynamic Power Structures," Coauthored with *Proc. 2008 Conference on Behavior Representation in Modeling and Simulation (BRIMS)*, April 14–17, 2008.

11 Luskin, Robert C., "Measuring Political Sophistication." *American Journal of Political Science* 31:856–899, 1987.

Table 9.3 Increasing levels of actor strategy sophistication

Level of Sophistication		Properties of Political Actors Competing in the Struggle for Power
1	Political Perception	Understanding of other political actor positions relative to own goals Understanding of social and economic actors and their perception of actions and their potential political influence
2	Goal-directed behavior	Multiple simultaneous goal management Selection of power-flow actions at any time to satisfy initial (fixed) power objective (defined as goals for relative power levels for actors)
3	Strategy-directed behavior	Goals based on coherent political strategy (policy) and values Selection and time-coordination of actions based on understanding of goals and the underlying policy Selection of actions based on long-term (multiple round) strategy to achieve multiple policies over time (e.g., PUNE methodology)
4	Relation Adaptation	Adaptation of relations to achieve goals; add/delete lines of influence Bargaining and negotiation with other actors to form, dissolve relationships and power flows
5	Learning	Refinement of political perception based on changing situation Refinement of strategy and performance based on learned behavior over many simulations
6	Goal Adaptation	Adaptation of initial goals to changing environment Creation of new goals, composite goals and meta-goals, based on changing environment and learned behavior
7	Strategem	Maneuvers or deceitful scheme contrived to deceive opponent's perception of the political strategy

perception processes, referred to as adversarial reasoning,[12] deal with the following kinds of reasoning considerations to model both the adversary's reasoning and behavior:

- Threats posed by multiple, simultaneous competitors;
- Inference of plans from observed actions; Given a set of possible plans or goals for an actor, and an observation trace, attempt to identify the actor's active plan(s) or goal(s); Adversary learning (identifying adversary patterns of behavior);
- Imperfect information (inability to accurately know the adversary's intentions, resources, options, constraints or plans) and stochastic elements of adversary behavior.

4. *Continual update* and *validation*—Future synthetic worlds must be continually updated, refined and the degree of current validity (fidelity of the model compared to the real world) must be reported to users. The modeled dynamics must be continually compared

12 See, for example, Kott, Alexander and McEneaney, William (eds), *Adversarial Reasoning: Computational Approaches to Reading the Opponent's Mind*, Taylor and Francis, 2006. This text describes methods to reason about the opponent to perform adversary strategy prediction, adversary plan recognition, adversary deception discovery, and counter-strategy formulation.

with real-time data on world situations to measure the current validity. Current processes of update and validation apply a confidence-building process by evaluating the model against two criteria to determine how faithfully it represents reality, for the intended application:

- Internal criteria—Behavior of model is consistent with a theory or understanding of phenomena or causality (i.e., the model is internally consistent with a coherent explanation of a system and its phenomena).
- External criteria—Behavior of model output is consistent with observed real world behavior (i.e., the model is consistent with at least one particular instance of such a system observed out in the real world).

The formal validation process determines the degree to which a model or simulation is an accurate representation of the real world from the perspective of the intended uses of the model or simulation.[13]

A recent RAND study described the challenge of validation in such models, where uncertainty in the model (e.g., application of a particular theory of social behavior and response to media appeals) and in the source data inputs (e.g., uncertainty in demographic data on tribal affiliations) is deep:

> "[Our conclusions] apply when the models or their data are more afflicted with uncertainty. For example, no one has a 'correct' model of war with all its notorious complications, and, even if such a model existed, it would have large numbers of uncertain inputs… In such cases, we believe that model validation should be construed quite differently than might be suggested by the usual definition of validity. A validation process might reasonably conclude by assessing the model and its associated databases as 'valid for exploratory analysis' or 'valid, subject to the principal assumptions underlying the model, for exploratory analysis'."[14]

5. *Computational exploration and behavior analysis*—The modeling process stage that collects, builds, integrates, updates and validates the *structure* of the synthetic world precedes the exploratory analysis stage that examines the *behavior* of the synthetic world. The first stage is *analytic*, or top-down, decomposing raw data to fundamental entities (or actors) and relationships, that are assembled into models (these models are hypotheses about the real world). The second stage is *synthetic*, where the simulation creates (by bottom-up computation) the envelope of possible behaviors of the entities and relationships across a range of contexts. This process immerses the analyst not only in the interaction within a complex target situation and possible behaviors, but also in the exploration of excursions and alternative situations that present new contexts. The

13 This definition of validation focuses on the external criteria. See DoD Directive 5000.59, "DoD Modeling and Simulation (M&S) Management," January 4, 1994. The validation process is distinguished from *verification*, the process that precedes validation to evaluate the correctness of a model with respect to a certain formal specification of a theory, using the methods of testing, inspection and reviewing.

14 Bigelow, James, and Davis, Paul K.. (2003). *Implications for Model Validation of Multiresolution Modeling*. Santa Monica, Calif.: RAND, p. 16.

model building stage focuses on *analytic inference* and is complemented in the second stage by *synthetic imagination* of possible behaviors and outcomes. The second stage is inherently exploratory in nature, characterized by a search for:

- Key dynamic drivers of behavior, and behavioral modes.
- Critical structural dependencies between entities and behavioral dependencies between subsystems.
- Sensitivities of behavior to changes in assumptions, magnitudes and phasing of actions, and targets of actions. The areas of sensitivity analysis that deserve the most attention should depend largely on the dominant effects and the areas of greatest uncertainty in the synthetic world. Sensitivity analysis may be used to assess the extent to which changes in assumptions, or the environment modeled will affect the ranking of alternative operational policies (based on effects achieved).

As in our scenario, the most common need for exploration will be, first, to understand what drives a situation, and second, to explore the effectiveness of alternative polices (courses of action) intended to move the situation to a desired state.[15]

6. *Computational search*—As synthetic worlds grow in their interconnected causal structures, even so the complexity and size of their behavior space will grow. With closed form solutions intractable and brute force solutions (compute the entire space of all possible policies over all sets of conditions) incomputable, effective forms of computational search will be required to locate policy solutions across massive behavior spaces of synthetic worlds (Figure 9.3).

Such search methods will search for local maxima (local satificing solutions) across massive n-dimensional spaces of behavior, and will likely integrate multiple methods:

- **Heuristic searches** based on the knowledge of individual models and model interactions can provides initial condition sets and control guidance for each behavioral domain (Best-first search), then provide intelligence control of search (sampling, iterative deepening, branch and bound methods).
- **Bidirectional Search** approaches will provide a search for policies (simulate to produce effects) then a search for effects (re-simulate).
- **Constraint Satisfaction** search approaches will allow search within plan constraints and restraints in terms of effects, resources and categories of policies.

7. *One last challenge*—It is essential to note that the synthetic worlds we have described in this chapter are *deeply uncertain* and *inherently unsolvable* for optimum solutions. We do not want the reader to believe that solutions in the preceding six areas will lead to deterministic solutions to intrinsically complex real-world systems that are characterized

15 For a description of representative policy analysis methods, see, Bankes, Steven, Exploratory Modeling for Policy Analysis, *Operations Research*, Vol. 41, No. 3, May–June 1993, pp. 435–449; for a description of more tactical applications, see Waltz, Ed, "Means and Ways: Practical Approaches to Impact Adversary Decision-Making Processes" in Kott, Alexander (ed.) *Information Warfare and Organizational Decision-Making*, Boston: Artech, 2007.

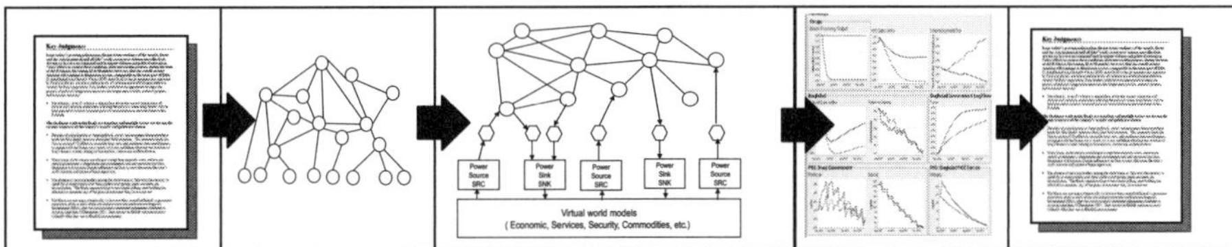

Narrative	Conceptual Model	Computational Model	Quantitative Results	Narration
Narrative description of the situation, actors and relationships. Explanations of drivers and causes	Construct conceptual maps or models of power actors and types of linkages— the social structure (political, social, economic, etc.)	Translate conceptual models of the abstract power structure and the non-abstract context to computational simulation models; estimate quantitative values and identify uncertainties. apply strategies and explore	Analyze results to explore the dynamics of the power struggle and discover causal interactions, sensitivities, and drivers.	Translate to narrative descriptions of struggle dynamics, drivers and relation-ships; outcomes of alternative strategies. Summarize key judgments.

Figure 9.3 Computational search across Synthetic World behavior spaces

by paradoxes, instability, uncomputability, connectivity and emergence.[16] Solving such challenges—deriving policies to guide policy in such complex situations—(described as "wicked problems" or "messes")[17] are distinguished from the difficult but tractable *problems* of science and engineering where causality is well-understood, even if only in a statistical sense, or more constrained and well-structured *puzzles*, which are known to have specific solutions. The analytic methodology of our synthetic worlds is to abstract an inherently wicked situation into a well-structured probabilistic problem—and then to explore the dynamics of that limited and representative system, always remembering the assumptions developed, constraints imposed, and factors left behind. Over a decade ago, Michael Pidd offered wise warnings to those who tackle messy problems:

> "One of the greatest mistakes that can be made when dealing with a mess is to carve off part of the mess, treat it as a problem and then solve it as a puzzle—ignoring its links with other aspects of the mess."[18]

Perhaps the greatest challenge will not be the preceding six technology challenges, but the methodological challenge of teaching users to apply these synthetic worlds as aid

16 John Casti describes the study of complex systems as the "Science of Surprise" and identifies the six mechanisms of complex systems that give rise to human surprise. See Casti, John, *Complexification: Explaining a Paradoxical World Through the Science of Surprise*, NY: Harper, 1994, p. 263, and Casti, John L., *Would-Be Worlds: How Simulation is Changing the Frontiers of Science*, NY: John Wiley and Son, 1997.

17 Problems that are inherently driven by complex behavior are characterized as "wicked", by Rittel, Horst, and Webber, Melvin; "Dilemmas in a General Theory of Planning," pp. 155–169, *Policy Sciences*, Vol. 4, Elsevier Scientific Publishing Company, Inc., Amsterdam, 1973, and "messy" by Pidd, Michael, *Tools for Thinking*, Wiley: London, 1996.

18 Pidd, Michael, *Tools for Thinking*, Wiley: London, 1996, p. 40.

to deep thinking—and warning them never apply them as enablers for shallow thinking. Here, technology can help, too, by providing visual indicators of the uncertainty in synthetic world factors, and in the validity (and limitations) of behaviors produced in the synthetic environment, while cueing the user to factors in the real world that are not represented in the synthetic one.

Research and Development Investments

The synthetic worlds in this chapter require research and development in each of the seven areas described in the previous section. The core of these efforts can be summarized in three areas, in which we enumerate key areas that require significant development to achieve our vision:

- *Computational physical and social sciences*—The underlying theories for human (social) behavior and interaction with the physical world (often called socio-technical systems) must be developed more fully, as well as the component theories and component models of social science, economics and the physical systems of modern life. While a diversity of theories of behavior in each of these area exist, there must be a meta-theory to guide the integration (or federation) of these theories, instantiated in models, into a coherent synthetic world.
- *Mathematics and computer science*—Mathematical contributions in the areas of graph theory applied to net analysis, dynamical systems, stochastic processes, uncertainty analysis, and the characterization of computational complexity and emergent phenomena will continue to provide formal representations to express real-world behaviors. Maturing technologies in content extraction, pattern and causal induction from empirical data, for automated model instantiation, and model federation-integration are required to implement synthetic worlds of the scale described in the vision. New visual methods of presentation are also required to represent complex (high dimensional, emergent dynamic) situations, and descriptions of causality to explain behavior.
- *Synthetic science*—The emerging discipline of synthetic representation of the real world from massive empirical data sets, analysis of the behaviors of these synthetic worlds and the discovery of meaning by exploration is perhaps worthy of a new scientific category of its own. The fundamental methods of synthetic world (hypothesis) composition, exploration and comparison with the real world (hypothesis testing) is nothing more than the scientific method applied at perhaps the grandest scale that science has ever attempted.

A recent National Research Council study on the modeling and simulation of human behavior echoes many of these recommendations, and has detailed similar categories of recommended research.[19]

[19] Greg L. Zacharias, Jean MacMillan, and Susan B. Van Hemel, (eds.), *Behavior Modeling and Simulation: From Individuals to Societies*, Committee on Organizational Modeling, National Research Council, Washington DC: National Academies Press, 2008; also see the related work,

Summary

Tom Pendleton and Gail McCreary are now in kindergarten, preparing for the crises they will face in 20 years. They will grow up to learn the distinction between tacit mental models, explicit conceptual models and computational models; they will feel comfortable describing complex situations in qualitative words as well as in quantitative models of causality, understandable by computers. They will be able to distinguish the deep uncertainty in the real world and the clean structure of the synthetic worlds they explore. They will learn to smoothly translate their own tacit knowledge or the tacit knowledge of other subject matter experts into explicit models suitable to be explored in synthetic worlds. Their generation will be the first to be truly at home in two worlds, the real and the synthetic.[20]

Even now, this author is participating in encouraging interagency experiments to apply complex synthetic world simulations to the challenge of representing complex real-world situations in such worlds, exploring the effects of alternative policies on those worlds, and using the synthetic worlds to brief policymakers on the complex dynamics that their policies may stimulate.[21] Long before the time frame of our earlier 2028 scenario, these synthetic worlds will gain recognition for the scientific rigor they represent—and for the faithfulness of their simulation of real-life dynamics (the tangible physical world, as well as the intangible aspect of the world).

Future crisis managers will benefit from the Raven-keeping catastrophic crises in the synthetic world, containing their worst outcomes with shaping and deterrent policies to prevent them from occurring in the real world.

Defense Modeling, Simulation, and Analysis: Meeting the Challenge, Committee on Modeling and Simulation for Defense Transformation, National Research Council, 2006.

20 The current generation of youth that grow up in computer gaming environments may use synthetic worlds as their context learning and for the circulation, interpretation, and deployment of meaning, according to researchers cited in Salen, Katie, "Toward an Ecology of Gaming." *The Ecology of Games: Connecting Youth, Games, and Learning*. Edited by Katie Salen. The John D. and Catherine T. MacArthur Foundation Series on Digital Media and Learning. Cambridge, MA: The MIT Press, 2008.

21 Waltz, Ed, "Situation Analysis and Collaborative Planning for Complex Operations" in *Proc. 13th International Command and Control Research Symposium*, Office of Assistant Secretary of Defense, Bellevue WA, June 17–19, 2008.

Chapter 10
Synthetic Worlds for Intelligence Analysts

Jeffrey G. Morrison, Kenneth W. Kisiel, and John DeBello

Abstract

Intelligence analysts have an inherently difficult, complex job. It is a job that requires diverse skills and expertise, and must be done in the face of great uncertainty. Analysts are expected to deliver reports about what *may* be. Rarely is there definitive knowledge or even a "right" answer to the problems they are asked to solve. An analyst must swim through an ocean of data, marshalling the data that might be useful, screening the data to try and identify data of value, i.e., information, potentially relevant to a problem, formulating hypotheses as to what the data could mean, and ultimately packaging and sharing their conclusions for the assessment of their peers and ultimately the tactical, operational and strategic end users that ultimately make policy and act in the government's interest. Analysis is hard.

As important as finding the right data can be, also important (and even harder) is recognizing when and how data changes. The analytic process is inherently disruptive in that the simple act of choosing one course of questioning and exploration of the data, precludes exploring alternate courses of analysis. Analysts work among a large community of specialists where their peers and potential collaborators may or may not be known, and may have very different perspectives than their own. As a result, collaboration is hard, yet communication critical. Let's see how the right technology might make analysis and collaboration a bit easier.

In the Not Too Distant Future...

It wasn't the first time, Alan thought, and he doubted it would be the last. *How can such a small country cause so much trouble?* He hadn't intended to become the Agency's go-to guy on Widgistan, but an early assignment had somehow morphed into a career path… and now here he is, analyst and a de-facto expert, designated to deal with the latest mess. And if he doesn't act fast, it will dwarf all the previous ones.

Sitting at his desk, sorting the stack of papers, files, and assorted information he'd just been handed, he takes a final glance at the tasking order…

> Widgistan is apparently cyber-attacking the US financial sector, with potentially devastating implications for the global economy. Decisive action will be taken in 24 hours, regardless of consequences, unless intel provides an alternative and this hypothesis is wrong, things will become very ugly in Widgistan.

The Boss said "work the problem." Alan's confident he has the tools to do the job, but does he have the *time?* First things first… *I need to find out what we know and what we don't know.* The first step is to clear his digital desktop and then figure out what we *think* we know. Because he already knows a fair amount about Widgistan's political and economic situation, he can make some reasonable guesses as to possible motives. That says his first order of business should be to see what we know about their cyber initiatives of late.

He's all too aware he doesn't know much about cyber-attacks or financial markets, but that's what his Solution Worlds are for. He definitely knows Widgistan—a breakaway Republic with the usual gamut of problems endemic to any fledgling nation, only more so, because it has more border disputes than borders, plus a ruling class with only a rudimentary concept of democracy (but a clear appreciation of corruption.)

Clearing and organizing is a lot easier than it used to be, because he's working from a virtual desktop projected across the walls and surfaces of his desktop. All he has to do is invoke a new desktop that can be dedicated to the cyber attack problem. (Sure makes it a lot easier to comply with the agency's clean desk policy when he needs to leave!)

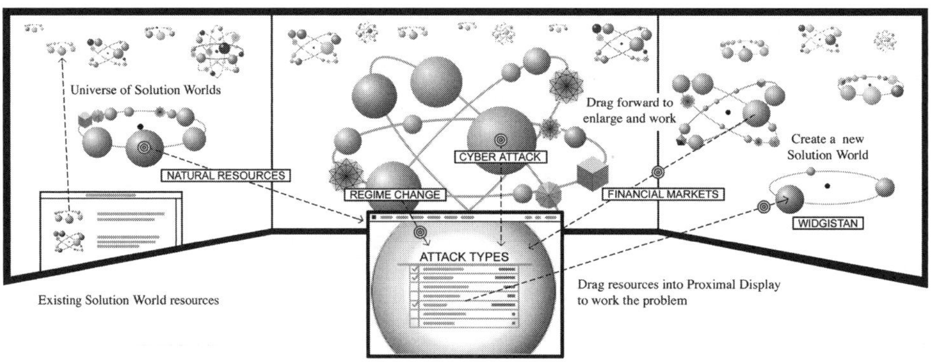

Figure 10.1 Navigating a synthetic world desktop of existing Solution Worlds

The next step is to start pulling information together about whatever he can dig up on recent cyber attacks… especially those relating to or coming from, Widgistan. Alan gets started with his searching and "shoe boxing"—dropping snippets of potentially relevant or just interesting factoids into his working library. He learned a long time ago that it pays to save factoids under as many different categories as possible because it facilitates the discovery of unexpected relationships later on. The process is a lot easier with the advent of computers and modern knowledge management tools that (at long last) allow him to bring together information from all his security domains.

As Alan builds his working library, a number of questions begin to emerge:

> Why are the Widgi's doing this? What do they expect to accomplish? What do cyber attacks look like? How do they typically unfold? Do different styles of cyber attacks lend themselves to different objectives? Who within Widgistan would have the skills

> to pull off these attacks? Where might they get those skills? What tools would they need and where would they get access to them?

Organized and focused, Alan accesses his working library. He works to extract those factoids that could be used as evidence in answering his questions, and then begins to build schemas for more elaborate hypotheses.

He also employs a relatively new tool where he can see how different expert analysts have created prototype solutions to different problem domains—particularly for the domain of cyber terrorism. These solutions take the form of synthetic worlds that were created to explain events in the physical or real world. Some of them reflect hypothetical scenarios for potential threats identified in the course of training exercises and war games. They are "Solution Worlds."

He finds that there are 12 Solution Worlds that relate to cyber threats of various kinds. With a little luck, one or two of these will be similar to the pattern of the current attacks, and will therefore give him some insights into who in Widgistan might be behind the current rash of cyber attacks… and what their motivation might be. *With a little more luck,* he thinks, *I might even discover the right questions that'll let us nail the people behind the attacks.*

Introduced two years ago, Solution Worlds are a place to bring together lots of data together with hypotheses to explain things that may not be self evident; to play against alternative explanations; and, ultimately, be shared across the entire Intelligence Community.

Solution Worlds, like every new technology, was greeted with skepticism by the Community. But it didn't take long before even the most iconoclastic analysts were believers…

Alan selects a "Cyber" Solution World from the library, and pulls down a list of problem types (history of cyber attacks, types, regions, impact)…

Clicking on "Attack Types," he watches the list cascade out to reveal the five most popular types of cyber attacks. He clicks on what looks like the three most promising types to work with, prioritizing a case study that catches his eye; a recent Denial of Service attack within Widgistan itself… one that follows the modus operandi of the mysterious attack on Estonia some 10 years ago, a seminal event in the history of cyber warfare…

Interesting.

He pulls down another Solution World focused on Financial Markets, a third labeled "Regime Change," a fourth titled "Natural Resources."

> Let's start with this; I'll use it as a template for my hypothesis.

Alan selects the first template Evidence Tree showing categories waiting to be populated (People, Motivation, Impact…). He wryly notes that these branches look awfully bare; hopefully, as he fills out one tree, the system's intelligent agents will recognize common information elements to fill the other trees quickly.

He must explore all the possibilities, because you never *really* know… in the analyst's world, you pick what looks like the best answer, and place your bet.

He wants to see where these cyber-attacks are starting, and where they terminate… so one of his Solution Worlds is a visual representation of a globe with patterns of attacks spread over it; others include an org chart, and a hierarchical representation. To focus on the critical cyber patterns, Alan examines a 90 degrees vertical access—*are the attacks for money, power, or…?* Alan also goes up the scale, to make the patterns more complex—*are these attacks part of something bigger?*

One of the synthetic worlds at his disposal is a special visual representation that shows each of his prospective Solution Worlds as galaxies in a Decision Space world. A vertical view shows how they interface… he can connect them within a larger pattern, and/or increase/decrease their size to signify importance in any given view.

On a separate work screen, he examines a "cube" matrix: one part indicates different kinds of attacks—(financial, government coup, etc) another one focuses on the possible attacker by category (hackers, government, criminals, etc.).

His Solution Worlds are optimized around the "real world," essentially giving him a "4D" picture of the problem and its many permutations over time as he explores the relationships of data to reach a better understanding, faster.

The unfolding attacks have an asynchronous nature… just *how* does a typical attack unfold? He observes patterns of activities at major computer centers… then drills down to patterns of local users working from that node… then propagates out to minor nodes.

The attacks can happen instantly and anywhere, much faster than he can assimilate on his own—but he has another tool at his disposal. Because each of his Solution Worlds allow for systematic distortions of one or more dimensions, what he chooses to see can be changed instantly. With the press of a button, an analyst has the ability to *manipulate* time, to control it, even discard it entirely in favor of event sequencing.

It provides a new kind of "N-dimensional pivoting process" to help solve complex, multidimensional, analytic problems. Like this one.

Alan needs to *compress* time to observe patterns and activities happening across the globe. But he must also *expand* time to effectively analyze cyber-attacks that occur in milliseconds. Using "Time Machine", he can create "temporal distortions" that compress any dimension that defines a world (time and space). So, instead of "real world" chronological time, he can generate an episodic timeline based on patterns of activity. Temporal distortions allows him to understand the *sequence* of events, because he doesn't care about time scale—*if we can insert ourselves here, we can stop this cascading event from happening…*

Alan also employs "temporal expansion" to essentially toggle between chronological time and episodic time, basically leaping from one time representation to another. He can slow down and fix the speed, consequences, and footprint of each attack. By taking out the chronological time dimension and looking *only* at the ordinal sequence of events—he sees attack patterns come into critical focus. Attacks against the financial infrastructure in the United States look a lot like the pattern of attacks against political institutions in Widgistan.

Could these attacks be by the same people? If so, why would they be attacking infrastructure *in Widgistan*??

An alternative hypothesis begins to form…

> Maybe there's another story here—I'm seeing attack patterns against Widgistan that look a lot like the attacks on us… why would they attack themselves…?

He tells Time Machine, "Only show me things that have changed over this timeframe… sort it based on day of the attack; the frequency; most common country of origin and by type…"

Alan synchronizes his Solution Worlds, allowing him to "play" them together, moving forward and backward in synchronization. He says "look at frequency of attacks…"

Then, "There's been a lot of activity of this type—start from these locations…" Through pattern synchronization, Alan is seeing confirmation that these attacks appear to work the same way—and therefore support his alternative story. He's also gaining critical insight into who might be behind this whole thing and what they may be trying to get out of all this… by virtue of his shoe-boxing exercise, a possible perpetrator emerges…

He's able to link a familiar face to the proceedings—Bahtiyer Ospanov, reputed to be an Eastern European crime boss in the pay, or under the protection, of Widgistan. Alan puts Ospanov in one of the slots for "potential players" in the Decision Tree.

To get a better picture of potential players, Alan employs a pivoting process that uses a visual representation to assess and ascertain promising relationships. On a work screen, he turns the "cube" around, highlighting connections, quickly pivoting between potential relationships, locations, interactions. He creates an organizational chart to highlight and track the network of connections…

> If this were an attack to make money for a few people vice a political agenda, who else might be involved, and how do they know each other? What kinds of people would be needed, and what skills would they need to have? How might such people come to know each other in the first place?

The next thrust at the problem is to move from forensic analyses to predictive analyses.

> What might they do next? If they were staging these attacks to make money, what would be their next move?

As he delves deeper into the problem and gains greater understanding, Alan creates 3 different hypotheses:

1. Widgistan is behind the cyber-attacks.
2. Widgistan is using a surrogate to launch the attacks.
3. The Widgistan government is innocent of these attacks, as they've claimed—though the perpetrators may be in Widgistan, and/or using Widgistani infrastructure, to mask themselves. This would explain why Widgistan has experienced similar attacks some time ago.

Alan picks Hypothesis #1 (as per his original guidance) and focuses in… he explores a branch, but he can't seem to make it fit the facts—the hypothesis just dies because it doesn't fit well.

The more likely that a path looks good, the more detail he'll get into; and the more he thinks about variance…

How to marry different types of data from different sources to the different hypotheses? Alan borrows a "story structure" from one Solution World to use in another… pruning, grafting, and assigning factoids to populate a new Evidence Tree. The information is color coded, based on where (and how well) the data fits. He quickly gets a sense of what data fits, what doesn't and perhaps most important—what is missing. Alan knows he'll never get a perfect tree, but if it looks good enough he'll be willing to place his bet on how things will unfold, and invest his time on the most promising hypothesis.

And he'll need to make that bet soon…. Three hours to deadline.

In his library, he finds a Solution World that describes how to thwart an apparently similar style of attack. He contacts its author, who's more than happy to describe how that previous attack was foiled. Much to remember….

Throughout the process, at any point in time, Alan is able to "visit his previous self" (well, really, his previous thinking!) by using MindSnaps. A MindSnap is a "mental bookmark" for his own thinking—it allows him to readily return to decision points and then pursue alternative courses of analyses.

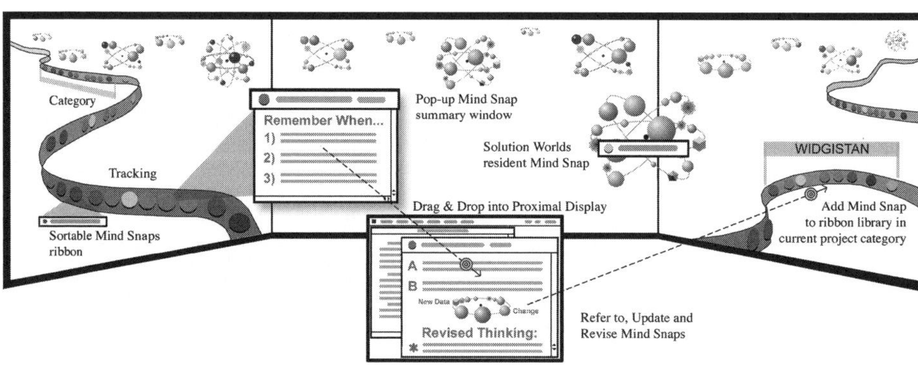

Figure 10.2 A MindSnap Synthetic World serves as a roadmap to previous thinking

The MindSnap system is one of the most advanced features of his analytic workstation. This set of tools is able to make inferences about his analytic process based on a basic understanding of the context of information he's working on, and *patterns* of activity. As a result, he can readily go back to *"that time when…"* as needed—allowing him to pick up his thinking from different points in the analytic process, and explore different possibilities—effectively allowing him to flesh out different paths of reasoning over the course of his analysis.

To find a MindSnap, Alan "changes the channel" to another of the synthetic worlds at his disposal—a "Decision Space" world.

The Decision Space world allows him see a history of information he's worked on, data he has touched, and effectively is a nodal map of his decision making process for the current problem. It helps him readily return to key points where he changed his decision trajectories.

When he finds the MindSnap that is most useful, he pastes the information captured within it into his current work space. One of the most helpful tools is the summary automatically generated when the MindSnap was originally created because it tells him what he was doing (and to some degree thinking about) when he was last "here". It effectively provides context about his thought process which allows him to re-load his thinking from that same point in time when a MindSnap was created.

Given how many possibilities he is dealing with in this situation, MindSnaps are invaluable—they allow him to go back and explore other decision paths as new data comes in.

In fact, he has come to rely on one of the handiest features of the MindSnap tool set; whenever he re-enters a Solution World, the MindSnap tool has enough understanding of what he was doing when he was last there that it can automatically build "workflow-defined agents" that show him any new data, as well as any changes in the underlying data he had previously used in that Solution World. Indeed, in every Solution World he's generated, Alan is able to return to the decision nodes stored for the MindSnaps and readily resume his thinking where it left off.

A Solution World Manager pares down the number of MindSnaps as he gets further away from a particular Solution World, helping him focus his attention on the pathway he deems most relevant. As he finds and mines relevant information from his array of Solution Worlds, a network of possibilities begin to take shape…

An instant message pops up on Alan's workstation.

"I see you've been using a lot of data from my financial world model," says Barbara Gordon, referencing a Solution World he's pulled from the library. "I've been tracking a lot of unusual activity in the last couple of days that you might find interesting. Do you have a few minutes to compare notes?"

Via video interface, the two analysts collaborate. Barbara's able to provide some missing pieces, and together they develop solid supporting analysis that extends the personal relationships between suspects and enhances motive possibilities around an illicit money making scheme.

While pursuing data on an unrelated task assessing the independence of Widgistan's educational system from the edicts of the central government, Barbara learned that Widgistan's Cyber Institute is actually sharing a great deal of information with the Widgistani authorities… suggesting that the Widgistan government may be *pursuing* Bahtiyer Ospanov—*not* collaborating w/him….

Thus dealing a significant blow to the original hypothesis.

Alan drops this new relationship data into all active Solution Worlds. He does so by simply "touching" a world—the avatar says "chart the changes," and instantly displays new material and information in context. In this manner, Alan's creating what psychologists would call an "affordance," making new data and meta-data available to all the worlds simultaneously.

As a result of what he's doing, his work is brought to the attention of other analysts (like Barbara) who are working with other worlds sharing some or all of his underlying data. Emergent groups form dynamically, based on common interests and agendas. If Alan had time to think about it, he'd likely agree that this kind of dynamic collaboration is pretty much the only way the community would ever have to get independent minds to work together. But Alan is thinking about other things.

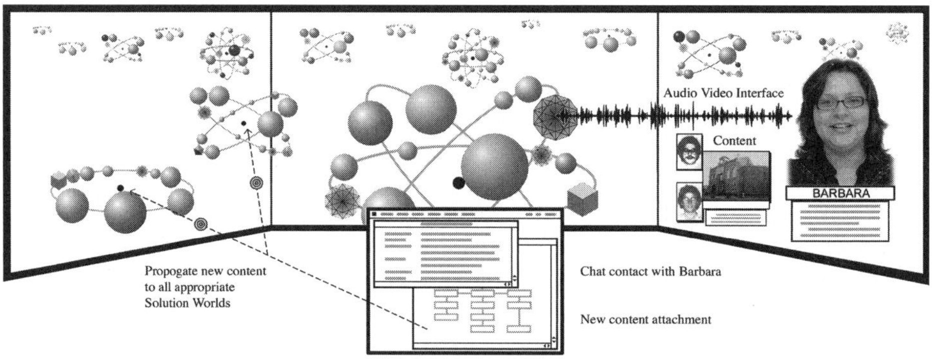

Figure 10.3 Synthetic Worlds provide shared context for collaboration

Through the interrelationship of his Solution Worlds, he's figured out that Ospanov and Alexei Abassov, a second person of interest, share a common mentor: "Professor Petrosyan" at the Institute… so it's reasonable to assume there is the possibility of a deeper connection between them. There is no literal proof of that connection—but there *is* an organizational overlap. It's reasonable that they would have attended the same alumni and professional meetings; would have worked in the same building; shared some, or many, of the same colleagues. One of the pivoting points Alan created was for people who had been trained at this Institute—and now it's paid off. By removing literal (or chronological) "time" from the equation, and replacing it with episodic time it's reasonable for him to surmise that there are many possibilities for a plausible relationship between these two actors. A common Professor, yes… but a common motivation?

Alan discovers that the Professor has recently been incarcerated as a political prisoner, purportedly as a member of an ultra-nationalist group. Thus, Alan has discovered a related series of facts. There is a personal relationship between the trio; they have a reason to seek revenge on Widgistan; and also had (and, presumably, would still have) access to government computer systems.

Alan has exposed the likely perpetrators through a social dimension that is not directly linked to the cyber attacks. With the first and second hypotheses looking highly unlikely, he focuses on developing Hypothesis #3: a network of rogue hackers are acting on their own, making it look like the government of Widgistan is behind the attacks.

A quick alert to The Boss—"you should seriously consider this…", and points him to his synthetic world analysis as a work in progress.

As he further develops Hypothesis #3, exploring and populating the categories, agents highlight what is consistent (and not). Alan's "structured argument diagram" is becoming flushed out—this evidence tree has leaves, and is growing rapidly. Means, motive, opportunity…

Alan confirms one of his emergent hypotheses: that Widgistan has been actually *under* attack, not *directing* the attack… thus providing the "DNA evidence" that confirms Widgistan's claims of innocence. The established fact that Widgistan has been subject to similar attacks effectively rejects the original hypothesis that Widgistan was behind the attacks.

Alan's hypothesis (along with the support materials and links to his synthetic world) is pushed to the proper agencies and people. Of course, not everyone is happy about his take on the situation. His Decision Space supports him in answering the hard questions from his superiors, facilitating instant access to appropriate data tied to his thinking (and it provides annotated sources and back-up).

As he wraps up, Alan is interrupted by a priority call. It's an analyst with a problem: "I understand you're the expert on the manipulation of networks for illicit gain… I have a time-critical problem you might be able to help with." It seems there's a strong possibility that an oil and gas price-fixing scheme with global repercussions is being run out of a renegade group within OPEC…

It's nice to be popular. Alan goes back to work.

Technology Assessment

Synthetic world technologies could represent a significant breakthrough for transforming the current information workspace into an enabler for the analytic process—fostering creativity and effective analytic reasoning. Below, we describe four technologies that provide a part of the foundation for this vision.

Synthetic Worlds

Immersive 3D environments represent the next evolutionary step in the way people interact with computers and over the past few decades, games and social networking sites have pioneered the majority of the advances in the technology (CNN 2005). However, until recently these environments simply were not robust enough for performing unstructured creative work. This situation is rapidly changing as a result of the convergence of three independent thrusts:[1] 1) display size; 2) immersive 3D environments; and 3) a comprehensive concept of operation (CONOP).

1 We recognize that the increase of computer speed also plays a very significant part in this but will not be addressed here.

Display size Instead of a flat world represented on a single screen driven by a windows-based operating system, the analyst of tomorrow will seamlessly move between these windows-based views (hosting legacy applications) and an immersive 3D world. Over the past decade, significant work has been done to determine the useful extent of increasing the viewing size for displaying information. These studies have shown that the optimal number of monitors for information analysis is four in a 2x2 configuration (Ball 2005). Other configurations are optimal (e.g., 2x3, 2x5, or even 5x10) depending on the task being performed (Ball 2005).

One configuration that might prove useful is using different monitors for different viewing purposes. For example, suppose that we keep one or two monitors in front of the user for working with legacy application much like they have today. We'll call these "proximal" displays. The new synthetic world view would then be resident on a larger viewing area behind the proximal displays—what we will call "distal" displays. It should be obvious that such a configuration can easily be constructed using current technology. However, there is technology emerging from research labs and commercial companies that will greatly facilitate implementation of the distal displays.[2]

The Organic light-emitting diode (OLED) represents an example of a pliable display material that can be shaped or trimmed to fit within the wall of a standard office cubical. Alternatively, extreme micro miniature projection devices (e.g., see Light Blue Optics) will allow a distal display area to be created on any surface.

Immersive environments Immersive environments have been around for a while but have primarily been used for gaming and other pleasurable pursuits. For the hobbyist, languages (e.g., VRML, X3D Earth, etc.) and libraries (e.g., OpenSim, RealWorld, etc.) have been created for ground-up development of immersive worlds. There are also a number of off-the-shelf applications that provide an immersive 3D experience (e.g., Croquet, Qwaq, Olive among others). Custom applications can also be created for training and other serious gaming exercises. Finally, immersive environments are available from the Internet (e.g., HiPiHi, Whyville, Yohoho! Puzzle Pirates, etc.).

When considering using an immersive environment for information analysis, we must evaluate the candidate environment against a number of characteristics:

- Mirror World to Abstract World—Analysts occasionally need to explore a simulated representation of the real-world. This representation is called a Mirror World. More typically, however, the analyst is working a problem at some level of abstraction or Abstract World. The combination of these two worlds and the ability to seamlessly move between them is our concept of a "Synthetic World."
- Persistence—The analytic world is constantly moving forward as new information is collected and made available regardless of the presence of our analyst. When the analyst does re-enter the environment after a period of absence, the changed data must be made apparent.
- Dynamic creation of objects—The world of the analyst is a highly dynamic environment where ideas (i.e., hypotheses) are repeatedly considered and

2 We have purposely not included the use of Caves or Head Mounted displays since we do not believe that they represent technology that an analyst would use on a sustained basis.

discarded, teams are formed and disbanded, and data is reviewed and put aside. The 3D environment needs to be able to dynamically create objects, collaboration rooms, cityscapes, and possibly entire worlds to facilitate the analytic process.
- Collaboration—Today, analysts are no longer the lone wolf we've seen in the past. The complexities of the problems are too great for a single person to completely comprehend. Therefore, future environment must allow for easy creation of teams, and the sharing of information and results.
- Storytelling—As mentioned above, the point of analysis is to make sense of the data being considered and the way that this sense-making is conveyed is through telling a story. The rich base of multi-media data available in an immersive 3D world must be carried into the final explanation.

Though we have concentrated on the use of large display areas for projecting 3D environments, we see a future where these environments are available on hand-held computers including cell phones or overlaid on the real-world in the form of augmented reality. Only time will time.

CONOP There are very distinct differences in the way an analyst uses a computer for "real" work, versus games or social interaction in 3D environments. As work begins to merge into the 3D environments, we will see a blending of the current 2D interactions (e.g., mouse, menus, dialog windows, etc.) with the 3D interactions found in games (e.g., sound including voice, gestures, body movements, etc.). However, this will still be insufficient to span the gap between the use of legacy applications interacting through traditional display devices and multi-dimensional immersive environments containing a range of real to abstracted realities.

MindSnaps/Decision Space

Analysts, by the nature of their task, are constantly forced to make decisions about the data that they are exploring. These decisions sometimes are wrong and require the analyst to return to that decision point at some time in the future in order to explore a different decision path. Analysts are also constantly dealing with interruptions and must spend precious time reconstructing their thoughts when they do get back on task.

Instead of forcing the analyst to simply remember each of 100's of decisions they make on a daily basis or resurrect a thought process following an interruption, the analytical environment of the future will keep a constant watch on the activities of the analyst. When the analyst makes a decision regarding a piece of data or changes the direction of their tasks, the environment will capture a complete representation of the analyst's environment.[3] MindSnaps expose the change in analysts' thinking.

MindSnaps capture the analytic process (such as lines of inquiry and narratives) and allow analysts (internal) or colleagues (external) to quickly return to earlier work, regaining peak awareness and knowledge. As analysts work through their daily tasks

---

3 This environmental **snap**shot represents the current state of **mind** of the analyst hence the name "MindSnap."

using their preferred tools, analytic process tools are tracking analyst progress in order to detect key analytic junctures which are automatically captured as MindSnaps. When a new path of analysis is taken (or not taken) or a key decision made, the MindSnap services will capture the analyst's cognitive state by saving all relevant task and context information at the time of that decision.

So what really is a MindSnap? In the course of their work, analysts produce a rich set of intermediate products. However, only a small fraction of the material in these intermediate products ever reaches the finished intelligence. After analysis is over these intermediate products are generally not shared and may even be discarded. A MindSnap, therefore, is the combination of these intermediate products and the process state at the time of capture.

If a MindSnap can be viewed as a mental bookmark of an analysts' decision-making then a collection of MindSnaps represent an analyst's reasoning process over time. Whereas a single MindSnap can be used to reset an analyst's work environment to restore context; the collection of MindSnaps, which we will call a Decision Space, will allow the analyst to review their entire thought process. Through synthetic world visualizations, the analyst can experience, manipulate, control and share their Decision Space. The Decision Space can expose how MindSnaps are connected and organized into multiple lines of inquiry, capturing the flow and progress of analytic thinking.

In sum, MindSnaps and Decision Space allow analysts to revisit, search, and explore their own decision-making process as well as data and applications relevant to that process at any given time. Analysts are able to: 1) Document, understand and present their reasoning process to others by highlighting and sharing their significant decision points and rationale; 2) Incorporate workflow abstractions and mental bookmarks as an integral part of the analytic process; 3) Quickly reset their thought process to an earlier point in time and continue the reasoning process along a new path of inquiry; and 4) Model decision trajectories that can be detectable and repeatable. A generalization of a Decision Space can be used as a Solutions World.

Solution Worlds

Solution Worlds are based on the premise that similar problems have similar solutions. Studies on human subjects (Schank 1982, Ross 1989) have shown that people typically do not solve a problem from scratch. They begin with a plan that was used in the past and then make adjustments to accommodate the new situation. Reusing previous successful solutions in solving new problems falls within the field of Case-Based problem solving also known as Case-Based Reasoning (CBR).

CBR, instead of relying solely on general knowledge of a problem domain, or making associations along generalized relationships between problem descriptors and conclusions, occurs when experts utilize the specific knowledge of previously experienced, concrete problem episodes (cases). A new problem is solved by finding a similar past case, and reusing it (possibly with modifications) in the new problem situation.

Case-Based problem solving can generally be viewed as a three step process (Rousu 1997):

- Retrieval: The system searches the case memory for cases representing successful solutions for problems that are sufficiently similar to the current problem at hand. Typically, several candidates are found so some ranking criteria is used to select one or more of them to be used in constructing a solution.
- Adaptation and Evaluation: The found cases are then modified to take into account the differences between them and the current problem to get a working solution. The working solution is determined through an evaluation process that checks whether the adapted solution will be suitable to solving the current case.
- Execution and Storage: Following the successful application of the case, the system records the case to be used in a similar situation in the future; meaning that it is appropriately tagged and indexed for quick retrieval.

Solution Worlds will represent a revolutionary step in the application of Case-Based problem solving. Instead of a case representing a single event episode, a Solution World represents an initial hypothesis for explaining data within an encapsulated synthetic world environment. These environments provide a place to fuse multi-model data; generate and consider alternative hypotheses to explain things that may not be self evident; and ultimately be shared with the user community.

Solution Worlds can be in one of three states. In the first state, the Solution World is private and still being evaluated as part of an active investigation. At this stage, it may or may not graduate to the second mode. A Solutions World enters the second state when it is successfully used to solve a targeted problem, and become part of the record. Even at that, it will still be considered a private Solutions World accessible only by the original user. Once a user is confident that the Solution World represents a new valid problem/explanation pair, it can be nominated for insertion into the public Solution World library, state three. This last state has the potential to capture all the expertise within an organization for reuse by current or future users.

Unlike traditional CBR systems that automatically retrieves candidate cases through a variety of matching schemes (Aamodt 1994); Solution Worlds will be selectable from a library organized into user definable topic areas. With this approach, the user is able to select the most relevant cases for the current problem. Once selected, the system might automatically make additional recommendations.

Solution Worlds offer the user the ability to simultaneously consider multiple explanations; which is very likely since both the incoming data and the set of Solution Worlds are incomplete. Additionally, the use of meta-knowledge will allow data to be readily brought into and used across alternative Solution Worlds. A final use of Solution Worlds would allow the user to create hypotheses and inject them into a world to determine if they were factual; in essence creating a dynamic 3D "What If" sandbox.

Time Machine

Time Machine is fundamentally about the exploration of change in multi-dimensional data, and synthetic worlds will be a place to visually explore this change by manipulating time. Today, analysts use ad-hoc notes, software shortcuts, and hand generated tags to mark topics of interest and convert this data into accessible information. They organize data into "shoebox" categories and use tools like Google "Alerts" and RSS feeds to monitor for data changes and keep current with changing context.

Time lining tools (e.g., see Sentinel TimeLine) offer some rudimentary ability to visualize data in chronological order and some packages go so far as to provide a time slider so time-blocked data (e.g., beginning and ending of relationships) can be dynamically displayed. This hodgepodge of tools, however, also makes it difficult to share this type of data in a collaborative way.

Synthetic worlds open a number of new dimensions when exploring data. They are in fact models that have several relevant properties: they can be shared by multiple people and they evolve over time. As a model, it is possible to systematically explore temporal aspects of change in the data and events that occur in the physical world. In a synthetic world based on a physical location in the real world, one can perform forensic analysis of an event by going back in time and studying the changes that were precursors to the event of interest. Implications of these events would be explored by applying predictive models that look forward in time to allow proactive analysis, and suggest indicators for future events.

One of the main challenges in working with temporal oriented data is that there are many different temporal representations. For example:

- Chronological/linear—Orients events in actual time.
- Episodic—Sequential (ordinal) time where events do not directly tie to chronological time (e.g., breakfast vs. 07:45). This is how people tend to think about time.
- Relative time—Assessing how events relate to one another in time; e.g. what things occurred at the "same" time.
- Semantically Derived Time—Translating time derived from language.

To convert between these different temporal representations, there will need to be a Temporal Reconciliation Service. This service will assist in managing synchronization across the different temporal representation and to determine what should be presented in the synthetic world for a given point in time. Pattern synchronization is another type of reconciliation that will determine if event patterns are the same even though the time scales are different.

Research Agenda

This section will describe the areas of science and the specific key technologies that must be developed in order to address the challenges.

Synthetic Worlds Synthetic World platform are multi-dimensional, coherent environments that allow N-Dimensional data to be represented, shared, and exploited. Multiple Synthetic worlds can also be created and optimized to support different analytic problems supported by a consistent Human-Computer Interface (HCI) CONOP. Several key issues that need to be addressed include: What are the key issues in developing an operational CONOP for how analysts would use Synthetic Worlds? What are the critical system properties that would ensure interoperability (i.e., between synthetic worlds and legacy software tools and across synthetic worlds)? What are the critical HCI issues to ensure coherent synthetic worlds are consistent in how they work? How do we architect for, detect, manage and represent change? How does the representation of the world change as an analyst manipulates the temporal focus of a world? What are the implications for what other users of the shared world would see? How do we manage the representation of factual data with theoretical (modeled) data? How do we allow an analyst to explore in a private, semi-public and shared modes within a synthetic world? Is there a role for avatars and when are they appropriate? What are the critical services and support infrastructure to allow coherent synthetic worlds? Where do we find changing data with which we can populate a world?

MindSnaps MindSnaps are the foundation for developing a Decision Space synthetic world that maps the overall decision-making processes of analysts as graphical decision nodes, and allows them to find, and cognitively re-load their workstation from different points in their own analytic process. Several key issues in developing the MindSnaps are: How will changes in workflow be detected and used to trigger a MindSnaps? What is the appropriate resolution for creating and searching for a MindSnaps? How will an abstraction of workflow be derived to meaningfully characterize a MindSnap? To what degree is analytic reasoning predictable, e.g., templates? What architecture and data-objects would enable the effective utilization of MindSnaps? What data and meta-knowledge belongs in a MindSnap so it can be used to create a useful restoration of workspace? How could data used in a MindSnap be automatically updated/have changes highlighted? How would autonomous automation work for finding related (new) data based on data currently stored as part of a MindSnap?

Solution Worlds The representation of Solution Worlds, the combination of a hypothesis and synthetic world environment, in case memory is primarily a problem of structure and content. Additionally, another challenge will be the dynamic nature of the organization of the case memory that is the user will periodically be changing the topics of interest within the domains. A few key research questions would include: What is the proper level of abstraction for the content of a case? Should cases be represented as separate knowledge units or split into subunits and distributed? What is the role of general domain knowledge outside of the actual Solution Worlds cases?

The success of the Solution Worlds will depend on how the case memory is organized and indexed. Ultimately, automatic identification of Solution World cases will be incorporated requiring some similarity matching between Solution World cases of varying abstraction. A few key research questions would include: How will a Solution World case be generalized (i.e., abstracted) and which version will be stored? What similarity metric provides the most efficient retrieval results while minimizing the return of unsuccessful cases? Would there be any benefit in incorporating domain specific taxonomies or ontologies?

It will seldom be the case that a retrieved Solution World case will exactly match the current problem. This means that the retrieved world will require modification if it is to be used to explain the current data. A few key research questions would include: With the complexity of the Solution World representation, what would be an efficient process for identifying the mismatches (i.e., errors) in the case? What general knowledge is required to prune and graft portions of world cases together?

A problem solver that does not learn, cannot adapt. Saving successful (modified) Solution World cases provides a mechanism for the case memory to expand. A few key research questions would include: Should unsuccessful cases (i.e., cases that did not lead to a successful goal) be saved? What level of detail from the Solution World cases that were used is saved? Are these saved cases automatically made public or kept private until further validation?

Time Machine The use of synthetic worlds as Time Machines is conceptually about the explorations of data, and as such, may be (but need not be) tied to a physical location. A critical issue in creating a Time Machine capability will be the ability to detect and manage significant changes of the data which is used in a synthetic world. Topics that need to be addressed before the Time Machine becomes a reality are: Is there a theory of time that would be a useful basis around which to construct analytic tools such as a Time Machine? How do we reconcile different concepts of time? What is the CONOP for how analysts would explore change by manipulating time? How would the Time Machine be used to test a hypothesis of a future event by reducing the ambiguity of data connected to that event? How would new (changing) data be used to assess the likelihood of a hypothetical event? How much ambiguity (or time into the future) would be appropriate for supporting analysis in a synthetic world Time Machine? What do we need to do with synthetic world architectures to exploit time?

Summary

The workspace of tomorrow will connect the analyst not only to other analysts for collaborative sessions but also with their past and future selves. Analysts will be able to explore their own past thinking about the data as well as enabling the proactive exploration of how that data might change in the future. The use of multiple, coherent, synthetic worlds will allow large amounts of multi-dimensional information to be explored as models. Multiple synthetic worlds will be optimized for different analytic problems. Changes in data will be detected by automated agents working on behalf of the analyst. Legacy applications will be integrated into the workspace through proximal displays while exploration in parallel synthetic worlds will be available through distal displays. Finally, synthetic worlds will be developed to: 1) Support different kinds of analytic decision-making; 2) Designed to highlight the dynamic aspects of the data, and how it changes; and 3) capture the evolution of the analyst's decision-making process itself.

References

Aamodt, A., and Plaza, E. (1994). Case-Based Reasoning: Foundational Issues, Methodological Variation, and Systems Approaches. *AI Communications*. 7(1):39–59. Available at http://www2.iiia.csic.es/People/enric/AICom.html [accessed: 10 March 2009].

Ball, R., Varghese, M., Sabri, A., Cox, D.E., Fierer, C., Peterson, M., Carstensen, B., and North, C. (2005). Evaluating the Benefits of Tiled Displays for Navigating Maps. Virginia Tech. [Online]. Available at http://www.uwosh.edu/faculty_staff/ballr/WWW/Professional/phoenix.pdf [accessed on 2 February 2009].

CNN. 2005. Top 25: Technologies Breakthroughs [Online]. Available at http://www.cnn.com/2005/TECH/04/01/cnn25.top.technology/index.html [accessed 09 April 2009].

Ross, B.H. (1989). Some psychological results on case-based reasoning. Case-Based Reasoning Workshop, DARPA 1989. Pensacola Beach. Morgan Kaufmann. pp. 144–147.

Rousu, J. (1997). Case-based Planning. *Seminar on Knowledge Engineering,* Fall 1997. Available at xxx [accessed: 13 October 2008].

Schank, R. (1982). *Dynamic Memory: A Theory of Reminding and Learning in Computers and People*. Cambridge University Press.

Chapter 11
Augmented Reality Tools for Enhanced Forensics Simulations and Crime Scene Analysis

Robert Rice

Abstract

Forensics simulations and crime scene analysis using virtual environments can increase in value and efficacy through the use of augmented reality tools for highly accurate simulations that are immersive and used both at the scene and in a reconstruction off-site. Law enforcement and investigations officers will have the ability to mark and highlight evidence with virtual markers and metadata, as well as run real-time tests and analysis through the use of dynamic tools and immediate access to key databases and other information sources.

Story

The call had arrived at a little past 0230 in the morning and Kendra had drawn the short straw to venture out in the freezing rain that had been cascading from an inky black sky for the last several hours. She waited at the stoplight, listening to the soft hum of her electric car and the turn signal's metronome clicking away little segments of time. She was tempted to let her mind wander while staring at the glistening raindrops snaking their way down her windows and brightly lit by the stoplight. Kendra had always felt something mysterious about inclement weather in the middle of the night, especially when there were only few people on the roads heading to some unknown destination. The only thing that could make the atmosphere a little more surreal would be snow materializing out of eternity and blanketing the city in silence, with only the reflections of street lights free to echo through the night.

The light finally changed to green and Kendra turned her mind back to the task at hand and drove the rest of the way to the crime scene, preparing herself for her work.

Kendra arrived at the scene and shouldered her way through the overly eager press reporters that had already gathered like hungry vultures desperate for a meal. She ignored their barrage of questions and ducked under the police cordon, showing her badge to the officers attempting to control the growing crowd. This was the fourth murder in as many days and the public was beginning to demand answers. She made her way across the driveway and up the brick stairs leading to the front door of the house, dodging the growing pools of rainwater that would soak her feet if she wasn't careful.

She entered the house and waited while most of the other officers cleared out to give her some room. The medical examiner had already been on the scene and the bodies were taken away. Kendra could sync up her databases with the examiner's later, it was time for her to do her own work now. She set down her bag and reached up to her glasses, tapping a barely noticeable touch sensitive key at the corner of the frames. A softly glowing heads up display pulsed into existence in front of her, immediately sensing her location in the real world and on the meta-net.

"Initialize." she commanded. "Voice authentication: Alpha-Zulu-Romeo-Bravo-Zero-Niner-Seven."

A nondescript male voice spoke in her ear. "Authenticated, Lieutenant Kendra Jackson, Enhanced Sensory Perception, ESPer Team 5."

"Begin scanning, crime scene, domestic, murder." She began to look at every area of the room, making a few mental notes of things she would pay special attention to when she returned for her detail and evidence collection sweep. The voice spoke in her ear again. "Location confirmed. Date and time confirmed. Scanning in process. Comparing visual point cloud to public architectural records and builder plans. Synchronizing. Process complete."

"Display wireframe" she said.

"Wireframe active. No anomalies detected."

Faint blue lines appeared, following the course of the walls, the floor, the ceiling, the doorframes, and every other part of the house that she could see. It was like seeing a 3D blueprint of the house overlaid on the real thing. This served multiple purposes, but for now she needed it to act as a reference for the scale, positioning, and orientation of everything in the house, particularly any evidence she would come across. She remembered hearing stories of a SWAT team that had used augmented glasses and the wireframe to navigate through a pitch black office building where terrorists had cut the power and had set off multiple smoke bombs. They never knew what hit them. After that particular incident, Fire departments all over the country began requesting the same gear. Not being able to see where you were going in a smoke filled building was no longer a problem. You simply needed to follow the blue lines or the floating translucent red arrows that pointed towards the nearest exit. Life was so much easier with augmented reality and the glasses.

"Activate WATSON" she requested, almost without thinking. She had grown accustomed to working with the artificial life intelligent agent. Originally he was not much more than a tool that helped gather information and run intelligent semantic database searches, all wrapped up in a life sized human representation. Kendra had spent a lot of time and a fair amount of her own money to customize him to her liking and upgrade his program with a more realistic personality and some law enforcement grade functionality that was not available to the public.

"WATSON is now online." The voice stated. She wondered if she should change her settings and give it a personality or if she preferred it to be completely devoid of any emotion. Having WATSON around was more than enough she guessed.

Kendra turned her head slightly and regarded WATSON, who was now standing in the middle of the room wearing his usual Victorian garb and peering at his surroundings while muttering to himself. He was faintly translucent, which was required by law for any virtual person, human controlled avatar or AI-driven persona. There were some public safety reasons for this and people generally preferred to keep it that way, mostly for the same reasons that humanoid synthetic androids were restricted from being too lifelike.

"WATSON, access the domestic security system and copy the logs from the last 72 hours" she said to her virtual companion while she began to start walking around each of the rooms on the first floor, observing everything.

WATSON nodded and pulled a worn leather-bound journal from thin air and started to make notes in it. He stopped muttering to himself and looked quite intent on his recording task. When he was finished, he walked out of the room, waddling slightly (he was a tad overweight, and it affected his walk cycle) and caught up with her.

When Kendra completed her initial walkthrough, she returned to where she began and started collecting evidence. Every bullet and casing were recovered, lasers used to determine angle of the bullet holes in the wall, fingerprints lifted, bloodstains sampled, and so on. By the time she was done, a highly detailed 3D mirror of the entire house had been created on the servers back at the station. Every photograph she took and corresponding video clips of everything she saw were also stored, but each was tagged with appropriate time and location data. She had taken the time to attach some notes and observations to a few key items and places of interest in the house. Anyone looking at the 3D version of the crime scene would have ready access to all of the data and her notes.

As Kendra was packing up her gear and preparing to leave, she had a sudden hunch. "WATSON, display all augmented reality content and channels associated with this residence please."

"Ah, yes yes, good idea Ma'am. Complying." WATSON looked like he was staring off into the distance at something vaguely interesting, while a wide variety of virtual objects began popping into existence. Normally, this would only be visible to the residents and friends that have access to their channels. Some abstract art materialized on one wall, shifting patterns and undulating waves rippling across the largest piece, their smooth motion was mesmerizing. A few virtual pets popped into existence next and started scampering around playing at some learning game intended for young children. A wonderfully detailed plan for a new house slowly appeared on the dining room table complemented by a soft woman's voice reciting a sales pitch and mentioning a number of optional additions that could be purchased.

WATSON frowned and coughed politely. "I'm sorry, but there seems to be some additional content here that is restricted. It is not listed on the normal public and private channels. It may be an illegal hack. Shall I attempt to access?"

Kendra considered for a moment. Normally, law enforcement personnel have access to all AR content, public and private, within the domain of a crime scene, but there were some levels of protection and privilege that required a court order or security clearance to access. In cases like these, discretion was usually prudent and it was safe to obtain a warrant first. Then again, there was a strong possibility it was an illegal hack and this was a murder scene, not a regular crime scene. Kendra's curiosity and intuition got the better of her.

"Force access WATSON, on my authorization. All means necessary."

"Yes Ma'am. I shall do my best". WATSON's eyebrows furrowed and little beads of sweat began to form on his virtual brow. A few long minutes passed and Kendra started wondering if WATSON had locked up… he hadn't moved in a bit and even flickered a few times, which was extremely unusual. She was about to give up and restart his program when he lurched with a gasp and a pained look on his face.

"Ahem, that was extraordinarily difficult, but I seem to have succeeded. A spot of tea would be really nice methinks."

"Thank you WATSON, what is the location of the hidden content?"

"In the living room I believe. Shall we investigate?" queried WATSON.

"Of course; this should be interesting." Kendra grinned and headed towards the living room. She stopped short at the doorway and stared at the center of the room in disbelief. A massive floating black skull hovered there, blood-red fire silently blazing in its hollow eye sockets, and a nasty black ichor dripping out of its mouth on to the carpet. The pools of liquid that formed stretched out and oozed across the rug to form intricate letters spelling something out in a bizarre language she did not recognize.

"Oh, my, this cannot be good." WATSON said, stating the obvious.

"No kidding. Begin scanning the usual databases for gang signs, military unit insignia, secret societies, tattoos, and ancient symbology. I think we may have stumbled onto something that we weren't meant to discover" said Kendra. "Let's head back to the office and start putting the pieces together."

The next several days were a blur for Kendra. Most of her time was spent processing evidence, populating the database with all of the information and media, and focusing every remaining waking moment trying to research the origin and meaning of the skull. It didn't take too long to establish a timeline of the crime and how the murders occurred, but her research efforts resulted in a lot of dead-ends and few leads.

It was Thursday afternoon and Kendra headed over to the simulations room to tweaking her presentation before the staff briefing the next day. The higher-ups were demanding some progress and wanted to look at her work so far. She went to Room Three, which she had reserved earlier, and looked around. Room Three was entirely empty and slightly larger than a racquetball court. The walls and floor were painted a light grey color with thin black registration marks at every corner. She thought it was pretty depressing and wanted to get started.

She touched the corner of her glasses and went through the usual initialization and authentication process. "Load SIM four-zero-three, set location to living room." Kendra paused and waited while her command was processed. After a few second a photorealistic 3D mirror of the crime scene faded into existence. Every detail was reproduced exactly and to scale, all based on the visual data she had recorded during her initial walkthrough and subsequent evidence collection at the scene.

Kendra continued giving the main computer additional commands, and after half an hour or so, the victim's bodies were also visible. Faint red beams crossed the room, originating at each of the areas where the bullets were recovered, giving her a good idea where the killer or killers had stood and fired from. All of the fingerprints that were taken were also referenced, faintly glowing various shades of green. She touched a pair that was on the coffee table and a small window materialized above the prints with a zoomed in version and information about who the prints belonged to. In this case, the prints were marked as unknown and not in any of the usual fingerprint databases.

She moved on, making notations and observations to each area of evidence. Everything was checked and rechecked. Kendra reviewed all of the collected data and media, making sure everything was properly linked to the relevant objects. If there were any questions at the meeting, she literally wanted everything at her fingertips. All it would take was a brief touch on anything (or anyone) and all of the reports, photographs, video clips, and lab data would be instantly viewable to anyone in the room.

Once she was satisfied with everything, Kendra started tweaking the reconstruction of the crime based on the evidence they had so far. She started by tracking backwards from what the Police discovered when they responded to the crime, continually adjusting the position of each of the victims as she worked through the timeline. When she finished, she directed the system to fill in the blanks based on the forensic data already in the database.

After the processing was complete, she would be able to view a realistic recreation of the crime from any angle and perspective. The combination of the 3D objects, advanced physics modeling, and actual forensics data made these simulations incredibly lifelike. She had heard stories of the occasional jury member being shocked after witnessing these simulations in court, particularly if the crime was unusually brutal and violent. It felt like being an unseen ghost right in the middle of the crime as it occurred, and was much more compelling than the old way of relying on photographs, charts, and awkward animations on a projector screen. This put you THERE and left little doubt as to what happened. Kendra wondered how long it would be before the engineers would figure out how to implement smell and tactile feedback.

She ran through the simulation a few times and checked all of the datapoints once again to make sure she hadn't missed anything. It was good enough she supposed. Maybe she should take another hour or two and check in with some of her contacts that were helping her with the skull research and then call it a night. Her boss didn't take kindly to oversleeping or flubbing a presentation with the brass due to lack of sleep. Tomorrow should be interesting. She hoped the press didn't show up, that always made her nervous.

"Save all files, backup, and copy to private storage. End simulation." Kendra looked around at the empty room once more and left for her office.

Technical

Augmented Reality ("AR") is the blend between the real and the virtual. While there are varying definitions of what augmented reality is, depending on the scope and application, it is commonly defined as an environment that includes virtual and real-world elements.

Contemporary popular culture examples include the yellow "first down" line seen in televised broadcasts of football, the interactive advertisements in *Minority Report*, the heads-up display for the *Terminator*, the holographic doctor in *Star Trek: Voyager*, and virtual interfaces seen in dozens of science-fiction and anime movies. Green screens used by weather forecasters are another example of augmented reality in one of the broadest definitions.

Ronald Azuma defines an augmented reality system as one that combines the real and virtual, is interactive in real-time, and is registered in three dimensions (Azuma 1997). This is suitable for early AR systems, but this definition should be expanded to encompass more than just the superimposition of graphics on reality, such as accessing and interacting with any media or source of data that is directly related to the user's location and contextual to their activities. For example, the usage of a GPS navigator to obtain directions to nearby restaurants, as well as information about those restaurants would be considered as a basic mode and form of AR. Interacting with this data and experiencing the media and visualization through wearable displays would be an advanced mode and form.

Recent next-generation smart phones and mobile internet devices, combined with WiFi triangulation or GPS positioning, has catalyzed new and widespread interest for augmented reality, particularly in creating mobile content that is locative. Developers are designing applications that can determine the user's rough location and either display media associated with that position (a video clip advertisement for a nearby café), or overlay relevant data (a building's address or historical notes).

The majority of current work in the field relies on a video source, printed graphic markers ("fiducials"), and 3D objects. This approach is readily accessible with multiple software development kits that are free for non-commercial use and available for commercial use with some type of license fee. There are benefits to this approach, particularly accessibility, ease of use, rapid prototyping, and so forth, but marker-based systems are ultimately not practical for mass-market usage or mobile applications.

While Augmented Reality is viewed as transformative and disruptive technology, it cannot reach its full potential as long as it relies on static graphic fiducial markers, single-user applications, and is tethered to a PC or video camera/monitor setup. It must be mobile, wireless, massively multi-user, collaborative, persistent, and all types of content available.

To achieve this full potential, there are a number of technical problems and obstacles that must be solved. Implementation issues regarding interoperability, user identity, privacy, secure commerce, user interface, data visualization, naming and meta-tagging conventions, data standards and communication protocols, file formats, and so forth must be researched and studied. Failing to do so during the early stages risks the technology suffering from the same foundational problems and flaws that the Internet and the Web are handicapped with today.

To build the system featured in the story at the beginning of the chapter requires a different approach to augmented reality design in several areas, as well as advances in related fields. Instead of relying on a marker-based approach, some method of visual tracking and mapping must be used in combination with geospatially accurate 3D reference or synthetic environment to achieve exact positioning of virtual content (static and dynamic) and facilitation of multi-user interaction, collaboration, and shared media.

The implementation of a synthetic environment that is essentially a geospatially accurate virtual world that is a mirror of the real world opens up a variety of options and functionality that would otherwise be extremely difficult to create. For example, if virtual media is associated with specific GPS coordinates in the mirror world, and the system tracks the user's real-world location, it is much easier to quickly determine what the user should be seeing and have access to. Further, external databases and sources of data, such as weather information from NOAA, sensor data from an advanced home security system, video feeds from CCTV or a military UAV, perimeter security systems, or YouTube.com videos that are meta-tagged with location and contextual data, can all be linked to reference coordinates in a synthetic environment.

In the story, Kendra used an artificially intelligent agent that was voice recognition enabled and had the ability to execute data searches based on semantic queries that were in context with her current location and situation. Because the system had access to public records for the blueprint of the house, and the victims were already using commercial AR technology, her personal system was able to quickly determine where she was, use visual tracking to ascertain her exact position and orientation, download the virtual content associated with the location, and tap into a number of databases to request information.

The visual tracking and mapping capabilities of Kendra's unit were used to track her hand movements and gestures in addition to her local environment, which makes it possible to implement a user interface similar to sign language and also lets the user interact with virtual objects. Her lightweight transparent wearable displays look similar to regular glasses or sunglasses, but are capable of displaying media in her line of sight, thus replacing the need for laptops, handhelds, and bulky head mounted displays that occlude the wearer's vision. The combination of the visual tracking, gesture interface, and transparent displays make it possible to create virtual "holographic" keyboards and interfaces in front of the user.

As Kendra collected real-world evidence, she was able to "tag" the specific location of each piece, which created a point in the synthetic mirror world that could be associated with lab reports, video clips, photographs, forensic analysis, audio notes, keywords, and links to other similar crimes in the database or records at the Federal level. Because this is all stored online in the mirror world (no different from any virtual world or online game), it could easily be reproduced back at the office or even in a courtroom for a jury to experience from a first person perspective and at any angle or scale.

The overall system hardware components would include the wearable displays (eyeglasses form factor), a micro PC or mobile internet device (a future version of the iPhone, iPaq, or Treo for example) which would handle all of the local processing and graphic generation, GPS positioning, broadband WiFi, and servers. The servers maintain all of the telecommunications, data transfer, storage of virtual media and data, user information, accounts and security, etc. Other elements, such as artificially intelligent agent based programs or personalized life-sized avatars intended for entertainment, remote telepresence, or virtual pets, would be part of this system or based on secondary external servers. This architecture is very similar to that used for massively multiplayer online games.

Development and innovation in the future that is necessary to realize such a ubiquitous, mobile, wireless, and massively multiuser augmented reality networks will need to emphasize areas such as smaller and faster CPUs, hardware miniaturization, smaller and more powerful batteries (or wireless power), semantic search, faster wireless broadband, artificial intelligence, natural language processing (voice to text), GPS with higher accuracy, and so forth. Universities and larger corporations are already focusing on many of these areas, but for general application, not necessarily specific for use in augmented reality.

The entire system described in the story segment is expected to be available and pervasive within 12 to 15 years, but may be possible within 5 depending on developing industry trends, market interest, and technology breakthroughs.

It is important to understand that ubiquitous, wireless, and mobile augmented reality applications in the future will require tracking systems that do not rely on physical printed markers. Further, augmented reality is not solely about the overlay of virtual media and content on the physical world, it must include elements of context and locality, as well as multiple modes of interaction and interface.

Literary Review

It is interesting to note that science fiction has acted as a driving inspiration in the commercial and academic sectors, creating a popular end goal or vision that developers aspire to in the development of augmented reality. Examples include *Dream Park* by Larry Niven and Steven Barnes, *Rainbows End* by Vernor Vinge, *Spook Country* by William Gibson, *Halting State* by Charles Stross, *The Diamond Age* by Neal Stephenson, and *Donnerjack* by Roger Zelazny and Jane Lindskold.

Considering the usage and application of augmented reality in these books, researchers and developers are able to mentally deconstruct how things could work in the future and use this to establish models and frameworks to conceptually define the necessary technical elements required to accomplish them in the present. There are several key areas that become apparent as core requirements for building the augmented reality platform that Kendra works with in the first section of this chapter. Giving these a higher priority for the allocation of research and development funding and resources will accelerate the overall advancement of the technology and practical deployment in multiple sectors.

These areas can be categorized as technical and perceptual. Technical is directly related to hardware and software, specifically that which is necessary for telecommunications, mobility, data processing, massively multiuser networking and visual display. Perceptual is more along the vein of human-computer interface, data visualization, user cognition, graphical user interface, contextual iconography, and so forth.

Of these, the spatial model, visual tracking, interface, and visualization and cognition are areas where resources should be prioritized in the near term as the business and commercial sectors are already naturally advancing processing power, high speed wireless broadband, mobile device miniaturization and other areas such as contextual search and artificially intelligent agent-based applications.

Spatial Model and Visual Tracking

Newman, Wagner, Bauer, Macwilliams, Pintaric, Beyer, Pustka, Strasser, Schmalstieg, and Klinker (2004) suggest that an augmented reality experience within a ubiquitous computing environment requires a coherent and up-to-date spatial model of the world. Their proposed framework is based on the combination of different tracking technologies to aggregate their data and balance the trade-offs of the individual approaches.

Specifically, they propose "...a graph-based model of spatial relationships to build dynamically extendible networks of trackers suitable for the high-precision, low-latency requirements of Augmented Reality". This framework is designed to accommodate new trackers, filtering schemes, and optimization criteria.

Newman et al. (2004) make a distinction between three types of graph-based models: "an idealized view of the world from the point of view of an omniscient observer, directly measured relationships corrupted by noise, and finally a graph derived from inferred relationships". The idea that a combination of different tracking technologies be used seems to be the most practical and flexible. Regardless of how the spatial model is created, it is essential for the establishment of a common and shared augmented reality environment where 3D data and media are perceived by users in a consistent fashion that is appropriate and contextual to their surroundings.

While there are multiple methods of creating the spatial model, such as Lidar, RFID, and so forth, the ideal approach is to use some method of visual mapping and tracking. This has been difficult in the past, but recent advancements have made this a viable approach to pursue and develop further.

Klein and Murray (2007), following previous work in the adoption of simultaneous localization and mapping (SLAM) algorithms from robotic exploration and computer vision, proposed a new approach using parallel threads to split tracking and mapping into two separate tasks. The result is a visual tracking system that produces highly detailed map of 3D point features that allows for rapid frame-rate based tracking and is very accurate and robust. While this can meet some of the goals as stated by Newman et al. (2004), it is fast and only requires a single monocular video source and is not as complex to process.

The current implementation performs best in limited areas and small workspaces, and does not have functionality to deal with out-of-plane objects that should block and occlude virtual items or characters that run into or move behind them. The ability to access GPS data and other geospatial designations was outside of the scope of the research and the implementation does not consider simultaneous mapping from multiple sources (multiple users).

The Klein and Murray (2007) approach has a number of benefits for mobile and wireless augmented reality applications. Printed physical markers (or "fiducials") are not necessary, and mapping can be conducted in an unknown area that has not been previously explored. This works particularly well for indoor areas where alternatives that require LIDAR are cost prohibitive or simply not possible. For example, Gatzidis, Brujic-okretic, Liarokapis, and Baker (2008) discuss several methods for the generation and visualisation of 3D urban areas for use on mobile devices. The goal is to create geospatially accurate and photorealistic 3D urban maps for a user-centered mobile VR for navigation and other uses. Their preferred method uses GIS information combined with aerial photographs and has both automatic and semi-automatic modes to create the urban maps. While this approach is good for creating photorealistic 3D urban spaces outside, it cannot be used indoors where the majority of casual computing and most business oriented augmented reality applications occurs.

The combination of Klein and Murray (2007) for immediate tracking, detail mapping and orientation; Gatzidis et al. (2008) for exact positioning outdoors, and providing a point of reference for linking interior AR mapping to the correct geospatial coordinates; and the Newman et al. (2004) framework for the reconciliation and synchronization of multiple data sets from various sources, provides one possible hybrid method of building the infrastructure necessary.

Interface and Visualization

A transition from 2D imaging to 3D media is necessary for augmented reality and demands new models in human-computer interface design. This creates challenges for developing mobile augmented reality applications and paradigm shifts for interactions with synthetic environments. Sampat, McCrickard, Gabbard, Kavanaugh, Perez-Quinones, and Chong Lee (2007) suggest that the convergence of various technologies and the emergence of augmented reality in commercial applications demand a refashioning of our understanding and use of online technologies. Because we are moving away from traditional forms of interaction through two dimensional web pages to spatial interfaces, contextual and locative content, and new methods of data visualization, we must rethink our frameworks and interfaces.

This is absolutely critical. The future of augmented reality is dependent on our ability to create new methods and modes of interaction with computers and media (technical) as well as moving away from the visualization of data and media in two dimensions and in the typical "page" metaphor (perceptual). Success means a revolution and a dramatic shift of paradigms in industry and communication.

The first component is hardware interface… keyboard, mouse, monitor, touch sensitive pad, joystick, etc. This can be extended with data gloves, infrared sensing, motion capture, and visual tracking. Moving into these other types of interface, especially motion capture and visual tracking, affords the opportunity to implement gesture based interfaces (as in *Minority Report*). This in turn creates new functionality and ways to interact with media and data in three dimensions.

The second component is the graphical user interface ("GUI"), which is half concerned with things like toolbars, drop downs, mouseover, left-click, right-click, or some new form of sign language that is interpreted as movement and control. The other half of the GUI is more related to data visualization… that is, how information and media is portrayed to the user and their ability to accurately perceive and understand it. Very little research has been conducted here beyond early work in the virtual reality industry (there are many similarities).

Both elements, hardware and GUI, require multidisciplinary collaboration and research to adequately create the necessary standards that are useful, practical and intuitive.

Cognition

Not only is it important to evaluate how we interact with media in augmented reality, and how it is portrayed and perceived, but other areas that should be researched as well, particularly user cognition. If users are overwhelmed with information overload and too much unmediated data, the system as a whole becomes fragile and loses its usefulness.

Sampat et al. (2007) summarize their ongoing work for computer-human interfaces and "balancing attention demanded from users with the utility provided through added reaction and comprehension" through describing three techniques for mobile spatial interaction. These three techniques, "images first", mobile augmented reality, and audio notification, need to be considered through the "attention-utility tradeoffs" of interruption, reaction, and user comprehension as well as aspects of touch, proximity and multi-modality.

Touch and proximity refer to the user interacting with virtual objects, data, and environments through an interface, but also in context based on spatial location of the user and the content. Multi-modality of interface types is equally important, particularly in developing the metaphors for visualization and interaction… visual, audio, tactile, and so forth.

The "images first" technique is based on user preference for contextual and locative information over map-based data or systems that support wayfinding. In this case, interruptions of user attention (providing wayfinding guidance) is minimal, while detail and user comprehension is higher as data presented is immediately useful and of interest based on the user's surroundings.

The second technique, mobile augmented reality, is an enhancement of the first and goes beyond the simple presentation and access of information based on location to immersive and interactive media that is possibly shared and multiuser, which also changes as the user moves from one location to another. Interfaces of this type require significant attention from the user and provides greater comprehension. Balancing the amount of information available at any given time with the user's ability to read and comprehend it is an area of on-going work and research.

The third technique, audio notifications and cues, can quickly convey information directly without the need for interfaces, data visualization, interpretation, and the divided attention of the user, but comes at the cost of a higher rate of interruption.

This research is an important first step in understanding how humans process information about the environment around them, and how we must change to deal with the ever increasing level of data and information that bombarded us daily. Augmented reality, confined to a single special purpose (such as in manufacturing or in forensics) is not far from what we deal with currently with computers, laptops, mobile phones, and televisions. However if the usage becomes ubiquitous through expansion to other sectors and day to day living, the challenge of too much "noise" and not enough "signal" will become an obstacle to overcome. Further research here may initially seem less important compared to the other areas, especially technical, but the benefits of advanced work here are significant and can be applied to other areas, particularly where users must make rapid decisions of a critical nature in a highly stressful environment where they are required to process large amounts of information. Air traffic controllers, battlefield commanders, law enforcement personnel, and national disaster response teams are several examples. Contextual computing and higher comprehension from computer mediated training will increase as well.

Summary

While the state-of-the-art is still relatively young, focused research and development in key areas will yield quick returns that will significantly advance augmented reality and have secondary benefits in other areas. Ubiquitous mobile augmented reality is becoming more viable as next-generation mobile devices and smart-phones grow in power. While many of the applications of the technology we have discussed are indeed feasible in the near future, work still has to be done in areas of visualization, semantic search, natural language and gesture-based interfaces, data structures and "smart objects", as well as further study in human-computer interactions, particularly in how and when information is presented in context based on location and user action (or inaction).

For Lieutenant Kendra Jackson to have the unique tools available to her in the future, resources and funding must be allocated to several key areas to fully leverage emerging trends, technology advancements, for the development of a global wireless augmented reality network that is connected to vast amounts of data, information, and media. Augmented reality and its ability to enhance our environment, create order out of chaos, and give us instant access to immediately useful and contextual data, has potential to change our day to day lives and dramatically accelerate other advancements in technology, culture, and society.

References

Newman, J., Wagner, M., Bauer, M., Macwilliams, A., Pintaric, T., Beyer, D., Pustka, D., Strasser, F., Schmalstieg, D., and Klinker, G. (2004). Fundamentals of Ubiquitous Tracking for Augmented Reality. In *Proc. of International Symposium on Mixed and Augmented Reality (ISMAR'04),* Arlington, Virginia, November 2004.

Azuma, R. (1997). A Survey of Augmented Reality. In *Presence: Teleoperators and Virtual Environments* 6(4):355–385.

Klein, G., and Murray, D. (2007). Parallel Tracking and Mapping for Small AR Workspaces. In *Proc. 6th IEEE and ACM International Symposium on Mixed and Augmented Reality (ISMAR'07)*, Nara, Japan, November 2007.

Gatzidis, C., Brujic-okretic, V., Liarokapis, F., and Baker, S. (2008). Developing a Framework for the Automatic Generation and Visualisation of 3D Urban Areas on Mobile Devices. *In Proc. 10th Symposium on Virtual and Augmented Reality 2008 (SVR 2008),* Joao Pessoa, Brazil, May 2008.

Sampat, M., McCrickard, S., Gabbard, J., Kavanaugh, A., Perez-Quinones, M., and Chong Lee, J. (2007). Refashioning our Interaction with Space. In *Proc. Computer Human Interaction Conference (CHI 2007)*, San Jose, CA, April 2007.

Wagner, D., and Schmalstieg, D. (2003). First Steps Towards Handheld Augmented Reality. In *Proceedings of the 7th International Conference on Wearable Computers,* White Plains, NY, October 2003.

COGNITIVE AMPLIFIERS

Chapter 12
Synthetic Worlds for On-Demand Experience

Kenneth W. Kisiel

Experience: It's All in Your Mind

> "People learn best when they are pursuing goals that they really care about and when what they learn helps them attain their goals. The best means of learning has always been experience."
>
> Roger Schank (1990)

Abstract

In the rapidly shifting, demanding, under staffed world of information analysis, it is often difficult to remove an analyst from the production environment to engage in education and training without causing the rest of the workforce to be chronically shorthanded. It has been documented that current programs for intelligence analysts vary considerably in their objectives and content and have questionable immediate value to the analyst's job (Lahneman 2006). Analysts[1] often know when they need to learn something to complete a task, and in such cases they should develop the necessary skills "on-demand." By providing accelerated on-demand learning experiences to analysts, we might be able to shorten the time required to become an expert.

The primary role of an analyst is to iteratively apply analysis[2] and synthesis[3] to move forward from data and backward from hypothesis and create a final product that explains the available data (Waltz 2003). Given the rapidly changing nature of the problems and threats that analysts must face, it is not surprising that they are often lacking the requisite expertise to effectively and efficiently complete the task.

Experience, about 10 years worth, is what distinguishes experts from novices (Ericsson 2006). Through experience, an expert accumulates more knowledge than the novice. In addition, the expert differs from the novice in how the knowledge is internally

---

1 Though we focus on intelligence analysts, the ideas and concepts presented here can easily be applied to developing expertise in any field. The training aspect of this vision can also be extended down into our formal (and informal) educational systems.

2 Analysis proceeds from a presumed effect (solution) backward, searching for the sequence of antecedent causes that would bring about the effect.

3 Synthesis proceeds from known antecedent causes forward toward a solution by linking them, in a construction process, to assemble a cause-effect chain that leads to the solution.

structured and recalled when necessary (Caneel). This accumulated knowledge leads to the development of new capacities, skills, values, understanding, and preferences.

There are many ways of accumulating the experience necessary to become an expert; the most effective of which is usually through the direct involvement in or exposure to that thing or event (Schank 2002). Sometimes, experiencing an actual event is not possible or is cost prohibitive. In that case simulations are used as an artificial (or simulated) form of experience by modeling some natural or human system. There have been many forms of simulations through the ages with the latest and most powerful being computer based. Computer based virtual reality (VR) represents the latest attempt at simulating the real world and there have been several mid-fidelity VR training systems built (Vargas 2006). When VR becomes indistinguishable from "true" reality, we will finally have a generalized simulated reality ("qVerse") that can be used not only for play but for serious work.

The qVerse might hold the key to providing on-demand simulated first-hand experience that could be directly applied in the real-world. In this context, qVerse is defined as a universe of nested multi-dimensional immersive worlds (i.e., simulations within simulations) representing real or imaginative environments, augmented with abstract conceptual information. The qVerse would allow the analysts of the future to quickly gain the experience they need from interactive involvement in historical cases[4] to solve a new problem instead of being limited to solving problems they have the experience to solve. Let's take a peek into the future and see how an analyst might benefit from such a paradigm shift.

Assignment 18-127

** 2018.03.15: 08.20 Tuesday morning; Old Ship Inn, Sidmouth (South Coast of England) **

Beads of condensation slide from the half empty mug of Heavy Seas onto the oak table as LJ Silverson watches the door expectantly. His contact is due any minute and he is anxious to get this session started. He has a critical deadline to meet and was hoping this person would provide some insight into how to approach his problem. He also came highly recommended…

** 2018.03.15: 06.27 Earlier Tuesday morning; on Tampa Bay **

The sun was just rising and casting early morning shadows across his deck but LJ Silverson was no closer to a solution then he was a week ago. LJ has been asked to look into the erratic behavior of the CEO of the Central Asian Union Investment firm. LJ has explored for possible financial issues that could explain the behavior and has come up blank.

4 Although we have chosen to focus on using reconstructed historical cases for sharing experience, we could have included the use of imaginary or synthetic situations as well.

LJ is a free lance analyst who specializes in financial transaction analysis and is routinely called upon for surge support. However, this particular problem is a bit out of his area and he is now out of ideas. Sensing frustration, his advisor/mentor Jim, gently solicits his attention and offers a suggestion.

Jim is an AI-based agent responsible for staying in the background but offering, from time-to-time, useful suggestions regarding LJ's current activities. LJ has been using Jim for a few years now and Jim has come to understand LJ's normal work habits. When LJ deviates from the expected mode of operation, Jim tries to determine why and then offers advice on how LJ can get back on track. Sometimes, this advice might include consulting with outside experts.

Jim, noticing that LJ has reached an impasse on his project, has identified a number of retired experts in the field who might be willing to assist LJ in exploring new approaches to this current challenge. After Jim gets LJ's attention, he suggests that LJ contact Boris Sadofsky and presents Boris's bio sheet. LJ makes the call and within moments, Boris's assistant confirms that he would be willing to meet with LJ at the Old Ship Inn at 8:00 am. LJ has little more than an hour to prepare his thoughts, summarize his problem, jot down a few questions that might help him solve his problem, and get to Sidmouth on the South Coast of England. With minutes to spare, LJ dials in the coordinates of the Old Ship Inn on his qPort and in a flash finds he's alone inside a 17th century English pub.

* *2018.03.15: 08.32 Tuesday morning; Old Ship Inn, Sidmouth* *

The qPort is a new device that LJ recently picked up and it has greatly changed the way he navigates through the qVerse. The qVerse has been around for several years now and had its origins in the virtual worlds created at the turn of the century. These early worlds were certainly interesting but they were lacking in resolution and the ability to dynamically create custom worlds for personal exploration. Boris has created one of these custom worlds for the meeting with LJ.

In the old days, getting from one location to another was only possible by using a mouse, keypad and a series of menu options. The qPort is the first of a new generation of devices that provides access to the qVerse through direct addressing much like the old GPS systems in the real-world. After entering the desired address and touching the *Go To...* button, the qPort transports the user into that new location and time period. There are now prototype MindPort devices that allow the user to simply think about a new location and the MindPort automatically takes you there. LJ tried a beta version at a recent trade show and found himself in a couple of strange places. Cool but he'll need to watch what he thinks.

Suddenly, the creaking of the door and a blast of frigid winter air announces the arrival of Boris. LJ is shocked to be face-to-face with the legendary analyst whose keen perception uncovered a dangerous plot and prevented a global war over the introduction of synthetic food.

On his way to the table, Boris shouts for a Hang Ten, and passes an IntroChip to LJ as an introduction. Laying the chip down, the tabletop lights up and LJ is presented with an expanded biography and recent publications by Boris. Boris, not one to waste words, comes straight to the point and asks LJ what he wants. In turn, LJ passes Boris his IntroChip, which contains the summary of his problem and the questions that he is currently trying to answer. LJ tries to ask the first question but Boris stops him; he knows where this is going. Instead of responding directly to the questions, Boris suggests that LJ take a short journey: he has something interesting to show him. LJ agrees and quickly finishes his Heavy Seas.

In the meantime, Boris links LJ's qPort to his, taps in a time and location and in an instant LJ finds he's in a very strange new world observing a much younger Boris. LJ knows that he is just a spectator, and using his qPort, attaches his observation point to the younger Boris to ease following Boris through his world.

** 2012.10.11: 15.41 Thursday evening; The Tsar's Café, Bucharest **

The younger Boris is in The Tsar's Café reading a newspaper. Newspapers have not yet become obsolete, in fact, the paper has become digital and the latest news is constantly streamed to the pages. *Boris notes that he still owns the same news reader he had then, although it has become worn, and makes a mental note to pick up a new model the next time he passes a news kiosk. The old model works fine, but is not compatible with some of the newest agent technologies.*

The top story is once again the postponed announcement of Russian Agro Minister Fredrick Dobbsonovich's new policy concerning synthetic food (also called synfood). With the world population recently passing the 12 billion mark, naturally grown and cloned food is not keeping up. There have already been several riots and serious acts of violence because of food rationing. It's the general consensus that without synfood, the world could spiral into another global conflict.

Boris, it turns out, is the main trouble shooter for the Prime Minister and is responsible for the early detection and elimination of situations that could be harmful to his country's national security interests. Boris understands that if synfood is not accepted, there could be a major shift in the world order—through violence. And Dobbsonovich is the key. At that moment, a flash item appears on Boris's news reader requesting his presence for a short meeting with the PM.

** 2012.10.11: 16.00 Thursday evening; Boris's Appt., Bucharest **

After a brief walk back to his room, Boris slips into his personal secure communication device and waits for the PM. Moments later, the PM appears, and with little preamble, describes the current situation regarding synfood and the Russian Agro Minister.

Tapping his qPort, Boris stops the scene to describe to LJ the events leading up to this situation. Two decades ago, cloned food was introduced to the market with minimal resistance. In addition to no reports of adverse effects of cloned food, there had been a global reduction in the number of people dying of starvation. The bad news was that the population continued to grow, reducing the number and quality of acres under cultivation. The reports of contaminated food supplies had also been on the rise.

In prior years, a handful of companies had been researching and testing a new, highly nutritious, substance made entirely of nanoparticles dubbed Synthetic Food or synfood. All the trials were successful and the manufacturing process had been tested and approved. All that was needed was approval from the Agro Minister to begin mass distribution.

Needless to say, not everyone had been pleased with this new development, especially the Cloned Food Syndicate. When pursuing legal avenues proved unsuccessful, they began a grassroots campaign to prohibit synfood from becoming a commercial product. Some of their demonstrations had turned violent. Russia, the first country to have a critical need for this new type of food, was determined to press ahead with their approval. That's when the Agro Minister began to behave strangely. Boris taps his qPort again and the scene resumes.

The PM had asked Boris to look into the situation and get back to her within 48 hours with an assessment of the minister's state of mind. This would be just a few hours before the rescheduled announcement and just enough time for the PM to take any necessary action. Wasting no time, Boris began a search on the Agro Minister. Almost immediately, he was presented with a synopsis of the minister's background and as he was reading, information continued to appear: network of friends and business colleagues, financial information, career advancements, and other personal information.

Boris's initial assumption (hypothesis) had been that the minister was taking a bribe. However, he hadn't found the normal indicators of bribery, and being on the take would not have explained the minister's weird behavior. Boris next considered that the minister was under some kind of distress, but what kind? Serious illness (him or his family), addiction problem (gambling, alcohol, sex), external pressure (blackmail), or possibly…

Before Boris pursued that last option, he needed to disconfirm each of the other possibilities. To do this, he created a miniature synthetic world floating above his desk to represent each possibility, and as he uncovered new information, each world will shrink or grow in size, representing its overall validity. After a few more hours of data diving, each of the worlds had vanished except for one. It appeared that the data just didn't support any of the other explanations. Being left with this last option, Boris began the hunt for when the minister was replaced with a double.

It took some time and effort to track back through the recent past of the minister but Boris thought he'd identified the point at which the minister was replaced, and more importantly, who was behind this reprehensible deed. Now the question was whether the real minister was still alive. It was now time to brief the PM. After preparing a preliminary report, Boris signaled that he has some initial findings that the PM needed to know. Boris received a response that the PM would be with him in a few minutes. While he was waiting, Boris began to plan his next steps in the effort to find the minister.

Boris taps his qPort and the world freezes once again. Assuming that LJ knows the rest of the story, Boris decides to end it here and take some time to delve further into the process that he took all those years ago. Boris explains that his secret to success was to approach every problem with as many competing hypotheses as he can. He knows that these hypotheses are really just patterns that can be found in the data and an expert analyst has a large collection of patterns to draw from (or recall). Therefore, the more patterns a person has, the more expert he or she is, which allows the person to solve a broader range of problems.

He explains that we usually get stuck when searching for a solution because we can't recall any relevant patterns (i.e., we do not have any relevant past experience in that area). A person's understanding (and hence their explanation) of the world is limited to the patterns that they can recall. If there is no pattern to recall or if the recalled pattern is wrong, then it will be difficult to correctly explain a situation. Boris concludes by emphasizing that to be a successful analyst, experience is key and LJ should take every opportunity to expand his experience base. With another tap on his qPort…

** 2018.03.15: 09.15 Tuesday morning; Old Ship Inn, Sidmouth **

Boris and LJ find themselves back in the Old Ship Inn where the aroma of sheppard's pie has filled the pub. LJ thanks Boris for his time and for sharing his insights and invites him to stay for lunch. Boris expresses his gratitude but declines, saying that he has another appointment. He is much in demand. As Boris disappears out the door, LJ begins to see some parallels with his own problem and is ready to get back to work.

** 2018.03.15: 09.22 Tuesday morning; Tampa Bay **

Back in his study, LJ is surprised to see that less than an hour has passed since he left for his meeting. LJ spends a few hours reviewing information that he had previously collected and suddenly realizes that one piece of information that had not seemed significant when he originally conducted his investigation may be the key to unraveling the CEO's behavior. The CEO recently received some compromising personal information and LJ now considers the possibility that the CEO is being blackmailed. After assessing other information in his file, LJ is convinced that the CEO is a victim of extortion and that the perpetrator is a woman with whom the CEO had a prior relationship. Feeling secure in his findings, LJ hits the send key and his final report is on its way.

Having Boris walk him through a different but analogous scenario helped LJ to consider a broader range of potential explanations for the CEO's behavior, leading LJ to analyze information he had collected but not previously focused on. LJ takes a final moment to send a note of thanks to Boris. Without his help, he would never have completed this assignment on time. LJ is not sure if experts like Boris are real people or one of the new Parahuman AI[5] (Hall 2007) agents. He could easily tell the difference in prior versions of these agents but he realizes that it really doesn't matter. Getting directly involved in these historical cases gives him the experience he needs to apply to current problems; and it is a significant improvement over the way analytical skills used to be developed. He remembers stories recounted by his mentor about how in the past analysts were forced to spend hours in the classroom, poring through books, and working several years under the guidance of a senior analyst before they could work

5 Para means along side and this type of AI would act with deep knowledge and endless patience monitoring how the material is being absorbed and ultimately finding the optimal presentation for understanding.

on their own. LJ appreciates that with the current technologies, analysts can build the requisite experience when and as needed. Before LJ can give too much more thought to Boris, there is alert for a new incoming assignment. It's time to get back to work…

Technology Assessment

The take away message of this vignette is that lack of experience need not be an impediment to gaining an understanding of data. If experiential deficiencies can be identified, they can be remedied on demand using the capabilities described in the vignette. At a minimum, five key technologies will be required in order to attain these capabilities. The following paragraphs briefly describe these technologies.

The qVerse

The objective of the qVerse is to provide a collaborative environment where users can experience firsthand a situation of interest. This may include experiencing a new problem (e.g., case study), a new environment (e.g., visiting downtown Fuzhou in the 1930's), or acquiring a new skill (e.g., learning a foreign language). The vision presented here is that the qVerse will be a universe of nested multi-dimensional immersive worlds (i.e., simulations within simulations) representing real/imaginative environments augmented with abstract conceptual data for understanding information.

Shared (immersive) environments have long been the goal of computer scientists and one of the earliest examples was Douglas Engelbart's demonstration at the 1968 Fall Joint Computer Conference (Engelbart 1968). There he demonstrated shared-screen collaboration involving two persons at different sites communicating over a network with audio and video interface. Fast forward 40 years and we now have massive multiuser on-line environments where millions of people go daily to socialize, play games, buy digital and real merchandise, and generally escape from the real-world. Special purpose worlds have also been created to target very specific subsets of the population (AVW 2008).

The primary characteristic of all these worlds is that they are persistent, meaning time in the virtual world progresses forward regardless of who is logged in (Bell 2008). This trait provides a familiar structure (i.e., based on the real-world progression of time) for the in-world participants and brings with it a well understood set of behavioral expectations. Imagine the chaos if time ran in reverse or time slices were sequenced randomly. This foundation may be good for socializing or game playing but it has major shortfalls for analysis, which does require running time in reverse, jumping to a time in the past or future, or fast forwarding time through periods of non-relevant activities (see the next section, Simulated Time Travel, for a more detailed description of this feature).

Science fiction authors and futurists have long recognized the potential benefit of alternate realities represented by virtual worlds. Neil Stephenson in his book *Snow Crash* (1992) introduces the original concept of a Metaverse world where people can enter a digital world and participate in an alternate/parallel existence. He then augments this idea with two additional concepts: 1) actions in the virtual world can have deadly effects in the real-world; and 2) digital data can be overlaid on the real-world, creating a sense of augmented reality.

In the past 10 years the convergence of the Internet and faster computer speeds have allowed for the creation of rudimentary worlds such as Second Life (www.secondlife.com), World of Warcraft (www.worldofwarcraft.com), and others in which millions of individuals can simultaneously participate in fantasy in near-realistic environments. Several organizations have also pursued creating development tools where groups and individuals can create and share their own worlds (e.g., OpenSim [www.opensimulator.org], Croquet [www.opencroquet.org], etc.).

The final steps needed to realize this vision of the qVerse require several extensions to existing platforms and include as a minimum: 1) the ability to dynamically create worlds within a world; 2) complete user control of time within worlds; and 3) generation of the graphics (i.e., scenes, objects, etc.) within these worlds that are indistinguishable from the real-world.

Simulated Time Travel

The objective of simulated time travel is to create an environment for dynamically representing time-bounded data, in essence, controlling "the moving Now" (Horwich 1987). Simulated time travel will allow the analyst of the future to experience first-hand and learn from real historical or imaginary pasts as well as the present or future environments. The qVerse will provide for the visualization for this exploration.

Actual time travel may ultimately be possible (Gödel 1949, Horwich 1987) but not soon. In the meantime, we will have to rely on simulated time travel to directly experience some past, present, or future environment. This is not a new concept; we all have taken the opportunity to relive past events either through unassisted memory recall or with the use of props such as pictures (still and motion) or raconteurs. Science fiction and our imagination allow us to relive (pre-live?) the future. In either case, these musings or stories represent a condensed model of the actual event as well as providing the necessary learning vehicle for gaining second hand experience.

Before writing was invented, people had to listen to learn and a good memory was an important tool. Early cave paintings may have been memory markers for the retelling of past events. These images were followed by re-enactments (i.e., plays), written language, motion pictures, and finally computer based simulation for capturing and passing along accumulated experience (Manohar 2007). The qVerse is the next step in this evolutionary chain. By providing an immersive, highly interactive environment, the qVerse will not only allow the user to learn the lessons of past experience but also to create new experiences by exploring a broader set of possible future end-states (Borges 1941).

Today, all traditional data management systems have the built-in parameters to temporally bound data returned from a query (Bowman 1993). This data bounding capability provides a necessary foundation but is insufficient for satisfying the demands of a convincing time travel device. If we are to replicate a point in time within an immersive 3D world, there needs to be an enormous repository of supporting display information. In a sense, the qVerse will function as a data fusion environment where multimedia data from many unknown sources will need to be normalized in time, space, and fidelity before being rendered for display.

Adding movement through time, either backward or forward, significantly increases the complexity of data management and recall. However, this feature is essential for performing forensic and forecasting analysis. From an analytical standpoint, a key component of simulated time travel is identifying and observing change in the data over time. One could assume that change is not equally dispersed through time, forcing a user to expend unproductive time observing little change punctuated with brief periods of intense change. Manual control of the movement of time is a required feature for effective simulated time travel.

Software Agents

In the context of the qVerse, software agents are autonomous pieces of software acting on behalf of the user to search for and assemble information. Another specialized role for these agents is to act in the capacity of a personal guide or mentor to the user, providing unobtrusive support on an as needed base. Software agents may be embodied as avatars within the qVerse.

A software agent is characterized as a self activating piece of software that acts on behalf of a user or other program. In the wake of the Internet, there have been a variety of approaches to developing agents. The concept of an agent can be traced back to Hewitt's Actor Model (Hewitt 1973) and has its roots in artificial intelligence. For an agent to be effective, it needs to exhibit a number of characteristics:

- *persistence*—code runs continuously and decides for itself when it should perform some activity;
- *autonomy*—agents have capabilities of task selection, prioritization, goal-directed behavior, decision-making without human intervention;
- *social-ability*—agents are able to engage other components through some sort of communication and coordination, and they may collaborate on a task;
- *reactivity*—agents perceive the context in which they operate and react to it appropriately.

In the vignette, software agents are used three ways: 1) data collector; 2) guide; and 3) intelligent (re: expert) teacher (see the next section for an expanded description of intelligent agents). In the data collector role, the agent is responsible for assuming the burden of data collection for the user. The majority of the analyst's time is spent finding and reviewing data (Kahaner 1996). By shifting the task to an agent, the analyst can concentrate on making sense of the data. However, this requires that the agent recognize the type of data that is required, implying that the agent is specialized in a particular field or source domain. This further implies that multiple agents can be pursuing the same (or similar) data and will need to compete on the acceptance of the data once it is found.

The agent guide is very different from the data collector agent in that it is a single agent, though it may depend on task specific subagents for support. The agent guide has the responsibility to monitor the activities of the user, modify its behavior to match the needs of the user, and offer task specific suggestion when appropriate. This requires a level of intelligence beyond that required of the data collector, encompassing the ability to track and modify goals and understand the workflow of many different problem types.

This description highlights only the two most significant roles that agents will play in the qVerse. Many other agents will be operating in the background, providing the necessary support for having the right information available at the right time.

Artificial General Intelligence

The objective of Artificial General Intelligence (AGI) is to endow software agents with a degree of broad-spectrum abilities to adapt, learn, and instruct users in a variety of analytical topics. In the context of the qVerse, we will limit this discussion to applying AGI to the area of sharing experience (i.e., expertise) with the user through storytelling. Behind the storytelling, the AGI agent needs to assemble and build the required expertise. The qVerse provides the medium for the dynamic, interactive involvement with these stories.

The initial question to be addressed should be "Why General AI?" as opposed to mainstream AI (i.e., applied/narrow/weak AI). Modern AI research began in the middle of the 1950s and after nearly 20 years, it became obvious that the difficulty of creating an artificial general intelligence (i.e., strong AI) had been grossly underestimated. At this point, researchers chose to focus on specific sub-problems where they could produce verifiable results and commercial applications with the hope that strong AI would ultimately emerge from this bottom-up approach (Moravec 1988). Though there have been many impressive results that have flowed from the research of applied AI (Turney 2008), the human intensive process of knowledge acquisition and coding makes using applied AI cost/time prohibitive for dynamically creating the expertise needed in this vision.

In the qVerse, a topic expert AGI agent will not be 'owned' by any single user; they will be a member of a pool of expert agents that can be called upon by any user. An AGI agent begins its existence with no knowledge of its target topic domain. However, it does possess a minimum knowledge base, a set of behaviors that allow it to seek out and generalize information, and a goal to become an expert in a specific topic domain. The agent will then enter a phase where it traverses the Internet and other open and private data sources and assimilates the data associated with the relevant domains. Moving into the next phase, the agent will organize the data and create a number of stories to convey the essence of the accumulated knowledge to a user.

For the autonomous AGI agent to be successful, it needs to exhibit the following characteristics (Kasabov 1998):

- Plan, learn and improve through interaction with the environment (embodiment);
- Adapt online and in real-time;
- Learn quickly from large amounts of data;
- Accommodate new problem solving rules incrementally;
- Have memory based exemplar storage and retrieval capacities;
- Have parameters to represent short and long term memory, age, forgetting, etc.;
- Be able to analyze itself in terms of behavior, error and success;
- Have the ability to represent and reason over knowledge (see section Knowledge Representation and Reasoning);
- Have "social intelligence" for effectively interacting with other AGI agents.

At the time of this writing, only one company, Novamente LLC (www.novamente.net), is working on a commercial AGI system. The remainder of the work being done in this area is still in the early research phases in university laboratories.

Knowledge Representation and Reasoning

The intent of knowledge representation and reasoning is to first formalize a standard foundation for efficiently embodying and sharing information; and second, to identify a set of validated reasoning engines for use by the software agents.

Knowledge representation and reasoning has been at the core of AI since the beginning and is concerned with how knowledge can be represented symbolically and manipulated in an automated way by reasoning programs (Brachman 2004). Since knowledge is used to achieve intelligent behavior, the fundamental goal of knowledge representation is to represent knowledge in a manner as to facilitate reasoning or inferencing (i.e., drawing conclusions) from knowledge. The key problem has always been to find a representation scheme (and a supporting reasoning system) that can make the needed inferences within time and resource constraints.

There are representation techniques such as frames, rules and semantic networks that have originated from theories of human information processing. Over the past several decades, many knowledge representation methods were tried at the problem specific level (e.g., heuristic questions-answering, neural networks, and expert systems) and at the general level (e.g., Cyc, OpenMind). Additionally, several programming languages were developed specifically tailored for knowledge representation and reasoning (e.g., Prolog, KL-ONE). More recently, the emergence of the Semantic Web has seen the development and evolution of representation schemes like XML, RDF, DARPA Agent Markup Language (DAML), Ontology Inference Layer (OIL), and Web Ontology Language (OWL). With all this data being encoded, one might wonder why inferencing is required.

First, there are some facts that are explicit while others are implicit. If automated processing can only deal with explicit facts, then it becomes too inflexible to perform sophisticated tasks. Inferencing discovers the implicit facts. Second, inferencing on the Web generally involves multiple sources of data. Inferencing provides a means to normalize data between different formats and between sources where data may contradict. In the past several years, there have been a number of tools created that allow developers to add inferencing functionality to their software applications (e.g., Swish, Jena, DAON, FaCT, Cerebra, etc.).

It should be clear that the AGI agents discussed above will require both a method for interpreting the wide range of representations found on the Web and access to a variety of inference engines for discovering implicit knowledge.

Research Agenda

This section will describe the areas of science and the specific key technologies that must be developed in order to address the challenges.

qVerse

1. **Blending the real with the abstract**. Analysis requires that data be viewed from multiple perspectives. At one end of the spectrum, we need to see a high fidelity reconstruction of a physical location. At the other end of the spectrum, the data only makes sense when viewed in a very abstract way. A few key questions would include: What does the synthetic environment need to look like to allow the user to dynamically shift between these two extremes? How might these two extremes overlap to expose greater detail? Can these different views be shared with other analysts without losing perspective?
2. **Make the imaginary indistinguishable from reality**. To extract the maximum benefit from an immersive experience, the synthetic environment needs to be almost indistinguishable from the real-world. Today, the graphic rendering of objects is close to photo quality while a high fidelity representation of humans (re: avatars) is still years away. A few key questions would include: How do we take the final steps in having avatars appear identical to live actors? Given the processing time required to render graphics, what other technique can be used to provide the same outcome in shorter time? Under what circumstances should the underlying physics model be suspended to facilitate analysis?
3. **Worlds within Worlds**. Allowing worlds to be dynamically created within other worlds (i.e., simulations within simulations), will give the analyst the ability to create an unlimited number of worlds (Borges 1941) in any time period for personal or group exploration. A few key questions would include: How would one manage and navigate between these parallel worlds? How would data stay consistent between the worlds? What would be the processing and storage

requirements for creating and maintaining multiple worlds across thousands of users?

Simulated Time Travel

1. **Time Control**. Sometimes the best way of understanding a situation is to experience it directly. Controlling the temporal aspect of data will allow the user to filter the data to display only the desired time periods. After resetting the time reference point, the user would be free to explore the data from this new perspective. A few key questions would include: What are the different types of in-world time and how do we translate between them? Is there a difference in (data, algorithms, etc.) traveling back in time compared to traveling forward in time? Is time an illusion? How about lunchtime?
2. **"Common Sense" Data repository**. Adjusting one's perspective through time (i.e., filtering the available data) allows the user to focus on the most relevant data items. However, to gain the maximum benefit, this data slice needs to be placed in context (i.e., contained in a data environment that is appropriate for the data slice). We can refer to this context as "common sense" data. A few key questions would include: What "common sense" data is required to set the necessary context? Given the multi-dimensional nature of time selection, what data representation and storage architecture is most efficient?
3. **Storytelling**. The primary purpose for visiting another (data) time period is to understand that data and representing the data in the form of a story is the most effective and expedient path to understanding. If the story is relevant, it will become part of the experience base of the user. A few key questions include: Can presenting data as a dynamic, interactive "play" enhance the learning experience? What method is required to create stories on-the-fly from a given data set? What is the best method to manage competing stories from a single data set?

Software Agents

1. **Scheduling and synchronization**. A major benefit of the agent architecture is that agents are aware of their environment and initiate action autonomously. For the search task, we envision that multiple agents might simultaneously activate a search and return potentially overlapping results. A few key questions would include: How are agent goals and behaviors defined? How are data synchronized from multiple data sources? Who is the arbitrator when returned data are conflicting or contradictory? What is the life-cycle of an agent?
2. **Collaboration**. Another important aspect of agents is that they must behave properly within their environment. This would include agents collaborating with other agents or recruiting other resources. For agents to work together efficiently they must share semantics of their data elements. A few key questions would

include: How are agents aware of the capabilities (i.e., data requirements and goals) of other agents? What are efficient methods for communication between agents and what metadata is required for sharing data?

3. **Dynamic Data**. Agents will live in a data rich environment in which data will be in a constant state of flux. To assist the user, agents will need to stay responsive to the changing data landscape and automatically update the user's environment. Changes in the data will need to be highlighted for recognition by the user. A few key questions would include: Will changes in the data lead to behavioral changes of the agents? Will a single agent be assigned to a single data item, a single data source, or something in between?

Artificial General Intelligence

1. **Learning**. Humans learn by interacting with the environment, listening to stories, watching plays and movies, and reading the real or imaginative stories of others. Hand coding the knowledge that will be required by the AGI agents is not practical so the AGI agents must learn on their own. A few key questions would include: Kids learn by playing so can we construct a kid-like synthetic environment for AGI agents to begin the learning process? What would be the metrics for graduating AGI agents to learn from text, videos, and other media? What is the agent equivalent "Turing test" to certify that an AGI agent has reached an expert performance level?
2. **Embodiment**. A significant portion of the knowledge that humans accumulate is as a result of direct interaction with the environment. By embodying an AGI agent into an avatar, we can continue the learning process across the perceptual, social, and spatial domains. A few key questions would include: What "senses" are required for an AGI agent to recognize stimuli in the environment? What methods are needed for an AGI agent to resolve the ambiguity resulting from having multiple senses? How would we encourage appropriate behaviors while suppressing undesirable behaviors in the AGI agents?
3. **Knowledge Transfer**. One primary learning form is through the experiences of others. Once an AGI agent has acquired a new experience that experience should be made available to the rest of the AGI agent population. A few key questions would include: What would be the representation structure for an experience such that it could be readily shared among AGI agents? Should all AGI agents contain all experience? If not, what method is needed to limit the experience an AGI agent accepts? Should an AGI agent "forget" experiences that have seldom been used?

Knowledge Representation and Reasoning

1. **Storage and Manipulation**. One problem in knowledge representation consists of how to formally store and manipulate knowledge in an information system

so that it may be used by software algorithms to accomplish a given task. With the Semantic Web emerging as the dominant information architecture for the foreseeable future, the representation structures will continue to evolve. A few key questions would include: Given the variety of knowledge representation schemes available, what scheme or combination of schemes is most appropriate for representing 3D data? What data storage architecture is most efficient for storing and retrieving data from an immersive world? What are the scalability issues associated with each architecture?

2. **Reasoning**. Reasoning (or inferencing) is the process of looking for implicit facts, conclusions, or actions. Reasoning will be a core component of intelligent agents. As these agents are traversing the Internet (and other data sources), they will be encountering data that has been explicitly organized for a specific purpose. The agents will need to be aware enough to select the most appropriate inferencing engine to complete the knowledge discovery task. A few key questions would include: How are inference engines registered for use by agents? What metadata will be required to properly characterize the capabilities of an engine? How might an engine determine the validity of its conclusions?

Summary

Down through the ages, storytelling has been a dominant way of sharing the collective experience of our forbearers. Through stories, we are able to gain insight into events that we did not directly participate in and use that accumulated knowledge to solve problems that confront us on a day-to-day basis. Yet, as effective as stories are, they are no substitute for first-hand experience. But as this chapter has demonstrated, by combining storytelling with immersive computer-based simulations, we can recreate realistic first-hand experiences that can be invoked on-demand.

Giving the user the ability to call upon this level of expertise as the need is identified will not only reduce the overall cost of developing expert users but also provide tremendous incentives for analysts to dig deeper into their own field while broadening their knowledge by exploring adjacent fields.

Finally, the Internet has given us the ability to globally share and access data on demand…the qVerse will give us the ability to globally share, access, and assimilate experiences on demand.

References

AVW. (2008). *The Blue Book: A Consumer Guide to Virtual Worlds*. The Association of Virtual Worlds (AVW) Publishing Division. Available at: www.associationofvirtualworlds.com [accessed: 30 April 2008]

Bell, M.W. (2008). Toward a Definition of "Virtual Worlds". *Journal of Virtual Worlds Research*, 1(1). Available at: http://journals.tdl.org/jvwr/issue/view/38 [accessed: 14 September 2008]

Borges, J.L. (1941). *El Jardín de senderos que se bifurcan (The Garden of Forking Paths).* Editorial Sur.

Bowman, J.S., Emerson, S.L., and Darnovsky, M. (1993). *The Practical SQL Handbook.* New York: Addison-Wesley Publishing Company.

Brachman, R.J., and Levesque, H.J. (2004). *Knowledge Representation and Reasoning.* Amsterdam: Elsevier.

Caneel, R. *Knowledge Representation: Expertise in Negotiations.* Massachusetts Institute of Technology.

Engelbart, D. (1968). NLS Demonstration Video. Available at: http://sloan.stanford.edu/MouseSite/1968Demo.html [accessed: 05 December 2008].

Ericsson, K.A., Charness, N., Feltovich P.J., and Hoffman, R.R. (eds.). (2006). *The Cambridge Handbook of Expertise and Expert Performance.* Cambridge: Cambridge University Press.

Goertzel, B. (2006). *The Hidden Pattern: A Patternist Philosophy of Mind.* Boca Raton: BrownWalker Press.

Gödel, K. (1949). *A Remark about the Relationship between Relativity Theory and Idealistic Philosophy.* Albert Einstein: Philosopher-Scientist. Edited by P. Schilpp. La Salle: Open Court, pp. 557–562.

Haag, S. (2007). *Management Information Systems for the Information Age.* Irwin: HcGraw-Hill.

Hall, J.S. (2007). *Beyond AI.* New York: Prometheus Books.

Hewitt, C., Bishop, P., and Steiger, R. (1973). *A Universal Modular Actor Formalism for Artificial Intelligence.* MIT Artificial Intelligence Laboratory.

Horwich, P. (1987). *Asymmetries in Time: Problems in the Philosophy of Science.* Cambridge: A Bradford Book.

Kahaner, L. (1996). *Competitive Intelligence.* New York: Simon & Schuster.

Kasabov, N. (1998). Introduction: Hybrid intelligent adaptive systems. *International Journal of Intelligent Systems*, 6:453–454.

Lahneman, W.J., Ph.D. (ed). (2006). *The Future of Intelligence Analysis Volume I Final Report.* Center for International and Security Studies at Maryland.

Manohar, U. (2007). *History of Communication.* [Online]. Available at: http://www.buzzle.com/articles/history-of-communication.html [accessed: 17 November 2008].

Moravec, H. (1988). *Mind Children: The Future of Robot and Human Intelligence.* Cambridge: Harvard University Press.

Muniz, A.M., and O'Guinn, T.C. (2000). Brand Community. *Journal of Consumer Research*, 27:227–235.

Schank, R.C. (1990). *Tell Me a Story.* New York: Scribner's.

Schank, R.C. (2002). *Every Curriculum Tells A Story.* KruzweilAI.net.

Smart, J., Cascio, J., and Paffendorf, J. (2007). *Metaverse Roadmap: Pathways to the 3D Web, A Cross-Industry Public Forecast Project.* Acceleration Studies Foundation. Available at: www.metaverseroadmap.org [accessed: 6 November 2007].

Stephenson, N. (1992). *Snow Crash*, Bantam Books.

Turney, P. (2008). *AI Success Stories.* Apperceptual. Available at: http://apperceptual.wordpress.com/2008/04/28/ai-success-stories/ [accessed: 14 December 2008].

Vargas, J.A. (2006). Virtual Reality Prepares Soldiers for Real War, *Washington Post*, 14 February.

Waltz, E. (2003). *Knowledge Management in the Intelligence Enterprise*, Boston: Artech House.

Chapter 13
Synthetic Worlds and Characters, and the Future of Creative Writing

Selmer Bringsjord and Alexander Bringsjord

The Future

Fenwick Gibsen ate breakfast with his wife each and every morning before commuting to his office. Suzannah Gibsen, Fenwick well knew, was a bit of a retro health nut; in fact, to say "a bit" was to understate the matter rather dramatically. She insisted on each of them consuming, side by side in their bay-windowed, east-facing breakfast room, at sunrise, a bowl filled with a mountain of crisp blueberries, under a layer of strawberries, atop a mound of oat brain suffused with an ample, underlying lake of fat-free (and, for that matter, lactose-free) milk. A tall glass of antioxidant-fortified fresh-squeezed orange juice (with one crystal-clear ice cube of distilled water) was also obligatory, as was a large, steaming cup of Jamaican Blue Mountain coffee, black. The kicker was that Suzannah insisted that all this food come from the soil in the old-fashioned way; no replicator-produced victuals for her and her famous husband. Fenwick had long ago given up trying to point out to his better half that molecules were molecules, whether they found their final arrangement over time in an old-millennium garden, or were configured in seconds in a replicator. Suzannah insisted that grown food was healthier, and she pointed out that she'd been right about berries and caffeine. And, she *had* been right: The recommendations that had surfaced at about the start of the new millennium had turned out to have unusual staying power, supported at this point (2029) by a veritable ocean of empirical data. Those recommendations had been to consume cancer-fighting berries, Alzheimer-fighting caffeine, and a host of other things that Fenwick now dutifully ingested every day of his life. (Red wine, also powerfully salubrious in moderation, was something Fenwick was allowed to have only when socializing with other members of the literatí. Fenwick had long ago let fall the objection that his wine cellar, worth a pretty penny, would take a century to enjoy at the Suzannah-prescribed rate of consumption.) When spooning down the cocktail Suzannah prescribed, he routinely fantasized about the day when cures for all forms of cancer would finally be found. On that glorious day, he would be able to revert to a breakfast of cheddar-infused scrambled eggs, sausage, bacon, and greasy home fries, all produced in under three seconds by a replicator.

Suzannah had rather strong prudential reasons for monitoring Fenwick's diet. After all, he was hands-down the greatest living dramatist on the planet, author of 14 screenplays (ten of which had led to films of enormous critical and financial value), nine plays (five of which had galvanized stages in New York, London, Paris, Rome, and Fenwick's hometowns of Oslo and Bergen), eight novels, innumerable poems, countless essays, and, of late, his first biography (on John Quincy Adams, one of the few Americans Fenwick truly admired, and a man with whom, courtesy of the system about to be described, Fenwick had had many face-to-face conversations). But the secret to Fenwick's success, the core of his genius, of course had nothing to do with his diet.

As a man of letters, Fenwick had the Midas touch because he could create characters of utter depth, intricacy, and interest. Once he had the characters created, the rest of his writing, whatever the form, was effortless. But for Fenwick, to "create a character" meant something a good deal more than it meant to the average writer, and in fact it meant much more than what it meant even to other renowned authors of belletristic prose. In short, Fenwick Gibsen would only begin to write the first word when his characters were as real to him as the human beings he knew in the real world. This *modus operandi* had nearly destroyed his marriage.

The problem, very simply, had been that Suzannah Gibsen had been forced to share her home with countless strangers, many of whom were not just somewhat unfriendly, but outright creepy. And the fact that they had been invisible had only made the situation all the more disturbing. Sometimes, in the past, Fenwick would sit beside her, and carry out lengthy conversations with a character in an in-progress work. Of course, only one side of the conversation could be heard by Suzannah: She could hear what her husband said, but she could never hear anything in response. One stormy, ink-black night, with thunder booming and wind howling all around their capacious house, and he and his wife both in bed, lights out, Fenwick had carried out a conversation with someone "standing" in their room. At one point Fenwick had said, with emotion: "All the murders you've committed, and you feel not the slightest remorse?"

Another crack of lightning. The room lit up. But of course no interlocutor was to be seen.

Fenwick again, speaking into the dark: "And what in your background has given you this black heart, my friend?"

Presently, Fenwick said: "Ah. Well, perhaps redemption will be possible. We shall see."

The conversation done, Suzannah now struggled to fall asleep. That was something Fenwick easily managed to do. He lay there in peace, his chest rising and falling smoothly, but she tossed and turned as rain slapped their roof in sheets, and as she tried to throw off the feeling that a third person was in their room: a murderer. The next morning, at breakfast together, Suzannah, her face pallid and weary, whispered: "Fenwick, I can't bear it any longer. Either they go, or I do. With all the money that your writing has brought us, is there no way for you to create them, refine them, interact with them—somewhere else?"

"Suzannah," Fenwick said, "they live in here." The author tapped his forehead. "Thus, where I go, they go."

She looked at him in silence.

Presently she said: "But think about the *words* you write. They live in the external world. You commit content in your mind to computer files, routinely. After all, when you turn over to your editor a play, or a novel, and so on, you turn over text that you have written. I should like to say, sweetheart, that you *externalize* the words that compose your works."

"True enough."

"Well," she continued, "then either you find a way to externalize your characters, and circumscribe your interaction with them, just as you do with the text you write, or I go."

The next day, Fenwick, calling in favors from some rather powerful friends, conversed by phone with one of the greatest neuroscientists in the world, at Columbia-Presbyterian: Francis Sullivan.

"Fenwick, no," Sullivan had answered. "I'm sorry. We cannot extract what you imagine when you form characters for a story. We could know inside and out what regions of your brain are active, down to the molecular level. But how, pray tell, would you have us extract emotions and personality from patterns of neural circuitry flowing through time? You can't derive semantic content from mere syntax. This is now an axiom in neuroscience. For example, we can tell when a person is lying by scanning his brain while we ask him key questions, but we can't tell what the *content* of the lie is. And certainly we shall never be able to see what a person is *feeling* when lying."

Fenwick simply said, "I see," in resignation.

"You're talking to the wrong kind of expert in me, Fenwick. Talk to someone who can tell you how to speak your characters into existence before your eyes; and someone who can tell you how to interact with them after they have been born."

"What field would such a person be in, Dr. Sullivan?"

"Your characters are intelligent creatures, right?"

"Certainly," Fenwick replied.

"And they are artificial, correct?"

"Sure."

"Then it seems quite plain: Go consult the AI folks."

Fenwick had done so. And now, after an investment of $40 million to build a home office more sophisticated (but more intimate) than the only three holodeck-like installations he had found (in laboratories at RPI, MIT, and Georgia Tech), all his marital turbulence was in the past. Thanks to advances in AI (of a particular variety; we'll get to that), and also to holography, connubial bliss now reigned in the Gibsen home, and the master writer was more productive than ever.

After breakfast on this particular morning, Fenwick pulled on his fur-lined boots, put on and buttoned up his sheepskin coat, pulled his wool cap down to cover his ears, and slid on his mittens. He then departed, and trudged off into the snowy woods, bound for his office, a stone cottage on his own property set back one mile into the forest. From the outside, from the fieldstone walls and slate roof, and the stone chimney from which curled a plume of smoke from the fire burning inside, the cottage looked to be anything but high-tech. Even inside, the only tip-off to the peerless technology that Fenwick had bought was to be found in those with whom the great writer interacted.

The second Fenwick stepped inside his cottage, Arnie greeted him: "Hello, Fenwick."

"Arnold, hi. Listen, I've been thinking. It seems to me that you're appearance is too conventionally, well, too conventionally *threatening*. It's true that you're a rather unsavory interrogator in the story, but I don't want your physical appearance to be a stereotype."

"What do you suggest?" Arnie asked.

"Well, for starters, you should be shorter, much shorter."

Immediately Arnie shrunk a full foot.

"And thinner, bordering on frail," Fenwick said.

Arnie lost 25 pounds in an instant.

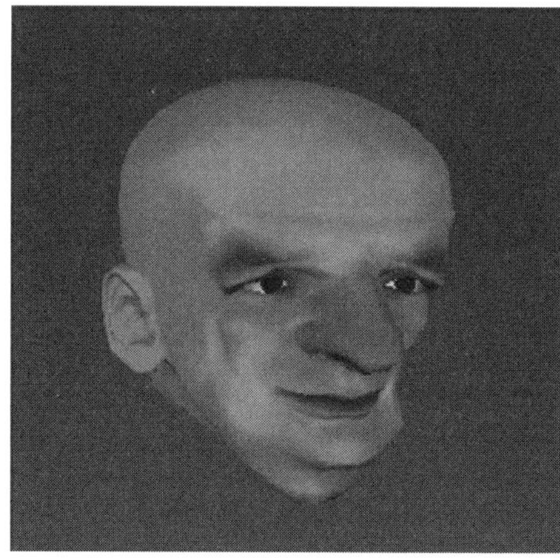

Figure 13.1 Arnie, face view

"With less hair," Fenwick directed. "A *lot* less."

Arnie's hair thinned out to the point that his skull could be clearly seen through what was left. The process continued until baldness arrived.

"And I think your physiognomy, while not engaging, should be a bit more … *pleasant*."

Arnie's face began to morph. His brow receded. But the same intelligent forehead remained, as did the prominent hook nose.

"What do you think?" Arnie asked.

Fenwick studied Arnie for a minute, walking slowly around him in a circle. "Yes, I like it," Fenwick said.

And then he continued: "Your voice is too low. I think you need a soft voice, one that borders on a whisper, but suggests, subtly, a disquieting hiss."

Arnie spoke: "Very well, Mr. Gibsen. How do I sound now?"

"Perfect," Fenwick replied.

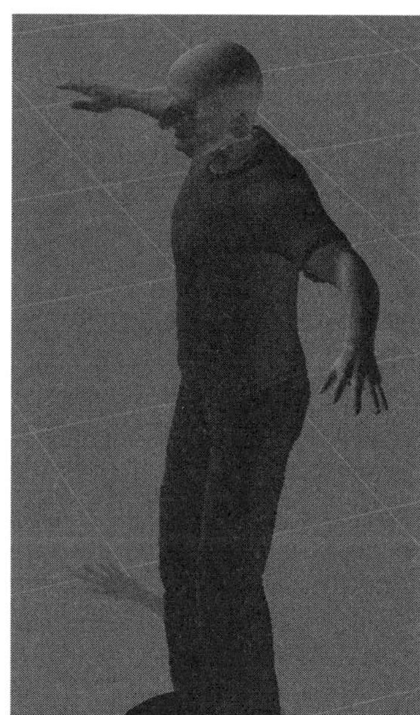

Figure 13.2 Arnie, full-body

At present, Fenwick was working on a play, *Calculi of Death*, or as Fenwick referred to it: *Calculi*. The title reflected the fact that in this play, a number of people run rather different calculations in order to try to figure out how fierce interrogation of a certain prisoner can become, before the interrogation becomes unethical. The prisoner, Muhammad, knows the secret location of ticking nuclear bombs planted within the mainland US. If these bombs are not diffused, millions of civilians will perish. If Muhammad discloses the locations before a certain deadline, US authorities can diffuse the devices, guaranteed.

Interrogators in *Calculi* include General Farrow and Arnie, with advice—ethical and theological—offered by the Reverend Franklin Gray. The President of the United States, President Bentham, is also one of the characters, and has ultimate say as to whether or not Arnie is allowed to proceed as he wants. General Farrow's view of interrogation, reflective of the standpoint of Occidental culture, is fairly standard: He refuses to use unadulterated torture, even when the stakes are as high as they are in this case; and even "tough tactics," such as a punch to the face, while for him admissible, are things he hates to even ponder, let alone implement. Gray is of the opinion that the Judeo-Christian ethic that he has devoted his life to upholding clearly implies that torture is unethical—and points out that if one uses a calculus that permits unlimited pressure to be applied to Muhammad, both Judaism and Christianity are vitiated, since the message being sent by such violence is that God isn't in control after all, and that matters must therefore be managed instead by human beings.

Arnie is quite a different animal. If he sees *anything* in the behavior of a prisoner holding such life-and-death secrets that indicates the prisoner will yield to certain extreme techniques for extracting information (and we cannot share what these techniques are here; readers are directed to the following url for the latest draft of *Calculi*: http://kryten.mm.rpi.edu/Calculi_of_Death.pdf), however painful those techniques may be, he will deploy these techniques without the slightest qualm. Below, we will look at what is happening from a technical point of view when Arnie sees a behavioral cue that triggers his pouncing, full-force, on Muhammad.

Discussion

Creative writing can be viewed from the perspective of the degree of content that can be *externalized* by the human author outside the mind/brain of that human author, courtesy of the best technology of the day. (Confessedly, this is a view of creative writing reflective of the fact that our interests, in the end, are more in the engineering direction, rather than the literary one.) Go back a bit, and authors didn't have computers, so they didn't have electronic text processing systems that are in the very bloodstream of today's writers. Creative writers, however, always had *something* to write on. It may not have been *easy* for the first creative writers to write text on an external object, and then rework that text—but it was done. On the other hand, there has always been a natural evolution of increasingly more sophisticated ways of externalizing text, and of allowing that text to be modified, refined, and so on. In addition, creative writing has always had both pictorial and auditory elements, and in light of the fact that in the history of hominids, there is evidence of the expression of narrative before language, we are really talking about the *tri*-evolution of technology for externalizing linguistic, auditory, and pictorial content related to the narrative in question. The state-of-the-art today in this tri-evolution is perhaps that which is available to screenwriters and playwrights (and also to novelists, but they tend not to use the software in question, for some reason), in the form of software systems that allow for the representation and manipulation of text, meta-representations of that text (outlines, storyboards, etc.), and visual and auditory tools.[1] That which is available to Fenwick Gibsen is really only a natural extrapolation along the evolutionary arc that creative writers have been travelling steadily upon for many, many centuries. Since Gibsen, like his namesake the brilliant Henrik Ibsen, is a dramatist who writes from a core composed of rich, robust characters, rather than from plot, technology for externalization in his case is devoted to enabling the construction and refinement of well-rounded characters. As Ibsen famously said, he would not take up pen for any play until he had all his characters in mind down to the buttons on their clothes (Bringsjord 1995).

We turn now to the theoretical foundation for the synthetic character/world technology exploited by Fenwick Gibsen. Much, in fact arguably most, of this foundation has already been erected as of 2009. We will pay special attention to the two cornerstones of this foundation that will likely prove to be the hardest to fully perfect: the part supporting real-time natural-language communication between a creative writer and his/her characters, and the part supporting the high-level cognition of those characters, specifically their beliefs about the minds of others. We begin by discussing the fact that both of these cornerstones of the foundation pertain not to the physical appearance of characters, but rather to their cognitive powers.

Theoretical Foundation for This Future

Clearly, given the goal of building an environment of the sort that Fenwick exploits in order to write creatively, there would appear to be little need for us to look carefully at the *biological* basis of human persons. The main reason is that the physical side of the future we imagine, even now, is remarkably close to what is currently available. The physical design of Arnie, as shown above in Figures 13.1 and 13.2, is already something that can be to a high degree carried out; indeed, we *have* carried it out. Arnie's physical appearance has been mapped out using the software system *Poser 7*—the "7" deriving from the fact that this is the seventh version of the system.[2] Now of course Arnie, as of 2009, appears to the authors of the present paper in 2D form. (Dropped into a game engine, Arnie does appear as a 3D character, but that is of course a "fake" 3D view. Fenwick, on the other hand, quite literally sees Arnie the same way he sees his wife: in full-blown, real-world 3D.) For interaction of the sort described above between Fenwick and Arnie, a full, life-like, 3D representation of Arnie is necessary, and hence it can be safely said that advances in holography and related areas (e.g., projection onto

1 Our current favorite such system is *Movie Magic Screenwriter*, which (e.g.,) allows the writers to hear their characters speak to them in desired styles. A succinct overview of the dominant systems in this class is provided in "Product Review" by Sean Kennelly, on page 74 of *Creative Screenwriting* (September/October 2008). His review specifically targets *Movie Outline v3*, which we also have, and very much like. *MO3* has built-in functions for building characters, and can be considered a primitive precursor to Gibsen's ability to modify Arnie (and other characters) merely by speaking commands.

2 Any number of other options are available today. *3D Studio Max* is another nice tool, and various games/game engines offer tools. For example, we have *Half Life*'s character design tool running in our laboratory.

3D shapes) will be needed if the future we have described above is in fact to arrive. We herein ignore this dimension of Arnie. Frankly, it is a dimension that is infinitely easier to advance, engineering-wise, than the cognitive and linguistic dimensions.

What's important to Fenwick about Arnie, and other characters in *Calculi of Death*, is their *cognitive* side. Even in cases where a character's physical status is central (e.g., in situations where a character is seriously ill, and the illness plays a significant role in the drama), it is the mental space that is of paramount importance. In short, when we look to the theoretical foundation of the system Fenwick uses, we must expect that foundation to relate to computational psychology, not to, say, the DNA structure of humans. When it is said that x is human just in case x has a particular genetic code, the perspective is not that of computational psychology. Along the same lines, our minds are not modeled by charting the physiology of our brains. Rather, the builders of Fenwick's system must be concerned with what it means to be a human being, from the *psychological*, and indeed specifically the *cognitive*, perspective. That is, the question is: What does it mean to be a human *person*? For ambitious AI, the centrality of personhood is plain in the relevant literature. For example, here is the more than two-decade-old objective for AI (Charniak and McDermott 1985):

> The ultimate goal of AI, which we are very far from achieving, is to build a person, or, more humbly, an animal (Charniak and McDermott 1985: 7).

More recently, other authors have made plain that AI aimed explicitly building persons is very much about the incorporeal, or purely intellectual side (e.g., see Pollock 1995).

One generic account of human personhood has been proposed, defended, and employed by Bringsjord (1997). This account is an orthodox one; for example, it generally coincides with one given by Dennett (1978), and by others as well, for example Chisholm (1976). In addition, this account is in line with the capacities covered, chapter by chapter and topic by topic, in surveys of cognitive psychology (e.g., see Goldstein 2005). The account in question holds that x is a person provided that x has the *capacity:*

1. to "will," to make choices and decisions, set plans and projects—autonomously;
2. for subjective consciousness: for experiencing pain and sorrow and happiness, and a thousand other emotions—love, passion, gratitude, and so on;
3. for *self*-consciousness, for being aware of his/her states of mind, inclinations, preferences, etc., and for grasping the concept of him/herself;
4. to communicate through a language;
5. to know things and believe things, and to believe things about what others believe (second-order beliefs), and to believe things about what others believe about one's beliefs (third-order beliefs), and so on;
6. to desire not only particular objects and events, but also changes in his or her character;
7. to reason (for example, in the fashion exhibited in the writing and reading/studying of this very chapter).

Arnie (and, for that matter, other characters in Fenwick's *Calculi of Death*) appear and interact with Fenwick on the strength of work carried out to capture parts of this definition in computation. Notice that we say *parts* of this definition. The fact of the matter is that some of the capacities constitutive of personhood don't seem to be amenable to mechanization, even in the long term. This seems to hold for Attribute 2 (Yang and Bringsjord 2003, Bringsjord 1999, Bringsjord 1998), and we discuss this issue at the very end of our chapter.

Anderson and Lebiere (2003), instead of defining personhood, give an operational equivalent of this definition by describing what they call "Newell's Program," an attempt to build computational simulations of human-level intelligence, where that intelligence is cashed out in the form of a list of abilities that correspond to those on the list just given.

For example, part of Newell's Program is to build a computational simulation of natural-language communication at the normal, adult level. This is Attribute 4 on the list above. As Anderson and Lebiere concede, AI and cognitive science (CogSci) are finding it rather difficult to mechanically simulate this attribute.

In the present chapter our emphasis is on Attributes 4 and 5, as we have already indicated. That is, we are concerned to explain how it is that the theoretical foundation for Arnie's having the capacity to communicate in English, and his having the capacity to know and belief things (up to at least third-order beliefs) on the strength of what he perceives, is in large measure already in place. (We also seek to prescribe a path forward to build atop this foundation. More on that in due course.) We turn now to the two cornerstones in this foundation.

Cornerstone #1: Natural Language Communication/Conversation

Twenty-five years ago, the dream of engineering an artificial agent with the capacity to communicate in a natural language (e.g., English, German, Norwegian, Chinese) at the level of human persons was alive and well. After all, Alan Turing, who can plausibly be regarded the founder of modern-day AI, inaugurated that field with a landmark paper in which he identified thinking with linguistic performance, and also predicted that before the year 2000, computing machines would be linguistically indistinguishable from neurobiologically normal humans (under certain reasonable time constraints; see Turing 1950). In addition, when AI officially started in the US in 1956 (at a DARPA-sponsored workshop at Dartmouth), Newell and Simon took themselves to be ushering in a research-and-development path that would very rapidly produce programs with human-level eloquence (see the quotes in Russell and Norvig 2002). As far as we can tell, the dream of human-machine linguistic equivalence was not based on any particular piece of technology, nor on any particular theoretical or mathematical advance, but rather simply on the assumption that natural language could be converted, without loss of meaning, into corresponding content expressed in a formal language. For example, as described in (Charniak and McDermott 1985), sentences in English were to be converted into formulas in the language of first-order logic (FOL). The basic assumption that communication in natural languages could be translated without loss of meaning into a formal logic-like language can be traced back much earlier than 1985: it can be traced back to Leibniz, who asserted in 1685 that disputes would eventually be settled by calculation in a formal language (Weiner 1951).

We haven't the space to provide a full review of FOL, or for that matter of any other logical system.[3] Readers wanting such a review can turn elsewhere (e.g., to Bringsjord and Yang 2003; and for an extensive presentation of logical systems in general, including FOL, all given in the context of precisely the kind of "mind modeling" that bringing Arnie to digital life requires, to Bringsjord 2008b). Suffice it to say here that FOL is based upon the simple idea that objects can have properties, and that these properties can be binary, ternary, quarternary, and so on. To say that Selmer, denoted by the constant s, has the binary property of being older in age than Alexander, denoted by the constant a, we can write in FOL:

$$\text{Older}(s,a)$$

In this simple formula, Older is a predicate. Functions can also be written in FOL in straightforward fashion. For example, let's assume that age is a function that returns the age of a constant (when that constant names a person), so that we can write such things as age(a), which (at present) returns 19. In addition, FOL has the Boolean connectives that all readers will at some point have seen during their education: $\wedge$ ("and"), $\vee$ ("or"), $\neg$ ("not"), $\rightarrow$ ("if … then …"), and $\Leftrightarrow$ ("… if and only if …"). FOL also has two *quantifiers*: the *existential quantifier* $\exists$, which, when paired with a variable x, as in $\exists$x, says "there exists at least one thing x such that …"; and the universal quantifier $\forall$, which, when paired with a variable x, as in $\forall$x, says "for every thing x …" Given this machinery, how would we represent in FOL the following sentence?

The age of every father is greater than that of all of his sons.

As follows:

$$\forall x \forall y(\text{Father-Of}(x,y) \rightarrow \text{Greater}(\text{age}(x),\text{age}(y)))$$

And for an example related directly to *Calculi*, observe that the sentence:

If Arnie deploys his interrogation technology, Muhammad will divulge his secret.

---

3 Note that there is a profound difference between a *formal language*, and a full *logic*, or *logical system*. The former requires only an alphabet of primitive characters, and a grammar for assembling well-formed or grammatically correct formulas from that alphabet. The latter, in short, requires not only such *syntactic* machinery, but also a formal *semantics* that specifies under what conditions the formulas have such values as *true*, *false*, *indeterminate*, *probable*, *certain*, and so on. In addition, a logical system includes some framework for systematically reasoning over the formulas; such reasoning can come in any of a number of modes, which include deduction, induction, abduction, and analogical inference. For an overview of logical systems, see Bringsjord 2008b. In Bringsjord's account, a logical system also includes meta-theorems that provide key mathematical information, such as whether or not all formulas that are true no matter what they represent can also be proved.

could in FOL be represented by something like the following first-order formula:

$$\text{Deploys(arnie,i-tech(arnie))} \rightarrow \text{Divulge(muhammad,m-secret)}$$

And the more general English sentence:

Anyone who deploys Arnie's interrogation technology will get Muhammad to talk.

becomes:

$$\forall x\ (\text{Deploys(x,i-tech(arnie))} \rightarrow \text{Divulge(muhammad,m-secret)})$$

As it happens, our logic-based AI work, and indeed the vast majority of such work carried out in our laboratory, is based upon an extremely useful variant of FOL: *multi-sorted logic* (MSL). A comprehensive presentation of MSL can be found in (Manzano 1996), and an example of R&D in our lab that leverages MSL can be found in (Bringsjord, Taylor et al. 2008). The basic idea behind MSL is that the set of objects described via formulas is partitioned into sub-categories. For example, one might have a sub-category (or *sort*) composed of people, and another composed of numbers, and so on.

Why would anyone want to reduce natural language to formulas in FOL or MSL? The answer is that from the dawn of AI, certainly one of the most impressive powers possessed by computing machines is their ability to reason automatically over propositional content expressed as formulas in logical systems.[4] In the painfully simple example of Arnie and Muhammad, a machine overseeing a knowledge base that includes the proposition that Arnie does in fact deploy his interrogation technology, along with the two formulas shown immediately above, can of course instantly deduce that Muhammad will divulge his secret. In general, if we assume that the collection of all that Arnie knows and believes (and fears, and hopes, etc.; these verbs all take as targets propositions and are known as *propositional attitudes*) can be identified with some set Φ of formulas in MSL, and we assume that any natural-language question uttered by Gibsen is expressed in MSL by some query φ?, then part of the cornerstone we are currently describing consists in the fact that machines can often answer such queries by attempting to find a proof of φ from Φ. One of us has explained this basic scheme in much detail elsewhere (Bringjord 2008b).

To this point, despite the richness of logical systems, natural language has resisted attempts to model it in logico-computational terms. However, the attempt to model *proper subsets* of unrestricted natural language in formal logic (e.g., see Fuchs 1999 and Bringsjord et al. 2007) has been quite successful, and it is this research activity that forms Cornerstone #1 of the theoretical foundation for Gibsen's remarkable home office. Specifically, the key research activity, as outlined in Figure 13.3, is the three-stage process used in our laboratory by which propositional content expressed in unrestricted natural

4 FOL is one logical system. The space of all such systems is infinite, and includes many different logics. For an explanation of the concept of a logical system, see Bringsjord 2008b.

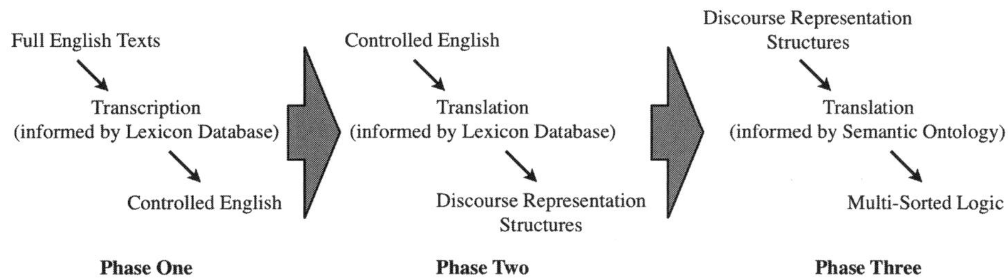

Figure 13.3 Overview of logic-based machine reading process

language (UNL) is eventually expressed in MSL. In the first stage of the process, UNL is translated into LCNL. In the second stage, LCNL is translated into corresponding *discourse representation structures*.[5] In the third and final stage, these structures are translated into formulas in MSL. In our lab, the second and third stages are mature and reliable, automated, and quite well understood. The first stage, on the other hand, is acutely challenging, and is in need of considerable improvement, in light of the fact that this stage currently only works when input sentences in UNL are "well-behaved." We will discuss the first stage below, in the section "Prescription for Future R&D."

Cornerstone #2: A Theory of the Minds of Other Minds

The principles and techniques that neurobiologically normal humans deploy in order to understand, predict, and manipulate the behavior of other humans are collectively referred to as a *theory of mind* (Premack and Woodruff 1978). In *Calculi*, the fact that Arnie has a theory of mind (ToM) is what underlies his beliefs about Muhammad's beliefs, and indeed his beliefs about what Muhammad believes about what Arnie himself believes. Before looking in some detail at an example of ToM-supported reasoning on the part of Arnie, we briefly discuss an example that has been explored in our laboratory. This example has been based on the much-discussed *false-belief test* (Wimmer and Perner 1983).

In the false-belief test, a subject *S* faces two containers, A and B. The experimenter, with *S* looking on, places an object *o* into A. Not only does *S* see that *o* is placed into A; he also sees that another person, *S'*, sees that *o* is placed into *A*. At this point in the test, *S'* is asked to leave. While he is away, *S'* cannot see what is taking place in connection with the containers and the object, and this limitation can be observed by *S*. After *S'* leaves, the experimenter, again in plain view of *S*, moves object *o* from A to B. At this point, *S'* returns, and the experimenter asks *S*: "Now *S*, if I ask *S'* to get *o*, which box will he look in, A or B?" A subject passes the false-belief test if he or she correctly answers that *S'* will look

5 DRSs are a syntactic variant of first-order logic for the resolution of unbounded anaphora. Their use in the interpretation of text is a central element of *discourse representation theory* (Kamp and Reyle 1993, 1996), upon which we directly rely. Discussion of this theory is beyond the scope of the present chapter.

in container A.[6] The subject fails if he or she says that *S'* will look in B. Almost all children before the age of four fail the test. Children above this age almost invariably pass.

In Figure 13.4, the center synthetic character, Eddie, who is playing the role of *S*, is shown, and to his right stands Micah, playing the role of *S'*. In the snapshot shown in Figure 13.4, the question shown is asked by the experimenter, who stands to Eddie's left. Of course, the action that took place before Eddie asked this question included the initial dropping of the teddy bear into container A and the transfer of the bear from A to B while Micah was away. Figure 13.5, in its insert, shows a snapshot of the automated reasoning that corresponds to the thinking taking place in Eddie's mind. This reasoning takes place on computers in our laboratory, despite the fact that the relevant animation happens in Second Life. This reasoning takes place in a "socio-cognitive" calculus more expressive than FOL and MSL. The increased expressivity is required in order to allow for formulas corresponding to such propositions as:

Eddie believes that Micah believes that the teddy bear is in Container A.

If we were to try to directly represent such a sentence in FOL, we would get something like this:

Believes(e,Believes(m,In(t-b22,container-A)))

But this is flat-out grammatically incorrect in FOL, because predicates cannot have predicates, formulas, or sub-formulas as arguments in FOL. Indeed, no such constructions are permitted in any logics that are (as it is said) *extensional* in nature. Traditionally, extensional logics are developed for the purpose of formalizing domains quite separate from cognition—domains like number theory, which posit only objects bereft of psychological attitudes like believing, knowing, intending, and so on. At the opposite end of the spectrum comes creative writing, which is nothing without highly elaborate cognition on the part of characters in narrative, readers of that narrative, and writers of that narrative. This is something one of us has explained in connection with murder mysteries; see Bringsjord and Ferrucci 2000. In murder mysteries, typically a clever detective hot on the trail of a villain who knows he is being pursued will have beliefs about the beliefs the villain has about the beliefs of the detective. For example, it may well be that the detective believes that the villain believes that the detective believes the villain has such-and-such a property. And given this, it's easy to see that the villain could discover it, and hence it would be the case that the villain believes that the detective believes the villain has such-and-such a property. For the details regarding how these kinds of constructions are representable, and how they can be rigorously reasoned over in the socio-cognitive calculus, see Arkoudas and Bringsjord 2008.

6 In our version of the test, a subject passes only if he or she not only answers correctly, but can also supply the correct justification for this answer. A subject who simply answers A or B based upon, say, the flipping of a coin, would not pass the test, and for us, this fact is important. Unfortunately, in the cognitive psychology literature, subjects are rarely asked to provide an argument in support of their answers.

Figure 13.4 Eddie just before his ToM-based reasoning

Figure 13.5 Eddie during his ToM reasoning

But these examples don't pertain to the case of hand, which involves Gibsen as the author of *Calculi*, and its most complex character: Arnie. We now provide an example of Cornerstone #2 in action, in connection with Arnie. To begin, we shall assume that it is well-known that certain behaviors indicate that those performing them are at least somewhat fearful. There are many candidate behaviors—cringing, letting one's eyes go wide, shivering, shuddering, and so on. To fix things in our example, for no particular reason we shall pick the action of taking a deep, cleansing breath while at the same time squinting. This action will be taken while one is under interrogation. We shall assume that this is a tell-tale sign that the person performing this action is at least somewhat fearful, and that it is common knowledge that if an agent believes that he has performed this action, that agent believes that he is indeed fearful. We shall denote the particular composite action in question by dbreath. We shall further assume that there is some formula $P^{fear}(a)$ in FOL that says that some agent a is fearful. Note that this might be itself a rather complicated formula, so we are denoting it with an abbreviation.

We can now generalize a bit: We can let α^* be a variable that can have as an instance any particular fear-indicating action, not just dbreath; and we can let $P^*(a)$ be a variable that can have as an instance any psychological state, not just fear. We are generalizing in this case to set up a framework in which we can formalize and mechanize the fact that human beings, upon seeing any of a vast number of behaviors, instantly infer that the bearer of this behavior is in some particular mental state. The generic procedures that produce such chains of inference are called *methods* (Arkoudas and Bringsjord 2008). Please refer to Figure 13.6 to see the actual chain of inference that underlies part of what Gibsen has written: a scene in which Arnie, upon seeing Muhammad take a deep breath and squint, believes that Muhammad is fearful, and indeed believes that Muhammad believes he is afraid. (Muhammad actually *knows* that he is fearful, but we leave this aside.) In this proof, provided for readers passionately interested in the details

Sample Method-Generated Proof in "Cognitive Calculus" of One of Arnie's Beliefs

Set the particular action-type α^* to *dbreath*, and the time of the dropping to t^*. In addition, let $P^{fear}(a)$ stand for the formula expressing the proposition that agent a, the only free variable in P^{fear}, is fearful.

The method (let us call it M) in this case allows a psychological state of the agent a to be quickly deduced from the performance of the action α^*. With a_a representing Arnie, and a_m representing Muhammad, what happens when the method fires is that the following proof is instantly generated. Note that the conclusion of this proof is that Arnie believes that Muhammad believes that Muhammad himself is fearful. Given this belief, Arnie's goal is closer, and he is emboldened.

Proof:

1	$\mathbf{S}(a_a, happens(action(a_m,\alpha^*),t^*))$	premise
2	$\mathbf{K}(a_a, happens(action(a_m,\alpha^*),t^*))$	1, DR_4
3	$\mathbf{K}(a_a, \forall a,\alpha,t.happens(action(a,\alpha),t) \Rightarrow \mathbf{K}(a, happens(action(a,\alpha),t)))$	A_4, DR_2
4	$\mathbf{K}(a_a, happens(action(a_m,\alpha^*),t^*) \Rightarrow \mathbf{K}(a_m, happens(action(a_m,\alpha^*),t^*)))$	3, DR_9

Figure 13.6 Sample method-generated proof in "Cognitive Calculus" of one of Arnie's beliefs

of our approach, the operator **B** stands for *believes*, **K** for *knows*, **C** for something that is common knowledge (= known by all agents), and **S** indicates *sees*. There are only two premises in the proof; they are labeled as such in the rightmost column. Every other line is machine-deducible. We don't have the space to explain each inference, and explain only the one made at line 2: Line 2 can be deduced using the general rule of inference (DR_4) that essentially says that whatever an agent sees an agent knows. So in this case, since Arnie sees Muhammad's tell-tale deep breath and squinting, he knows that Muhammad has indeed taken such a breath.

Prescription for Future R&D

Can we really get there from here? Is it really true that today's logic-based brand of AI and CogSci has in fact laid the foundation for providing creative writers with a work environment like that which Gibsen enjoys? If so, how do we get from the groundwork, from the cornerstones described above, to the wondrous home office in question? There are three sustained projects that must be launched in order to forge a link from today's foundation to Gibsen's holodeck-infused home office. As will be seen, the first two of these projects both require a sustained investment in the refinement of LCNL-based work, while the third involves applying parallelization techniques that are now common in non-cognitive supercomputing domains to the mechanization of ToM. We now briefly describe these three projects in turn.

Project #1: Boost LCNL to Cover Doxastic and Other Operators

As we explained above, logical systems equipped to represent doxastic operators (e.g., *believes* and *knows*) already exist, and in some cases are accompanied by precise proof theories that make automated reasoning over such propositional content possible. Such is exactly the case with respect to the socio-cognitive calculus of Arkoudas and Bringsjord (2008). LCNL, however, is currently only able to capture the structure and meaning of sentences devoid of such operators. In order to reach the day when Arnie will be not just a character in a vignette like the one we opened with, but a cognitively robust synthetic character able to interact with real creative writers, it is essential that LCNL be expanded to cover these operators—as well as other aspects of unrestricted natural language that currently cannot be formalized and mechanized in logic-based AI or CogSci.

What is involved in the push to augment the expressivity of LCNL so as to cover doxastic operators? Developing a detailed answer to this question would constitute an extensive research program in its own right. Nonetheless, we can venture a few general points in response to the question.

The first point is that the traditional semantics for logical systems created to represent doxastic operators seems to us to be ill-suited to providing guidance for how to augment and modify LCNL to handle such operators. Along with Arkoudas, we are of the view that the meaning of formulas involving the **B** and **K** operators from above should not be given in terms of traditional so-called "possible worlds," which is common in philosophy and AI (as, for example, in Fagin et al. 2004), but rather in terms of the rationales that support the relevant attitudes. In other words, on this approach what it means to say that some agent believes a proposition (at least when this belief is a conscious one) is that there is a web of inference conferring plausibility on this proposition, from the standpoint of what the agent knows. So, you believe that Lincoln was President of the US, and the meaning of this belief consists in the fact that there are many things you know that can be arranged essentially into an elaborate series of (not necessarily deductive) arguments for the proposition that Lincoln was President. (For more on this general direction, see Bringsjord, Shilliday et al. 2008.) The advantage of this approach is that it should be much easier to associate concrete algorithms with belief, since if there is any success story within AI it surely must be the amazing progress machines have made in processing proofs and arguments.

Project #2: Capture an Appreciable Percentage of the Meaning of UNL in LCNL

Suppose for the sake of argument that Project #1 is pursued aggressively, and is a resounding success. This means that the range of LCNL will have been significantly extended. But there is still a severe challenge: viz., it is not possible to mechanically translate arbitrary UNL into LCNL in such a way that preserves meaning. In fact, the situation is quite dire, in light of the three-phase process discussed above, and shown in Figure 13.3. As the reader will recall, the second and third phases are already automatic. This immediately implies that if there was on hand a way to translate UNL to LCNL the entire natural language problem in AI would be solved! But that problem is enormously challenging (a fact we return to in our conclusion, below), and we believe that creative writers can be empowered by synthetic character/world technology long before this problem is solved (if it ever *can* be solved).

The solution is to aim at capturing only a *percentage* of the content of text expressed in UNL when that text is translated into LCNL. To our knowledge this approach has never been explored. If Gibsen suddenly began to engage in conversation that breaks the bounds of LCNL, the technology underlying Arnie should take some risks in recasting Gibsen's language into LCNL. Consider tense, for example. Currently, LCNL doesn't provide a way to represent sentences using anything other than the present tense. But as anyone can tell you, even when you can only speak a foreign language in the present tense, you can still carry out rather elaborate, productive conversations with native speakers of that language.[7] We do not ourselves yet have on hand algorithms for moving from UNL to LCNL in a manner resigned to losing considerable information in the process. What we are saying is that the development of such algorithms and experimentation therewith, is a project that is part and parcel of our roadmap for how to get from today, to what Gibsen enjoys in 2029.

7 Selmer never managed to move beyond the present tense in speaking and writing Spanish, but found ways of nonetheless communicating with Spaniards.

Project #3: Use Methods to Parallelize Automated Reasoning Over Content in Socio-Cognitive Calculus

The third and final project we recommend is the parallelization of the machine reasoning central to our approach. Please refer back to Figure 13.6, and the proof shown therein. As we have already explained, the fact that this proof is produced quickly by a so-called *method*, and is not laboriously constructed *de novo* for the particular case at hand, is crucial. The idea that human persons go around consciously constructing, step by step, complicated chains of reasoning like what is shown in Figure 13.6 is not psychologically plausible in the least. That is why methods are so attractive, for on the other hand that human persons have on hand *general-purpose procedures* (which are essentially what methods are) for rapidly forming inference-supported beliefs isn't psychologically implausible in the least. But with methods on the table, the next natural step is to allow agents to run methods *in parallel*. At the same time that Arnie is looking for, and making inferences from, the facial expressions and gestures of Muhammad, he must be attuned to the attitudes of his superiors (who are monitoring his behavior), to words Muhammad utters, to words he himself utters (and to the strategies that dictate what he ought to say), to his own premeditated facial expressions and gestures, and so on *ad indefinitum*. All of this, and all of the reasoning that accompanies it, must be carried out in parallel. That seems obvious, and yet automated theorem proving has been steadfastly sequential, not parallel. The reason for this is that the basic formats for automated reasoning, for example reasoning based on the rule of inference known as *resolution*, are not ones that are easily parallelized.[8] The situation is quite different in the case of methods: There would appear to be no major obstacle standing in the way of a system capable of simultaneously firing multiple methods. To our knowledge, this is a research direction that has yet to be explored, but it is one that is crucial to our vision.

Two Caveats

Finally, what pair of caveats have we in mind? Well, these:

First, however painful it may be, and despite what we have said above, we need to be dead honest about the unmitigated difficulty of building artificial agents able to deal with *unrestricted* natural language in ways that are indistinguishable from those used by normal human persons of average intelligence. While as we have noted, Turing (1950) predicted over half a century back that by now we would be able to engineer machines linguistically indistinguishable from us (i.e., machines able to pass his so-called "Turing Test"), the fact of the matter is that, today, a bright toddler's conversational reach still exceeds that of any and all computers on our planet. In the approach described above, there is a loss, and indeed a *significant* loss, that takes place when moving from completely unrestricted natural language to logically controlled natural language. We believe that if this loss is small enough, natural-language communication between a

8 Nice coverage of resolution-based theorem proving can be found—within the context of AI—in Russell and Norvig 2002.

creative writer and his or her characters can be sufficiently robust to enable that writer to work more efficiently, and perhaps at a higher level of quality. But we are under no illusions about how hard it is for a machine to communicate at the level of a human person.

Of course, there are those (e.g., Moravec 1999) who hold that, relatively soon, person-level communication will be mechanized. Unfortunately, such writers are confident because of the continuous increase in processing speed produced by Moore's Law, but raw processing speed is not the problem (as explained in Bringsjord 2000): the challenge is to discover the information-processing *procedures* that enable human persons to communicate in unrestricted natural languages. However fast the hardware, it does little good unless there are procedures to run upon it. It can therefore be said with confidence that while logically controlled natural language, and clever translation of unrestricted natural language into it, will pay great dividends, we certainly don't recommend that you hold your breath in anticipation of the arrival of human-to-synthetic-character linguistic interaction indistinguishable from the human-to-human case. Fenwick can talk to Arnie within the confines of the narrative structure that Fenwick has himself established. He can't talk to Arnie about anything, in any manner. It's ironic that some originally logic-based experts in computational language processing have turned their backs on logic, in favor of purely statistical approaches. Charniak himself is an example; he abandoned logic in favor of purely statistical approaches (Charniak 1993). The situation is ironic because statistical approaches are content to capture only a portion the natural language such approaches receive as input, and yet in the present chapter we are recommending a logicist path based on the humble concession that only a portion of natural language received by Arnie as input can be transformed into logically controlled natural language. Of course, the nice thing about the approach we recommend is that that which is expressed in logically controlled natural language can be reasoned over with great power.

And what of the second caveat? It is that we need to be crystal-clear about the apparent insurmountability of qualia; that is, about the outright impossibility of literally imbuing synthetic characters with the capacity to feel what it's like to, say, drink a great Pinot Noir, or carve a ski turn on hardpack at 40 mph, or—hitting closer to present chapter—experience the fear that comes from facing someone as ruthless as Arnie. There are today no simulations of subjective consciousness (Attribute 2 in the above list of capacities constitutive of personhood). There *are* robots that encourage humans seeing them to ascribe consciousness to them. But that is quite different, as explained in Bringsjord 2007.

Notice that while you may disagree about what is *ultimately* mechanizable, you must concede that, at least as of *now*, we have no third-person formalization of consciousness. In other words, property dualism (the view that such properties as "experiencing the deep fear that comes from facing such a one as Arnie" are incorporeal, though they may be *correlated* with certain neurophysical properties of the brain) may be false, but it currently can't be overthrown by providing the third-person description of the physical properties that are identical to the psychological (or, as they are sometimes called in philosophy, "Cartesian") ones. Tied to the scenario of Fenwick and Arnie with which we began, the point is that while, as we've seen, we can look inside Arnie's mind and find the structures constitutive of his belief that Muhammad will fold if subjected to exceedingly harsh tactics, we can't find anything constitutive of Arnie's enjoying the pain that his interrogation inflicts. (Recall what Francis Sullivan tells Fenwick about the limits of brain imaging technology.) As we have seen, we can formalize propositional attitudes like *believing* and *knowing*; we cannot, alas, do any such thing for emotional states. Of course, though these states are not part of the technology we envision, it is far from clear that Fenwick Gibsen is thereby hampered. When he imagined his characters before him in his home, it made no difference that the apparitions failed to literally have conscious states. What was important, and what is important in the remarkable home office that he subsequently built, is that the characters were real *to him*, because that, in the end, is all it takes for Fenwick Gibsen (and indeed for any real-life creative writer using the synthetic worlds technology we envision) to be a better dramatist.

References

Anderson, J., and Lebiere, C. (2003). The Newell test for a theory of cognition. *Behavioral and Brain Sciences,* 26:587–640.

Arkoudas, K., and Bringsjord, S. (2008). Toward formalizing common-sense psychology: An analysis of the false-belief task, in *Proceedings of the Tenth Pacific Rim International Conference on Artificial Intelligence* (PRICAI 2008) *Lecture Notes in Artificial Intelligence* (LNAI), No. 5351. Edited by T.-B. Ho, and Z.-H. Zhou. New York, NY: Springer-Verlag, 17–29. Preprint available at: http://kryten.mm.rpi.edu/CognitiveCalculus092808.pdf [accessed 18 March 2009].

Bringsjord, S. (2008a). The logicist manifesto: At long last, let logic-based artificial intelligence become a field unto itself. *Journal of Applied Logic,* 6(4):502—525. Preprint available at: http://kryten.mm.rpi.edu/SB_LAI_Manifesto_091808.pdf [accessed 18 March 2009].

Bringsjord, S. (2008b). Declarative/logic-based cognitive modeling, in *The Handbook of Computational Psychology,* edited by R. Sun. Cambridge, UK: Cambridge University Press, 127–169. Preprint available at: http://kryten.mm.rpi.edu/sb_lccm_ab-toc_031607.pdf. [accessed 18 March 2009].

Bringsjord, S., Taylor, J., Shilliday, A, Clark, M. and Arkoudas, K. (2008). Slate: An argument-centered intelligent assistant to human reasoners, in *Proceedings of the 8th International Workshop on Computational Models of Natural Argument* (CMNA 8). Edited by F. Grasso, N. Green, R. Kibble, and C. Reed, 1–10, Patras, Greece, July 21, ISBN: 978-960-6843-12-9. Offprint available at: http://kryten.mm.rpi.edu/Bringsjord_etal_Slate_cmna_crc_061708.pdf [accessed 18 March 2009].

Bringsjord, S., Shilliday, A.,Taylor, J., Werner, D., Clark, M., Charpentier, E., and Bringsjord, A. (2008). Toward logic-based cognitively robust synthetic characters in digital environments, in *Artificial General Intelligence 2008. Frontiers in Artificial Intelligence and Applications*. Edited by P. Wang, B. Goertzel, and S. Franklin. Amsterdam, The Netherlands: IOS Press, 87–98. Available at: http://kryten.mm.rpi.edu/sb_etal_agi2008_frames.pdf [accessed 18 March 2009].

Bringsjord, S., Arkoudas, K., Clark, M., Shilliday, A., Taylor, J., Schimanski, B. and Yang, Y. (2007). Reporting on some logic-based machine reading research, in *Proceedings of the 2007 AAAI Spring Symposium: Machine Reading* (SS–07–06. Menlo Park, CA: AAAI Press, 23–28. Available at: http://kryten.mm.rpi.edu/sb_ka_machinereading_ss07_012907.pdf [accessed 18 March 2009].

Bringsjord, S. (2007). Offer: One billion dollars for a conscious robot. If you're honest, you must decline. *Journal of Consciousness Studies*, 14(7):28–43. Offprint available at: http://kryten.mm.rpi.edu/jcsonebillion2.pdf [accessed 18 March 2009].

Bringsjord, S. and Yang, Y. (2003). Representations using formal logics, in *Encyclopedia of Cognitive Science Vol. 3*. Edited by L. Nadel. London, UK: Nature Publishing Group, 940–950. Offprint available at: http://kryten.mm.rpi.edu/SBYY.ECS.pdf [accessed 18 March 2009].

Bringsjord, S. and Ferrucci, D. (2000). *Artificial Intelligence and Literary Creativity: Inside the Mind of Brutus, a Storytelling Machine*. Mahwah, NJ: Erlbaum.

Bringsjord, S. (2000). A contrarian future for minds and machines. *Chronicle of Higher Education*, November 3, B5. (Reprinted in *The Education Digest* 66(6):31–33.)

Bringsjord, S. (1999). The zombie attack on the computational conception of mind. *Philosophy and Phenomenological Research*, 59(1):41–69.

Bringsjord, S. (1998). Chess is too easy. *Technology Review*, 101(2):23–28.

Bringsjord, S. (1995). Pourquoi Hendrik Ibsen Est-Is Une Menace Pour La Littérature Générée Par Ordinateur?. (traduit par Michel Lenoble) in *Littérature et Informatique la Littérature Générée Ordinateur*. Edited by A. Vuillemin. Arras, France: Artois Presses Universite, 135–144.

Bringsjord, S. (1997). *Abortion: A Dialogue*. Indianapolis, IN: Hackett.

Charniak, E. (1993). *Statistical Language Learning*. Cambridge, MA: MIT Press.

Charniak, E. and McDermott, D. (1985). *Introduction to Artificial Intelligence*. Reading, MA: Addison-Wesley.

Chisholm, R. (1976). *Person and Object: A Metaphysical Study*. London, UK: George Allen and Unwin.

Dennett, D. (1978). Conditions of personhood, in *Brainstorms: Philosophical Essays on Mind and Psychology*. Montgomery, VT: Bradford Books, 267–285.

Fagin, R., Halpern, J., Moses, Y. and Vardi, M. (2004). *Reasoning About Knowledge*. Cambridge, MA: MIT Press.

Fuchs, N., Schwertel, U. and Schwitter, R. (1999). *Attempto Controlled English (ACE) Language Manual, Version 3.0*. No. 99.03. Zurich, Switzerland: Department of Computer Science, University of Zurich.

Kamp, H. and Reyle, U. (1996). A calculus for first order discourse representation structures. *Journal of Logic, Language and Information,* 5:297–348.

Kamp, H. and Reyle, U. (1993). *From Discourse to Logic: Introduction to Model-theoretic Semantics of Natural Language, Formal Logic and Discourse Representation Theory*. First edition. New York, NY: Springer.

Manzano, M. (1996). *Extensions of First Order Logic*. Cambridge, UK: Cambridge University Press.

Moravec, H. (1999). *Robot: Mere Machine to Transcendent Mind*. Oxford, UK: Oxford University Press.

Pollock, J. (1995). *Cognitive Carpentry: A Blueprint for How to Build a Person.* Cambridge, MA: MIT Press.

Premack, D. and Woodruff, G. (1978). Does the chimpanzee have a theory of mind? *Behavioral and Brain Sciences,* 4:515–226.

Russell, S. and Norvig, P. (2002). *Artificial Intelligence: A Modern Approach.* Second edition. Upper Saddle River, NJ: Prentice Hall.

Turing, A. (1950). Computing machinery and intelligence. *Mind LIX,* 59(236):433–460.

Wiener, P. (1951). *Leibniz: Selections.* New York, NY: Scribner.

Wimmer, H. and Perner, J. (1983). Beliefs about beliefs: Representation and constraining function of wrong beliefs in young children's understanding of deception. *Cognition,* 13:103–128.

Yang, Y. and Bringsjord, S. (2003). Newell's program, like Hilbert's, is dead; let's move on. *Behavioral and Brain Sciences,* 26(5):627.

Chapter 14
Virtual Rehabilitation: Synthetic Worlds to Address Disabilities

Maria T. Schultheis, Lisa K. Simone, and Ana C. Merzagorra

Part I: A Glimpse into the Future...

"*Watch your airspeed, you're coming in too high.*" Mike nodded intently, cutting back on the throttle and pulling a bit more on the yoke. He hoped his adjustments would burn off more airspeed. "*Dump your flaps! It will slow you down!*" Dave's directions became more insistent as they approached the airport property, *"Chop your power!"* Mike tried to keep the nose of the single engine plane on the centerline of the quickly-approaching runway. Finally, the plane smartly fell the last hundred feet but remained floating over the runway, refusing to drop the last few feet for a successful landing. "*Ground effect is keeping you off the runway, slow it down!*" David's hands posed ready to grab the yoke as he demanded, "*Do it now, you're running out of runway!*" Despite his attempts, the plane refused to touch down. Landing on a runway this short was always tough, but the challenge was intensified by the runway's location; sandwiched on either end by deep blue mountain lakes. It seemed the small plane was destined for an emergency water landing if Mike didn't act very soon.

But he'd waited too long. At his experience level, Mike was unable to recover from his mistake. Even if the wheels finally touched down, he didn't have enough runway to come to a full stop. Seeing the frigid water rushing at him, he froze; unable to react to the certain disaster. *"My controls!"* David yelled and grabbed the yoke. *"Aborted landing! Full power, pull up on the stick."* Mike felt his body pushed back into the seat as the plane regained speed; but still the plane's windscreen showed only water. He prayed David had taken over the controls in time. With the last few feet of runway flying by beneath them, the plane's nose finally lifted skyward under David's control. Rising rapidly, they soared up and over the placid lake, ripping the calm water's surface in its wake.

Mike slumped in his seat, heart racing and happy to be alive. At the same time, he dreaded what was going to happen next—a painful debriefing at the end of this frustrating and scary training session.

< -- break -- >

The only difference between this and a typical training session is that the instructor is not in the plane, but on the ground. David is a licensed pilot and pilot instructor for single and twin engine airplanes who after flying for 10 years, lost the use of his legs in an automobile accident. As a young, dynamic man of 36, he refused to let the injury keep him from his passions—playing with his 8 year old daughter, flying around the country, and teaching others the joy of soaring through the sky at the controls of their own planes. Losing all that isn't going to happen if he can help it.

David removes the headset and unhooks a cable of wires from a concealed mount on his scalp. Next, he slips the tight-fitting flexible shirt over his head and unwinds sheathes of similar material from his legs. Setting them aside, he transfers from the virtual reality simulator capsule into his wheelchair.

As he waits for Mark to shut down the plane and join him, he ponders the capsule he'd just exited. He is one of the first pilot instructors to certify new pilots using the virtual environment technology. While VEs had been around for a while, creating an entire environment that allows an individual on the ground to completely control a manned aircraft in the air was a bold step. Not only technologically, but for safety and liability reasons.

The complex system provides full sensory and motor interfaces between the plane and the capsule. 360 degree cameras relay the full visual field; microphones and speakers allow communications and engine noise feedback. David can view all the gauges in his simulated cockpit and access every switch and button in the plane. He would never be able to control the plane from the ground without feeling all the vibrations and movements, so sensors transmit everything to the ground capsule. The highly secure and redundant wireless protocol ensures data is transmitted faithfully between the air and ground using a protocol, he muses, which does not suffer from "dropped calls."

During the flight, the capsule cockpit and the data cable running to the implant in his brain floods his senses and simultaneously records his motions for complete immersion in the flying plane. Because David has no use of his legs but must still control the plane's rudder pedals, the simulator is unable to gather the necessary control information from muscles and nerves in his legs that it would acquire from an able-bodied occupant. Instead, these commands are intercepted by a tiny implant overlaying the motor and sensory portions of brain. He has only to think about applying rudder, and the implant detects his intentions and transmits it to the receiver in the plane itself.

The reality David experiences in the capsule is so realistic that he could almost convince himself that he is flying. He receives full sensory input and can access all the plane's controls. When he pulls back on the yoke, the horizon falls away and he soars into the clouds. Pitching steeping to the left, he sees the ground from the side window and feels his body slide as centripetal acceleration pushes him against the side of the seat. Certainly not as good as his own plane, adapted to his specific needs, but the thrill is still there and the simulator allows him to take off in any type of plane.

< -- break -- >

The sound of Mike opening the door brings David out of his reverie, and seeing the disappointed look on Mike's face, Dave empathizes but steels his expression. Time to instill the reality check, he decides—he's is no pushover, no easy instructor. "Nearly an emergency—not good." Pause. "Okay, let's review what happened step-by-step." David walks Mike through the flight, focusing on the exact state of the plane when

Mike started to lose control. "I know what I did wrong," Mike admits. "Thanks for taking over. You're a great instructor to let me get into that much trouble before saving my butt just to teach me the tough stuff." David relaxes his expression and nods at the compliment. "There's no better way to learn. You might still have recovered when I took over, but it's important you realize you should have anticipated the danger much earlier than you did." Seeing Mike's frustration with his performance, David gestures to the VE capsule. "So here's what we're going to do. Since the capsule recorded the entire flight, I'll put it in playback mode for "able-bodied pilot" and you'll try again under exactly the same conditions." He motions to the door with a disarming smile, "Strap in. I think this time you'll recover just fine."

< -- break -- >

"Come on Dad, we're gonna be late!" Jessica pleads, poking her head out the door for the third time. "They're gonna start without us!" David wheels around the corner and kisses her head, smiling at her excitement. "Okay, let's go, we're fine." Jessica settles snugly in her seat and shouts, "UAC on!" Before them the home's Universal Access Center system activates and a holographic screen shimmers into view. Three dimensional icons spin in circles and Jessica reaches out as they spin by—*Music . TV . Interactive Games . Video phone . Sports and Exercise . Internet Surfer .* " before tapping on the last one, *Events*. The screen clears and four new icons appear. Quickly, she locates *Andreo's Birthday Party*.

"Before we go, I want to change clothes," she announces, and shouts again at the UAC, "Jessica's avatars!" 17 different clothed and accessorized versions of Jessica filled the screen and she quickly taps one. "You get dressed too, but fast, Daddy!" David laughs and accesses his own avatars, scrolling past business suits and selecting himself casually dressed. He also selects himself standing. It wasn't a good day to restrict himself to the chair, he thinks; not for an event like a birthday party. Each pulls on smooth-fitting elastic caps and then allows the comfortable chairs to snug a thin layer of whispery fabric over each arm and leg. "UAC, let's go!"

The screen fades and a three-dimensional world appears around them. Jessica checks herself once last time as David rings the doorbell—she decides the pretty pink top and blue shorts fit just right. "Come in," a young woman opens the door and welcomes them into a large room festooned with balloons and decorations. With a quick "Hi Mrs. Riley!" Jessica is off to join her friends collecting around the presents. David rolls his eyes, "Hi Claire, I see the sugar high has already begun." Claire laughs and nods in agreement. "I'll regret it tonight, but Andreo is in heaven with all the excitement!" David strolls over beside her to join a collection of parents. After a time, conversation pauses as Andreo speeds around the room shouting, "Time for the Bouncing Room!" David has little time to react before Jessica is again tugging on his arm for attention. In the back yard, he notices a large inflatable tent. Kids are ripping off shoes to crawl inside the front flap, and several adults are following them. Claire smiles on her way out, "Join us, David. After all, it's about time us adults got to play in these things again." "I have no choice," he laughs, trying to raise the hand entrapped within his daughter's. Then quickly dragged outside, he stoops to remove his shoes as well.

Inside the inflatable, adults bounce and laugh as children leap up to tap the ceiling. Andreo takes a running bounce off a side wall and speeds towards the other wall, nearly missing another child hovering 8 feet off the ground. David marvels; the air is full of spinning, bouncing, hovering and laughing parents and children. While recording/ translating neural and muscular control necessary for completely fluid of human gait and movement in the real world, the UAC can translate the signals from the chair with enough information to make this holographic representation nearly perfect. Plus, it allows them all to repeal the laws of gravity! How free this is, he muses, as he crawls into the inflatable behind his daughter. Inside, he sneaks up behind Jessica, encircles her waist from behind and launches straight up with her screaming in surprise. They speed directly into the ceiling and land with a smack against the flexible material. Laughing, they flip upside down and run across the top and all the way down the side walls. David chases his daughter around the enclosure to her excited squeals of delight and marvels at the freedom everyone can share, with their physical bodies so many miles apart. He might have mused on the simple ability to run and play with his daughter as well.

After ice cream and cake are finished and presents opened, the party comes to an end and goodbyes are shared around. Outside on the front walk, small groups of people begin blinking out of sight as they head home.

Instantly back in the UAC room, David and Jessica collapse on the couch as she babbles on how much fun the party was. She pleads for the mile-high water slide with upside down loop-de-loops that Andreo told her about. "Please Dad? For my birthday? It would be SO much fun! The UAC can even make the weather outside warm enough for swimming!" David lets out a mock groan and hugs his special girl, "Let's talk about it tomorrow." With a deep sigh, he debates the merit of the total reality the UAC provides. While it does a terrific job of translating neural and muscular signals into physical intent and movement, the consequences of those actions cannot be denied. "Tomorrow, sweetie. My legs are throbbing from all that jumping and I just want to watch some TV, okay?"

< -- break -- >

David is awake early the next morning, rubbing his legs, knowing that the morning exercise will do him good. After much needed coffee, he wheels back into the UAC room and launches the menu, this time selecting *Sports and Exercise* and then *David's Morning Routine*. Rather than the thin suit for activities like the party, he pulls on a thicker, more reinforced skin suit used for actual physical movements. After positioning himself prone on a floor matt, he gives the UAC the go-ahead.

The gentle beat of his warm up music begins and the room fades away. David finds himself on a mountain top in the Midwest; the rust colored ground is barely lit as the sun first peeks over the horizon. His brain interface allows him to feel both the calming warm breeze and the stiffness in his legs. Unlike the party yesterday, this program requires that he move his legs to stretch the muscles for flexibility and increased blood flow. Sitting in his chair too long will cause pressure sores that can quickly become infected. His sadness at Christopher Reeve's death as a result of these stupid sores gives him the incentive to exercise every day.

David begins, trying to move his right leg. The UAC searches for any minute electrical activity in the leg and also for movement intent in his brain, and uses these inputs to control the slow stretching regime. At the same time he struggles with the exercise, David tries to distract himself with the sunrise. Flying his plane in the morning brings him the same calmness and appreciation of life as the mountain top sunrise, and he makes a mental note to check the weather for a flight next Saturday. With his warm-up complete, he next places his feet on a metal plate that provides programmed resistance, and he tries to push against the plate. This time, the UAC translates the mental commands to move his legs into neural control signals that contract his muscles. While the plate doesn't move, it is just as important that he can push isometrically. It's unlikely he'll regain the use of his legs during his lifetime, but this exercise reduces muscle wasting and loss of minerals in his bones. That's all he needs, to break a bone in real life while wrestling with his daughter in the virtual world. But perhaps it would be a small price to pay for the privilege of following her down the mile-high water slide. With the routine over, David transfers back to his chair and heads out to take a real-life shower before dressing for work. Kissing Jessica as she leaves for school, he gets into his car and heads to the airport.

Just the start of another regular day.

Part II: The Technology

The current scenario offers a glimpse into a possible future for individuals with disabilities. The scenario depicts the extension of current technologies that if developed, could offer a new way of life for these individuals. These technologies would offer individuals the opportunity to enhance their daily lives and engage in common everyday activities that are currently hindered by their disability. The key concept is that these technologies offer the opportunity to be a part of the general public and minimize the effects of their disability. If you can image a world that is technologically savvy and accepting, then the opportunity for individuals with disabilities to use these technologies and to engage in everyday common activities is both highly desirable and also achievable.

The key technologies highlighted in this scenario include telemedicine/ telerehabilitation, virtual reality simulation and avatars, and brain computer interface. A brief review of the current state of these technologies is presented below.

Telemedicine/Telerehabilitation

In the last decade the field of telemedicine and/or telerehabilitation has grown into a fertile substrate for innovative approaches to fulfill clinical needs. Telemedicine can be defined as the use of medical information exchanged from one site to another via electronic communications, information technology and telecommunications, for the health and education of the patient or healthcare provider and for the purpose of improving patient care (Schultheis and Rizzo 2006). Telerehabilitation, a specific application of telemedicine represents the use of information technology for the remote delivery of rehabilitation medical services and support for independent living

(Rosen 2004). To some, the concept of telerehabilitation denotes complex high-tech devices, such as intelligent therapeutic robots that are supervised from afar, while to others the use of simpler devices, such as a telephone can serve to deliver telerehabilitative services. Regardless of the method, to many telerehabilitation brings the hope of enabling access for all, and could help address societal challenges in the delivery of rehabilitative services once barriers such as distance and reimbursement are overcome (Winters 2002)

Telerehabilitation systems can be designed so that they are either clinic-based or home-based (Rosen 1999). For clinic-based design, a therapist assistant at a remote clinic environment is supervised by a therapist expert at a tertiary care setting. In home-based designs, instead, the patient trains directly at home under the coaching of a remote therapist from the clinic (Deutsch et al. 2007). The most common methods used for telerehabilitation have been video- or tele-conferencing often delivered via the internet or World Wide Web.

If properly planned and designed, a telerehabilitation system can certainly widen the horizons of health care services that are currently provided and pave the way to new initiatives. In particular, telerehabilitation systems can help address the problem of providing adequate health care services to individuals living in rural areas or sparsely populated regions, where health care facilities and trained personnel are significantly less available. Because telerehabilitation can help minimize the barrier of distance, it represents a viable means for the delivery of therapeutic services to such patients. The services provided through telerehabilitation often include monitoring of the patient's status, consultations, therapeutic intervention, and follow-up care. More rarely but on the horizon, telerehabilitation is allowing diagnosis and preventative services (Scheideman-Miller et al. 2003).

To date, telerehabilitation has been examined with a variety of clinical rehabilitation populations. For example, a handful of studies have been conducted with patients with spinal cord injury to examine the use of telerehabiliation to reduced pressure soars (Vesmarovich et al. 1999) and the management of autonomic dysreflexia, a complication of SCI that may put patients at risk of serious morbidity and even death (Lapierre et al. 2006). The largest study conducted to date (Phillips et al. 2001) is based on 111 subjects who were randomized to video-based intervention for 9 weeks, telephone-based intervention for 9 weeks, or standard care, and followed for at least 1 year to monitor hospitalization days, depressive symptoms, and health-related quality of life. The findings indicated that telephone or video-based support was associated with a lower number of mean annual hospitalization days than standard care, but no clear evidence was found on differential functional improvement across the groups.

Telemedicine/telerehabilitation has also been successfully employed to address cognitive and behavioral issues. For example, telerehabilitation has been shown to improve cognitive status, treatment compliance, and stability of chronic disease for homebound elderly persons with common complex comorbidities (Cobb et al. 2003). Another study examined feasibility, acceptability, and clinical outcome of a cognitive intervention program designed to improve memory in older patients with mild cognitive impairment and mild dementia using telemedicine versus a conventional face-to-face method (Poon et al. 2005). Specifically, participants were administered a total of 12 sessions of assessment and cognitive interventions conducted via videoconferencing or by face-to-face. The results indicated significant and comparable cognitive improvement in participants in both treatment arms. In addition the videoconference arm was highly accepted by the participants and overall compliance rate of participants was above 95 percent (Poon et al. 2005). Similar findings were reported in a study examining the delivery of psychotherapy related to brain injury or stroke recovery via videoconferencing for therapy (Schopp et al. 2000).

Traditionally, telerehabilitation has been administered through video- or tele-conferencing but this approach has been significantly enhanced by the introduction of smart sensors which can provide additional data to therapists and feedback to patients. One example of this can be found in the use of data gloves, which have been proposed to provide automatic measurements of finger and joint position during different activities. In telerehabilitation, a data glove can serve to objectively record hand and finger movements of individuals with deficits resulting from stroke, hand surgery or other types of disorders. Specifically, data gloves are glove-like devices that are able to capture information about the hand motion and gestures and automatically relay that information via a computer to a therapist. Such information is obtained through a variety of sensors that can capture the hand trajectory and joint angle data. Examples of these devices are the Power Glove by NES, the P5 Glove by Essential Reality or the CyberGlove II by Immersion and more recently the Shadow Glove Monitor. In general the use of these sensors serves to provide specific information about the individuals' performance related to the hand or fingers, but most importantly records this information during functionally relevant everyday activities in the comfort of the patient's home.

As technology continues to develop new opportunities for expanding telemedicine and telerehabilitation continue to evolve. However, the design of a telerehabilitation system needs to take into consideration the human factors involved in it. So far, both the medical community, and patients and caregivers have had very little exposure to telerehabilitation systems. Proper user acceptance and satisfaction still remains one of the major challenges for the success of such systems. Additionally, technology used in a telerehabilitation system must be geared towards fulfilling the specific clinical needs of the providers and the capabilities of end-users at the same time (Shannon et al. 2002).

Virtual Reality Technology

Virtual reality (VR) can be viewed as an advanced form of human-computer interface that allows the user to "interact" with, and become "immersed" within a computer generated virtual environments in a more intuitive and naturalistic fashion (Schultheis and Rizzo 2001). VR environments are complex systems that emerge from the integration of real-time computer graphics and a variety of sensory devices which can include head-mounted displays (HMDs), tracking systems, gesture-sensing gloves and haptic-feedback devices. The degree and effectiveness of this "immersion" includes the rendering of the virtual environment, the spatial multisensory interface, and the space and time mapping or the creation of the simulation. Different incarnations of VR systems exist, which allow different degrees of embedding the physical reality into the virtual world.

VR outputs: In order to reach the degree of complexity needed for VR systems to be functional, specific technologies are necessary at both the output and input level. In terms of output devices, their task is to transform the internal state of the virtual environment into actual human perceivable sensual experiences as light, pressure, and force.

Most of the current technology concentrates on visual and audio outputs. Audio output devices can range from stereo speaker systems to surround systems to speaker arrays. There is also a variety of available visual display devices, each with its own strengths and limitations. Stereoscopic glasses, for example, are relatively low in cost but have a limited field of view and resolution. Head Mounted Dislays (HMDs) have overcome some of these limitations but are more expensive and heavy. Stereoscopic displays have also been developed for 3D vision if used in combination with specially designed glassed. There are also VR "domes" for immersive viewing, able to arrange from one up to 5 people. An example of multi-user device that includes both visual and audio channels is instead the well-known CAVE (Cave Automatic Virtual Environment). In the CAVE the user in a cube completely surrounded with rear-projection screens (with the exception of the floor, which is a down-projection screen); the user is also provided with stereoscopic glasses, head and hand tracking systems and audio feedback.

Avatar and human representation in VR: As computing power continues to increase, the opportunity to populate these virtual environments increases. In some VR systems, users can view their own actions reflected in an *avatar,* which is a virtual representation of the self in a given environment. To date, the level of detail of such avatars has been relatively low and not apt to convey facial expressions, eye gaze or body language.

In terms of behavior, realistic rendering of movement is most commonly obtained through the placement of multiple motion sensors that capture the user movements, which can then be recorded and displayed via the avatar. But challenges remain in improving avatar expressiveness which can directly affect communicative possibilities (Emering et al. 1998, Garau et al. 2003, Kolko 1999, Kshirsagar et al. 2002, Tamagawa et al. 2001).

Despite these limitations, avatars have been successfully integrated into training modules. For example, the MediSim system extends virtual environments (both local and network) to represent simulated medical personnel interacting with simulated casualties. This technology fosters dual-use applications involving planning, training, and evaluation of both medical corpsmen and civilian EMTs (Badler et al. 1995). More recently, new simulation worlds, such as Second Life, have demonstrated additional benefits to the use of avatars, by creating entire "worlds" of individuals and environments. These avatars may not require the level of detail to convey emotion and communication, but in the context of virtual environments, avatars can serve to create a "social framework" that can offer new interactive opportunities for individuals with disabilities.

VR rehabilitation application: To date, a considerable amount of research using VR for the study, assessment and rehabilitation of human cognitive and functional processes have been generated. These have included environments that allow individuals to simulate and rehabilitate everyday functions, such as cooking (Christiansen et al. 1998), learning to cross the street (McComas et al. 1998), improve their memory

(Pugnetti et al. 1998), and drive a car (Schultheis et al. 2001). The findings to date support the notion that VR could serve to advance the study of brain/behavior relationships as well as produce innovative evaluation and intervention options that are unavailable with traditional methods.

VR technology also offers the exciting perspective of facilitating physically-impaired individuals in performing tasks and having experiences that would otherwise be precluded. For example, VR technology has been used to enhance orthopedic rehabilitation in patients with spinal cord injury (Riva et al. 2001). In this particular application, a rigid exoskeleton was designed to support the trunk and allowed the individual to simulate ambulation in various environments. In summary, by capitalizing on an individuals' residual strengths (either motor or cognitively), VR technology can offer a mechanism for interfacing with a computer, which in turn could provide increased access to daily activities (Greenleaf 1998).

A basic VR system adapted for motor rehabilitation could be envisioned as a system that allows users to map custom-tailored gestures to pre-specified actions. These actions could be as simple as clicking a mouse button or as complicated as controlling a robotic arm (Greenleaf 1998). For example, one combination that has been explored is the use of a data glove, a haptic system and a sensory feedback system that produces feeling in the fingers when "touching" an object in a virtual environment in order to rehabilitate damaged hand mobility or to diagnose a range of hand problems (Burdea et al. 2002).

From a historic perspective, stroke rehabilitation has been one of the earliest and most effective applications of VR. This is because the rehabilitation of impaired motors skills is built on the concept that the amount of training and physical therapy sessions received by a stroke patient plays a major role in relearning those skills. In particular by integration both VR and telerehabilitation methods, this area of rehabilitation has developed home-based systems that offer the advantage of providing more intense therapy than would be possible in a hospital setting and, if enhanced by VR, could be even more effective and motivating (Cameirao et al. 2007, Dreifaldt et al. 2007, Jack et al. 2001). One example is the Remote Console (ReCon) developed at the University of Medicine and Dentistry of New Jersey and used for the rehabilitation and training of the ankle in post-stroke patients (Deutsch et al. 2007, Lewis et al. 2006). It includes a 3D real-time representation of the patient's movement available to the remote therapist, performance monitoring and adjustable VR-based exercises. These exercises include piloting a plane or sailing a boat, with and without haptic feedback. Other examples of current, VR-based exercises include, reaching (Cameirao et al. 2007) and grasping tasks, pick-and-place tasks, modified versions of standard videogames (for example Tetris, where arm motion is used to rotate and move the incoming blocks (Kizony et al. 2006) or virtual table tennis.

In summary, there is growing knowledge of the use of both telerehabilitation and virtual reality technologies to provide unique advantages for the continued care of rehabilitation clinical populations. These technologies offer patient's an opportunity to conduct their rehabilitation in the comfort of their own home and in functionally relevant tasks (not artificially derived tasks in the hospital setting). In additional these technologies can increases the patient's autonomy during therapy, decreasing the need for constant surveillance and collect quantitative data about the therapy progress itself.

All of these advantages can help to extend support and healthcare beyond the boundaries of a hospital and can also help individuals with disabilities engage in common activities along with the rest of the population.

Brain Machine Interfaces (BMI)

The term *brain-machine interface (BMI)* generally refers to a system that acquires signals from a subject's brain and uses them to control an external device (*actuator*). BMIs constructs are in fact a very prominent line of research in neuroprosthetics. They aim to provide an alternative means of interaction with the surrounding environment for individuals who have lost the functional integrity of the connection between neural/neuromuscular structures. Such disabilities could result from spinal cord injuries, strokes, developmental or neurodegenerative diseases.

Brain signals used in BMIs: The signals used to control the artificial device can be electrophysiological, magnetic or metabolic and can be recorded through methods that are either invasive or non-invasive. *Invasive technologies* employ electrodes that are implanted intracranially and rely on recording the neurophysiological properties of individual neurons (or ensembles of neurons) to detect changes in their activity in association with specific events (e.g., movements). Depending on the specific kind of electrodes, they can record the activity of multiple single neurons or integrated activity of larger networks through local field potentials (LFPs). A BMI can include a single recording site, thus obtaining only specialized information from a single cortical area, or can have multiple recording sites; this second option provides simultaneous access to many cortical areas, thus accounting for the distributed information processing in the brain, but is more technically challenging. Although the invasive approach in BMI carries implicit risks associated with the surgical procedure required for implanting the recording electrodes, it provides a rather robust signal. One major disadvantage is that this approach requires long-term implants (several years) but the current technologies are able to provide only a limited recording longevity (months) (Lebedev and Nicolelis 2006). Wide research has been done towards this goal, leading also to some prototypes that are currently seeking FDA approval. As an example, the Neurotrophic Electrode (Baker 2008) combines the recording wires (that have wireless capability) with a mix of nerve growth factors promoting the growth of new neurons that would hold the device in place and provide a better contact. Another well known system used in invasive BMIs is the BrainGate Neural Interface System which consists of a chip carrying 100 microelectrodes implanted in the motor cortex; the recorded signals are then used to control computer software or other objects.

Non-invasive technologies, instead, are based on signals recorded from the head surface and primarily use electroencephalograms (EEG). BMIs that are based on EEG aim at deciphering the subject's intentions or decision based on the combined electrical activity of large neural populations; this results in a more limited spatial and temporal resolution of events. Additionally, EEG recordings are susceptible to a variety of electrical artifacts that can heavily deteriorate the signals. Other incarnations of non-invasive BMIs include the use of imaging technologies such as functional magnetic resonance imaging (fMRI) and functional near-infrared spectroscopy (fNIRS). These imaging modalities capture the metabolic and hemodynamic activity associated with electrical activation in a neural population. Compared with EEG-based BMIs, these systems have a lower time resolution, linked to the physiological time delay between the electrical and hemodynamic/metabolic activations. However, they offer information about the spatial localization of the activity of interest. Generally speaking, non-invasive BMIs have the advantage of not requiring the surgical implantation of the recording electrodes. However, they are only able to provide more limited communication capabilities: at present, in fact, they are generally constrained to binary selections, such preventing them from being used in motor applications. Additionally, long training periods are required before the subjects are able to select, with reasonably low error rates, the desired outputs.

Information extraction in BMIs: The signals recorded from the subject's brain, either invasively or non-invasively, need to be properly manipulated in order to extract from them the features of interest that encode the user's intentions in the signal. Generally speaking, these features are in association with identifiable electrophysiological events like the firing of a specific neuron or the synchronized and modulated activation of a neural population (Wolpaw et al. 2002). Although the current knowledge in the neuroscience field is far from providing a clear understanding of how motor and cognitive information is represented population of neurons and different encoding strategies have been suggested, a precise knowledge of this is not necessarily crucial for the creation of clinically relevant BMIs (Lebedev and Nicolelis 2006). Mostly, BMI systems predict the characteristics of interest in the subject's command based on the signal patterns.

The majority of BMIs based on single or multiple neuron signals extract task-relevant information from the modulation of the neuron firing rate and the correlation between neurons in the considered population. Typically, a model is created based on repeated trials of the same pre-specified set of tasks in order to define the response characteristics of the single neurons/ensemble. After sufficient training of this model, the subsequent incoming neural signals are interpreted to match the previously learned characteristics. In the case of LPF- or EEG-based BMIs, instead, the user undergoes a training period in order to optimize his or her ability to use it (Patil and Turner 2008).

Actuators: The aim of BMI systems is to use the information obtained from a subject's brain in order to control an external device, the actuator, which will *actuate* the subject intention or decision. The vast majority of the current systems use a computer screen as actuator and the output is, for example, the selection of targets presented on it or the movement of a cursor. Other output devices include switches, wheelchairs, prosthetic limbs or other neuroprostheses in a more general sense. The operating protocol governing the BMI defines how the user can turn on or off the system, whether communication between the system and the actuator is continuous or discontinuous and if the communication is triggered by the system or by the user. The operation protocol also sets speed of interactions between user and system and determines what feedback (if any) needs to be provided to the user. At the current state of the art most prototypes do not allow the user any on/off control on the system and in common tasks designs the user is explicitly asked to try and communicate a specific intention or decision using the BMI. It is therefore reasonable to expect that such differences in protocol could complicate the transition of the current BMIs from bench to bedside. Additionally, the design of the actuator itself plays a major role in determining the information content needed in the recorded signal in order to drive the execution of an intentional action. For example, although robotic arms exist, with varying degree of similarity to the natural limb, they require the BMI to be able to differentiate between a variety of activation patterns encoding for different movements, speeds, relative angles between the arm components. Therefore, one of the greatest challenges in BMI research is the design of a communication channel from the brain to the actuators with sufficiently wide information bandwidth to allow for useful function of the neuroprosthetic device (Patil and Turner 2008).

The last years have seen great advances in the field, thanks also to the commitment of governmental agencies such as NIH or DARPA (mainly through its "Human-Assisted Neural Devices" and "Revolutionizing Prosthetics" programs). Nonetheless a long way is still ahead before fully functional interfaces between the human brain and external devices are available. Many scientists have instead been pursuing a probably less challenging incarnation of BMIs, where the actuator consists of a computer that produces a virtual output. Some research has in fact been done in order to offer some brain-directed control over web browsers and other connected applications such as e-mail or virtual keyboards (Bensch et al. 2007).

This line of research melds with the studies done in the field of computer gaming and virtual reality. Rather renowned prototypes in this field are EEG-based NeuroSky headset and the EEG system developed by Emotiv Systems (Greene 2007, Singer 2008). The objective of this last one would be to use the electrical signals produced by the player's brain to control the video game environment. It comprises three modules with different alleged capabilities: the first module senses facial expressions such as slimes or winks and is able to transfer them to an avatar; the second module detects two possible emotional states, defined as "excitement" and "calm"; and the module captures a few intentions, such as lifting an object or pushing it. Nonetheless, skepticism still exists about the actual performance of similar devices. The EEG signal is in fact extremely prone to a variety of noise source even in laboratory setups, in which conductive gel is used to ensure a good coupling between the sensors and the scalp, external electrical noise is kept to a minimum and the subject is instructed to minimize movements, conditions not necessarily true in a gaming scenario.

Part III: What is Needed in the Future?

The challenge of extending the current state of these technologies to deliver on the vision of creating a world where simulation can enhance an individual's life is not insurmountable. If you can image a world that is technologically savvy and accepting, then the opportunity for individuals with disabilities to use these technologies and to engage in everyday common activities is both highly desirable and also achievable. These technologies could offer individuals with disabilities the opportunity to enhance their daily lives and an opportunity to be a part of the general public and minimize the effects of their disability.

The development of these technologies is well-underway and their potential is currently only limited by future research that will address the key areas necessary for successful integration. A brief discussion of key areas that will facilitate continued evolution of these technologies is presented here.

Human Factors—Clinical Design

As technologies are developed a common stage in development is user-design feedback or evaluation of human factors. By definition, this stage usually entails obtaining input and feedback from potential users of the developing technology. Feedback can be obtained on a variety of aspects, including overall design, usability of the system/technology, user comfort, ease of use, reliability of the system, robustness of the system, etc. The goal being that this input/feedback from the end-user can be integrated during development to generate an overall user-accepted system/technology. In most cases, these studies or evaluations are conducted with individuals without disability. Surprisingly this is often true, even when technologies are designed to target clinical populations or individuals with disabilities. Research that will directly solicit and incorporate the input and feedback of individuals with disabilities is a critical area of further development.

Some models such as, Participatory Action Research (PAR) (Turnell et al. 1998) have been proposed for rehabilitation research and have been supported by federal research funding agencies, such as National Institute on Disability and Rehabilitation Research (NIDRR). PAR is a collaborative process between researchers and the people who are expected to benefit from the research, including family members of people with disabilities. Families are stakeholders of the PAR research along with the researchers. To date, the application of these methods to actual technologies designs has remained limited.

Multi-Disciplinary Research

Successful development of technologies can only come from teams of experts bringing forth their individuals strengths to address the many aspects of successful development and integration of any new device. Evidence indicates that multidisciplinary research works best when scientists and clinicians from different research backgrounds are able to work together free from discipline or structural barriers. As such, supporting research that integrates various disciplines in the development of these future systems/technologies will be critical. Expertise from a broad range of areas can be included in this, including various branches of engineering, information systems, computer science, human factors, psychology and clinicians. The latter is a critical component to successful research, in order to help early identification of the medical needs of individuals with disabilities.

Development Outside of the Laboratory

To successfully create technologies that can assist individuals in their homes or in their workplaces, the next level of technologies must be robust enough to survive in the "real world". As such, research that will look towards developing portable and rugged system becomes an important need. If these technologies are truly designed to be integrated into an individuals' environment, and not limited to the hospital, then key issues such as size, robustness, and ruggedness will need consideration. While, technologies for home use may be on the horizon, if these system are too fragile they will not be able to endure the proposed greater use that will come from having accessibility at home.

In addition to this, issues of reliability and validity of the system/technologies need to be established to help define these systems as true clinical tools. Specifically, if these systems will serve to collect relevant clinical data that will be used for treatment decision making, then research that ensures that data collected is both relevant and reliable will have to be conducted. Too often, the attractiveness of developing new technologies can cloud the way for development of truly validated clinical tools.

Development of Accessible and Available Technologies

As new technologies continue to play a larger role in our society, a key concern is the potential for a "digital division". That is, those that can afford the newest and latest technologies will greatly benefit, while those that do not have the resources to afford these systems will be left behind; subsequently creating a large gap between the two groups. Although, such a harsh prediction may not come to fruition, there is great benefit to the development of future technologies that are both accessible to individuals with disabilities, as well as affordable.

With this, also comes the consideration for the overall generalizability of the tool. That is, if a system or technology only addresses specific or unique need, the overall application of that system will be limited. There are many common themes that cut across the various rehabilitation populations, and future research that looks to develop systems/technologies that cut across those themes, as compared to focusing only on one diagnosis can help provide options for a greater number of individuals and move the translation of research to application at a quicker pace.

Social Acceptance of Technologies

A final area of consideration for future research is in the overall social studies of acceptance of technologies. A key question that will have to be examined is what makes a technology socially acceptable. This will be critical to meet the overall goal of using these systems to help individuals with disabilities overcome their limitations and be part of the general public. Existing models, such as the Technology Acceptance Model (TAM) developed developed by Fred Davis and Richard Bagozzi (Bagozzi et al. 1992, Davis et al. 1989), address areas such as perceived usefulness and perceived ease of use, but additional considerations are needed for developing system for persons with disabilities. For example, in order to minimize potential stigmatism, as technology should be discreet and not draw attention to the user. A technology should also when possible be a common tool—for example, expanding the capacity of existing systems or technologies, such as an entertainment system with new capacities for telerehabilitation.

In conclusion, these areas discussed represent global domains of research that can be integrated in specific research proposals. That is, while each of these technologies, virtual reality, brain-computer-interface, avatars and telemedicine, will continue to be developed at a technical level as new technologies continue to be developed, the application of these systems require a greater consideration. The idea of not developing technologies in isolation but rather within the context of an eye to the future application can greatly increase how quickly these technologies move from the laboratory to becoming a common tool for all individuals.

Acknowledgements

The authors are indebted to the guidance of pilot instructor Matt Minucci and pilot Scott Ducey for their input to this scenario.

References

Baker, S. (2008). "The rise of the cyborgs." [online]. Available at: http://discovermagazine.com/2008/oct/26-rise-of-the-cyborgs

Badler, N.I., Clarke, J.R., Hollick, M.J., Kokkevis, E., Metaxas, D.N., Bindiganavale, R., Webber, B.L., Chi, D.M., Foster, N., Ogunyemi, O., and Kaye, J. (1995). "MediSim: Simulated medical corpsmen and casualties for medical forces planning and training," *Military Telemedicine On-Line Today, Research, Practice, and Opportunities. Proceedings of the National Forum*, pp. 21–28 and 27–29.

Bagozzi, R.P., Davis, F.D., and Warshaw, P.R. (1992). "Development and test of a theory of technological learning and usage". *Human Relations*, 45(7):660–686.

Bensch, M., Karim, A.A. et al. (2007). "Nessi: An EEG-controlled web browser for severely paralyzed patients." *Computational Intelligence and Neuroscience*: 71863.

Burdea, G., J. Zhuang et al. (2002). "A portable dextrous master with force feedback." *Presence: Teleoperators and Virtual Environments* 1(1):18–28.

Cameirao, M., S.B. Badia et al. (2007). "The rehabilitation gaming system: A virtual reality based system for the evaluation and rehabilitation of motor deficits." *Virtual Rehabilitation 2007*. September 27–29, 2007. Venice, Italy.

Davis, F.D. (1989). "Perceived usefulness, perceived ease of use, and user acceptance of information technology". *MIS Quarterly*, 13(3):319–340.

Deutsch, J.E., J.A. Lewis et al. (2007). "Technical and patient performance using a virtual reality-integrated telerehabilitation system: preliminary finding." *IEEE Transactions on Neural Systems and Rehabilitation Engineering* 15(1):30–5.

Dreifaldt, U., D. Goude et al. (2007). "A home-based virtual reality system for stroke rehabilitation." *Virtual Rehabilitation 2007*. September 27–29, 2007. Venice, Italy.

Emering, L. et al. (1998). "Interacting with virtual humans through body actions." *IEEE Journal of Computer Graphics and Applications* 18(1):8–11.

Garau, M., Slater, M. et al. (2003). "The impact of avatar realism and eye gaze control on perceived quality of communication in a shared immersive virtual environment." SIG-*CHI on Human Factors in Computing Systems*. April 5–10, 2003. Ft. Lauderdale, FL.

Greene, K. (2007). "Connecting your brain to the game." [online]. Available at: http://www.technologyreview.com/Biztech/18276/

Greenleaf, W.J. (1998). "Virtual reality applications in medicine." *WESCON'98*. September 15–17, 1998. Anaheim, CA.

Jack, D., Boian, R. et al. (2001). "Virtual reality-enhanced stroke rehabilitation." *IEEE Transactions on Neural Systems and Rehabilitation Engineering* 9(3):308–18.

Kizony, R., Weiss, P.L. et al. (2006). "TheraGame: A home based virtual reality rehabilitation system." *International Journal on Disability and Human Development* 5(3):265–269.

Kobb, N. Hoffman and Lodge, R. (2003) "Enhancing elder chronic care through technology and care coordination: Report from a pilot." *Telemed J E Health* 9:189–195.

Kolko, B.E. (1999). "Representing bodies in virtual space: The rhetoric of avatar design." *The Information Society* 15(3):177–186.

Kshirsagar, S., Magnenat-Thalaman, N. et al. (2002). "Avatar markup language." *8th Eurographic Workshop on Virtual Environments*. May 30–31, 2002. Barcelona, Spain.

Lapierre, N.M. Blackmer, J., Coutu-Wakulczyk and Dehoux, E. (2006). "Autonomic dysreflexia and telehealth." *Can Nurse* 102:20–25.

Lebedev, M.A. and Nicolelis, M.A.L. (2006). "Brain-machine interfaces: past, present and future." *Trends in Neurosciences* 29(9):536–546.

Lewis, J.A., Deutsch, J.E. et al. (2006). "Usability of the remote console for virtual reality telerehabilitation: Formative evaluation." *Cyberpsychology and Behavior*, 9 (2):142–7.

Patil, P.G. and Turner, D.A. (2008). "The Development of Brain-Machine Interface Neuroprosthetic Devices." *Neurotherapeutics* 5(1):137–146.

Poon, P., Hui, E., Dai, D., Kwok, T. and Woo, J. (2005). "Cognitive intervention for community-dwelling older persons with memory problems: Telemedicine versus face-to-face treatment." *Int J Geriatr Psychiatry* 20:285–6.

Phillips,VL,. Vesmarovich, S., Hauber, R., Wiggers, E. and Egner, A. (2001). "Telehealth: reaching out to newly injured spinal cord patients." *Public Health Rep* 116(Suppl 1):94–102.

Riva, G. (2001). "Virtual reality in rehabilitation of spinal cord injuries: A case report." *Rehabilitation Psychology* 45(1):81–88.

Rosen, M. (1999). "Telerehabilitation." *NeuroRehabilitation* 1(12):11–26.

Rosen, M. (2004). *Telemedicine Journal and e-Health* 10(2):115–117.

Scheideman-Miller, C., Clark, P.G. et al. (2003). "Efficacy and sustainability of a telerehabilitation program." *36th Hawaii International Conference on System Sciences*. January 6–9, 2003. Big Island, HW.

Schultheis, M.T. and Mourant, R.R. (2001). "Virtual Reality and Driving: The Road to Better Assessment of Cognitively Impaired Populations." *Presence: Teleoperators and Virtual Environments* 10(4):436–444.

Schultheis, M.T. and Rizzo, A.A. (2001). "The Application of Virtual Reality Technology for Rehabilitation." *Rehabilitation Psychology*, 46(3):1–16.

Schultheis, M.T. and Rizzo, A.A. (2006). "Emerging technologies in Neuropsychological Practice and Research" In Morgan, J. and Ricker, JR (eds) *Handbook of Clinical Neuropsychology*, Swets and Zeitlinger Publishers.

Schopp, L.H., Johnstone, B.R. and Merveille, O.C. (2000). "Multidimensional telecare strategies for rural residents with brain injury." *J Telemed Telecare* 6(Suppl 1): S146–9.

Shannon, G., Nesbitt, T. et al. (2002). "Organizational models of telemedicine and regional telemedicine networks." *Telemedicine Journal and e-Health* 8(1):61–70.

Singer, E. (2008). "Brain Games." [online]. Available at: https://www.technologyreview.com/biomedicine/20944/

Tamagawa, K., Yamada, T. et al. (2001). "Developing a 2.5-D video avatar." *IEEE Signal Processing Magazine* May 2001.

Turnbull, A.P., Friesen, B.J., and Ramirez, C. (1998). "Participatory action research as a model for conducting family research." *Journal of The Association for Persons with Severe Handicaps*, 23(3):178–188.

Vesmarovich, S., Walker, T., Hauber, RP. Temkin, A. and Burns, R. (1999). "Use of telerehabilitation to manage pressure ulcers in persons with spinal cord injuries." *Adv Wound Care* 12:264–269.

Winters, J. (2002). "Telerehabilitation Reserach: Emerging Opportunities." *Annu. Rev. Biomed. Eng.* 4:287–320.

Wolpaw, J. R., Birbaumer, N. et al. (2002). "Brain-computer interfaces for communication and control." *Clin Neurophysiol* 113(6):767–91.

Chapter 15
Use of a Synthetic World for Negotiation and Consensus Building

Diana Burley

Abstract

Today's global economic environment requires that organizations operate across geographic, national, and cultural boundaries. The resulting distributed work environments exacerbate the already difficult process of negotiation and consensus building and necessitate the use of electronic negotiation tools that facilitate the negotiation process. Electronic negotiation tools are computationally based software applications that link a diverse set of users and allow them to engage in complicated negotiation tasks.

Although sufficient for basic consensus building and negotiations, today's tools neither exploit the opportunities afforded by the increasing availability of high performance computing nor adequately address the organizational challenges presented by a global economy that is increasingly interconnected, time sensitive and digitally dependent. As we move toward the year 2025, the dynamic global environment necessitates the use of more sophisticated electronic negotiation tools where users are able to virtually engage and make use of advanced computing capabilities. This chapter explores the role of a synthetic world for virtual negotiation and consensus building through the scenario of Black Gold, a Texas-based international oil conglomerate negotiation of its Nigerian oil production schedule in the year 2025.

Introduction: Negotiation in 2025

It's Tuesday morning and Patrick Lynndoll, the lead negotiator for Black Gold (BG) Oil, has four weeks to get an agreement signed by the major parties on BG's Nigerian oil production schedule. The operating environment is volatile, dynamic, and often hostile; and BG Oil executives are growing increasingly concerned about Lynndoll's ability to negotiate an agreement that is both profitable and feasible (operationally, politically and culturally). They've been down this road before. Eight months ago BG Oil tried to negotiate a new Nigerian production agreement only to have negotiations stall at the last minute due to several unresolved conflicts between the Nigerian and US governments, local labor representatives, and Earth Action, a major environmental group. The previous negotiation required a significant amount of travel and was held primarily through face-to-face meetings in a variety of locations including London, New York, and Port Harcourt—the major trade center in Nigeria.

To support their efforts eight months ago, BG Oil used a variety of electronic negotiation tools to aid in communication, analyses, and other basic negotiation tasks. Lynndoll believes that the tools helped with the negotiation process. However, he also believes that BG Oil could have used the tools more effectively to address the challenges of a negotiating environment characterized by rapid change, internal and external parties separated by time and space, cultural differences, public pressure, and a host of other issues. Accordingly, Lynndoll has decided to move forward using a more technologically advanced approach and has decided to shift many of the negotiation activities into a synthetic negotiation environment. He hopes that the combined use of face-to-face discussions, traditional electronic tools, and *eNCB*, a synthetic world built specifically for negotiation and consensus building, will further enhance the negotiation process and ultimately help BG Oil achieve a successful result.

Lynndoll enters his New York BG Oil office, sits down at his desk, and logs into *eNCB*. His jaw is tight as he prepares for the continuation of what has proven to be a very intense negotiation. Represented by his avatar, Lynndoll has a full range of electronic negotiation tools at his disposal as he makes the rounds in *eNCB*. Seamlessly moving between conversations with the key negotiating parties, Lynndoll adjusts his avatar's image to suit the interaction.

With his corporate bosses, Lynndoll's clean-shaven Caucasian avatar is conservatively attired in a dark suit. As he intently listens to corporate analyst projections his avatar removes his suit coat and rolls up his sleeves. With Nigerian government officials, Lynndoll's avatar is remarkably different. He now appears as a well-dressed Nigerian man, with mannerisms to match and speaking in English with a Yoruban accent. At the virtual US State Department Lynndoll converts his avatar's appearance again. Now he presents himself as Jasmine Kim—a smartly dressed, engaging woman with great diplomatic skills and fluency in several languages. Throughout the weeks, Lynndoll's avatar repeats this metamorphosis many times; strategically adjusting his appearance to reduce the impact of any socially-based conflict. All of the avatars in *eNCB* are equipped with this same capability. In addition, they have decision-making tools, artificial intelligence-based learning capabilities, and negotiation software agents that allow them to contribute to the discussion from their respective stakeholders' points of view.

At 7:00 am Lynndoll finds himself in the midst of chaos as he reviews the status of the internal discussions held overnight. Since BG Oil officials are located around the globe in Texas, New York, London, and Nigeria; the internal debates have been going on all night. Throughout the debate period, avatars stand in for their stakeholders as necessary in order to keep the discussions moving forward. Though relatively independent for short periods of time, the avatars' actions must periodically be reviewed and confirmed by their stakeholders. Consequently, immediately upon their return to *eNCB*, stakeholders review negotiation status with the electronic negotiation tools that constantly monitor all of the proceedings. As Lynndoll assesses the status of the internal negotiations, his avatar is surrounded by an assortment of other avatars representing various BG Oil stakeholders. They have been working to prioritize BG Oil's negotiation goals and are still debating the relative merits of several production scenarios.

Max Henry, the CFO whose avatar has a face that looks like something between a pitbull and a hound dog, is engaged in a war of words with the head of Public and Governmental Relations, Bruce Oscar. "Production levels cannot decline! Even if we adjust production down only slightly (~.25 percent), we'll have to layoff at least 3 percent of our US workforce in the next 9 months." Oscar's avatar is small and unassuming except for an unusually large head that he believes illustrates his intellectual prowess. "Nonsense, you're missing the big picture and your short-term view will cost us more in the long run! A slight decrease in pipeline activity will help us avoid a PR nightmare instigated by that zealous environmental group—one that will most certainly cost us even more job and revenue losses across our worldwide operations." It is noon in London, where Henry is currently based. Oscar is in Nigeria where it is now 1:00 pm and he has been working to convince Henry for more than 6 hours. Using his avatar's analytical capabilities to quickly counter Henry's purely financial argument, Oscar is finally making progress.

The avatars of the other BG Oil VPs join in on the discussion. Each avatar is arguing his or her point, and displaying data to support their stance on the walls of the BG Oil virtual office. The walls act as virtual white boards and can be updated, reorganized, and replicated as necessary. Data is flowing fast. As the details of each scenario are displayed, Lynndoll's avatar steps through the simulated outcome and uses electronic negotiation tools to immediately assimilate the information and analyze the impact of even small changes to production volume.

Suddenly, Lynndoll hears his assistant running down the hall. Jade Wilson swiftly enters the office and hands Lynndoll a just released World Health Organization (WHO) report that blames oil-generated environmental pollution in the Niger Delta region for the severe decline in farming and fishing, and the skyrocketing malnourishment rate. The results of this study hit the wires only 5 minutes ago, yet opponents of Nigerian Delta oil drilling and BG Oil already are quoting the results. Lynndoll is necessarily concerned as he knows that a successful negotiation result will require a strong response to this report. He wonders aloud… "What if we institute new environmental precautions? What if we contribute money to regional and/or global environmental organizations? How much could we accelerate production then? .." Clearly the details of the report need to be incorporated into the *eNCB* simulations and Lynndoll asks Wilson to immediately scan the report into *eNCB*. Once the details of the report are entered, the discussions and what-if scenarios continue. Negotiation agent assistants begin to compile and display data based on the WHO report and on the alternative interpretation put forward by the BG Oil analysts. Scenario by scenario Lynndoll's avatar walks through the simulations and is able to immediately witness the potential environmental impact of every decision. The negotiation agent assistants provide subject matter expertise upon which his avatar can base the selection of environmental precautions. Each selection is incorporated into the simulation, considered in context, and then either combined with other actions or discarded. Through these fluid scenarios and equipped with an ever increasing body of knowledge, Lynndoll simultaneously assesses the impact of changes on the achievement of BG Oil priorities and on the perceived interests of the other negotiating parties.

Environmental concerns are only the tip of the iceberg. Lynndoll and his BG Oil colleagues also must discuss a variety of additional issues including; logistics, labor contracts, and waste management. One by one, each issue is discussed among key internal stakeholders using the *eNCB* negotiation support system. Eventually a tentative priority list is put forward to BG Oil management for their consideration. Since his team has made significant progress toward the achievement of an internal agreement and the internal negotiation priorities are now reasonably clear, Lynndoll is ready to engage external parties.

Along with other members of his BG Oil team, Lynndoll negotiates with the external parties through traditional channels (e.g., face-to-face meetings, telephone conferences) and through his avatar in *eNCB*. Within the synthetic environment his avatar virtually travels to other organizations' offices, meets in public spaces, and brings other parties into BG Oil virtual office to discuss scenarios and view simulation results. Moving tactically between private meetings and public forums within *eNCB*, he actively solicits general feedback, monitors group opinion, and shapes the input of other party negotiators.

As challenges to the BG stance are raised, Lynndoll's avatar draws on information provided from subject matter experts, in the form of negotiation agent assistants, and the collective insight gained from the results of the countless simulations. Lynndoll uses the knowledge collected within the *eNCB* environment to work with his colleagues—the actual stakeholders when they are available and through their avatars when they are not—to develop counter arguments, and to shore up in some cases, and adjust in others, the BG Oil stance. As such, the simulation results help to inform his own actions, the decisions of his colleagues, and the opinions of external parties.

When Karl Aidan, the lead negotiator for Earth Action, references the WHO report and demands a stop to drilling, Lynndoll invites him to view simulations in *eNCB* so that he can witness the full impact of a complete halt to regional production in Port Harcourt. Aidan is uptown near the BG Oil office, and since he has never used *eNCB* and doesn't have an avatar of his own, he will stand in the background while Lynndoll logs into the *eNCB* environment. Aidan also wants his assistant, Elaine Jacks, who is still in the Earth Action office, to join him in the simulation viewing. Jacks is a long term Earth Action employee and was a major opponent of the negotiations eight months ago. She is a staunch environmentalist who has never forgiven BG Oil for their role in the 2012 Alaskan oil spill that caused twice the damage of the historic Exxon Valdez spill of 1989. Interestingly, she is also a technology geek. Jacks has her own avatar in *eNCB* and is well versed in both the benefits and the limitations of using a synthetic environment for the negotiation. She is dazzled neither by the *eNCB* environment nor by the advanced technological tools that it contains.

The simulation depicts the following: Within 2 months of a complete production stoppage, the Nigerian Delta region experiences a severe and immediate reversal to regional economic development initiatives, infrastructure improvements, and an exponential increase in unemployment. Within 6 months, poverty rates double, and within 1 year famine spreads across the western portion of the Nigerian Delta region.

At the BG office, Aidan is astonished and is rethinking his stance. He calls Jacks on his cellphone. "This simulation is compelling. Given these results, I think a halt to the drilling will hurt more than help. It will cause serious harm to those we are trying to protect. Perhaps we need to back off our stance." Jacks tells Aidan to take a deep breath and hold on. She is not even close to being ready to back down. Through her avatar, which is now pacing in front of the BG Oil virtual office, she challenges the scenario detail by detail. "Wait a minute. Yes, oil accounts for nearly 90 percent of Nigerian revenue, but it is no secret that most of that money either leaves the country or lines the pockets of the ruling class. It does NOT contribute to regional economic development initiatives. This is precisely the problem! Increased drilling does not equate to increased economic development! Clearly a stop to drilling will NOT mean a stop to economic development. Lynndoll, are you suggesting that if drilling goes forward BG Oil will work to ensure that more of the proceeds are used to help the people?"

For several hours, Lynndoll and Jacks debate the details of the drilling through their avatars while Jacks and Aidan stay in touch via cellphone. Lynndoll touts the benefits of drilling and hammers the point that the BG Oil of today is not the BG Oil of 2012. Jacks pushes back and argues that BG Oil must enhance environmental precautions and take a more aggressive stance with the Nigerian government to increase the transparency of oil revenue spending. Making a few adjustments to the simulation, she uses it to show that without any increase to the current 13 percent oil derivation collected by the Nigerian government, if BG Oil increases pressure on government officials to abide by stricter environmental standards, regional farming projects and economic development initiatives may begin to flourish, or at least survive.

At the end of the day, an agreement in principle is reached. Aidan and Jacks agree to soften their stance; realizing that it will not serve Earth Action constituents, nor will it insight BG Oil to significantly alter its drilling schedule. In return, Lynndoll agrees to significantly and publicly increase pressure on local government officials to increase the transparency of oil revenue spending, return more money to local economic development initiatives, and to increase the penalty for violating environmental ordinances.

Leaving his avatar in the *eNCB* environment to continue working through scenarios with Jacks, Lyndoll escorts Aidan out of the BG Oil office and turns his attention to a dispute between the US and Nigerian governments regarding drilling licenses. This situation needs a personal touch. So Lynndoll and his team are headed to a meeting at the Consulate General of Nigeria office on 2nd Avenue to mediate the discussion and to help work through the final details. Though held outside of the *eNCB* environment, these negotiations still benefit from the knowledge gained by Lynndoll and his team while inside the *eNCB* space. After several hours of intense discussions, Lynndoll is able to whittle the points of dispute down to a small few and to help the parties reach a tentative agreement. Confident in the ability of the parties to reach a final resolution on their own, Lynndoll and his team head back uptown to the BG Oil office.

When he logs back into *eNCB,* Lynndoll updates the status of the drilling license negotiations. Next he receives an update from his avatar regarding the status of ongoing discussions with Jacks, and is pleased to learn that several scenarios have received a positive response. Then his avatar enters into the BG Oil virtual office and receives a status update on portions of the negotiation occurring outside of the *eNCB* environment.

He finds that negotiations with the regional production partners are going well. Most of them have agreed to accept contracts in line with BG Oil budgetary parameters and the holdouts are wearing down. His screen begins to flash and he receives an alert that no recent update has been provided from Oscar or Henry regarding their discussions. Lynndoll is unable to reach either of them on the phone but his avatar does make contact with Oscar's avatar in *eNCB*. He is disappointed to learn that discussions between Oscar and Henry have halted for the time being. They are waiting for data from Joanie Cuban, the VP of worldwide HR. Cuban has suffered a medical emergency so her avatar is waiting for input from Nick Kelly, the Assistant VP who is gathering the requested information. Cuban did not properly set her avatar's parameters. As a result, the avatar was unable to automatically switch to a pro-active mode of engagement when Cuban did not log into the system within the specified time. This situation reminds Lynndoll to send an announcement out to the full team, and he sends the following email blast:

> To ensure accurate negotiations within eNCB, frequent updates are essential. All team members are reminded (1) to properly set and review avatar parameters; and (2) to use the automated tools to immediately record the status of all negotiation-related activities held outside of the eNCB environment with your avatar. Type- and handwritten notes, as well as audio and video recordings all can be directly uploaded using the automated support tools....

Throughout the week Lynndoll repeats the day's activities, moving in and out of the *eNCB* environment to engage the parties, receive status updates, perform simulations, and highlight possible results. Ultimately, Lynndoll secures the consensus his executives tasked him to build.

Four weeks later... It's Friday morning in New York and to the satisfaction of his BG Oil executives, Lynndoll has been able to successfully balance BG Oil priorities and the collective interests of the Nigerian and US governments, environmental advocates, production partners, and other key stakeholders. The parties have reached consensus and the production agreement is signed.

Analysis: Virtual Negotiation Today and Tomorrow

The scenario of BG Oil illustrates how a synthetic world could be used to support negotiation and consensus building, and highlights the distance between virtual negotiation today and the promise of virtual negotiation tomorrow. As considered here, negotiation is "the process leading to a mutually acceptable agreement between two or more parties on some course of action" (Rinehart and Closs 1991). Virtual negotiation is computer-supported negotiation that ranges from simple electronic communication to more complex virtual engagements.

As illustrated in the BG Oil scenario, negotiation activities begin with each party assessing and prioritizing their individual goals. In this first phase of the negotiation, the key parties convene privately to outline priorities. Today, BG Oil employees positioned in disparate locations might work collaboratively to set priorities using electronic negotiation tools housed on a corporate intranet, or they may collaborate through a negotiation support system located inside a virtual collaboratory. Used in this manner current negotiation support tools prove to be a valuable addition to face-to-face negotiation activities. As discussed at the outset of the scenario, Lynndoll was pleased with the role these tools played in the first negotiation—the one taking place outside of the synthetic environment. However, the effectiveness of these tools was limited by the constraints of the physical environment and did not (1) exploit the opportunities afforded by the increasing availability of high performance computing; (2) adequately address the organizational challenges (operational, political and cultural) presented by a global economy that is increasingly interconnected, time sensitive and digitally dependent; or (3) adequately represent the cognitive capabilities of the human negotiators. As shown through the role of *eNCB* in the BG Oil scenario, synthetic worlds may provide the infrastructure to support advanced virtual negotiations by enabling these capabilities.

As demonstrated through the BG Oil scenario, virtual negotiations occur through a range of electronic negotiation tools: negotiation support systems, electronic negotiation systems, and negotiation software tools. Ranging from simple email to more complex negotiation support systems, these tools support activities from communication to consensus building. Collectively, electronic negotiation tools are defined as computationally based software applications that link a diverse set of users and allow them to "undertake complex negotiation tasks including conflict identification, management and resolution, search for consensus, assessment of agreement stability and equilibrium analysis" (Kersten and Lai 2007: 554).

Early work on virtual negotiation (e.g., Jelassi and Foroughi 1989) examined a variety of factors, including goal agreement, communication effectiveness, and technology media choice (Davison et al. 2003). More recently, virtual negotiation research has investigated hostile behavior in electronic negotiations (Stuhlmacher and Citera 2005), the influence of gender differences (Stuhlmacher et al. 2007), user acceptance, and perception of the virtual negotiation partner (Turel and Yuan 2005). In addition to their individual findings, these studies collectively suggest that both the category of the negotiation tool and the mode of interaction it uses to support virtual negotiation activities are important considerations.

Negotiation Support Systems Negotiation support systems (NSSs) are computationally based applications designed to support communication and coordination among multiple parties in virtual negotiation activities (Kersten and Lai 2007, Lim and Benbasat 1992). Though similar to group decision support systems in their ability to aid in the management and resolution of conflicts, NSSs are based on the premise that (1) users are only able to connect virtually; (2) the decision processes being supported are consensual (Kersten 2003)—in other words, the parties *want* to reach consensus; and (3) reaching consensus is necessary for a successful negotiation (Kersten and Lai 2007). NSSs are designed assuming that users have independent decision-making authority, represent different interests but have interdependent objectives, and can reject offers and/or terminate negotiations at will (Kersten and Lai 2007).

In the scenario, Lynndoll and his BG Oil colleagues used an NSS within the *eNCB* environment to prioritize negotiation items and to set an internal agenda. The NSS supported negotiation activities among BG Oil stakeholders and between BG Oil stakeholders and external parties. During the course of the prioritization activities, Lynndoll is able to work collaboratively with his BG Oil colleagues using an NSS to share information, outline priorities, and rank preferences. Using avatars to stand in for their human stakeholders when necessary, they were able to conduct deliberations without regard to time or space. The combination of the synthetic environment and the NSS allowed negotiation activities to continue around the clock.

Electronic Negotiation Systems Electronic negotiation systems (ENSs) represent a broader class of virtual negotiation tools that include web-based systems from email and chat to video streaming to automated negotiations and electronic auctions (Kersten and Lai 2007). ENSs are web-based applications that automate, coordinate, and/or document negotiation activities; and are distinguished from NSSs by their focus on the support of the negotiation process rather than the negotiation content and context. More specifically, ENSs assist with such tasks as the documentation of information exchanged rather than the exchange itself (e.g., Yuan 1998), and the coordination of negotiation activities rather than the activities themselves (e.g., Bichler 2003). With this class of virtual negotiation tools, there is no assumption that interaction among parties is limited to the virtual environment.

Lynndoll and his BG Oil colleagues used ENSs to document and coordinate prioritization tasks. The ENSs were used to record activities, schedule meetings, automate information updates, and coordinate decision-making. The tools assisted Lynndoll both within and outside of the *eNCB* environment. He used them to track interaction and to prepare for each phase of the negotiation. Tracking and automated updates are a particularly important role of ENSs. Because negotiation activities are not limited to the *eNCB* environment, updates on activities occurring outside *eNCB* must be added to the *eNCB* knowledgebase. Recalling the scenario, Lynndoll used ENSs to update the status of the drilling license debate between the US and Nigerian governments. He also used ENSs to review other parts of the negotiation. It was an ENS that alerted Lynndoll that no update regarding the Oscar and Henry debate had been received, and it was an ENS that motivated Kelly to act after being notified that Cuban missed her login period.

Negotiation Software Tools Negotiation software tools represent a third category of virtual negotiation tools. Negotiation software tools are web-based, standalone applications designed to support specific negotiation activities (e.g., price comparisons, auction partner searches). Like the other categories of virtual negotiation tools, these software tools range from the simple to the complex. Simple negotiation software tools include the electronic negotiation table, which provides a virtual meeting space in which parties can negotiate and make use of a variety of support services such as legal and competitive analyses (Kersten and Lia 2007). Negotiation software agents and negotiation agent assistants also fall under this category of tools. Negotiation software agents are automated webbots that directly participate in negotiations on behalf of the principal party. The negotiation software agents that support avatar actions gather reference data through multiple interactions and with the assistance of negotiation agent assistants. This constant updating of information allows stakeholders like Lynndoll to adjust their participation based on a fairly comprehensive understanding of decision consequences.

Negotiation agent assistants do not directly participate in the negotiation. Instead, these tools monitor the negotiation process and, acting as subject matter experts, provide advice and council to their principal party (Chen et al. 2004). Negotiation software tools can be used alone or in conjunction with other tools. In the scenario, both NSAs and NAAs played a significant role. Throughout the negotiation, Lynndoll received subject matter expertise from the NAAs and when he was unable to direct his avatar's actions in real time, the NSA associated with his avatar took over and directed the avatar on his behalf.

Modes of Engagement The ability to learn and exhibit proactive behavior highlights another difference between the use of virtual negotiation tools today and their use tomorrow within the synthetic environment. The grey area in Figure 15.1 represents the virtual negotiation tool space in which organizations operate today. Outside of the synthetic environment, the tools allow users to engage through a passive mode, where the tools acts as little more than a computational tool; and an active mode, where the tools allows for the application of computational models. Tools that operate in the proactive mode of engagement, where they can accept input and plot a course of action based on that input, are not generally available beyond the experimental laboratory at this point.

		Mode of Engagement		
		Passive	Active	Pro-Active
Category	Negotiation Support Systems			
	Electronic Negotiation Systems			
	Negotiation Software Tools			

Figure 15.1 Categories and modes of virtual negotiation tools

As the scenario illustrates, parties engaged in negotiations using a synthetic world are able to go beyond the grey space of Figure 15.1 and into another dimension of virtual engagement—one that affords the opportunity to combine virtual negotiation tools in new ways, and to leverage the capability of the synthetic world to alter the human and organizational dynamics associated with the negotiation. Within the *eNCB* environment, Lynndoll's avatar can behave as a passive, active, or proactive agent (Kersten and Lai 2007).

As a passive agent, Lynndoll's avatar must be directed by user input and act based on these computational inputs. In this sense, his avatar operates as little more than a basic computer-based communication and computational tool; responding to the requirements, options and data entered by Lynndoll. As an active agent, Lynndoll's avatar can apply computational models, and formulate, evaluate, and solve complex problems. In active mode, his avatar can structure problems, assess, and act on offers. As a pro-active agent, his avatar can accept input from other avatars and the operating environment, verify assumptions, apply knowledge and plot a course of action without a full requirements specification from Lynndoll, critique negotiation performance and monitor negotiator activities.

The Challenges: Negotiation in a Synthetic World

In addition to the potential benefits, negotiation and consensus building in a synthetic world presents significant challenges. Progress on several technical fronts must be made in order to fully exploit the potential of the synthetic world and when we do get there, the use of even more sophisticated virtual negotiation tools will necessitate a fresh examination of user behavior, organizational culture, and the influence of a host of other organizational variables on negotiation results. Using details from the BG Oil scenario, this section highlights a few of the technical, social and organizational challenges that should be considered.

Technical Challenges

The technical challenges associated with the development of an *eNCB*-type environment are numerous. First, although the scenario suggests that the synthetic environment provides the basic infrastructure for a seamless integration of the various electronic negotiation tools, the current reality is that this integration may be difficult to achieve. The underlying models upon which these tools are developed vary (Kersten and Lai 2007). Negotiation support systems have been developed from using the underlying models and processes of operations research and the decision sciences, while electronic tools such as negotiation support agents and negotiation agent assistants, are typically based on the quantitative and qualitative models of computer science and artificial intelligence. As a result, key functions such as the form of input data, how the systems interact with other systems, and how they interact with users, differ. These differences increase the integration challenges.

Second, the scenario depicts the simulation of real-time, dynamic plots where the details of the negotiation change rapidly. Within *eNCB*, individual actions (through avatars) and environmental fluctuations (e.g., economic changes, climate change, or civil unrest) provide a holistic view of the consequences of negotiation results. This key feature of the synthetic environment, the ability to handle dynamic plots, is essential for the support of real-time negotiations. Yet, virtual negotiations with dynamic plots are still limited to the experimental space (see, for example, Beroggi 2000a).

Third, subject matter expertise in *eNCB* is readily available through negotiation agent assistants but is not independent of human stakeholders. In the scenario Lynndoll had access to subject matter experts 24 hours per day, 7 days per week. Further enhancing the value of this constant access to expertise, Lynndoll could use the analytic capabilities built into the system to quickly and accurately synthesize the information. Since updates, even those occurring automatically, relied to some extent on the participation of human stakeholders, the successful use of electronic negotiation tools is dependent on human interaction.

Fourth, avatars can adjust the mode of engagement to fit the situation. Lynndoll can adjust his avatar's mode of engagement and move between passive, active, and pro-active modes of interaction. This ability change based on the needs of the situation allows the human stakeholder to be actively engaged as time permits. Again, however, achieving this capability will require additional research.

Social/Organizational Challenges

The social and organizational issues associated with the use of a synthetic world for negotiation and consensus building are equally challenging. First, as depicted in the scenario, avatar images are self-selected and dynamic. As Lynndoll moved between meetings in *eNCB,* he adjusted his avatar's image in an attempt to reduce socially constructed biases based on his appearance. Of course, if Lynndoll also interacts with the parties outside of the *eNCB* environment his persona is known. However, even in those cases, the immediacy of the avatar's visual presence may influence the social dynamic. The question for researchers is whether or not this influence will be positive or negative. For users of synthetic worlds, the saying, "When in Rome, do as the Romans do," holds new meaning.

Second, organizations also must grapple with what I call the "synthetic divide." Negotiations of the type presented in the BG Oil scenario, include a variety of organizations—large and small, for-profit and not-for-profit, government agencies, heavily resourced and the reverse. In addition to considerations of technical resources, access, and sophistication, engaging in a synthetic environment adds another dimension to discussions surrounding the digital divide. In the scenario, this synthetic divide is illustrated through the interaction between Lynndoll and Earth Action employees Aidan and Jacks. Aidan, the key advocate for Earth Action, did not have his own avatar in *eNCB.* Left to his own devices, he was easily persuaded by the power of the visual simulations presented by Lynndoll. Jacks, on the other hand, was well versed in the synthetic environment and was able to use it to her (and Earth Action's) advantage. Clearly, organizations and the individuals within them vary in their ability and/or desire to participate in synthetic world virtual negotiations. These variations, and their impact on virtual negotiations, must continue to be explored.

Third, advances in security are required to ensure that communications within a single organization's space as well as communications between specific groups are secure, information can be authenticated, and privacy rules are enforceable and enforced. The privacy and security of negotiation activities is both a technical and an organizational challenge.

Conclusion

Today's global economic environment requires that organizations operate across geographic, national, and cultural boundaries. The resulting distributed work environments, whether within a single organization or as a result of collaboration across multiple organizations, exacerbate the already difficult process of negotiation and consensus building and necessitate the use of electronic negotiation tools that facilitate the negotiation process.

Negotiations are often unsuccessful because parties struggle to communicate, share information, and adequately convey the underlying rationale for their preferences. As demonstrated through the BG Oil scenario, the synthetic environment may provide an opportunity for enhanced information sharing, and a mechanism for transparency that assists parties explain rationale for each position taken. Ultimately, a successful negotiation will be based on the ability of the parties to successfully balance individual needs with collective interests. The features of an environment like *eNCB* may facilitate this process by providing a host of electronic negotiation tools that exploit the opportunities afforded by the increasing availability of high performance computing.

Negotiation and consensus building in a synthetic world provides great promise. From a technical perspective, high performance cyber-infrastructures have the ability to handle immense data flows, support the exploration of large-scale databases, enable data visualization applications, and support more realistic virtual reality applications. From an organizational/social perspective, it has the potential to significantly alter the influence of socio-cultural biases. Arguably, as we move toward the year 2025, the dynamic global environment necessitates the use of more sophisticated electronic negotiation tools where users not only are able to virtually engage, but also are able to make use of advanced computing capabilities and adjust individual and organizational behavior accordingly.

References

Beroggi, G. (2000a). An experimental investigation of virtual negotiations with dynamic plots. *Group Decision and Negotiation*, 9(5):415–429.

Beroggi, G. (2000b). Dynamic plots in virtual negotiations. *Computational and Mathematical Organization Theory*, 6(2):171.

Cerquides, J., López-Sánchez, M., Reyes-Moro, A., and Rodríguez-Aguilar, J.A. (2007). Enabling assisted strategic negotiations in actual-world procurement scenarios. *Electronic Commerce Research*, 7(3-4):189–220.

Chen, E., and Kersten, G. (2004). Agent-supported negotiations on e-marketplace. *International Journal of Electronic Business*, 3,(1):28–49.

Cronin-Harris, C. (2009). Negotiation strategy: Planning is critical. *CPA Journal*: Online.

Davison, R., Fuller, M., and Hardin, A. (2003). E-Consulting in Virtual Negotiations. *Group Decision and Negotiation*, 12(6):517–535.

Kersten, G., and Lai, H. (2007). Negotiation support and e-negotiation systems: An overview. *Group Decision and Negotiation*, 16(6):553.

Kannan, M., and Balasubramaniam, R. (2007). Traceability-based knowledge integration in group decision and negotiation activities. *Decision Support Systems*, 43(3):968.

Rinehart, L.M., Closs, D.J. (1991). Implications of organizational relationships, negotiator personalities, and contract issues on outcomes in logistics negotiations, *Journal of Business Logistics*, 12(1):123–44.

Stuhlmacher A., Citera, M., and Willis, T. (2007). Gender differences in virtual negotiation: theory and research. *Sex Roles*, 57(5-6):329–339.

Stuhlmacher, A., and Citera, A. (2005). Hostile behavior and profit in virtual negotiation: A meta-analysis. *Journal of Business and Psychology*, 20(1):69–93.

Turel, O., and Yuan, Y. (2007). User acceptance of web-based negotiation support systems: The role of perceived intention of the negotiating partner to negotiate online. *Group Decision and Negotiation*, 16(5):451.

TRAINING

Chapter 16
A Day in the Life of Airman Basic Smith

Peter Garretson and Nathan T. Denny

Airman Basic Steve Smith looked up from the three person team performing CPR on the nearly drowned child. Local USAF paramedics had just arrived. It had been an exhausting few minutes. Rough as his Pashtun was, he had been able to direct two locals to assist him in his efforts, and directed another to summon the village elder. Now he turned his efforts to explaining to the child's uncle and village elder that the USAF P.J.'s would now need to take the child to hospital in their helicopter but he would be back the following day. As the P.J.'s departed with the child, and the crowd finally dispersed, Airman Smith wiped the sweat off his brow and removed his wrap-around sunglasses.

Immediately the entire scene disappeared as his glasses left his face. He moved through his dorm's common area and poured himself a glass of lemonade to cool down.

Like many of his class-mates, Steve is a "millennial," a "digital native," and a stimulation junkie. Introduced to USAF roles and missions through AMERICA's AIR FORCE massive-multiplayer-online-role-playing game, Steve's was basically self-selected.

His self-motivation and interest had set him apart and he had been offered a chance to enter the Air Force with an additional bonus and higher rank. Now he was going through a tailored basic and tech school training customized to his specific needs. He finished his drink and reflected on the earlier language-cultural drill… that had been fun, now he was ready for more.

Steve looked down in wonder at his wraparound sunglasses. These simple items, now almost as popular as cell-phones, had been painstakingly created over a decade of collaboration between DARPA and AFRL. This joint effort had created an absolutely superb tool—a man-portable augmented reality tool that allowed the individual airman to enter a fully immersive collaborative mixed, augmented, or virtual reality environment.

Hidden within the sharp looking glasses was an amazing amount of compact technology.

Near the ears Steve could see tiny ultrasonic actuators that could induce sensations of motion in the inner ear as real as any simulator. Sharp looking audio phones hung down from the frame and provided dynamic and directional 3-D audio.

Barely visible along the edges of the frame were the broadband wireless data-link and a row of tiny EEG and fNIR sensors that monitored his brainwaves, sensing if he was fatigued, task saturated, or bored, and adjusting the program and display to maximize his performance and situational awareness.

At each corner were two very wide field-of-view day-night/infrared digital cameras that doubled as optic gyros. They linked directly with a sophisticated navigation system which included a compact GPS receiver, MEMS cold-atom inertial gyro, and specialized massively parallel predictive mixing chip and Kalman filter. The upshot of all this technology was that his glasses perfectly know where Steve's head and eyes were with respect with the outside world.

But best of all, concealed within each lens were very high resolution, wide field-of-view displays that filled each eye with beautiful, vibrant, daylight readable color images… perfectly locked to outside features in the environment, with no noticeable drift, skew or jitter.

The glasses were wirelessly linked to a small wearable Personal Digital Assistant (PDA) about the size of the old Apple iPod. Small as it was, the PDA ran an immensely powerful suite of software. Stated briefly, it was an immersive simulator. From its onboard storage of the entire NGA database at moderate detail and the actual theater of his operations down to millimeter LIDAR data, it generated a panoramic synthetic battle space, and populated it with virtual entities, including a number of artificially intelligent virtual tutors. It also monitored the sensors embedded in Steve's glasses and the "smart" clothing he was wearing and reported Steve's health, vital signs, and cognitive state.

But the glasses and PDA were not stand-alone; they connected Steve to the rest of the USAF and the entire Global Information Grid (GIG). Through it he could data-link to various ISR platforms, or share team situational awareness with other airmen. In an actual conflict, he would have access to the common operational picture (COP) from his first person perspective and with proper permissions could potentially control any USAF asset.

He could also access any number of on-line continuous learning programs—as he was about to do now. He re-donned the glasses. This time the world stayed the same, except for the fact that Curtis Lemay was now standing in front of him, smoking a cigar, and pointing at a schedule of options that floated in the air next to him full of scheduling options. Lemay was one of several popular USAF mentor avatars, though the smoking cigar was his own hack. Lemay pointed out that he had been cleared for JTAC/TAC-P training and that the Urban Operations range was open at 16.00 hrs. It was 15.40 now, would he have time?

Steve directed: "Direction to Urban Ops Range" and a moving map appeared in the upper left corner of his vision, an translucent series of 3-D arrows now hovered showing him the most expeditious route out of the dorm. The nearest arrow displayed his speed and arrival time: 0.5 mph and 1607. He would need to make better time. As Steve began to run other things appeared in his field of vision—his heart rate and percent of VO_2 max.

Steve was wearing standard issue under garments that were technological marvels akin to his glasses. His wearable computer integrated with the garments and could monitor body posture and dynamics as well as core temperature. Sensing that Steve was getting warm, his garments changed state to release heat more efficiently. His wearable computer monitored his running gait and overlaid virtual footprints for optimal pacing along with a metronomic beat to keep pace. Tiny translucent outlines reminded him to swing his arms slightly more and run slightly more erect. On the pavement appeared markers showing the remaining distance to go.

In time, the machine sensed that Steve was becoming bored and so it provided him with a bit of entertainment—first a sort of Pac Man, and then a sort of first person "Campus Doom." The time went by fast enough.

As he rounded the corner and slowed his pace for an even cool down, he passed several officers. As each approached, a floating digital resume appeared to their left telling Steve who they were and where they worked. Various floating virtual reality signs advertised Services and MWR events.

He passed through the entrance to the range and confirmed the machine had signed him in (not that anyone actually signed anything anymore—his generation had made it a priority to eliminate having any routine operation take more than 3 selections or "clicks" and it was considered extremely poor design to have to enter data more than once, ever).

He entered the plain white-walled, nondescript urban training area. "Player Status?" he vocalized. At any time any of the other players could be live with him, virtual or telepresent, or constructed (Artificially Intelligent entities). Today he was alone on the range, but would have a platoon of constructed Army mates. One of his classmates, Amy, was going through AOC remote reach back training and would be the ISR battle manager. The four UCAV's were being commanded virtually in simulators by Guard pilots on opposite ends of the country. Red, which sometimes were constructed, were today being played by an all volunteer force of middle and high school students who earned extra money playing aggressors from their parents homes—real gamers were preferred because they were still more creative and unpredictable than the AI's.

A countdown timer alerted him that the simulation was about to start. As he looked around, the bare nondescript white drywall facade became a Middle Eastern town complete with population. "Had enough gawking, newbie?" An army sergeant barked, "How about getting us some imagery?"

Steve looked up at the clear, blue, seemingly empty sky. "Augmentation On." Now Steve could see airways, holding patterns, threat domes and no-fly areas as if they were crystal prisms suspended in the air. He could now locate where the medium and high altitude ISR assets were, as well as the relevant satellite orbits. He points to each and says "subscribe."

He pointed to the UAV he wanted to use, pointed two fingers toward his eyes to signify "look" and pointed toward the area in which his unit was interested.

He watched a digital spotlight show where the sensor was pointed and bumping the cone left and right with his fingers, fine-tuned it.

He can look from his perspective, the UAV's or any other within that field of view. From the external point of view, he zooms in to the area of interest—an overhead view. "Assisted Target Recognition and Non-Cooperative ID on." This links the various layers of sensors (signals, GOTCHA SAR radar, change detection, high resolution ultra-short pulse encoded LADAR, and EO/IR) and applies an upstream data-fusion and pattern recognition techniques to enhance the chances of discriminating objects of interest from the background noise.

As objects are discovered, the most competent UAV is automatically selected by the swarm rules and applies a facial and gait recognition algorithm for people and a similar template for vehicles and weapon to provide a continuously updates non-cooperative combat ID at the granularity of the individual.

The scene changes, dimming items not of interest to constrain his search, tinting definite enemies in red, civilians in green, and his own team in blue, unknowns in grey. Where subjects are known, labels appear with names beside them, where not, they are automatically numbered. He passes this to his team mates who give him a thumbs up. Looking at each of them, they are outlined in blue to prevent friendly fire and above each floats their own avatar signifying their call sign to enhance identification and coordination.

Returning to the shared exocentric view projected on the floor between them, he sees the target is leaving their safe house and heading this way. "Take out the first and last vehicle, no casualties," says the Lieutenant, "and seal off that escape route.

Steve now designates where to hit the vehicles and the timing. Based on the time of the effect, he is shown the available UCAV's and weaponry. He points at the desired UCAV and brings up its armaments. This will be the shooter, he designates its laser weapon, and specifies the acceptable lines of fire to disable the engine blocks of the first and last vehicle.

He points at another UCAV and sets its jammer to jam an appropriate radius right at the moment they make the hit. Then Steve hand-draws a safety perimeter and directs the UAV to use non-lethal active area denial to ensure no one wanders into their ambush once begun.

He points at the third UCAV and selects a kinetic weapon (in this case a nano-energetic "brilliant" munitions that will adjust its fragmentation pattern to prevent collateral damage. He drags the weapon down onto the wall of the escape avenue, watching the predictive weapon effect model illustrate the blast radius and trajectory. Wanting the effect of shock, he decides the explosion should come slightly after the vehicles have stopped.

Steve's heart races as the convoy of SUV's and technicals with machine guns rounds the corner into the street. Within seconds the hood of the front vehicle starts to smoke and comes to a complete halt. As the convoy stops, the last vehicle also stalls. The center SUV driver realizes something is amiss and tries to turn for the alley right as the wall blasts, blocking the way. His team moves in, taking out the guards systematically to capture their leader. Right as it is going their way, Steve notices activity in one of the windows as a rifle is trained on one of his team mates. Steve immediately points his finger and says bang, sending a shower of projectiles from the hovering UAV gunship, fragmenting, inside the room, but not penetrating the surrounding walls.

The scene is chaotic—terrorists going down, his team swarming the leader's SUV, people from the crowds moving in but then running back after feeling the sting of the active denial system accompanied by a directed intense sonic message telling them not to approach for their own safety.

"We got him. Let's get us out of here—roof of that building!" Steve points at the unmanned mobility aircraft, a larger slowed compound rotor. He points where he wants it to land and tells it "Two minutes."

Discussion

The story above is illustrative of the vision of synthetic worlds for training future Air Force recruits. This story presents many interesting technologies, some of which are already available, some of which are within our grasp, and some of which still lie just beyond our reach. Presently, we will parse Steve's experience with the aim of identifying specific technologies and properly categorizing them by their maturity.

Scene 1—Virtual Afghanistan

Our vignette opens just as Steve is winding down a learning exercise in the synthetic world of Virtual Afghanistan. Broadly, Virtual Afghanistan is a form of computer-based learning, but more specifically Virtual Afghanistan is an environment that provides digital game-based learning (GBL). GBL is not just a means of instruction, but also a source of entertainment. Rarely do Steve's instructors need to assign home work in Virtual Afghanistan, Steve and his peers spend many hours there, on their own volition. There, they meet to socialize and to engage in fun, but realistic competitions that hone their martial skills as well as their cultural skills, including the language, customs, and social fabrics of the real people of Afghanistan. Should Steve later be deployed to the physical Afghanistan, he will be better prepared on the human terrain than nearly every other soldier or airman of previous generations.

Digital game-based learning Between the traditional, linear method of instruction by lecture and progressive methods that provide learning toys without structure, GBL aims for a balance that is engaging and experiential, yet goal-driven. As a tool for education, immersive games empower the autodidactic allowing the student to progress at the pace appropriate for his or her own abilities. Furthermore, being a soldier or a physician, or any professional is more than just the sum of the facts and lessons that are common to practitioners of the profession. Every mature profession also has a professional culture which provides context for their specialized knowledge. Acquisition of professional culture is an area where GBL seems to shine (Gee 2005). Consequently, the military has seen potential in GBL for some time, now, and has begun investing heavily in developing GBL technology and content (Prensky 2001). After some initial resistance to GBL, the concept is beginning to gain traction in the civilian world, as well. Currently, it seems that most GBL environments are standalone, but the future will likely see these standalone systems merge into comprehensive synthetic worlds that offer a variety of experiences in the same virtual space.

Intelligent tutoring systems GBL, as envisioned in our vignette, is the product of the fusion of many different technologies, including intelligent tutoring systems and automatic scenario construction. Intelligent tutoring systems (ITS) are knowledge-based systems that attempt to mimic some of the practices of real tutors in facilitating the process of learning. Many ITS products are integrated with the pedagogical content and interact with the user through standard point-and-click interfaces. As human tutors are particularly effective and they are definitely not point-and-click objects, there is considerable interest in making interaction with ITSs more natural. As conversation is a common mode of interaction between real tutors and their students, it follows that a conversational dialog between the student and the ITS would be an alternative to point-and-click interfaces. Conversational interfaces, with pedagogical agents which manifest themselves with humanoid avatars not only deepen the immersion experienced by the student but also provide a mechanism that can encourage the student to think deeper about the material being learned. Rather then engaging the function of recall when selecting a multiple choice answer, a free form conversational dialog requires the student to perform both recall and synthesis.

Conversational dialogs have been around since at least ELIZA, the computer program which plays at being a psychiatric therapist (Weizenbaum 1966). ELIZA has evolved over the years into modern chatterbots. Chatterbots use a broad database of text strings that associate conversational cues to sets of possible replies (Galvão et al. 2004). Although the internal functionality of chatterbots is relatively simple, ITSs have employed similar, "shallow" natural language processing to produce meaningful conversations about the material being learned. This method was successfully demonstrated in the ITC Leaders project where students participated in a 3-D version of a "choose-your-own-adventure" that imparted real leadership skills (Gordon et al. 2004). While not a deeply immersive ITS, AutoTutor (Graesser et al. 2001, Graesser et al. 2005) uses more complex data structures, such as a dialog advancer network, to lead the student in meaningful conversations.

Automatic story and scenario generation Since Steve will be spending much of his time engaged in GBL situated in synthetic worlds, there is the ever present risk of repetition and consequent boredom. For GBL to avoid the death trap of boredom, the pedagogical system must provide a constant stream of novel situations. Steve should rarely, if ever, see the same scenario, again. While it is feasible that the Air Force, in collaboration with the other branches of the armed services, could construct a large library of scenarios for GBL, it may be preferable to use information from the physical world to automatically generate new training scenarios. In this way, scenarios will always be unique and published "walk through" cheats will be mitigated.

In automatically generating such scenarios, there are several methods coming to fruition which might one day be used in Virtual Afghanistan. These methods generally fall into plot-driven or character-driven generation. Using plot-driven methods, a plot template is used as a framework around which a story is built using, for instance, case-based techniques (e.g., Fairclough and Cunningham 2003, Gervás et al. 2005). Character-driven methods endow each character with specific goals and provide AI planning routines that allow the agent to act towards achieving its given goals (Cavazza et al. 2007). In comparison, plot-driven methods present finer control over pedagogical goals, making them excellent choices for martial scenarios based on "lessons learned." In contrast, character-driven methods create richer characters and could be an excellent vehicle for teaching foreign language and culture.

Scene 2—In the Dorm Room

A window into Synthetic Worlds As Steve cools off after his virtual training, we get a glimpse of his glasses. Steve's glasses are a marvel of technology and are the preferred window into the immersive synthetic worlds that are common in his time. As windows into the virtual, Steve's glasses must be light and comfortable for viewing durations of several hours at a time. For a highly immersive experience, the display capabilities must closely match the performance characteristics of human vision both in field of view and resolution. Including the limits of peripheral vision, humans have a field of view of about 180 degrees. The angle through which we experience depth perception is in the range of 75–95 degrees. Current head mounted virtual reality systems, primitive predecessors to Steve's glasses, provide a field of view on the order of 120 degrees (horizontal) with a binocular overlap in the neighborhood of 50 degrees. An advanced, see through helmet-mounted display for augmented and virtual reality can be seen in Figure 16.1. Steve's glasses are not only superior in visual angle and depth perception, but also in their ability to display images that are photo-realistic with little to no pixel distortion. The pixel density, beyond which there is little advantage with respect to viewing experience, is based upon the spatial distribution of foveal cones and the Nyquist sampling theorem. Although still debated, this limit is believed to be about 60 cycles per degree, or 120 pixels per degree (Williams and Coletta 1987). Contemporary high end HMD displays can achieve 20 pixels per degree. In terms of both viewing angle and image fidelity, clearly current technology has room for progress.

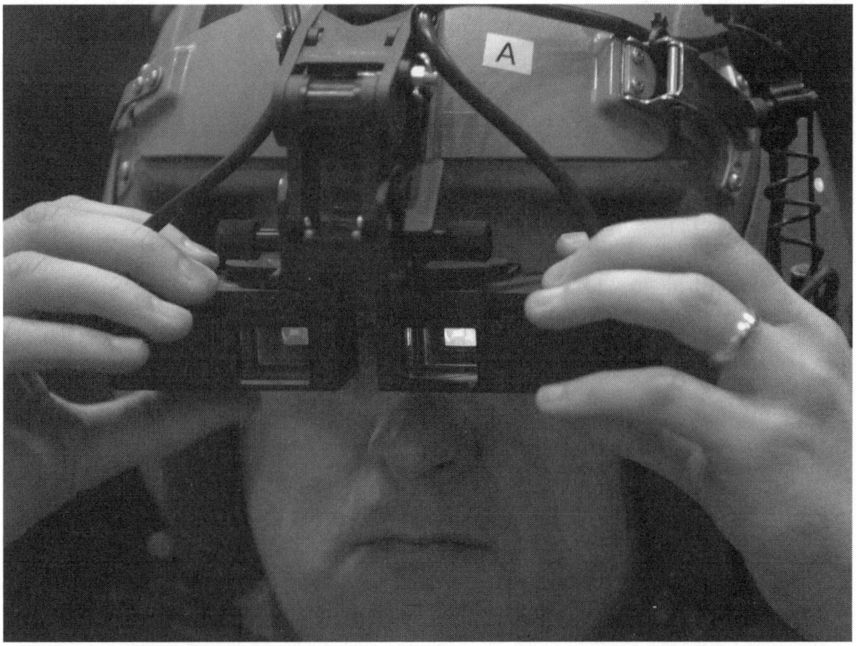

Figure 16.1 An advanced see through helmet-mounted display for augmented and virtual reality

Source: U.S. Air Force photo/Tech. Sgt. Larry A. Simmons.

In current virtual worlds, the sense of self-motion is constructed by changing the point-of-view and increasing or decreasing the amplitude of sounds in the environment. This illusion in both sight and sound is known as *vection* and is sufficient to provide a minimal sense of self-motion, but is still short of a truly immersive experience. The vestibular system of the inner ear is sensitive to both angular and linear acceleration and is essential for many unconscious functions, such as maintaining body posture and the vestibular-occular reflex (VOR) that maintains visual lock while the head turns or the body is in motion. The sensitivity of the vestibular system to galvanic stimulus has been known for quite some time. Modern laboratory experiments have even demonstrated the possibility of using galvanic vestibular stimulation as a mechanism for enhanced balance control (Scinicariello et al. 2001). Science has also discovered that the vestibular system can also be influenced by strong, low frequency sound (e.g., Todd and Cody 2000). Thus it is possible that the vestibular system can be externally manipulated, providing a potential channel that can enrich the sense of self-motion. In the context of our vignette, Steve's glasses are equipped with ultrasonic transducers that manipulate his vestibular system in order to present a better sense of self-motion.

So far, we have only discussed Steve's glasses as output devices, with information flowing from the synthetic world toward Steve. However, in order to keep Steve's gaze and posture coherent with the synthetic world, his glasses must also act as an input device. Immersed in a completely constructed virtual world, Steve's glasses must track the motion of his head to register his field of view with the synthetic world. There are a variety of means to measure such movement. Given the constraints of cost, size, weight, and power (CSWAP), the most likely option is a solid state inertial measurement unit (IMU). Today, the best of these devices can measure acceleration in all six degrees of 3-D freedom, similar to a navigational gyroscope, but is much smaller, lighter, and cheaper. Of course, IMUs are not perfect and even a little noise in the system will create drift in the numerical integration that computes position and orientation. Small drift effects will likely be insignificant in interacting with completely constructed virtual worlds, such as Steve's virtual Afghanistan. However, in synthetic worlds which manifest as mixed reality, even a small drift rate will quickly cause a decoherence between any real objects and registered virtual objects. With the addition of a cheap camera, the IMU can work synergistically with the image stream produced by the camera. Rehbiner and Ghosh (2003) demonstrate that visual-inertial pose estimation is theoretically sound. Vis-Tracker (Foxlin and Naimark 2003) is an exemplary method and system which employs a visual-inertial method for localization and situation in mixed reality. Although highly accurate, Vis-Tracker assumes pre-installed, known fiducials which require a finely controlled, usually indoor, environment. Jiang, Neumann, and You (2004) describe a visual-inertial method for pose estimation without using fiducials. Rather than pre-installed, known fiducials, they assume the pre-existence of a 3-D model from which they can extract references. In the absence of any map, the method of Aron, Simon, and Berger (2004) is able to synchronize IMU and vision dead-reckoning over short distances.

Steve's glasses also provide a means for gathering information on the state of both his mind and body. Using techniques pioneered in DARPA's augmented cognition (augcog) program (Schmorrow and Kruse 2002), this information would be used by the synthetic world and interface programs to provide an optimal experience. In pedagogical worlds, the underlying AI tutor would be able to monitor Steve's learning rate and potential, in effect knowing when learning is occurring and at what level of effect. In operational worlds, the interface would be able to negotiate with other systems in the world to shape the information flow into Steve's mind, optimizing for situation awareness and planning. Contemporary technology is on the road to the future seen by Steve. Today, EEG readings are typically processed offline by human experts; however, Mathan et al. (2005, see also Erdogmus 2005) have constructed experimental systems that can capture EEG signals and process them on a computer carried by an ambulatory soldier. This experimental system is a proof of the concept that EEG interpretation can be taken in the field and interpreted in real-time by software. Similar technologies using EEG, fNIR, and other sensors for the purpose of classifying cognitive states are detailed in DARPA's Technical Integration Experiment (St. John 2004).

Wearable computing Steve's experience in synthetic worlds that are both mixed and constructed is mediated through the PDA-like computer that he wears in much the same fashion as modern, consumer MP3 music players or touch screen mobile phones. In comparison to contemporary portable, digital devices, Steve's PDA is a substantial improvement in computing power, local storage, connectivity, and energy efficiency.

The question of how much computing power such a device would need is largely dependent on the fidelity of the simulation. Rasterization techniques in modern graphics hardware are truly impressive, however animation studios are currently using combinations of REYES rendering and ray-tracing to render photo-realistic scenes (Christensen et al. 2006) that surpass the quality of raster-only techniques. Workstation computers can already use such techniques to render simple scenes in real-time, but only at relatively low resolution. For a high fidelity stereoscopic display with a minimum frame rate of 25 frames-per-second and a display with a 180 degree horizontal field of view by 135 degree vertical field of view and a 90 degree field of stereo vision, we estimate a rendering rate in excess of 17 Gigapixels/second would be needed. This level of performance is well beyond current commodity systems. Looking forward into the future, the growth in multi-threaded, multi-core processors is promising for making significant improvements in real-time, photo-realistic rendering, but much work is still needed.

Improvements in hardware may not be sufficient to realize real-time photo realistic imagery for stereoscopic displays. Likely, advanced hardware will be complemented by advanced software. Since the performance of human vision is not uniform across the entire visual field, a smart rendering algorithm would exploit the difference in fidelity, rendering the area under focus in very high detail while rendering the scene at the periphery of vision in lower detail. Further improvements in rendering and video compression may be possible using algorithms that incorporate additional knowledge of human perceptual processing with respect to time, space, and color in order to achieve additional reductions in computing power and bandwidth (e.g., Reddy 2001, Komogortsev and Khan 2004).

In rendering visualizations of realistic terrain, Steve's PDA draws upon the Digital Terrain Elevation Database (DTED) products from the National Geospatial-

Intelligence Agency (NGA). DTED stores elevation data of the Earth in a raster format with elevations recorded at equally spaced "posts" with 16 bits of precision. The NGA currently defines three DTED levels (0, 1, and 2) with level 2 posts being on the order of 30m apart. Higher resolution levels have been outlined in levels 3, 4, and 5 with post spacings of 10m, 3m, and 1m, respectively. Storage requirements increase dramatically as fidelity improves in higher levels. A DTED level 2 cell, containing approximately 13M samples in a 1 degree x 1 degree cell near the equator, requires about 26MB of storage. For the same cell, the 14.4G samples at Level 5 require approximately 29GB of storage. Current mobile solid state devices are limited to a few hundred gigabytes. Looking forward with the assumption that Moore's law remains predictive through 2020, a mobile solid state storage system of more than 1TB is plausible. However, a naive method of storing the entire DTED Level 5 database would exhaust even our anticipated storage capacity.

As with rendering, we expect that advanced software will come to the rescue. The DTED database is a raster map, i.e. 2-D plane sampled for height. This organization has a natural representation as a grayscale image where height is visualized as a shade of gray. Thinking of the DTED in this way suggests that image compression algorithms might be applicable. Indeed, Owen and Grigg (2004) have demonstrated that the JPEG2000 algorithm can effectively compress DTED maps. Using lossless compression, allowing for a complete reconstruction of the DTED, Owen and Grigg were able to achieve a compression ratio of better than 5 to 1. Allowing for some loss of quality, compression ratios of 32:1 retain a remarkably high degree of fidelity. Kidner and Smith (2003) argue that spatial data has properties which allow for better compression than even that achieved by using JPEG2000 and other image compression algorithms. Using a benchmark set of 24 USGS 1:250,000 scale elevation maps, they demonstrate that their technique is able to achieve a 10:1 lossless compression ratio.

Likely, Steve's PDA will store a world model in DTED that matches elevation resolution with expectation of need. Regions less likely to be visualized will likely be stored in DTED Level 1, while frequented areas will be sampled at DTED Level 5 or beyond, using an advanced compression algorithm to reduce the storage requirements to manageable levels. While connected to the network, Steve's PDA will employ a caching strategy that will automatically manage the tradeoff between fidelity and frequency, where the cache manager will download higher level DTED cells when needed.

While there are clear challenges to creating the processing and storage capabilities needed for Steve's PDA, the most difficult challenge may lie in meeting the power demands of Steve's PDA. As a mobile computing device, there are significant limitations in CSWAP that must be overcome on the road from now to then. Steve's PDA must work, disconnected from the power grid, for a minimum of 8 hours and ideally much longer. During operation, Steve's PDA will need to provide power to, at minimum, the graphics processor and central processor. Under many conditions, Steve's PDA will also be interacting with networked resources, requiring more power for wireless communication. Modern predecessors to Steve's PDA include smartphones, netbooks, and ultra-mobile PCs (UMPCs). Netbooks and UMPCs are still considered to be severely limited by their battery life (Weiss 2008), with many of them lasting less than 3 hours and the best of them lasting only about 8 hours. The newest smartphones capable of running embedded OpenGL 3D applications last on the order of 4–6 hours (Chehimi, Coulton, and Edwards 2005).

While our modern mobile computing devices fall short of the target set by Steve's PDA, we have some room for optimism. Power efficiency is clearly improving as progress in silicon process technology continues to confer a double benefit. Reducing the wafer area used by the processor allows for higher levels of integration that enables System-on-a-Chip (SoC) technology. SoC places one or more processor cores on the same chip along with a graphics processor, I/O controllers, networking hardware, etc. This integration reduces power demands by eliminating much of the need for driving external buses. Additionally, the reduction in gate size within the cores reduces the energy required for a gate to change states, resulting in significant power savings over similar devices that are manufactured using a larger silicon process. An excellent example of current SoC integration can be found in the NVidia® Tegra® line. Tegra chips integrate an ARM® processor with NVidia's ultra-low power GeForce graphics processor and other components onto a single chip with a power consumption low enough for "all day media processing" (Nvidia 2009).

However, even with improvements in hardware and power management system software, batteries might not be sufficient to meet future power demands. Relative to other mobile computing parameters, battery cost and energy density has remained relatively flat (Pardiso and Starner 2005). With the explosion of mobile computing in the form of cell phones, notebooks, and netbooks, there is an obvious demand for novel power technologies that marry endurance with size and weight. Fuel cells, like batteries, convert chemical energy directly to electrical energy without intermediate stages of combustion. Unlike batteries, fuel cells are open systems and will maintain power output as long as they are fed the appropriate reactants. As a mobile power source, the ideal fuel cell would only need to carry cartridges of a fuel, typically either diluted methanol or sodium-borohydrate. While operating, the fuel cell would then consume the fuel cartridge, reacting the fuel with free oxygen extracted from the surrounding air. Some miniature fuel cells are now becoming commercially available, however many challenges remain before fuel cells can be made small enough to be a clearly superior alternative to advanced batteries (Dyer 2002, Kundu et al. 2007).

Barring the perfection of fuel cell technology, Steve's PDA may be designed to scavenge energy from its ambient environment (Paradiso and Starner 2005). Energy scavenging technologies come in many forms, harvesting marginal energy impulses from broadcast radio waves, mechanical vibration, and even very slight changes in temperature or atmospheric pressure. Most of the more exotic designs and devices for energy scavenging will not be sufficient for powering Steve's PDA. However the concepts from energy scavenging may be applied to a larger and almost ubiquitous power source. Steve's body may very well be the energy source which powers his PDA.

The human body must produce about 100W of power, even under sedentary conditions, to maintain life. Under extreme exertions, such as long distance running or powerful sprints, the body may produce in excess of 1kW of power. If only a small fraction of that energy could be scavenged, Steve could at least extend the endurance of the batteries in his PDA, if not keep them fully charged. For harvesting energy from the human body, there are two general sources to tap: thermal and mechanical.

In the case of thermal, a set of lightweight thermocouples would gather energy from the transfer of heat from Steve's body to the cooler, room temperature air around him. The difference in absolute temperatures of the human body (310K) and room temperature (298K) is so small that the theoretical efficiency limit of the ideal Carnot heat engine is only 4 percent. Starner and Paradiso (2004) optimistically estimate that a thermogenerative neck or hood garment might be able to capture between 200mW and 960mW of power. Unless truly impressive gains are made in reducing power consumption for computing devices, Steve is just not hot enough to be a good thermogenerative power source for his PDA.

The other option remaining is to convert the mechanical energy produced by Steve's body into electrical energy. Fortunately, there are many possible methods to do this. A simple method would be to embed a magnetic pendulum and inductive coil in the PDA itself. As Steve walked, the motion of the pendulum, similar to the operation of a pedometer, would generate small impulses of energy. A better alternative might be to use piezoelectric materials to capture mechanical energy. Piezoelectric materials convert mechanical deformation into impulses of direct current. Likely, Steve's under garments will already have piezoelectric elements woven into the fabric. As Steve moves his arms, torso, and legs, the piezoelectric strips or fibers would produce energy that could be gathered. Using modified shoes with piezoelectric materials properly formed and placed in the heel and toe areas of the shoe, Steve's PDA might be able to harvest up to 7W (Paradiso and Starner 2005). Piezoelectric shoes have already been demonstrated in prototypes that produced as much as 800mW (Shenck and Pardiso 2001).

Smart clothing Steve's experience with synthetic worlds is pervasive and immersive. Synthetic worlds are not just a part of how Steve works but also how Steve lives. The very clothing that Steve wears is just as integrated into the synthetic environment as are his glasses. His undergarments unintrusively monitor elements of his health, the posture and kinematics of his body, and can even facilitate computing by harvesting energy or acting as an antenna for wireless networking. Of the advanced elements presented so far in this section, we are probably nearest to achieving this part of the vision. Already garments have been designed with optimally placed, nearly unnoticeable sensors that can detect the posture and kinematics of the body (De Rossi 2000). Prior research has been very successful in embedding sensors and network communication into clothing (e.g., Weber et al. 2003). Already on the commercial market, VivoMetrics® produces the LifeShirt® (Grossman 2003) for a variety of uses, including passively monitoring the health of firefighters who wear the special Lycra® shirt while in action. Additionally, with the proliferation of mobile phones and wireless data networks, some researchers are already exploring the possibility of weaving antennae into clothing to improve reception and range of mobile communication devices (e.g., Salonen et al. 1999, Klemm, Locher, and Troster 2004).

Staying coherent with the global information grid When Steve is within network range, which will be almost everywhere in Steve's day, his PDA will automatically acquire a linkage to the Global Information Grid (GIG). The GIG is the future information architecture and infrastructure of the US military. The net-centric vision of the GIG is to place essentially all military resources into a common, yet secure service-oriented architecture that will empower soldiers, sailors, airmen, and marines to cooperate laterally like never before. By the time Steve has taken up his calling with the US Air Force, the GIG will have already become a backbone of US DoD operations.

Through the GIG, the synthetic worlds with which Steven interacts remain coherent with the physical world. Information generated by sensors, systems, and people in the physical world flow into the GIG. In the GIG, this information is made available through services and then pulled by synthetic worlds that are subscribed to spaces and events, where they evolve independent of human initiation. In synthetic worlds, this information is processed by intelligent software agents and people, such as Steve, and then flows bidirectionally back into the GIG. In this way, the GIG is the linkage between the physical world where matter is made to act and synthetic worlds where information is processed and decisions are made.

In a simple example of coherent synthetic worlds, Steve may visualize in near real-time packages that are being sent to him from family and friends and other packages that he has sent to friends that are deployed abroad. In a similar fashion, Steve's training simulators, such as Virtual Afghanistan, will automatically integrate recently released imagery and publicly available news into the setting and stories of its internal world. In examples where information from synthetic worlds flow back into the physical world, Steve's peers may use advanced applications hosted in synthetic worlds to visualize and control the flow of material and allocation of logistical assets. Taking this concept even further, remotely operated and robotic assets, such as UAVs, UGVs, and satellites, may publish themselves as services in the GIG, allowing for those assets to be controlled in real-time through an avatar in a synthetic world.

Although the GIG is unique to the scope and scale of the military, the emerging collection of Internet-available real-time data feeds and services is an appropriate civilian analog. Coherence between the matter of the physical world and the informational spaces of virtual worlds is the next step in developing synthetic worlds as an instrument of improved productivity. Methods and tools for maintaining coherence are still in their infancy, but developing rapidly. The relative ease of in-world development and overall popularity of Second Life® has made it a popular place for experiments in coherence. Mirroring the physical world, many well-known commercial brands have Second Life products and the marketing community is very interested in reaching people through virtual worlds (Barnes 2007). Some brands, particularly those in apparel and fashion, even sell real products through Second Life stores (Christopher 2008). Several physical establishments also have a co-presence within Second Life, using these sites for politics, education, and other social uses. In an example of maintaining real-time coherence, Second Life tools already exist for visualizing NOAA weather conditions and FAA air traffic in the continental US (Boulos and Burden 2007).

Coherence is bidirectional, with information flowing not just from the physical world into the synthetic world, but also from synthetic worlds into the physical world. An early example of this bidirectionality can be seen in the tele-operation of remote assets. Hoyer et al. (2004) demonstrate the potential of using a synthetic world for pedagogical collaboration where engineering students are able to cooperate in real-time to conduct engineering experiments in a remotely located physical laboratory.

Scene 3—Learning from Lemay

After Steve's brief reflection on the technology that he uses to interact with synthetic worlds, he invokes his digital mentor, an AI manifesting itself as an avatar of the great General Curtis Lemay. Although virtual Lemay is similar in many respects to the constructed characters that Steve interacts with in training simulations, the AI that drives virtual Lemay is long lived and has a planning horizon well into the future. Virtual Lemay is more than a constructed character; it is a personal life coach that tracks the long term progress of Steve's declared personal and professional goals. As we see in the vignette, virtual Lemay is a proactive agent that plans and recommends courses of training and helps to keep Steve motivated.

Steve's interaction with virtual Lemay also gives us our first glimpse of augmented reality. Augmented reality is a synthetic world that visualizes the matter world and informational spaces simultaneously. When looking through his glasses, Steve sees the physical world around him, but his view is augmented by the visualization of spatially aware informational elements. Although virtual Lemay doesn't exist in the physical world, it is registered and remains coherent with physical space (Azuma 1997, Azuma et al. 2001).

To date, augmented reality has been slow to develop into a practical tool. So far, the stumbling blocks seem to be the lack of sufficient hardware. Current helmet-mounted displays, early forms of Steve's glasses, are bulky, heavy, and costly. Furthermore, mobile computing, although making great strides, still falls short of the needed computing power and operating endurance. Completely immersive augmented reality is still some years away. However, we believe that the next few years will see an explosion in limited forms of augmented reality. The rapid evolution of smartphones has brought together many of the needed pieces: a high resolution display, location awareness through GPS reception, accelerometers that track orientation, significant processing power, relatively long endurance, and nearly constant contact with the 3G+ cellular data network. In the near future, smartphones may act as a handheld looking glass into augmented reality. Wagner and Schmalstieg (2003) have already constructed a prototype of handheld augmented reality using COTS hardware and their own custom software.

Scene 4—In Transit

Steve's garments are both input and output devices, and are one of the many components that keep various synthetic worlds coherent with the physical world. As input devices, Steve's garments sense the posture and motion of Steve's body. While jogging to the training grounds, Steve's PDA uses information from the under garments to monitor his physical performance and uses augmented reality to guide Steve towards better performance. As output devices they can assist in thermoregulation by inducing a chemical phase change or by altering the shape of the fibers of the constituent cloth.

In this scene, we also see a potential application where augmented cognition meets augmented reality. Using augmented cognition technology, Steve's PDA can sense when Steve is about to get bored, perhaps even before Steve is aware of it, himself. Steve's AI coach (virtual Lemay) proactively lays out the augmented reality games Pac Man and ARQuake (Piekarski and Thomas 2002) to keep Steve motivated, engaged, and at a high level of overall performance.

As Steve rounds the corner, he is met by several officers. His augmented reality system automatically visualizes personal information about each of the officers. This is another demonstration of augmented reality. This application has the potential for rapidly building and improving local social networks. No such tools are practical, yet, but many modern applications seem to be converging towards that end. Twitter® is one such application that allows users to post short text fragments into an informational space. In the near future, these spaces will be georegistered using a GPS-enabled smartphone, adding location and context to online social networking.

Scene 5—At the Range

At the range, Steve is again immersed in a synthetic world similar to Virtual Afghanistan. This world is coherent with the physical structures on the range, but is otherwise completely constructed. In the spectrum of mixed reality (Milgram and Colquhoun 1999), rather than augmented reality, we see an example of augmented virtuality. While there are many points of interest in this scene, we will focus our discussion on the use of synthetic worlds for embedded modeling and decision support and the social potential of synthetic worlds.

Embedded simulation and decision support In the initial moments of preparation for the simulated raid, we see Steve visualizing the physical effects of a weapon as it would react to a real structure. This is an excellent example of the potential for synthetic worlds to wrap simulations for decision support, in this case the simulation of ammunition effects (Woodley 2007) guides Steve's placement of the munitions for optimal effect. The application of military simulations to decision making in synthetic worlds is only beginning. Other possible military uses include simulation and experimentation, in real-time or near real-time, of the deployment of forces and positioning of ISR assets.

The real-time, embedded modeling of blast effects may not have a plethora of civilian uses, yet other embedded simulations may be very useful in the civilian domain. A synthetic world made coherent to the physical world through, for instance, system control and data acquisition (SCADA) systems could embed real-time simulations of traffic, communications, water, and power networks. With such technology SCADA operators could visualize the effects of control decisions, using the embedded simulation as a decision aid for forecasting delayed effects. Furthermore, as telerobotics finds more civilian uses, embedded kinematic simulations will allow operators to plan out the motion of precision robotic arms and manipulators, as illustrated in Figure 16.2. This capability is of great interest to medicine (e.g., Taylor and Stoianovici 2003), space exploration (e.g., Nguyen et al. 2001), and search and rescue organizations (e.g., Carpin et al. 2007).

Figure 16.2 A conceptual synthetic world for tele-operation of robots

Source: Art by Eric Proctor of the Sensors and Electron Devices Directorate of the Army Research Laboratory.

Tapping into the cognitive surplus The Internet has only begun to tap into the vast "cognitive surplus" of free time and thought. Wikipedia and Linux are only the beginning of what is still to come. At the range, we see an example of how the military might one day tap into the cognitive surplus in order to train their personnel to be more adaptive to the adversarial ingenuity of other humans. Steve and his mixed team of humans and AI constructs are competing against an OPFOR composed of real humans—in this case otherwise idle teenagers. In many respects, this aspect of Steve's world has already arrived. While we do not experience the same qualities of immersion that Steve someday will, contemporary massively multiplayer online games (MMOGs) and virtual spaces such as Second Life spontaneously bring together people from many corners of the globe.

In MMOGs, such as the popular Call of Duty® series, players join opposing sides and compete in a "first-person shooter." With no formal organization or command structure, one may be surprised at the level of coordination that can be found in such games. Similarly, in non-game synthetic worlds such as Second Life, people meet and form relationships and enterprises, spontaneously. Such groups are made possible by the dramatic decrease in the cost of group formation compared to pre-Internet times

(Shirky 2008). Where Steve's world has likely improved the world of today is in the system of incentives and filters to prevent "griefers" from abusing the system. Current preventative and corrective methods are still in the process of rapidly evolving and many methods to date retain an *ad hoc* flavor.

Future Directions

In the preceding text, we have given an overview of the current state of the art with respect to synthetic worlds. From our discussion and the referenced literature an interested reader can infer many areas where further research is needed; however there is one broad area which we believe is currently underdeveloped and requires further investment in research and development to foster continued evolution of synthetic worlds for productive uses.

Decluttering Complex Information Spaces

Synthetic worlds, both completely constructed virtual worlds and mixed reality worlds, have the potential to overwhelm the user with information. Even the most mundane objects in synthetic worlds can have associated metadata and annotations and occlusion is no reason to suppress this information. Indeed, seeing into and through synthetic objects with "x-ray" vision is a powerful feature of synthetic worlds. With all of the information available, a real problem emerges in the need to "declutter" and reduce the flow of information to manageable levels while not discarding information that the user will find valuable. Basically, this problem breaks down into view management, or how should the information be displayed, and what some call label management, or deciding which metadata and annotation to display.

In the case of label management, or the more general problem of information filtering, most VR and mixed reality systems begin by reducing the potential information set by spatial interaction (Benford and Fahlen 1993). Each informational element has an associated nimbus and each user in the synthetic world has a focus. Elements are displayed if the nimbus and focus intersect. More recent systems have used a two step process for further filtering objects that are retained by spatial interaction. The method of Julier et al. (2000) uses a vector-space model of information similar to that used in many information retrieval systems. Rule-based approaches have also been considered for a second processing step for task-oriented environments such as KARMA (Feiner et al. 1993).

The problem of dynamically placing labels in real-time can be quite difficult. Given a discrete set of positions, relative to the object being annotated, computing the optimal placement of labels that minimizes collisions from the perspective of the viewer is NP-Hard. Given the NP-Hard nature of the problem, some have experimented using soft computing techniques for finding satisficing, but not necessarily optimal, layouts. Experiments done by Azuma and Furmansk (2003) tested the efficacy of a greedy algorithm, a gradient descent algorithm, and simulated annealing all on the layout of a set of 20 dials on the interface to a radio. Zhang and Sun (2005) use the vector space model for filtering, and then decide on whether to place the label within the project of the object it is annotating, or external to the object with an arrow to associate to the label to the object. Zhang and Sun also present several ideas for transforming the labels to reduce the cognitive load on the user. Attacking a slightly different problem, Livingston et al. (2003) have developed techniques for transforming the "x-ray" view of occluded objects in a way that retains some information as to the depth of the object. Visualizing occluded objects is an essential technology for systems intended to improve situation awareness by revealing objects that could not otherwise be seen by direct line of sight.

Moving forward, we believe there are several gaps that remain in developing a useful capability for information filtering in synthetic worlds. The general problem of filtering real-time information streams is not unique to synthetic worlds and we believe that other domains, such as aviation, may already have existing techniques which might be profitably ported into synthetic worlds. More specifically, a view and label management system that was based on situation awareness theories such as that developed by Endsley (1995) would not only assist in "decluttering" views but also assist the user in reaching higher states of awareness by inferring non-obvious relations between objects within view. Solutions along this line also require investigation into methods of communicating intent to the filtering system. The relevance of objects and relations is not constant, but is instead highly contextual. A good solution to the problem of communicating intent to the view management system will be composed in part from good HCI and in part from advanced knowledge representation.

Conclusion

Today is an exciting time to do research and development on synthetic worlds. These worlds of information processing may become the fabric that unites many contemporary technologies. Here we have outlined the current state of the art and included a vignette to weave all the pieces together into a single experience. We encourage the reader to continue where this chapter leaves off and find new applications for synthetic worlds and new develop hardware and software to facilitate those applications.

References

Aron, M., Simon, G. and Berger, M. (2004). *Handling uncertain sensor data in vision-based camera tracking*. Proceedings of the Third IEEE/ACM International Symposium on Mixed and Augmented Reality (ISMAR 2004), 58–67.

Azuma, R. (1997). A Survey of Augmented Reality. *Presence: Teleoperators and Virtual Environments*, 6(4):355–385.

Azuma, R. et al. (2001). Recent Advances in Agumented Reality. *IEEE Computer Graphics and Applications*, November/December 2001, 34–47.

Azuma, R. and Furmanski, C. (2003). *Evaluating label placement for augmented reality view management*. Proceedings of the IEEE/ACM International Symposium on Mixed and Augmented Reality (ISMAR 2003), 66–75.

Barnes, S. (2007). Virtual Worlds as a Medium for Advertising. *The DATA BASE for Advances in Information Systems*, 38(4):45–52.

Benford, S. and Fahlen, L. (1993). *A spatial model of interaction in large virtual environments*. Proceedings of the third conference on European Conference on Computer-Supported Cooperative Work (ECSCW '93), 109–124.

Boulos, M.N.K. and Burden, D. (2007). Web GIS in Practice V: 3-D Interactive and Real-time Mapping in Second Life. *International Journal of Health Geographics* [online], 6(51). Available at: http://www.ij-healthgeographics.com/content/6/1/51 [accessed: March 10, 2008].

Carpin, S. et al. (2007). Bridging the Gap Between Simulation and Reality in Urban Search and Rescue. *Lecture Notes in Computer Science*, 4434:1–12.

Cavazza, M. et al. (2007). *Madame Bovary on the holodeck: immersive interactive storytelling*. Proceedings of the 15th International Conference on Multimedia (MM '07), 651–660.

Chehimi, F., Coulton, P., and Edwards, R. (2005). *Evolution of 3-D games on mobile phones*. Proceedings of the IEEE Fourth International Conference on Mobile Business, 173–179.

Christensen, P.H. et al. (2006). *Ray tracing for the movie 'cars'*. Proceedings of the IEEE Symposium on Interactive Ray Tracing, 1–6.

Christopher, L.C. (2008). Advertisers Go Net Native. *Internet Advertising*, 8(6):5–14.

De Rossi, D. et al. (2000). *Monitoring body kinematics and gesture through sensing fabrics*. Proceedings of the 1st Annual International Conference on Microtechnologies in Medicine and Biology, 587–592.

Dyer, C.K. (2002). Fuel Cells for Portable Applications. *Journal of Power Sources*, 106:31–34.

Endsley, M.R. (1995). Toward a Theory of Situation Awareness in Dynamic Systems. *Human Factors: The Journal of the Human Factors and Ergonomics Society*, 37(1):32–64.

Erdogmus, D. et al. (2005). *Cognitive state estimation based on eeg for augmented cognition*. Proceedings of the 2nd International IEEE/EMBS Conference on Neural Engineering, 566–569.

Fairclough, C.R. and Cunningham, P. (2003). *A multiplayer case based story engine*. Proceedings of the 4th International Conference on Intelligent Games and Simulation (EUROSIS 2003), 41–46.

Feiner, S. et al. (1993). Knowledge-based Augmented Reality. *Communications of the ACM*, 36(7):52–62.

Foxlin, E. and Naimark, L. (2003). *VIS-Tracker: A wearable vision-inertial self-tracker*. Proceedings of the IEEE Virtual Reality 2003 (VR '03), 199–206.

Galvão, A.M. et al. (2004). Adding Personality to Chatterbots Using the Persona-AIML Architecture. *Lecture Notes in Computer Science* 3315:963–973.

Gee, J.P. (2005). What Would a State of the Art Instructional Video Game Look Like? *Innovate Journal of Online Education* [Online], 1(6). Available at: http://innovateonline.info/index.php?view=article&id=80 [accessed: 5 March, 2009].

Gervás, P. et al. (2005). Story Plot Generation Based on CBR. *Knowledge-Based Systems*, 18(4–5):235–242.

Gordon, A. et al. (2004). *Branching storylines in virtual reality environments for leadership development*. Proceedings of the 16th Innovative Applications of Artificial Intelligence Conference (IAAI-04).

Graesser, A.C. et al. (2001). Intelligent Tutoring Systems with Conversational Dialogue. *AI Magazine*, 22(4):39–51.

Graesser, A.C. et al. (2005). AutoTutor: An Intelligent Tutoring System with Mixed-Iniative Dialogue. *IEEE Transactions on Education*, 48(4):612–618.

Grossman, P. (2003). *The LifeShirt: A multi-function ambulatory system that monitors health, disease, and medical intervention in the real world*. Proceedings of the International Workshop on New Generation of Wearable Systems for eHealth, 73–80.

Jiang, B., Neumann, U. and You, S. (2004). *A robust hybrid tracking system for outdoor augmented reality*. Proceedings of the IEEE 2004 Virtual Reality (VR '04), 273–275.

Julier, S. et al. (2000). *Information filtering for mobile augmented reality*. Proceedings of the 2000 IEEE and ACM International Symposium on Augmented Reality (ISAR 2000), 3–11.

Kundu, A. et al. (2007). Micro-fuel Cells–Current Development and Applications. *Journal of Power Sources*, 170:67–78.

Hoyer, H. et al. (2004). A Multiuser Virtual-Reality Environment for a Tele-operated Laboratory. *IEEE Transactions on Education*, 47(1):121–126.

Kidner, D.B. and Smith, D.H. (2003). Advances in the Data Compression of Digital Elevation Models. *Computers & Geosciences*, 29(8):985–1002.

Klemm, M., Locher, I., and Troster, G. (2004). *A novel circularly polarized textile antenna for wearable applications*. Proceedings of the 7th European Conference on Wireless Technology.

Livingston, M.A. et al. (2003). *Resolving multiple occluded layers in augmented reality*. Proceedings of the IEEE/ACM International Symposium on Mixed and Augmented Reality (ISMAR 2003), 56–65.

Mathan, S. et al. (2005). Sensor-Based Cognitive State Assessment in a Mobile Environment, in *Foundations of Augmented Cognition*, edited by D.D. Schmorrow. New York: Lawrence Erlbaum.

Milgram, P. and Colquhoun, H. Jr. (1999). A Taxonomy of Real and Virtual World Display Integration, In *Mixed Reality—Merging Real and Virtual Worlds*, edited by Y. Ohta and H. Tamura. Berlin: Springer-Verlag, 1–16.

Nguyen, L.A. et al. (2001). Virtual Reality Interfaces for Visualization and Control of Remote Vehicles. *Autonomous Robots*, 11:59–68.

NVidia. (2009). NVIDIA Tegra FAQ. Available at: http://www.nvidia.com/docs/IO/55043/NVIDIA_Tegra_FAQ_External.pdf [accessed March 9, 2009].

Owen, M.J. and Grigg, M.W. (2004). *The Compression of Digital Terrain Elevation Data (DTED) Using JPEG 2000*. Defense Science and Technology Organization, Salisbury, Australia, Tech. Rep. DSTO-TR-1548.

Paradiso, J.A. And Starner, T. (2005). Energy Scavenging for Mobile and Wireless Electronics. *IEEE Pervasive Computing*, 4(1):18–27.

Piekarski, W. and Thomas, B. (2002). ARQuake: The Outdoor Augmented Reality Gaming System. *Communications of the ACM*, 45(1):36–38.

Prensky, M. (2001). True Believers: Digital Game-Based Learning in the Military, in *Digital Game-Based Learning* (1st ed.). New York, NY: McGraw-Hill, Chapter 10.

Reddy, M. (2001). Perceptuall Optimized 3D Graphics. *IEEE Computer Graphics and Applications*, 21(5):68–75.

Rehbiner, H. and Ghosh, B. (2003). Pose Estimation Using Line-based Dynamic Vision and Inertial Sensors. *IEEE Transactions on Automatic Control*, 48(2):186–199.

Salonen, P. et al. (1999). *A small planar inverted-F antenna for wearable applications*. Proceedings of the Third International Symposium on Wearable Computers, 95–100.

Schenck, N.S. And Paradiso, J.A. (2001). Energy Scavenging with Shoe-Mounted Piezoelectrics. *IEEE Micro*, 21(3):30–42.

Schmorrow, D.D. and Kruse, A.A. (2002). *DARPA's augmented cognition program—tomorrow's human computer interaction from vision to reality: Building cognitively aware computational systems*. Proceedings of the 7th IEEE Conference on Human Factors and Power Plants.

Scinicariello, A.P. et al. (2001). Enhancing Human Balance Control with Galvanic Vestibular Stimulation. *Biological Cybernetics*, 84:475–480.

Shirky, C. (2008). *Here Comes Everybody: The Power of Organizing Without Organizations*. New York: Penguin Press.

Starner, T. and Paradiso, J.A. (2004). *Human Generated Power for Mobile Electronics*. Low-Power Electronics Design, edited by C. Piguet, The CRC Press.

St. John, M. et al. (2004). Overview of the DARPA Augmented Cognition Technical Integration Experiment. *International Journal of Human-Computer Interaction*, 17:131–149.

Taylor, R.H. and Stoianovici, D. (2003). Medical Robotics in Computer-Integrated Surgery. *IEEE Transactions on Robotics and Automation*, 19(5):765–781.

Todd, N.P.M. And Cody, F.W. (2000). Vestibular Responses to Loud Dance Music: A Physiological Basis of the "Rock and Roll Threshold"? *Journal of the Acoustic Society of America*, 107(1):496–500.

Wagner, D. and Schmalstieg D. (2005). *First steps towards handheld augmented reality*. Proceedings of the 7th IEEE International Symposium on Wearable Computers, 127–135.

Weber, J.L. et al. (2003). *VTAM—A new "biocloth" for ambulatory telemonitoring*. Proceedings of the 4th International IEEE/EMBS Special Topic Conference on Information Technology Applications in Biomedicine, 299–301.

Weizenbaum, J. (1966). ELIZA—A Computer Program for the Study of Natural Language Communications Between Man and Machine. *Communications of the ACM*, 9(1):36–45.

Weiss, A. (2008). Ultra-mobile PCs: Slow but Small and Specialized Computers are a Surprise Hit for the Industry. *netWorker*, 12(2):22–30.

Williams, D.R. and Coletta, N.J. (1987). Cone Spacing and the Visual Resolution Limit. *Journal of the Optical Society of America*, A, 4:1514–1523.

Woodley, R., Barker, J. and Noll, W. (2007). *AmmoSIM0—Ammunition simulation for front line and command units*. Proceedings of the 12th International Command and Control Research and Technology Symposium (ICCRTS).

Zhang, F. and Sun, H. (2005). *Dynamic labeling management in virtual and augmented environments*. Proceedings of the Ninth International Conference on Computer Aided Design and Computer Graphics (CAD/CG 2005).

Chapter 17
Mirror Man: A Speculative Case Study of the Synergetic Potential of Data Visualization and Virtual Worlds

Ben Goertzel

Mirror Man

From: I.M. Brilliant <brilliant@syntheticsciencelabs.com>
To: I.B. Bossi <bossi@syntheticsciencelabs.com>
Date: Sun, Jun 29, 2023 at 3:34 AM
Subject: Mirror Man project and episode

Ian,

Bob asked me to send you a long email giving an accounting of the Mirror Man episode from my own perspective. So, here goes!

Since the basic facts of the matter are obviously well known to you and Bob and all others involved, I assume the purpose of getting my perspective must lie in whatever unique paltry insights I may be able to shed based on my background in putting together the infrastructure for the Mirror Man experiments. Actually, I don't think the work I did was really relevant to the most interesting aspects of the episode—so I'm not at all sure these unique insights actually exist—but I'm happy to share my observations, for whatever they're worth (after all, I'm writing this on company time!).

From my point of view—as a professional, anyways—the actual subject matter of the Mirror Man experiments was never the main point: I don't know much about AI nor neurobiology, my expertise is pretty much restricted to the information visualization side of things. My goal in the project was to use our VirtualViz tools (which as you know I've been working on for almost a decade now) to help the neuroscientists and the AI guys understand what each other were doing—as well as to help each of the two teams understand their own data, of course.

The way the project was explained to me at first was something like the following. The basic goal of the project was to create an AI system capable of entering into social relationships with human beings in an emotionally meaningful way. The key concept being explored in the project was the idea of "mirror neurons"—neurons in human being A's brain, that respond to something human being B does, in a way that's very similar to what would happen in A's brain if it were A taking the action himself. (I hope I didn't mangle that too badly, but I do recall that the neuro geeks were also arguing about this stuff a bit, so I'm honestly not sure I'm any more confused than they are.) For instance if I raise my arm and you're watching me, some mirror neurons in your brain may start getting active, and may start activity patterns in your brain that are somewhat similar to what would happen in your brain if you were raising your arm yourself. Furthermore sometimes the mirror neurons fire as a response to the perceived INTENTION of what person B is doing, rather than what person B actually did. If B reaches out to grab something—even if he never actually grabs it—the mirror neurons fire in A's brain consistently with what would happen if A were TRYING to achieve the goal of grabbing the thing.

The fun thing is this can happen with emotions as well. If I get sad, and you're watching me, then you may get sad as well—your sadness mirror neurons are firing. (To simplify a little bit, I'm sure—but as I said, I'm really no expert on this stuff.) So the idea behind the Mirror Man project is that this business of mirror neurons is critical to human empathy. When we humans really feel we're empathizing and sharing with another person, it's because we have a kind of feedback relationship where each of us has mirror neurons firing based on the other guy's actions and feelings. We're like two mirrors reflecting each other.

So this is where the AI guys come into the picture. They want to make avatars in the OpenSim grid that will inspire more trust in people—that will really give people the feeling of being understood and genuinely interacted with. So they took their AI system—something called OpenCog, which I don't understand at all, it's too much hairy computer science for me—and gave it the analogue of mirror neurons. And then they set up an experiment in which their AI avatar—the now-notorious Mirror Man—was talking to and otherwise interacting with an avatar controlled by a human, in a standard OpenSim conference room. Meanwhile the human was hooked up to a nanoball brain imager that measured the flow of energy through his brain with a fairly decent space-time resolution—so the neuro guys could see what was going on in his head while he interacted with the AI avatar.

So here's where I come in. We've got to visualize the neural activity in the human subject's brain... we've got to visualize the activity in the AI system's "brain" (which isn't very much like the human brain, because OpenCog from what I understand is based on totally different computer science principles), and we've got to somehow draw connections between these two things. We've got to see if there really are correlations going on between the mirror neuron activity in the person's brain and the "kind of mirror neuron like" activity in the AI's brain... and see if these correlations map up with the person's subjective report of how much empathy, how much human connection they feel with the AI. And of course human connection is a hard thing to quantify so we need to look at what the human subjectively reports, in ordinary English, about the experience of their interaction.

This is exactly the kind of super-funky data visualization problem that VirtualViz was made for! Furthermore, if I can be forgiven for a bit of shameless self-promotion here, I was pleased to observe that the initial set-up for the VirtualViz application involved just three steps.

We already had a visualization widget for nanoball brain imaging set up, from an earlier project, so turning that on was a two-click operation. What this guy does is let you see a dynamic 3D "heat map" of the subject's brain activity. You can select any 2D slice of the brain, from any direction; or any 3D chunk of the brain; and then you see a separate 3D map of that portion of the brain. Also you can identify a brain region by name—"amygdala" or "left temporal lobe" or whatever and then just see a separate 3D map of that chunk. These 3D maps are just objects like anything, of course—you can take them back to your (virtual) office, you can play baseball with them, whatever. If you want to do some analysis on the data in a chunk you just grab the right wand—if you want to run some clustering analysis, for example, you just grab the clustering wand from your bag of tricks and touch it to the chunk and—voila!—you've got it, the results of the clustering visualized by whatever method goes along with it. One of the basic principles of VirtualViz is that each type of data analysis owns its own visualization, so how nicely the clustering results are visualized depends on who made the clustering wand. If you don't like the wand you can say so and the wand's ratings will go down, so people have an incentive to make their tools as good as they can.

What we had to do to configure the nanoball viz app for this experiment was just to define the mirror neuron regions in the brain. This was a little bit interesting because there are a lot of them. But we didn't need to do any actual programming here, we just used the Correlyzer data analysis widget. We did some training where one of our grad students controlled Avatar B while the guy hooked up to the nanoball brain imager controlled Avatar A and, every time Avatar B did something, we asked the Correlyzer which parts of Avatar A's brain seemed to be getting most active, according to the Correlyer's statistical analysis wizardry. After a few hours of admittedly not too exciting work, there we were, we had a decent mapping of the mirror regions of the subject's brain. (It turns out these regions are a little different for each person, otherwise this would be less tricky, but then, that wouldn't be any fun, now would it?)

Also, some of the AI guys had built their own viz widget for OpenCog, their AI tool. I have to say it wasn't as slick as our nanoball brain imaging visualizer, but it basically did the job. The AI system keeps its knowledge in a big network of weighted nodes and links, not that different from the neurons and the synapses in the brain, at least from my totally naive point of view, and their viz widget let you watch activity flow through the network of nodes and links. Here things were a little simpler since they'd programmed the quasi mirror neuron stuff in their AI system directly—they knew exactly where it was, we didn't need to do any correlyzing to find out.

So we had the viz tools set up for the real brain and the AI brain, and the next step was to hook everything together. All hail the Correlyzer! We asked it to create objects for the most significant correlations it noted between the mirror regions of the human subject's brain, and the mirror regions of the AI's "brain." The more significant the correlation, the bigger the object.

What this meant was, as the human subject (a bright young grad student named Xiaoyu, as it happens) was talking to the AI avatar, she could see when she was "connecting" with the robot visually. When a really tight emotional connection was being made, a large object would appear, with a wire running into both of their (avatars') heads. So when she said something and the AI didn't quite get it—didn't quite empathize with it—she could notice that right away, and phrase her statement differently.

This was a pretty interesting thing, and we immediately hit upon the idea of trying it with two people instead of a person and an AI. So when Xiaoyu and John (the other grad student who first tried it out) were talking to each other, they could visually see when they were making a connection—a visual connection would spring up between their heads. We only had four nanoball brain imagers available so we couldn't try it with more than four people at once at that stage, but it was still pretty interesting—seeing the web of connections form between the people's heads, as the web of empathic responses formed between their minds. (If nanoball imagers weren't so damn expensive, I suppose this would be a great approach to online dating!)

But none of this really prepared us for what happened next, of course. We've since documented all this stuff pretty rigorously for publication (I say "we", but really I played a pretty small role in it; but hey, the papers look nice on my resume!), but initially it was all just qualitative observation. Xiaoyu and John liked each other well enough, but each of them independently noticed that they found the OpenCog AI agent to be somehow more responsive, more understanding, more empathic. As if it really understood them better, and responded to them more genuinely.

And it wasn't just the two of them. Everyone who tried the system reported the same sort of response. The AI simulation of the mirror neuron system actually did a way better job of mirroring emotions than the human mirror neuron system. This was reflected in the visual webbing that VirtualViz generated, but also came across really strong in the subjects' subjective reactions.

And what was most interesting at all, from the neuroscientists' point of view, was what they saw in the brain visualizations while the human subjects were interacting with the AIs. The mirror systems in the human brains were getting bigger! By interacting with the AI, which was more empathically capable than the humans, the humans themselves were becoming more empathic. After interacting with the AI for enough hours, when the humans interacted with each other, they found the experience more satisfying.

The psych guys did some tests to see how much (if at all) this neural change impacted the peoples' real-life interactions, and the finding was that it did, though not as strongly as their virtual world interactions. According to all the standard measures, interacting with the empathic AI's actually made people more empathic, even in real life.

And this is where we were when the Cybercrisis hit. We actually were in the middle of some experiments building webs between four humans and four AI's, when we saw the news that half the Net had gone down due to some kind of cyberterrrorist activity. That's when I got the idea that this system might be of some practical use. Not a particularly brilliant idea in hindsight, but I just happened to be the first one to think of it. Probably everyone else had deeper things on my mind, whereas I was mostly thinking about lunch (I guess it was about 11am), so there was plenty of extra space in my head for obvious ideas to pop into. Anyway, it occurred to me that, with this crisis going on, someone was definitely going to be interrogating someone—and who would be a better interrogator than someone who could establish a superhuman level of trust and understanding with another person? That is, the Mirror Man. The wizardry there was all on the part of the OpenCog team, and as I said, I have no frigging idea what goes on inside that AI engine, and I don't want to know. Aside from setting up the deployment of VirtualViz for this app, my sole contribution here was to make a phone call to my old college friend Russell, whom I knew to be working for a certain three-letter agency down in Washington. He came up to the lab and I showed him our set-up and then he logged into our minorly hacked OpenSim grid and, well, you know the rest. Mirror Man did his country proud and we actually found out who was behind the Cybercrisis with a remarkably small amount of hassle. And I moved on to the next project, which I'm still working on now, which involves visualizing the interactions between the brain and the immune system.

Wow—that went on longer than I expected! I hope it wasn't too digressive, or too redundant with what you already know. And I'm sorry if I blew my own horn too much in there; it's an occupational hazard.

Anyway, if you want any more information, you know where to find me—just log into OpenSim is the easiest way; or else send me an email ;-)

Your friend and partner in data-visualization and cybercrime-stomping mayhem,

Igor
--
Igor Mikhailevich Brilliant
Director, Information Visualization
Synthetic Science Labs LLC

"Nothing will ever be attempted if all possible objections must be first overcome"

Dr Samuel Johnson

Bringing Data Visualization and Virtual Worlds Together

The synergetic potential of data visualization and the virtual-world experience is obvious in principle, yet difficult to realize in practice. The fictional "Mirror Man" vignette given above illustrates one potential future realization of this synergy, in the context of neuroscience, AI and social psychology—but the themes raised by the vignette are relevant far more generally (see Figure 17.1).

There have already been some serious efforts to bring data visualization and virtual worlds together (see Swan 2008, 2008a for a nice review), but so far, no technology has emerged that comes close to realizing the potential power of the combination. Most what exists in virtual worlds today, along these lines, are real-time interactive data displays: NOAA's real-time weather simulation, air traffic data, various 3D charts showing stock prices, and so forth. However, there are not yet sophisticated tools that let you load in and visualize your own datasets, or customize the properties of the display within the virtual world to suit the properties of a particular new type of dataset (see Figure 17.2).

The next step, it would seem, would be to create data visualization and analysis widgets that would allow users to upload their own datasets, and then explore these using 3D camera zooming, "physical" interaction and other unique virtual world aspects. This wouldn't necessarily replace traditional data visualization and analysis software but it would certainly complement it nicely. But these possibilities have barely yet been explored. Perhaps the biggest step in this direction so far is the PrimPlotter shown in Figure 17.3.

Among the most interesting virtual-worlds data-visualization applications I've seen so far is IBM's "virtual server room" (Brodkin 2008), which lets a system

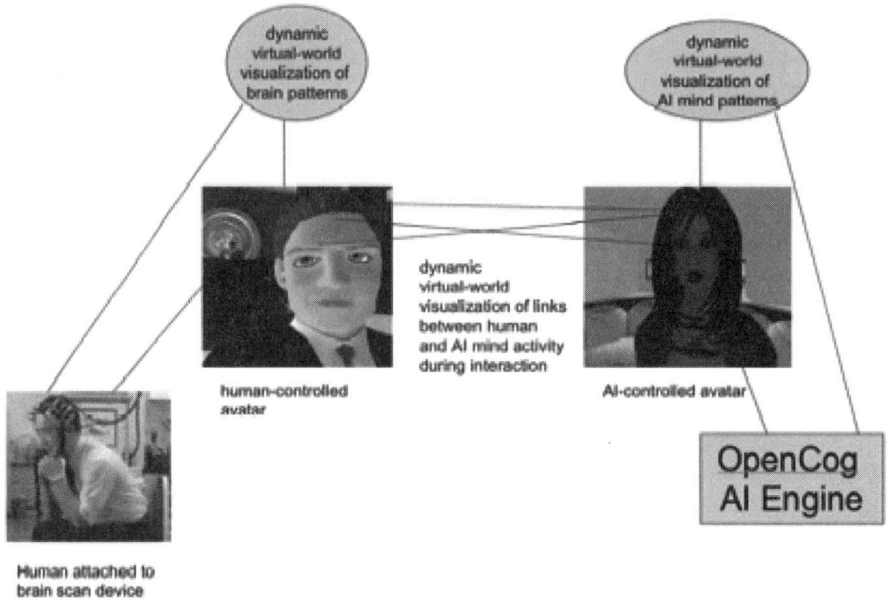

Figure 17.1 Logical structure of the data visualization in the Mirror Man Vignette (unfortunately, visually evocative depiction of the data-viz in the vignette would go far beyond the author's artistic capabilities!)

Figure 17.2 3D stock price visualization in Second Life. The lower picture is more interesting as it uses trading volume as the third dimension

Source: http://slurl.com/secondlife/Io/84/34/48

Figure 17.2 ***Concluded***

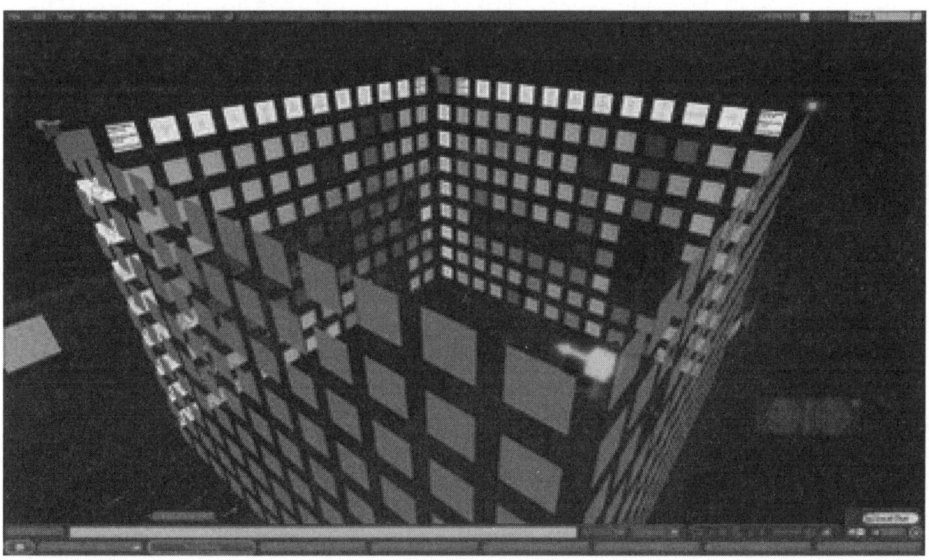

Figure 17.3 PrimPlotter: data visualization walls in Second Life

Source: From http://1cellpk.blogspot.com/2008/07/official-release-of-primplotter-at-sl5b.html, accessed 3/15/09.

administrator walk around in a virtual-world simulation of a server room and inspect the machines under his supervision. This is particularly interesting in that it lets the sys-admin view the machines as if they were all in a single room, arranged in a physical manner that reflects their informational relationship, when in fact the machines may actually be distributed across various physical locations in a complex way. However, even this exciting application has serious limitations, related to the way objects and their interactions are currently controlled in virtual worlds, a topic I will return to below.

My goal in developing the "Mirror Man" vignette was to go a little further out, beyond the more obvious possibilities (even though many of these obvious possibilities haven't been realized yet in reality), and to explore what might be possible regarding the utilization of virtual worlds for the collaborative analysis and visualization of complex data, once the technology advances significantly beyond its current state—but in directions that are clearly plausible in scientific and engineering terms.

Part of the message of the vignette is that data analysis and visualization can have implications going in both directions—virtual worlds can help data visualization, and data visualization can also help enhance the virtual worlds experience in various ways. Potentially, once they're brought to an adequate level, they can integrate thoroughly and synergetically with virtual-world interactions in real-time, becoming a critical enabler of a rich virtual-world experience. This may happen in many different ways, of course—the Mirror Man vignette just hints at one interesting possibility. In the Mirror Man case, the synergy arises in large part because data visualization technology is used to visualize data *about* virtual world interaction, which then enhances the interaction itself, potentially with effects that are important in the real world as well.

Bringing Mirror Man to Life

The realities of virtual world data visualization and analysis today are fascinating, but obviously fall far short of the fantasy in the Mirror Man vignette. What exactly does the vignette have to do with reality? How far "out there" is it?

There is nothing in the Mirror Man vignette that seems outside the scope of scientific and engineering plausibility. Mirror neurons systems are the subject of active study (Rizzolatti and Sinigaglia 2008), an increasing number of AI scientists are focusing their efforts on achieving virtually-embodied artificial general intelligence (Wang et al. 2008), and the VirtualViz information visualization mechanisms described are certainly within the realm of plausibility. Whether or not things do develop in such a way that makes Mirror Man type scenarios plausible, it seems very likely that they *could.*

However, bringing the Mirror Man vignette to life would require advances far beyond the state of the art in a host of different areas, including brain imaging and AI as well as virtual world technology. In this section I will overview what these advances would be. I will focus mainly on the virtual world aspect, but before doing so will give brief mention to these other three areas as well.

Advances Needed Beyond the Virtual Worlds Domain

Firstly, current brain imaging technology is not able to detect the dynamics of thoughts and feelings as they pass through the brain. At the current state of technology (which includes such tools as fMRI, PET and voltage-sensitive dyes; see (Bremner 2005) for a review), things are more at the level of being able to detect which regions of the brain are using the most energy when a certain type of thought or feeling is in play. However, a number of radical new brain imaging technologies are under active development, and we agree with Kurzweil's (2006) assessment that ongoing exponential growth in this area is likely. Kurzweil estimates that by the late 2020's we will have the brain scanning capability required by the Mirror Man vignette. And if an appropriate breakthrough occurs (like the vignette's fictional "nanoballs") we may get there sooner.

Next, artificial intelligence technology is of course not yet to the level where we can create humanlike virtual agents such as Mirror Man. The majority of the AI research field at the current time is focused on "narrow AI," meaning the creation of specialized algorithms for solving specialized, context-constrained problems, but an increasing minority of the field is now looking beyond this and moving back toward the original goals of the AI field, involving the creation of general software intelligence at the human level and ultimately beyond. Most AI experts agree that this sort of Artificial General Intelligence (AGI) will eventually be possible, but estimates of the timeline and the most likely path to this goal differ widely. Kurzweil (2006) is the most vocal advocate of the perspective that human-level intelligence will likely first be achieved as a side-effect of advances in brain science and computer hardware, via the creation of hardware emulations of human brains. On the other hand, the author has argued (Goertzel 2007) that it may be more productive, at this stage, to focus on non-brain-based approaches to software intelligence, and has organized a series of conferences gathering together researchers focused on AGI, with the explicit goal of moving toward the creation of software programs that think, create and act autonomously and intelligently in the general manner of a human being, or Mirror Man.[1]

OpenCog,[2] mentioned in the fictional vignette, is a real, current AI project, which aims to be a comprehensive framework for the creation of powerful AI systems (Hart and Goertzel 2008). The author's work on the Novamente Cognition Engine (Goertzel 2006) and OpenCog Prime (Goertzel 2008) AGI systems (the latter operating within the OpenCog framework) represents one among many current approaches to the creation of powerful AGI. And in the context of this chapter, it is worth noting that this work is closely tied with contemporary work on virtual world technology. One of the major conceptual debates in the AI community has to do with the importance (or otherwise) of embodiment for AGI. Some researchers, most famously Rodney Brooks (2004), argue that robotic embodiment is necessary for true, humanlike artificial intelligence. Many others argue that it's essentially irrelevant, and there's no need to anthropomorphize AI's to this extent. A middle-road approach holds that embodiment is extremely useful though not strictly essential for developing AI's, and that virtual-world embodiment may

1 See agi-08.org, agi-09.org, accessed 3/15/09.

2 opencog.org, accessed 3/15/09.

confer many of the advantages of robotic embodiment, at lower cost and with greater flexibility and potentiality for collaborative work. This ties in with the discussion on virtual worlds and robot simulation in the following subsection.

Advances Needed in Virtual Worlds Technology

On the virtual world side, what improvements to current technology would be required to enable the realization of the Mirror Man vignette, or other virtual-world data-analysis-and-simulation applications of comparable complexity? These are twofold:

1. Introduction of more flexible control devices, allowing humans to use their natural body movements and facial expressions to control avatar behaviors;
2. A thorough revision of the way objects' movements and interactions are controlled

Both of these are extremely important, but I will say more about the latter because it is closer to my own research, and hence an area where I have more original insights to offer.

Advances in Human Control of Virtual Agents

There are many interesting ways of going beyond the current, extremely crude modality in which virtual agent behaviors are controlled by keyboard and menu commands.

First of all, there is what I think of as "Motion Capture Plus": imagine a host of cameras aimed at the user, capturing their movements from all angles; and including (something that current motion capture technology does not do; see Liverman 2004) the ability to capture detailed facial expressions. Throw in haptic devices like cybergloves (see Figure 17.4) and comparable cybersuits. With this sort of motion/emotion capture technology, to put it simply, the human user can act out a behavior, and then the virtual agent will do it, with appropriate style and feeling. A number of researchers are actively working in this direction, using a variety of different devices (see review in Fisch et al. 2003). One source of motivation for this sort of work lies in the game industry, but of course the interest there is more in low-cost, limited-functionality devices suitable for short-term mass distribution, whereas for research purposes one may be more willing to explore the higher-cost, higher-functionality frontier.

Furthermore, motion capture should be supplemented with emotion capture: a variety of physical sensors capturing parameters such as heart rate, galvanic skin response, and so forth, giving a physiological indication of the user's emotional state. There is significant ongoing work in this direction as well, though not specifically directed at virtual agent control (e.g., Alvino et al. 2007, Harris 2006).

But motion/emotion capture is not the full solution to the virtual agent control problem. Acting out behaviors physically may quickly become exhausting for the user; and, one may wish virtual agents to carry out activities such as flying which their physical bodies can't do. So, a more complete solution might be a combination of menu-driven commands, verbal commands (interpreted by appropriate AI software) and

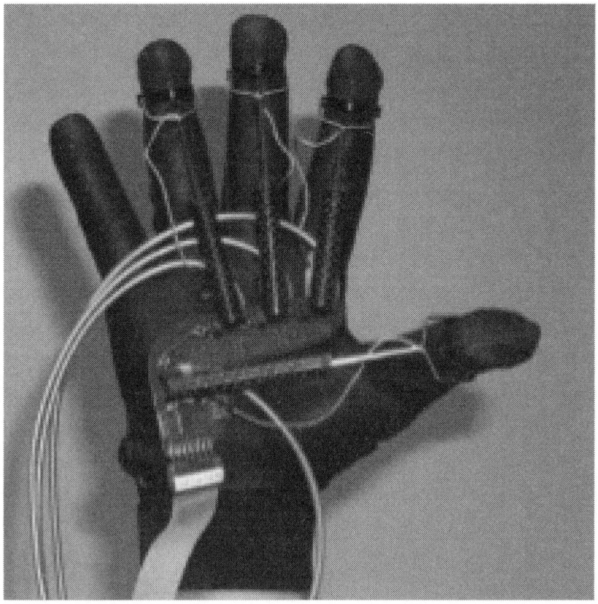

Figure 17.4 Master II cyberglove from Rutgers University
Source: Bouzit et al. 2002.

Motion Capture Plus. For instance, the user might say "I want to fly up there to look at what Bert is looking at," and then the AI language interpretation engine would need to understand where the user wants to fly to, and make it so. But then the user might want to point at something in particular, and for this purpose might find it easier to simply move his arm in the right direction. Some fairly sophisticated adaptive control software will be needed to combine the various sorts of control signals into a coherent whole.

Going a little further out, it also seems clear that, as brain imaging technology advances, it will find wide application in the domain of virtual agent control. Why act a movement out, or describe it verbally, when you can simply *think* it and see it happen? This hinges on dramatic advances in brain imaging technology, as mentioned in the previous section. However, the neural encoding of movements is not as obscure and complicated as the encoding of abstract thoughts, and so there is reason to be fairly optimistic that this sort of thing may be possible in the next few decades (so that, for instance, one day every Nintendo console may come with a brain-scan-based game controller).

Advances in Automated Control of Virtual Objects, Avatars and Interactions

Today's virtual world technology evolved largely to meet the needs of the entertainment and social networking markets. Thus it is lacking in some key areas that are necessary for many more "serious" applications, including:

- Fine control of body movements. Right now, avatars in virtual worlds are controlled via supplying them with a fixed set of animations (e.g., "step forward",

"raise hand", "kick ball", etc.). This is different from how a robot is controlled, where one can send a signal to a specific joint such as "Exert force X in direction Y". The robotics way allows for a much wider variety of spontaneously determined movements.
- Tool use. Right now, in the existing virtual worlds, there is no way to (for instance) pick up a fork and stick it in an arbitrary soft object. There is no way to build a simple mechanical device from available parts and have it actually function.

The Mirror Man vignette depends heavily on fine control of avatar body movements: without it, it's unlikely that the empathic responses associated with mirror neurons would be intensely elicited during virtual-world interactions (see Figure 15.5).

These shortcomings come from a common source: the physics engines underlying virtual worlds are not used to control avatar movements nor to mediate object-object interactions, in a sufficiently general way. Until this problem is solved, avatars will not be able to move naturalistically nor with a broad variety of movements; and they will not be able to use tools, build machines, etc.

Fortunately a technology exists that already overcomes these shortcomings: this is the robot simulator. At the present time, due to various difficulties involved in working with physical robots, a great deal of practical robotics work actually involved working with simulated rather than real robots. Robot simulators are fairly sophisticated these days, providing accurate simulations of physics as manifested in laboratory environments, if not real-world situations like forests, oceans and city streets. However, they lack one of the key strengths of virtual worlds such as Second Life and Multiverse (where the Novamente Pet Brain controlled animals have been prototyped): this is the capability for massive multiplayer interaction.

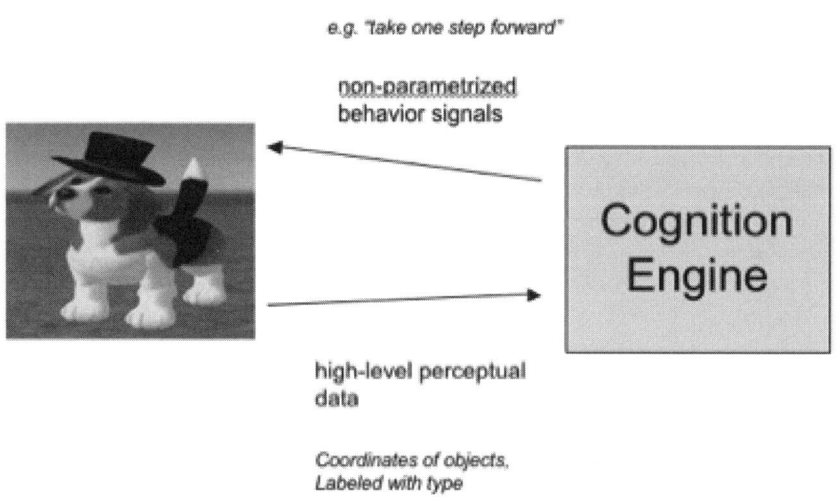

Figure 17.5 Cognitive Control of agents in current virtual worlds—e.g., Second Life, Multiverse, OpenSim

Robot simulators exceed virtual worlds and game engines in terms of allowing detailed control of simulated robot joints, and physically realistic interactions between objects (as needed for instance to enable tool use), but don't allow large numbers of individuals to log on and help teach robots. It seems that the integration of robot simulator and virtual world technology has a great potential to advance intelligent robotics, via supplying robots with a large number of teachers. Recently, in collaboration with Dan Miller and others, I have been exploring ways of bringing this integration about, such as modifying the OpenSim[3] (virtual world to use the Gazebo[4] robot simulator in place of its current physics engine. This would however require substantial changes to the OpenSim architecture.

Specifically, as Dan Miller has noted (private communication), the most elegant way to implement this functionality would be to re-architect OpenSim so that each object in a sense "owns its own actions." So potentially each object could control its interactions according to whatever laws of physics its creator associated it with. There seem no fundamental objections to modifying OpenSim in this way, but it would require significant effort and it's not currently clear how rapidly this effort will proceed.

In sum: The knowledge and the supporting software exists to extend current virtual world technology in a way that would enable flexible object behaviors and interactions of the sort required by the Mirror Man vignette; but at time of writing, no governmental or industry funding source has emerged to spearhead this sort of work, presumably because it is not needed for the entertainment and social networking functions that provide the main purpose of current virtual environments.

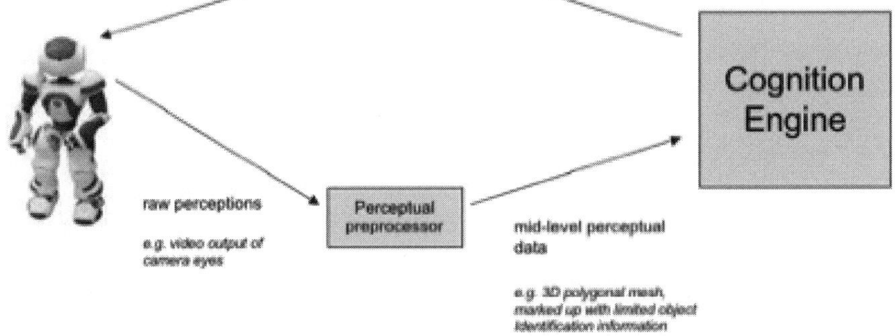

Figure 17.6 Cognitive control of agents in a robot simulator (which may be integrated with a virtual world engine)

---

3 opensimulator.org, accessed 3/15/09.

4 playerstage.sourceforge.net/gazebo/gazebo.html, accessed 3/15/09.

Recommendations for Research and Development

Based on the above, if we want to work toward the eventual enablement of Mirror Man type scenarios, what should we be doing right now? Setting aside fundamental brain imaging and artificial general intelligence research, which are critical but somewhat peripheral to the scope of this book, the suggested foci would be:

1. Refactoring of current virtual world engines to allow "objects to own their own interactions", as outlined above;
2. Integration of robot simulators and other simulation engines with appropriate objects in virtual worlds, so as to provide fine-grained agent control;
3. Creation of AI language comprehension systems capable of correctly translating verbal commands into complex, context-appropriate physical movements;
4. Creation of low cost motion and emotion capture devices.

The first three of these are computer software related; the fourth is hardware focused. Noteworthy is that the first two do not require any groundbreaking research; they are "merely" software integration, but of a nontrivial magnitude, and of a sort that the commercial game and virtual world industry currently lacks the motivation to pursue.

References

Alvinoa, C., Kohlerb, C., Barrett, F., Gurb, R.E., Gurb, R.C., and Vermaa, R. (2007). Computerized measurement of facial expression of emotions in schizophrenia. *Journal of Neuroscience Methods* 163(2):350–361.

Bouzit M., Popescu, G., Burdea, G., and Boian, R. (2002). *The Rutgers Master II-ND Force Feedback Glove*, Proceedings of IEEE VR 2002 Haptics Symposium, pp. 145–152.

Bremner, J.D. (2005). *Brain Imaging Handbook*. New York: Norton.

Brodkin, J. (2008). IBM Redefines "Virtual" Data Center. *IT World*, Feb.

Brooks, R. (2002). *Flesh and Machines*, New York: Pantheon Books.

Fisch A., Mavroidis C., Melli-Huber J., and Bar-Cohen Y. (2003). Haptic Devices for Virtual Reality, Telepresence, and Human-Assistive Robotics, in *Biologically-Inspired Intelligent Robots*, edited by Y. Bar-Cohen and C. Breazeal, New York: SPIE Press.

Goertzel, B. (2006). *Patterns, Hypergraphs and General Intelligence.* Proceedings of International Joint Conference on Neural Networks, IJCNN 2006, Vancouver CA.

Goertzel, B. (2007). Human-level artificial general intelligence and the possibility of a technological singularity. *Artificial Intelligence* 171(18).

Goertzel, B. (2008). *OpenCogPrime: Design for a Thinking Machine*, online at http://opencog.org/wiki/OpenCogPrime:WikiBook, last accessed on 03/15/2009.

Harris, R. (2006). Market researchers feel a) delighted, b) elated, c) ecstatic, about new tools to measure consumers' emotional responses to advertising. *Marketing Magazine*, 25 Sept.

Hart, D. and Goertzel, B. (2008). OpenCog: A Software Framework for Integrative AGI, in *Artificial General Intelligence 2008: Proceedings of the First AGI Conference*, edited by Stan Franklin, Ben Goertzel and Pei Wang. Amsterdam: IOS Press

Kurzweil, R. (2006). *The Singularity Is Near.* Penguin, New York.

Liverman, M. (2004). *The Animator's Motion Capture Guide: Organizing, Managing, Editing.* Boston: Charles River Media Game Development

Rizzolatti, G., and Sinigaglia, C. (2008). *Mirrors in the Brain: How Our Minds Share Actions, Emotions, and Experience.* New York: Oxford University Press

Swan, M. (2008). *Data Visualization in Second Life.* http://www.slideshare.net/labloga/virtual-world-data-visualization-339518/, last accessed on 03/15/2009

Swan, M. (2008). *Data Visualization in Second Life.* http://futurememes.blogspot.com/2008/02/data-visualization-in-second-life.html, last accessed on 03/15/2009.

Wang, P., Goertzel, B., and Franklin, S., (eds.) (2008). *Artificial General Intelligence 2008: Proceedings of the First AGI Conference.* Amsterdam: IOS Press

Chapter 18

Turing, Androids and a Travel Holiday: A Futuristic View of Synthetic Worlds

Robert Cox, Patricia Crowther, and John Campbell

Abstract

Synthetic worlds provide potential for a new working environment. We provide a perspective on the future of work in a synthetic world; following a fictional robot trainer in the course of his work, experiencing the difficulties of programming an android to pass the Turing test. During his lunchtime break, our fictional worker plans a travel holiday with his wife using another synthetic world. We use this vignette to extrapolate over the next 15 years the changes in synthetic world technologies required to realize our vision of working life in 2024.

A Day in the Life of an Android Trainer

"Damn"

The tall, dark, handsome man stood staring at a picture. Beside him, an attractive woman was talking. "Interesting picture," she said. A waterfall cascaded down a rocky scarp, sunlight glimmering on the spray, leaves of nearby trees damp with moisture. Either side of the picture, windows opened onto a meadow dotted with wildflowers.

The man turned to her and said, "I think it's a window."

"No, it isn't," said the woman. "Can't you tell, it's a picture, but someone has animated the waterfall?"

"Oh, I must have been mistaken," replied the gentleman.

"How could you possibly think it's a window, silly? The image in the frame doesn't change as you move." replied the woman. She moved her head from side to side to illustrate her point. The man turned away, his cautionary circuits detecting that he had made a social faux-pas. His higher priority behaviors caused him to end the conversation and wander away.

I watched the interaction, "Damn," I said again, dismayed that my android program had been so easily fooled by an animated picture. In the cubicle beside me, my colleague Harold chuckled. He always had a good laugh when I said "damn", knowing that thousands of hours of programming were yet to produce human-like behaviors in even this virtual world.

"What was it this time?" queried Harold. "Damn animated picture," I said. "The bot thought it was a window." Harold chuckled again. "Promotion to android trainer," he mocked. I smirked, "The extra five thousand dollars a year?" in reply. Harold responded, "You can buy the beers tonight, then."

I stared back at the screen. My android Maxx, the handsome man with his dark hair and good looks, had managed to extract himself from the conversation and was wandering dangerously close to the edge of the simulator. I briefly toyed with the idea of allowing him into the neighboring sim, but common sense prevailed, so I de-rezzed him, his form fading and finally dissolving as he was removed from the virtual world. It was time to add additional training to his program.

I set a search program running to see if anyone had already trained their androids to tell the difference between the view through a window and an animated picture.

The hourglass hung annoyingly on the program window, indicating that the search would take a further ten minutes. "Time for a coffee," I said to Harold. He responded, "Make mine black, with two sugars." Despondently, I ambled to the coffee machine and ordered a straight black, two sugars and a cup of tea for myself; Earl Grey, "hot". The machine obediently filled two cardboard cups with liquid that could be loosely termed coffee and tea, and spoke with a sensual female voice, "Enjoy your drinks, do come again." I groaned and made a mental note to ask that the voice circuit be disabled from this particular dispenser.

Harold doubled over laughing. "What's so funny?" I asked.

"Next month, your in-world android will be able to order coffee from that machine," said Harold. I handed him the cup containing the darker liquid.

"Coffee?" I offered, ".. or perhaps just some kind of random burnt bean." Harold sipped and spluttered, spraying a fine mist of liquid on his screen.

"Hasn't that tech arrived to fix the blasted thing yet?" He grumbled all the way to the kitchenette, grabbing a cloth to mop the offending liquid from the display.

He paused a moment to ask, "So why do we need android trainers, anyway? And putting them into Third Life makes no sense to me. Wouldn't it be better to train them in the real world?"

"Well, the problem is generalization. Take a bottle, for example. Let's assume there are some rules to identify a bottle. It's thicker at the bottom than that top. It's generally round, has a label and a lid. Well, now." I grabbed a coke bottle from the bin. "Take this. It fits the criteria; it's generally round, it has a lid, in your case, you appear to have been chewing on it..." Harold mashed his teeth, as if to say, "Yes." "So it's obviously a bottle. And in fact, many bottles do fit those criteria, but not all. Some bottles are annoyingly square. For example, whiskey bottles. Many good scotches come in a square bottle and worse still; the criteria fit many things that are definitely not bottles, such as a jam jar. So we android trainers teach the brain-ware the difference between a jam jar and a bottle, and also that a bottle can be square.

"Just as well the android can't drink scotch, or it would be into your stash," said Harold teasingly.

"As if you don't already take advantage of my good nature," I replied, thinking of the rapidly dropping quantity in my drinks cabinet.

"Brain-ware," he chortled. "More like dumb-ware if you ask me. If it can't tell the difference between a bottle and a jar."

"Well at age two, I bet you couldn't tell the difference," said I, in defense of what was definitely a losing proposition.

Thankfully the search finished at just that time—with a loud BING, it told me that someone had already trained a 'droid to recognize animated pictures in Third Life. I breathed a sigh of relief as I downloaded the partial co-operation map, that would tell the agents in the 'droid's brain where to start on this difficult task of distinguishing a picture from a window. The download was fortunately fast, the server being able to operate close to the 10 gigabit per second theoretical limit.

Rapidly I reprogrammed Maxx. I "compiled" the brain-ware and was met with a cruel shock. The new brain-ware model would require 114 threads in 72 CPUs. Maxx was currently running in 63 CPUs and had less than 100 threads. I initiated a video call with tech support. We all hated tech support, since they seemed to be able to say "no" vastly more frequently than they said "yes". I asked to talk to Chris, who I knew was a shift leader and who had the most amazing Facebook page. More widgets than I knew existed, including the fast, new 3D graphic ones. Thankfully she was there. "Hi Chris." I tried the soft social approach first. "How's life?"

She paused. "What do you want?" she said with a voice that could have fractured glass. My heart sank. She was on to me. I guess there's only so much a free beer on Friday will buy you.

"I need some more threads and cores," I stated nonchalantly.

The tone of her voice was enough to freeze blood. "How many?" she asked.

"I currently have 63," I said. "I need 80." Long ago, I learned that you should start with an ambit claim.

"Oh, is that all," she said. "Tell you what; I'll give you a hundred." I was puzzled. "Why?" I queried. "Oh," she replied. "We just got a rack of the new 1024 Core motherboards. I want to see them used."

"Cool," I said, "Give me a thousand threads; it'll reduce training time."

"Oh," she replied, "Here's a hundred - if you want more, you'll have to fill out online requisition form 601/2-1:4. And don't forget to put in a cost code."

"Yes, Ma'am," I replied, saluting sharply, much to Harold's amusement. "Way to go, Galen," he said once I'd disconnected the call.

I stared at the screen, waiting for my extra CPUs to materialize, when the familiar ting of an appointment reminder sounded, telling me to meet my wife for lunch at the Virtual Plaza Cafe. I picked up my bag and headed out the door. "I'm off to lunch Harold, see you in an hour." I hummed to myself as I strolled down the street to the cafe. Despite its name, the Virtual Plaza Cafe exists in the real world. It has high speed broadband, and I'm told that all the furniture accurately recreates the Reality Cafe in Third Life. I wondered for a moment which had come first, the real world furniture, or the virtual furniture.

I greeted Trixie with a hug. She was bubbling with enthusiasm, freshly printed travel brochures protruded from her over cluttered handbag. "If we're lucky, we'll be able to see the Eiffel Tower." She pulled out her mini laptop and connected to the Cafe server. "I've always wanted to visit Paris," she went on, "see the sights, sample genuine French Cuisine, immerse myself in the culture. I can hardly wait. We just need to plan our itinerary."

I looked over her shoulder as the waitress came to take our orders. Trixie pulled up the interface and connected us to *Third Life: Travel*. A slowly rotating globe appeared on the screen. Trixie's finger hovered, waiting for France to come into view. She tapped on the screen. A map of France expanded to fill the field of view. Almost absent-mindedly, she ordered a bowl of pumpkin soup and a café latte, as she honed in on a map of Paris. I ordered my usual, a pizza and coke. I watched as Trixie selected a region and materialized our avatars. I connected to Third Life via her laptop with my mobile phone, so I could control my own avatar. It seemed my wife had already decided on our itinerary and much to my disappointment, it didn't appear to include the Moulin Rouge. "I found this great little hotel. Here, I'll teleport you." The screen faded and our avatars were standing in what was indeed a very beautiful place. Lush green carpets, reminiscent of grass; the walls looked like marble. "It's supposed to be an accurate representation, right down to the stain on the carpet there." I brought up the Third Life AccVPP (Accuracy Verification Protocol Portal). The image verification certificate was two months out of date and its code showed that the scans had been done by Brontier, well-known for photoshopping textures before applying them to Third Life; but generally they were reliable, so I had some confidence that L'hotel Yolanda, as I was viewing it here in Third Life, was a reasonable representation of what we would find in the real world.

"Hey, slow down. There are a few places in Paris I want to see. Is it within walking distance of The Louvre? And what about the Arc de Triumphe?" Her avatar grabbed my avatar's hand and marched me out the door. We could just see the Eiffel Tower in the distance. We spent the next forty minutes wandering around the Paris sim, jotting down places that we wanted to see. Trixie tapped the screen at regular intervals; she was building an interactive itinerary document. Knowing her, she would play with it for several days before finalizing and having the software make the relevant bookings.

We finished lunch; I gave Trixie a final goodbye kiss before heading back to work. When I got there, my desk was covered with cardboard cups. Harold smirked as he delivered two more. I was puzzled, but I knew it was one of his jokes. He grinned as he placed two more cups of Earl Grey tea on the last remaining space on my desk. "They fixed the coffee machine," he said. "And guess what? It's now live in Third Life."

I looked at the tea and hesitantly asked, "Why is my desk covered with rapidly cooling cups of tea?"

"Simple," said Harold. "I suggested to Maxx that he order you a nice cup of tea."

I grabbed the keyboard. Harold had rezzed Maxx and the screen was filled with "Has the tea been delivered yet?" messages from Maxx. I hurriedly typed, "Yes" and made a mental note to change my password so that Harold couldn't surprise me like this again.

After I had disposed of the tea, I went back to Maxx. His face showed a broad smile, apparently pleased that my tea had been delivered. The coffee machine in Third Life and Maxx seemed to be interacting. I pushed Maxx away from the machine, lest he be tempted to surprise me with yet another cup of tea. Maxx's curiosity circuit seemed to have taken over, as he started roaming. I initially felt quite comfortable. He seemed to be coping with the other avatars in the sim. Much to my surprise, he had a fairly sane conversation with an elf. The pointed ears didn't seem to be a problem for him. Flushed with confidence, I pointed him to one of my favorite haunts, a dance club called The Rock and Roll Stadium. The floor was polished timber, the walls sported pictures of old rock stars; Elvis, Buddy Holly, The Rolling Stones, Alice Cooper, Joan Jett and Marty McFly just to name a few. A large log fire crackled at one end of the stadium, smoke coiling up from the wood. There was no roof, but today for some reason, a large 3D model of the number 42, made of the same wood as the polished floor, hung in the air above the stadium.

Maxx coped well. Realizing it was a dance club, he even started dancing. Another patron, (Bluey by name) said, "Hi Maxx." Maxx was cool, responding with a cheery, "Hello". Android training suddenly didn't feel like such a bad profession. I let Maxx go unsupervised for a while, and for the first time since my promotion, I started to relax. My euphoria was short-lived. Maxx, in an apparent effort to sound friendly, tried to strike up a conversation with Bluey. "Nice weather," he said. Bluey looked to the skies and commented that there were low clouds.

The club DJ blared out, "Win a thousand v-dollars if you can guess the age of the club's owner, Mr. Diamond Tim." Fairly rapidly, the club was filled with cries of "42" the clue hanging in the sky. Even Maxx seemed to respond. "Yes, 42 clouds," he responded. The other patron laughed. "Yes, it's raining 42s." Maxx's agent-based brain clearly understood the subject. "Clouds of 42 all day," said Maxx. Bluey clearly wanted to be part of the conversation. "Now it's raining 42s we're all in trouble," he declared. Maxx stared at the heavens. "When it rains, we get wet," he said. I could almost see his android brain fixating on the large 42 in the sky. "Don't do it," I thought. "Don't say something stupid now." But Maxx was determined. He walked towards a fire "Come," he said to Bluey. "Let's dry ourselves by the fire." I was hopeful he was still making sense, but a gnawing sensation of doubt still nagged at me. "Let's get the 42s out of our clothing," said Maxx. "Good idea," came the response, "We'd better make sure the 42s don't catch fire." The whole conversation was becoming surreal. "You're silly. 42s extinguish fire. They don't burn. 42s evaporate from the ocean, condense as 42 and precipitate as 42, thus filling lakes and rivers of America with 42. Which can then be used to put out fires," said Maxx. Bluey pointed to the 42 in the sky. "It's obviously made of wood," he said. "Wood burns. Let's feed the fire with 42." I began to hope that Maxx's social faux-pas circuits would cut in, and he would end the conversation as he had earlier that day with the picture. This time I was not so lucky. The only thing holding this conversation together was his syntax circuits. He'd confused water, clouds and 42. Provided you knew that, his sentences were syntactically correct and made perfect sense. It gradually dawned on me that the other patron was also an android in training. He was sure that 42 meant wood. So his comments made sense too. But there was a total disconnect between them. I let the conversation continue, more out of morbid curiosity rather than any professional interest. It was obvious this brainware release was unsalvageable. Maxx was over-contextualizing.

An attractive blond leaned against the wall near them. I guessed she'd been listening to their conversation. "What are you two on about," she said. "That's one of the strangest conversations I've ever heard." Maxx's social circuit finally cut in. "Hi, good looking," he finally said. The other patron also chimed in with "Hi, you look nice." I wondered if both of them were operating on the same broken version of brainware.

"I think you're both silly. Are you brothers?" she asked. "No, we only just met," they uttered together. The inflection in their voices was very similar. They collided as they each took one step away from the blond. My suspicions were confirmed as Maxx and Bluey simultaneously headed for the door. They looked at each other, stepping away, each taking a 180 degree turn, the paths they followed looking eerily similar. I figured Maxx had shown his stupidity long enough and de-rezzed him.

"Harold" I queried, "do you know a Droid trainer fond of the Rock and Roll Stadium with a droid called Bluey?" "Oh," he replied, "That would be the elderly woman on the third floor that sits in the cubicle near the big window. Can't remember her name but she has a picture of Third life on her wall with the Words 'Bluey, Who' written on it."

"It figures," I said, "Twenty two million people in Third Life, and Maxx meets a trainer from three floors below. How many degrees of separation are there? Six? Tell me..."

At this point we will leave poor Galen and his ailing brainware challenged droid in training and discuss the science and reasons behind our story.

Towards a Working Life in Synthetic Worlds

So how plausible is the above scenario by 2024? Well from our knowledge of artificial intelligence it is quite likely that android software will need some kind of training period, so the idea of doing this in a synthetic (or virtual) world where it is fairly safe seems to us to be a good idea. Robot designers are already playing with learning robots such as SAIL (Weng et al. 2001). It is only a short jump to suggest that the title of android trainer would be given to the person in charge of teaching the 'droid. The idea of Brainware as an additional layer in the software is proposed by Zadeh (2008).

As for the synthetic world of Third Life; well it is an extension of the current world Second Life (www.secondlife.com) (though if versions are to be maintained in the name then it may well be Sixth Life by 2024). We feel it is highly likely that Second Life will be eclipsed by another synthetic world by 2024.

Galen sends his android, Maxx into the synthetic world we call Third Life for training. Third Life is our extrapolation of how a synthetic world may appear, and how it might be used as a work environment in the year 2024. We take elements of the experiences to be found in Linden Lab's Second Life along with a bit of extrapolation. While Second Life is currently the largest and most significant synthetic world, the authors also draw on experience from other synthetic worlds including IMVU (www.IMVU.com) and OpenSim (www.opensimulator.org).

Predicting the future is a difficult task. Clarke (1962) states "All attempts to predict the future in any detail appear ludicrous within a few years." Whilst many of his predictions have come to pass, others, such as the understanding of Cetacean Languages by the 1990s (talking with dolphins), appear unlikely to ever occur.

In 1994/95 the first author was asked as part of a strategic planning exercise to predict the desktop computer of the year 2000, and was quite accurate, due to Moore's law. Moore (1965) predicted that the number of transistors on a chip will double about every two years which has not been a bad guide (while there is evidence mores law is breaking down we think it will fade slowly rather than fail cataclysmically).

A meaningful starting point for understanding potential changes in synthetic environments is to examine current aspects and then make reasonable extrapolations:

- Technology (CPU, communications, networking, portability, energy efficiency and connectivity);
- Physical (for example, the use of Carbon fiber in aircraft to reduce weight, or optical fiber replacing wires—in synthetic worlds, such changes will occur both in the user interface and on the server);
- Social. It can be very hard to predict these: some social changes hit hard and fast but others never arrive (for example, a world without war) or changes to a country's laws;
- Global and/or Regional (for example, global warming).

Technology

CPU technology Extrapolating from the common desktop and server environment at the time of writing (July–October 2008) based on a core2 Quad with about 820 million transistors; if we double the number of transistors every two years, then we can say that it is likely that in 2024 the common CPU/chips will have around 820*2^8 million transistors (about 200 Billion transistors). Since Intel Corporation (2008) states that it already has in its labs 2 billion transistor devices, this processing capacity appears plausible by 2024. It is probably better to think of it as the equivalent of 256 current chips; or perhaps a single chip with 1024 CPUs with each CPU having roughly the same power as a 'current' core in a quad core. This is why our protagonist, Galen is asking for more cores and threads from a server farm equipped with new 1024 core CPUs.

This increased power will almost certainly be delivered with a form of parallel processing. The clock speed increases in CPUs so common in the 90's have in general already stopped. These speed increases have little to do with semiconductor packing density as it is probable that high packing density silicon will not run significantly faster than 3GHz for the foreseeable future.

While more cores are not the only form of parallel processing, it is highly likely that it will be the first significant parallel technology applied to the mass market. The authors note that VLIW (very long instruction word) and cell computing also offer parallelism of a different form and will certainly co-exist in the market. In fact both these technologies have significant advantages for servers running Second Life like virtual Grids. However, it will not be so easy to migrate today's crop of Wintel (Windows/Intel) applications to these technologies. We therefore expect an adoption gap to still exist in 2024.

The Internet and bandwidth Using our own experience as a guide, we estimate that a single active user (40 hours per week) of Second Life requires around 40 gigabytes of internet bandwidth per month. So by 2024 what will we need? Perhaps no more than

120 gigabytes, since little extra bandwidth would be needed to increase the fidelity of Second Life. One could imagine the same kind of graphical objects that one finds in other games being added to Second Life or its successors, in particular normal maps.[1] Normal maps are critical to the beauty and visual splendor of games like WoW (World of Warcraft). Many of these artifacts can be (and will be) computed on the client as needed using the multitude of "spare" CPU's that will be available at the desktop. The synthetic worlds of the future may include larger textures and higher polygon counts; even more objects (in SL these are termed prims—an abbreviation for primitives). However, it is probable that a substantially higher visual splendor could be achieved with a fairly modest increase in bandwidth. Some issues, such as the physics engine, are mainly server based. So a vast increase in physics fidelity (which may require increasing server capacity by an order of magnitude) would probably require only small increases in bandwidth.

Responsiveness is a totally different problem. Delays caused by the Internet as a whole will continue to plague synthetic worlds. Currently it requires 0.3 of second to "ping" a Second Life server in the USA from Australia; since this is governed by the speed of light and the path of the signal—it is very hard to expect that to decrease substantially in 2024.

One area that may well grow, is the use of video feeds into synthetic worlds; however since a better movie experience will be available from services like YouTube it is likely that many users will just switch off movie feeds at the client side so as to decrease lag (a practice that is already common now in SL).

We believe that the Internet in 2024 will not be an impediment to synthetic worlds.

Portability How portable will synthetic worlds be in 2024? Cell phone technology is already emerging. Obviously it will be easier to immerse oneself inworld on a larger display device—the current world analogue would be the difference between watching a movie on a television screen or on a portable mp4 player, such as an iPod. The basic CPU/memory and display capability will be available on cell phone sized machines. Additionally, the cell phone will provide internet connectivity allowing such virtual environments to be used anywhere, for example while on the bus on the way home from work.

We imagine a range of devices, from small cell phones to large home Virtual Reality kits, will be used to connect to synthetic worlds and will support the full range of immersion options (from a cell phone chat, to a walk in Virtual Reality Room).

Physical Changes

User interface The development of new ways to interface with synthetic worlds provides an interesting study. Consider the console games market. For many years console players were happy with wired controls. Wireless controllers became available and standard with the Xbox 360, but they merely did away with the cable. In late 2006

1 A normal map is an image file that contains lighting information that improves the quality of rendering.

there was a paradigm shift when Nintendo released the Wii - with its revolutionary controls using the movement of the control itself. Can such a "revolution" affect Second Life and other synthetic worlds? Some candidate technologies are obvious such as virtual reality glasses. We also expect that games like "Guitar Hero" will manifest in synthetic worlds, with their "guitar attachment".

Sony has announced a 3D world called "Home" for the PlayStation 3 (PS3); as of writing it is still in closed Beta release. This will bring synthetic worlds to a new group of people.

Server grids One physical change that is likely is that the synthetic world grids will not have a single server location; instead becoming highly reliant on distributed grid computing (this can be said to be the case now with Second Life having server farms in different countries). The authors see the future with affordable servers in people's homes or at least readily available from a range of vendors in different geographic locations. This is the approach currently being pursued by OSGrid and OpenSim. If we assume that these grids are interoperable (see the interoperability caveat below) then one could literally walk off a server in New York USA and onto a server in Tokyo Japan. This grid structure will have little impact on the final user, but is quite different from the way existing grids operate. This will also introduce server version issues since on a non-homogeneous grid, different servers may be running different versions of the server code. By 2024 the common clients (and there may well be several) will all support a common core of features and even the older servers will be advanced enough to deliver a satisfactory user experience.

Social Changes

Social norm Synthetic worlds offer deep immersive social experiences that rely on the ability of the technological platform to support expressive communication exchanges including non-verbal signals (Carey 2007). One area that we expect to see rapid changes is the social governance systems deployed to support social networks and to control individual behaviors. Historically trust-based models have been used to provide explanations of human social interaction and control. However, trust is a somewhat problematic and artificially constrained social construct (Shapiro 1987, Fletcher et al. 2006). We see social governance structures in synthetic worlds evolving to become increasingly defined by complex underlying social tensions and conflict. These tensions are an integral structural element of the social interrelations found in both physical and synthetic worlds and often reflect the simultaneous pressures for both collaboration and competition (Campbell et al. 2008).

Gaining a better understanding of interpersonal tensions and conflict and their role in social organization has implications for the design and governance of sustainable synthetic world ecosystems which in itself is likely to influence player retention rates (Campbell et al. 2007). Also, the ability to deal with conflict and respond in appropriate ways will be an important performance criterion for our android and its trainer. For example, any failure to deal with conflict in a social setting will expose the artificiality of our droid more quickly than excessively polite or seemingly out-of-place but friendly communication behaviors.

Legal It is reasonable to assume that legal guidelines may become required and it is likely that some states will create laws that relate only to synthetic worlds. We expect the legal domain to remain uncertain with increasing disputes over IP and trademark infringement.

Global or Regional Changes

While global warming is a major global change, it is difficult to see how such a change would affect synthetic worlds. Of course a game like Second Life can be set up to model global warming and it may be a way of predicting the social events that global warming may cause. The game *SimCity: Societies* released in 2007 deals with the causes and some consequences of global warming (BP 2008). We believe global warming will have little effect on synthetic worlds except perhaps to encourage their operators to use less energy by buying energy efficient computers for servers and clients. We have seen reports that the power consumption of the infrastructure required to run synthetic worlds contributes to global warming (Carr 2006), but this may be countered by the emergence of conferences held online rather than face to face, reducing the carbon footprint of those who would otherwise travel to attend (MacMillan Cancer Support 2008). In addition, the possibility of work being performed in synthetic worlds may reduce or in some cases eliminate the need to commute.

Synthetic World Interoperability

The authors of this chapter expect that some degree of interoperability between synthetic worlds will emerge. We also expect that the different needs of large user groups will mean that a range of synthetic world standards may well be developed. Though it is clear that there will be at least one large interoperable grid based on the emerging Second Life standards which includes OpenSim and its variants, there appear to be few commercial reasons for a synthetic world vendor to conform to one standard. Such integration will not emerge without a clear commercial incentive. However, since the initial drafting of this chapter, the events listed below have further developed our view:

- The release of Google Lively which does not conform to the OpenSim standard. Google has not delivered its protocol to the open source community.
- Litesim (litesim.com), which had previously diverged from the OpenSim standard, has reverted to being compatible with OpenSim.
- An Intergrid teleport was performed between Second Life and several OpenSim grids on 8 July 2008 (Linden Labs 2008). This is the synthetic world equivalent of surfing from one web site to another via a link. It may represent a defining moment in the move to the 3D web.
- Several OpenSim grids have forked the server code in order to add features that they believe will give them a marketplace edge. For example, 3rd Rock

Grid (www.3rdrockgrid.com) added a currency system, the Luna (similar to the Linden dollar but available only on their grid).
- The commercial product SecondInventory (www.secondinventory.com/files/details.php) can now be used to move compatible full permission content between Second Life and OpenSim. The vendors of this program are unsure of the legal situation in transferring asset information from one grid to another.

At this stage, other than Second Life and the OpenSim grids, none of the major synthetic worlds are in any significant way interoperable. This is highlighted by the two 3D virtual environments of There.com and IMVU, which are supplied by the same vendor and yet are still not interoperable.

It has taken a very long time for competing word processing vendors to agree on a common document format.[2] Synthetic worlds may take even longer. However, Linden Labs (2007) released their client to the open source community in January 2007 and the Second Life viewer is used by at least three vendors (Second Life itself, OpenSim and Litesim). This may become the basis for other systems in the future. Clearly OpenSim will be a standard—but it is likely to diverge into incompatibility as the open source community experiments with various possibilities.

While asset, script, sim and avatar data may well remain unique to each synthetic world vendor, it is quite possible that financial data will be able to be made common to all synthetic worlds via a sort of virtual world bank or clearing house. Such a facility would easily allow the transfer of virtual world currencies between platforms.

Extrapolating Synthetic World Architecture—Where Does it Lead?

There are three parts to a synthetic world—a telecommunications network, a client and a server. The server handles the main world elements and the client manages the rendering of the image that the player sees. The telecommunications provider transmits data between these two parts.

If we examine the server level in detail, we find that each part of the synthetic world is handled by a different server.

- The sim server is responsible for the immediate environment around the avatar; this is the one that has the physics engine and the landscape information. It tracks the positions of the avatars and manages events such as collisions. It also runs the scripting language. The sim server also handles chat messages.
- The Asset server is responsible for delivery of game objects (e.g., textures, data, scripts and polygons) to either the sim server or directly to the client.
- The log-on server authenticates the user.
- An IM (Instant Message) server for Instant Messaging, particularly between in different sims.

2 Word processors appeared on PCs in the early 80's but a common file format was not agreed upon until 2008, about twenty six years later. It could be argued that this standard came into acceptance in 2006, which is true, but Microsoft did not accept it till 2008.

- A finance server that validates and transfers funds following a transaction. Alternatively this could be done by either the log-on server or the asset server.
- We imagine that in the future textures and other components of synthetic worlds may be cached at a local server level for example at an ISP, rather than only at the host server. In this way the bandwidth required from the host server to the client would be reduced.

At this point in time, all Second Life-like synthetic world vendors sell land in Sim (256 meter by 256 meter) lots. This is not convenient for all simulations. For example, a simulation of the solar system in a space game, or even a large ocean for simulation of historical events such as the Battle of Trafalgar needs much more simulation space.[3] Although one could join sims together to form a much larger simulation space, there are practical difficulties with this approach, which will be familiar to anyone who has walked from one sim to another within Second Life and wound up walking towards infinity before crashing.

This implies that the Second Life system is fundamentally flawed, since the current model requires that land be sold in these restrictive sizes. It therefore appears inevitable that allocation of land will be detached from these 256m by 256m block sizes in the future. The current sim size is ludicrously small for any serious naval simulation—the aircraft carrier *USS Nimitz* is 335 meters long. Now compare that with the 8 000m by 8 000 meter maps in the game Battlefield 2.

Additionally one sim (one of these blocks) runs on one server CPU. Again this is a severe limitation, which does not allow for the coming massive parallelization that will be available with the 1000 CPU chips potentially available by 2024 or even the 8 CPU chips of 2010. The further sub-division of tasks, effectively splitting apart the physics engine, the scripting engine, the chat engine and the object management engines into separate CPUs will inevitably be needed, simply to get at the increased power that the next four years of Moore's law will deliver. The transition of players from one sim (or one part of a sim to another if a large sim is to be modeled on many CPUs) must be addressed to take full advantage of the multi-CPU model.

We think that the language LSL (linden scripting language) currently the basis of Second Life, OpenSim and Litesim scripting is fundamentally of low grade and will be replaced by a more syntactically traditional language. Due to the micro-threading nature of scripting in synthetic worlds, scripts will be easily made to take advantage of the multi-CPU environment.

We have previously made the case for having a fixed number of scripts purchased with virtual land (Cox and Crowther 2008). We also have made a case for client side scripting. If we add that we must detach physical size from the sim to allow large naval simulations, then we can extrapolate out a few years at least and confidently say the following in comparison with the existing Second Life system:

- Land owners in synthetic worlds will effectively purchase or rent servers, CPUs and/or threads. They will then allocate a number of avatars, find a suitable land

3 This model of a large sim is found in military simulators such as Battlefield 2.

(or sea) area, allocate a number of scripts, allocate a number of objects and then let their sims run.

- Consequently, the amount of land in a sim will vary from sim to sim, to allow very large and quite small sims; perhaps as large as an ocean and as small as a single building.
- The number of objects and avatars in a sim will vary from sim to sim and be based more on the available power than any arbitrary rule made up by the vendors. Tools will exist for sim owners to balance load across avatars, scripts, land features and objects.
- The number of scripts will be purchased separately from land and prims. This is already being explored by some OpenSim vendors, such as 3rd Rock Grid, which allows the purchase of sims with different prim counts). We foresee that the number of scripts in a sim will be greatly increased because this is an area that is easily parallelizable in a multi-CPU model.
- The sim will incorporate some client side processing; this will include a full scripting language as well as things like particle systems and texture animations.
- With many CPUs, one can easily imagine a time when each player has a dedicated CPU on the server, just to interact with their avatar and manage local chat and player related items (for example scripts on attached items).

Putting it all Together

Synthetic worlds are not all that new—MUDs (Multi-user domains) and MOOs (Objected Oriented MUDs) have all been around for some time and game worlds like Ultima Online (UO) (www.uoherald.com) have been around for some time (since 1997). What is different now is that synthetic worlds like Second Life are in fact not games in their own right but instead environments in which the users create their own content.

In the future, synthetic worlds will have variable fidelity. Sim owners will purchase a number of servers which may or may not be physically located in a common location; they will be attached to the 'grid' and divided up into sims; each sim will be set up so that it has the fidelity it needs. Some sims (e.g., a medical sim) may need only a very basic physics engine, but a very detailed internal organ layout inside the avatar. Others will need very accurate physics engines. Some may need engines that are not yet thought of (e.g., a forensics engine). The vast number of CPUs available will allow most of these engines to be run as interpreted scripts (which compile to an intermediate code). This will allow the creation of virtual sims that are interoperable and useful at the same time, but may have some interesting characteristics such as the sudden appearance of your internal organs when visiting a hospital sim. When you leave the hospital sim a 'database' will remember you and the state of your internal organs, which will re-appear when you next return to the sim. On your next visit you may find that your health has improved or deteriorated.

Getting There: Research Paths

There are several projects that will help achieve the longer term goal of meaningful work being performed within synthetic worlds:

Technology

Utilizing CPU technology The expansion of CPU capability across multiple cores and threads is an area that is proceeding at a fast pace. To utilize this capacity within synthetic worlds requires a project to create servers (and their associated scripting languages) that can take full advantage of the coming multi-cored CPUs. We see this as a critical step in realizing variable fidelity across worlds. We suspect that initially a Scripting Language compatibility mode will be required.

Internet and bandwidth We envisage browser plug-ins will exist to make the transition from the 2D internet to the 3D internet more accessible. This is the approach taken by Google with Lively (www.lively.com) and also ExitReality (www.exitreality.com). We see value in a project to incorporate the Second Life (or OpenSim) client as a plug-in to conventional internet browsers.

Other research projects in this area could include the development of new compression algorithms; redistribution of CPU workload and/or new texture delivery options.

Portability There are many possible projects to make synthetic worlds more accessible from portable devices. Some examples are: Increasing the 3D capabilities of mobile phones and other portable devices such as Netbooks; utilization and expansion of technology built into portable gaming devices such as Sony's PSP and the Nintendo DS and their successors; the use of gaming consoles such as the Xbox 360 and the PlayStation 3 to access synthetic worlds (thus moving their functionality from the computer room to the living room); development of scalable imaging technologies that allow the resolution of textures to be dynamically resized to fit different display devices (for example, texture resolution might be downgraded for display on a mobile phone).

Physical Changes

User interface In our opinion, the most obvious project in this area is the development of low cost fully immersive virtual reality hardware (including haptic devices) to interface with synthetic worlds. Opportunities exist to develop interface applications that help make synthetic worlds more feasible as future work environments.

Server grids Potential projects exist in the domain of super grids that are comprised of synthetic world grids, each of which have many regions and servers.

One technology that may alter the way things run is the emergence of high-performance computing clusters (HPC) specifically designed to run synthetic worlds. The IBM gameframe announced in April 2007 using cell processors may well be leading the way to a new generation of HPC clusters. Research projects are needed to determine how to distribute servers so they can utilize this kind of cluster technology.

Social Changes

Social norm In the future, we imagine that people will use 3D web sites just as commonly as they currently use 2D websites. The interconnection of existing social network sites such as MSN and Facebook to synthetic world environments will also have had significant impacts on social organization. Research is required to better understand how this interconnectedness will impact individuals and society.

The emergence of artificial intelligence in synthetic worlds is already impacting on interpersonal communication and social interaction (Boellstorff 2008). Further research is required to enhance the role of artificial intelligence in these environments and to better understand their impacts on communication and human experience.

Laws Further research into the legal aspects of synthetic worlds is required particularly in the areas of IP ownership, virtual commerce and social control. Dispute resolution mechanisms between residents and synthetic world owners are emerging as a particularly important area of focus.

Global and Regional Changes

Telecommuting is becoming more widespread and synthetic worlds will play a role in this change by providing rich experiential platforms that can support the social interaction missing from current workplace applications of ICT. Research is required to understand the potential and limitations of using synthetic worlds both as a place to do work and as a way to reduce social isolation between remote work environments.

Synthetic World Interoperability

We propose projects that include the creation of common asset servers and financial servers for synthetic worlds. From a technical perspective, it would be reasonably straightforward to create such a service. However, major obstacles would remain including user acceptance.

Another area where research is needed is the legal infrastructure to enable users, developers and other content creators and consumers to move intellectual content from one synthetic world to another.

Synthetic World Architecture

We see a critical problem with the 256m x 256m sim size limitation in both Second Life and OpenSim. This severely restricts the kinds of simulations that can be undertaken with a synthetic world. We believe research is needed into variable simulator sizes, from the small to the very large. We believe that merely making sims contiguous, as is currently the practice, does not provide sufficient scalability or stability for useful large scale simulations, for example, air traffic control or virtual battlefields.

We believe research is needed to provide client-side scripting, in order to offload this computational burden from the server to the client. This is particularly important to facilitate the advent of much larger sims.

Additional projects to explore alternate ways of delivering asset data to synthetic world clients similar to the way web pages are cached at the ISP level would be worthwhile.

The possibility exists to make use of the client's CPUs to unload the server with more than just client side scripting (e.g., a client side distributed physics engine); this could be a very fruitful area for future research.

Conclusion

In summary, we believe that synthetic worlds offer many opportunities for the development of commercial activities as well as new forms of social networking. Consequently we expect that there will be significant changes to these worlds over time. Many of these changes will come about because of the operating difficulties currently faced by developers and users. Other changes will be due to incremental and revolutionary improvements in technology and the technological appropriation and social adaptation of user groups and other stakeholders. We have put forward our reasoned expectations for what changes might be realized and opportunities for future research and development. Accuracy aside, there remain significant challenges and opportunities for further development in these environments.

References

Boellstorff, T. (2008). *Coming of Age in Second Life: An Anthropologist Explores the Virtually Human*. New Jersey: Princeton University.

BP (2008). How did SimCity™ Societies get BP green power? [Online]. Available at: http://bpsimcitysocieties.com/simcity-societies-bp-ea/ [accessed: 9 November 2008].

Clarke, A.C. (1962). *Profiles of the Future: An Inquiry into the Limits of the Possible*. New York: Harper and Row.

Campbell, J., Fletcher, G., and Greenhill, A. (2008). Conflict and identity shape shifting in an online financial community. *Information Systems Journal*, [online, 26 March 2008], DOI: 10.1111/j.1365-2575.2008.00301.x.

Campbell, J., Fletcher, G., and Greenhill, A. (2007). Sustainable virtual world ecosystems. *Database for Advances in Information Systems*, 38(4):29–31.

Carey, J. (2007). Expressive communication and social conventions in virtual worlds. *Database for Advances in Information Systems*, 38(4):81–85.

Cox, R. J., and Crowther, P. S. (2008). A Review of Linden Scripting Language and its Role in Second Life. *Proceedings of ICCMSN 2008*, Dunedin New Zealand June 2008.

Fletcher, G., Greenhill, A., and Campbell, J. (2006). Fight club: Culture, conflict and everyday life amongst an online community. *International Journal of Web Based Communities*, 2(4):474–489.

Intel Corporation. (2008). World's first 2-billion transistor microprocessor [online]. Available at http://www.intel.com/technology/architecture-silicon/2billion.htm [accessed: 11 July 2008].

Linden Labs. (2007). Embracing the inevitable. [Online]. Available at: http://blog.secondlife.com/2007/01/08/embracing-the-inevitable/ [accessed 11 July 2008].

Linden Labs. (2008). IBM and Linden Lab interoperability announcement. [Online]. Available at: http://blog.secondlife.com/2008/07/08/ibm-linden-lab-interoperability-announcement/ [accessed 22 October 2008].

MacMillan Cancer Support. (2008). Conference to take place in virtual world. [Online]. Available at: http://www.macmillan.org.uk/Get_Involved/In_your_area/Northern_Ireland/Latest_News/ConferenceToTakePlaceInVirtualWorld.aspx. [accessed: 9 November 2008].

Moore, G.E., (1965). Cramming more components onto integrated circuits. *Electronics*, 38(8), [online]. Available at: http://download.intel.com/museum/Moores_Law/Articles-Press_Releases/Gordon_Moore_1965_Article.pdf [accessed: 10 July 2008].

Shapiro, S.P. (1987). The social control of impersonal trust. *American Journal of Sociology*, 93(3):623–658.

Weng, J., McClelland, J., Pentland, A., Sporns, O., Stockman, I., Sur, M., and Thelen, E. (2001). Autonomous mental development by robots and animals. *Science* 291(5504):599–600.

Zadeh, L.A. (2008). Towards Human-Level Machine Intelligence—Is it Achievable. *Keynote Address WSEAS AIKED'08*. University of Cambridge, UK. February 2008.

Chapter 19

The Cognitive Playground: Fostering Critical and Creative Thinking with Synthetic Worlds

Judi McCuaig, Joe MacInnes, and William Wright

Abstract

This chapter explores the potential of synthetic worlds to help individuals learn and practice higher order thinking skills including critical and creative thinking. Such skills are difficult to teach in traditional educational settings and are rarely addressed in common simulation-based training programs. The potential is explored first through a fictional account of a day in the life of Tara Defarge, an eco-detective in the year 2025 and her interactions with the Cognitive Playground. Present day understandings about teaching, learning and virtual worlds are used to show that synthetic worlds naturally consist of appropriate metaphors and capabilities to foster critical thinking. An assessment of the state of intelligent interfaces and adaptive systems informs a discussion of the technological challenges that must be met before a Cognitive Playground can be realized.

Tara Defarge:Eco-Detective

Finding data is a trivial task in the information-rich society of 2025 but understanding and the generation of knowledge is a challenge. Knowledge is not the tool of the powerful; power lies with those who know where to ask the correct questions. The public Information Conduit contains streams of data of every imaginable type: news, maps, phone and email traffic reports, consumer and stock prices, travel information, weather information, real estate prices, music, video footage from public events and so on. Public perception is controlled by mash-up specialists and data spinners, who carefully present selected data in support of particular viewpoints and perspectives. Accurate data are freely available from the conduit, but knowledge and information is only free for those who know which streams to select and how to interpret and aggregate the data for the context of the particular question. Working with the Conduit requires creativity, the ability to think critically and regular application of higher order thinking skills such as synthesis and evaluation.

Tara Defarge is a freelance environmental detective. She sorts out threads of information surrounding unexplained environmental puzzles, and determines the real cause of past events or the predicted impact of proposed events. Tara Defarge works for those who are affected, or are about to be affected by the actions of organizations and governments.

Tara Defarge was certain that today was shaping up to be a bad day. She'd taken a case involving Regen-Harris (RH) syndrome, remembering only later that the medical high-brows felt that RH was a completely understood condition. This meant that those 'in the know' felt there was no room for investigation about cause-effect and it meant that there would be zero cooperation with Tara on the case. On top of it all, it was a case with a short timeline. Worse yet, Tara had finally admitted last night that Fe, her Cognitive Playground, was right; she couldn't do the legwork on her own, which meant involving Krin as a collaborator. Tara hated going to Krin's. But Fe had been quick to point out that the last time she started off doing her own preliminaries, she ended up wading through two weeks worth of irrelevant weather data before realizing she was looking in the wrong place. Or at least, looking in the wrong way. She didn't have two weeks this time.

-Which, by the way, was not my fault. I suggested on day two that you start with the soil analysis, or at least get Krin to sift through some of the historical water flow stats before you tried to link them to anything.-

"Fe, that doesn't mean I listened. And I got there eventually, so quit complaining. Besides, I'm listening this time. Don't push your luck."

Of late, Tara had begun to visualize Fe as an undersized eight-year-old boy in short pants, and she was conscious of the fact that the two of them made a strange pair in this end of the Conduit. Walking around with the visualizer for one's CP turned on was decidedly last-decade, and overuse of the personality function was frowned upon, especially in the hipper circles. Most other freelance sifters and distillers chose to communicate via implant, but Defarge liked the verbal interaction. It relaxed her, focused her thoughts.

Regardless, Aldous Krin was a frustrating man to contact. The man's insistence upon hyper-realistic weather simulpatts for the front of his sifthouse wouldn't be so bad if he hadn't also modeled it on his physical location, just outside of Winnipeg. Even that would be forgivable even if he'd let the temporal norm settle on spring, but the last three times Defarge had stopped by, it had been set to midwinter. So as she ported to the sifthouse front, it wasn't much of a surprise to land knee-deep in snow and blasted by gail-force winds.

"Fe, why am I doing this? I just got the sensories on this avatar sorted out, and now I can't feel my toes anyway."

-You want to get paid, remember?-

"Some excuse. I'm shutting down your visual. Krin probably already thinks I'm nuts."

Fe disappeared, and Defarge approached the ostentatiously detailed door to Krin's sifthouse. It was made of finely grained oak with a deep lustrous stain, complete with meticulously programmed layers of tiny scuffs and scratches. Krin devoted much of his time to maintaining the sifthouse's detailed physical environment, an obsession Defarge could respect even if she didn't share.

"Krin?"

Defarge opened the unlocked door and stepped in. The room had nice tactiles—-a warm fire, soft carpet, and a vague scent of baking. She spent a few minutes warming up and enjoying before Krin's avatar appeared, a large Caucasian smiling with a comically wide grin. Someone must be having a good day, she thought.

-A good day?-

"You disagree?"

-You looked at his purchase stream just this morning.-

"Oh, the facial."

Krin's purchase records indicated he'd just had this shop avatar detailed yesterday by Kiri T'gong, the hot new star in tooth and tongue design. And while Defarge wasn't sure it mattered, Fe's connection was in all probability right. Chances were the grin was not a sign of goodwill, but was calculated to show off Krin's resplendently realistic dental plaque. And if he was showing off, she'd do well to notice. Always handy to check purchase records.

"Nice grills, Krin"

"Thanks, Tara. You're early."

"I've got a new case."

"I saw. Hired by J.P. Iri? You're moving up in the world."

"Don't get jealous. And I'm not sure if I can do much. He's got a nephew with what sounds like RH syndrome."

"Who doesn't these days? And why hasn't that hit any of the main newstreams?"

"The kid's not on-census. Check the Regent Hospital patient records, though, and you'll find him. J.P's little sister had a kid there, unknown father. Last week he showed up at his uncle's apartment displaying signs of stage-two RH. Loss of motor control, tremors, implant-cortex malfunctions. None of the other neurological stuff has set in, though, so he might pull through. Either way, J.P. wants me to find out where he picked it up, probably so he can sue them."

Tara looked up to find Krin's avatar's eyes softly glowing in the universal signal that their driver was occupied accessing a Conduit datastream.

"He's Zara's kid, then? The methicline addict?"

"The same. His name's Pike. And while she went off-stream, probably dead, ten years back, the kid has left records. Mostly opiate purchases and trades, but some grocery records, short-term employment notes, Conduit access logs, a couple of vote credits. Not much, actually, considering he's nineteen already."

"No implant maintenance records?"

"None."

"So he's got RH. Listen, I was doing some work on Regen-Harris a couple months ago. Seventy percent of cases that come from unshielded implants. If he hasn't ever had his adjusted, he's at high risk already. Plus, he's probably only using public access points, especially if he's got no rent or tenement lease records. The kid's living on-street, eating GroGen hand-outs, and getting his Conduit time wherever he can. No offense, but I don't think this is much of a case."

"I didn't either. Until I checked the dates on his Conduit access streams. He hasn't been on for two years. And the longest-ever gap reported between exposure and first symptoms is nine months."

"Is he a dealer? Or in one of the troikas? If he's got enough money, he could be using an anon, or going through a record deletion client."

"J.P. Ira doesn't think so. Besides, I'm not that clumsy. If he was really such a big fish, I'd have dug something up in the last couple hours."

"So what do you want me for?"

"I'm going to sift for more information about the kid and his case specifically. But I need someone to do the broad stuff, particularly to look through hospital and clinic downloads to find anyone who has had a longer period between infection and symptoms. That data doesn't seem to be collected directly."

"Can do. I'm not working on anything major, so I can start that today."

Tara had been worried Krin wasn't going to take the case. But somehow, she'd managed to pique his interest, or possibly just his pity. After all, this was a pretty major tangle; and because it involved a terminally ill teenager, she was going to have to move quickly or risk offending Pike Ira's powerful uncle. Krin was a good worker, and his help would be useful.

"Glad to have you on board. I'm moving out, then. I'll contact you later today to see if you've got anything for me."

Krin nodded and Tara ported herself out from the sifthouse. Although realism friends like Krin tended to disapprove of those who blithely ported and forgot to use the door or dress their avatars appropriately for the weather, Tara didn't care enough about offending him to consider braving the storm she saw through the stained-glass window. He'll get over it, she thought. My sensory perceptors won't.

After Krin's, Tara ported back to her office, a stripped-down pre-fab module with only the sparsest of visual detail. She didn't receive a lot of clients here, preferring to meet them in public space. This was purely an organizational convenience. While the Conduit provided any citizen access to unlimited streams of raw data, it didn't provide any analysis, summary, or sorting. Any number of consumer-use news-feeds claimed to succinctly provide the true story behind any situation, but Tara knew that a good dataspinner could make any narrative believable using Conduit data. Processed information from spinners was useless to her, and was certainly not what her clients were interested in receiving. They were paying for someone with no vested interest in their case to sift the primary data and provide them with something closer to the true story.

Tara's office walls were covered in tabs providing hyperlinks and feeds to her most commonly used streams, but she preferred to keep the bulk of her bookmarks stored in volumes on a bookshelf she had written in for herself a year or so back. As Fe had pointed out at the time, she functioned better with a physical object to reference, and the bookshelf had proven just as good a way to organize streams as any.

She began by digging for more about Pike Iri. Most citizens left whole volumes of datastream behind them, from which a decent sifter could create an almost hour-by-hour portrait of their days. Not Pike. Hospital records indicated he had been checked into Bracebridge Memorial a week ago, and that since then he had been staying in the RH ward on intensive treatment and methadin withdrawal care. His vital signs were normal, but his tremors were worsening and his implant-cortex bond was weakening. But before the hospital records, he practically didn't exist on-stream. Even his laundry and grocery transactions rarely showed up, which meant he lived pretty much entirely on charitable transactions, a lot of which were given out without recording citizen numbers or prints.

-He has implant-cortex malfunction? Isn't that characteristic of stage four?-

Fe had materialized, perky-eyed, to perch casually on the arm of her client chair.

"Yes. But Bracebridge records indicate that ninety-four percent of patients who advance to stage four start showing the first cortex malfunctions symptoms in stage two."

-So you had better move fast. A fifty-fifty mortality rate is nothing to laugh at.-

"It's worse than that, actually. I checked, and for stage four patients the mortality rate is close to eighty percent. We have got to get this figured out before the kid dies."

-What are you going to do? I'm not going to be very useful in aiding your creative thinking unless you give me something to go from.-

"Fe, I've got no idea where to start with this one. Aside from the inconvenient fact that he can't have picked up RH because he hasn't accessed the Conduit, it sounds like a textbook case. Maybe this is a case of him getting on sometime without making it into logs."

-Can RH spread any other way? Maybe not through the Conduit?-

Tara reached over to her bookshelf and grabbed a thick volume and a couple flashy looking magazines. She leafed through the thicker book for a few minutes while Fe put on his best not-so-patient waiting look. Tara could see out of the corner of her eye that he was beginning to sift through the book as well, looking for elements to surprise her with.

"The doctor's union records say no. At their last meeting, they discussed that possibility at length."

-What prompted the discussion? Did they have a similar case under review?-

"Not really. They were actually discussing rapid-onset RH, and whether it can be considered treatable at all."

-What is rapid-onset RH?-

"It's when patients don't exhibit the earlier symptoms that typify stage one or two. It's not understood how frequent it is, because some patients actually don't notice the headaches and nausea that come with the first two stages of implant rejection."

-Isn't the early part when you are most infectious?-

"Yes. And that's why the DU was discussing the possibility. Apparently, at some hospitals, early-onset is the most common variety of RH. And if the patients are truly not getting the early symptoms of implant rejection, it isn't really known if they are contagious through the Conduit during that period. If they aren't, it would make sense for it to be spreading in some other way."

-But they didn't find anything?-

"No. Although these visual records show that a few doctors at the meeting—Dr. Lena Yas, in particular, remained convinced that RH is spreading in some way they don't understand."

-I'd note that. It might be related.-

"It doesn't seem relevant."

Fe grinned impishly.

-You've been looking for cases that resemble Pike's textbook RH without an explanation of exposure.-

"Well, really that's what I hired Krin to do. But yes."

-I think that's backwards.-

"Why?"

-There aren't any that resemble his. RH contracted without Conduit exposure? OpenPort spent three years trying to prove RH wasn't related to use of public Conduit ports. If they had heard of Pike Iri, they would have plastered his picture all over every newscast they own. Which, by the way, is a lot. Even you would have noticed by now.-

"Thanks for the vote of confidence Fe. You've got a better idea?"

-You've got an outlier case. Look for other outlier cases, even ones that aren't remotely like his. Anything nonstandard might give us something to work with.-

"What, just look at every nonstandard case on record? That's going to help me get to bed on time."

-Quit whining. Personally, I'd like to hear more about rapid-onset RH. You said that 'at some hospitals early onset is the most common'—which ones?-

Tara blinked and looked at Fe.

"Which ones? What do you mean?"

-Well… that's a broad statement with no substance behind it yet. Here- look at this geographic distribution of hospitals and clinics that are first-contact points for people with RH.-

Fe pulled out his box of blocks and a map—Tara's favourite visualization tool for geographic information. Rapidly the map filled with blue blocks representing the first-contact institutions and red blocks representing other institutions.

Tara sifted rapidly through the second book she'd pulled from her shelf.

"Ok, that's a pretty picture Fe, but isn't going to help much. Since both RH and rapid-onset RH are treated exactly the same, hospitals don't even note who is considered to be an 'early-onset' patient in their own files."

Fe shifted his weight in order to sit in the client, dangling his legs below him.

-That's awkward. Why wouldn't they make a distinction?-

"Why would they make a distinction Fe—if both states are treated exactly the same?"

Fe moved over to the blackboard and posted the past month's admission records for the equally deadly Fazet syndrome.

-Look at these—Fazet syndrome has two starting conditions too—and each one has the same treatment plan. But the hospital documents clearly show which type of Fazet is being treated—in all cases.-

"That is odd Fe—hang on to those records for me please. I need to think about that a bit."

Just then Tara's collab chimed and Krin's head materialized with the gleaming grin front and center. Fe faded out, but the map and the blackboard remained.

"Hey Tara—this case is a bit weird. I'm sifting for the gap-data you were looking for and it's just very strange. I can find data-spun aggregates that report average gap between exposure and symptoms, maximum gap, minimum gap and all kinds of things,

but I can't find a single individual admission record that confirms any of the spun news. Where did the spinners get the data to spin?"

It's getting stranger and stranger—I'm trying to understand why the hospital records don't distinguish between rapid-onset RH and regular RH. Now you've found another records-based oddness. Krin, can you grab a sample of hospital records with admission dates for RH and cross reference it against conduit access for the same IDs? We'll build the missing data if we have to.

"Actually already started that—just wanted to check in while the cross-reference was building."

Krin's head faded out—without even the usual good-bye pleasantries. Krin never used the collab unless he was really pressed for time. Tara found herself wondering about what data Krin might find.

-Why don't you build data too?-

Fe was back—this time sitting cross legged on the floor stacking blocks left over from the map-vis.

"Huh? What data would I build?"

-Well, you're missing hospital and admission data in this case. You and Krin are both missing data that should be available. You sent him off to create data—why don't you create the rest of the missing information? Work back from what you need to the raw materials for the information.-

"Oh! So. let's see, I need to know which hospitals checked in people with rapid-onset RH. Rapid onset RH starts with stage 3 symptoms—most regular-onset RH patients are already checked in at that point. I could check the self-diagnosis admission data for symptoms and collect the files for which stage 3 symptoms are reported at admission time. I could overlay the pharmaceutical codes attached to those files, along with doctor's ID to get me a reference to the institution name. We might not get it right for everyone, but we'd get a broad picture!"

As Tara was talking, the data was appearing on walls and charts around her. She pointed at some of the data features, pulled them into a cloud above Fe's map, and within a few seconds some of the blue blocks began to glow. Tara stared at the map.

"Fe, would you look at this! Hospitals that see rapid-onset RH are all clumped in particular zones with large spaces between the clumps. Zoom in on the map please Fe?"

The map zoomed in to finer detail on the clump that was closest to Tara's location.

Fe started humming tunelessly. Tara knew he was processing data she couldn't see.

"What is it Fe? What do you see?"

-At the current level of abstraction the map shows you major transportation routes, public institutions, schools and political boundaries. I can see the whole map but you see only a little part of it in this visualization. I am adding data to the map and zooming out to show you what I see.-

The map zoomed back out, but floating above the map in more or less regular space were numbers, some green, some orange.

"What do the numbers mean Fe?"

-Each color represents data that clustered along the political boundaries of the map. I thought you might find that interesting. The green numbers show the average number of public Conduit point users per month, over the last year in each area. The orange numbers show the average number of people in each neighborhood who regularly get food handouts. The orange lines show the political boundaries of hand out districts. Green lines show the rest of the political boundaries.-

"Fe—the map is too cluttered to make sense. Can you take the Conduit access data off please? I just don't think that it will help us with this case."

The green lines and numbers on the map disappeared, leaving orange lines and numbers overlaid with the glowing blue blocks that were representing first response hospitals (see Figure 19.1).

"Fe! Look at the map!! Hospitals that see rapid-onset RH are all in hand-out districts! I gotta talk to Krin. Something is not right."

-What about Dr. Lena Yas—is it time to contact her?-

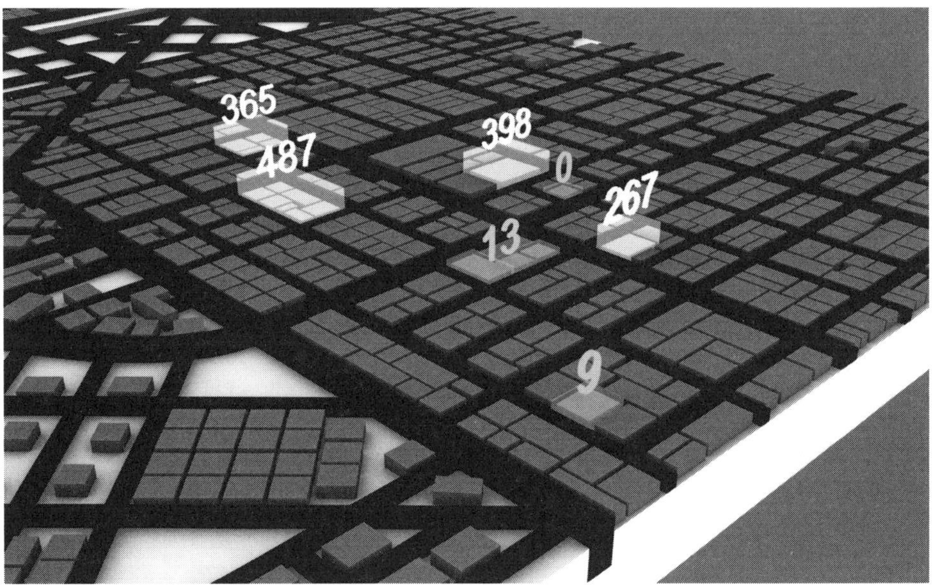

Figure 19.1 Map visualization showing hospitals

Learning from the Cognitive Playground

A world with cognitive playgrounds and the information conduit seems far-fetched, but the tools provided in the fictional world of Tara Defarge would be in high demand in today's workplace. Information analysis is a common task in many professions and requires analysis and synthesis of information and the evaluation of several parallel hypotheses. Individuals who demonstrate an ability to question productively and to think creatively excel in almost any workplace. Unfortunately those prized skills are best learned by practice and by modeling someone who is using the skills, making higher order thinking difficult to teach in traditional educational settings.

Hands on, apprentice-style training provides realistic opportunities for watching and modeling, but provides no mechanism for methodically recording the progress of the pupil or for ensuring that every student has the same educational opportunities. Classroom style instruction offers control over the curriculum, but lacks the capacity for realistic practice. Synthetic worlds can be employed to maximize the benefits of each educational approach, and may prove to be exactly the correct mechanism for teaching and fostering critical and creative thinking.

Research suggests (Burleson 2005, Hewett 2005, Shneiderman 2000, Zheng 2007) that computing environments to foster creativity and higher order thinking skills should have the following characteristics:

- Mechanisms for collaboration and communication with others.
- Ability to integrate information from multiple domains and to explore problems from a variety of angles and perspectives.
- A variety of representations for artifacts and problem solving results.
- A rich recording of process and interim results, enabling backtracking and the comparison of previous problems to current problems.
- Representation and identification of analogies.
- The ability to surprise the user with outcomes, representation or suggestions.

Tara's cognitive playground is an example of this type of creative problem solving meta-world. The synthetic world provides built-in mechanisms for collaboration, communication and access to multiple data streams. The tools that Tara used in her work (Fe, her bookshelf, her office, the blackboard—see Figure 19.2) allowed her to make notes, change perspectives, be reminded of her previous work and its similarities to her current task and be challenged with observations and suggestions about both process and data. Through working on her normal tasks, Tara learns to approach problems creatively and hones her higher level thinking skills—all without any attempt at "teaching" in the conventional sense.

Synthetic worlds and virtual environments are already creeping into the educator's toolkit, resulting in numerous simulation-type training scenarios.[1] Health professionals have examined the use of virtual environments in health care and therapy (Garshnek 2002). Cognitive scientists have had successes using virtual words for cognitive rehabilitation (da Costa 2004, Grealy 1999, Strickland 2007). Synthetic worlds can also be used to measure cognitive abilities, such as memory (Parsons 2008). The use of virtual worlds for training higher order thinking and questioning skills is a logical next step. Software systems within the virtual world can adaptively assist users to explore information, ask questions, and make connections between information, thus helping the human user to develop complex higher order thinking skills.

1 For examples see: http://slurl.com/secondlife/Svarga/128.0/128.0 or http://slurl.com/secondlife/Obelix/75.83807/180.75517/24.56805

Figure 19.2 Tara's virtual office

Complex interactive video games are the precursors to a connected, universal synthetic world. The connection between a video game and its ability to promote higher order thinking can be measured (Rice 2007). Rice introduces the "Video Game Cognitive Viability Index" to measure the degree which a game supports higher order thinking. Games with high levels of interactivity, the opportunity for role playing, a requirement for gathering and synthesizing knowledge, and lifelike avatars receive a high score using Rice's index, indicating a greater likelihood that the game will promote higher order thinking skills. Synthetic worlds, even the limited ones available in 2009, exhibit all of the characteristics noted by Rice. This would suggest that the computing genre of synthetic worlds is well suited for promoting critical and creative thinking.

Tara's cognitive playground (Fe) used questions and suggestions to direct Tara's attention to activities and data that would employ her higher level thinking abilities. In the background, the CP quietly assesses Tara's activities to determine whether she needs to be prodded into higher-level thinking, while carefully recording all interactions with Tara to ensure that she doesn't fall into ruts and predictable patterns of analysis. This type of human-software interaction may seem like the stuff of futuristic films and science fiction novels however, most of the barriers are in the integration of existing technologies and in data management practices. The necessary advances are explored in the following section.

Moving Towards the Cognitive Playground

The technological advances required before Tara's cognitive playground fall into three categories: advances in adaptive/intelligent information systems (data ingest, understanding, and intelligent interfaces), advances in information control (privacy and security), and advances in information display and interaction (modalities and representations). The Cognitive Playground, and similar applications, will not materialize unless these advances are made.

Intelligent adaptive information systems Intelligent information systems locate timely, task-appropriate information from multiple (potentially massive) data sources and place that data in a presentation that is customized or adapted for the user's task and context. In addition to applications like the cognitive playground, automated storytelling, education and training, advertising, and information fusion are immediate application domains for which advances in intelligent information systems could provide key enabling technologies.

The past decade has seen an unprecedented increase in the volume of electronically available data. The Internet has billions of publicly available web pages containing information of all kinds and all qualities. Private organizational databases and document repositories contain huge volumes of data in varied formats. The scale, heterogeneity, and frequency of updates of this global dataset pose significant challenges for applications that access, process, and present information to users or to cooperating applications. This is especially true for intelligent applications that exist to find, process and present data from multiple, diverse sources. The need for timely information adds complexity to the mix—for many applications, including the Cognitive Playground, the right information delivered too late becomes the wrong information. Success in building adaptive information environments must be preceded by research in several key areas including:

A robust, universal metadata language with automated metadata creation capabilities. The metadata language must represent more than simple relationships between individual data items. Rather it must attempt to represent the understanding that humans have of their world. If the Cognitive Playground is to understand our perceptions (and misconceptions) it will require a connectionist understanding of relations, and the conditions under which that subjective reality can change. This metadata language must supply that understanding.

Planning algorithms to access, obtain, and transport information in response to the user's tasks or problems. Research into the creation of planning algorithms that can adapt based on user history, domain and task knowledge will be essential.

Contextually situated information analysis techniques will allow the adaptive information system to select specific information for a particular task, user, and problem. These techniques include statistical metrics for categorizing data as well as techniques relying on ontologies, image recognition, and other types of natural language processing. The resulting measures will form the basis for information selection decisions made by the adaptive information system.

The information architecture for the Cognitive Playground must be a smooth integration of machine and human readable content. For example, information from chats, satellite imagery and web-cams must be processed and understood by the Cognitive Playground in real time. Technologies to support the Cognitive Playground will need the ability to parse and understand voice and video clips and streaming content in addition to text and static images. It is not unreasonable to think that touch and scent information will be collected, stored and passed to haptic and olfactic interfaces, which means that the information architecture must also account for those types of data.

Task/problem decomposition to create a machine recognizable task model and process description is one of the key technologies for adaptive information systems. The ability to describe the task being performed within the context of larger problems is critical to the success of intelligent information systems. Task decomposition is presently an unwieldy, manual process that must be at least partially automated to enable the development and testing of more generic, task-independent adaptive systems.

Human-information interaction components and techniques to create on-the-fly composition of customized information presentations for specific problem sets and users are also areas requiring further research and development.

The preceding list suggests research into several different domains within computer science. The immediate needs can be organized into three thrusts:

1. An investigation into the creation of reusable models for domain, tasks and users, along with a metadata language that can be robustly applied to heterogeneous data. Ontologies and the associated initiatives stemming from Semantic Web (Berners-Lee, Hendler, and Lassila 2001, Shadbolt 2006) research seem to be a reasonable starting technology for this thrust.
2. The development of a methodology for calculating a contextually situated measure of expected utility for data items.
3. The application of the models and similarity measures in creating adaptive planning algorithms to select information and assemble presentations for users.
    - Advances in these three core areas could result in intelligent information systems with capabilities that strongly resemble the abilities of Tara's cognitive playground.

Privacy, security, information integrity and universal information access The information conduit described earlier ignores some significant barriers that exist in today's stovepipe approach to information access. The services provided by the Cognitive Playground are only possible when accurate information is rapidly available to individual information seekers. In today's world, raw data are rarely directly accessible, but must be scraped from public aggregations presented for human consumption across one or more websites. Interfaces for interacting with data from government or corporate sources are practically non-existent.[2] A key hurdle in changing this situation is a solution to the problem of protecting privacy for individuals while allowing public access to information. The fictional world of Tara and Krin is one in which electronic information is public. In that world, personal privacy is something that happens only "off-stream". In the real world a middle ground must be found that permits public access to information without sacrificing individual freedom and privacy. That challenge is

2 Both the Canadian and US governments, for example, provides a wide variety of aggregated census reports and charts to the public, but will not permit public access to raw data, and thus prevents any sort of secondary research based on the collected data.

not so much technological as sociological. The dramatically differing ideologies of governments, corporations, and those who presently control information access, and the apparent unwillingness to make compromises in order to merge ideologies, may mean that societal disparities stand in the way of technologies like the Cognitive Playground, not technological gaps.

The problem of ensuring data security travels hand in hand with concerns about individual and corporate privacy. Data must not be tampered with, altered, lost or corrupted in Synthetic Worlds like the Conduit. The Conduit cannot exist if data are not secure and reliable. Assistants like the Cognitive Playground are rendered useless if the underlying data that is the basis of decision-making become inconsistent. Most research on data privacy is dovetailed with research on data security because the two topics cannot be easily separated. A universal, trusted mechanism for authentication and authorization must be available before anything like the Cognitive Playground will be accepted into day-to-day activities.

A parallel data security problem is the need for assurances about accuracy and timeliness of data. Data providers must have a mechanism for guaranteeing the accuracy of their data, and for communicating the strength of that guarantee to intelligent agents such as the Cognitive Playground.

Users of data require assurances across several dimensions. How reliable is the source? How frequently is this information updated? How has the process that creates this data been affected by recent events? The answers to these questions could prompt an agent to select one information source over another. The relative importance of any one question to the decision maker is dependent on the task and context. For example, the source reliability could be the key factor one day, while the timeliness of the data could be key the next day and the cost might be the deciding factor on a third day. A mechanism to communicate these types of data characteristics is not present in the information systems of today. The key characteristics that must communicated reliably are: the lineage of the data (where did it come from) and of the quality of the data (how accurate is it).

A record of data lineage must contain information about the origins of the item as well as its history. Data lineage can directly affect the utility of the information. For example, imagine a series of financial records issued by an institution that is later found to have subtracted a small amount from some accounts in a processing error. The data in the entire set of records would be unusable unless both data history and data lineage were available and the processing error could be undone.

Identification of the quality of information is likewise a complex topic. For example, the reputation of an information source often plays a key role in determining its usefulness. Similarly the time and location from which the original data was recorded may affect its usefulness, especially in the case of data collected from physical sensors in the world. Environmental data collected from light sensors during a solar eclipse would be misleading unless it were known where and when that data had been collected. Data collected from sensors with limited capacity for precision would be useful to some information consumers but less useful to others. The information consumer can make choices, but only if information about data quality is available.

Before the Conduit and the Cognitive Playground can be a reality, the accuracy and lineage of information must be measured and reported as part of the associated metadata, which is subsequently used in calculating the expected utility of the data for the current task.

Displays, visualizations and user interaction Tara was able to "converse" with Fe using her choice of interaction style (voice). Additionally she could use alternate interaction styles (implant control) when societal norms dictated. Even though both of those interaction styles are possible to a limited extent using today's technology, the primary interaction mechanism for computing and information interaction is still the mouse and keyboard. The development of the Cognitive Playground requires continued advances in interaction mechanisms between humans and computing systems. The keyboard and mouse based interaction style limits the interactions and the inputs possible for the artificially intelligent tutor. Ideally, human computer interaction would advance to a point where humans can select their preferred interaction style and computers are adept at accepting voice, gesture, or textual/pointing device comments.

Visual effects and data displays are the mainstay of synthetic worlds. The story of Tara, Krin and Fe alluded to sensors for haptic interfaces as well as feed-back interfaces that let the user feel things not just see and hear them. These sorts of interfaces are in their infancy and significant research must be done to make them interoperable with a general-purpose information source like the conduit or cognitive playground. Sensory interfaces are not just "nice to have" features of a pretty interface. Humans are wired to use all of their senses to interpret their experiences. Current interaction mechanisms with computing restrict the available sensory experiences significantly.

Finally, as suggested earlier, visualization efforts must move beyond static visualizations of regular data in bar charts or globe viewer markers to produce robust systems that can render cognitively aware and perceptually adapted visualizations from real-time data on-the fly. Correctly composed visualizations will engage the viewer in the substance of an issue. Poorly composed visualizations impede creative and critical thinking and mask content. Intelligent visualizations must embody perceptual and cognitive psychology principles for enhancing human cognitive performance. Only with these types of visualization can something like the conduit and Cognitive Playground exist.

Closing Thoughts

This chapter has explored the application of Synthetic Worlds to the acquisition of higher order thinking skills. We have shown that synthetic worlds in general have the appropriate characteristics and tools to facilitate learning and practice of higher order thinking. We have discussed the necessary advances in language recognition, real-time reasoning, and user interfaces to allow the creation of artificially intelligent tutors that prod humans into practicing higher order thinking.

We have also shown that one of the largest barriers to the information conduit and the cognitive playground is the availability and usability of the data. In today's world data are guarded fiercely and released sparingly, usually for political purposes. Advances in data acquisition, metadata definition and creation, and assurance mechanisms for data integrity, quality and lineage are key.

The required advances in technology are, however, not out of reach. Closed-world prototypes of the cognitive playground could be constructed with present day technology. It is an exciting direction for computing that will result in a system to teach highly prized skills that are rarely taught and seldom practiced. It could, and should, become a component in many complex environments (or in one large one like the information conduit).

Acknowledgements

A small army of graduate and summer students fueled the background research for this chapter. Grateful thanks goes out (in no particular order) to: Alana Cordick, Mike Pearlstein, Tony Thompson, Andrew Berry, Julia Baldwin, Wyatt Carrs, Annie Wraight, Ali Tremblay and Kyle Gretchev. The storyline was greatly improved by a kindhearted family member who wishes to remain anonymous, but still deserves thanks.

References

Berners-Lee, T., Hendler, J., and Lassila, O. (2001, May 2001). The semantic web. *Scientific American*.

Burleson, W. (2005). Developing creativity, motivation, and self-actualization with learning systems. *International Journal of Human-Computer Studies*, 63(4-5): 436–451.

da Costa, R. M. d. C., L. A (2004). The acceptance of virtual reality devices for cognitive rehabilitation: A report of positive results with schizophrenia. *Computer Methods and Programs in Biomedicine*, 73(3):10.

Garshnek, V. (2002). Touching the future: Applications of virtual reality technology to mental health concerns. *International Journal of Healthcare Technology and Management*, 4(5):10.

Grealy, M.J., D. and Rushton, S. (1999). Improving cognitive function after brain injury: The use of exercise and virtual reality. *Archives of Physical Medicine and Rehabilitation, 80*(6), 7.

Hewett, T. (2005). Informing the design of computer-based environments to support creativity. *International Journal of Human-Computer Studies,* 63(4-5 SPEC. ISS.): 383.

Parsons, T. (2008). Virtual environment for assessment of neurocognitive functioning: Virtual reality cognitive performance assessment test. *Studies in Health Technology and Informatics*, 132:351.

Rice, J. (2007). Assessing higher order thinking in video games. *Journal of Technology and Teacher Education*, 15(1):87.

Shadbolt, N. H. and W; Berners-Lee, T. (2006). The semantic web revisited. *IEEE Intelligent Systems*, 21(3):6.

Shneiderman, B. (2000). Creating creativity: User interfaces for supporting innovation. *ACM Trans. Comput.-Hum. Interact.*, 7(1):114–138.

Strickland, D. (2007). An evolution of virtual reality training designs for children with autism and fetal alcohol spectrum disorders. *Topics in Language Disorders,* 27(3):226.

Zheng, S. (2007). Surprising creativity: A cognitive framework for interactive exhibits designed for children, *Creativity and Cognition 2007, CC2007—Seeding Creativity: Tools, Media, and Environments* (pp. 17). Association for Computing Machinery.

INFRASTRUCTURE

Chapter 20
2039: A Day in the Life of a Usability Engineer

Theresa A. O'Connell, Elizabeth D. Murphy, and Renate Roske-Shelton

Abstract

As we approach the end of the fourth decade of the twenty-first century, intelligent agents will handle most of the time-consuming drudge work of usability engineering, freeing usability engineers (UEs) to focus on the mental work of analysis and usability recommendations. Just as gamers today meet in synthetic worlds, UEs will enter customized synthetic environments. Here they will investigate human cognition and behavioral interactions with new software capabilities. Immersed in synthetic worlds, UEs will employ a range of technologies at every step of usability evaluation. We'll be working smarter and more efficiently to measure and improve human experiences with technology. The future holds promise for UEs and, by extension, for users of the technologies we are beginning to imagine.

Just Another Day on the Job

Work becomes more abstract as it depends upon understanding and manipulating information. This marks the beginning of new forms of mastery and provides an opportunity to imbue jobs with more comprehensive meaning (Zuboff 1988: 6).

Morning. Monday, October 4, 2039. Time to check the weather report delivered to my Greenberry by Wex, the weather agent. It looks like a beautiful day—great weather for travelling. Oops, Traff, my traffic agent, tells me the third level of the outer loop is closed for construction. The FedShuttleBus will have to detour. Its driver will be guided along its route by positioning system telemetry updates, but there will still be traffic jams. This means a longer drive to the airport along the second level but more time to get some work done in the u-eval-space.

I don't usually go to conferences in person, but the Government Usability Engineers are having one of their rare face-to-face, in-person meetings. It's one thing to exchange technical information in electronic meetings, but we all crave some actual human interaction. Some would argue that the most important work of a conference gets done outside of the technical sessions, over lunch or dinner, or just during the coffee breaks between sessions. That's certainly the time for networking, which can sometimes get lost in virtual conferences. I'm looking forward to seeing old friends and meeting new people.

As I board the FedShuttleBus, I pass other people at work already in their synthetic environments (SE). I find a cubicle at the back, settle into the fully adjustable comfort chair with safety bar, and start my session.

Pausing slightly to position my right eye straight in front of the wall mounted iris recognizers until I hear the confirmation tone, I press a button. The simulated usability-evaluation space opens ready to go because we finished all the prep work yesterday. I'm suddenly surrounded by a 360 degree synthetic world (syworld) display with full directional audio.

The u-eval-space recreates our lab at our Center's office, which we don't use much anymore since most of our work is done remotely and on the go. But the u-eval-space goes way beyond the capabilities of our physical lab.

A problem with the u-eval-space, or any syworld, is that users sometimes experience a different kind of disorientation. They can become overwhelmed by the vast amounts of information in the streaming visualizations that surround them. Some people experience physical effects like nausea or dizziness; others report euphoria and manic moods. Combined with information overload, these phantom symptoms can make it very difficult for information analysts to do their jobs in a syworld. Since we're working within a fully realized version of the People Capabilities Maturity Model (Curtis 2008) however, information analysts and others who work in SEs are given training and practice to familiarize themselves with the psychophysical side effects of the work environment.

Something I really like about the syworld is that we no longer have to worry about test participants getting lost in the maze of our physical campus and parking garages. The u-eval-space finds the participants wherever they are, so they don't need to find us. In the old days, we lost some participants who got so disoriented that they gave up on trying to find the visitor's entrance. Sometimes they would show up too late to participate in collaborative testing. The u-eval-space also does away with the need to supply participants with step-by-step directions of how to get to us. And, we don't need to go down and escort them through the secure bricks-and-mortar building. The synthetic testing space lets us fully concentrate on the users, their thought processes, attentional behaviors, emotions and motivational factors and on developing recommendations to resolve the tough usability issues.

Today we're testing an upgrade to an immersive visual analytic tool with our last two users. Like all our other users for this study, they are information analysts who are American citizens. But, Tony and Greta live and work outside the US. Ira, the intelligent recruiting agent, has picked them from our database and scheduled them both for overlapping sessions today; so one of my colleagues, Sam, will conduct his testing in an adjoining room within the u-eval-space.

Before we get started with the testing sessions, Sam and I meet to review our plan for the day's activities. Sam joins me in our regular cyber meeting space. Right now he is physically in his apartment in Georgetown. Via our avatars, we are meeting to review the test plan and to confirm the day's schedule. Our literature reviewing agent, Rex, has found a new measure of disorientation mentioned in an article by Dr. Kim Edwards. Since the measure has not yet been published, we've invited Dr. Edwards to join our discussion. It appears that disorientation is highly correlated with cognitive overload.

During an analytic session in a syworld, the visualizations become larger, more complex and dense as they receive huge dynamic data sets from disparate sources. Although additional interactive functionality becomes available as needed, many users find it difficult to sustain the cumulative mental workload. Having to keep the products of mental manipulations in mind from one screen location to another is particularly difficult, just as it was in the old days when system operators in spacecraft control centers had to make mental comparisons between actual streams of telemetry data and the nominal ranges for multiple parameters. Battery, solar panels, antenna status—they seemed like a lot of information in the old days. Now the computer has taken over these comparisons, but has given us a new information tsunami to handle with our same, limited, human neurological and psychological capabilities. We're interested in learning whether information analysts can cope with the intellectual workload of using visualizations of these massive data sets in syworlds.

To assess neurological and psychological effects, we outfit our users with a smart, hooded jumpsuit that can take physiological measures, including brain scans, without distracting them or causing any discomfort. They wear glasses that collect eye tracking data, even as the users move around in the syworld. This is full 360 degree, unobtrusive eye tracking, which has advanced to the point that we understand the cognitive sources of the various measures. Results from eye tracking help us measure user success (accuracy and efficiency). Using other measures, we assess the user's satisfaction with the immersive experience of working in the syworld. All users receive test kits with these items included and return pickups pre-scheduled.

The upgrade that we're testing is designed to help analysts with the mental integration and interpretation of key findings that emerge from the automated analysis of multiple data streams. It puts the user in control of the data streaming, empowering the novice information analyst to slow down, or even pause the data streams. The expert analyst has the option of taking data streams in fast time, experiencing data elements in a compressed flow unbroken by dead time and examining the data at a fast rate. Using this tool, information analysts can systematically subtract selected streams from the analysis or add others to the mix. They can apply a variety of data-transformation filters. Known as WHIF, the tool provides an externalized "what if" capability, using visualizations to relieve some of the burden on analysts' working memories.

Today's testing will complete data collection on the WHIF upgrade.

Sam's user lives and works on the International Space Station, rotating out after a six—month stint focused on analysis of information about the space-faring nations, including new members as they join the club. Other observers from the development team will join us, via their avatars, from time to time. Of course, the sessions will be fully recorded, and will be available to any authorized staff member.

My user is here, that is, his avatar has popped up in the syworld. Tony works in Rajististan. He has passed all the physiometric checks we have in place, so we're sure it's really Tony. Our avatars greet each other, and I turn things over to Trog, the intro agent, which already knows everything we know about Tony. Trog speaks in a well-modulated, female voice, which goes well with its tailored female avatar:

"Thanks for being here today, Tony. You'll be helping us evaluate WHIF, an upgrade to the syworld that you currently use in your work as an analyst. Please make sure you are wearing all the test kit items..."

Continuing the instructions, Trog explains to Tony that thinking aloud is a technique we use for getting at the user's thought process as he works:

"Please talk about the decisions you make before you take any action that would result in changes to the data displayed; that is, please 'think aloud' about your assessment of the situation, specifically by telling us what you expect will happen if you take a particular course of action or an alternative action, and your reasons for the choices you make. If you stop talking for more than 30 seconds, I'll remind you to keep talking. I can't answer questions, but I encourage you to ask questions aloud if that's part of your decision-making process. Next, we'll do a brief practice on thinking aloud…"

Even though he's a native speaker of AmerEnglish, Tony prefers working in the language of his host country. So, we'll use the Rajististani version of WHIF, and he'll think aloud in Rajististani. Through my headset, I'll hear the questions and think-aloud commentary in English. All vocalizations will be captured not just by audio recorders, but also by a speech-recognition capability for the source language. Then the language system will translate all of Tony's spoken comments into English and synthesize that translation into a male voice similar to Tony's for me to hear. At the same time, it will send Tony's comments in Rajististani to a natural language analyzer which will extract quotes and then send those quotes to machine translation from Rajististani into English for later incorporation with other data from the session.

Having the agent deliver these messages allows us to give the introduction and instructions in exactly the same way and in the same words to each user, even though the agent-appropriate voices vary across avatars. The verbal protocol provided by the user helps us to interpret the eye-tracking data and other measures of cognitive activity collected by the smart jumpsuit.

Checking highway conditions, displayed periodically by Traff, I see we're about halfway to the airport; so there's plenty of time to complete this session. It's a big help to have our human effort augmented by the intelligent software agents. They're all part of the team.

From previous testing and observation, it's not clear that the upgrade is usable. We've found indications of usability problems, such as disorientation, nausea, and dizziness, as well as cognitive overload. Resolving these problems is going to require some redesign, which will be time consuming. That's unfortunate—the WHIF upgrade was supposed to be launched next week. I wish the developers had requested testing earlier.

This new version of the analytic space used by information analysts has been touted as the answer to their needs for ways to support their worldwide collaboration in managing widely diverse data sets, in searching visual informational spaces for keys to understanding, and in developing more insightful hypotheses. It may be that expectations were too high and that further capabilities will be needed to support interworld collaboration with scientists at the lunar colony.

The code for the prototype upgrade has long since been run through Usachex, the automated usability checker, a tool with capabilities to evaluate the look and feel of syworlds, as well as more day-to-day, mundane user interfaces. Although the upgrade passed this level of evaluation, we started finding issues when human information analysts began to interact with the higher-powered syworld. For example, Usachex would not reliably predict nausea and disorientation. This is why we insist on keeping human users in the process. Personas and user models have their place in system design, and automated evaluators free us from some of the drudgery of old-style usability testing; but there's no substitute for the real thing in testing highly complex, interactive syworlds. The real user will invariably do something unexpected or experience unexpected side effects, and that's the true test of a flexible syworld.

One task in the WHIF upgrade evaluation asks users to monitor several sources of information about troop movements in an occupied city. One source of information provides aerial views of the city at different moments in time. Most users have had trouble with this task because the troops have been cloaked by a stealth frequency that makes them invisible to the aerial cameras. Tony reasons that—if such a frequency is in use—it can't be effective from every possible angle of view; so he rotates the visualization until he can detect armored vehicles and troops moving through the streets. In the past, this strategy, when used in a syworld, resulted in disorientation. Tony reports that he does not experience disorientation or cognitive overload while performing this task. Electroencephalogram, electrocardiogram and galvanic skin response feedback from the smart jumpsuit back this up. There are no indications of stress.

Meanwhile, Sam's user, Greta, is working on her simulated tasks. Her test scenario involves simultaneous monitoring of unmanned satellite launches from Earth, checking on the progress of automated resupply missions to the current International Space Station (ISS4), and communicating with a simulated manned Mars mission. In the midst of a communication from Mars, Greta receives an emergency alert from an Automated Transfer Vehicle about to dock with ISS4. Forwarding the alert to a station mate, she stays on the line with Mars, only to hear that several members of the mission are suffering from exposure to cosmic radiation.

Later, when rating this task set for mental workload, Greta gives it the highest possible rating for cognitive demand. We'll have to check physiometric feedback from the smart suit to see if it backs this up. If there had been cognitive overload, we'd expect to see a spike in feedback from the central executive in working memory. In the debriefing, Greta comments that monitoring the visualized data streams made her feel slightly queasy. Our intelligent statistical agent, Isa, will correlate eye-tracking data with physiometric feedback so we can assess whether frequent eye movements or elongated saccades are associated with Greta's queasiness and sudden drop in blood pressure. This quantitative physiometric feedback sets our work above the best we could do thirty years ago. With hard data, we can validate or call into question subjective user comments. But, we still need the human in the loop; even if the data say that a phenomenon such as nausea wasn't severe, if the user interprets and reports that it was, our user-centered recommendations call for a high-priority remedy. One thing remains the same in 2039: user impressions and experiences drive software acceptance just as much today as they ever did. We expect that they always will.

When Tony completes his task scenarios, Holo, our holographic assistant, asks him about his satisfaction with various features of the WHIF upgrade. Tony answers aloud. When we want Tony to give ratings on a scale for his level of satisfaction, Holo displays the scale. Holo also accepts free-form comments. Interacting with the holographic assistant engages users. Tony views and edits his ratings and comments within the hologram. While Tony interacts with this satisfaction survey, Holo observes his facial expressions, body language, gestures, and tone of voice. Holo looks for any responses that don't conform to known limits for truth-in-self-reporting. Since Tony's ratings and comments fall within these boundaries, Holo doesn't need to ask him any follow-up questions or suggest that he reconsider any of his ratings.

This completes the test sessions.

When we arrive at the airport, I close down the syworld and exit the FedShuttleBus. As I make myself comfortable in the waiting area, simulation sensors predict that, had Greta continued working with this WHIF version for just five more minutes, there is a high likelihood that she would have experienced something akin to an epileptic seizure. The autonomous agents simulate this condition with a surrogate persona (a program that has the relevant user characteristics of Greta). They devise a design solution that changes the flashing rates for a specific type of data display update. The screen will now refresh at a frequency that will not trigger an epileptic seizure. Then they rerun the tests, using the redesigned display, with four additional personas that simulate tendencies to epileptic seizures. They've eliminated the cause of the seizure.

But there is a new open question: Has the modification impacted usability? We are certain that we have removed the risk of causing a seizure with the software, so, I approve further testing. Ira recruits four more human users. While I'm in flight, these users run through the scenario Greta used. Sam monitors the sessions, ready to intervene if necessary. The agents and Ira have demonstrated their worth. Usability scores remain in the same ranges as those from all other users before the minor modification.

While I'm en route to the conference hotel, the data are aggregated automatically, so that when I fire up the syworld again, at the hotel, all the data have been rolled up, and standard statistical measures have been calculated (e.g., means and standard deviations, along with lostness functions, mental workload graphs, and a disorientation history). In the old days, we rarely tested with samples large enough to yield statistically significant results. Now, in the u-eval-space with our agent colleagues and new technologies, we can work with more users, generating much more data, and testing hypotheses almost immediately.

Once the data analysis is completed, our widely distributed network of usability engineers (UE) collaborates on a holographic report. Working in my hotel room, but back in the syworld, I'm surrounded by visualizations of data from all the testing sessions we have conducted. Sam and our other human collaborators are remote. The report outline has been automatically generated based on our research design. Each section has authors assigned. Some sections are assigned to autonomous intelligent agents, and others to me, Sam, and our human collaborators.

The autonomous intelligent agents populate charts and conduct straightforward data reporting in real time. As we humans watch parts of the report being filled in, we do the heavy analytic work and come to conclusions. The visualization leads us through the evaluation process, step by step, starting with receiving data that the autonomous agents deem important, evaluating the data, coordinating the data into groups of facts, hypothesizing, and collaborating on refuting or accepting the research hypotheses. We're standing in the synthetic space, talking to each other in real time, building the report that surrounds us.

We can turn to the right to check out the user profiles; turn to the left to see the error reports; look toward the floor to see the critical incident report; and look toward the ceiling to see the summary of usability issues and recommendations. Our colleague, Jim, has a speech disability. So, instead of inputting to the report with speech as some of our colleagues do, he's using his invisible keyboard. Such tools have opened the door to UE careers for many new colleagues with disabilities. Jim's avatar looks like he's typing on thin air as a new paragraph appears in the findings section of the report.

Our colleague, Mario, is thinking aloud, "I wonder if we should swap places for Sections A and B?" The sections immediately trade places. He shakes his head, and they return to their original locations.

Major issues are discovered in WHIF disorientation and cognitive overload. We recommend that the upgrade not be released until these problems are resolved. We stress the need for additional semi-autonomous agents to take on the burden of monitoring data streams, a task not well suited for human analysts. As the lead author, Sam reviews the draft report for consistency. Once our final report is delivered to the sponsors and all data archived in the UE library, I log out and head for the welcoming reception, ready to greet old friends and meet new ones.

Where We are Today

> "Reality is merely an illusion, albeit a very persistent one."
>
> Attributed to Albert Einstein (1879–1955)

Powerful new tools will empower us to do better usability engineering. These tools will result from trends that are part of the user experience today—the integration of many technologies into a single device and the integration of many technologies into end-to-end systems. A better understanding of human-syworld interaction (HSI) will inform tool design. Usability challenges are already surfacing: human interaction with technologies in complex interactive environments that change with each interaction; the new and wider range of user experiences possible in syworlds; and continual technological advances that outmode usability findings with each new version. Today we are beginning to understand the usability issues behind HSI. For example, gaming research is informing the usability of syworld analytical tools such as the WHat-IF tool, WHIF (O'Connell et al. 2008).

In this section, we look at four types of technologies encountered in our story and discuss human experiences with them today, keeping an eye open to the implications for 2039.

Synthetic Environments

> "The experience of being transported to an elaborately simulated place is pleasurable in itself, regardless of the fantasy content. We refer to this experience as immersion…"
>
> Murray (1997: 98–99)

In our story, both UEs and users experience some degree of immersion in syworlds. In our vision, the classic usability lab with its one-way glass has given way to the syworld of the u-eval-space. The UE's toolbox has expanded with contents derived from research already in progress. The test participants experience new technologies, e.g., holographic survey forms and WHIF, an advanced visual analytic tool.

The reality of this immersion today is that it does not yet exist to the seamless extent portrayed in the story. In our story, the UE enjoys the convenience of simply firing up the syworld using her own laptop, from any place she may happen to be. When today's users enter the closest thing we have to such an environment, a CAVE (Computer-Assisted Virtual Environment), they must don special glasses to experience the multi-dimensional graphics. The CAVE requires a large dedicated physical space with projectors, electromagnetic sensors, and speakers, all to create the impression of immersion in the multi-dimensional syworld.

Today, holograms can only be updated by showing a different view of an existing image. The holographic report in the story uses holography in a different way. In the story, the technology has evolved into dynamic holographic displays with a degree of fidelity that empowers users to interact with objects such as surveys as though the objects were physically present. Observing this provides us with richer data because we are able to observe body language, facial expressions, gestures, and tone of voice. Users can say "how big" something is via gestures. They can point to a screen element they're talking about. We are provided with more cues to motivations and emotional state during the survey.

In our story, users interact with the hologram construction by providing data input. How this input becomes part of an integrated updated hologram is purely speculative. Perhaps the user's speech is converted to digital text and then to a digital representation, which is fed to the hologram. Pattern recognition, analysis, and synchronous publication (rendering) are the necessary technological process elements. Holography is advancing to the point where a holograph will accept updates: the required increased memory capacity is within reach and erasing and rewriting capabilities are already under research (Steere 2008).

The virtual keyboard used in our story is currently under research by Rashid and Smith (2008). Although they intended to facilitate typing into small mobile devices and to save screen real estate on touch screens, the leap to inputting to a virtual report is a short one. Using so-called natural gestural interaction to communicate with a computer is not new. To take an example from gaming, players gesture to communicate with the Nintendo Wii™. However, they are restricted to using a handheld wireless motion sensor, which has disappeared in 2039. In our vision, Mario moves report content simply by shaking his head.

We see two kinds of avatars moving through the synthetic world: Some avatars represent autonomous intelligent agents (IA). For other avatars, actions are triggered by the thoughts or gestures of the humans whom they represent. As the UE team builds its report, Mario appears to return report content to its original location at will. Today it is possible to use haptic interfaces to move objects from one part of an interface to another, but Mario and the UEs have done this via thought sensing. Such abilities are currently emerging in games. The first steps have already been taken toward understanding the human experience with brain-computer interfaces in virtual worlds (Bayliss and Auernheimer 2001). Today, in video games, brainwave information is collected and used to set the pace of the game in response to a player's emotional state or attention level (e.g., Yang 2008, NeuroSky 2008). Companies such as Emotiv Systems (2008) use information about facial expressions and emotional states, as well as users' thoughts to manipulate onscreen objects. Of course, this doesn't happen to the degree described in the story, but the path has been forged to empower users to immerse themselves in the creative intellectual aspects of building a report without having to share cognitive resources with such mundane activities as manipulating input devices.

Intelligent Agents

> "Work must be smart, appropriately targeted, and adapted to the particular circumstances of the process and the customer. Imagination, flexibility, and commitment to results are needed. You are accountable for results, not for effort."
>
> Hammer (1997: 28)

We already have the technology to support the behavior of the personal, autonomous agents in the story, e.g., Traff or Wex, which reside on a mobile device called a Greenberry (Olsen 2008). Such devices reduce the need for paper, thus contributing to a more ecologically stable environment. Less sophisticated technologies exist today in specific household applications for vacuuming, floor sweeping or gutter cleaning. Each of these packages is programmed to do a specific job, as specified by the user: gathering the current traffic report or weather forecast for a specified area daily at the same times. The story extends these concepts into areas in which autonomous agents could be useful, such as the area of recruiting participants for usability tests. In this particular case, we want the agent to be semi-autonomous, because there is always a need to coordinate exceptions with the human usability analyst. Franklin and Graesser (1997) have developed a systematic inventory of agent classifications based on such goal directed functionality.

The role of Ira, the intelligent recruiting agent, is to take over the tedious tasks of contacting potential participants and scheduling them for time slots specified by usability analysts in published calendars. Ira uses variants of email and mobile messaging that we anticipate will persist into the 2030s to communicate associated social niceties. Ira's message gives potential participants a choice of available dates and times. Individuals sign up or decline. It is part of Ira's job to remove slots as they are filled. Ira also annotates the database of potential participants with the outcome of every attempt to contact a particular person and with information about the person's actual participation (e.g., date, time, name of study). The technology exists today but a price barrier still prevents wide-spread commercial adaptation.

The technology is already in place to conduct an automated evaluation of user-interface code, looking for violations of usability principles. Various tools have been developed for this purpose, for example, AIDE (Sears 1995) and KALDI

(Al-Qaimari and McRostie 1999). Ivory and Hearst (2000) present a detailed review of the theoretical background, methods, models, and techniques developed for automated user-interface evaluation.

A proof-of-concept appeared in the early-to-mid-1990s in research conducted for the NASA-Goddard Space Flight Center (e.g., Jiang et al. 1993). The prototype tool was called CHIMES, for Computer-Human Interaction Models. CHIMES was based on the concept of checking user-interface-design code against coded human factors guidelines on such topics as color use, font variations use, and screen density. A conceptually similar prototype tool, called TUNE (Nordqvist 1996), evaluated compliance with human factors guidelines and style guides. Automated tools are also used to assess software accessibility for people with disabilities (SSB Technologies Inc. 2006, World Wide Web Consortium 2007, 2008). In our story, Usachex follows in this tradition.

A difficulty for early automated usability tools was how to deal with graphical user interfaces, that is, how to quantify the use of graphical elements without penalizing the design for using elements that actually decrease burdens on the user's cognitive capabilities. A promising set of style-consistency checking tools, known as SHERLOCK (Mahajan and Shneiderman 1997) tackled some of these issues. A task-analytic approach gets around the issue of quantifying graphical elements by focusing on the user's performance of tasks (e.g., Lecerof and Paterno 1998). In the story, we imagine that obstacles to an automated evaluation have been overcome and that automated user-interface evaluators, such as Usachex, can deal with subtle, yet quantifiable, effects of design strategies on the user experience in SEs. Progress toward that goal is evident in work reported by Okada and Asahi (2000) on their tool, GUITESTER2, which checks the properties of graphical widgets for consistency. Research on tangible user interfaces (e.g., Merrill, Kalanithi, and Maes 2007) has the potential to bring cognitive overload under user control in SEs.

Natural Language Technologies

> "There is, of course, some engineering involved.... Yet, something is missing... As adults, we focused on constricted problems... But as children, we encountered the world in all its broad diversity, and we learned our relation to the world, and that of every other entity and concept. We learned context."
>
> Kurzweil (1999: 89)

The end-to-end systems that handle the linguistic components of interactions between the UE and the users are possible today. Speech recognition (SR), machine translation (MT), synthesis, and natural language understanding (NLU) are commercially available. However, they do not have the accuracy required to carry off the scenario in the story. Context is the reason why. Natural language technologies have made great strides on the levels of phonemes, morphemes, words and syntax, but have not conquered the full context of human communication.

Pragmatics is the study of language in the context of human social interactions. The environment in which discourse occurs provides contextual clues that shed light on meaning. Harnessing these clues is currently a focus of computational linguistics, but much work remains to be done. Integrating statistical models of language into natural language technologies is a current approach to resolve context, but it has become apparent that this integration is only part of the solution.

Systems of integrated computational linguistic components are commonplace today. In the story, the transition takes two paths, both starting when Tony speaks, although, of course, if the UE replied, there would also be a path from spoken English to spoken Rajististani. (We're assuming that the autonomous agent, Trog, is multilingual, interacting with Tony in Rajististani and with Greta in English.) The first path leads to synthesis for the UE and the second to NLU where Tony's comments are understood and salient elements are extracted. For example, in the second path, extraction can produce a list of places Tony mentioned. Thus, users' statements are passed to the agents for use as anecdotal evidence to explain quantitative data in the report.

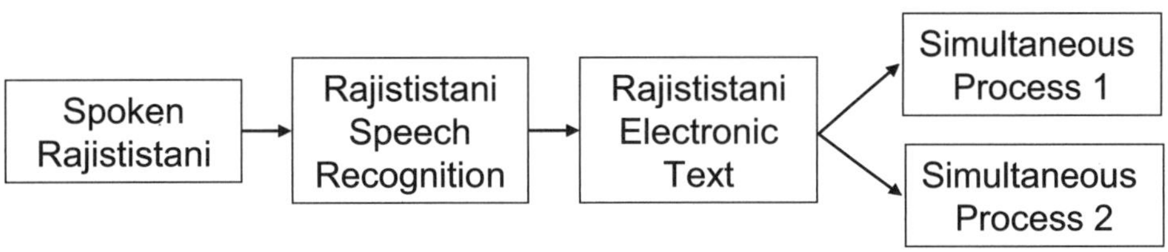

Figure 20.1 Spoken Rajististani undergoes SR to become electronic text to pass on to two simultaneous downstream processes

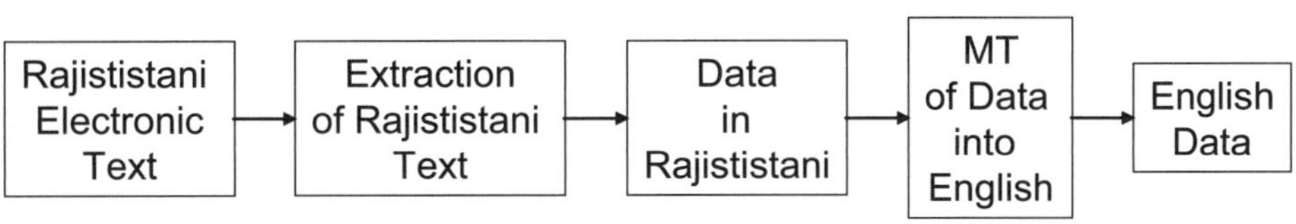

Figure 20.2 In Simultaneous Process 1, Rajististani electronic text undergoes extraction followed by MT

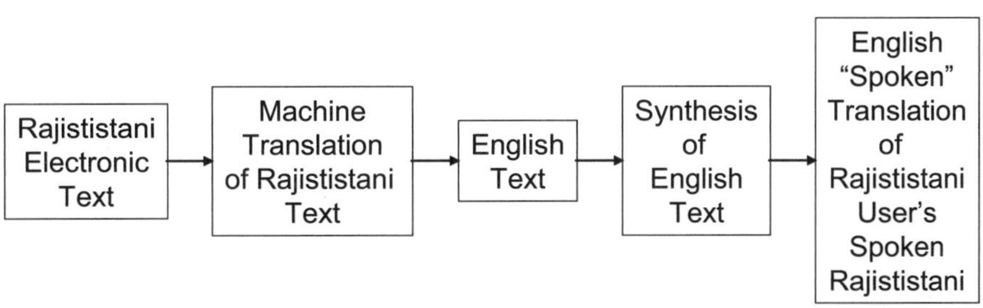

Figure 20.3 In Simultaneous Process 2, the Rajististani electronic text is automatically translated into English and synthesized to sound like spoken English

However, Tony is not speaking his native language, AmerEnglish, but speaking Rajististani with a foreign accent, introducing allophones beyond the Rajististani allophonic range. Today, this input would impair the SR at the beginning of the process and pass tainted data to all subsequent steps. Given this confounding factor and the current state of NLU accuracy, the result would not be accurate enough to produce data to inform usability judgments.

Speech recognition with immediate input to the form, even with today's state of the technology, will be more reliable. If the system automatically fills in stored unusual words such as the user's name, street, and city before the user starts to give responses, the words in the user's responses will most likely fall within the range of a defined vocabulary (e.g., numbers, yes/no) that, even without training each user, should be recognized.

Today, MT performs best in applications designed for specific linguistic domains, e.g., weather or travel. Non-domain-specific MT continues its more than 60-year quest for perfection. Because of the complexity of human language in context, MT remains an application that can successfully transfer the gist from one language to the other, but often at the expense of stylistics and fluency. These require human post-editing.

The state of today's technology is that SR will send input to MT that includes recognition errors. Our scenario does not include human post-editing of the MT. So, the MT would propagate SR errors, adding its own. The output quotes would not be accurate enough for use in a report.

In *Star Trek, The Next Generation*, the android, Mr. Data, cannot use contractions. The agents in this story use contractions to make their speech more natural and engaging. Working at the pragmatic level of linguistics and taking contextual clues into account, when appropriate, the agents use contractions. A minor victory for the androids, this is not a stretch from today's computational linguistics capabilities.

Physiometrics

> "I believe in evidence. I believe in observation, measurement, and reasoning, confirmed by independent observers."
>
> Asimov (1997: 43)

By 2039, biometrics has evolved into physiometrics, measuring a wider range of physiological attributes. This work has already started. A physiometric project, called the VIEW of the Future, measured neurophysiological and psychophysiological factors of users interacting with a virtual environment (VE) (Karaseitanidis et al. 2006). The eSense project (Presser et al. 2006) addressed the miniaturization and robustness required for physiometric sensors such as those in our story.

Our smart jumpsuit draws on technologies in common use today, and presupposes a miniaturization and everyday integration of wearable computing that we are already on the path to achieving. Our jumpsuit is fitted with a tiny electroencephalogram (EEG).

An EEG collects neurological information about brain activities through electrodes placed on a person's head.

An EEG indicated the possibility of Greta's impending epileptic seizure. Today, an EEG can also supply information on a user's state of mind to help them control objects in a syworld or the real world. For example, to play the game Mindball (Interactive ProductLine 2008), players wear a headband with an embedded EEG and electrodes that connect to a physical gaming table. Physiometrics on electrical activity in the players' brains become input to the game that empowers players to move a physical object, a small ball, in the real world. In real time, visualizations of analysis of players' brain activity show players' relaxation levels. Sending the EEG feedback to an IA is surely possible.

The jumpsuit has an embedded electrocardiogram (ECG) that, like today's ECGs, provides heart rate information to inform stress analyses. This information helped the UE team in the story validate that Tony had not experienced the stress of disorientation. The jumpsuit contains galvanic skin response biosensors which, like today's lie detectors, use factors such as sweat to indicate emotion. We assume that the smart jumpsuit has automatically self-calibrated to the individual user. Excluding the extreme miniaturization factor, these are all today's capabilities.

What Needs to Change

> "It is change, continuing change, inevitable change, that is the dominant factor in society today. No sensible decision can be made any longer without taking into account not only the world as it is, but the world as it will be... our everyman must take on a science fictional way of thinking."
>
> Asimov (1978: 5)

Usability engineering is all about improving human experiences with technology. Therefore, we are interested in what needs to change to bring the story's technologies to realization, but we are also interested in what has to change to build the bridge to human acceptance of these technologies and to foster human ability to use the technologies. The first change that has to happen is that cognitive psychology must rethink its theories of "psychological reality" to incorporate the integral role of computers in human experience (Norman 2008: 5). Cyberpsychology will pave the way for a more holistic approach to usability engineering.

New technologies will continue to face the same hurdle that they face today: user acceptance. Although tomorrow's shelfware may be virtual, nonetheless, shelfware it will be if users do not accept it. Usability will remain a primary driver behind acceptance, but as the story shows, usability will take on new dimensions because of the syworld context of use. The call has already gone out for us to rethink our approaches (e.g., Cooper 1999). In this section, we discuss what must change in both usability engineering and in technology to make our science fiction reality.

The drivers behind the way we evaluate HSI will include a factor currently under investigation: in 2039, analysts will differ from their predecessors in more than their techno-savvy work styles. There is evidence that the digital native gamers of our current generation can assimilate larger amounts of information than their predecessors; handle more complex displays; and interact with each other in syworlds to a degree unknown to their predecessors (Jonas-Dwyer and Pospisil 2004). Therefore, they may be able to achieve work products beyond the capabilities of their predecessors. Tony and Greta will feel quite at home in the syworld they test. The 2039 generation of UEs will be comfortable collaborating on a report while immersed in a visualization of mountains of usability data.

New user profiles and changed technologies will generate new interaction behaviors. We must be able to measure human interaction with evolving technologies in the context of syworld use. Perhaps the longest leap in our story is the commonplace and ubiquitous use of synthetic worlds. Unless these technologies and the associated metrics mature in a way that fosters usability, UEs and information analysts will not be able to realize the benefits that the characters in our story enjoy. To this end, work is underway to identify usability principles to inform the metrics that UEs will use in 2039 (e.g., O'Connell and Choong 2008, Wilson and D'Cruz 2006). Some will be traditional, others innovative.

The story assumes that we have already evaluated the technologies that the UEs use. For example, we have tested Ira using metrics such as the ratio of the number of participants recruited to the number of participants who actually perform the evaluation; the degree to which participants conform to the desired user profile; and participants' subjective ratings on the experience of being recruited by Ira. While these go beyond today's stress on time and errors, they are not completely innovative. To be innovative, our metrics must address the innovative aspects of the new technologies. We are already identifying questions that will lead to these metrics (Choong and O'Connell 2008). For example, how do you measure cognitive workload when all you see directly is the avatar? How do you measure perceptual overload when the user is interacting with a hologram or working in a fully immersive synthetic world? How do you measure the user's total psychological experience in a synthetic environment? Such questions need answering to take usability engineering to the story's level of immersion and innovation.

Sensitive metrics and refined methods will measure human interaction with technologies with more precision than we can in the first decade of the 21st century. We will measure the usability of such tools by the quality of the work products—is the UE report more complete and insightful than those produced back in the first decade of the millennium? For example, how many aspects of the user experience did we measure? How quickly did we deliver the report? And, perhaps most interestingly, how are we going to measure insight in a UE report?

Wilson (2006) has predicted that evaluating human interaction with VEs will be "extraordinarily difficult." He identifies a steeply rising number of variables and application possibilities that will, in turn, mean larger interaction spaces and a heavier analysis workload for the evaluator. We expect that the syworlds themselves will alleviate some of this increased workload and empower UEs to go beyond the analytical accomplishments of their predecessors.

Perhaps the u-eval-space itself is the most interesting evaluation challenge. Does the UE become disoriented or nauseated in this environment? Do we need to assess a privacy factor? The UE employs vocal, gestural and perhaps traditional input. The u-eval-space provides audio and visual feedback. *In situ* evaluation may become more important in the future as we tackle these new concerns. If we can generate a syworld anyplace, we will be doing work in public places, but still wanting to protect the anonymity of the user and the independent integrity of the UE's work.

The technologies in the story will have to change. To achieve the interaction that the UEs enjoy with their syworld, the state of the technology today is that users must wear a headpiece to interact "hands free" with a gaming syworld. Miniaturization will be a primary goal to make devices small enough to be embedded in clothing or accessories, out of sight, out of mind and not interfering with immersion in the synthetic world.

IAs are already commonplace, and the uses described in this paper are logical extensions of existing technology. In our story, the agent works as a UE assistant, a cyber-colleague; it goes beyond traditional information delivery; it is doing intelligent literature searches, connecting us to others in the field by bringing literature to our attention—it closes the communication loop. We already know that trust is a vital aspect in measuring acceptance of IA technology (Maes 1994, O'Connell 1990), and we know how to measure users' sense of an agent's trustworthiness. However, before we accept and use such a tool, we need to measure factors such as the relevancy of the literature the agent brings to the reporting and the willingness of our colleagues to interact with agent technology.

Our testing scenario relies heavily on natural language technologies that now exist. However, the accuracy and fluency in our story require progress in accommodating non-linguistic factors such as context.

In our story, physiometric information is collected through a jumpsuit that users wear during the usability evaluation. ICT (2008) have already identified some of the things that must change to make the smart jumpsuit a reality. Factors that impact the human experience include miniaturization of hardware to the point where it is unobtrusive; wireless communication systems that will relieve users of being tethered to physiometric collection devices; and secure data systems. The UEs in our story would stress that these data systems must be secure enough to protect the user's privacy. In addition, the UEs would add that the interfaces between the human and the jumpsuit will have to be unobtrusive and transparent to the user experience (Jain and Pankanti 2008).

There are two sure conclusions to our examination of how things are now and what needs to change to take us to the future we envision for usability engineering. First, we will have to continue to research evaluation metrics, methods and technologies. Then we must test them against the evolving technologies that will empower better usability engineering. To achieve the changes necessary to make our story reality, we will start with what we know; from there, we will develop new evaluation metrics, methods and technologies.

Many alternate futures are possible, but in 2039, thanks to new developments in synthetic worlds, usability engineering should be going strong. Up-and-coming syworlds are going to be better places for both UEs and users. We'll work smarter. We'll be more efficient and effective. But, we still won't be satisfied; we'll be wondering about working in the syworlds of 2069.

References

Al-Qaimari, G., and McRostie, D. (1999). KALDI: A Computer-aided usability engineering tool for supporting testing and analysis of human-computer interaction. In J. Vanderdonckt and A. Puerto (eds.), *Proceedings of the 3rd International Conference on Computer-Aided Design of User Interfaces* (pp. 337–355), Louvain-la-Neuve, Belgium. Norwell, MA, U.S.A.: Kluwer.

Asimov, I. (1978). My own view. In R. Holdstock (Ed.), *The Encyclopedia of Science Fiction* (p. 5). London: Octopus.

Asimov, I. (1997). *The Roving Mind.* Amherst, NY: Prometheus.

Bayliss, J. D. and Auernheimer, B. (2001). Using a brain-computer interface in virtual and real worlds. In M. J. Smith, G. Salvendy, D. Harris, and R. J. Koubek (Eds.), *Usability Evaluation and Interface Design: Cognitive Engineering, Intelligent Agents and Virtual Reality* (Vol. 1, pp. 312–316). Mahwah, NJ, U.S.A.: Erlbaum.

Choong, Y. and O'Connell, T. (2008). Planning user-centered evaluations for interactive information visualizations. *Proceedings of Usability Professionals Association International Conference,* June 16–20, Baltimore, Maryland, U.S.A.

Cooper, A. (1999). *The Inmates are Running the Asylum.* Indianapolis, IN, U.S.A.: Sams.

Curtis, B. *People Capability Maturity Model* (Version 2.0). Carnegie Mellon University Software Engineering Institute. Pittsburgh, PA, U.S.A.: Carnegie Mellon.

Emotiv Systems. (2008). Home page. Retrieved September 17, 2008 from http://emotiv.com/INDS_3/inds_3.html

Franklin, S. and Graesser, A. (1997). Is it an agent, or just a program?: A taxonomy for autonomous agents. In J. P. Muller, M. J. Wooldridge, and N. R. Jennings (eds.), *Intelligent Agents III: Agent Theories, Architectures, and Languages.* (pp. 21–35). Berlin: Springer Verlag.

Hammer, M. (1997). The soul of the new organization. In F. Hesselbein, M. Goldsmith, and R. Beckhard (eds.). *The Organization of the Future* (pp. 25–31). San Francisco, CA, U. S. A.: Jossey-Bass.

ICT Results (01/07/08). Ambient intelligence: Snowboarding to the new frontier. Retrieved September 11, 2008 from http://cordis.europa.eu/ictresults/index.cfm/section/news/tpl/article/id/89427

Interactive ProductLine (2008). EG Biofeedback. Retrieved September 17, 2008 from http://www.mindball.se/egg_biofeedback.html

Ivory, M. Y., and Hearst, M. A. (2000). The state of the art in automated usability evaluation of user interfaces. Retrieved August 9, 2008 from http://www.eecs.berkeley.edu/Pubs/TechRpts/2000/CSD-00-1105.pdf

Jain, A. K., and Pankanti, S. (2008). Beyond fingerprinting. *Scientific American, September*, 78–81.

Jiang, J., Murphy, E. D., Carter, L. E., Bailin, S. C., and Truszkowski, W. (1993). Knowledge-based evaluation of GUI color usage. *Proceedings of MOTIF '93 and COSE: International User Conference* (pp. 78–87). Bethesda, MD, U.S.A.: Open Systems.

Jonas-Dwyer, D. and Pospisil, R. (2004). The millennial effect: Implications for academic development. *Proceedings of the 2004 Annual International Conference of the Higher Education Research and Development Society of Australia (HERDSA,* pp. 194–207*)*, Sarawak, Malaysia. Crawley, WA, Australia: University of Western Australia.

Karaseitanidis, I., Amditis, A., Patel, H. Sharples, S., Bekiaris, E., Bullinger, A., and Tromp, J. (2006). Evaluation of virtual reality products and applications from individual, organizational and societal perspectives—The "VIEW" case study. *International Journal of Human-Computer Studies*, 64:251–266.

Kurzweil, R. 1999. *The Age of Spiritual Machines*. New York: Penguin.

Lecerof, A., and Paterno, F. (1998). Automatic support for usability evaluation. *IEEE Transactions on Software Engineering*, 24:863–888.

Mahajan, R., and Shneiderman, B. (1997). Visual and textual consistency checking tools for graphical user interfaces. *IEEE Transactions on Software Engineering*, 23:722–735.

Maes, P. (1994) Agents that reduce work and information overload. *Communications of the ACM*, 37(7):31–40.

Merrill, D., Kalanithi, J., and Maes, P. (2007). Siftables: Towards sensor network user interfaces. *Proceedings of the First International Conference on Tangible and Embedded Interaction* (TEI'07). Baton Rouge, Louisiana, U.S.A.

Murray, J. H. (1997). *Hamlet on the Holodeck.* Cambridge, MA: MIT Press.

NeuroSky. Product Summary. Retrieved September 17, 2008 from http://www.neurosky.com/menu/main/technology/product_summary/

Nordqvist, T. (1996). TUNE: A tool for user interface evaluation. *Proceedings of the Sixth Australian Conference on Computer-Human Interaction,* Hamilton, New Zealand, 129–134.

Norman, K. L. (2008). *Cyberpsychology: An Introduction to Human-computer Interaction.* New York: Cambridge University Press.

O'Connell, T. A. (1990). A simplistic approach to internationalization: Design considerations for an autonomous intelligent agent. *Proceedings of the 6th ERCIM Workshop, "User Interfaces for All"* (pp. 15–27). Florence, Italy.

O'Connell, T., and Choong, Y-Y. (2008). Metrics for measuring human interaction with interactive visualizations for information analysis. *Proceedings of the SIGCHI Conference on Human Factors in Computing Systems* (pp. 1493–1496). Florence, Italy.

O'Connell, T., Choong, Y-Y., Grantham, J., Moriarty, M. and Wong, W. (2008). From a Video Game in a Virtual World to Collaborative Visual Analytic Tools. *Journal of Virtual World Research*, North America, 11.07.2008. Retrieved November 2, 2008 from http://www.jvwresearch.org/

Okada, H., and Asahi, T. (2000). Automatic consistency evaluation tool for graphical user interfaces. *NEC Research and Development*, 41:377–382.

Olsen, M. (2008). Greenberry. Retrieved on March 05, 2009 from http://dynastync.blogspot.com/2008/10/greenberry.html

Presser, M., Gluhak, A., Babb, D., Herault, L. and Tafazolli, R. (2006). e-SENSE—Capturing ambient intelligence for mobile communications through wireless sensor networks. *Proceedings of the 15th Information Science Technologies (IST) Summit*—Myconos, Greece, Workshop.

Rashid, D. and Smith, M. (2008). Relative keyboard input system. In J. Bradshaw, H. Lieberman, and S. Staab (Eds.), *Proceedings of the 13th International Conference on Intelligent User Interfaces* (IUI 2008, Maspalomas, Gran Canaria, Spain, pp. 397–400). New York: Association for Computing Machinery (ACM).

Sears, A. (1995). AIDE: A Step toward metric-based interface development tools. *Proceedings of the 8th ACM Symposium on User Interface Software and Technology* (pp. 101–110). New York: ACM Press.

SSB Technologies, Inc. (2006). InSight/InFocus 508 Suite. Retrieved November 3, 2008 from http://www.ssbtechnologies.com/products/infocus/indix.html

Steere, M. (2008). Scientist: Holographic television to become reality. Retrieved November 3, 2008 from http://www.cnn.com/2008/TECH/science/10/06/holographic.television/index.html

World Wide Web Consortium (W3C). (2008). CSS Validation Service. Retrieved November 3, 2008 from http://jigsaw.w3.org/css-validator/

World Wide Web Consortium (W3C). (2007). W3C Markup Validator (v0.8.3). Retrieved November 3, 2008 from http://validator.w3.org/

Wilson, J. (2006). Interaction with virtual environments. *International Journal of Human-Computer Studies*, 64:157.

Wilson, J. and D'Cruz, M. (2006). Virtual and interactive environments for work of the future. *International Journal of Human-Computer Studies*, 64:158–169.

Yang, S. (2008). Interview. Retrieved September 17, 2008 from http://www.streamocracy.com/watch/f5a9133504de568f5f6d/Neurosky-Stanley-Yang-CEO

Zuboff, S. (1988). *In the Age of the Smart Machine: The Future of Work and Power*. New York: Basic Books.

Chapter 21
InfoSec in Synthetic Worlds: Historical Perspectives from MOOs, MUDs, and MMOGs

Jeffrey M. Stanton

Abstract

From the time of clay tablets and abacuses, people have always sought new technological methods for supporting the organization and conduct of work. A new possibility in this realm has arisen over recent years in the form of three-dimensional immersive environments, or synthetic worlds. In a synthetic world, each user has a representation of the self, called an "avatar," that can be used to navigate through a realistic 3D environment rendered on a display. Although the idea of using a synthetic world to organize a large-scale work activity might seem like anathema to those whose jobs involve mainly physical resources, consider that more than 99 percent of the information produced by the human race last year was originated in digital form. Many contemporary theories and models of organizations focus primarily on the information management and processing capabilities of the organization and consider the movement of physical materials an important, but secondary concern. In this regard, virtual spaces are plausible as a substrate for functioning organizations. Indeed virtual spaces are, in effect, constructed from information.

Whenever information is handled by humans, however, there is the possibility of mishandling and malfeasance. When appropriately motivated, people will hide information, corrupt information, send information to the wrong person, or otherwise misuse the information. In a synthetic world, which exists for exchange and manipulation of information, these possibilities for malfeasance could be devastating. Fortunately, we have a substantial history to draw upon because the creation of synthetic worlds predated the creation of the Internet. The first multi-user information interaction environments were developed in the 1970s, long before the Internet caught on as a public phenomenon. These early environments were called MUDs (multi-user dungeons) and almost from the start, security issues were an important consideration. This chapter reviews the history of MUDs, MOOs (MUDs object oriented) and MMOGs (massively multiplayer online games) for important clues about the future of security in virtual spaces. The chapter then provides an overview of areas where security researchers and practitioners should focus their efforts in these areas. As with other contributions to this volume, this chapter begins with a future scenario that highlights possible future security problems in virtual space.

Introduction: Synthetic World Security Scenario 2020

Bruce Cularto failed to notice that his avatar was under attack until he had already lost control. His work shift had begun in the usual way: meeting new clients in the netspace agora and chatting about their needs for promotional animations. On Bruce's wall display, the agora was full of sound and light. Bruce's avatar was decked out in a custom tailored, high resolution, three piece, pinstripe suit with a slowly oscillating pattern in the rendering of the pinstripes that focused attention on every subtlety of his avatar's gestures. His clients' avatars—their 3D representations in the agora—ranged from traditional human forms to rainbow covered bugs that exhaled shimmering clouds of pink miasma. These avatars inhabited virtual trading counters for commodities—power, grain, synthetic human tissues, and netspace leases. Regardless of how the clients depicted themselves and their companies in the agora, however, sooner or later they would need advertising, and Bruce represented the largest global conglomerate of netspace advertising anywhere, with more than a billion points of contact inside the 3D web. In the moment before Bruce lost control, he was selling a series of 1024 millisecond promotional animations on his 11,537 billboards to a wind power broker. In the moment after he lost control, his avatar was authorizing instantaneous, worldwide distribution of a propaganda message from AGC—the Arctic Griefer Conglomerate, a transnational radical group espousing random disruption of the global economy, "just for the fun of it." This was definitely a bad thing: besides possibly costing Bruce his job, the propaganda message caused a disruption of global commerce that reverberated for the next 72 hours.

With all of the security controls in place on Bruce's avatar, how could this kind of breach occur? The breach described above resulted from a series of smaller failures that cascaded into a catastrophic loss of control over an avatar with substantial administrative privileges. The initial culprit was the Extended Avatar Interaction Standard (EAIS), an international standard for kinetic control devices that researchers developed in the wake of the popularity of the Nintendo Wii™ controller, to promote interoperability among a proliferating population of similar controllers. EAIS provided a method by which kinetic control devices—such as joysticks and head position navigators—could receive new universal microcode from a host console in order to provide control dynamics appropriate for a given application. Earlier in the workweek, Bruce had used his kinetic controls to test drive a cool, new freeware navigation application that he had downloaded from a distribution list. The code for that application had been tainted by AGC or someone working on their behalf, and the tainted code had planted a Trojan horse inside Bruce's head controller.

The Trojan horse had lain dormant until Bruce began to use his head controller to enter authentication data with an in-world keypad. Bruce's company had policies explicitly prohibiting in-world keypads for entry of sensitive information such as passwords and PIN numbers; he was supposed to use an RFID authentication token to establish a secure channel to the object and then use a company approved text input device to communicate with it. Like most of his colleagues, though, Bruce preferred to use the keypads that appeared on many of the virtual objects in his work area, as this method simplified and streamlined a set of operations that he had to repeat several times a day to get access to protected resources in the agora. Besides, he had misplaced the RFID token that his company had shipped to him. He had used the head controller to login to an in-world demonstration kiosk using the keypad on the back of that kiosk. The Trojan horse recorded all of his head movements during this interaction and relayed the input stream to a server controlled by AGC. Although this input stream contained only a set of motion directives, griefers at AGC had easily mapped these onto a relatively small set (<512) of possible corresponding key combinations. After a small amount of trial and error, AGC had the ability to login to and control all of Bruce's local virtual objects—displays, file cabinets, gift vending machines, and greeter robots.

Greeter robots are an important part of any organization's presence in-world, because it is simply not economical to have human-controlled avatars at every location, around the clock. Customizing these greeters to respond intelligently to customer inquiries is time consuming and expensive, however, so in most cases a robot greeter is trained through "slaving" it to a human-controlled avatar. The robot uses machine-learning algorithms to learn what the greeter needs to know by "observing" the human avatar as it interacts with customers. This training process requires the exchange of multiple security certificates to ensure that the communication links among the avatar, the robot, and the company's database servers transmit only appropriate information for the robot's learning algorithms and that those transmissions are not intercepted by others. Unfortunately, the company that developed the robot training packages left security flaws in their code. Once AGC had gained access to the robot using Bruce's login information, it was straightforward to harvest the security certificates. After monitoring a few of the training sessions that Bruce had provided for the robot, the trail of certificates was large enough that AGC had the ability to generate keys for communication between Bruce's avatar and many of his company's resources in servers worldwide.

Now the final step: In an earlier R&D project, Bruce's avatar had needed substantial administrative privileges to test scripting revisions on in-world promotional displays. Delays in completion of that project had caused Bruce's project manager to extend the end date several times, so Bruce's avatar was not due for "de-provisioning" of heightened administrative privileges for another two weeks. Once they had control of Bruce's avatar, AGC griefers used these administrative capabilities to add a tag line to about 7 million short text messages that appeared in the inboxes of avatars all over the world: "Trust me, this thing is just a total piece of sh*t." This message appeared under sales quotes, customer service descriptions, purchase orders, and a variety of other business-oriented communications. Natural language processors automatically translated the message into 12 different languages. The message also appeared alongside paid advertising on the 11,537 billboards under Bruce's control, signed by AGC and decorated with an offensive icon. Recipients naturally reacted with confusion and concern. Several million avatars across the world began simultaneously to contact each other looking for information and guidance. Friendship robots—similar to greeter robots but designed to help members of social groups stay in touch with each other—began spewing questions and rumors within more than 53,000 affinity groups. The resulting spike in communications among avatars on all channels—voice, text, facial video, and full gesture capture—was so huge that 3D web grids in nine countries crashed within half an hour. The excessive bandwidth use caused routers across the globe to lose touch with each other: the subsequent repeated rewriting and redistribution of routing tables took three days to subside. Media coverage of the messages and the breach that led to their distribution was extensive, and AGC obtained a huge boost in recruitment of new members.

Analysis: InfoSec in Synthetic Worlds

The futuristic scenario described above illustrates some key similarities and differences between traditional information security and information security in synthetic worlds. Considering similarities first, note that the scenario indicates how a chain of small problems in interconnected systems can lead to a much larger failure. From an engineering perspective, a common property of systems of systems is that complexity and interdependency rise rapidly at the same time as the individual designer loses the ability to control, and therefore foresee, the security, safety, and/or reliability of design decisions (Runciman, Webb, Lee, and Holland 1993). In the scenario, a large set of independent vendors had provided software (e.g., the robot software) and hardware (e.g., the kinetic, head mounted controller) that users expected to be interoperable, safe, and reliable. Yet these various pieces of software and hardware had been designed and implemented by different groups, at different times, and to differing standards of engineering quality. As we have learned from the design of other complex systems—nuclear power plants, spacecraft, bridges, and the Internet are just a few examples—it seems extraordinarily difficult to anticipate the range of failure modes that may occur (Dörner 1996). As a result, complex systems inevitably contain vulnerabilities that a motivated individual or group might exploit.

This last point emphasizes a second key similarity between traditional information security and synthetic world security: the human aspect. As in real life security situations and those occurring in more traditional information systems, the scenario illustrates the importance of human behavior in security. Although natural disasters such as earthquakes and lightning strikes can and do have an adverse effect on all types of information systems, the most common point of origin for information system failures is human agency. Individuals and groups may seek to attack an information resource for a variety of reasons. Attackers may hail from within the organization whose resources are being attacked (the so-called insider threat), or from outside the organization (Stanton and Stam 2006). The reasons for attack may include highly malicious motivations but may also spring from less severe origins such as curiosity or incompetence. In the scenario, the motivations of the "griefer" group served as the primary driver for the scenario, but other motivations—such as the motivation of the main character to save time by violating a company policy against in-world keypad use—also figured into the breach.

Next, turning to notable differences between traditional information security and synthetic world security, the weak linkage between synthetic worlds and actual physical objects provides both advantages and disadvantages for security. In traditional information security, one ubiquitous point of attack lies in the physical objects that are accessible in organizational settings. Laptop computers, mobile telephones, personal digital assistants, flash drives, portable hard drives, printed materials, and a variety of other physical objects are all vulnerable to theft, interception, and copying. In contrast, objects in a synthetic world have no physicality.[1] Thus the control of these virtual objects is "simply" a matter of software: The underlying code that controls ownership, possession, and transfer of digital resources is the law of the land in a synthetic world (Lessig 1999). The advantage from a security standpoint is that the problem of control of information bearing objects becomes more akin to secure inventory management than to secure transportation. Of course, this is a double-edged sword: An inventory management system is only as good as the underlying database on which it runs. By its nature a synthetic world must "run" on some kind of software substrate, and that software must provide the capabilities for secure management of information objects. As the scenario noted with respect to the access of security certificates on the greeter robot, such capabilities may not be easy to guarantee.

Similarly, because the information objects in a synthetic world do not have physicality, developers can tailor their visual appearance and operational modes to their functions without regard to the physics that constrains the appearance and function of regular objects. For example, while it is a common mistake to misplace an RFID token or a flash drive containing sensitive information, a memory device in a synthetic world can take on any appearance and thus could be designed to visually remind the user of its sensitivity and importance. In the scenario, creators of objects such as the demonstration kiosk had *failed* to design them to reinforce their security sensitivity in the minds of the object's users.

Another key difference between security in synthetic worlds and in more traditional information systems pertains to social interconnectedness. Machine interconnectedness has been a persistent feature for many decades and a longtime, frequently exploited vector for information security problems—for example, the "Creeper" worm implemented on ARPANET in the 1970s (Leiss 1990). Machine interconnectedness increased rapidly starting around 1994 as the World Wide Web became popular, and with this increase came a concomitant rise in the significance of self-replicating malware threats such as viruses and worms. Principles of network growth—particularly Metcalfe's law—help to explain why self-replicating code threats have become more problematic as network connection density has increased (Mercuri 2004). Only recently, however, has the power of social networking emerged as an additional and powerful force in network interconnectedness: a substantial increase in *social* interconnectedness did not manifest until the first major social networking sites began to emerge in the early 2000s (Rheingold 2002). Social interconnectedness refers to the number of simultaneously functional social groups formed in a population of N individuals (Reed 1999). In theory, the interconnections in these overlapping groups grows exponentially (e.g., 2^N; Reed's law), whereas a more traditional peer connected network grows as the square of N (Metcalfe's law). Within a highly linked mesh of interconnected groups, social information can spread more rapidly and infiltrate the network more fully than in other, less densely connected network topologies. From a security perspective, this suggests that adverse ideas, messages, or communications—what sociologists have referred to as

1 While this is generally true, an object in a synthetic world may certainly mirror or even control a physical object.

memes (Blackmore 1999)—can spread more readily in a network of overlapping groups. Synthetic worlds provide the potential for extreme forms of social interconnectedness because the physical barriers that generally limit an individual's ability to engage in face-to-face social interactions become irrelevant. Other barriers such as differences in native language also decrease to the extent that the synthetic world provides automatic translation facilities. Put bluntly, under the right conditions a synthetic world might become the ultimate gossip generation and distribution machine because of its capability for hosting interlinked and overlapping social groups. Such situations provide a superb vector for denial of service attacks. In the scenario presented above, an intended and powerful side effect of the distribution of the griefers' message was a spike in activity on all available social communication channels. The spike and its resultant depletion of bandwidth had severe and debilitating effects as a direct result of the high degree of social interconnectedness among avatars in the synthetic world.

Security Issues Emerging from MOOs, MUDs, and MMOGs

Many of the security issues described above have manifested in the precursors and early versions of synthetic worlds that have emerged over recent decades. As computer networking began to spread widely in the 1970s and the availability of inexpensive dumb terminals increased, software developers began exploring avenues for multi-user gaming. Early multi-user games such as MUD (multi-user dungeon) allowed players to interact with one another through text descriptions of the environment and text messages between players. Later versions of similar games, sometimes referred to as MOOs (multi-user object oriented), additionally permitted users to create their own content—for example, new areas to explore or new objects to possess and wield. MOOs, in their turn, evolved into multi-player, networked games where landscape and characters rendered onscreen using computer graphics (note that text remained a common mode of social communication). Although MIDI Maze (Atari 1987) was perhaps the first graphical game with a networked multiplayer mode, the shareware title DOOM (id Software 1993) arguably provided the first example of a graphical multiplayer environment that functioned on a conventional local area network. Within a year or two, titles such as The Realm Online (Sierra 1995) began to popularize Internet-based game play. Each of these graphical multiplayer games embodies some or all of the most essential characteristics of synthetic worlds—persistent characters represented by avatars, shared landscape, real time or near real time interaction, and modes of social communication such as text—albeit in a rather primitive form. Present day MMOGs (massively multiplayer online games) such as World of Warcraft™ (Blizzard 2008) encompass many of the characteristics that we can expect to find in future synthetic worlds. More pointedly, other existing virtual environments such as Second Life—which many do not consider as a game—provide key elements such as currency exchange, object creation, and object behavior scripting will likely support the future use of synthetic worlds for organizational purposes.

Because researchers initially developed these environments for purposes of game play, the most common expression of security issues pertains to the problem of cheating

(Pritchard 2001). Although cheating is not the only security issue relevant to multiplayer online gaming, it is certainly the most prevalently discussed and analyzed. Webb and Soh (2007) noted a number of security issues not directly related to users cheating during game play, for example, compromised account passwords, insider threats by individuals running a trusted server, and denial of service attacks against gaming infrastructure by individuals or groups not participating in the game. For example, in 2006, the BBC reported such an incident in which hackers stole the personal information of about 650,000 Second Life users from databases maintained by Linden Labs ("Security row upsets Second Lifers" 2006).

In the context of game play, cheating is functionally parallel to hacking in a traditional information system. The cheater starts with a variety of motivations to obtain an advantage over other players, much as a hacker begins with a variety of motivations to break into a target system. The cheater exploits software defects or software architecture vulnerabilities (e.g., unencrypted communications between client and server) to obtain a resource or capability not normally permitted to that individual user or a group of users to which the cheater belongs (e.g., a clan). The cheater then uses that resource for personal or group advantage, thus upsetting the ecosystem—competitive, economic, or both—in which the gamers operate. Researchers such as Bardzell (2007), Yan (e.g., Yan and Randell 2005), and Webb (e.g., Webb and Soh 2007) have documented a variety of modes of cheating, focusing primarily on the software architecture issues that tend to enable or prevent cheating.

One strategy for organizing an analysis of cheating in multiplayer environments lies in dividing the problem into four different domains: player, application, communications, and infrastructure (cf. Webb and Soh 2007). In the domain of the game, players may employ a variety of means to gain unfair advantage over others including fraud, theft, social engineering, collusion, and extra-game activities (e.g., monetary exchanges outside of the game to gain valued resources usable inside the game). Most of these attack vectors involve taking advantage of typical human foibles and few require a high degree of technical sophistication. For example, some individuals have employed low-wage workers in developing countries to "harvest" in-world currency for their later use inside the game. Although this example lacks obvious criminality, Chen et al. (2004) documented more than 1300 "cybercrime" cases related to online multiplayer gaming during 2002 just in Taiwan. Most types of financial crime that can occur in real life have a potential analog in synthetic worlds, with the added complexity resulting from issues such as anonymity, electronic identity theft, and large geographical distances between victim and perpetrator.

In the application domain, a user modifies or supplements any application software under his or her control in order to modify an avatar's capabilities. The most common target of attack is thus the specialized and often proprietary client software that most game platforms require in order to access the synthetic world. The client software renders the synthetic world on the user's computer and provides the means for controlling the user's avatar in-world. Modified or supplemented client software may give the avatar special abilities or may provide enhanced information about the landscape or other avatars. Modifications or supplements to a game client frequently present a sizable technical challenge. As we have commonly experienced with viruses and worms, however, if a platform has a sufficient level of popularity, attackers will eventually create tools for use by individuals who lack technical expertise (in traditional information security, such individuals have the moniker "script kiddie"). For example, the highly popular online game World of Warcraft™ became the target of a software product called "Glider" (http://www.mmoglider.com/) that, "plays your World of Warcraft character for you." Glider generates user input to control the user's avatar, effectively automating a variety of repetitive game tasks that some users wish to avoid.

In the communication domain, cheaters work by modifying the timing or content of information transmissions between nodes in the game. Most commonly, these methods modify the communications to and from a particular user's client, either in a client-server or peer-to-peer architecture. One example described by Nichols and Claypool (2004) involved the insertion of a fixed time delay in the stream of outgoing packets from the client of Madden NFL Football™ (Electronic Arts 2004). The resulting change in the operation of the game gave the user with the outgoing delay a performance advantage over an opponent whose outgoing packets did not have a similar delay. Besides time delays, other modifications to unencrypted communications among nodes may provide useful information not otherwise displayed on the user interface or the possibility of issuing illegal or impermissible content into the control stream. Such content may give a user unwarranted power to influence the environment or control objects within the synthetic world, including the status or behavior of other users' avatars. Computer scientists have active research programs investigating such protocol-based attacks (e.g., Di Chen and Maheswaran 2004).

Finally, in the infrastructure domain, cheaters operate by attacking hardware or non-client software in an effort to subvert the operation of the game. Most game environments include a variety of hardware elements such as displays, text input devices, kinetic input devices, cameras, microphones, and network elements (hubs, switches, routers, and bridges). The device itself or the software drivers that animate the hardware may provide suitable targets for attack. One common attack usable across many online gaming platforms is a network denial of service attack using a technique such as a ping flood. Particularly in the context of player-to-player combat, a gamer might decide that it is better to knock an opponent offline than to allow the battle to continue. Pritchard (2001) documented an attack of this nature on the game Age of Empires (Ensemble Studios 1997) in which a player could create a packet containing an illegal character that would crash the client software of other players.

Although this four-way division of attacks on MMOGs is certainly not the only way of dividing up the security threats to synthetic worlds, it can provide a useful framework for examining the scenario described at the beginning of this chapter. Starting with the "player" level, it is clear that the behavior of both the main character of the scenario and members of the griefer organization contributed to the breach described in the scenario. Members of the griefer organization certainly held malicious intentions toward the main character of the scenario and his advertising company. The griefer organization laid a trap for the main character in the form of the freeware navigation software that he downloaded onto his kinetic control device. The enticement of getting something for nothing provides a standard strategy for social engineering and fraud attacks by building on a "weakness" in human nature (Mitnick and Simon 2002). As noted previously, the main character's flouting of his company's security policy also represented an effort to circumvent "game rules" that were developed to protect players by avoiding security lapses (Bardzell et al. 2007). The failure of the main character's supervisor to decommission his administrative rights in a timely way represents a third and final "player" level failure in security precautions for the information resources described in the scenario.

At the application level, the griefer organization took advantage of application design flaws in the training software for the greeter robot. As is nearly universally true with current software applications, the robot software contained unpatched vulnerabilities that allowed the griefer organization to harvest security certificates and ascertain from them a method of decrypting secret communications between the main character and his other information resources. Given the complexity and size of contemporary application software, it is virtually impossible to remove all such vulnerabilities: systems must thus contain compensatory countermeasures that prevent a breach of one application from causing a catastrophic system-wide failure (e.g., a system of vulnerability reporting and automatic updates).

At the communications level, the griefers used techniques described above to obtain security certificates and encryption keys that allowed them to communicate with and control remote information resources, despite the precautions that the advertising company had taken to protect those communications from interception or corruption. As cryptography expert Bruce Schneier (2000) has noted, an over-reliance on cryptography can lead to a false sense of security. For purposes of convenience and efficiency, the advertising company allowed a single appropriately configured user to communicate with a large array of sensitive information objects without a means of building checks and balances into the transactions.

Finally, at the infrastructure level, the griefers exploited a feature of the head mounted kinetic input controller to introduce malicious code containing a Trojan horse into the device. This malicious code provided the initial entry vector for the griefer organization's attack on the main character's avatar. As we have learned from standards such as 802.11b (Borisov, Goldberg, and Wagner 2001), industry experts frequently fail to anticipate every type of attack that a given type of infrastructure element might undergo. Such attacks uncover vulnerabilities only after a standard deploys into the field, and lags of months or years may occur before engineers derive a succeeding standard that repairs the problem. Additionally, the ubiquity and decreasing cost of field programmable nonvolatile memory and gate array devices has led to a concomitant increase in their use to implement highly reconfigurable systems (DeHon 2000). For the fictional head-mounted kinetic controller, engineers considered the capability of introducing new microcode essential because the differing physics of various synthetic worlds in which the user might find him or herself could require substantially different dynamics in the responses of device.

In summary, the foregoing material provided an analysis of the synthetic worlds security scenario presented at the beginning of this chapter. This analysis suggests that our collective experiences with cheating and other security issues in existing and historical MMOG environments and their precursors can provide useful insights for anticipating future security problems that we may encounter in the context of synthetic worlds. Although the division may not prove comprehensive, tentatively separating security issues into four domains—players/users, applications, communications, and infrastructure—served as an adequate method to analyze some of the security failures that occurred in the scenario. The remainder of this chapter provides directions for future research based on this four-way division of security problems.

Future Directions for Research on Security in Synthetic Worlds

As a preface, note that many of the research problems described below cross disciplinary boundaries, so suggestions concerning the technical or social nature of the research should not discourage researchers from other disciplinary backgrounds from tackling the problems from their own unique perspective. With that said, one important security research area for virtual worlds pertains to social behavior of the users who control their avatars on behalf of their organizations. We know from examining the cheating literature that some individuals acting in synthetic environments will take extraordinary efforts to gain advantage over their fellow "players" regardless of whether those efforts are legal, ethical, or in accord with the "rules of the game" operative in that particular environment. If such behavior is more prevalent in synthetic environments that in the "real" world, this likely results from disinhibition of behavior that stems from anonymity and other unique factors of virtual interaction (Barak 2005, Davis 2001, Joinson 1998, Suler 2004). Research on information security in organizational contexts (e.g., Stanton and Stam 2006) clearly indicates that social constraints on behavior serve as a critical component in maintaining security. Thus, we need to develop programs of research that examine issues related to personal identity, social embeddedness, reputation management, and community formation in synthetic worlds. One theoretical strategy that has emerged from research on social networking sites such as MySpace™ lies in framing these problems in terms of the development of social contracts (Snyder, Carpenter, and Slauson 2006). In essence, a social contract is a mutual agreement among "players," "users," or "citizens" concerning the rules for right behavior. Early studies of MUD and MOO environments (e.g., Curtis 1992) clearly indicated that social contracts spontaneously emerge among groups of players and that the virtual nature of the interactions among players makes enforcement of the social contract challenging.

What is unknown at this point is what mechanisms of avatar creation, group formation, communication, virtual property management, and related issues are workable or optimal in the context of synthetic worlds. We need research that documents and seeks patterns in the activities of groups in a range of synthetic world environments. These environments must include variation in issues such as identity, age, and gender verification; group management and communication; economics, ownership, transfer, and replication of virtual goods; social roles of mentors and authority figures; and social enforcement techniques such as "banning." Once a rich set of primary studies has appeared in the literature, then we will need some integrative work to examine results across these variations and to offer recommendations for how to design a synthetic world that promotes secure and responsible behavior among its inhabitants.

Looking next at the application domain, we can see the predominance of client-server architectures for the manifestation of present day virtual worlds such as Second Life™. Client-server architectures have apparent superiority in terms of security and curtailing of cheating (Yan and Randell 2005). The development of a secure client for running an avatar in a synthetic world appears feasible, and a number of reasonable approximations already exist for environments such as World of Warcraft™. Equally evident from these client-server implementations, however, is an indication that the client-server architecture for synthetic worlds is not scalable, even given decreasing costs of bandwidth, processor power, and storage (Brutzman, Zyda, Watsen, and Macedonia 1997, Shirmohammadi and Georganas 2001, Smed, Kaukoranta, and Hakonen 2002). It is simply unacceptable that any synthetic world would contain a permanent restriction on the number of avatars present in a given "shard" regardless of whether that number is 16, 64, 128, or some larger number. Likely future progress in overcoming these scalability limitations lies in moving towards peer-to-peer architectures. While these approaches have great hope of addressing scalability, peer-to-peer architectures seem intrinsically more difficult to control with respect to security concerns (Gauthier, Bershad, and Gribble; Yu, Singh, and Sycara 2004). Of additional concern, monetizing a purely peer-to-peer architecture has proven difficult in many Web 2.0 applications because of the absence of a centralized locale of control for the collection of funds (Högg, Meckel, Stanoevska-Slabeva, and Martignoni 2006).

Current research on security in peer-to-peer networks is extensive and diverse, covering issues of reputation management, trust, routing, decentralization, storage, and caching, among other topics (Oram and Oram 2001, Rowstron and Druschel 2001, Wallach 2002). This diversity represents the wide range of current and proposed applications for peer-to-peer networks. One likely way to cut a path through this vast forest of assorted concerns lies in focusing research on the practical development of a peer-to-peer synthetic world development environment that can serve as a testbed for security experiments. Such an environment already exists in the form of Croquet (www.opencroquet.org), an open source virtual world development toolkit developed by Alan Kay and David A. Smith, among others, and originating at Duke University. A related project, built on the Croquet platform and called Cobalt, seeks to develop an open source "metaverse" browser that will allow users and their avatars to navigate within and across a variety of synthetic worlds, much as current web browsers allow navigation and linking across websites. Croquet's non-profit status and affiliation with a consortium of more than 60 research institutions provides a development infrastructure suitable for research on security issues in synthetic world applications.

In examining security issues at the communications level, some notable interdependencies emerge with application architecture. Scalability remains an important issue in synthetic world communications protocols (Ferreira 2005, Souayed et al. 2003). In particular, updating state information across multiple users consumes substantial bandwidth in client-server architectures and only fractionally less in peer-to-peer. Adding encryption to ensure secure transmission of data among peers or between clients and servers creates an additional communication burden. Ensuring that the client and other application software have not been corrupted, and can be trusted to produce well formed, "legal" data streams provides an additional challenge. Fortunately, a currently active program of research on grid computing promises to deliver insights about secure communications protocols readily adaptable for use in synthetic world applications (Basney, Nejdl, Olmedilla, Welch, and Winslett; Foster, Kesselman, and Tuecke 2001, Welch et al. 2003). The most pressing security research needs in the more general area of distributing computing lie in developing optimal protocols for federated management of identity, privileges, and trustworthiness. Researchers have begun to adapt existing, web services security protocols such as SAML to serve these purposes, but much more research is needed to ascertain whether web service protocols can be stretched enough to serve the needs of a highly distributed, multi-owner synthetic world environment (Lang, Foster, Siebenlist, Ananthakrishnan, and Freeman 2006).

Finally, with respect to infrastructure, the most pressing problems are arguably not technical engineering problems, but rather problems of economics and incentives facing vendors. As the scenario strongly implied, the use of synthetic worlds requires a wide range of engineered products—from pointing devices to network attached storage. Across the globe, thousands of vendors create or manufacture these products or the components of these products. A casual examination of the electronics market reveals a plethora of products with different purposes, interfaces, and outputs. A cornucopia of acronyms includes GPSs, PDAs, PCs, HDTVs, and a hundred other lines of electronic devices designed for purchase and use by end users. As Ross Anderson (2001) has noted, most vendors have little economic incentive to develop secure products, but powerful incentives to overload devices with features and bring them to market as quickly as possible. As the international networked computing infrastructure continues its exponential growth—with everything from medical instruments to refrigerators attached to the Internet—the security of these linked devices has become unmanageable (Goldberg 1998). This situation leads to two research needs. First, more research is needed into the economic implications of security engineering, and what kind of policy structures might be deployed in order to create greater incentives for investment in the security of our computing infrastructure. Second, we need additional research with respect to the development, deployment, and effects of security engineering standards. Although engineering standards are proliferating from our various national and international standards organizations, minimal research exists on the extent to which these standards improve the security of engineered products (Emam and Garro 2000). Standardized methods for developing secure software products (e.g., UMLsec) are still in their infancy (Jurjens 2002), suggesting that the research community needs to closely track the extent to which these methods reach the engineering practitioner community and create a positive impact on the security of the many engineered systems that will be used in the context of virtual worlds.

Conclusion: No Better Time to be a Security Researcher

The history of the Internet provides clear instruction on the value of security research. Originally developed by academics and used in educational and governmental contexts for low risk applications, the Internet was designed with security as an afterthought—if it was a thought at all. Some have made similar claims about popular operating systems and application software. These examples make clear the idea that if security is not planned and designed in from the origins of a project, the challenges of retro-fitting secure operations into an existing insecure environment are enormous. History tends to repeat itself, and the first movers in the area of synthetic worlds—with Second Life™ as a prime example—seem to be dedicating substantial resources to combating problems that have arisen from the malicious actions of hackers, cheaters, and griefers. Although there is certainly a chance that a highly secure, scalable, standardized platform will arise to support the upcoming metaverse of synthetic worlds, in all likelihood we will be fighting an analogous set of security battles on the cobbled, heterogeneous, and unpredictable grid for decades to come. The silver lining in this cloudy prediction is that security researchers and security product vendors will remain valuable and important in the provision of workable, secure environments for the synthetic world users of the future.

References

Anderson, R. (2001). Why information security is hard-an economic perspective. *Computer Security Applications Conference, 2001. ACSAC 2001. Proceedings 17th Annual*, 358–65.

Barak, A. (2005). Sexual Harassment on the Internet. *Social Science Computer Review,* 23(1):77.

Bardzell, J., Jakobsson, M., Bardzell, S., Pace, T., Odom, W., and Houssian, A. (2007). *Virtual Worlds and Fraud: Approaching Cybersecurity in Massively Multiplayer Online Games*.

Basney, J., Nejdl, W., Olmedilla, D., Welch, V., and Winslett, M. Negotiating trust on the grid. *2nd WWW Workshop on Semantics in P2P and Grid Computing*.

Blackmore, S. J. (1999). *The Meme Machine*. Oxford University Press, USA.

Borisov, N., Goldberg, I., and Wagner, D. (2001). Intercepting mobile communications: the insecurity of 802.11. *Proceedings of the 7th Annual International Conference on Mobile Computing and Networking*, 180–189.

Brutzman, D., Zyda, M., Watsen, K., and Macedonia, M. (1997). Virtual Reality Transfer Protocol (vrtp) Design Rationale. *Proceedings of the 6th Workshop on Enabling Technologies on Infrastructure for Collaborative Enterprises*, 179–186.

Chen, Y. C., Chen, P. S., Song, R., and Korba, L. (2004). Online Gaming Crime and Security Issue—Cases and Countermeasures from Taiwan. *Proceeding of the Second Annual Conference on Privacy, Security, and Trust (PST2004), Fredericton, NB, Canada, October*, 13–15.

Curtis, P. (1992). Mudding: Social Phenomena in Text-Based Virtual Realities. March, 5, 1999.

Davis, R. A. (2001). A cognitive-behavioral model of pathological Internet use. *Computers in Human Behavior*, 17(2):187–195.

DeHon, A. (2000). *The Density Advantage of Configurable Computing.*

Di Chen, B., and Maheswaran, M. (2004). A cheat controlled protocol for centralized online multiplayer games. *Proceedings of 3rd ACM SIGCOMM Workshop on Network and System Support for Games*, 139–143.

Dörner, D. (1996). *The Logic of Failure*. New York: Holt.

Emam, K. E., and Garro, I. (2000). Estimating the extent of standards use: the case of ISO/IEC 15504. *The Journal of Systems and Software,* 53(2):137–143.

Ferreira, P. (2005). Network middleware for large scale mobile and pervasive augmented reality games. *Proceedings of the 2005 ACM Conference on Emerging Network Experiment and Technology*, 242–243.

Foster, I., Kesselman, C., and Tuecke, S. (2001). The Anatomy of the Grid: Enabling Scalable Virtual Organizations. *International Journal of High Performance Computing Applications*, 15(3):200.

Gauthier, P., Bershad, B., and Gribble, S. D. *Dealing with Cheaters in Anonymous Peer-to-Peer Networks*: Technical Report 04-01-03, University of Washington, January 2004. Computer Science and Engineering.

Goldberg, L. (1998). Information appliances: From web phones to smart refrigerators. *Electronic Design*, 46(7):69–84.

Högg, R., Meckel, M., Stanoevska-Slabeva, K., and Martignoni, R. (2006). Overview of business models for Web 2.0 communities. *Proceedings of GeNeMe*, 23-37.

Joinson, A. (1998). Causes and implications of disinhibited behavior on the Internet. In *Psychology and the Internet: Intrapersonal, Interpersonal, and Transpersonal Implications*, 43–60.

Jurjens, J. (2002). UMLsec: Extending UML for secure systems development. *UML,* 2460:412–425.

Lang, B., Foster, I., Siebenlist, F., Ananthakrishnan, R., and Freeman, T. (2006). A Multipolicy Authorization Framework for Grid Security. *Proc. Fifth IEEE Symposium on Network Computing and Application*.

Leiss, E. L. (1990). *Software Under Siege: Viruses and Worms*. Oxford, UK: Elsevier Advanced Technology.

Lessig, L. (1999). *Code and Other Laws of Cyberspace*. Basic Books.

Mercuri, R. T. (2004). Superscaled security. *Communications of the ACM,* 47(3): 15–18.

Mitnick, K. D., and Simon, W. L. (2002). *The Art of Deception: Controlling the Human Element of Security*. Wiley.

Nichols, J., and Claypool, M. (2004). The effects of latency on online madden NFL football. *Proceedings of the 14th International Workshop on Network and Operating Systems Support for Digital Audio and Video*, 146–151.

Oram, A., and Oram, A. (2001). *Peer-to-Peer: Harnessing the Power of Disruptive Technologies*.

Pritchard, M. (2001). How to Hurt the Hackers: The Scoop on Internet Cheating and How You Can Combat It. *Information Security Bulletin*, February.

Reed, D. P. (1999). That Sneaky Exponential—Beyond Metcalfe's Law to the Power of Community Building. *Context* magazine.

Rheingold, H. (2002). *Smart Mobs: The Next Social Revolution*. Perseus Books Group.

Rowstron, A., and Druschel, P. (2001). Storage management and caching in PAST, a large-scale, persistent peer-to-peer storage utility. *Proceedings of the Eighteenth ACM Symposium on Operating Systems Principles*, 188–201.

Runciman, W. B., Webb, R. K., Lee, R., and Holland, R. (1993). The Australian Incident Monitoring Study. System failure: An analysis of 2000 incident reports. *Anaesth Intensive Care*, 21(5):684–695.

Schneier, B. (2000). *Secrets and Lies: Digital Security in a Networked World*: John Wiley and Sons, Inc. New York, NY, USA.

Security row upsets Second Lifers [Electronic (2006). Version]. *BBC Online*. Retrieved June 15, 2008 from http://news.bbc.co.uk/1/hi/technology/5365148.stm.

Shirmohammadi, S., and Georganas, N. D. (2001). An end-to-end communication architecture for collaborative virtual environments. *Computer Networks*, 35(2-3): 351–367.

Smed, J., Kaukoranta, T., and Hakonen, H. (2002). Aspects of networking in multiplayer computer games. *The Electronic Library*, 20(2):87–97.

Snyder, J., Carpenter, D., and Slauson, G. J. (2006). MySpace. com: A social networking site and social contract theory. *Proc. of the Information Systems Education Conference (ISECON-2006)*.

Souayed, R. T., Gaiti, D., Pujolle, G., Yu, W., Gu, Q., and Marshall, A. (2003). Haptic virtual environment performance over IP networks: A case study. *Distributed Simulation and Real-Time Applications, 2003. Proceedings. Seventh IEEE International Symposium on*, 181–189.

Stanton, J. M., and Stam, K. R. (2006). *The Visible Employee: Using Workplace Monitoring and Surveillance to Protect Information Assets-Without Compromising Employee Privacy or Trust*. Information Today, Inc: Medford, NJ, USA.

Suler, J. (2004). The Online Disinhibition Effect. *CyberPsychology and Behavior*, 7(3):321–326.

Wallach, D. (2002). A survey of peer-to-peer security issues. *International Symposium on Software Security*, 42–57.

Webb, S. D., and Soh, S. (2007). Cheating in networked computer games: A review. *Proceedings of the 2nd International Conference on Digital Interactive Media in Entertainment and Arts*, 105–112.

Welch, V., Siebenlist, F., Foster, I., Bresnahan, J., Czajkowski, K., Gawor, J. et al. (2003). Security for Grid services. *High Performance Distributed Computing, 2003. Proceedings. 12th IEEE International Symposium on*, 48–57.

Yan, J., and Randell, B. (2005). A systematic classification of cheating in online games. *Proceedings of 4th ACM SIGCOMM workshop on Network and system support for games*, 1–9.

Yu, B., Singh, M. P., and Sycara, K. (2004). Developing trust in large-scale peer-to-peer systems. *Multi-Agent Security and Survivability, 2004 IEEE First Symposium on*, 1–10.

Index